Advanced Microsoft® Word 97 Desktop Publishing

NITA HEWITT RUTKOSKY
PIERCE COLLEGE AT PUYALLUP
PUYALLUP, WASHINGTON

JOANNE MARSCHKE ARFORD
COLLEGE OF DUPAGE
GLEN ELLYN, ILLINOIS

JUDY DWYER BURNSIDE
COLLEGE OF DUPAGE
GLEN ELLYN, ILLINOIS

Developmental Editor	Lisa McGowan
Copy Editor	Susan Trzeciak Gibson
Proofreader	Margaret A. Marr
Indexer	Nancy Sauro
Art Director	Joan D'Onofrio
Cover & Text Designer	Jennifer Wreisner
Desktop Production Specialist	Jennifer Wreisner

Permissions—Microsoft Publisher clip art is used by permission of Microsoft Corporation. The following people have generously given permission to use their materials: Dane and Mary Beth Luhrsen, Ride Safe Inc., Wheaton, Illinois; Edward Hospital, Marketing Department, Naperville, Illinois; Edward Cardiovascular Institute, Naperville, Illinois; Floyd Rogers, Butterfield Gardens, Warrenville, Illinois; and Crowe, Chizek, and Co. LLT. Material has been excerpted from *Microsoft Word 7* by Nita Hewitt Rutkosky, Paradigm Publishing Inc., 1997; *Microsoft Word 97* by Nita Hewitt Rutkosky, Paradigm Publishing Inc., 1998; and from *Telecommunications: Systems and Applications* by Robert Hendricks, Leonard Sterry, and William Mitchell, Paradigm Publishing Inc., 1993.

Acknowledgments—The author and publisher wish to thank the following instructors for their technical and academic assistance:

•Deborah C. Clear, Virginia Highlands Community College, Abingdon, Virginia
•Diana R. Hrynchuk, Northern Alberta Institute of Technology, Edmonton, Alberta
•Peggy Maas, College of DuPage, Glen Ellyn, Illinois
•Janet C. Sheppard, Collin County Community College, Plano, Texas
•Nancy Stanko, College of DuPage, Glen Ellyn, Illinois

Dedication— To my husband, Michael, and my children, Audrey, Ryan, and Ian.—Nita Rutkosky

To my husband, Frank, and our children, Rachel, Lisa, and Kaitlin.—Joanne Arford

To my family and friends, for all their support.—Judy Burnside

---

Library of Congress Cataloging-in-Publication Data
Rutkosky, Nita Hewitt
Advanced Microsoft Word 97 desktop publishing / Nita Hewitt Rutkosky, Joanne Marschke Arford, Judy Dwyer Burnside.
p. cm.
Includes index.
ISBN 0-7638-0105-4 (text). — ISBN 0-7638-0106-2 (text & disk)
1. Microsoft Word 2. Word processing. 3. Desktop publishing.
I. Arford, Joanne Marschke. II. Burnside, Judy Dwyer. III. Title.
Z52.5.M52R867 1998 97-40893
652.5'5369—dc21 CIP

Text + 3.5" disks: ISBN 0-7638-0106-2
Order number: 04305

Published by **EMC**Paradigm
875 Montreal Way
St. Paul, MN 55102
(800) 535-6865
E-mail: publish@emcp.com

Printed in the United States of America
10 9 8 7 6 5 4 3 2 1

contents

unit 2 PREPARING PROMOTIONAL DOCUMENTS, WEB PAGES, AND POWERPOINT PRESENTATIONS 207

preface

Microsoft Word, one of the best-selling word processing programs for microcomputers, includes a wide variety of desktop publishing features. The scope and capabilities of these features have expanded with each new version of Word. *Advanced Microsoft Word 97: Desktop Publishing* is designed to address specific desktop publishing features included in Microsoft Word 97, along with general desktop publishing concepts.

Word's desktop publishing features allow the user to create very professional-looking documents. Desktop publishing eliminates the need for a typesetter and page designer, greatly reducing the cost of publishing documents. Desktop publishing produces immediate results and offers the computer user the ability to control the production from beginning to end.

Advanced Microsoft Word 97: Desktop Publishing is designed to be used by students already familiar with word processing. This textbook focuses on advanced Word features along with desktop publishing terminology and concepts. Most of the key desktop publishing concepts addressed in this textbook are presented in chapter 1. Applications of these key concepts are presented in the remaining 11 chapters. The applications are designed to develop skills in critical thinking, decision making, and creativity. Many applications in this textbook are designed to reinforce collaborative learning in planning, designing, and evaluating business documents. In numerous applications, basic information is given for a task just as it may be given in a real life situation.

The text contains three units with a total of 12 chapters. Each chapter contains the following elements:

- Performance objective
- Desktop publishing concepts
- Word features used
- Desktop publishing pointers used to reinforce concepts
- Word and desktop publishing terms and definitions
- Hands-on exercises interspersed within each chapter demonstrating key concepts and features
- Chapter summary
- Commands review
- Student study guide (Check Your Understanding)
- Hands on computer applications (Skill Assessments)
- Additional applications promoting collaborative learning and critical thinking as well as individual creativity (Creative Activity)

In addition, a unit objective summarizes the key goals emphasized in each unit. Each unit also ends with Performance Assessments that evaluate students' mastery of both the desktop publishing concepts and the Word skills presented in the unit.

SCANS (Secretary's Commission on Achieving Necessary Skills) standards emphasize the integration of competencies from the areas of information, technology, basic skills, and thinking skills (see the back of the first page of each unit). The concepts and applications material in this book have been designed to coordinate with and reflect this important interdisciplinary emphasis. In addition, learning assessment tools implement the SCANS standards. For example, the end-of-chapter exercises called Skill Assessments reinforce acquired skills while providing practice in decision making. Performance Assessments at the end of each unit offer simulation exercises that require students to demonstrate their understanding of the major skills and technical features taught in the unit's chapters within the framework of creativity, decision making, and writing. Optional exercises related to SCANS standards are included in the Performance Assessments and in selected Skill Assessments.

Students who successfully complete this course will have achieved the following competencies:

- Use basic type-oriented design techniques available with Microsoft Word 97 to enhance the readability of multiple-page, portrait or landscape documents such as letterheads, business cards, personal documents, flyers, brochures, promotional documents, presentational materials, newsletters, reports, and manuals.
- Enhance the visual appeal of business and personal documents with variable page layouts using standardized type and graphic design techniques along with Word templates and clip art.
- Use Microsoft Word 97 to manage desktop publishing files and document templates.

READ THIS BEFORE YOU BEGIN

Using Microsoft Word 97

Whether you are using the standalone version of Microsoft Word 97 or using Word within Microsoft Office 97, the following information is important to your success in using Word to complete the exercises in this textbook:

System Requirements

- Personal computer with at least a 486 processor; a Pentium processor is recommended
- Microsoft Windows 95 operating system or Windows NT Workstation 3.51 with Service Pack 5 or later
- At least 8 MB of memory (RAM); 16 MB of memory is recommended and is also necessary for use with Windows NT Workstation
- Large capacity hard disk or file server; 20-60 MB of hard disk space is required; 46 MB required for a typical installation; more may be needed depending on the type of installation and your system's configuration
- VGA or higher-resolution video adapter compatible with Windows 95; Super VGA, 256-color recommended
- At least a 1.44 floppy disk drive or a double- or quad-speed CD-ROM drive
- 4 megabytes or more of free disk space at all times for temporary files
- Mouse (not all features are available through the keyboard)
- Laser printer or good quality inkjet printer supported by Windows 95; color printer if available
- Internet access to fully complete the exercises in chapter 8

Word Folders/Directories

By default, Word is installed in a folder named *Office*. The default pathname to this folder is *C:\Program Files\Microsoft Office\Office*. The *Office* folder contains the essential files and subfolders (containing additional files) necessary to run Word 97. Additional subfolders of the *Microsoft*

Office folder, such as *Clipart* and *Templates*, contain files that are necessary to complete the exercises in this textbook. The *Clipart* folder contains subfolders, such as *Popular* and *Backgrounds*, that include files of clip art images that can be inserted into documents. The *Templates* folder contains subfolders, such as *Letters & Faxes* and *Reports*, that include the template document files available through Word 97. In addition, some necessary Word program files are classified as shared files. Shared files can be used by other programs contained in Office 97, such as PowerPoint or Excel. Some of these shared files can be found in the *Microsoft Shared* folder or any of its subfolders. The path to this folder is usually *C:\Program Files\Common Files\Microsoft Shared*.

Installing Microsoft Word 97

To properly install Word, please refer to the Word 97 documentation (or Microsoft Office 97 documentation) and to the information that follows.

The type of installation selected when installing Word 97 as a standalone or as part of Microsoft Office 97 determines the Word components available. The default installation type, known as *Typical,* installs the most commonly used Word 97 options. To see a list of the components that are installed with Word 97 as part of a Typical installation, complete the following steps:

1. Click Help on the Word Menu bar.
2. Click Contents and Index, then make sure the Index tab is selected.
3. In the text box following *1 Type the first few letters of the word you're looking for.*, key **Word components**.
4. Click Display.
5. Read the topic on the screen or click Options, then Print Topic to print a hard copy of the Word components installed as part of a Typical installation.

The best approach to installing Word 97 is to choose the *Custom* installation. The Custom option lets you install other components in addition to the default options that are included in a Typical installation. If you are installing Microsoft Word 97 for the first time, select Custom as the type of installation and include the following components, in addition to the default options already selected, to successfully complete the exercises in this textbook:

1. Select the *Microsoft Word* option and change this option to include the following (some of these options may already be selected):
   a. From the *Wizards and Templates* component, all selections (*Faxes, Memos, Reports, More Wizards, Resumes* and *Letters)* except *Macro Templates*.
   b. From the *Proofing Tools* component, all selections (*Grammar, Hyphenation,* and *Thesaurus)*.
   c. From the *Text Converters* component, the *Text with Layout Converter* option.
2. Select the *Microsoft PowerPoint* option and change this option to include the following (some of these options may already be selected):
   a. *Content Templates*.
   b. *Design* Templates.
   c. From the *Help* component, the *Help for Microsoft PowerPoint*.
   d. *Animation Effect Sounds*.
3. Select the *Web Page Authoring (HTML)* component.
4. Select the *Office Tools* component and change this option to include the following (some of these options may already be selected):

a. *Spelling Checker.*
b. *Microsoft Graph.*
c. *Microsoft Graph Help.*
d. *Microsoft Photo Editor.*
e. *Popular Clipart.*
f. *Clip Gallery.*
g. *Find All Word Forms.*

5. Select the *Converters and Filters* component and change this option to include *Text Converters* and *Graphic Filters.*

Adding Additional Word Options

If Microsoft Word 97 has already been installed on your computer, you can install the additional components mentioned in the previous section by completing the following basic steps (refer to the Word documentation for more specific information):

1. Close all programs.
2. Click the Windows Start button, point to Settings, then click Control Panel. (Or at the Desktop, double-click the *My Computer* icon, then double-click the Control Panel folder.)
3. At the Control Panel dialog box, double-click the *Add/Remove Programs* icon.
4. At the Add/Remove Programs Properties dialog box, make sure the Install/Uninstall tab is selected. Click Word 97 or Microsoft Office 97 in the list of available software, then click Add/Remove.
5. At the next screen, insert the Word or Microsoft Office setup disk in the appropriate drive.
6. At the Microsoft Office 97 or Word 97 Setup dialog box, click Add/Remove.
7. At the Microsoft Office 97 or Word 97 Maintenance dialog box, include the components listed in steps 1–5 above in the section titled *Installing Microsoft Word 97.*
8. Exit Setup when you are finished installing the additional components.

Defaults

All default formatting settings, such as font, margin settings, line spacing, and justification; toolbars; templates; and folders used in this textbook are based on the assumption that none of the original defaults have been customized after installation.

Using This Book

As you work through the desktop publishing information presented in this textbook, you need to be aware of the following important points:

- Instructions for all features and exercises emphasize using the mouse. Where appropriate, keyboard or function key presses are added as an alternative.
- As you complete the exercises, view the completed figure following each exercise to see what the document should look like.
- Be aware that the final appearance of your printed documents depends on the printer you use to complete the exercises. Your printer driver may be different from the printer driver used for the exercises in this textbook. Not all printer drivers interpret line height the same, nor do they all offer the same font selections. Consequently, you may have to make some minor adjustments when completing the exercises in this book. For instance, if you have to select a different font from the one called for in the instructions, you may need to change the type size to complete the exercise in the space allotted. You may also need to adjust the spacing between paragraphs or specific blocks of text. As you will see in the chapters that follow, creating desktop published documents is a constant process of making small adjustments to fine-tune your layout and design.

Most of the fonts specified in the exercises are common, but it is possible that some of the fonts used may not be supported by your printer. In that case, you will have to select an alternate font. When substituting another font, your documents will look slightly different from what you see in this text, and you may need to make minor adjustments.

Using Files from the CD-ROM Version of Office 97

The *ValuPack* folder located on the CD-ROM version of Office 97 contains many additional useful files that may be used in Word 97. Some exercises in this textbook require that you use template files located in related *Valupack* subfolders (*D:|Valupack|Template|Word*). To access these additional template files easily within Word 97, copy all the template files from the *Valupack* folder into Word's default *Template* folder. Complete the following steps to copy the template files from the *ValuPack* folder:

1. Access the Save As dialog box, then change the active folder to Word's default *Templates* folder (*C:|Program Files|Microsoft Office|Templates*).
2. Click the Create New Folder button and create a new subfolder named *ValuPack*.
3. Click Cancel to close the Save As dialog box.
4. Access the Open dialog box, then change the active folder to the *ValuPack* subfolder named *Word* containing the Word template files on the CD-ROM (*D:|ValuPack|Template|Word*).
5. Select all of the file names in the Look in: list box.
6. Right-click one of the selected file names, then click Copy.
7. Change the active folder to the newly created subfolder (*C:|Program Files|Microsoft Office|Templates|ValuPack*).
8. Right-click anywhere within the white area in the Look in: list box, then click Paste.

To use the template files copied from the CD-ROM:

1. Click File, then New.
2. Click the *ValuPack* tab, then select the desired template file.

Some additional template files are located in a folder (or related subfolders) named *Template* (*D:|Template|Letters, Memos,* etc.). These files can be copied to the default *Templates* folder by following similar steps to the ones just described.

Using the Student Data Disk

Advanced Microsoft Word 97: Desktop Publishing is packaged with two student data disks containing keyed documents and some extra graphics that you will use to complete various exercises. The most efficient and easiest way to use the student data disk files is to copy them into their own folder on the hard drive or network file server. When you need a specific file, open the file from the folder holding the data disk files instead of repeatedly reinserting the student data disk into your floppy drive.

If you experience any difficulty inserting graphic files from the student data disk, you may be missing some graphics filters. Make sure you have installed the *Graphic Filters* component of the *Text and Converters* option as referred to in the *Installing Microsoft Word 97* section. Refer to chapter 11 for a more detailed discussion of graphics filters.

The remaining disk space on the student data disk will not be enough to store all the exercises in this textbook. To be on the safe side, allow at least 10 extra disks to completely store all the exercises in this textbook. Your instructor may suggest that you delete specific exercise files once you have turned in the documents and they have been graded. Check with your instructor about this procedure.

Understanding File Extensions

File names with extensions such as *.doc, .dot, .wmf,* and *.html* are frequently used throughout this textbook. A filename extension commonly identifies the file format of the associated file. The filename extensions referred to in this textbook and their corresponding file formats are as follows:

Extension	File Format
.doc	Microsoft Word
.dot	Word template
.wmf	Windows Metafile
.bmp	Windows Bitmap
.cgm	Computer Graphics Metafile
.html	Hypertext Markup Language
.gif	Graphics Interchange Format
.ppt	PowerPoint
.pot	PowerPoint template

By default, file name extensions do not automatically display. To display filename extensions, complete the following steps:

1. At the Windows 95 Desktop, double-click the My Computer icon.
2. Click View, Options, then select the View tab.
3. Remove the check mark from the Hide MS-DOS file extensions for file types that are registered check box.
4. Click OK.
5. Close the My Computer dialog box.

photo credits

The following photos are courtesy of:

Page	
2	Intel Corporation (second from top)
3	Peter Fox/Apple Computer, Inc.
29	Hewlett-Packard Company
81	Hewlett-Packard Company
151	Apple Computer, Inc.
209	Frank Pryor/Apple Computer, Inc.
263	Apple Computer, Inc.
329	Hewlett-Packard Company
369	Peter Fox/Apple Computer, Inc.
409	Peter Fox/Apple Computer, Inc.

Unit one

CREATING BUSINESS AND PERSONAL DOCUMENTS

In this unit, you will learn to define and incorporate desktop publishing concepts in the design and creation of business and personal documents.

scans

The Secretary's Commission on Achieving Necessary Skills

DECISION MAKING

TECHNOLOGY

PROBLEM SOLVING

COMMUNICATIONS

chapter ONE

Understanding the Desktop Publishing Process

PERFORMANCE OBJECTIVE

Upon completion of chapter 1, you will be able to evaluate design elements in a desktop published document for the appropriate use of focus, balance, proportion, contrast, directional flow, consistency, color, and page layout.

Desktop Publishing Concepts

Planning	Symmetrical design	Directional flow
Designing	Asymmetrical design	Consistency
Focus	Proportion	Color
Thumbnail sketch	Contrast	Page layout
Balance	White space	Grid

Word Features Used

Open a document as Read-Only	Templates
Save As	Viewing multiple pages

Defining Desktop Publishing

Since the 1970s, microcomputers have been an integral part of the business environment. Businesses use microcomputers and software packages to perform a variety of tasks. For many years, the three most popular types of software purchased for microcomputers were word processing, spreadsheet, and database.

During the past decade, another type of software program called *desktop publishing* has gained popularity with microcomputer users. With the introduction of the laser printer and its ability to produce high-quality documents, desktop publishing software became the fastest growing microcomputer application of the 1980s, and its widespread use continues well into the 1990s. Desktop publishing involves using desktop publishing software or word processing software with desktop publishing capabilities, a computer system, and a printer to produce professional-looking documents. The phrase "desktop publishing," coined by Aldus Corporation president Paul Brainard, means that publishing can now literally take place at your desk.

Until the mid-1980s, graphic design depended almost exclusively on design professionals. But desktop publishing changed all that by bringing graphic design into the office and home. Faster microprocessors, improved printer capabilities, an increased supply of clip art, CD-ROMs, and access to the Internet continue to expand the role of desktop publishing. Everything from a flyer to a newsletter to a Web page can be designed, created, and produced at a computer.

In traditional publishing, several people may be involved in completing the publication project. This may be costly and time-consuming. With the use of desktop publishing software, one person may be performing all of the tasks necessary to complete a project, greatly reducing the costs of publishing documents. The two approaches have a great deal in common. Both approaches involve planning the project, organizing content, analyzing layout and design, arranging design elements, typesetting, printing, and distributing the project.

Desktop publishing can be an individual or a combined effort. As an individual effort, desktop publishing produces immediate results and offers you the ability to control the production from beginning layout and design to the end result—printing and distribution. However, desktop publishing and traditional publishing work well together. A project may begin on a desktop, where the document is designed and created, but an illustrator may be commissioned to create some artwork, or it may end up at a commercial printer for printing and binding.

Initiating the Desktop Publishing Process

The process of creating a publication begins with two steps—planning the publication and creating the content. During the planning process, the desktop publisher must decide on the purpose of the publication and the intended audience. Although the design of a publication is important, the content of a publication must convey the intended message to the reader.

Planning the Publication

Initial planning is probably one of the most important steps in the desktop publishing process. During this stage, the following items must be addressed:

- **Clearly identify the purpose of your communication.** The more definite you are about your purpose, the easier it will be for you to organize your material into an effective communication. Are you trying to provide information? Are you trying to sell a product? Are you announcing an event?
- **Assess your target audience.** Whom do you want to read your publication? Are they employees, co-workers, clients, friends, or family? What will your target audience expect from your publication? Do they expect a serious, more conservative approach, or an informal, humorous approach?
- **Determine in what form your intended audience will be exposed to your message.** Will your message be contained in a brochure enclosed in a packet of presentation materials for a company seminar? Or will your message be in the form of a newspaper advertisement, surrounded by other

DTP POINTERS
Consider your audience when planning your publication.

advertisements? Will your message be in the form of a business card that is to be distributed when making sales calls? Or will your message be tacked on a bulletin board?

- **Decide what you want your readers to do after reading your message.** Do you want your readers to ask for more information? Do you want some kind of a response? Do you want your readers to be able to contact you in person or over the telephone?
- **Collect examples of effective designs.** Decide what you like and do not like. Try to determine why one design is more appealing than another. What elements attract your attention? Let the designs you like be a catalyst for developing your own ideas.

Creating the Content

The most important goal in desktop publishing is to get the message across. Design is important because it increases the appeal of your document, but content is still the most important consideration. Create a document that communicates the message clearly to your intended audience.

In analyzing your message, identify your purpose and start organizing your material. Establish a hierarchy of importance among the items in your communication. Consider what items will be important to the reader, what will attract the reader's attention, and what will spark enough interest for the reader to go on. Begin to think about the format or layout you want to follow. Clear and organized content combined with an attractive layout and design contribute to the effectiveness of your message.

Designing the Document

If the message is the most significant part of a communication, why bother with design? A well-planned and relevant design sets your work apart from others, and it gets people to read your message. Just as people may be judged by their appearance, a publication may be judged by its design. Design also helps organize ideas so the reader can find information quickly and easily. Whether you are creating a business flyer, letterhead, or newsletter, anything you create will look more attractive, more professional, and more convincing if you take a little extra time to design it. When designing a document, you need to consider many factors:

DTP POINTERS
Take the time to design!

- What is the intent of the document?
- Who is the intended audience?
- What is the feeling the document is meant to elicit?
- What is the most important information and how can it be emphasized?
- What different types of information are to be presented and how can these elements be distinguished and kept internally consistent?
- How much space is available?
- How is the document going to be distributed?

Answering these questions will help you determine the design and layout of your communication.

An important first step in planning your design and layout is to prepare a *thumbnail sketch*. A thumbnail sketch is a miniature draft of the document you are attempting to create. As you can see in figure 1.1, thumbnail sketches let you experiment with alternative locations for such elements as graphic images, ruled lines, columns, and borders.

Thumbnail Sketch
A rough sketch used in planning a layout and design.

figure 1.1

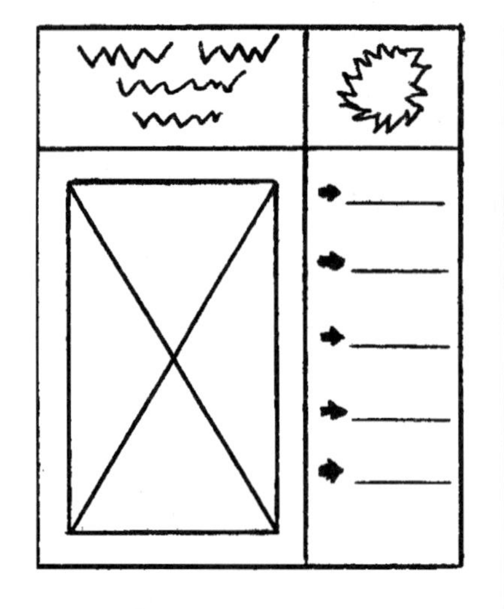

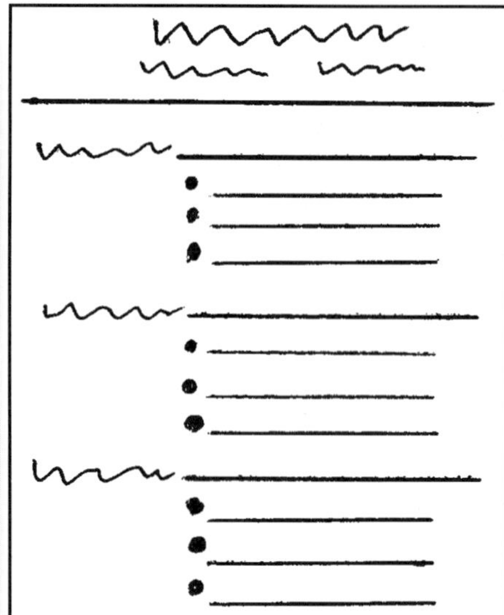

A good designer continually asks questions, pays attention to details, and makes well-thought-out decisions. Consider examples A and B in figure 1.2. Which example attracts your attention, entices you to read on, looks convincing, and would most likely encourage you to take action?

figure 1.2

PRIVATE
MUSIC LESSONS

Contact Kim Diehl at:

The Music Store
(708) 555-7867

A

Private
Music
Lessons
Contact Kim Diehl at:
The Music Store
(708) 555-7867

B

Overdesigning is one of the most common tendencies of beginning desktop publishers. Design should be used to communicate, not decorate. Although there are no hard-and-fast rules on how to arrange elements on a page, there are some basic design principles that can be used as guidelines to help you get started. To create a visually attractive and appealing publication, some concepts to consider are focus, balance, proportion, contrast, directional flow, consistency, and color.

Creating Focus

The *focus* on a page is an element that draws the reader's eyes. Focus is created by using elements that are large, dense, unusual, and/or surrounded by white space. Two basic design elements used to create focus in a document are:

- Titles, headlines, and subheads created in larger and bolder typefaces
- Graphic elements such as ruled lines, clip art, photographs, illustrations, logos, or images created with a draw program or scanned into the computer

Focus
An element that draws the reader's eyes.

Titles, Headlines, and Subheads. Untrained desktop publishers often create publications that are essentially typewritten documents that happen to be set in proportional type. With desktop publishing features, however, choice of typeface, type size, and positioning are highly flexible and can be used to create focus on the page.

In a text-only document, primary focus is usually created by using large or bold type for titles and headings, surrounded by enough white space to contrast with the main text. *White space* is the background where no text or graphics are located. The amount of white space around a focal element can enhance its appearance. The size of a headline in proportion to surrounding text is an indicator of its importance. A headline or title set in a larger type size is easily identified and immediately informs the reader of the nature of the publication. A well-designed headline not only informs, but it also attracts the reader's attention. It can play a big part in whether a reader continues reading your publication. A title/headline needs to be precisely stated and easily understood. *Legibility* is of utmost importance. Readers must be able to clearly see and read the individual letters in the headline/title. Your selection of an appropriate font (typeface, type size, and type style), the alignment of the text, and the horizontal and vertical white space surrounding the text affect the impact of your headline/title as a focal element in your document.

White Space
Background space with no text or graphics.

Legibility
The ease with which individual characters are recognized.

In any type of communication—a semi-annual report, company newsletter, advertising flyer, or brochure—subheads can be used to provide a secondary focal element. A headline may be the primary focal element used to attract the reader's attention, but the subheads may be the key to luring the reader in. Subheads provide order to your text and give the reader further clues about the content of your publication. Content divided by subheads appears more manageable to the reader's eye and lets the reader focus in on a specific area of interest. Like titles and headlines, subheads need to be concise, legible, and easy to understand. Appropriate font selection, spacing above and below the subhead, length, and alignment must be taken into consideration also.

Look at document A in figure 1.3. Can you find any focal element? Does any particular location on the page attract your attention? Now look at document B. Are your eyes drawn to a certain spot on the page? The headline, set in a larger and bolder type, definitely serves as a primary focal point. Your eyes are immediately drawn to the headline and an important question is answered for the reader; namely, what is this all about? After viewing the headline in figure 1.4, what area of the page are your eyes drawn to next? Notice how subheads set in a type bolder and larger than the body text but smaller than the heading provide secondary focal points on the page.

figure 1.3

Desktop Publishing Newsletter

November 1995 Volume 2, No. 5

Knowledge Is Power!

How can one have the up-to-date knowledge needed to keep on the cutting edge of desktop publishing? One way to have knowledge is to read some of the periodicals, newsletters, and books now available that address all aspects of desktop publishing.

Two basic types of periodicals are available. The first type is based on technological development to communication arts. These periodicals contain useful information about current and new products. The second type contains knowledge of technique, style, and applications.

Many newsletters and books are available. Listed below are some magazines, newsletters, and books that can help you as a desktop publisher.

Publish is a monthly magazine with information of interest to those involved in all areas of print and multimedia productions. The focus is on print design and production and addresses emerging technologies.

PC Publishing covers information on desktop publishing and presentation graphics for those using IBM and compatibles. Each issue addresses specific subjects with in-depth discussion.

Desktop Communications covers hardware/software, design, typography, and useful tips. Industry professionals provide extensive knowledge from their experience.

WordPerfect Magazine is a practical periodical dedicated to WordPerfect users and published by WordPerfect Corporation. It contains how-to graphic design and typographic guidance.

Before and After, a bimonthly newsletter, gives down-to-earth advice with graphic design and desktop typography.

Newsletters from the Desktop by Roger Parker has tips on saving time and money on design and layout.

The Makeover Book has 101 design solutions for desktop publishers. "Before" and "after" examples are given to show you how to make your documents more interesting and persuasive.

Training Techniques

Two types of training are available for those just beginning in desktop publishing.

The first type is a content-based program. This program is based on a typical college program and the information is presented in a classroom situation. Instructional books and videos are frequently utilized.

Skill-based training is another type of training. This training is useful to businesses as skill-based training produces capable people quickly. Productive skills are put to use on the type of job the person will be expected to fulfill.

Both types of training produce workers with equal productivity and confidence. The best equipment is wasted if people are not trained to use it efficiently. Good training, regardless of which type, is essential to desktop publishing.

A

Desktop Publishing Newsletter

November 1995 **Volume 2, No. 5**

Knowledge Is Power!

How can one have the up-to-date knowledge needed to keep on the cutting edge of desktop publishing? One way to have knowledge is to read some of the periodicals, newsletters, and books now available that address all aspects of desktop publishing.

Two basic types of periodicals are available. The first type is based on technological development to communication arts. These periodicals contain useful information about current and new products. The second type contains knowledge of technique, style, and applications.

Many newsletters and books are available. Listed below are some magazines, newsletters, and books that can help you as a desktop publisher.

Publish is a monthly magazine with information of interest to those involved in all areas of print and multimedia productions. The focus is on print design and production and addresses emerging technologies.

PC Publishing covers information on desktop publishing and presentation graphics for those using IBM and compatibles. Each issue addresses specific subjects with in-depth discussion.

Desktop Communications covers hardware/software, design, typography, and useful tips. Industry professionals provide extensive knowledge from their experience.

WordPerfect Magazine is a practical periodical dedicated to WordPerfect users and published by WordPerfect Corporation. It contains how-to graphic design and typographic guidance.

Before and After, a bimonthly newsletter, gives down-to-earth advice with graphic design and desktop typography.

Newsletters from the Desktop by Roger Parker has tips on saving time and money on design and layout.

The Makeover Book has 101 design solutions for desktop publishers. "Before" and "after" examples are given to show you how to make your documents more interesting and persuasive.

Training Techniques

Two types of training are available for those just beginning in desktop publishing.

The first type is a content-based program. This program is based on a typical college program and the information is presented in a classroom situation. Instructional books and videos are frequently utilized.

Skill-based training is another type of training. This training is useful to businesses as skill-based training produces capable people quickly. Productive skills are put to use on the type of job the person will be expected to fulfill.

Both types of training produce workers with equal productivity and confidence. The best equipment is wasted if people are not trained to use it efficiently. Good training, regardless of which type, is essential to desktop publishing.

B

figure 1.4

Desktop Publishing Newsletter

November 1995 **Volume 2, No. 5**

Knowledge Is Power!

How can one have the up-to-date knowledge needed to keep on the cutting edge of desktop publishing? One way to have knowledge is to read some of the periodicals, newsletters, and books now available that address all aspects of desktop publishing.

Two basic types of periodicals are available. The first type is based on technological development to communication arts. These periodicals contain useful information about current and new products. The second type contains knowledge of technique, style, and applications.

Many newsletters and books are available. Listed below are some magazines, newsletters, and books that can help you as a desktop publisher.

Publish is a monthly magazine with information of interest to those involved in all areas of print and multimedia productions. The focus is on print design and production and addresses emerging technologies.

PC Publishing covers information on desktop publishing and presentation graphics for those using IBM and compatibles. Each issue addresses specific subjects with in-depth discussion.

Desktop Communications covers hardware/software, design, typography, and useful tips. Industry professionals provide extensive knowledge from their experience.

WordPerfect Magazine is a practical periodical dedicated to WordPerfect users and published by WordPerfect Corporation. It contains how-to graphic design and typographic guidance.

Before and After, a bimonthly newsletter, gives down-to-earth advice with graphic design and desktop typography.

Newsletters from the Desktop by Roger Parker has tips on saving time and money on design and layout.

The Makeover Book has 101 design solutions for desktop publishers. "Before" and "after" examples are given to show you how to make your documents more interesting and persuasive.

Training Techniques

Two types of training are available for those just beginning in desktop publishing.

The first type is a content-based program. This program is based on a typical college program and the information is presented in a classroom situation. Instructional books and videos are frequently utilized.

Skill-based training is another type of training. This training is useful to businesses as skill-based training produces capable people quickly. Productive skills are put to use on the type of job the person will be expected to fulfill.

Both types of training produce workers with equal productivity and confidence. The best equipment is wasted if people are not trained to use it efficiently. Good training, regardless of which type, is essential to desktop publishing.

Graphic Elements. Graphic elements provide focus on a page and can enhance the overall appearance of a publication. Graphic elements such as ruled lines, clip art, illustrations, photos, charts, graphs, diagrams, tables, reverse text, pull quotes, and sidebars, can be used effectively to establish focus in your document.

When considering using a graphic element as a focal point, remember the following two points:

DTP POINTERS
Graphics should enhance your message, not decorate the page.

- **Communicate; don't decorate.** Let your message dictate the use of graphic elements. Does the graphic element enhance your message or does it overshadow your message? Is it relevant, meaningful, and appropriate? Do not use it just for the sake of using it.

DTP POINTERS
Keep your design simple.

- **Less is best. Simplicity rules.** Owning a CD-ROM with 10,000 clip art images does not mean that you should find as many pictures as you can to insert into your document. One simple, large, and effective graphic image provides more impact than using several smaller images. Your goal is to provide focus. Too many images create visual confusion for the reader.

If all other factors are equal, publications containing graphic elements will be noticed and perused before text-only publications. The flyer illustrated in figure 1.5 uses two graphic clip art images, one of a paint splatter and one of an artist, as focal points. The impact of the paint splatter image is enhanced by the use of color. The impact of the artist is emphasized as a solid black silhouette. Both of these images are very effective and relate well to the message within the flyer. The use of gray shading behind the picture of the artist creates the look of a framed portrait, further enhancing the graphic image and its use as a focal point. The varying typeface, type size, and density accent the information's order of importance and establish secondary focal points on the page.

figure 1.5

Four Corners Gallery

Art Studio/Gallery

- Colored Pencil Drawing
- Mixed Media
- Watercolor
- Oil Painting
- Open Workshop

203 Shore Road • Kennebunkport, ME 04104 • (207) 555-6787

6 Sessions • $60.00

Creating Balance

Balance
The equal distribution of design elements on a page.

Symmetrical Design
Balancing elements of equal weight on a page.

Asymmetrical Design
Balancing contrasting elements on a page.

Balance is attained by equally distributing the weight of various elements, such as blocks of text, graphic images, headings, ruled lines, and white space on the page. Balance can be symmetrical or asymmetrical. A *symmetrical design* contains similar elements of equal proportion or weight on the left and right sides and top and bottom of the page. Contemporary design favors *asymmetrical balance*, which is a balance of dissimilar elements on a page, such as two smaller blocks of text balanced by one larger graphic image. Asymmetrical design is more flexible and visually stimulating. In asymmetrical design, balance is created by moving, resizing, and positioning opposing elements on a page with enough contrast to be noticeable.

The Four Corners flyer in figure 1.5 illustrates an asymmetrical design that achieves balance through the use of contrasting elements. The shaded rectangular box enclosing the headline, *Four Corners Gallery, Art Studio/Gallery*, provides opposing balance to the square box containing the purple paint splatter set on a contrasting white background. Even though these two boxes and their contents are different, the weight of these contrasting elements provides a pleasing balance. The box containing the high-contrast black and white artist image effectively balances the shaded box to the right containing a bulleted listing of services offered. Although the box on the right is narrower, balance is achieved with high contrast bullets, dense type, and white space. The type size is smaller than the main heading but large enough to distribute more weight down the length of the column. An appropriate amount of white space in and around each line of text in this column adds weight and balance to the column itself.

As you can see, a block of text set in a larger and denser type can be used to offset a graphic image. A number of small graphic images can balance a large graphic or large headline. A small graphic or small block of type surrounded by white space can have the same weight as a large graphic or block of body text.

Beginning designers have a tendency to set everything centered in single-page publications and to set everything in even columns in multipage publications. This type of design results in an overall gray look to the page and is a carryover from typewriter formatting. When learning to take advantage of the great expressiveness that type and graphics can convey, viewing pages that will face each other when opened as one unit (called a two-page spread) is essential. Balance must be achieved among the elements on both pages.

Providing Proportion

Proportion
Sizing elements in relation to one another.

When designing a communication, think about all the individual parts as they relate to the document as a whole. Readers tend to view larger elements as more important. Proportionally size the visual elements in your publication according to their importance. This way you can make sure your readers see the most important information first. Readers also are more likely to read a page where all the elements are in *proportion* to one another. Appropriate typeface and type size selection for headlines, subheads, and body text can set the proportional standards for a document.

When viewing the documents in figure 1.6, look at the headline size in proportion to the body text. Think about this relationship when selecting the type size for any headlines, subheads, and body text.

figure 1.6

TOO LARGE!

When designing a page, think about all the parts as they relate to the big picture. Readers tend to view larger elements as more important.

Proportionally size the visual elements in your publication according to their importance. This way you can make sure your readers see the most important information first.

Readers also are more likely to read a page where all the elements are in proportion to one another. Appropriate typeface and type size selection of headlines, subheads, and body text can set the proportional standards for a document.

A

TOO SMALL!

When designing a page, think about all the parts as they relate to the big picture. Readers tend to view larger elements as more important.

Proportionally size the visual elements in your publication according to their importance. This

B

JUST RIGHT!

When designing a page, think about all the parts as they relate to the big picture. Readers tend to view larger elements as more important.

Proportionally size the visual elements in your publication according to their importance. This way you can make sure your

C

White space is also important in establishing proportion in your document. Margins that are too narrow create a typing line that looks long in relation to the surrounding white space. Too much white space between columns makes the line length look short. Too little space between columns makes the text harder to read. Excess white space between lines of text creates gaps that look out of proportion to the type size. Not enough white space between lines of text makes the text hard to read. Proportion must be achieved consistently throughout your whole project. A whole, integrated, unified look is established when elements are in proportion to one another.

Creating Contrast

Contrast is the difference between different degrees of lightness and darkness on the page. More conservative and formal types of documents, such as an annual report, a legal contract, a research paper, or minutes from a meeting, will have less visual contrast than an advertising flyer, a newsletter, or an announcement. Text with a low level of contrast gives an overall appearance of gray to your page. While appropriate for some situations, a higher level of contrast is more visually stimulating and can serve to keep your reader's interest longer. Sharper contrast enables the reader to distinctly identify and read all the elements on the page.

Contrast
The difference in degrees of lightness and darkness.

Consider using contrast as a way to achieve some emphasis or focus. High contrast graphics can create a powerful image or focal point. Depending on the colors used in the image, a color graphic can provide great contrast. A solid black image against a solid white background produces a sharp contrast. A graphic image in varying shades of gray or a watermark can produce contrast on a lower level. Graphic rules, whether gray shaded or 100% black, can also provide visual contrast when used alone, as part of a heading, or as a visual separator in your text.

DTP POINTERS
To create contrast, set heads and subheads in larger, denser type than the text.

Headlines and subheads set in a larger and denser type can help to create contrast on an otherwise "gray" page. Using a reverse technique for a headline or subheadings, such as white text on a black background, can create a higher level of contrast.

DTP POINTERS
Use bullets to organize information and add visual contrast.

Special characters used as bullets to define a list of important points, such as •, ■, ▼, ◆, ●, ✦, ★, ❑, ➤, ☛, ✔, and ✧, not only serve as organizational tools, but also contribute visual contrast to your page. Placing these special characters in a bolder and larger type size provides a higher level of contrast. Look at the quill pen tip bullets in figure 1.5. These high-contrast symbols help to neatly organize the services offered, provide visual contrast, and add weight and emphasis to each item listed.

White space is an important tool in achieving contrast. A more open and light feeling is projected with the increased use of white space on a page. A more closed and darker feeling is projected when use of white space is limited. Think of white space as the floor space in a room. The more furniture and accessories in the room, the more closed or crowded the room becomes. Rearranging or removing some of the furniture can provide more floor space, producing an open, lighter feeling. Your page design, like a room, may need to have some elements rearranged or removed to supply some visually contrasting white space.

DTP POINTERS
Use plenty of white space to convey an open feeling.

The use of color in a heading, a logo, a graphic image, a ruled line, or as a background can also add to the contrast level on a page. When using more than one color, select colors that provide a pleasing contrast, not colors that provide an unpleasant conflict. In addition, consider whether the color(s) being used increases or decreases the legibility of your document. Color may look nice, but it will confuse the reader if there is not enough contrast to easily identify the text. Look at the examples in figure 1.7. The level of contrast is obvious in the first two figures. In example C, notice how the text is more difficult to read with the shaded background. Use high contrast for the best legibility.

figure 1.7

LOW CONTRAST
Consider using contrast as a way to achieve some emphasis or focus. High contrast in graphics can create a powerful image or focal point. A solid black

A

HIGH CONTRAST
Consider using contrast as a way to achieve some emphasis or focus. High contrast in graphics can create a powerful image or

B

C

Creating Directional Flow

Directional Flow
A pattern that leads the reader's eye down a page.

Directional flow on a page is created by a pattern that leads the reader's eyes. This pattern can be established with the use of ruled lines, lines of type, or paths created by the placement of focal elements.

By nature, graphics and display type (larger than 14 points) act as focal elements that attract the eye as it scans a page. Positioning focal elements on a page so that the eye moves from one focal point to the next creates directional flow within a document.

Strictly symmetrical design (all elements centered) is static because the directional flow is limited to movement down the visual center of the page. If the design is asymmetrical but balanced, dynamic flow can be created with the placement of focal elements and white space, leading the eye through the text and to particular words or images that the designer wishes to emphasize. Focal elements may include a well-designed headline, logo, subheadings, ruled lines, graphic images, boxes with text inside, a chart, reverse text, or a shaded background.

When scanning a page, the eye tends to move in a Z pattern. The eye begins at the upper left corner of the page, moves to the right corner, then drops down to the lower left corner, and finally ends up in the lower right corner of the page. In text-intensive publications such as magazines, newspapers, and books, visual landmarks are frequently set in these positions. In an advertisement, the lower right corner is often where important information, such as a company name, address, and phone number, is placed.

The Low Income Housing flyer shown in figure 1.8 positions elements on the page to provide directional flow down the page. The title, serving as the focal element, is located in the upper left corner of the page, where the reader's eye is most likely to look first. The subheadings and bulleted items draw the eye down the page. The date and location of the conference, positioned in the lower left corner of the page, draw the reader's eye along the bottom and to the right with additional information about the conference. The name and telephone number of a contact person is positioned in the lower right corner of the page where the reader's eye is likely to stop.

The Z pattern is only a guideline. Since there are no hard-and-fast rules, not all designs fit exactly into this pattern. Take another look at the art studio/gallery flyer in figure 1.5. The eyes are drawn to the vivid purple paint splatter in the upper right corner. The eyes then gravitate to the left toward the headline and down toward the artist image. The eyes are then led to the right—the direction the artist is facing. The quill pen tip bullets help to supply the directional flow to the right and down the column, ending in the lower right corner.

figure 1.8

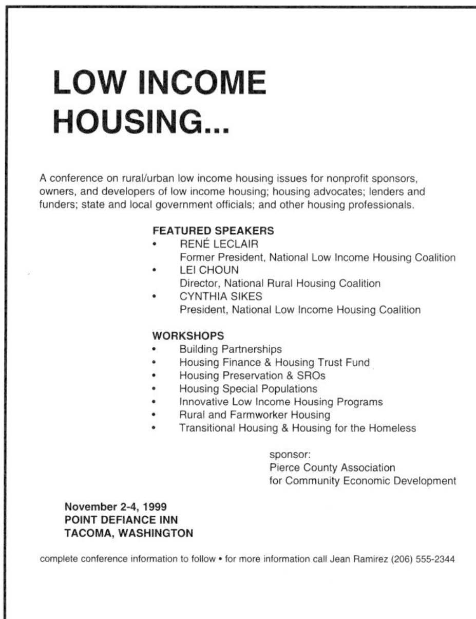

LOW INCOME HOUSING...

A conference on rural/urban low income housing issues for nonprofit sponsors, owners, and developers of low income housing; housing advocates; lenders and funders; state and local government officials; and other housing professionals.

FEATURED SPEAKERS

- RENÉ LECLAIR
  Former President, National Low Income Housing Coalition
- LEI CHOUN
  Director, National Rural Housing Coalition
- CYNTHIA SIKES
  President, National Low Income Housing Coalition

WORKSHOPS

- Building Partnerships
- Housing Finance & Housing Trust Fund
- Housing Preservation & SROs
- Housing Special Populations
- Innovative Low Income Housing Programs
- Rural and Farmworker Housing
- Transitional Housing & Housing for the Homeless

sponsor:
Pierce County Association
for Community Economic Development

November 2-4, 1999
POINT DEFIANCE INN
TACOMA, WASHINGTON

complete conference information to follow • for more information call Jean Ramirez (206) 555-2344

DTP POINTERS
Center align only small amounts of text.

Just as headlines and subheads set in larger and bolder type create focal points for your reader, they also serve as direction markers. The reader knows when to start and stop and what comes next. Directional flow can also be aided by vertical and horizontal ruled lines. Ruled lines are effective for drawing the eye across or down the page. Text alignment can also affect directional flow. Left-aligned text is the easiest to read, with all lines aligning on the left side, leaving the right margin ragged or uneven. The reader has no difficulty finding the beginning of each line. With right-aligned text—text with a ragged left margin because all lines align on the right—and centered text—text centered around a specific point, leaving both margins ragged—the reader has to spend more time finding the beginning of each line. Headers and footers, text that appears repetitively at the top or bottom of each page, also contribute to directional flow in a publication. Chapter name, chapter number, title of a report, and page numbering are common items included in headers or footers. These page identifiers direct the reader to specific locations in a document.

As in the design of balanced pages, the design of pages with good directional flow is best accomplished by experimenting with variable placement of elements on the page. Position elements on the page so the reader is directed to information in a logical order. For single-page display publications, you can consider each element, or group of elements, as a separate focus in establishing directional flow on the page. For multipage publications, you can consider body text and white space as the landscape in which focal elements are set to establish directional flow.

Establishing Consistency

Uniformity among specific design elements establishes a pattern of consistency in your document. Design elements such as margins, columns, typefaces, type sizes, spacing, alignment, and color should remain consistent throughout a document to achieve a degree of unity. In a single-page or multipage publication, consistent elements help to integrate all the individual parts into a whole unit. In a multipage publication, consistency provides the connecting element between the pages. Repetitive, consistent elements can also lend identity to your document and provide the reader with a sense of familiarity.

Consider the consistent components of this textbook. Find the first page of each chapter. The chapter titles and chapter numbers are consistent in typeface, type size, color, and position throughout the book. This consistency lets you easily identify the end of one chapter and the beginning of the next. Look at the top, bottom, and side margins on each page. For the most part, they are consistent throughout the book. Notice the headings and subheadings. Consistency exists in the typeface, size, color, and position. Examine the footers on the odd and even pages. They are consistent in their placement on the page and in the information they supply. You, as the reader, become familiar with the footers as consistent elements and depend on them for the information they provide. Glance at the captions identifying the illustrations throughout this book. The figure numbering format is consistent in every chapter. The end of the chapter sections, such as Chapter Summary, Check Your Understanding, and Skill Assessments, are also unifying elements that appear at the end of each chapter.

DTP POINTERS
Consistency establishes unity within a document.

Inconsistency can confuse and frustrate the reader. Reader frustration can lead to a reduction in your readership. Consider the following scenario. In this textbook, what if the chapter number on the chapter opening page was placed at the top of the page in one chapter, at the bottom of the page in the next, and somewhere on the left side of the page in the next chapter? What if the margins were different from page to page? What if the headings and subheadings changed typeface, size, color, and position from chapter to chapter? What if a footer existed in one chapter that contained the chapter name, number, and

DTP POINTERS
Inconsistency confuses and frustrates the reader.

page number and then was changed to a header in the next chapter? What if some figure captions were positioned at the bottom left, outside of the border, while some captions were positioned at the top right, inside the border? Does this scenario totally confuse you? Of course it does! Consistency not only establishes unity *within* a chapter (or a newsletter, or an advertisement), but it also establishes unity *among* the chapters (or a series of newsletters or advertisements).

When trying to design consistent parts of a publication, keep it simple and distinct. Simplicity is important since consistent elements are repetitive elements. Elaborate repetitive elements, such as a chapter opening page, have their place but can be distracting. Unfortunately, simple, consistent elements can sometimes be boring. Make your consistent elements distinct as well. The use of color can set some consistent elements apart. Page numbering in color, a color horizontal ruled line in a header, a color background for a reverse text heading, or color subheadings are all ways to achieve distinct consistency. Distinctiveness can also be achieved with black and white. A solid black ruled line in a header, a reverse text heading, or a contrasting typeface and type size are also effective.

Using Color

Color is a powerful tool in communicating a message and portraying an image. Color on a page can help organize ideas and highlight important facts. Publications that use color appropriately have a professional look. Color can be used to create focus, organize information, organize documents, and add emphasis to bar graphs and pie charts. Color can even elicit an emotional response from the reader. Word provides many ways of inserting color into your documents. You may use graphic pictures, borders, backgrounds, bullets, and lines of a specific design and color. You may also create your own color shapes, lines, borders, text boxes, and text.

DTP POINTERS
Use color to create focus, organize ideas, and emphasize important facts.

If a color printer is not available, consider using color paper to complement your publication. Color paper can match the tone or mood you are creating in your document. Orange paper used for a Halloween flyer is an inexpensive alternative to color graphics and text. Your audience will recognize the theme of the flyer by associating the paper color with the event. The color paper provides contrast and adds vitality and life to the publication.

You can also turn plain white documents into colorful, attention-grabbing documents by purchasing preprinted letterheads, envelopes, brochures, or presentation packets from paper supply companies or your local office supplies store. Color, emphasis, and contrast can all be achieved through an assortment of colorful page borders, patterned and solid color papers, as well as gradient color, marbleized, and speckled papers. Many of these paper suppliers provide free catalogs and offer inexpensive sample paper packets.

Even though laser printers have become more affordable, the color laser printer remains rather expensive. A less expensive alternative is the ink jet color printer. The printer uses a color ink cartridge(s) to produce the color. The copy may be slightly damp when first removed from the printer. The resolution can be improved by using specially designed ink jet paper. Some ink jet printers are capable of achieving near-photographic quality with a resolution of 720 dpi (dots per inch).

Another option for color is to send your formatted copy to a commercial printer for color printing. You can get almost any color you want from a commercial printer, but it increases the cost of the project.

DTP POINTERS
Use color sparingly.

Here are a few guidelines to follow when using color in documents:

- Use color sparingly—less is best! Limit your use of colors to two or three, including the color of the paper.
- Remember that the message is most important; color can add emphasis and style, but do not let color overpower the words!
- Text printed with light colors is difficult to read. Use light colors for shaded backgrounds or watermarks. Black text is still the easiest to read.
- Color can be used to identify a consistent element.
- Remember to use color to communicate, not decorate!

Evaluating Documents

Up to this point, you have learned the importance of carefully planning and designing your publication according to the desktop publishing concepts of focus, balance, proportion, contrast, directional flow, consistency, and color. In exercise 1, you will evaluate the document illustrated in figure 1.9. You will open a copy of the Document Analysis Guide, which is saved to your student data disk as *document analysis guide.doc*. The Document Analysis Guide will be used to analyze your intentions, decisions, and any processes you used in designing and creating your desktop documents. In addition, a Document Evaluation Checklist has been saved to your student data disk as *document evaluation checklist.doc*. The focus of this evaluation tool is directed toward the finished document. The Document Evaluation Checklist will be used in units 2 and 3. Both forms will be used to analyze your own documents, existing commercial publications, and/or other students' desktop publications.

Opening a Document as Read-Only

In Word, options exist that eliminate the risk of saving over the original copy of a document. One such option is to open a document as a *read-only* document. The words *[Read-Only]* will appear after the filename in the Title Bar. A document opened as read-only may be read, printed, or edited. However, when a read-only document is saved with the Save command, Word displays the message, *This file is read-only.* Click OK for Word to lead you to the Save As dialog box so you can enter a new name for the document. This option protects the original copy of a document from being saved with any changes. Many of the documents you will open from your student data disk will be retrieved as Open Read-Only files. To open a document as read-only, complete the following steps:

1. Click File, then Open; click the Open button on the Standard toolbar; or press Ctrl + O.
2. At the Open dialog box, click the drive, folder, or Internet location in the Look in list box that contains the desired document.
3. At the Open dialog box, click the filename of the document that you want to open as read-only.
4. Click the Commands and Settings button (the last button to the right of the Look in list box).
5. From the drop-down menu that displays, click Open Read-Only.
6. After reading or making changes to the file, choose File, then Save.
7. Click OK at the dialog box that displays the message, "This file is read-only."
8. At the Save As dialog box, key a name for the document, then choose OK.

Saving a Document with Save As

Another option that eliminates the risk of saving over the original copy of a document is to save a document using Save As. To do this, open the original document, then immediately choose File, Save As before making any editing changes. Give the document a new name, then click OK. You will be instructed to use Save As in several of the exercises in this textbook.

Saving Documents

You should periodically save your work to avoid losing it if a power or system failure occurs. This is particularly important when creating desktop published documents that involve many steps.

exercise 1

Evaluating a Document

Evaluate the flyer illustrated in figure 1.9 by completing the following steps:

1. Open as a read-only document *document analysis guide.doc* from your student data disk. This file is the Document Analysis Guide.
2. Print one copy of the Document Analysis Guide.
3. Close *document analysis guide.doc.*
4. Turn to figure 1.9 in your textbook.
5. Complete an analysis of the flyer in figure 1.9 by writing short answers to the questions in the Document Analysis Guide.
6. When completed, fill in the exercise number, located at the top of the guide, as c01ex01.

To gain more experience in analyzing documents, you will evaluate a report title page in exercise 2. To create the report title page, you will use a Word template. Templates are a wonderful feature made available in Word to assist you in creating documents when you do not have a great deal of time to create or customize your own documents from scratch. After completing this document, you will be asked to evaluate the report title page based on the Document Analysis Guide.

figure 1.9

Skyline Communications, Inc.

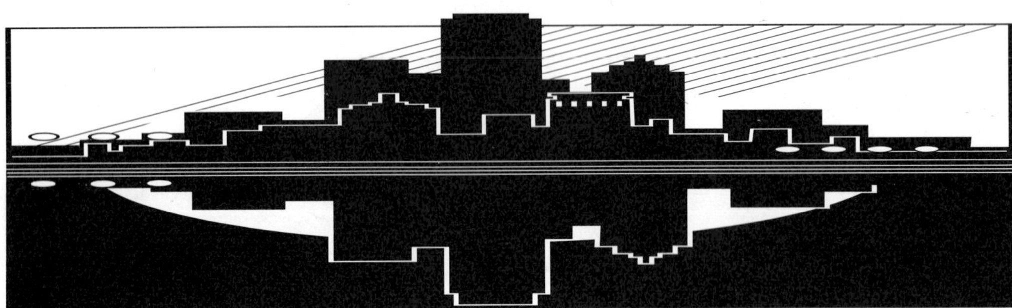

For 1998, we are offering three different formats to meet your scheduling needs:

- ➢ One-day hands-on workshops
- ➢ One-day seminars
- ➢ One-day conferences

Networking
"Establishing Relationships"

- ➢ One-day seminar
- ➢ Morris Inn, Rosemont
- ➢ May 15, 1998

Presentations
"Using Word for Windows 95"

- ➢ One-day conference
- ➢ Palmer House, Chicago
- ➢ June 5, 1998

Team Building
"Building Trust and Mutual Respect"

- ➢ One-day hands-on workshop
- ➢ Holiday Inn, Lisle
- ➢ June 19, 1998

Managing Time
"How to Get Things Done"

- ➢ One-day seminar
- ➢ Hyatt, Oak Brook
- ➢ June 19, 1998

Read over the enclosed information for details, times, and fees.
Mail or fax the attached reservation form.

Skyline Communications, Inc. ▾ 73 West 22nd Street ▾ Oak Brook, IL 60555 ▾ (708) 555-5647 ▾ Fax: (708) 555-6521

exercise 2

Producing a Report Title Page with a Word Template

1. Open as read-only *document analysis guide.doc* from your student data disk.
2. Print one copy and then close *document analysis guide.doc*.
3. At a clear editing screen, display the report title page as illustrated in figure 1.10 using the Contemporary Report template by completing the following steps:
   a. Click File, then New; or press Ctrl + N.
   b. At the New dialog box, click the Reports tab. (If the Reports tab does not display at the New dialog box, Word was installed using a typical installation and some components that you need have not been installed. Refer to the Preface and a Word reference manual to add uninstalled components.)
   c. At the New dialog box with the Reports tab selected, double-click *Contemporary Report.dot*.
4. Make sure the title page is displayed on the screen, then click the Print Preview button on the Standard toolbar.
5. With the title page displayed in the Print Preview screen, complete the Document Analysis Guide and fill in the exercise number as c01ex02, title page.
6. If you want to print the title page of the report, position the insertion point on the title page, then select the Current Page option at the Print dialog box. (Even though the globe is visible on the screen, it may not print due to the lightness of the shading. Increasing shading or changing the color of a picture will be discussed in later chapters.)
7. Close the report document without saving it.

[Type Address **Here**]

blue sky associates

FilmWatch Division
Marketing Plan

Trey's Best Opportunity to Dominate
Market Research for the Film Industry

figure 1.10

Creating a Page Layout

DTP POINTERS
Use the same margin settings throughout your entire publication.

Planning your margins is one of the first steps in designing a page layout. Using wider margins is an excellent way to add white space or breathing room around text and graphics. Margins can also be a means of creating consistency in your document. Use the same margin settings throughout your entire publication. To apply an asymmetrical design to your document, try varying the width of your margins to create a more interesting use of white space. The width of your margins is also dependent on the type size you have chosen to use. Large type sizes demand wider margins.

In addition to establishing margins for your page layout, you also need to consider the amount of text needed to express your message, the paper size desired, and the number of pages you plan to use. If you are producing a multipage publication, remember that basic elements such as margins, headers and footers, page numbers, and borders should stay consistent from page to page. Typically, when you work at a computer, you are creating and viewing one page at a time.

In designing a page layout for a multipage document, think in terms of what is called a *two-page spread* or a *two-page layout*. Pages that are viewed opposite each other when opened, as in a book or brochure format, need to be looked upon as one unit. Remember that your readers will see both pages at the same time so certain elements must remain consistent.

In Word 97, you can view your document in a two-page spread. To do this, make sure the viewing mode is Page Layout, then click the Zoom Control button on the Standard toolbar. At the drop-down menu that displays, click Two Pages. The pages appear in reduced size, but you should be able to see placement of elements, the use of white space, and certain consistencies (or inconsistencies!) between the two pages.

Word also lets you view more than two pages at a time. To do this, click View, then Zoom. At the Zoom dialog box, select Many Pages. Click the monitor icon under Many Pages and then click the page icon representing the number of pages you want to display. If you point to one of the page icons and click and drag the mouse to the right or down and to the right, you can extend the number of pages offered. The maximum number of pages that may be displayed at the same time is twelve pages displayed in two rows containing six pages in each row. The Preview box shows the number of pages that will be displayed horizontally and vertically across the screen at one time. Click OK when done. Notice the two-page and six-page spread views illustrated in figures 1.11 and 1.12. The display in figure 1.11 was achieved by selecting the second icon in the first row to display one row of two pages. The display in figure 1.12 was achieved by selecting the third icon in the second row to display two rows of three pages each.

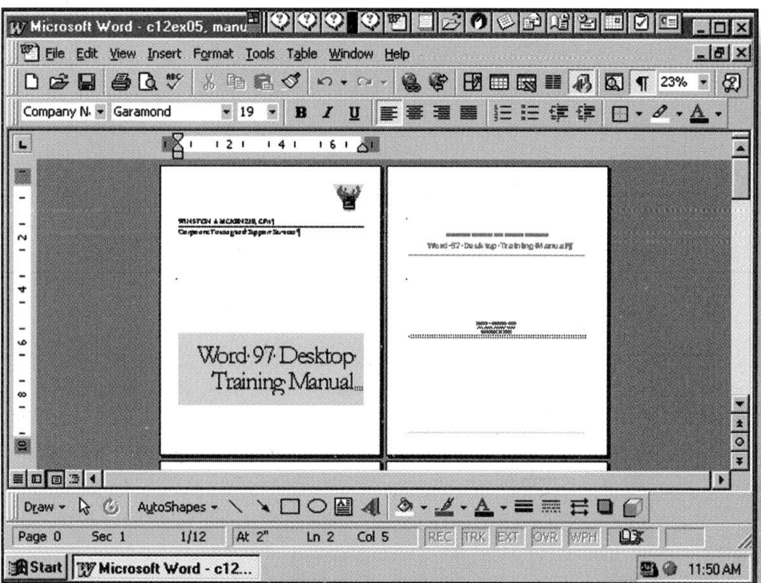

Two-Page Spread View

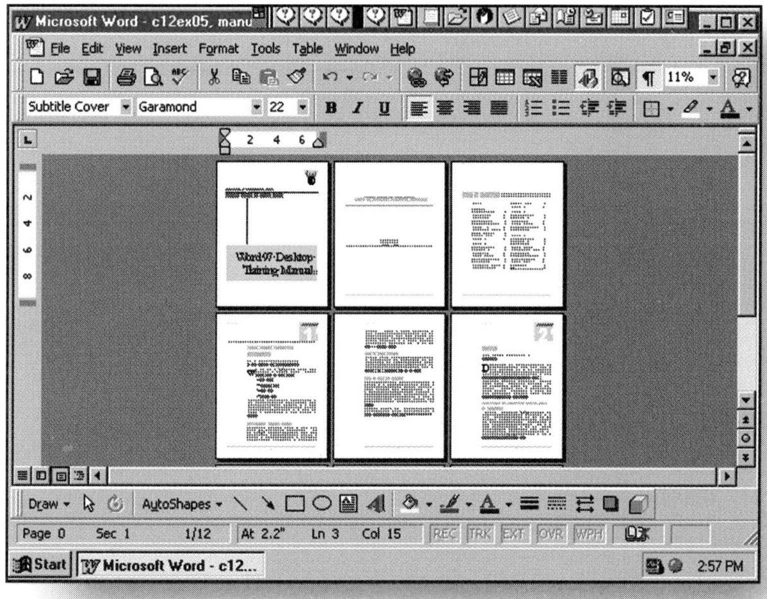

figure 1.12

Six-Page Spread View

In planning page layout, a column format is commonly used. Laying out text in columns adds visual interest and makes the text easier to read. The *gutter*, which is the space between columns, creates additional contrasting white space and serves as a separator between the columns. Text in full justification needs more column space than left-justified text. Also, text created in a larger type size demands more space between the columns than text in a smaller type size.

Gutter
The white space between columns.

The line length of each column affects the readability of your publication. Long lines of text are difficult to read because the eye can get lost reading along the line or trying to get to the next line. As a general rule, lines should be under 70 characters long but no less than 30 characters in length.

Too many columns can decrease readability and confuse your readers. In portrait orientation (when the paper's short side is the top of the paper), use no more than three columns on standard-sized paper. With a landscape orientation (when the paper's long side is the top of the paper), you can use four or five columns on standard-sized paper.

Grid
The underlying structure of a document.

In determining the exact placement of columns and varying elements on the page, a *grid* is a helpful tool. A grid is the underlying structure of a document. In some software programs, a grid appears on the screen as a non-printing framework to assist you in laying out the page. A grid can be created on a sheet of paper using a ruler and pencil. Notice the grid illustrated in figure 1.13. A grid consists of vertical and horizontal lines to be used as a guide in the placement of elements on the page. Grids enable the desktop publisher to be consistent with the location of elements and the size of columns. However, the number of columns actually used does not have to match the number of columns in the grid as long as the underlying framework is maintained. For example, notice the three-column layout with the clock graphic in figure 1.13. Even though you can only see two columns, it has an underlying structure of three columns. Notice the grid lines in the background.

The centered one-column page layout is commonly used for more formal, conservative documents such as letters, a financial report, a legal document, or a wedding invitation. Multicolumn layouts, whether equal or unequal, include such items as sales brochures, advertisements, résumés, and newsletters.

figure 1.13

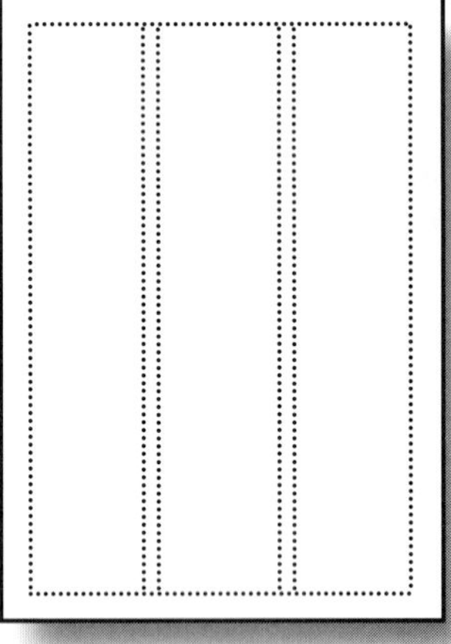

Grid

Xxxx Xxxxx

XXXXXXXXXXXXXXX
XXXXXXXXXXXXXXX
XXXXXXXXXXXXXXX
XXXXXXXXXXXXXXX
XXXXXXXXXXXXXXX
XXXXXXXXXXXXXXX
XXXXXXXXXXXXXXX

One-Column Layout

XXXXX

XXXXXXXX XXXXXXXX
XXXXXXXX XXXXXXXX
XXXXXXXX XXXXXXXX
XXXXXXXX XXXXXXXX
XXXXXXXX XXXXXXXX
XXXXXXXX XXXXXXXX
XXXXXXXX XXXXXXXX
XXXXXXXX XXXXXXXX

Two-Column Layout

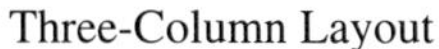

Three-Column Layout

Three-Column Layout (Left column equal to twice the width of the third column—notice the extended grid)

Three-Column Layout (Right column equal to twice the width of the first column)

Two-Page Spread

Using Word 97 in Desktop Publishing

Microsoft Word, one of the best-selling word processing programs for microcomputers, includes a wide variety of desktop publishing features. In Word 97, the scope and capabilities of these features have been expanded to include creating and designing Web pages to be placed on an Intranet or the Internet. Word 97 is a highly visual program providing an efficient means of editing and manipulating text and graphics to produce professional-looking documents and Web pages. Some of the desktop publishing features include a wide variety of fonts and special characters; drawing, charting, and text design capabilities; graphics, graphic manipulation, and image editing tools; predesigned templates; template wizards; and much more.

Putting It All Together

DTP POINTERS
Experiment with different layouts and designs.

Design can be learned by studying good design and by experimentation. Analyze what makes a specific design and layout unique and try using the same principles or variations in your publications. Take advantage of the special design and layout features that Word 97 has to offer. Take time to design. Layout and design is a lengthy process of revising, refining, and making adjustments. And above all else, *EXPERIMENT, EXPERIMENT, EXPERIMENT!* Start with small variations from the default formats to create designs that are attractive and visually interesting.

The rest of the chapters in this book will take you through the steps for creating specific business and personal desktop publishing applications, such as letterheads, business cards, résumés, flyers, brochures, Web pages, presentations, and newsletters. In addition to step-by-step directions for completing the applications using Word 97, each application will introduce guidelines relevant to that particular application as well as reinforce the design concepts introduced in this chapter.

Remember: **Take the time to design!**
Communicate; don't decorate!
Less is best!

exercise 3

Creating a Portfolio

Begin a "job-hunting" portfolio of the documents you will create in the exercises and assessments throughout this book. Exercises marked with the portfolio icon should be included in your portfolio. These documents have been chosen to show a prospective employer a wide range of your desktop publishing skills. You may also include additional documents from the chapter and unit assessments. Since the assessments are less structured than the exercises, your creativity can really shine.

You will create a title page for your portfolio in the Unit 3 Performance Assessments. As an optional assignment, you may create a table of contents after completing Unit 3. Your instructor will determine a due date and any other specific requirements for your portfolio. If possible, purchase plastic protector sheets for your documents and a binder to hold them.

chapter summary

- When creating a publication, clearly define your purpose, assess your target audience, establish where your audience will see your message, and decide what outcome you are expecting.
- Effective design involves planning and organizing content. Decide what items are most important to the reader. Design concepts such as focus, balance, proportion, directional flow, consistency, and the use of color are essential to creating a visually attractive publication.
- Focus can be created by using large and/or bold type, such as for titles and subheads; by using graphic elements, such as ruled lines, clip art, and photographs; and by using color for emphasis.
- Balance on a page is created by equally distributing the weight of elements on a page in either a symmetrical or asymmetrical manner. Symmetrical design balances similar elements of equal proportion or weight on the left and right sides and the top and bottom of the page. Asymmetrical design balances contrasting elements of unequal proportion and weight on the page.
- In establishing a proportional relationship among the elements on a page, think about all the parts as they relate to the total appearance. Proportionally size the visual elements in your publication according to their importance.
- Contrast is the difference between varying degrees of lightness and darkness on the page. A higher level of contrast is visually stimulating and can serve to keep your reader's interest longer. Sharper contrast enables the reader to distinctly identify and read all the elements on the page.
- Directional flow can be produced with ruled lines, type, or paths created by the placement of elements. A reader's eye tends to scan a page in a Z pattern.
- In determining page layout, consider the width of the margins, the amount of text in the message, the desired length of the publication, and the desired paper size.
- Pages that are viewed opposite each other when opened, as in a book or brochure format, need to be looked upon as one unit.
- Most documents are laid out in some type of a column format ranging from one column to several columns.

commands review

	Mouse/Keyboard
Open document as Read-Only	File, Open, click desired filename, click Commands and Settings button, then click Open Read-Only
Templates (New dialog box)	File, New, then click desired tab
Viewing multiple pages	View, Zoom, Many pages, then click the monitor button below and select the number of pages

check your understanding

Terms: Match the terms with the correct definitions by writing the letter of the term on the blank line in front of the correct definition.

- **A** Asymmetrical design
- **B** Balance
- **C** Consistency
- **D** Contrast
- **E** Desktop publishing
- **F** Directional flow
- **G** Focal point
- **H** Grid
- **I** One-column
- **J** Proportion
- **K** Symmetrical design
- **L** Thumbnail sketch
- **M** Traditional publishing
- **N** White space

_____ 1. Areas in a document where no text or graphics appear.

_____ 2. Page design containing similar elements of equal weight distributed evenly on the page.

_____ 3. Process of creating publications with the cooperation of several people, each performing specific tasks.

_____ 4. An element that draws the reader's eye to a particular area in the document.

_____ 5. The difference between varying degrees of lightness and darkness on the page.

_____ 6. Pattern established by the use of ruled lines, lines of type, or paths created by the placement of focal elements.

_____ 7. Process where one person can accomplish the tasks of several people by using a computer, a software program, and a printer to design, create, and print a document.

_____ 8. A preliminary rough draft of the layout and design of a document.

_____ 9. Uniformity among specific design elements in a publication.

_____ 10. The sizing of various elements so that all parts relate to the whole.

_____ 11. Contemporary design where balance is created by positioning opposing elements on the page with enough contrast to be noticeable.

_____ 12. The underlying structure of a page layout.

_____ 13. Common page layout used for more formal, conservative documents.

skill assessments

Assessment 1

In this skill assessment, you will begin a *presentation* project. The purpose of this assignment is to provide you with experience in planning, organizing, creating, and making a class presentation using Microsoft Word or PowerPoint. Specific instructions are provided for you in the document named *presentation.doc* located on your student data disk. To print this document, complete the following steps:

1. Open as read-only *presentation.doc* from your student data disk.
2. Print one copy and then close *presentation.doc*.

Begin researching a topic for your presentation. You may compose and create a presentation on a desktop publishing or Web publishing article or concept, a Word or PowerPoint desktop publishing or Web publishing feature(s) or process used to create a specific document, or an instructor-approved topic that you would like to share with your class. Include any Word or PowerPoint tips or techniques you may have discovered while creating your presentation. Use any one of the many desktop publishing, Word, and PowerPoint resources available at your local library or bookstore. You may consider using any of the topics presented in this textbook. Your instructor will notify you of a scheduled date for your presentation.

Assessment 2

The information highway is littered with well-designed and poorly designed documents. Looking critically at as many publications as possible will give you a sense of what works and what does not. In this skill assessment, find three different examples of documents—flyers, newsletters, résumés, brochures, business cards, announcements, certificates, etc. Evaluate these documents according to the desktop publishing concepts discussed in this chapter using the Document Analysis Guide located on your student data disk. To do this, complete the following steps:

1. Open as read-only *document analysis guide.doc* from your student data disk.
2. Print three copies of this form and then close *document analysis guide.doc*.
3. Complete the evaluation forms and attach them to the front of each example document. Write the exercise number as c01sa02 on the front of each form.

Assessment 3

In this assessment, you will evaluate a poorly designed flyer according to the items listed on the Document Analysis Guide located on your student data disk. On a separate piece of paper, list three suggestions to improve this flyer.

1. Open as read-only *document analysis guide.doc* on your student data disk.
2. Print one copy, then close *document analysis guide.doc*.
3. Open as a read-only document *cleaning flyer.doc* on your student data disk.
4. Print one copy, then close *cleaning flyer.doc*.
5. Complete the Document Analysis Guide and name the exercise c01sa03. List your three suggestions for improvement on the back of this form.

creative activity

You have been asked to create flyers for the situations described below. Draw two thumbnail sketches, using lines, boxes, and rough drawings to illustrate the placement of text and graphics on the page. You decide how to include focus, balance, proportion, contrast, white space, directional flow, and consistency in your thumbnail sketches. Be sure to consider the purpose and target audience for each situation. Designate areas in your sketches for such items as time, date, location, and response information. Label your sketches as c01ca01.

Situation 1: Annual office golf outing

Situation 2: Software training seminar

chapter TWO

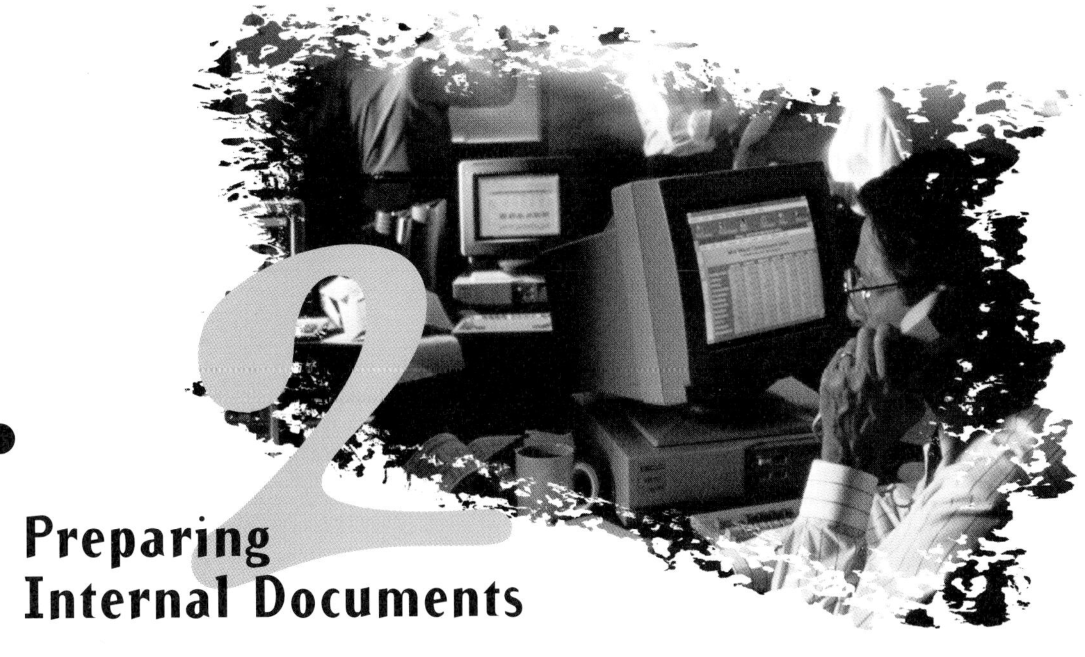

Preparing Internal Documents

PERFORMANCE OBJECTIVE

Upon successful completion of chapter 2, you will be able to produce internal business documents such as memos, agendas, press releases, and fax cover sheets with a variety of typefaces, type styles, type sizes, and special symbols.

Desktop Publishing Concepts

- Font selection
- Typeface
- Type size
- Type style
- Readability
- Spacing after end-of-sentence punctuation
- Using special characters and symbols
- Em dash
- En dash
- Quotation marks
- Apostrophe
- Watermark
- Bullets

Word Features Used

- Templates
- Wizards
- Special characters
- Smart Quotes
- AutoFormat
- Headers and footers
- Watermark
- Text boxes
- Send Behind Text
- Image Control
- Borders and shading
- Tables

Understanding Basic Typography

A document created on a typewriter generally contains uniform characters and spacing. A typeset document may contain characters that vary in typeface, size, and style and that are laid out on the page with variable spacing.

In this chapter, you will produce internal business documents using Word's Template feature and produce and format your own business documents. An important element in the creation of internal business documents such as memos, agendas, and press releases is the font used to format the text.

Information on the elements of a font as well as how to choose a font is presented in this chapter. You will use this information to prepare documents in this chapter as well as documents presented in the remaining chapters. To choose a font for a document, you need to understand basic typography and the terms that apply.

As you learned in chapter 1, a professional graphic designer considers many factors when creating a document, including the intent of the document, the audience, the feeling the document is to elicit, and the important information that should be emphasized. These factors help the graphic designer determine the layout of the document and the type specifications. With Word, which contains desktop publishing features, the originator of the document rather than a graphic designer can make these decisions. The person creating the document chooses the type specifications, determines the layout, and produces the final product.

Before selecting the type specifications to be used in a document, the terms used in desktop publishing need to be defined. Terms that are used to identify the type specifications are typeface, type size, and type style.

Choosing a Typeface

Typeface
A set of characters with a common design and shape.

A *typeface* is a set of characters with a common general design and shape. One of the most important considerations in establishing a particular mood or feeling in a document is the typeface. For example, a decorative typeface may be chosen for invitations or menus, while a simple block-style typeface may be chosen for headlines or reports. Choose a typeface that reflects the content, your audience expectations, and the image you want to project.

Baseline
An imaginary horizontal line on which type characters rest.

There are characteristics that distinguish one typeface from another. Type characters rest on an imaginary horizontal line called the *baseline.* From this baseline, parts of type may extend above the baseline and/or below the baseline. Figure 2.1 illustrates the various parts of type.

Parts of Type

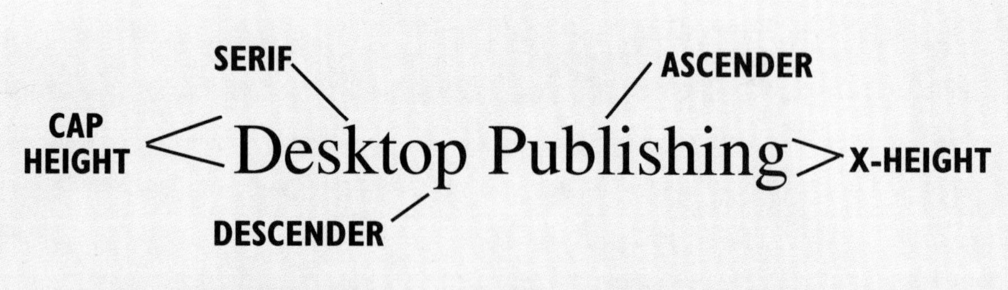

x-Height
Height of lowercase x.

Serif
A small stroke at the end of a character.

The *x-height* is the height of the main body of the lowercase characters and is equivalent to the lowercase *x*. The cap height is the distance between the baseline and the top of capital letters. Ascenders are the parts of lowercase characters that rise above the x-height, and descenders are parts of characters that extend below the baseline. *Serifs* are the small strokes at the ends of characters.

There are many typefaces, and new designs are created on a regular basis. A variety of typefaces are popular with desktop publishing programs, including Arial, Times New Roman, Bookman Old Style Bold, Garamond, Century Gothic, Impact, Matura MT Script Cap, and more.

Typefaces are either monospaced or proportional. A monospaced typeface allots the same amount of horizontal space for each character and is rarely used in professional publications. Courier is an example of a monospaced typeface. Proportional typefaces allow a varying amount of space for each character. For example, the lowercase letter *i* takes up less space than an uppercase *M*. Also, different proportional typefaces take up different amounts of horizontal space. The same sentence in Times New Roman, for example, takes up less horizontal space when set in the same size Century Gothic.

Proportional typefaces are divided into two main categories: serif and sans serif. As mentioned earlier, a serif is a small stroke at the edge of a character. Traditionally, a serif typeface is used with documents that are text intensive (documents that are mainly text, such as business letters) because the serifs help move the reader's eyes across the page.

A *sans serif* typeface does not have serifs (*sans* is French for *without*). Sans serif typefaces are often used for headlines and advertisements that are not text intensive. In modern designs, sans serif typefaces may also be used for body text. Figure 2.2 shows examples of serif typefaces. Figure 2.3 shows examples of sans serif typefaces.

Sans Serif
Without a small stroke at the end of a character.

Book Antiqua
Bookman Old Style Bold
Footlight MT Light
Garamond
Century Schoolbook
Times New Roman

figure 2.2
Serif Typefaces

Arial
Arial Narrow
Arial MT Black
Arial Rounded MT Bold
Century Gothic
Impact
Kino MT

figure 2.3
Sans Serif Typefaces

DTP POINTERS
Use a sans serif font for headings.

DTP POINTERS
Use a serif font for text-intensive documents.

The field of desktop publishing has a set of general guidelines, or conventions, that provide a starting point for designing documents. A guideline for selecting typefaces is to use no more than two different typefaces in the same document. Too many typefaces and styles give the document a disorderly appearance, confuse the reader, and take away from the content of the document.

For publications, especially those that are not text intensive, one typeface with different type sizes and type styles used to distinguish elements is usually adequate. To emphasize headings and other important elements, a typeface that is distinct from the body text typeface may be used.

Display type (titles and headings) are sometimes set in a sans serif typeface and the body text in a serif typeface, since the uniform strokes of a sans serif typeface give the appearance of greater density than a serif typeface. For example, an Arial typeface may be used for headlines, headings, and subheadings, with a Garamond typeface used for the text within the body. Fonts such as Arial MT Black, Braggadocio, Colonna MT, Impact, and Wide Latin would be appropriate choices for display text.

Script fonts resemble handwriting and are frequently used in formal documents, such as invitations and social announcements. Avoid using all caps with script fonts because they will not be legible. Figure 2.4 displays fonts that match the mood and tone of your message.

Fonts That Match the Tone of Your Message

Calling All Students!	Braggadocio
25th Anniversary	Brush Script MT Italic
Four Corners Art Gallery	Matura MT Script Cap
FUNFEST '97	Impact
DESIGN 2000	DESDEMONA
Antique Auction	Colonna MT
Line Dancing Classes Available	Playbill

Choosing a Type Size

Point Size
A vertical measurement; a point is approximately 1/72 of an inch.

Pitch
The number of characters that can be printed in 1 horizontal inch.

Type size (font size) is defined by two categories: *point size* and *pitch*. Proportional typefaces can be set in different sizes. The size of proportional type is measured vertically in units called *points* (measured vertically from the top of the ascenders to the bottom of the descenders). A point is approximately 1/72 of an inch. The higher the point size, the larger the characters. When keying a point measurement in a Word dialog box, you must use the abbreviation *pt* to indicate a point increment.

There are common point sizes used in typesetting. Some common sizes are 6, 8, 9, 10, 11, 12, 14, 18, 24, 36, and 48. These sizes date back to the time when typesetters cut blocks of wood for each character in a particular typeface, size, and style. The use of standard sizes reduced the number of wood blocks required. Figure 2.5 shows Garamond and Arial typefaces in a variety of point sizes:

8-point Garamond
12-point Garamond
18-point Garamond
24-point Garamond

8-point Arial
12-point Arial
18-point Arial
24-point Arial

figure 2.5

Varying Garamond and Arial Point Sizes

Monospaced typefaces are measured by the number of characters that can be printed in one horizontal inch. This measurement is known as *pitch*. For some printers, the pitch is referred to as *cpi*, or characters per inch. Examples of monospaced fonts include Courier and Courier New.

Choosing a Type Style

Within a typeface, characters may have a varying *type style (font style)*. The standard style of the typeface is referred to as *Roman* for some typefaces and as *regular* for others. In addition to the standard style, other styles include *bold*, *italic*, and *bold italic*. Figure 2.6 illustrates two type styles in 12-point type.

Type Style
Variations of the basic type design, including regular or normal, bold, and italics.

Century Schoolbook Regular
Century Schoolbook Italic
Century Schoolbook Bold
Century Schoolbook Bold Italic

Century Gothic Regular
Century Gothic Italic
Century Gothic Bold
Century Gothic Bold Italic

Type Styles in 12-Point Type

Choosing a Font

The term *font* describes a particular typeface in a specific style and size. Some examples of fonts include 10-point Arial, 12-point Times New Roman Bold, and 12-point Century Gothic Italic. Types of fonts available depend on the printer and soft fonts or cartridges you are using.

Font
A particular typeface in a specific style and size.

Choosing a Printer Font

The printer that you are using has built-in fonts. These fonts can be supplemented with cartridges and/or soft fonts. The types of fonts you have available with your printer depend on the type of printer you are using, the amount of memory installed with the printer, and the supplemental fonts you have. A font cartridge is inserted directly into the printer and makes more fonts accessible. To install a font cartridge, refer to the documentation that comes with the cartridge.

Soft fonts are available as software on disk or CD-ROM. Before you can use soft fonts, the fonts must be installed. Many TrueType soft fonts were installed with Microsoft Word. Fonts can also be copied from the Word 97 and the Office 97 CDs. (See your program manual for information on copying these fonts to your hard drive.)

All these fonts are displayed in the Font dialog box. Some other fonts also may be listed in the Font dialog box. These fonts are a shared resource from other Windows-based software programs already installed on your hard drive. You will use many TrueType typefaces as you create documents in this book. If your printer does not support a font or size you are using to format your text, Word may substitute the closest possible font and size. If the textbook calls for a particular font and you do not have this font, select a similar one.

Using the Font Dialog Box

The fonts available with your printer and with Word are displayed in the Font list box at the Font dialog box. To display the Font dialog box shown in figure 2.7, click Format, then Font or click the down arrow to the right of the Font list box at the Formatting toolbar.

Font Dialog Box

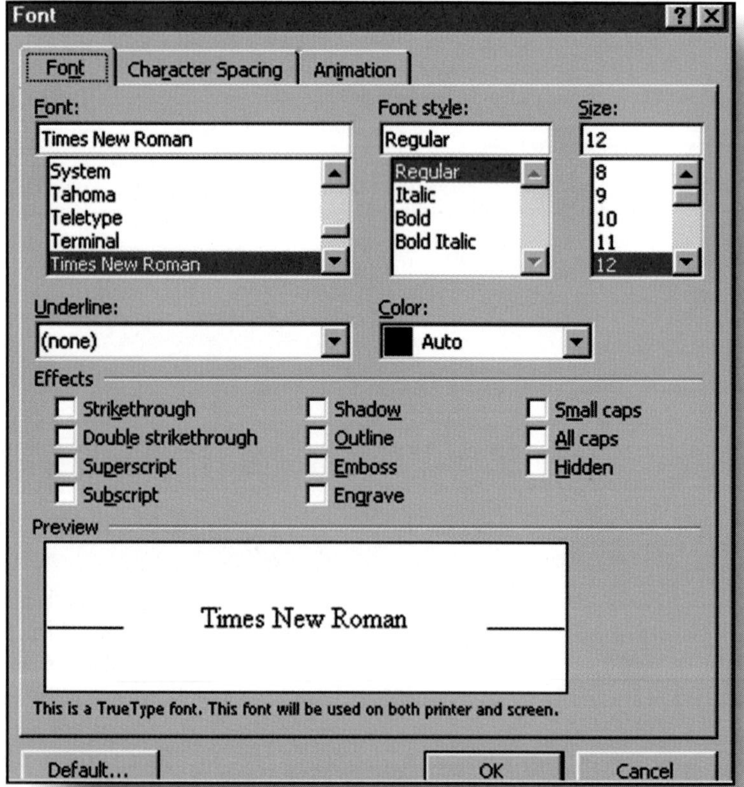

Changing the Default Font

Each printer defaults to a specific font. The default font setting dictates the font Word defaults to every time the program is loaded or a new blank document is opened. The default font is 10-point Times New Roman. To change this, click Format, then Font. At the Font dialog box, select the new defaults you want to use, then click the Default button. At the dialog box stating that the change will affect all new documents based on the NORMAL template, click Yes. (The Normal template will be explained later in this chapter.)

When you exit Word for Windows, you may see a message box asking whether you want to save changes to Word for Windows. At this message box, click Yes. When you change the default font, the change is in effect for all documents you create. Font selections made within a document through the Font dialog box will override the default font settings for the current document only.

For this textbook, use 12-point Times New Roman as the default font.

Changing Typefaces

The Font list box at the Font dialog box displays the typefaces available with your printer. The printer or printers you install determine what fonts are available. An HP LaserJet printer, for example, may include CG Times, Times New Roman, Palatino, Bookman, and Avant Garde.

DTP POINTERS
Use a typeface that reflects the tone of the document.

An icon may display before the typefaces in the Font list box. TrueType fonts are identified with the TT icon. TrueType typefaces are *graphically* generated and may take a little longer to print. The fonts that display without a preceding icon are usually nonscalable fonts, printer-generated fonts, or various other types of fonts.

To choose a typeface in the Font list box, select the desired typeface, then click OK or press Enter. You can also double-click the desired typeface. When you select a typeface in the Font list box, the Preview box in the lower right corner displays the appearance of the selected typeface. A message at the bottom of the Font dialog box provides information about the type of font selected. Often documents created in Word are keyed first and then formatted later. In these instances, you need to select the text first, then change the font and any of its attributes.

DTP POINTERS
Text set in a large, dense font adds weight, balance, and contrast to a document.

In addition to the Font dialog box, a typeface can be chosen from the Font drop-down menu. To display this drop-down menu, click the down arrow to the right of the Font list box on the Formatting toolbar. To choose a typeface from the list, click the desired typeface. As you choose typefaces, Word displays the most recently chosen typefaces at the top of the drop-down menu.

Changing Type Size

The Size list box at the Font dialog box displays a variety of common type sizes. Decrease point size to make text smaller or increase point size to make text larger. To select a point size, click the desired point size. You can also key a specific point size. The Font Size drop-down list displays various sizes ranging from 8 points to 72 points. However, you may key a point size not listed. For instance, to create a font size of 250 points, position the arrow pointer on the number immediately below Size, click the left mouse button, then key 250.

In addition to the Font dialog box, you can use the Font Size button on the Formatting toolbar to change type size (third button from the left). To change the type size with the Font Size button, click the Font Size button, and then from the drop-down menu that displays, click the desired point size or key a point size.

The point size of selected text can also be increased by one point by pressing Ctrl +]. The shortcut key combination to decrease the point size is Ctrl + [.

Changing Type Style

The Font style list box at the Font dialog box displays the styles available with the selected typeface. As you select different typefaces, the list of styles changes in the Font style list box. To choose a type style, click the desired style in the Font style list box.

Selecting Underlining

In desktop publishing, underlining has become somewhat dated with the availability of many other text attributes. In place of underlining, consider enhancing your text with italics, bold, a different font size, all caps, or small caps. To use the underline feature in the Font dialog box, first select any desired text, then at the Font dialog box, click the down arrow to the right of the Underline list box. From the list that displays, select one of the following choices: (none), Single, Words only, Double, Dotted, Thick, Dash, Dot dash, Dot dot dash, and Wave.

The AutoFormat feature (click Format, AutoFormat, then Options) will automatically apply underlining to text if you key an underline immediately followed by text and another underline. You must first select the *Bold* and _underline_with real formatting check box at the AutoFormat and AutoFormat As You Type tabs of the AutoFormat feature as shown in figure 2.8.

AutoFormat Feature

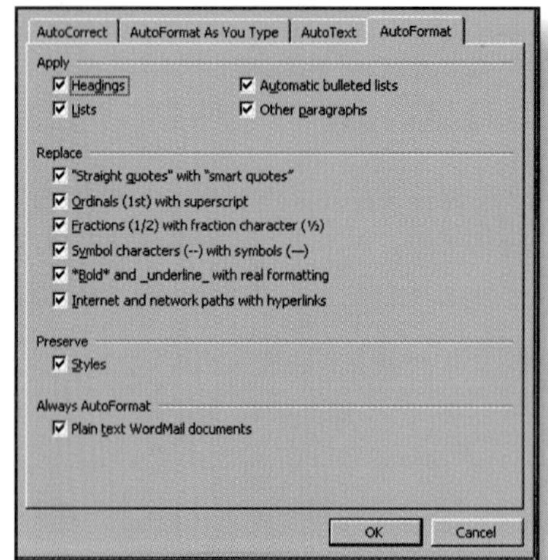

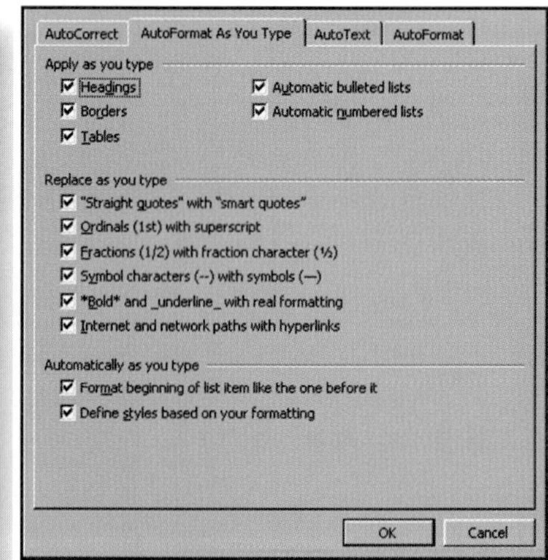

Changing Effects

The Effects section of the Font dialog box contains a variety of options that can be used to create different character formatting, such as Strikethrough, Double strikethrough, Superscript, Subscript, Shadow, Outline, Emboss, Engrave, Small caps, All caps, and Hidden. To choose an effect, click the desired option. The text in the Preview box will reflect the change. If the text already exists, select the text before applying these formatting options. Figure 2.9 illustrates a few of the new font effects now available in Word 97.

DTP POINTERS
Use italics or small caps to emphasize text instead of all caps or underlining.

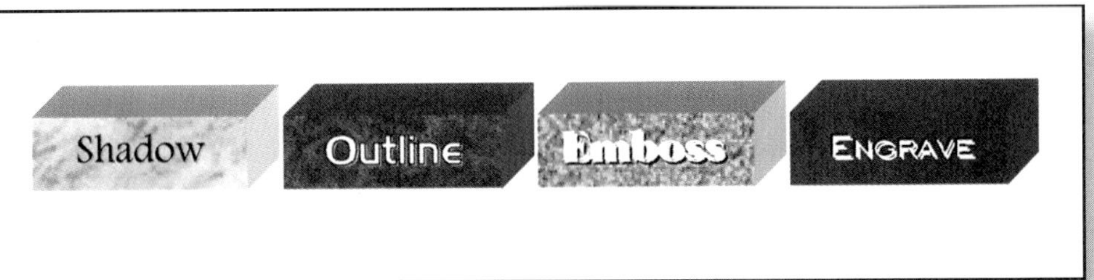

figure 2.9

Four New Font Effects (Displayed in 3-D Text Boxes with Textured Fill Color)

Changing Font Color

Font Color

Select the text you want to change to another color. At the Color section of the Font dialog box, click the down arrow to the right of the Color list box. At the drop-down list, select a font color that will enhance the appearance of your document. Font Color can also be accessed by clicking the Font Color button on the Formatting toolbar or on the Drawing toolbar. Clicking the down arrow to the right of the Font Color button will provide you with a palette of 16 font color choices.

Bold

Italic

Enhancing Text Using the Formatting Toolbar

Underline

In addition to the character enhancements available to you in the Font dialog box, the appearance of your text can also be changed using bold, italics, underlining, highlighting, and font color from the Formatting toolbar, as shown in figure 2.10. Highlighting lets you call attention to a specific area of text. Click any one of these features, then key your text; or if the text already exists, select the text you want to format, then click the buttons that correspond with the formatting you want to apply.

Highlight

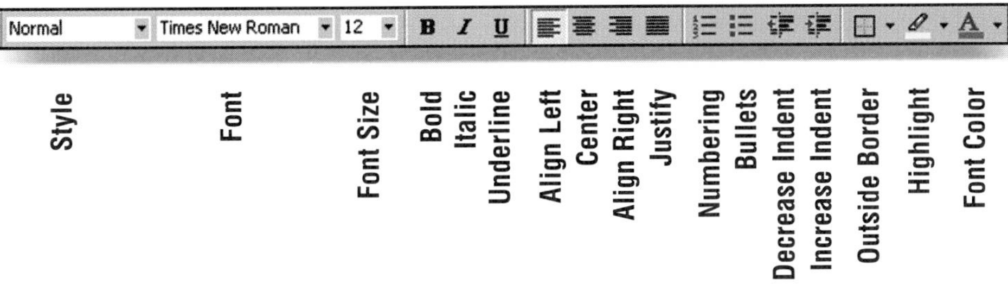

figure 2.10

Formatting Toolbar

You can also use the following keyboard commands to activate formatting commands: Ctrl + B for bold, Ctrl + I for italics, and Ctrl + U for underlining. To change the color of the highlighting, click the down arrow to the right of the Highlight button. At the drop-down list of colors that displays, click the desired color.

The AutoFormat feature (click Format, AutoFormat, then Options) will automatically format text with bold and underlining if the *Bold* and _underline_with real formatting check box has been selected on the AutoFormat and AutoFormat As You Type tabs.

Spacing Punctuation

DTP POINTERS
When using proportional fonts, space once after end-of-sentence punctuation. Do not use the space bar to align text.

When keying a document in a monospaced font, such as Courier, end-of-sentence punctuation such as the period, exclamation point, and question mark is followed by two spaces. When creating a document set in a proportional typeface, space only once after end-of-sentence punctuation as well as after a colon (except a colon used to indicate a ratio, such as 1:3). Proportional type is set closer and extra white space at the end of sentences is not needed. If the extra white space is added, the text will appear blotchy.

With Word's Replace feature, you can search for ending punctuation followed by two spaces and replace it with the same punctuation followed by one space. Click Edit, then Replace. At the Find what text box of the Replace dialog box, key a period then press the space bar twice. At the Replace with text box, key a period, then press the space bar once. Click the Find Next button, then click the Replace button. To automatically replace all occurrences of the correction, click the Replace All button.

Creating Documents Using Templates and Wizards

Template
A preformatted document layout that can be used again and again.

Every document created in Word is based on a *template*. When you create a document at a clear document screen, you are using the default template. This default template, called the *Normal.dot* template, establishes the formatting for the document, including margins, tabs, font, etc. Besides the *Normal.dot* template, the most commonly used templates are the memo and report templates.

Time spent designing and formatting basic documents is not productive. You can save time by creating a variety of documents using Word's predesigned templates, such as agendas, awards, brochures, business reports, calendars, fax cover sheets, letters, memos, newsletters, résumés, and more. To display the types of templates available, click File, then New. The predefined templates are organized on different tabs in the New dialog box. The Memos tab is shown in figure 2.11. (Similar template types are available through the Memo Wizard.)

figure 2.11

New Dialog Box with the Memos Tab Selected

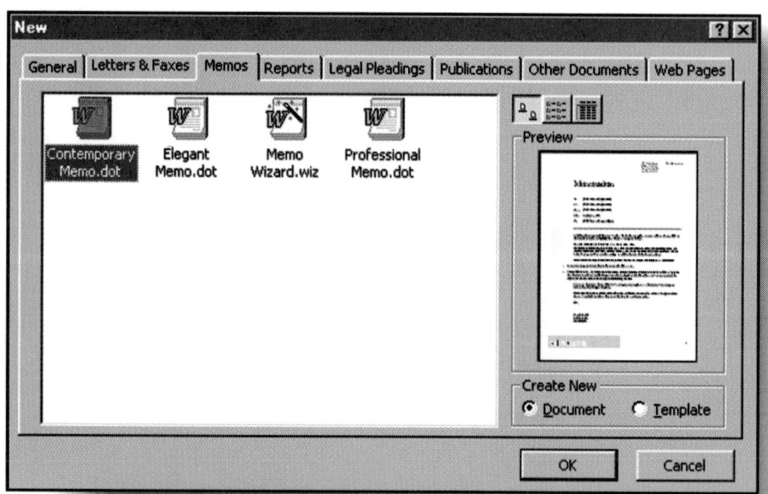

If you select the Memos tab, Word displays Memo icons representing *Contemporary Memo, Elegant Memo,* and *Professional Memo* templates. Figure 2.12 shows the three types of memo templates and the formatting used for each. The use of consistent formatting within each category lends a harmonious, professional appearance to your documents. For instance, use the same category of template for a cover letter, résumé, and follow-up letter to show consistency.

The memo templates contain "Click **here** and type" features that make creating memos easier. To fill in areas containing this prompt, click and then key text between the brackets. Select the placeholder text in the memo body location, then key your memo. Prompts will suggest that you use styles such as Heading 1-3, Body Text, and List Bullet in the Style button on the Formatting toolbar. More information on styles will be presented in later chapters.

Each tab in the New dialog box corresponds to the name of a subfolder (subdirectory) in the template folder (directory). To change the folder Word uses for templates, click Tools, then Options. At the Options dialog box, click the File Locations tab. At the Options dialog box with the File Locations tab selected, click Modify, then choose a new template folder.

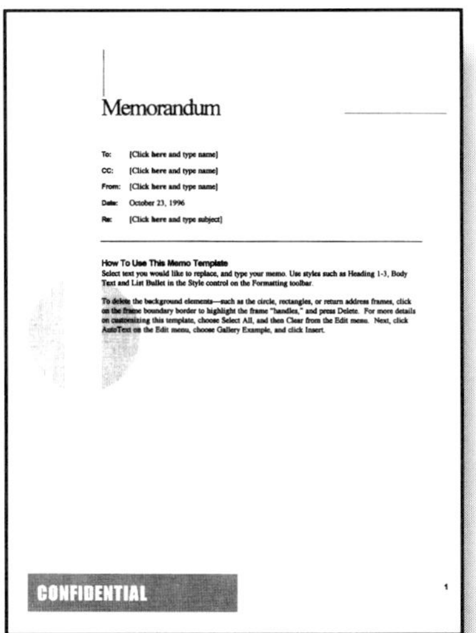

Memorandum

To: [Click here and type name]
CC: [Click here and type name]
From: [Click here and type name]
Date: October 23, 1996
Re: [Click here and type subject]

How To Use This Memo Template
Select text you would like to replace, and type your memo. Use styles such as Heading 1-3, Body Text and List Bullet in the Style control on the Formatting toolbar.

To delete the background elements—such as the circle, rectangles, or return address frames, click on the frame boundary border to highlight the frame "handles," and press Delete. For more details on customizing this template, choose Select All, and then Clear from the Edit menu. Next, click AutoText on the Edit menu, choose Gallery Example, and click Insert.

CONFIDENTIAL

1

CONTEMPORARY

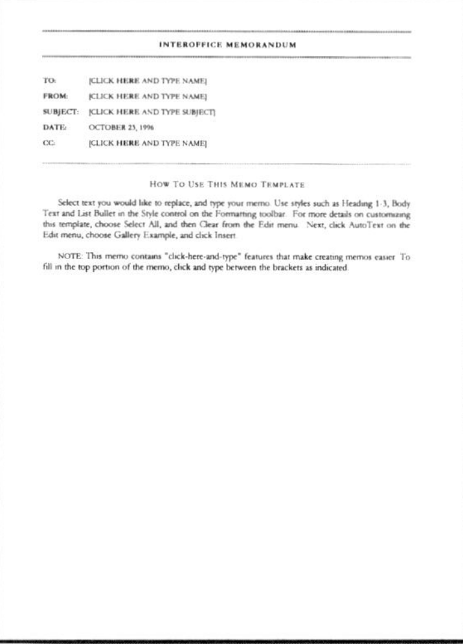

INTEROFFICE MEMORANDUM

TO: [CLICK HERE AND TYPE NAME]
FROM: [CLICK HERE AND TYPE NAME]
SUBJECT: [CLICK HERE AND TYPE SUBJECT]
DATE: OCTOBER 23, 1996
CC: [CLICK HERE AND TYPE NAME]

HOW TO USE THIS MEMO TEMPLATE

Select text you would like to replace, and type your memo. Use styles such as Heading 1-3, Body Text and List Bullet in the Style control on the Formatting toolbar. For more details on customizing this template, choose Select All, and then Clear from the Edit menu. Next, click AutoText on the Edit menu, choose Gallery Example, and click Insert.

NOTE: This memo contains "click-here-and-type" features that make creating memos easier. To fill in the top portion of the memo, click and type between the brackets as indicated.

ELEGANT

figure 2.12

Memo Templates

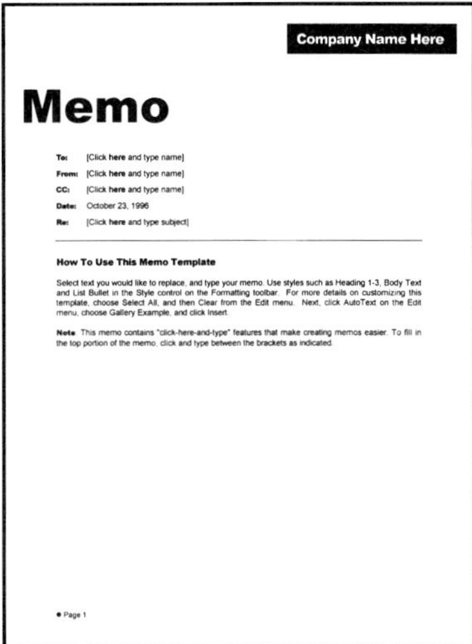

Company Name Here

Memo

To: [Click **here** and type name]
From: [Click **here** and type name]
CC: [Click **here** and type name]
Date: October 23, 1996
Re: [Click **here** and type subject]

How To Use This Memo Template

Select text you would like to replace, and type your memo. Use styles such as Heading 1-3, Body Text and List Bullet in the Style control on the Formatting toolbar. For more details on customizing this template, choose Select All, and then Clear from the Edit menu. Next, click AutoText on the Edit menu, choose Gallery Example, and click Insert.

Note: This memo contains "click-here-and-type" features that make creating memos easier. To fill in the top portion of the memo, click and type between the brackets as indicated.

• Page 1

PROFESSIONAL

Wizards walk you through a series of steps in which you add or select information to set up formatting, content, and layout of your document. When you finish the wizard, the Office Assistant provides interactive assistance in making changes to your document, sending the document via E-mail or fax, or selecting from many other options.

Office Assistant

Copying and Downloading Additional Templates

If a template used in an exercise is not available to you, check with your instructor to make sure that all the templates included in the ValuPack folder on your program disks or CD have been copied to your hard drive or network. If you installed Microsoft Word from a CD, insert the disk and double-click on the ValuPack folder to see what other templates and wizards are available. Copy the files you want to the Templates folder for Word 97 on your hard drive or create your own folder for the templates. The selected templates and wizards will display in various tabs at the New dialog box. For instance, to copy the Webpage.wiz located on the Office 97 CD-ROM, follow this path: Office97pro (D:)\Valupack\Template\Word\Manual.dot or Office97pro (D:)\Template\Webpages \Webpage.wiz., then copy the templates to C:\Program Files\Microsoft Office \Templates\Publications (or another specific template folder or create your own folder).

Additionally, you may download free templates and wizards from the Microsoft Office Web Site. (Many of the same templates are available in the ValuPack folder.) To find the templates, first make sure you are connected to the Internet, then click Help, point to Microsoft on the Web, and then click Free Stuff. Follow the on-screen prompts to load these items. They also will display in the New dialog box. (Free Stuff may include: Microsoft Word 97 HR/Ops Template Pack, Microsoft Word 97 Sales & Marketing Template Pack, and Microsoft Word 97 Time Management Wizard Pack.)

Customizing Templates

Templates and wizards can help you create great-looking documents. But if you do not want your documents to look the same as the next person's documents or if you want more variety in your formatting, consider some of the following suggestions (many of the features listed below will be discussed in greater detail in later chapters):

- Change fonts, font styles, and/or font sizes
- Add font color
- Add font effects—bold, underlines, color, small caps, shadow, emboss, engrave, etc.
- Use expanded or condensed character spacing
- Use raised or lowered character spacing
- Use reverse text
- Add fill color and fill effects—gradient, texture, or pattern
- Add text box shading, shadows, or 3-D
- Use special characters
- Use unique bullets
- Add borders and shading

- Add a picture
- Use drop caps
- Draw your own picture
- Create a logo
- Create a watermark
- Delete background elements in templates—circles, rectangles, etc.
- Delete unnecessary information in template headers and footers

Finding Additional Suggestions for Customizing Templates

The AutoText feature in Word provides helpful suggestions on how to customize each predesigned Word template. For more details on customizing a template, open a specific template, click Edit, Select All, then click Edit again and Clear. Next, point to AutoText on the Insert menu, then click AutoText at the side list. Select the AutoText tab, click the down arrow to the right of the Look in: list box, and make sure the name of your template along with *(global template)* displays in the Look in: list box. Select Gallery Example, and then click Insert. Read the template text and experiment with the suggestions given in the template. If you like the way your document looks, save it as a template and use it again.

Using Desktop Publishing Concepts in Customizing Templates

When customizing a template to meet your specific needs, as well as when creating a document from scratch, remember to apply the basic design concepts discussed in chapter 1. Always begin a document with the end in mind. Plan your text carefully to achieve your desired results without unnecessary wording. Identify your audience. Consider how the document will be distributed. Emphasize important information. Consider what you want the document to accomplish. Evaluate your document for appropriate choices in fonts, font sizes, font effects, graphics, colors, focus, consistency, balance, proportion, and directional flow.

When choosing a font for a memo, readability of the document should be considered. *Readability* is the ease with which a person can read and understand groups of words. In a text-intensive document such as a memo, readability is a primary consideration since multiple paragraphs of text are set in large blocks of type. Generally, a serif typeface in approximately 12-point size is appropriate in the body of the memo.

Readability
The ease with which a person can read and understand groups of words.

In the template documents, Word chooses fonts for each template. Word may use more than one font within a template document to add variety to the document.

Each of the memo templates is distinctive in design. As an example, the Contemporary memo attracts attention through the use of a lightly shaded geometric shape in the left margin and subtle gray vertical and horizontal lines that tend to lead the reader's eyes down and over to the right margin. Also, the placement of the shaded box containing the word "CONFIDENTIAL" in the bottom left corner of the memo balances the darker and stronger weight of the word "Memorandum" in the top left corner of the memo. This is a good example of asymmetrical design—the left margin is wider than the right margin and the left side of the memo is balanced by the weight of the body text.

Saving a Document as a Template

Typically, you would not spend a great deal of time customizing a memo document unless you wanted to show consistency among many company documents or reinforce a company or department identity with a logo, graphic, colored text, or other design elements. In these cases, you may want to save the memo, which may have been based on an existing template, as a new template to be used over and over again.

To save a document as a new template that does not replace the original, complete the following steps: (If your instructor does not want you to add your template to the network or hard drive, delete any unnessary text, graphics, etc., then save your new template as a document on your student data disk and retrieve it when needed.)

1. Click File, then Save As.
2. In the Save as type box, select *Document Template*.
3. Make sure *Templates* displays in the Save in: option. (If you are working on a network, consult your instructor as to the location of the template files.)
4. If the new template is a memo, double-click the Memo folder.
5. Key a new name in the File name: list box (Example: *your last name, hospital memo*). Word automatically adds *.dot*.
6. Click Save. (Ask your instructor if you should delete the template at the end of the chapter.)

exercise 1

Creating and Customizing a Professional Memo from a Word Template

1. At a clear document screen, create the memo in figure 2.13 by completing the following steps:
   a. Click File, then New.
   b. At the New dialog box, select the Memos tab. Make sure Document is selected in the Create New section.
   c. At the Memos tab, double-click the Professional Memo icon.
   d. Select *Company Name Here* in the shaded box in the upper corner of the memo, then key **Denver First Bank**.
   e. Select *Denver First Bank* and change the font to 18-point Garamond Bold with the Shadow and Small caps effects.
   f. With the insertion point still positioned inside the shaded box, click the Center button on the Formatting toolbar.
   g. Change the shading of the box by completing the following steps:
      (1) Select the box. (Eight sizing handles should display).
      (2) Click Format, then Borders and Shading.
      (3) At the Shading tab, select Dark Blue in the first column and the seventh row of the Fill palette. (The dark blue color is a good choice for a conservative business such as a bank.)
      (4) Click the down arrow to the right of the Style list box in the Patterns section and select Clear, then click OK or press Enter.
   h. Select *Memo* and click the down arrow to the right of the Font Color button (last button) on the Formatting toolbar. Select the dark blue color in the first row and in the second column from the right of the color palette.

i. Click inside the placeholder text following To: [*Click* **here** *and type name*] and key **All Supervisors**.
j. Click inside the placeholder text following From: and key your name.
k. Select, then delete the entire line beginning with CC:.
l. Make sure the date defaults to the current date.
m. Click inside the placeholder text following Re: and key **Relationship Building Workshop**.
n. Read the sample text in the body of the memo template, then select the sample text.
o. Click Insert, then File.
p. At the Insert File dialog box, select *memo01.doc* located on your student data disk, then click OK or press Enter.
q. Key your initials in lowercase in place of the xx in the reference initials line.
r. Select the body text and reference initials line and change the font to 12-point Garamond.
s. Highlight the important text in the memo—date, time, location, and to whom you should repond by completing the following steps:
    (1) Click the down arrow to the right of the Highlight button (second button from the right) on the Formatting toolbar.
    (2) Select the bright yellow color, then drag the highlighting through the important text.
    (3) Click the Highlight button again to turn it off. (Highlighting is particularly effective if you send your memos electronically!)

2. Save the completed memo and name it c02ex01, memo.
3. Print and then close c02ex01, memo.

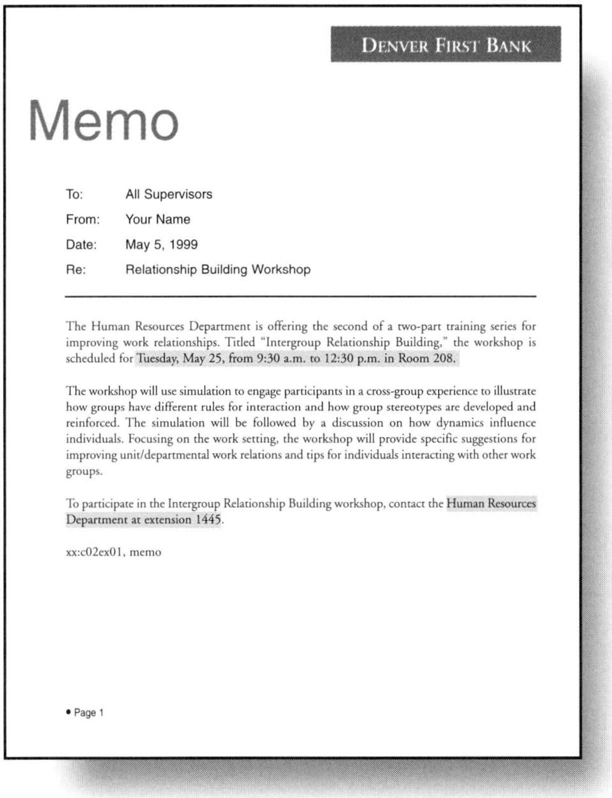

figure 2.13

DENVER FIRST BANK

Memo

To: All Supervisors
From: Your Name
Date: May 5, 1999
Re: Relationship Building Workshop

The Human Resources Department is offering the second of a two-part training series for improving work relationships. Titled "Intergroup Relationship Building," the workshop is scheduled for Tuesday, May 25, from 9:30 a.m. to 12:30 p.m. in Room 208.

The workshop will use simulation to engage participants in a cross-group experience to illustrate how groups have different rules for interaction and how group stereotypes are developed and reinforced. The simulation will be followed by a discussion on how dynamics influence individuals. Focusing on the work setting, the workshop will provide specific suggestions for improving unit/departmental work relations and tips for individuals interacting with other work groups.

To participate in the Intergroup Relationship Building workshop, contact the Human Resources Department at extension 1445.

xx:c02ex01, memo

• Page 1

Using The Memo Wizard

The memo templates and the Memo Wizard (as shown in figure 2.14) both produce professional-looking, ready-to-complete memos. The difference between the two is that the wizard lets you choose layout options step by step while the templates have a preset layout. The memo wizard will automatically insert names on the To and Cc lines if you use an electronic personal address book, as well as include tips that will give you advice on making other selections. To use the Memo Wizard, click File, then New. Select the Memos tab, then double-click the Memo Wizard icon.

Memo Wizard

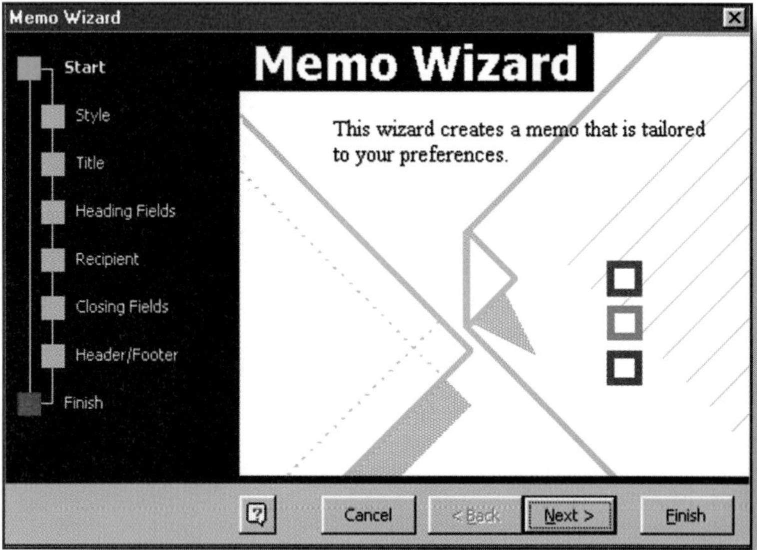

Adding Symbols and Special Characters to a Document

You can insert many symbols and special characters into your Word documents. Symbol fonts such as Monotype Sorts, Wingdings, and Symbol include decorative characters that may display in the form of bullets, stars, flowers, and more. Other symbol fonts may be built into your printer. For example, most PostScript printers include Zapf Dingbats. Other character sets may be available from other software installed on your hard drive.

DTP POINTERS
Special characters add visual contrast to a document.

Special characters can also be used to add interest and originality to documents. ANSI symbols are the regular character set that you see on your keyboard plus many more characters, including a copyright symbol, registered trademark symbol, scientific symbols, and foreign language characters such as umlauts (¨) and tildes (˜). Special characters include em and en dashes, smart quotes, ellipses, nonbreaking hyphens, and more. These characters are used to add a polished, professional look to your documents.

Inserting Symbols Using the Symbol Dialog Box

To insert symbols using the Symbol dialog box with either the Symbols tab or the Special Characters tab selected, as shown in figures 2.15 and 2.16, complete the following steps:

1. Position the insertion point in the document where you want the symbol to display.
2. Click Insert, then Symbol. (The Symbol dialog box will appear.)
3. Select either the Symbols tab or the Special Characters tab.
4. At the Font list box, select the font for which you want to see the symbols. (Click a symbol to see it enlarged. You can press the arrow keys to move around the screen. If a shortcut key combination is available for a particular symbol, it will appear below the Font list box.)
5. Click the Insert button. (At the Symbol dialog box, you can click Insert to insert the symbol in the document and not close the dialog box. This might be useful if you are inserting more than one symbol in the document at the same time.)
6. Click Close.

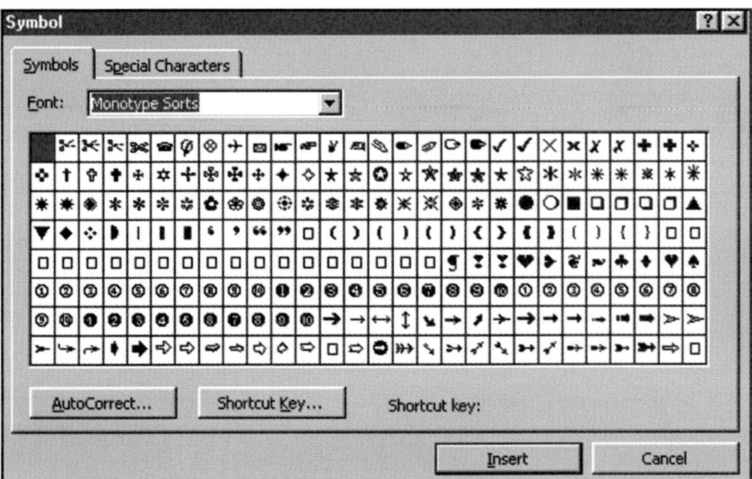

Symbol Dialog Box at the Symbols Tab

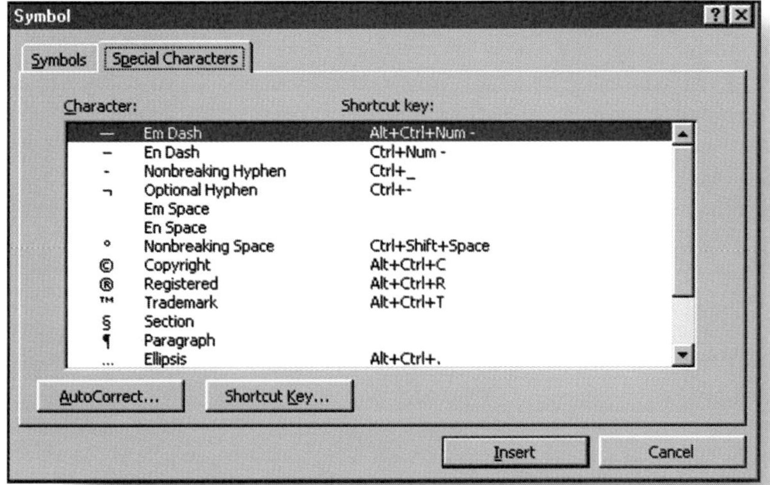

Symbol Dialog Box at the Special Characters Tab

Inserting Special Characters Using the Keyboard

To insert special characters at the Symbol dialog box using the keyboard, press the up, down, left, or right arrow key until the desired character is selected, then press Alt + I. Press Enter to close the Symbol dialog box.

Special characters can also be added by using shortcut keys. The shortcut keys are listed in the Symbol dialog box. For example, to insert a copyright symbol in a document, you would press Alt + Ctrl + C. To create é (as in résumé) hold down the Ctrl key, press the single quotation mark key, press the "e" key, then release the Ctrl key, and the symbol will display. You can also assign shortcut key combinations to frequently used symbols—for instance, you could assign Alt + H to a heart symbol if this shortcut key combination has not been assigned to another symbol. (Word will prompt you if it has already been used.)

You can add frequently used symbols to AutoCorrect by selecting each symbol, clicking the AutoCorrect button at the Symbol dialog box, then assigning a keystroke to the symbol at the AutoCorrect dialog box. Make sure *Replace text as you type* is selected.

Creating Em and En Dashes

The Symbol dialog box with the Special Characters tab selected contains two symbols that are used with proportional type—an em dash and an en dash. An em dash (—) is as long as the point size of the type and is used in text to indicate a pause in speech. An em dash is created on a typewriter by typing two hyphens. In typesetting, an em dash is one character. An em dash can also be created at the keyboard by pressing Alt + Ctrl + Num -. An en dash (–) indicates a continuation, such as 116–133 or January–March, and is exactly one-half the width of an em dash. An en dash can be inserted at the keyboard by pressing Ctrl + Num -. Generally, you do not space before or after an en or em dash. However, a space may be added before and after an en dash when used in duration of time to show more white space around the times.

En and em dashes display automatically if the Symbol characters (–) with symbols (—) check box is selected on both the AutoFormat As You Type and the AutoFormat tabs of the AutoFormat feature as shown in figure 2.8.

The AutoFormat feature is accessed by clicking Format, AutoFormat, and then Options. You control which automatic changes Word makes as you type by selecting or clearing options you want. Word automatically inserts an en dash when you key text followed by a space, one hyphen, and then one or no space, followed by more text. For example, May 2 - 7 becomes May 2 – 7. Word automatically inserts an em dash only when you type text followed by two hyphens followed by more text.

Using Smart Quotes

DTP POINTERS
Use vertical quotation marks only to indicate inches.

In typesetting, the open quotation mark is curved upward (") and the close quotation mark is curved downward ("). The quotation mark used on the standard keyboard creates a vertical mark ("). This is commonly used in documents created on a typewriter but is not appropriate for typesetting. In typesetting, the vertical mark is used to indicate inches.

The Smart Quote option in the AutoFormat feature is on by default and causes quotation marks entered around text to change to proper open and close quotation marks. Additionally, AutoFormat automatically converts single quotation marks around text to the proper open and close quotation marks and inserts the appropriate symbol for an apostrophe (').

In exercise 2 you will create a hospital memo using the Memo Wizard. Even though the wizard allows you to make some formatting decisions, you may want to make additional changes. You will make changes that will reinforce the identity of the hospital and promote consistency among other hospital documents. Assume this memo will be sent through the hospital's Intranet.

exercise 2

Creating a Memo with the Memo Wizard

1. At a clear document screen, use the Memo Wizard to create the memo in figure 2.17 by completing the following steps:
   a. Click File, then New.
   b. At the New dialog box, select the Memos tab. Make sure Document is selected in the Create New section located in the bottom right corner of the New dialog box.
   c. Double-click the Memo Wizard icon.
   d. At the Start screen of the Memo Wizard, click Next>.
   e. At the Style screen, select the *Contemporary* template, then click Next>.
   f. At the Title screen, select Yes, then key **hospital memorandum** in the Title text box. Click Next>.
   g. At the Heading Fields screen, select Date and make sure the current date displays. Select From, then key your name. Select Subject, then key **Children and Hospital Week**. Click Next>.
   h. At the Recipient screen, key **All Hospital Staff** in the To text box. Click No to create separate pages. Click Next>.
   i. At the Closing Fields screen, do not select any of the items. Click Next>.
   j. At the Heading/Footer screen, select Date in the footer section. Click Next>.
   k. Click Finish.
   l. If the Office Assistant appears, click Cancel if no changes are needed. (If you want to send the memo via E-mail or fax, click *Send the Memo to Someone*. If you selected Fax, the Fax Wizard will display, where you will be prompted to access your own fax software and make various customizations. Selecting E-Mail will activate your E-mail Internet program, where you can send your document through your Internet connection.)
   m. Select *hospital memorandum* and change the font to 36-point Colonna MT with a Shadow effect and change the font Color to Teal. Click OK or press Enter.
   n. Customize the line separating the subject line from the memo body text by completing the following steps:
      (1) Position the insertion point anywhere in the subject line (RE:) of the memo heading. Click Format, then Borders and Shading.
      (2) At the Borders and Shading dialog box, select the Borders tab.
      (3) Click the down arrow to the right of the Color list box and select *Teal*.
      (4) Click the down arrow to the right of the Width list box and select *3 pt*.
      (5) Click the bottom line in the Preview box to apply these changes to the original line, then click OK or press Enter.
   o. Create the logo (cross symbol) as shown in figure 2.17 by completing the following steps:

(1) Click Insert, then Text Box.
(2) Drag the crosshairs into the area to the right of the memo headings and draw a text box approximately 0.75 inches square. (Make sure the insertion point displays inside the text box.) Verify this setting by selecting the text box, then clicking Format, then Text Box. Select the Size tab and key **0.75** inches in the Height and Width text boxes in the Size and rotate section.
(3) Select the Colors and Lines tab, click the down arrow to the right of the Color list box located in the Fill section, and click the Teal color in the second row and the fifth column of the color palette.
(4) Click the down arrow to the right of Color in the Line section and click *No Line*.
(5) Select the Wrapping tab, then select None in the Wrapping style section. Click OK or press Enter.
(6) With the text box still selected and the insertion point positioned inside the text box, click Format, then Paragraph.
(7) Key **0** in the Left and Right Indentation text boxes, then click OK.
(8) Click the Center align button on the Formatting toolbar.
(9) Change the font to 50-point Times New Roman in White.
(10) Click Insert, then Symbol.
(11) At the Symbol dialog box, select the Symbols tab.
(12) Click the down arrow to the right of the Font list box and select *Monotype Sorts*.
(13) Click the cross symbol in the first row and the second to the last column, then click Insert, then Close.
(14) If necessary, select the text box and drag it to a position similar to figure 2.17. (The arrow pointer will display as a four-headed arrow, drag the box to a desired location, and then release the left mouse.)

p. Create the initials (CMH) in a text box and drag the box to a position similar to figure 2.17 by completing the following steps:

(1) Create a text box with measurements of **0.4** inches in Height and **0.9** inches in Width. Verify the measurements by clicking Format, then Text Box. Select the Size tab and key the measurements if necessary.
(2) Select the Colors and Lines tab, then select White at the Fill Color list box and select *No Line* at the Line Color list box.
(3) Select the Wrapping tab, then select None in the Wrapping style section. Click OK or press Enter.
(4) With the text box still selected, click Format, then Paragraph and change the Left and Right Indentations to **0**. Click OK or press Enter.
(5) Click the Center align button.
(6) Change the font to 24-point Colonna MT in Teal and in All caps, then key **CMH**.
(7) Select the text box containing *CMH* and drag it to the circular gray shape to the left of the memo text and then release the left mouse.
(8) With the text box still selected, click Format, then Text Box.
(9) Select the Position tab and clear the check mark before Move object with text and select the check box before Lock anchor to turn this feature on. Click OK or press Enter.

q. Save the customized document as a new template by completing the following steps:

(Check with your instructor if you should save this document as a template to your hard drive or as a document to A:\ drive.)

(1) Click File, then Save As.

(2) In the Save As dialog box, change the Save as type: option at the bottom of the dialog box to *Document Template (*.dot)*.

(3) Click the down arrow to the right of the Save in: option, then change to the *Templates* folder. (If you are working on a network, consult your instructor as to the location of the template files.)

(4) Double-click on Memos.

(5) Key **(your last name), hospital memo** in the File name text box. Word will automatically add a .dot extension.

(6) Click Save, then close the document.

r. Click File, then New.

s. Select the Memos tab (make sure Document is selected in the Create New box), then double-click on *(your last name), hospital memo.dot* template or open *(your last name), hospital memo.doc* document if you saved it to your student data disk.

t. Click inside the memo text placeholder, then click Insert, then File.

u. At the Insert File dialog box, select *memo02.doc* located on your student data disk.

v. Key your reference initals in place of the xx.

2. Save the completed memo and name it c02ex02, memo.
3. Print and then close c02ex02, memo.

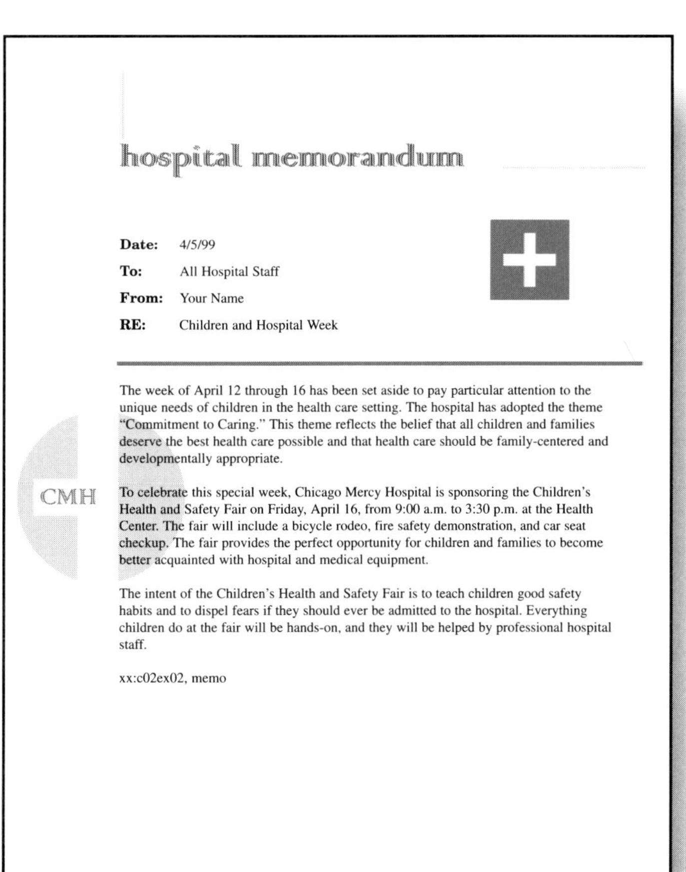

hospital memorandum

Date: 4/5/99

To: All Hospital Staff

From: Your Name

RE: Children and Hospital Week

The week of April 12 through 16 has been set aside to pay particular attention to the unique needs of children in the health care setting. The hospital has adopted the theme "Commitment to Caring." This theme reflects the belief that all children and families deserve the best health care possible and that health care should be family-centered and developmentally appropriate.

To celebrate this special week, Chicago Mercy Hospital is sponsoring the Children's Health and Safety Fair on Friday, April 16, from 9:00 a.m. to 3:30 p.m. at the Health Center. The fair will include a bicycle rodeo, fire safety demonstration, and car seat checkup. The fair provides the perfect opportunity for children and families to become better acquainted with hospital and medical equipment.

The intent of the Children's Health and Safety Fair is to teach children good safety habits and to dispel fears if they should ever be admitted to the hospital. Everything children do at the fair will be hands-on, and they will be helped by professional hospital staff.

xx:c02ex02, memo

CMH

figure 2.17

Using Word Layers in Documents

In exercise 3, you will customize a memo by adding a watermark for visual appeal. A basic understanding of the unique four-level layers of text, pictures, and drawing objects in Word will be helpful in understanding how to create watermarks in documents. Word's four layers include Foreground, Text, Background, and Header and Footer layers as illustrated in figure 2.18.

2.18

Word's Four Layers

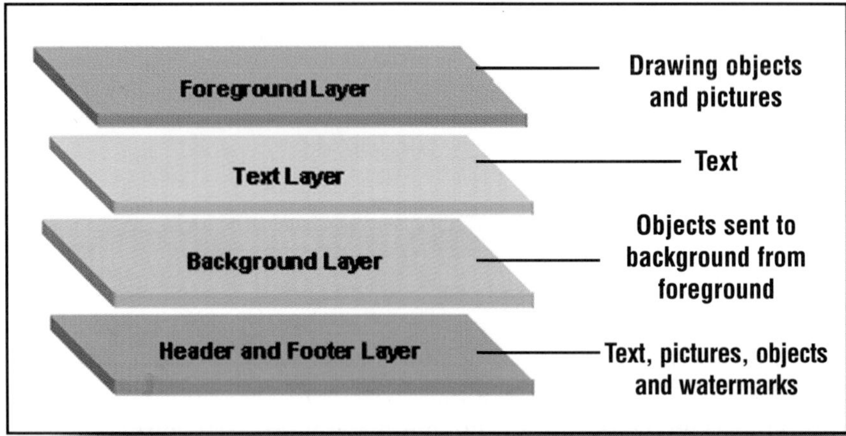

Every Word document is composed of these four basic layers. Also, within each one of these layers you may create additional layers of text, objects, or pictures. You may think of a document created in Word as a sandwich.

Figure 2.19 illustrates Word's unique layering process in a memo document. Document text exists in the middle layer or text layer. This layer is the one you may be most accustomed to working with in word processing. Word also includes the foreground layer or drawing layer above the text layer where drawing objects and pictures display by default. Drawing objects include all AutoShape forms, WordArt objects, rectangles, ovals, lines, 3D objects and shadowed objects created with tools on the Drawing toolbar. Watermark images that are sent behind the text layer exist in the background layer along with any other drawing objects, text or pictures sent behind the text layer. Text, pictures, and watermarks that are created in the header and footer pane are positioned below the background layer.

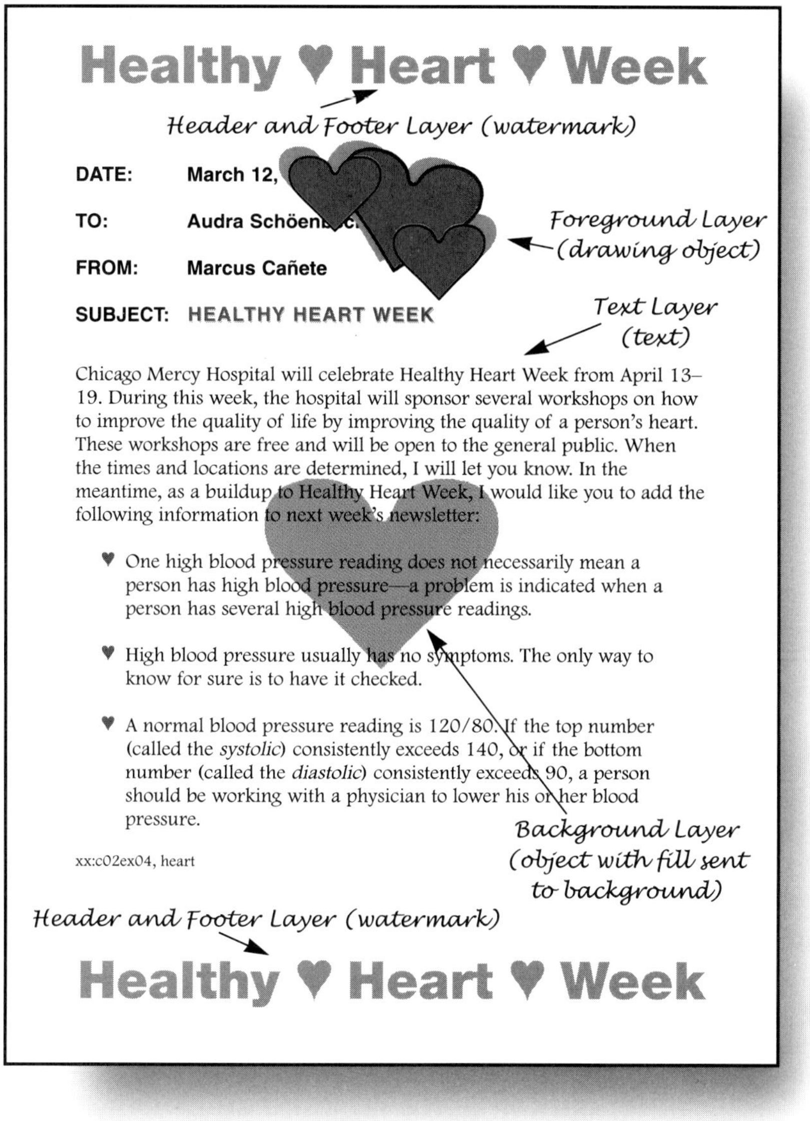

Healthy ♥ Heart ♥ Week

Header and Footer Layer (watermark)

DATE: March 12,

TO: Audra Schöen...

FROM: Marcus Cañete

SUBJECT: HEALTHY HEART WEEK

Foreground Layer (drawing object)

Text Layer (text)

Chicago Mercy Hospital will celebrate Healthy Heart Week from April 13–19. During this week, the hospital will sponsor several workshops on how to improve the quality of life by improving the quality of a person's heart. These workshops are free and will be open to the general public. When the times and locations are determined, I will let you know. In the meantime, as a buildup to Healthy Heart Week, I would like you to add the following information to next week's newsletter:

- ♥ One high blood pressure reading does not necessarily mean a person has high blood pressure—a problem is indicated when a person has several high blood pressure readings.
- ♥ High blood pressure usually has no symptoms. The only way to know for sure is to have it checked.
- ♥ A normal blood pressure reading is 120/80. If the top number (called the *systolic*) consistently exceeds 140, or if the bottom number (called the *diastolic*) consistently exceeds 90, a person should be working with a physician to lower his or her blood pressure.

xx:c02ex04, heart

Background Layer (object with fill sent to background)

Header and Footer Layer (watermark)

Healthy ♥ Heart ♥ Week

figure 2.19

Four Layers as Shown in a Document

If an object is drawn using a button on the Drawing toolbar in a document containing text, the object is positioned above the text. It can also be positioned below the text by changing the Order of the object. To change the order of an object, click the Draw button on the Drawing toolbar, point to Order, then click an option to position the object above or below text. If you want the text in the document to wrap around an object, you may select a wrapping option at the Format Text Box dialog box or Format AutoShape dialog box depending on how the object was created.

In earlier versions of Word, you used frames to wrap text around a picture, text, or object. In Word 97, you can wrap text around a picture, text, or object of any size or shape without first inserting it into a text box or frame by changing the wrapping style through the corresponding dialog box with the Wrapping tab selected. Wrapping styles include: Square, Tight, Through, None, and Top & bottom as shown in figure 2.20. Objects—AutoShapes, text boxes, etc.—default to the None Wrapping style. Pictures default to the Top & bottom wrapping style.

figure 2.20

Wrapping Styles

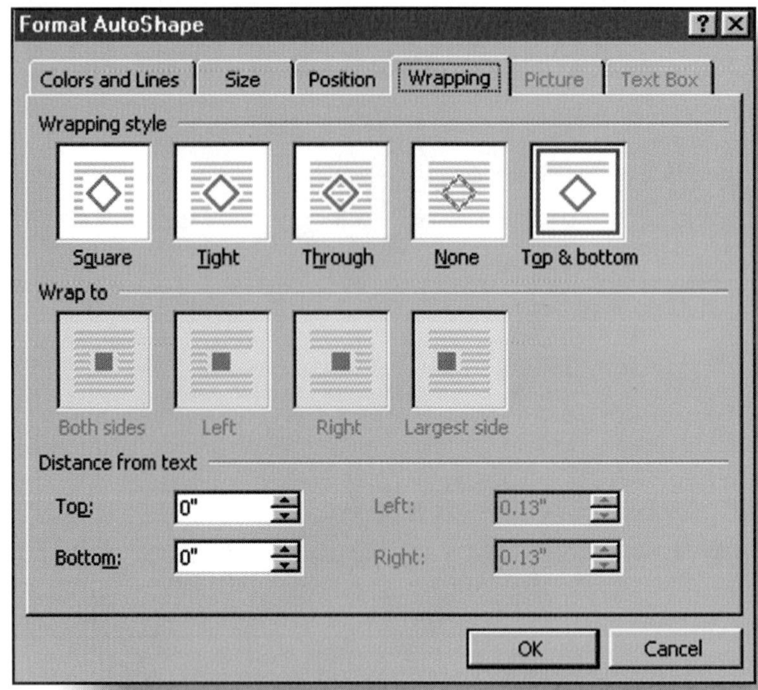

Adding a Watermark for Visual Appeal

Watermark
A lightened graphic or text image displayed behind text on a page.

A *watermark* is a lightened image that appears either on top or behind document text. For example, you may use a watermark when you want a graphic, such as a company logo, or text, such as "Confidential," to display in the background of a printed page. Traditionally, a watermark is a design impressed in high-quality paper stock. This design can be seen more clearly when the paper is held up to the light.

Creating a Watermark in a Header and Footer

One of the easiest ways to create a watermark, which will appear on every page of your document, is to insert the image or text you want to use in the watermark into a header or footer. Placing the watermark into a header or footer automatically positions the object in the appropriate layer below the text layer. At the Header and Footer pane, the watermark may be inserted into a text box and placed anywhere you want it placed on the page—not confined to the typical area of a header or footer at the top or bottom of the page.

You do not have to place an object inside a text box; however, it is easier to control the size and location of the object if you use one. A text box is not necessary, since Word inserts pictures as floating pictures—pictures that are inserted in the drawing layer so you can position them on the page or in front of or behind text or other objects.

Drawing

Text Box

To create a text box, display the Drawing toolbar by clicking the Drawing button on the Standard toolbar (fourth button from the right), then click the Text Box button on the Drawing toolbar as shown in figure 2.21. Alternatively, you can click Insert, then Text Box as discussed earlier. Drag the crosshairs on the page to draw a box that will hold a graphic image or text. You can later size and position the text box more precisely by accessing the Size and Position tabs at the Text Box dialog box or size the box by dragging the sizing handles or dragging the box to position it. Figure 2.22 displays a watermark inside the header and footer pane.

Image Control

Key any text inside the text box or insert a picture. To insert a graphic, click Insert, point to Picture, then click Clip Art or From File; or display the Picture toolbar as shown in figure 2.23 and click the Insert Picture button. Choose an appropriate picture that relates to the subject of your document.

More Contrast

If you inserted the picture inside a text box, be sure to remove the border surrounding the text box by selecting No Line at the Colors and Lines tab of the Format Text Box dialog box.

Less Contrast

To reduce the shading of the picture, display the Picture toolbar, then click the Image Control button as shown in figure 2.23. Select Watermark from the drop-down list that displays. This option automatically reduces the shading of the picture. Additional changes can be made to the image by clicking the More Contrast, Less Contrast, More Brightness, and Less Brightness buttons on the Picture toolbar as shown in figure 2.23.

More Brightness

Once you are satisfied with the shading, size, and location of the watermark image in the Header and Footer pane, click the Close button on the Header and Footer toolbar.

Less Brightness

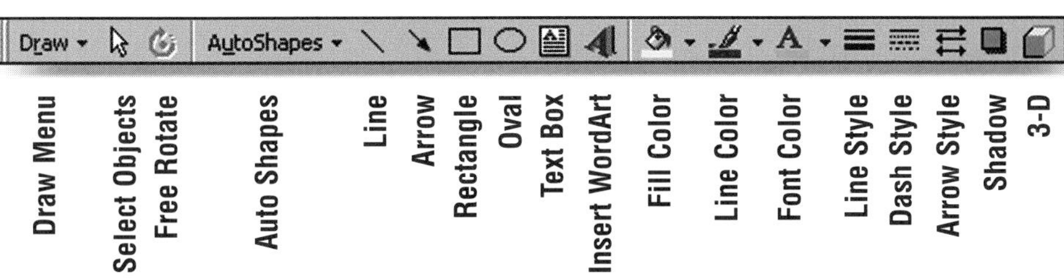

figure 2.21

Drawing Toolbar

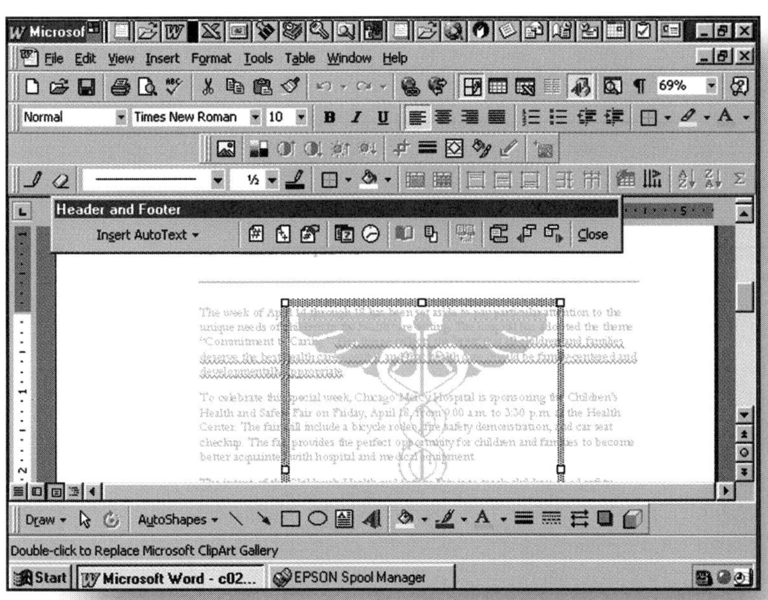

figure 2.22

Watermark in the Header and Footer Pane

figure 2.23

Picture Toolbar

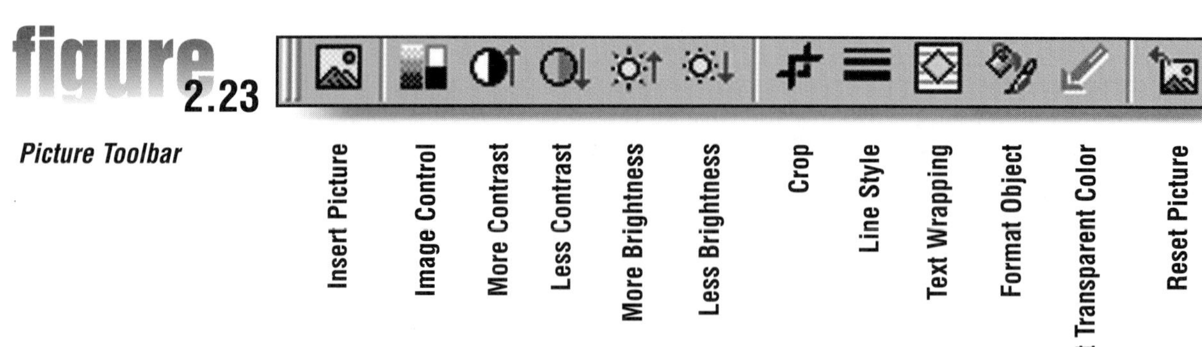

To create a watermark in a header and footer, complete the following steps:

1. Click View, then Header and Footer.
2. Draw a text box as a container for your picture. (Not necessary, but helpful in controlling the size and location of the picture in the text.) Draw a text box by either clicking Insert, then Text or by clicking the Text Box button on the Drawing toolbar.
3. Remove the border around the text box.
4. Position the insertion point inside the text box, then click Insert, point to Picture, and then click Clip Art or From File.
5. Display the Picture toolbar.
6. Click the Image Control button, then select Watermark.
7. Click the Close button on the Header and Footer toolbar.

Creating Watermarks Using Send Behind Text

Text Wrapping

Another method may be used to create watermarks. This method involves inserting a picture into a document, reducing the shading of the image, then sending it behind the text layer of the document as shown in figures 2.24 through 2.26. Before moving and sizing the picture, make sure to change the Picture Wrapping style to None at the Format Picture dialog box, or click the Text Wrapping button on the Picture toolbar and select None.

Alternatively, a picture may be inserted into a text box, the shading altered, and then sent behind text. Placing the object inside a text box helps you control the size and position of the picture in the document. However, make sure the Left and Right paragraph indentations are set at 0 inches before inserting the picture into a text box.

Complete the following steps to create a watermark with the Send Behind Text option:

1. Display the Drawing toolbar and the Picture toolbar.
2. Insert a picture. (You could insert the picture inside a text box to control its size.) If you use a text box, remove the border surrounding it.
3. Select the text box.
4. Click the Text Wrapping button (fourth button from the right) on the Picture toolbar and make sure None is selected.
5. Select the picture (solid black sizing handles will display inside the frame of the picture).
6. Resize and move the picture if necessary.

7. Click the Image Control button (second button from the right) on the Picture toolbar.
8. Click Watermark.
9. Select the text box.
10. Click the Draw button on the Drawing toolbar.
11. Point to Order at the side menu.
12. Click Send Behind Text.

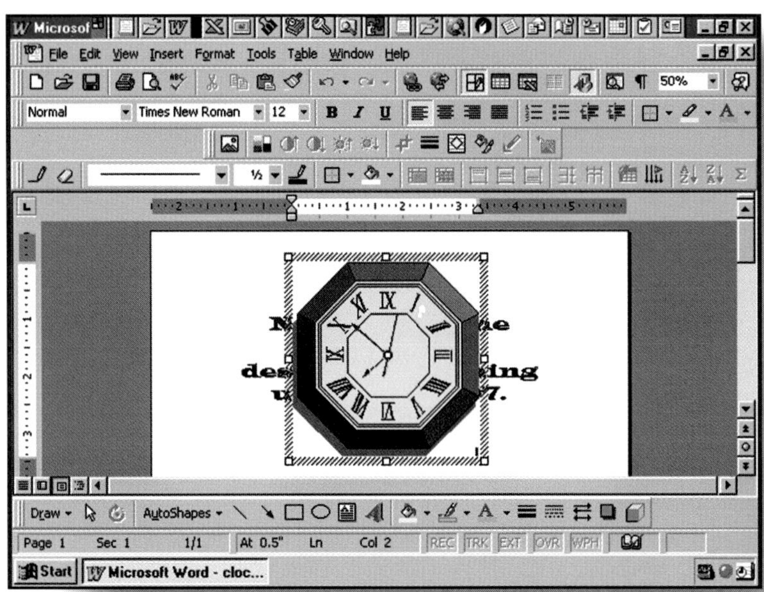

figure 2.24

Picture with None Wrapping Style

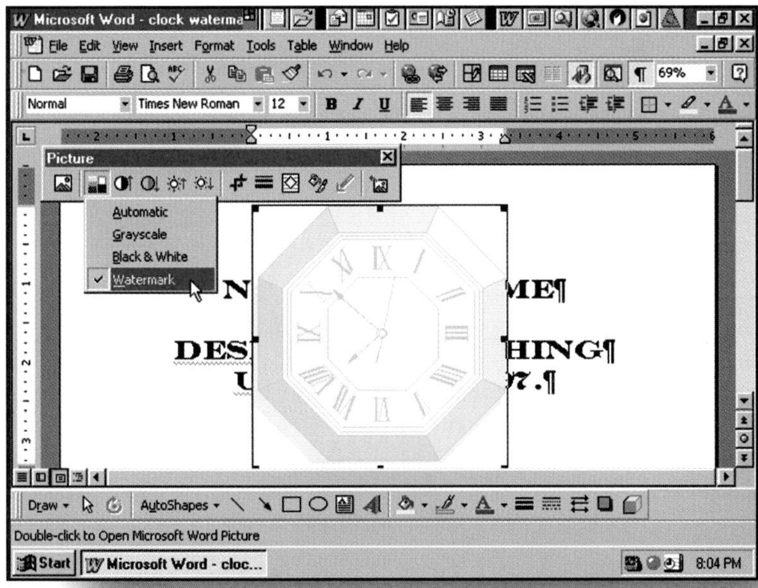

figure 2.25

Watermark Option at Image Control

Sending a Picture Behind Text

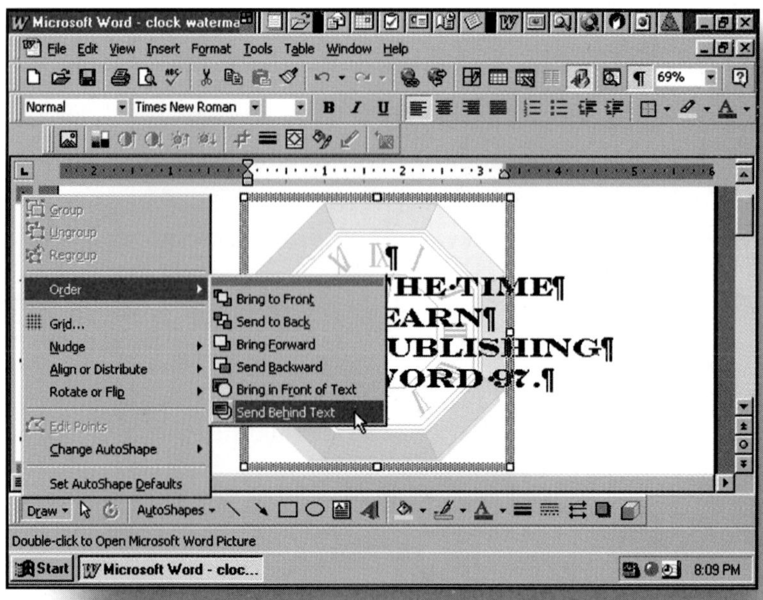

Working with Watermarks

To view a watermark, switch to page layout view or print preview. If a watermark interferes with the legibility of the text on the page, lighten the watermark by following one of the following suggestions:

- To lighten text, click Format, then Font and select another color such as light gray.
- To lighten WordArt objects, click Format, then Object. Select the Colors and Lines tab, then change the fill color to a lighter gray or color shading.
- To lighten drawing objects, such as AutoShapes, click Format, then AutoShapes. At the Colors and Lines tab, change the fill color to a lighter gray or color shading. To add text to an AutoShape, click Add Text on the shortcut menu, then key your text.
- To lighten a picture, use the Picture or Object command at the Format command. At the Colors and Lines tab, change the fill color to a lighter gray or color shading. At the Picture tab, under Image Control, click the down arrow to the right of the Color list box, then click *Watermark* from the Color box to format the picture with preset brightness and contrast settings, or adjust these settings manually using the Brightness and Contrast slide controls. Alternatively, display the Picture toolbar as shown in figure 2.23 and click the Image Control button and then click Watermark. Increase or decrease the contrast or brightness of the image by clicking the More Contrast, Less Contrast, More Brightness, or Less Brightness buttons on the Picture toolbar.
- To remove a watermark, click View, then Header and Footer or double-click on the dimmed header or footer, then select the text or graphic and press Delete.
- To access a watermark that has been sent behind text, click the Select Objects button (second button from the left) on the Drawing toolbar and draw a dashed border around the picture. When you release the left mouse, sizing handles should display around the image. Then, you can move or resize the picture.

Select Objects

exercise 3

Creating a Memo with a Watermark

1. At a clear document screen, create the memo shown in figure 2.27 by completing the following steps:
   a. Open *medical memo.doc* from your student data disk.
   b. Click File, then Save As, and name the document c02ex03, watermark.
   c. Select *Memorandum* and change the font to 30-point Times New Roman Bold in Violet with the Outline effect, then key **Chicago Mercy Hospital Memorandum**.
   d. Change the line style and color preceding the memo text by completing the following steps:
      (1) Position the insertion point anywhere in the subject line (*Re.*) and click Format, then Borders and Shading.
      (2) At the Borders tab, click the down arrow to the right of the Style box and select the three-line style.
      (3) Click the down arrow to the right of the Color list box and select *Violet*.
      (4) Make sure the Width displays at 1/2 pt.
      (5) Click the bottom line in the Preview box, then click OK or press Enter.
   e. Remove the gray-shaded circle on the left side of the memo by selecting it, then pressing the Delete key.
   f. Create the medical watermark as shown in figure 2.27 by completing the following steps:
      (1) Display the Drawing toolbar and Picture toolbar by choosing View, then Toolbars, and then clicking *Drawing* and *Picture* from the drop-down list.
      (2) Click View, then Header and Footer.
      (3) Scroll downward until the first few parargraphs of text display. Change the Zoom to 50%.
      (4) Click Insert, then Text Box, or click the Text Box button on the Drawing toolbar (ninth button from the left).
      (5) Drag the crosshairs into the memo text, hold down the left mouse button and draw a text box beginning slightly above the first paragraph and approximately one inch from the left margin of the memo. Continue dragging the crosshairs to the right, ending approximately one inch from the right margin and dragging downward ending at the reference initials, then release the left mouse button.
      (6) Position the insertion point inside the text box. Notice that the insertion point is positioned approximately one-half inch from the left edge of the box. Remove the embedded formatting that is causing this indentation by completing the following steps:
         (a) Click Format, then Paragraph.
         (b) At the Paragraph dialog box, select the Indents and Spacing tab.
         (c) Change the Left and Right Indentation settings to **0** inches.
         (d) Click OK or press Enter.
      (7) Click the down arrow to the right of the Line Color button on the Drawing toolbar and select *No Line* to remove the border around the text box.
      (8) With the insertion point positioned in the upper left corner of the text box, click Insert, point to Picture, then click From File.
      (9) At the Insert Picture dialog box, make sure A:\ or the drive where your student data disk is located displays in the Look in: list box.
      (10) Select *Medstaff.wmf* from the list box, then click Insert.
      (11) If necessary, drag to move or resize the image.

(12) Change the shading of the picture by completing the following steps:
   (a) Select the picture so that small black sizing handles display inside the border of the picture. (If hollow sizing handles in a diagonal border display around the picture, you have selected the text box and not the picture.)
   (b) With the picture selected, click the Image Control Button (second button from the left) on the Picture toolbar, then select Watermark from the drop-down menu.
   (c) Click the Close button on the Header and Footer toolbar.

g. View the document at Print Preview.

2. Save the memo again with the same name, c02ex03, watermark.
3. Print and then close c02ex03, watermark.

figure 2.27

Chicago Mercy Hospital
Memorandum

To: Fred Médard

From: Juliette Danner

Date: May 17, 1999

Re: PREOPERATIVE PROCEDURES

At the last meeting of the medical team, concern was raised about the structure of preoperative procedures. In light of recent nationwide occurrences in some city hospitals, members of the team decided to review written procedures to determine if additional steps should be added. A meeting of the surgical team has been set for Tuesday, May 25. Please try to arrange surgical schedules so a majority of the surgical team can attend this meeting.

Please review the following items to determine where each should be positioned in a preoperative surgical checklist:

- ✔ Necessary operative forms are signed—admissions and consent for surgery.
- ✔ Blood tests have been completed.
- ✔ Blood type is noted in patient chart.
- ✔ Surgical procedure has been triple-checked with patient and surgical team.
- ✔ All allergies are noted in patient chart.
- ✔ Anesthesiologist has reviewed and initialed patient chart.

I am confident that the medical team will discover that the preoperative checklist is one of the most thorough in the region. Any suggestions made by the medical team will only enhance a superior checklist.

xx:c02ex03, watermark

CONFIDENTIAL

Formatting a Memo

Besides using a template or wizard to create a memo, you can also create a memo at a clear editing window. Use the default margin settings of 1-inch top and bottom margins, and 1.25-inch left and right margins. Double space between the memo headings and triple space after the last memo heading. Single space the body text, but double space between paragraphs. Double space before the reference initials.

Creating a List in a Memo

You can insert a special character as a bullet preceding a list by using one of the following methods. One method involves inserting a special character from the Symbols dialog box, pressing the Tab key, then keying the text. Word automatically converts your text to a Bullet List item when you press Enter, if the Automatic bulleted lists feature has been turned on. To check if this feature is active, click Format, AutoFormat, then Options. Make sure a check mark appears in the check box preceding the Automatic Bulleted Lists in the Apply As You Type section at the AutoFormat tab.

In addition, this feature will not work if you press the Enter key twice after each line to create a double space between each entry. Press Shift + Enter to create a blank line. Pressing the Enter key twice will actually turn off the Automatic Bulleted Lists feature. After the list has been keyed, additional formatting can be applied to the selected list. For instance, a paragraph indentation may be applied to the text by accessing the Paragraph dialog box.

Inserting Bullets

Bullets can be inserted into a document at the Bullets and Numbering dialog box or with the Bullets button on the Formatting toolbar. To insert a bullet with the Bullets button, position the insertion point where you want the bullet to appear or anywhere within a paragraph that you want proceeded by a bullet, then click the Bullets button. A bullet is inserted at the left margin of the line or paragraph where the insertion point is positioned.

Bullets

By default, a small circle bullet is inserted in the document. This can be changed at the Bullets and Numbering dialog box shown in figure 2.28. When a bullet is inserted with this dialog box, the insertion point is also automatically indented to the first tab setting to the right. Each time you press the Enter key in the document, another bullet or the next number in the sequence is inserted in the document.

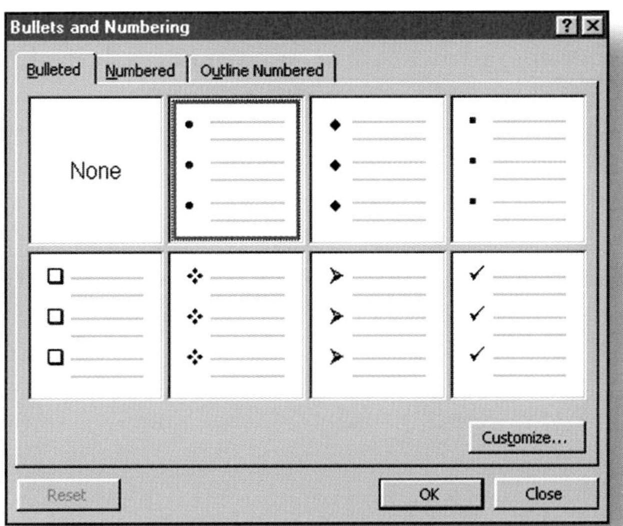

figure 2.28

Bullets and Numbering Dialog Box

DTP POINTERS
Use bullets to organize lists.

To display the Bullets and Numbering dialog box, click Format, then Bullets and Numbering. The Bullets and Numbering dialog box contains three tabs: Bulleted, Numbered, and Outline Numbered. If you click the Customize button at the right side of the dialog box, the Customize Bulleted List dialog box displays. At this dialog box, you can select a different Bullet character, Font, and Bullet.

DTP POINTERS
Use special characters as customized bullets to add interest and contrast.

The bullet and text positions can also be changed. For instance, to insert a different bullet character, click the Customize button, click the Bullet button, and then select a character at the Symbol dialog box. Change the size and color of the bullet by clicking the Font button. See figure 2.29 for the Customize Bulleted List dialog box.

figure 2.29

Customize Bulleted List Dialog Box

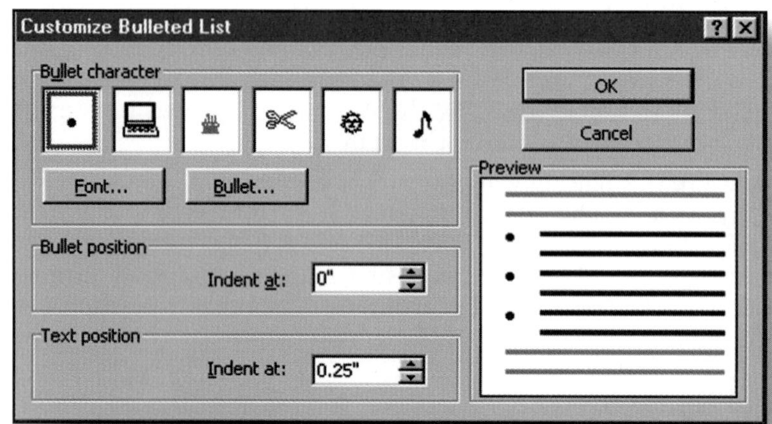

Creating Text in a Watermark

DTP POINTERS
Use spot color to add contrast and impact to a document.

In exercise 4, you will create two watermarks from text created in a header pane and in a footer pane. Text watermarks can also be created in text boxes and positioned anywhere in the document. The text color will be changed to a light gray in the Font dialog box.

exercise 4

Creating a Memo with Text in a Watermark

1. At a clear document screen, create the memo from the text in figure 2.30 by completing the following steps:
   a. Position the insertion point approximately two inches from the top edge of the paper. (Press Enter until the status bar indicates 2 inches.)
   b. Change the font to 14-point Arial Bold and key the memo headings and the information after the headings as shown in figure 2.30. Tab two or three times after each memo heading to align the heading text. To create the special symbol ö, press Ctrl + :, then o; or complete the following steps:
      (1) Click Insert, then Symbol.
      (2) At the Symbol dialog box, select the Symbols tab, then select *[normal text]* in the Font list box.

(3) Click the ö symbol in the seventh row and the twelfth column from the left.
(4) Complete similar steps to create the ñ. (This symbol is located in the *[normal text]* font, in the seventh row and the seventh column from the left.)
(5) Key **Healthy Heart Week** in Red and select the Emboss effect.

c. Triple space after the last line of the memo heading.

d. Change the font to 14-point Footlight MT Light Regular and turn off the Emboss effect and change the font color to black. Key the first paragraph of text. Use en and em dashes where needed—click Insert, then Symbol; select the Special Characters tab; then select the en or em dash and click Insert, then Close.

e. Press the Enter key twice after the first paragraph.

f. Create the heart bullet by completing the following steps:
(1) Click Format, then Bullets and Numbering.
(2) At the Bullets and Numbering dialog box, select the Bulleted tab.
(3) Select the last bullet in the second row, then click the Customize buttom.
(4) At the Customize Bulleted List dialog box, click the Bullet button.
(5) At the Symbol dialog box, click the down arrow to the right of the Font list box and select the Monotype Sort font.
(6) Click the heart symbol located in the fifth row and the eighth column from the right, then click OK.
(7) Click the Font button.
(8) At the Font dialog box, click the down arrow to the right of the font Color list box and select *Red*, make sure *14 pt* displays in the Size list box, then click OK or press Enter.
(9) At the Customized Bulleted List dialog box, change the Bullet position in the Indent at: text box to 0.25 inches, then change the Text position in the Indent at: text box to 0.5 inches. Click OK.
(10) After inserting the first heart bullet, key the remaining paragraphs in the body of the memo in figure 2.30. Press Shift + Enter to create a blank line between each paragraph in the list, then press Enter to activate the bullet feature. (Pressing the Enter key twice will turn off bullets.)
(11) Press the Enter key twice after the last paragraph.

g. Create two watermarks by completing the following steps:
(1) Click View, then Header and Footer.
(2) At the Header pane, click the Center align button on the Formatting toolbar.
(3) Change the font to 32-point Arial MT Black and the Color to Gray-25%.
(4) Key **Healthy ♥ Heart ♥ Week**. Use the same heart as in step 1f (6).
(5) Select **Healthy ♥ Heart ♥ Week**, then click the Copy button on the Standard toolbar.
(6) Click the Switch Between Header and Footer button (fourth button from the right) on the Header and Footer toolbar.
(7) With the insertion point positioned inside the Footer pane, click the Center align button on the Standard toolbar, then click the Paste button on the Standard toolbar.
(8) Click the Close button on the Header and Footer toolbar.

h. Key your reference initials and the exercise number in 11-point Footlight MT Light a double space below the last paragraph.

2. Save the memo and name it c02ex04, heart. (*Optional:* Delete any unnecessary text from the memo, then save it as a template.)
3. Print and then close c02ex04, heart.

figure 2.30

Healthy ♥ Heart ♥ Week

DATE: March 12, 1999

TO: Audra Schöenbeck

FROM: Marcus Cañete

SUBJECT: HEALTHY HEART WEEK

Chicago Mercy Hospital will celebrate Healthy Heart Week from April 12–18. During this week, the hospital will sponsor several workshops on how to improve the quality of life by improving the quality of a person's heart. These workshops are free and will be open to the general public. When the times and locations are determined, I will let you know. In the meantime, as a buildup to Healthy Heart Week, I would like you to add the following information to next week's newsletter:

- ♥ One high blood pressure reading does not necessarily mean a person has high blood pressure—a problem is indicated when a person has several high blood pressure readings.
- ♥ High blood pressure usually has no symptoms. The only way to know for sure is to have it checked.
- ♥ A normal blood pressure reading is 120/80. If the top number (called the *systolic*) consistently exceeds 140, or if the bottom number (called the *diastolic*) consistently exceeds 90, a person should be working with a physician to lower his or her blood pressure.

xx:c02ex04, heart

Healthy ♥ Heart ♥ Week

Preparing an Agenda

Before a meeting in a business, an agenda is generally prepared that includes such information as the name of the group or department holding the meeting; the date, time, and location of the meeting; and the topics to be discussed during the meeting. In Word, an agenda can be created with the Agenda Wizard or created at a clear document screen in a table. Agendas created with the Agenda Wizard may be sent through E-mail and fax connections. An agenda created at a clear document screen may be sent to an E-mail recipient or fax recipient by clicking File, then Send to.

Preparing an Agenda with the Agenda Wizard

Some templates and wizards are installed through a Typical setup, some can be installed through a Custom setup, and some are available in the Office 97 ValuPack on CD-ROM and on the Microsoft Web site. If the Agenda Wizard is not available to you, do one of the following:

- Run Setup again and select more templates and wizards.
- If you have the CD-ROM version of Microsoft Office, copy the appropriate wizard or template you want from the ValuPack\Templates folder to the appropriate subfolder of the Templates folder on your hard drive (for example: C:\Program Files\Microsoft Office\Templates\Publications).
- If you have access to the World Wide Web, point to Microsoft on the Web on the Help menu, and then click Free Stuff. Follow the instructions on the Web page to download the templates or wizards you want.

exercise 5

Preparing an Agenda with the Agenda Wizard

1. At a clear document screen, create the agenda shown in figure 2.31 using Word's Agenda Wizard by completing the following steps:
   a. Click File, then New.
   b. At the New dialog box, select the Other Documents tab. Make sure Document is selected in the Create New section.
   c. Double-click the Agenda Wizard icon.
   d. At the Agenda Wizard Start screen, click Next>.
   e. At the Agenda Style screen, select the Boxes style and then click Next>.
   f. At the Agenda Details screen, select the current date in the Date text box, then key **April 22, 1999**.
   g. Select the current time in the Starting time text box, key **8:00 AM**, then click Next>.
   h. At the Agenda Headings screen, exclude the following headings by clicking inside the check box to remove the check mark: *Please bring* and *Special notes*, then click Next>.
   i. At the Agenda Name screen, exclude the following names on the agenda by clicking inside the check box to remove the check mark: *Meeting called by*, *Timekeeper*, *Observers*, and *Resource persons*, then click Next>.
   j. At the Agenda Topics screen, click the Add button after keying each of the following lines:

Agenda topic:	Person:	Minutes:
1. **Meeting Overview**	**Becky Peterson**	**30**
2. **Introduce Facilitator**	**Stanley Barnett**	**10**
3. **Quality Care Timeline**	**Gail Zinn, Consultant**	**60**
4. **Area Reports and Discussion**	**Ellen Heitz, Hui Lenzi, Geoffrey Benn, Wendy Mitaki**	**60**
5. **Summary**	**Becky Peterson**	**20**

k. Click Next>.

l. At the Agenda Minutes screen, select No, and then click Next>.

m. At the Agenda Finish screen, click Finish.

n. When the Office Assistant appears, click the blue bullet to the left of *Enter text*.

o. Read the information about entering text, then click OK.

p. Click Table, then Show Gridlines.

q. Key the following information in the sections listed below:

Type of meeting:	**Presentation and Discussion**
Facilitator:	**Gail Zinn, Consultant**
Note taker:	**Katrina O'Dell**
Attendees:	**Hospital Timeline Committee**
Please read:	**Area Summaries**

r. Customize the agenda by completing the following steps:

(1) Select the checkmark picture located in the upper left corner on the first page of the agenda.

(2) Click Insert, point to Picture, then click From File.

(3) At the Insert Picture dialog box, make sure *Clipart* displays in the Look in: list box.

(4) Double-click the *Popular* folder at the Insert Picture list box.

(5) Select *Meeting.wmf* from the list of files.

(6) Click Insert.

s. Cancel the Office Assistant if you do not need any additional help. (*Optional:* If your classroom is setup for E-mail or fax, click the option to *Send to someone* at the Office Assistant prompt. Send your agenda to one of your classmates for her/his approval. In return, have your classmate E-mail or fax back to you any additions, corrections, or comments.)

2. Save the agenda and name it c02ex05, agenda.

3. Print and then close c02ex05, agenda.

figure 2.31

April 22, 1999
8:00 AM to 11:00 AM

Type of meeting:	Presentation and Discussion	**Facilitator:**	Gail Zinn, Consultant
Note taker:	Katrina O'Dell		
Attendees:	Hospital Timeline Committee		
Please read:	Area Summaries		

----- Agenda Topics -----

Meeting Overview	Becky Peterson	30
Introduce Facilitator	Stanley Barnett	10
Quality Care Timeline	Gail Zinn, Consultant	60
Area Reports and Discussion	Ellen Heitz, Hui Lenzi, Geoffrey Benn, Wendy Mitaki	60
Summary	Becky Peterson	20

Other Information

Creating an Agenda Using a Table

An agenda can be prepared at a clear document screen with *side-by-side columns*, which are similar to parallel columns. Word does not include a parallel column feature where text is grouped across a page in rows. However, the same effect can be accomplished by using a table to format an agenda as shown in figure 2.32.

Side-by-Side Columns
Column format that groups text horizontally across the page in rows.

2.32

Agenda Created Inside a Table

CHICAGO MERCY HOSPITAL

QUALITY CARE PROJECT

❖ AGENDA ❖

9:00 – 9:30 a.m.	Call to order and introduction of new project members.	Becky Peterson, Chair
9:00 – 9:30 a.m.	Presentation of project mission statement	Stanley Barnett

A table can be created with the Insert Table button (eighth button from the right) on the Standard toolbar or the Table option from the Menu bar.

To create an agenda similar to the one shown in figure 2.32, create a table with three columns and six rows. The number of rows will depend on the number of entries in your agenda. To create a table using the Insert Table dialog box, you would complete the following steps:

1. Click Table, then Insert Table.
2. At the Insert Table dialog box, key **3** in the Number of Columns text box.
3. Click Number of Rows.
4. Key **6**.
5. Click OK or press Enter.

Entering Text in a Table

Cell
The intersection between a row and a column in a table.

Information in a table is keyed in cells. A *cell* is the intersection between a row and a column. With the insertion point positioned in a cell, key or edit text as you would normal text. Move the insertion point to other cells with the mouse by positioning the arrow pointer in the desired cell, then clicking the left mouse button. If you are using the keyboard, press Tab to move the insertion point to the next cell or press Shift + Tab to move the insertion point to the previous cell. If you want to move the insertion point to a tab stop within a cell, press Ctrl + Tab.

If the insertion point is located in the last cell of the table and you press the Tab key, Word adds another row to the table. If you have added too many rows to your table, select the unwanted rows then press Delete. When all the information has been entered into the cells, move the insertion point below the table and, if necessary, continue keying the document, or save the document in the normal manner.

An agenda is a practical example of a document that could be sent to employees through the Intranet of a company. Alternatively, an agenda could be sent as an attachment to an E-mail message. (If your class has E-mail access, create exercise 6 and send it to a recipient in your class as an attachment to an E-mail message.)

exercise 6

Preparing an Agenda with Tables

1. At a clear document screen, create the agenda shown in figure 2.33 by completing the following steps:
   a. Position the insertion point at approximately 1.5 inches from the top of the page. (Press Enter until the status bar displays approximately 1.5 inches.)
   b. Change the font to 36-point Colonna MT (or a similar font) in Small caps with a Shadow effect and in the Teal Color.
   c. Click the Center alignment button on the Standard toolbar.
   d. Key **CHICAGO MERCY HOSPITAL**, then press Enter twice.
   e. Change the font to 18-point Book Antiqua Bold in Small caps and change the font Color to Auto. (Turn off the Shadow effect.)
   f. Key **QUALITY CARE PROJECT**.
   g. Press Enter twice, then key ❖ **AGENDA** ❖. (Insert the ❖ symbol at the Symbol dialog box with the Monotype Sorts font selected. The symbol is located in the fourth row, third column. Press the space bar three times before and after **AGENDA**.)
   h. Press Enter twice, then click the Align Left button on the Standard toolbar.
   i. Change the font to 12-point Book Antiqua Regular (or a similar font) and turn off Small caps.
   j. Create a table to hold the agenda text by completing the following steps:
      (1) Click Table, then Insert Table.
      (2) At the Insert Table dialog box, change the Number of columns to **3**.
      (3) Change the Number of rows to **6**.
      (4) Click OK.
      (5) With the insertion point positioned inside the table, click Table, then Cell Height and Width.
      (6) At the Cell Height and Width dialog box, select the Column tab.
      (7) Change the Width of column 1 to **2** inches.
      (8) Click the Next Column button.
      (9) Change the Width of column 2 to **2.8** inches.
      (10) Click the Next Column button.
      (11) Change the Width of column 3 to **2** inches.
      (12) Change the Space between columns to **0.6** inches.
      (13) Select the Row tab.
      (14) Change the Height of rows 1–6 to **At Least** and change the At: measurement to **54 pt**.
      (15) Click OK.
   k. Position the insertion point inside the first cell.
   l. Press the space bar once, key **9:00 – 9:30 a.m.** in the first cell, then press Tab. (Add a space before a single digit number to align the times. Use the en dash between the times—to create an en dash, check to see if the en and em dash option has been turned on at AutoFormat; then press the space bar, key a hyphen, press the space bar, then key a number.)
   m. Key **Call to order and introduction of new project members.**, then press Tab.
   n. Continue keying the text and pressing Tab until the agenda is completed. (If a cell contains three lines of text, press the Enter key after the last line to provide consistent spacing between the cells.)

o. With the insertion point positioned inside the table, click Table, then Table AutoFormat.
p. At the Table AutoFormat dialog box, click the down arrow to the right of the Formats list box, select *Contemporary*, and then click OK.
q. After keying the text for the last column (*Becky Peterson, Chair*), position the arrow pointer below the table, then click the left mouse button.
r. Change the font to 18-point Book Antigua Bold, then press Enter three times.
s. Click the Center alignment button on the Standard toolbar.
t. Create the three symbols (❖) and press the space bar three times between each symbol.

2. Save the agenda and name it c02ex06, table. (*Optional:* If your classroom has access to E-mail, send this agenda to a classmate—the WordMail E-mail program allows you to select Word as your E-mail editor; in which case, you may be able to send the agenda by clicking File, pointing to Send To, and clicking Mail Recipient.)
3. Print and then close c02ex06, table.

CHICAGO MERCY HOSPITAL

QUALITY CARE PROJECT

❖ AGENDA ❖

9:00 - 9:30 a.m.	Call to order and introduction of new project members.	Becky Peterson, Chair
9:30 - 10:00 a.m.	Presentation of project mission statement.	Stanley Barnett
10:00 - 11:00 a.m.	Determination of project goals timelines.	Katrina O'Dell, Geoffrey Benn, and Wendy Mitaki
11:00 - 11:45 a.m.	Brainstorming on public relations activities.	Ellen Heitz and Hui Lenzi
11:45 - 12:00 Noon	Scheduling of next project meeting.	Becky Peterson, Chair
12:00 Noon	Adjournment.	Becky Peterson, Chair

❖ ❖ ❖

Preparing a Press Release

A press release is prepared by a business for submission to a public agency such as a newspaper. It announces something special or new that is being offered by the business, or it may announce accomplishments or promotions of businesspeople. In exercise 7, you will be creating a press release for Chicago Mercy Hospital announcing the construction of a new pediatrics wing.

Word contains three press release templates—Contemporary, Elegant, and Professional Press Releases. However, these templates must be copied from the ValuPack CD included with your Word program or downloaded from the Microsoft Web Site. In exercise 7, you will create a press release with the Elegant Press Release. (When creating documents for an organization, consider using the same colors and basic designs to reinforce identify and continuity; however, you have been asked to use different colors in this chapter for the purpose of learning how colors can affect the overall look of a document.) If you completed a typical installation, you may not have the Publications tab. In which case, you will need to create the Publications folder in C:\Program Files\Microsoft Office\Templates.

exercise 7

Preparing a Press Release

1. At a clear document screen, create the press release shown in figure 2.34 using a Word template by completing the following steps:
   a. Click File, then New.
   b. At the New dialog box, select the Publications tab. Make sure Document is selected in the Create New section.
   c. Double-click the Elegant Press Release icon.
2. Read the information below the heading *HOW TO CUSTOMIZE A PRESS RELEASE* located in the body of the Elegant Template.
3. Position the insertion point in the upper left corner of the press release form at the beginning of the default name, then press Tab. Select the default name, then change the font to 18-point Colonna MT Bold, and then key **CHICAGO MERCY HOSPITAL**.
4. Select the default text in each of following areas and then key the text shown in figure 2.34: Address, Contact, Phone, and For Immediate Release.
5. Select the text from the heading *HOW TO CUSTOMIZE A PRESS RELEASE* to the end of the document, then insert the file, *press release.doc*, from your student data disk.
6. Change the shading behind the heading text by completing the following steps:
   a. Select the text box containing *CHICAGO MERCY HOSPITAL* (eight sizing handles should display), then click Format, Borders and Shading.
   b. Select the Shading tab.
   c. Select the fifth color in the first row of the Fill color palette (Gray-12.5%). The Style list box should read 12.5% and the Color list box should read Auto.
   d. Click OK or press Enter.
   e. Position the insertion point on *Press Release*, then click Format, Borders and Shading.
   f. Select the Shading tab.
   g. Select the Dark Blue color in the seventh row and first column of the Fill palette. The Style list box should read Clear and the Color list box should be inactive. Click OK or press Enter. (*Notice:* The text automatically changes to white!)

   h. Select each text box containing *Contact:...* and *FOR IMMEDIATE...* and change the shading to Gray-20% found in the second row and second column of the Fill palette.
   i. Select the text in each box and apply bold.
7. Add a watermark by completing the following steps:
   a. Position the insertion point in the first line of the body text.
   b. Click Insert, point to Picture, and then click From File.
   c. Select the *medstaff.wmf* file from your student data disk.
   d. Select the picture (sizing handles should display).
   e. Click Format, then Picture.
   f. Select the Wrapping tab, then make sure the None Wrapping style is selected.
   g. Select the Picture tab. Then click the down arrow to the right of Color in the Image Control section and click Watermark.
   h. Click OK or press Enter.
   i. Select the picture and drag it to the center of the memo, then drag one of the corner sizing handles outward to increase the size of the image. Refer to figure 2.34 for an approximate size and location.
   j. Click the Drawing button (fourth from the right) on the Standard toolbar.
   k. Click the Draw button (first button) on the Drawing toolbar.
   l. Point to Order, then click Send Behind Text.
8. Save the press release and name it c02ex07, press release. *(Optional:* Delete any unnecessary text, then save the customized press release as a template.)
9. Print and then close c02ex07, press release. (*Optional:* Send the press release as a fax—in Word, click File, point to Send To, then click Fax Recipient.)

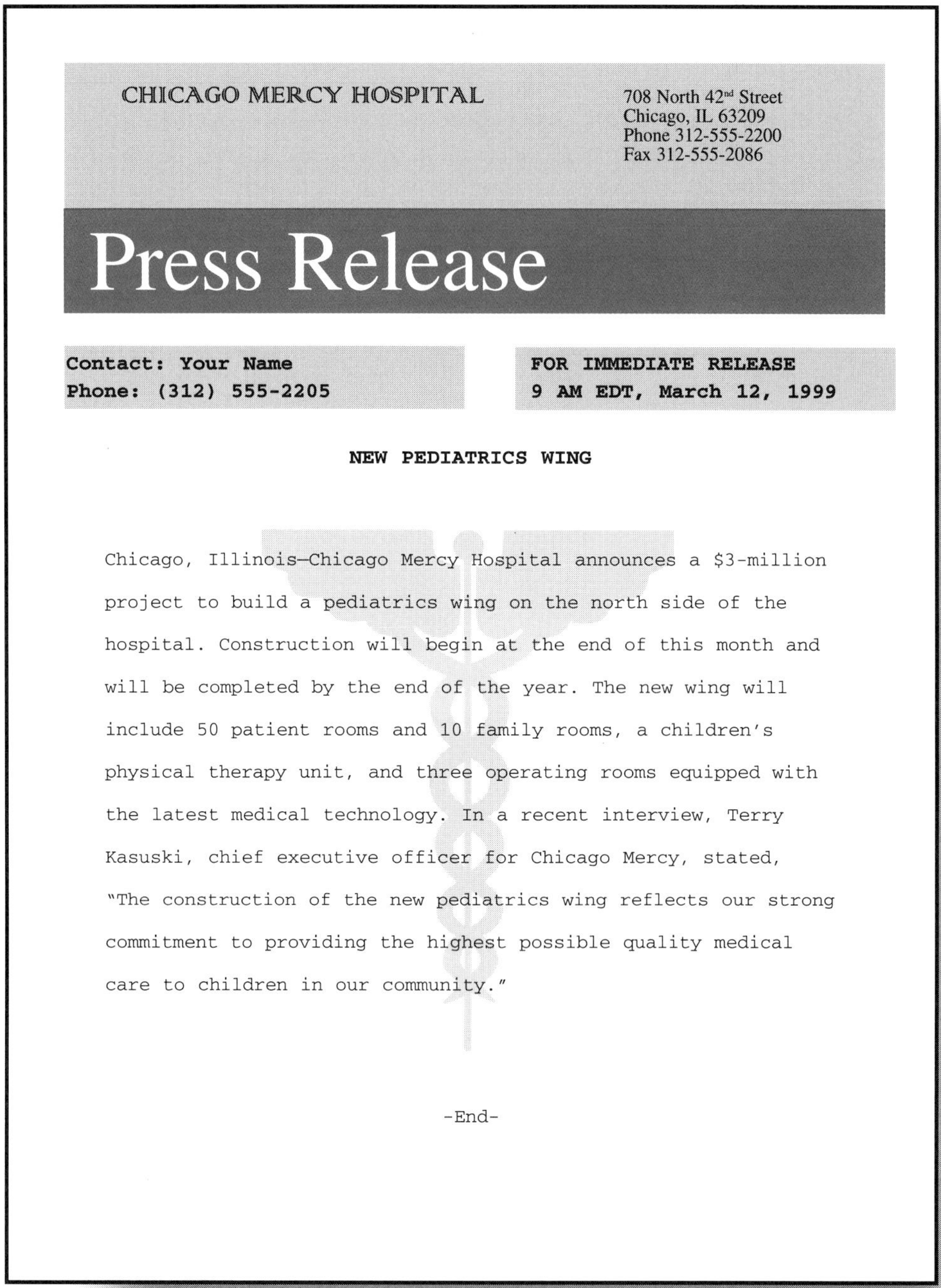

CHICAGO MERCY HOSPITAL

708 North 42nd Street
Chicago, IL 63209
Phone 312-555-2200
Fax 312-555-2086

Press Release

Contact: Your Name
Phone: (312) 555-2205

FOR IMMEDIATE RELEASE
9 AM EDT, March 12, 1999

NEW PEDIATRICS WING

Chicago, Illinois—Chicago Mercy Hospital announces a $3-million project to build a pediatrics wing on the north side of the hospital. Construction will begin at the end of this month and will be completed by the end of the year. The new wing will include 50 patient rooms and 10 family rooms, a children's physical therapy unit, and three operating rooms equipped with the latest medical technology. In a recent interview, Terry Kasuski, chief executive officer for Chicago Mercy, stated, "The construction of the new pediatrics wing reflects our strong commitment to providing the highest possible quality medical care to children in our community."

-End-

figure 2.34

Preparing a Fax Cover Sheet

Assume you are working for a lending company and you want to send a contract to a client; one of the fastest ways is to fax it. Because time is critical, you may not want to spend much time customizing the fax or cover sheet, so you decide to use Word's Fax Wizard. The Fax Wizard provides a ready-made cover sheet along with an option to have the wizard send your document.

Word contains three fax cover sheet templates—Contemporary Fax, Elegant Fax, and Professional Fax, along with the Fax Wizard.

exercise 8

Creating a Fax Cover Sheet

1. At a clear document screen, create the fax cover sheet shown in figure 2.35 using the Fax Wizard by completing the following steps:
   a. Click File, then New.
   b. At the New dialog box, select the Letters & Faxes tab.
   c. Double-click the Fax Wizard icon.
   d. At the Fax Wizard Start screen, click Next>.
   e. At the Document to Fax screen, select Just a cover sheet with a note. (To send a document with the fax cover, open the document first, start the Fax Wizard, and then select the appropriate options.)
   f. At the Fax Software screen, select the Microsoft Fax program, then click Next>. (If your classroom has access to a fax, select the appropriate software program.)
   g. At the Recipients screen, key **Marie Finney** in the name text box and **(612) 555-4711** in the fax text box. Click Next>.
   h. At the Cover Sheet screen, select the Contemporary style. Click Next>.
   i. At the Sender screen, key the following: Then click Next>.

Name:	**Your name**
Company:	**Commercial Lending**
Mailing Address:	**1308 East River Road**
	St. Paul, MN 55101
Phone:	**(612) 555-2300**
Fax:	**(612) 555-4711**

   j. At the Finish screen, click Finish.
   k. Read the Office Assistant's message.
   l. Position the insertion point at the beginning of *1308 East River Street* in the text box at the top of the facsimile transmittal form, then key **Commercial Lending**. Press Enter to force *1308...* down one line. (The Fax Wizard failed to add the company name to the fax form.)
   m. Click each of the placeholders listed below, then enter the following information:

Phone:	**(612) 555-2300**
Pages	**14**
Re:	**Legal Contract**
CC:	**Kathy Nixon and John Shea**

   n. Place a (✔) in the check boxes corresponding to Urgent, Please Reply, and Please Recycle. (The ✔ will replace the check box symbol.) Use the check mark symbol from the Symbol dialog box with the Monotype Sorts font selected. The symbol is located in the first row and the eighth column from the right.
   o. Key the following in the Notes section:
   Please read the legal document, sign both copies, then return one copy to me. Thank you.
   p. If your classroom has access to a fax, click the Send Fax Now Button. Otherwise, click the close button (X) at the Send Fax dialog box.
2. Save the fax cover sheet and name it c02ex08, fax.
3. Print and then close c02ex08, fax.

figure 2.35

Commerical Lending
1308 East River Road
St. Paul. MN 55101
Phone: (612) 555-2300
Fax: (612) 555-4711

facsimile transmittal

To: Marie Finney **From:** Your name

Fax: (612) 555-4711 **Date:** September 8, 1998

Phone: (612) 555-2300 **Pages:** 14

Re: Legal Contract **CC:** Kathy Nixon and John Shea

✓ Urgent ☐ For Review ☐ Please Comment ✓ Please Reply ✓ Please Recycle

Notes: Please read the legal document, sign both copies, then return one copy to me. Thank you.

CONFIDENTIAL

chapter summary

- A font consists of three characteristics: typeface, type style, and type size.
- The term *typeface* refers to the general design and shape of a set of characters.
- The typeface used in a document establishes a particular mood or feeling.
- Characteristics that distinguish one typeface from another include x-height, cap height, height of ascenders, depth of descenders, and serifs.
- A serif is a small stroke on the edge of characters. A sans serif typeface does not have serifs.
- Typefaces are either monospaced or proportional. Monospaced typefaces allot the same amount of horizontal space to each character, while proportional typefaces allot a varying amount to each character.
- Pitch is the number of characters that can be printed in one horizontal inch.
- Point size is a vertical measurement and is approximately 1/72 of an inch. The higher the point size, the larger the characters.
- Printer fonts are the built-in fonts and the supplemental fonts that are available to your printer. Supplemental fonts can be added to your printer in cartridge form or as soft fonts.
- At the Font dialog box you can change the typeface, type size, and type style of text.
- For text set in a proportional typeface, space once after end-of-sentence punctuation.
- A number of template documents are provided by Word that can be used to produce a variety of documents. The default template document is the *Normal.dot*.
- A number of memo templates are available including Contemporary, Elegant, and Professional. A memo wizard is also available that guides you through the creation of a memo.
- A watermark is a lightened image that can be added to a document to add visual interest.
- One of the easiest ways to create a watermark in Word is to insert the watermark into a header or footer.
- Another method to create a watermark is to insert a picture into a document, select the Watermark option at the Image Control, and then select the Send Behind Text option.
- Special symbols can be inserted in a document at the Symbol dialog box with the Symbols tab or the Special Characters tab selected.
- Bullets can be inserted in a document at the Bullets and Numbering dialog box or with the Bullets button on the Formatting toolbar.
- Word contains an agenda template that can be used to prepare an agenda.
- Tables can be used when formatting an agenda into side-by-side columns.
- Three press release templates are available in Word—Contemporary, Elegant, and Professional Press Releases.
- Three fax cover sheet templates are available in Word—Contemporary, Elegant, and Professional Faxes.
- The Fax Wizard helps you send a fax through your computer.

commands review

	Mouse/Keyboard
Font dialog box	Format, Font; or press Ctrl + D
New dialog box	File, New
Header and Footer	View, Header and Footer
Format Text Box dialog box	Format, Text Box
Borders and Shading dialog box	Format, Borders and Shading
Picture dialog box	Click Format, point to Picture, then click Clip Art or From File
Watermark	View, Header and Footer. At the Header and Footer pane, create a text box, insert picture, click Image Control on the Picture toolbar, then select Watermark. Close Header and Footer pane. Or, create text box, insert picture, click Draw on Drawing toolbar, Order, then Send Behind Text. (You do not have to insert picture into a text box—the text box helps control the picture size and location.)
Symbol dialog box	Insert, Symbol
AutoFormat	Click Format, AutoFormat, then Options
Bullets and Numbering dialog box	Insert, Bullets and Numbering
Insert Table dialog box	Table, Insert Table

check your understanding

Matching: Match the terms with the correct definitions by writing the letter of the term on the blank line in front of the correct definition.

A Baseline	F Cap height	K Type style
B Monospaced	G Point size	L Sans serif
C Serif	H x-height	M Typeface
D Descenders	I Roman	N Ascenders
E Point	J Proportional	O Font

_______ 1. A set of characters with a common design and shape.

_______ 2. Imaginary horizontal line on which text rests.

_______ 3. Height of the main body of the lowercase characters and equivalent to the lowercase *x*.

_______ 4. Distance between the baseline and the top of capital letters.

_______ 5. Parts of lowercase characters that rise above the x-height.

_______ 6. Parts of characters that extend below the baseline.

_______ 7. Approximate distance from the top of the ascenders to the bottom of the descenders.

_______ 8. A small stroke at the edge of characters.

_______ 9. A typeface that does not contain serifs.

_______ 10. Approximately 1/72 of an inch.

_______ 11. Varying style of a typeface, including bold and italic.

_______ 12. A typeface in a specific size and style.

True/False: Circle the letter T if the statement is true; circle the letter F if the statement is false.

T F 1. Proportional typefaces allot the same amount of horizontal space for each character in a typeface.

T F 2. An em dash is used to indicate a duration of time.

T F 3. When text is set in a proportional typeface, space once after end-of-sentence punctuation.

T F 4. The default template document is the *Main* template.

T F 5. Click the New button on the Standard toolbar to display the New dialog box.

T F 6. A watermark exists in the text layer of a document.

T F 7. Click Format, then Bullets and Numbering to display the Bullets and Numbering dialog box.

T F 8. Press the Tab key to move the insertion point to the next cell in a table.

skill assessments

Assessment 1

1. At a clear document screen, create a memo using one of the memo templates or the memo wizard. Include the following information in the memo heading:

To:	**Amanda Wong**
From:	**Your name**
Date:	**Current date**
Re.:	**Outpatient Survey**

2. Key the text shown in figure 2.36 in the memo.
3. Customize the memo to match the tone of the memo text.
4. Save the completed memo and name it c02sa01, survey.
5. Print and then close c02sa01, survey.

figure 2.36

For the past six months, the members of the Outpatient Survey Team have been preparing a survey to gather data on the quality of patient care in the Outpatient Clinic. The information gathered from this survey will help us make positive changes in the services offered by the clinic. We are also interested in why patients pick the Outpatient Clinic rather than the traditional Surgical Unit.

Please read the enclosed survey and let me know what you feel should be changed or added. I would like to present the final draft of the survey to the team by next week. I will schedule a meeting with you later in the week to get your feedback.
xx:c02sa01, survey
Enclosure

Optional: Create an appropriate watermark for the memo in Assessment 1. If your classroom is setup to fax documents, send the memo as a fax to one of your peers.

Assessment 2

1. At a clear document screen, create the agenda shown in figure 2.37 with the following specifications:
   a. Change the top margin to 1.5 inches and the left and right margins to 1 inch.
   b. Change the font to 24-point Colonna MT Bold.
   c. Set a right tab at 6.5 inches.
   d. Key **✧✧✧ L. & D. Inc.** (Create the special symbol ✧ at the Symbol dialog box with the Wingdings font selected. The symbol is located in the seventh column, sixth row.)
   e. Press Tab then key **Agenda ✧✧✧**.
   f. Press Enter three times, then key **BOARD OF DIRECTORS' MEETING** centered.
   g. Turn off bold and change the alignment to Align Left. Press Enter twice, then change the font to 14-point Book Antiqua.
   h. Create a table with three columns and seven rows. Adjust each column width to 2.22 inches with 0.15 inches in between. Change the Height of Rows 1–7 to At Least and At 56 points.
   i. Key the agenda text shown in figure 2.37. (Align the times and use an en dash.)
   j. Position the insertion point inside the table, then click Table, Table AutoFormat.
   k. Select *Subtle 1* from the Formats list.
   l. Select Shading, Color, and AutoFit and deselect the rest of the options in the Formats to apply and Apply special formats to sections.
   m. Click OK or press Enter.
   n. Position the arrow pointer below the table, click the left button, then press Enter three times.
   o. Change the font to 24-point Colonna MT Bold then key the remaining symbols.
2. Save the agenda and name it c02sa02, agenda.
3. Print and then close c02sa02, agenda.

BOARD OF DIRECTORS' MEETING

8:00 - 8:15 a.m.	Introduction of Members	Scott Ingram, Chief Executive Officer
8:15 - 9:30 a.m.	Discussion of expansion into Canada	Suzanne Reiser, Director of Facilities Planning
9:30 - 10:15 a.m.	Discussion of expansion into Europe	Ryan Keyes, Assistant Director of Facilities
10:15 - 10:45 a.m.	Break	Refreshments served
10:45 - 11:30 a.m.	Review of short-term and long-term goals for 1999	Lucinda White, Vice President
11:30 - 12 :15 p.m.	Short-term and long-term goal setting for 1999	Francis Lewellyn, President
12:15 p.m.	Adjournment	Scott Ingram, Chief Executive Officer

Optional: Delete the Table AutoFormat from the agenda and insert an appropriate watermark that will enhance the appearance of the agenda.

Assessment 3

1. Use Word's Help feature to learn more about WordMail and Word as an E-mail editor. (*Hint:* Use Contents and Index, and key **E-mail**, then select using Word as your editor as shown in figure 2.38.)
2. Click on each topic displayed in a text box with a red marker. Read the information, then right-click the mouse to access the print command. Print each topic.
3. Write a memo describing what you have learned about WordMail and Word as an E-mail editor.
4. Consider adding enhancements to the memo such as bold and/or italics, bullets, varying font attributes, symbols, and a watermark.
5. Save the memo and name it c02sa03, email.
6. Print and then close c02sa03, email.

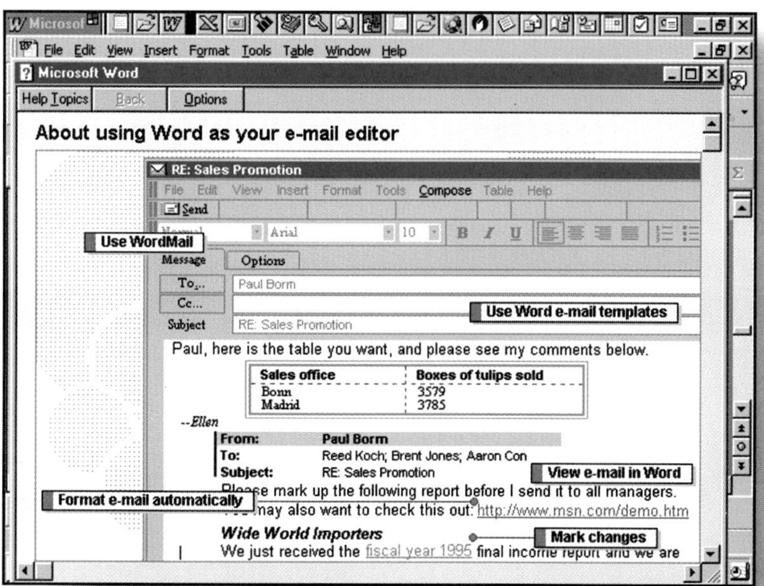

figure 2.38

Using Word as an E-mail Editor (Help Screen)

creative activity

Situation: You work for a desktop publisher called Desktop Designs located at 4455 Jackson Drive, Raleigh, NC 27613. You have been asked by your supervisor to develop a press release describing the services performed by Desktop Designs. Use a Word template to create this press release and include the following information in your own words:

- Desktop Designs has been operating in the Raleigh area for over 12 years.
- The employees of Desktop Designs have over 30 years of combined graphics design and typesetting experience.
- The company provides a variety of services, including creating personal documents such as cover letters, résumés, invitations, programs, cards, envelopes and labels; creating business documents such as letterheads, envelopes, business cards, forms, logos, and slides; and creating promotional and marketing documents such as newsletters, flyers, and brochures.
- The company is open Monday through Saturday from 7:00 a.m. to 6:00 p.m.

After creating the press release, save it and name it c02ca01, press release. Print and then close c02ca01, press release.

chapter THREE

Creating Letterheads, Envelopes, and Business Cards

PERFORMANCE OBJECTIVE

Upon successful completion of chapter 3, you will be able to produce business letterheads, envelopes, and business cards using a variety of templates, fonts, and ruled lines.

Desktop Publishing Concepts

Identifying purpose
Design
Appropriate font selection
Templates
Styles
Use of horizontal and vertical lines
Exact placement of elements on a page
Kerning
Tracking
Consistency

Word Features Used

Fonts
Letter template
Template styles
Template folder
Letter Wizard
Drawing toolbar
Lines
Text boxes
Format text box
Borders and shading
Symbols
WordArt
Automatic and manual kerning
Character spacing
Envelopes and Labels feature
AutoText
Business card label definition

In this chapter, you will produce business letterheads, envelopes, and business cards using your own design and creative skills as well as Word's Template feature. Although Word provides a variety of letter templates to choose from, they do not meet the needs of all situations. Information on how to customize an existing template and how to create your own design and layout from scratch are presented in this chapter. Ruled lines, kerning (the spacing between specific pairs of letters), and tracking (character spacing), along with Word's Envelopes and Labels, Text Box, and AutoText features, are also discussed.

Identifying the Purpose of Letterheads

In planning your letterhead, clearly identify its purpose. While the content of a letter may vary, the purpose of any letterhead is generally the same—to convey information, to establish an identity, and to project an image.

Conveying Information

Consider all the necessary information you want to include in your letterhead. Also, consider what items your readers expect to find in your letterhead. Although the information provided may vary, letterheads commonly contain the following:

- name of company or organization
- logo
- very brief business philosophy statement, marketing statement, or slogan
- address
- shipping or mailing address, if different from street address
- telephone number, including area code (include actual numbers if your phone number incorporates a catchy word as part of the number; include extra phone numbers, such as a local number and/or an 800 number, if any)
- fax number, including area code
- E-mail address

The information in a letterhead supplies the reader with a means of contacting you in person, by phone, or by mail. Leaving out an important component in your letterhead can affect your company's business and project a careless attitude.

Establishing an Identity

DTP POINTERS
A letterhead conveys information, establishes an identity, and projects an image.

Oftentimes a business relationship is initiated through one or more business letters. For example, a buyer from one company may write to another company inquiring about a certain product or asking for a price list; a real estate agent may send out a letter explaining his or her services to residents in surrounding communities; or, your volunteer organization may send thank you letters to local businesses. Whatever the reason for the letter content, a letterhead with a specific design and layout helps to establish your organization's identity. When readers are exposed to the same pattern of consistent elements in your letterhead over a period of time, they soon begin to establish a certain level of familiarity with your organization's name, logo, colors, etc. Your letterhead is recognizable and identifiable.

You can further emphasize your company's identity by using some of the design elements from your letterhead in your other business documents. Many direct mail paper suppliers offer a whole line of attractively designed color letterheads, along with coordinating envelopes, business cards, brochures, postcards, note cards, disk labels, and more. All you have to do is design and lay out your letterhead text to complement the existing design and then print on the preprinted papers. Purchasing a coordinating line of preprinted papers can save on the high costs of professional designing and printing. It also provides a convenient way to establish your identity among your readers. Some paper suppliers offer a sample kit of their papers for purchase at a reasonable price. This is a great opportunity to see and feel the papers and to test some of them in your printer.

Projecting an Image

Along with establishing an identity, you need to think about the image that identity projects to your readers. As mentioned in chapter 1, assess your target audience. Who are your readers? Whom do you want to be your readers? What image do you want to project and what image do your readers expect you to project? Pretend that you have a folded letter in your hand from a bank. Without even looking at the letter, what image do you expect that letter to portray? Pretend, again, that in your other hand you have another folded letter from an old country inn. Without looking at that letter, what image comes to your mind? Are the two images the same or different? Most likely, you expect the bank's image to be more serious, conservative, formal, and businesslike. And you probably expect the old country inn's image to be more casual, informal, comfortable, and cozy. Figures 3.1 and 3.2 show examples of company names in different fonts.

figure 3.1

First Bank of Dupage

First Bank of DuPage

figure 3.2

Salem Country Inn

Salem Country Inn

However, giving your readers what they expect can sometimes lead to boredom. Your challenge is to create a design that gives the readers what they expect and, at the same time, sets your letterhead apart from the rest.

Printing your letterhead on high-quality paper may add to the cost, but it certainly presents a more professional image. An off-white, ivory, cream, or gray paper is a better choice than plain white. You may have to go to a commercial printer to purchase this kind of paper. Many print shops let you buy paper by the sheet, along with matching envelopes.

DTP POINTERS
Printing on high-quality paper presents a professional image.

Using Word's Letterhead Templates

As discussed in chapter 2, Word includes a variety of predesigned template documents, including letterheads. At the New dialog box, select the Letters & Faxes tab to display the following Word letter templates:

Letter Wizard.wiz (Helps you create a letter)
Contemporary Letter.dot
Elegant Letter.dot
Professional Letter.dot

DTP POINTERS
Establish identity and consistency among your internal and external business documents.

Notice that the descriptive letterhead names coordinate with the descriptive names for the memo and fax templates introduced in chapter 2. This is an easy way for you to establish identity and consistency among both your internal and external business documents. For example, select Professional for your memo, fax, and letter template choices and all your documents will have matching elements. Even though you can view a template in the Preview box at the New dialog box, printing samples of your template documents lets you see firsthand what is available. The body of the template document may contain some valuable user information. For example, when you select the *Contemporary Letter* from the New dialog box, the body of the letter contains a brief paragraph that includes the following sentence: *For more details on modifying this letter template, double-click* ✉. When you double-click the envelope icon, the letter is replaced with a completed sample letter. The body of this sample letter provides more specific information on how to use the existing template and how to customize the letterhead for your own use. To create a business letter based on the *Professional Letter* template, complete exercise 1.

exercise 1

Creating a Letter Using Word's Professional Letter Template

1. At a clear document screen, create the business letter shown in figure 3.3 using the *Professional Letter* template by completing the following steps:
   a. Click File, then New.
   b. At the New dialog box, select the Letters & Faxes tab.
   c. Make sure that Document is selected in the Create New section, then double-click the *Professional Letter.dot* icon in the Letters & Faxes tab (or click the template name, then click OK).
   d. Double-click the envelope icon in the first line of the placeholder body text, then print a copy of the completed *Blue Sky Airlines* sample letter.
   e. Read the sample letter for future reference. Close the sample letter without saving any changes.
   f. With the original *Professional Letter* template document letter displayed on the screen, select *Company Name Here*, then key **Chicago Mercy Hospital**.
   g. Position the I-beam pointer (not the arrow pointer) anywhere in the prompt that reads *[Click* ***here*** *and type return address]*, click once to select this section, then key the following in the return address location (*Note:* The "nd" in 42nd Street will automatically superscript once Enter has been pressed.):

780 North 42nd Street
Chicago, IL 63209
312.555-2035
Fax: 312.555-2086

h. Position the I-beam anywhere in the prompt that reads [Click **here** and type recipient's address], click once to select this section, then key the following as the inside address:

Sylvia Hensley, M.D.
Quality Care Program Director
Allenmore Clinic
1005 Seventh Avenue
Chicago, IL 65145

i. Select *Sir or Madam* in the salutation, then key **Dr. Hensley** in its place.
j. Select the placeholder paragraph below the salutation, then key the body of the letter as shown in figure 3.3. Select *(your last name)* in the last paragraph, then key your last name. (*Note:* Press the Enter key once after each paragraph, except the last paragraph. The body text in the Professional Letter template contains a paragraph spacing instruction that provides 11 points of spacing after each paragraph. Pressing Enter two times would result in too much white space between paragraphs.)
k. After keying the body of the letter, create the complimentary close by completing the following steps:
   (1) Position the I-beam anywhere in the prompt that reads *[Click **here** and type your name],* click once to select this section, then key your name.
   (2) Position the I-beam anywhere in the prompt that reads *[Click **here** and type job title],* click once to select this section, then key **Health Care Director**, then press Enter.
   (3) Select *Normal* from the Style list box located on the left side of the Formatting toolbar, and then press Enter.
   (4) Key your initials followed by **:c03ex01, letter**, then press Enter two times.
   (5) Key **Attachments**.
2. Save the completed letter and name it c03ex01, letter.
3. Print and then close c03ex01, letter.

3.3

Chicago Mercy Hospital

780 North 42nd Street
Chicago, IL 63209
312.555-2035
Fax: 312.555-2086

June 7, 1999

Sylvia Hensley, M.D.
Quality Care Program Director
Allenmore Clinic
1005 Seventh Avenue
Chicago, IL 65145

Dear Dr. Hensley:

I am excited about the potential benefits of a community-oriented health care program and look forward to working with you. Attached is a copy of the letter of intent that we submitted for the health care program. Also attached is the response we received notifying us that we had been selected to receive further consideration for this special funding.

There is a meeting on June 10, from 1:30 to 3:00 p.m., in the conference room at Chicago Mercy Hospital. If you cannot personally attend the meeting, please send a designated representative from your clinic. After the meeting, we will pull together a work group to define the particular health care issues to be proposed in our grant application.

If you have any questions or comments on the attached material or the process being contemplated, please give me a call at 555-2035, extension 347 or you may e-mail me at (your last name) @mercynet.hosp.com.

Sincerely,

(Your name here)
Health Care Director

xx:c03ex01, letter

Attachments

Understanding Template Styles

A template may include several components, such as styles, text, graphics, AutoText entries, and macros. As mentioned in the previous chapter, Word automatically bases a new document created at a blank screen on the *Normal.dot* template. This template initially contains five styles, including one called the *Normal* style. The Normal style contains formatting instructions to use 10-point Times New Roman as the font, English (US) as the language, character spacing scaled to 100%, flush left alignment, single spacing, Widow/Orphan control, and body text as the default outline level. Word automatically applies the Normal style to all paragraphs in your documents unless you give it other formatting instructions. Depending on the type of document that is being created, templates often have additional styles. For example, the *Professional Letter* template used to create the letter in exercise 1 contains many styles. Styles are included for the body text, closing, date, enclosure, inside address, reference initials, salutation, and more. For example, if you open *c03ex01, letter,* and position the insertion point within the inside address, the Style box on the Formatting toolbar displays *Inside Address* as shown in figure 3.4. This means that a style named *Inside Address*, containing formatting instructions for the inside address, has been applied to this section of text. Additionally, if the insertion point is positioned in other sections of text in *c03ex01, letter,* you will see different style names displayed in the Style box on the Formatting toolbar. You may override any style formatting instructions by selecting text and making the desired changes at the normal editing window or by modifying the style itself. Styles are discussed in greater detail in chapter 6.

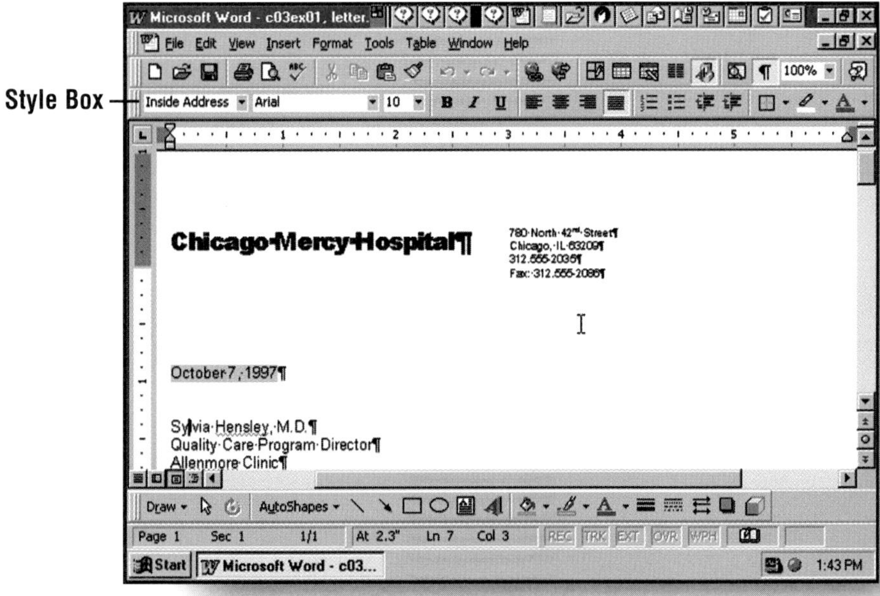

figure 3.4

Style Box on the Formatting Toolbar

Using the Letter Wizard

Word provides a Letter Wizard that guides you through the steps for creating a single business or personal letter using the Contemporary, Professional, or Elegant Letter template or any other letter template that you may have created. The difference between accessing the letter templates directly through the New dialog box versus the Letter Wizard is that the wizard allows you to make various decisions on the letter style, the recipient and sender information, the wording used in the salutation and the closing, and the inclusion of specialized letter elements before the letter even displays on the screen. In addition, the Letter Wizard gives you the opportunity to make an envelope or label for the letter being created.

Word's User Information feature is a way to store the name, initials, and address of the primary user of your Word program. Word automatically inserts this information in specific documents, such as letters, memos, and résumés, that are constructed with a Wizard. For example, the Letter Wizard uses the Name listed in User Information in any of the letter closings it helps you create. However, it does not use this information if you select one of the letter templates from the New dialog box instead of using the Letter Wizard to create your letter. Word uses the Mailing Address from User Information as the default return address on envelopes. The Initials are used in conjunction with Word's Annotation feature—a feature that lets you leave notes to yourself or others in your document.

After constructing a document with a wizard or template, you can customize that document by adding or replacing text, inserting or replacing graphic images, and including formatting instructions to fit your needs. Complete exercise 2 to create a Contemporary letter using the Letter Wizard. You will then customize the letter by changing the shading of some of the graphic elements included in the template.

exercise 2

Creating a Contemporary Letter with the Letter Wizard

1. At a clear document screen, enter User Information by completing the following steps:
   a. Click Tools, then Options.
   b. At the Options dialog box, select the User Information tab.
   c. Key your name at the Name list box. (Do not take the time to change the Initials or Mailing Address. This information will not be used by the Letter Wizard.)
   d. Click OK.
2. Use the Letter Wizard to create the business letter shown in figure 3.5 using the Contemporary Letter style by completing the following steps:
   a. Click File, then New.
   b. At the New dialog box, select the Letters & Faxes tab.
   c. Make sure that Document is selected in the Create New section, then double-click the Letter Wizard icon in the Letters & Faxes tab (or click the wizard, then click OK).
   d. When the Office Assistant appears, select *Send one letter*.
   e. At the Letter Wizard dialog box with the Letter Format tab displayed, complete the following steps:
      (1) Make sure there is a check mark in the Date line check box and the current date displays in a *month, date, year* format, such as *June 10, 1998*.
      (2) Click the arrow in the Choose a page design list box, then select *Contemporary Letter*.
      (3) Make sure Full block displays as the letter style, then click Next>.

f. With the Recipient Info tab displayed, complete the following steps:
   (1) In the Recipient's name text box, key **Mr. George Peraza**.
   (2) In the Delivery address text box, key the following (*Note:* The "nd" in 42nd Street will automatically superscript once Enter has been pressed):

   Assistant Director, Health Services
   Chicago Mercy Hospital
   780 North 42nd Street
   Chicago, IL 63209

   (3) In the Salutation section, select *Formal*.
   (4) Click Next>.
   (5) With the Other Elements tab displayed and no options checked, click Next>.

g. With the Sender Info tab displayed, complete the following steps:
   (1) Make sure your name is displayed in the Sender's name text box.
   (2) In the Return address text box, key the following:

   Director of Human Resources
   Worldwide Health Services
   893 Renquist Avenue
   Chicago, IL 65068

   (3) In the Closing section, click the down arrow to the right of the Complimentary closing list box, then select *Yours truly,* as the closing.
   (4) In the Job title text box, key **Director of Human Resources**.
   (5) In the Writer/typist initials text box, key your initials in lowercase.
   (6) Click Finish.

h. When the Office Assistant asks if you would like to do more with the letter, click Cancel.

i. Click File, Page Setup, then change the bottom margin to 0.5 inches. If Word displays the message *One or more margins are set outside the printable area of the page. Choose the Fix button to increase the appropriate margins.*, click Fix. Word will adjust the margin to the minimum amount allowed by your printer.

j. With the letter displayed on the screen, position the insertion point to the left of the date, then press Enter six times. (The spacing will be more than normal because the *Date* style, which is active at this point, includes 13 points of spacing after each paragraph.)

k. Insert the company name on top of the gray shaded rectangle (which is an AutoShape inserted in the header pane) by completing the following steps:
   (1) Click View, then Header and Footer.
   (2) Position the mouse in the shaded rectangle until it displays as an arrow with a four-headed arrow attached, then right-click one time.
   (3) Click Add Text.
   (4) Change the font to 24-point Times New Roman Bold, Small caps, then key **Worldwide Health Services**. (The text will not completely fit in the box.)
   (5) Change the size of the AutoShape rectangle by completing the following steps:
      (a) With the rectangle still selected, click Format, then AutoShape.

(b) At the AutoShape dialog box, select the Size tab. In the Size and rotate section, change the Height to 0.48 inches and make sure the Width displays as 7.5 inches.
(c) Click OK or press Enter.

l. Darken the shading of the rectangle by completing the following steps:
   (1) With the rectangle still selected, make sure the Drawing toolbar is displayed. If not, position the arrow pointer anywhere within the Standard or Formatting toolbar, then right-click one time. Click *Drawing* from the toolbar drop-down menu. (A check mark should display to the left of the Drawing option.)
   (2) Click the Fill Color arrow on the Drawing toolbar, then click Gray-25%, located in the fourth row, the last column.

m. Click Close on the Header and Footer toolbar.

n. Select the one paragraph of body text, then key the three paragraphs as displayed in figure 3.5, pressing Enter one time between paragraphs.

o. Position the insertion point after your reference initials, then key **:c03ex02, letter**.

p. Insert the slogan on top of the shaded rectangle (which is an AutoShape inserted in the footer pane) located at the bottom of the page by completing the following steps:
   (1) Click View, then Header and Footer.
   (2) Click the Switch Between Header and Footer button on the Header and Footer toolbar.
   (3) Position the mouse in the shaded rectangle until it displays as an arrow with a four-headed arrow attached, then right-click one time.
   (4) Click Add Text.
   (5) Turn on bold and italics, then key **Serving those in need around the globe!**.
   (6) Click Format, Paragraph, then change the Spacing Before to 10 points.

q. Darken the shading of the rectangle by repeating steps 2l(1-2) above.

r. Darken the shading of the globe by completing the following steps:
   (1) With the header and footer screen still displayed, use the vertical scroll bar to locate the globe graphic image.
   (2) Position the arrow pointer within the globe until it displays with a four-headed arrow attached, then double-click to enter the image into Word's Picture Editing feature.
   (3) Click once inside the globe to select it.
   (4) Click the Fill Color arrow on the Drawing toolbar, then click Gray-25%, located in the fourth row, the last column.
   (5) Click File, then Close & Return to ...(followed by a document number or the name of the file if it has already been saved).
   (6) Click Close on the Header and Footer toolbar.

3. Save the completed letter and name it c03ex02, letter.
4. Print and then close c03ex02, letter.

figure 3.5

Director of Human Resources
Worldwide Health Services
893 Renquist Avenue
Chicago, IL 65068

WORLDWIDE HEALTH SERVICES

June 17, 1999

Mr. George Peraza
Assistant Director, Health Services
Chicago Mercy Hospital
780 North 42nd Street
Chicago, IL 63209

Dear Mr. Peraza,

Thank you for your inquiry about employment opportunities at Worldwide Health Services. We appreciate your interest in our company.

Although your background is impressive, we currently have no openings that match your skills and qualifications. We will keep your résumé on file for six months for review should we have an opening for which you are qualified.

Again, thank you for your interest. Best wishes for success in your career search.

Yours truly,

(Your name here)
Director of Human Resources

xx:c03ex02, letter

Serving those in need around the globe!

After printing the Contemporary style business letter created in exercise 2 (figure 3.5), compare it with the Professional style business letter created in exercise 1 (figure 3.3). In exercise 1 (Professional style), the company name, set in 16-point Arial Black, provides the only real focal point on the page. The reader is able to readily identify the name of the company. Notice how this focal element draws the reader's eyes to the natural starting position for reading (upper left corner of the page) and initiates the directional flow in the letter. The larger and bolder company name leads the eye to the block of text containing the return address, set in 7-point Arial. The date, inside address, body text, and closing continue to direct the flow down the page. Word's Professional style letter is very straightforward and conservative in its layout and design.

In contrast, the letter created in exercise 2 employs more contemporary design elements. The eye is immediately drawn to the gray shaded rectangle containing the company name, which is set in 24-point Times New Roman Bold Small Caps. The rectangular box provides directional flow to the right side of the page. The globe watermark acts as a secondary focal point that draws the eye back over to the left side of the page and to the body text. The gray shaded rectangle located in the bottom left corner of the page leads the reader down to the bottom of the page and over to the right. The horizontal dotted line provides a finishing touch, leading the reader to the bottom right corner of the page. Can you visualize a form of the Z directional flow pattern mentioned in Chapter 1 in this letter's design and layout? Consistent elements are exemplified by the repeated use of the same typeface, the gray shaded rectangles, the gray shading of the watermark, and the dotted lines. This letter utilizes several examples of asymmetrical design. The vertical dotted line at the top left of the page and the accompanying white space help to balance the block of text containing the return address. Also note that the white space provided by the wider left margin and the globe watermark extending into the left margin counterbalance the larger block of letter text. In addition, the horizontal dotted line and the surrounding white space located at the bottom of the page serve as balancing contrasting elements to the gray shaded rectangle containing the slogan.

DTP POINTERS
Asymmetrical design adds interest and impact.

Word's template documents are definitely an easy and convenient way to create a variety of professional-looking documents, but they cannot meet the needs of all people, companies, or organizations in all situations. However, templates can serve as the framework for creating customized documents. A document created from a template can be individualized (as in exercise 2), an existing template can be edited permanently, or a whole new template can be created from an existing document or from scratch. For example, the customized letterhead created in exercise 2 could be saved as a totally new template to be used over and over again. Since text was automatically inserted into the letter through the Letter Wizard options, you would need to delete any information that may vary from letter to letter, such as the inside address, the salutation, the body text, the closing, etc., then save your document as a template into the Letters & Faxes folder following similar steps as those mentioned in chapter 2.

Designing your own letterhead is also possible. Designing your own letterhead lets you create your own identity and image while cutting costs at the same time. In upcoming exercises, you will have the chance to create a letterhead from scratch and to convert the letterhead into a template.

Designing Your Own Letterhead

When it comes to designing a letterhead, you might ask yourself, "Isn't this where the commercial printer takes over? Doesn't everyone have their letterhead designed and created by a commercial printer?" Obviously, a lot of businesses have their letterheads created professionally. However, there are distinct cost-saving advantages to creating your own letterhead.

Smaller businesses and newly created businesses may not have the financial resources to purchase a letterhead designed by a graphic designer and created by a printer. Not only is a custom design costly, but using more than one color on a page adds to the expense (and black is counted as one color!). With the lower-cost laser and color ink jet printers available today and your Word software, you can create very professional-looking letterheads at a much lower cost. In addition, when working with a commercial printer, you would probably be required to meet a minimum purchase order. If you produce your own letterhead, you can print any amount you need and save yourself the upfront costs of purchasing a large number of letterheads. Also, as long as you have a supply of paper (and your equipment is not temperamental!), your letterhead is always only a few keystrokes away. Second sheets to go along with your letterhead are readily available, too. All things considered, designing and producing your own letterhead is a cost-effective alternative to having it created through an outside source.

Designing and producing your own letterhead takes some time and practice. When you have completed the planning stage for your letterhead and you are actually ready to "create" the design, get out pencil and paper and make some thumbnail sketches. This is a great way to experiment with your layout and design without your software interfering with the creative process, as we all know it can from time to time!

DTP POINTERS
Designing takes time and practice.

When creating your thumbnail sketches and, ultimately, your letterhead, think of the following design concepts, as presented in chapter 1:

- *Focus:* What is the focal point(s) in your letterhead? What is the most important information? What is the least important information? Is there more than one focal element? If so, is there a natural progression from one to the other?
- *Balance:* Is your layout and design symmetrical (similar elements distributed evenly on the page, such as a horizontally centered layout)? Or is it asymmetrical (dissimilar elements distributed unevenly on the page in such a way as to balance one another out)?
- *Proportion:* Are the design elements used in proportion to one another? Is the type size of the company name in proportion to the company logo? To the other letterhead information? To the type size that will be used for the body text? Is the size indicative of importance?
- *Contrast:* Are there varying degrees of lightness and darkness? Is there enough surrounding white space assigned to darker elements on the page? Does the typeface used in the letterhead provide a complementary contrast to the typeface that will be used in the body text? Does the use of color provide a pleasing contrast?
- *Directional flow:* Are the design elements strategically placed to create a natural flow of information? Is the reader able to logically progress from the more important information to the less important information? Do text, special characters, ruled lines, and graphic images direct the flow rather than impede the flow of information?

- *Consistency:* Are there any elements of your page layout and design that are consistent? Is a particular typeface consistently used in your letterhead even though it may vary in type size, type style, or color? Is one color repeated sparingly to emphasize important or distinctive elements (called "spot" color)? Is there some repeating element that ties the letterhead to subsequent pages, such as a ruled horizontal line that is repeated as a footer on each page?
- *Color:* Does the use and intensity of color relate proportionally to the importance of the item? Is color used sparingly to provide emphasis and contrast? Does the color used meet readers' expectations?

Creating Horizontal and Vertical Ruled Lines Using Word's Drawing Toolbar

Ruled Lines
Horizontal or vertical lines.

In Word, several methods may be used to set horizontal and/or vertical lines anywhere on a page. In addition, you can adjust the length and width, color, and shading of the lines. In typesetting, these horizontal and vertical lines are called *rules, ruling lines,* or *ruled lines* to distinguish them from lines of type. Horizontal and vertical ruled lines are used in a document to guide readers across and/or down the page, to separate one section of text from another, to separate columns of text, or to add visual interest.

DTP POINTERS
Ruled lines act as boundaries to surrounding text.

Remember that ruled lines act as boundaries to the surrounding text. A thicker line serves as more of a barrier than a thinner line. For example, a thin vertical line separating columns of text tends to keep the reader's eyes from jumping over to the next column. Alternately, a thicker ruled line between columns tends to tell the reader that the information in one column is entirely separate from the information in the next column. Keep this same idea in mind when considering using ruled lines with headings. Ruled lines should be placed above the heading rather than below the heading. This way the reader knows that the heading belongs to the text that follows it. In addition, when using ruled lines, be consistent in their purpose and their appearance.

You can use Word's Drawing toolbar to create horizontal and vertical ruled lines at any location on a page. The Drawing toolbar is one of the predefined toolbars provided by Word. To turn on the display of the toolbar, choose one of the following methods:

Drawing

- Click the Drawing button on the Standard toolbar.
- Choose View, then Toolbars, click Drawing (this inserts a check mark in the check box), then choose OK or press Enter.
- Position the arrow pointer in any gray area of any currently displayed toolbar, click the right mouse button, then click *Drawing* in the drop-down menu.

When you select the Drawing toolbar, the toolbar appears at the bottom of the screen above the Status bar. The Drawing toolbar and the names of each button are shown in figure 3.6.

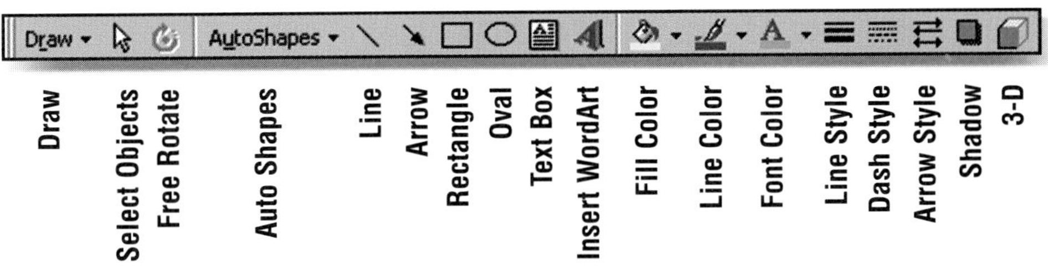

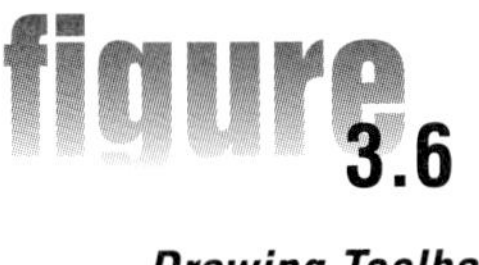

figure 3.6

Drawing Toolbar

Drawing Horizontal or Vertical Lines

Line

To insert a horizontal or vertical line using the Drawing toolbar, click the Line button (the fifth button from the left). Word automatically changes the viewing mode to Page Layout view if this view has not already been selected. Position the crosshairs at the desired starting point of your horizontal or vertical line. To create a perfectly straight horizontal or vertical line, hold down the Shift key and the left mouse button, drag the mouse horizontally or vertically to create the line length of your choice, then release the mouse button and the Shift key when done. (Ragged or imperfect lines are created when the Shift key is not pressed during the drawing process.) To create horizontal or vertical arrow lines, follow the same basic procedure but click the Arrow button (the sixth button from the left) on the Drawing toolbar instead of the Line button. To display the crosshairs continuously to draw additional lines, double-click on the Line (or Arrow) button, and then draw any number of lines. Click the Line (or Arrow) button again to discontinue line drawing.

Arrow

Sizing Horizontal and Vertical Lines

Horizontal and vertical ruled lines (or any other shapes) created with the Drawing tools are called *objects*. Objects can be customized as to their size, position on the page, style, and color. To edit or change an object, you must first select it. To do this, position the I-beam pointer on the line to be edited until it turns into an arrow pointer with a four-headed arrow attached, and then click the left mouse button. This causes the line to be selected and to display with sizing handles (white square boxes) at each end of the line.

Using the Mouse

Once the line is selected, you can use the mouse to change the length and location of the line. To change the length of a straight line, position the arrow pointer on either sizing handle (depending on the direction you want to increase or decrease the line) until it turns into a double-headed diagonally pointing arrow. Hold down the Shift key and the left mouse button (cross hairs will display), drag the cross hairs in the appropriate direction until the line is the desired length, and then release the mouse button.

Using Options from the Format AutoShape Dialog Box

The length of a line may be controlled more precisely at the Format AutoShape dialog box. To do this, position the I-beam pointer on the line until it turns into an arrow with a four-headed arrow attached, and then double-click the left mouse button. At the Format AutoShape dialog box, choose the Size tab. In the Size and rotate section, key the desired length of the line in the Width list box. You can also access the Format AutoShape dialog box by selecting the line first, then choosing Format, and then AutoShape.

Positioning Horizontal and Vertical Lines

Using the Mouse

To change the location of a line with the mouse, position the I-beam pointer on the line until it turns into an arrow with a four-headed arrow attached. Hold down the left mouse button, drag the outline of the line to the new location, then release the mouse button.

Using Options from the Format AutoShape Dialog Box

To precisely position a line (or object) on a page, use options from the Position tab in the Format AutoShape dialog box. To change the horizontal and/or vertical location of a line or any other object, you must provide Word with two pieces of information. First, you must tell Word the point from which you want to position the selected line (or object). Second, you must tell Word the distance the line (or object) is to be positioned from this point.

In the Position on page section, use the horizontal From option to tell Word the point (page, margin, or column) from which you want to position the left edge of the line (or object). Alternately, you must use the vertical From option to set the point (margin, page, or paragraph) from which you want to position the top edge of the line. When these options are selected, Word automatically changes the horizontal and vertical measurements to reflect the current location of the selected line. Therefore, it is best to change the "from" options first, then enter the specific horizontal and vertical measurements.

If the horizontal From option is set at *Column,* the left edge of the line is horizontally placed the specified distance from the left edge of the column. (In a one-column format, which is the default, the left edge of the column and the left margin are the same.) If *Margin* is selected, the left edge of the line is horizontally placed the specified distance from the left margin. Choosing *Page* horizontally places the left edge of the line the specified distance from the left edge of the page. For example, to place a horizontal line 1.35 inches from the left edge of the page, select *Page* in the From option, then key 1.35 in the Horizontal option.

If the vertical From option is set at *Paragraph,* the top edge of the line is vertically placed the specified distance from the top edge of the paragraph to which the line is anchored. If *Margin* is selected, the top edge of the line is vertically placed the specified distance from the top margin. Choosing *Page* vertically places the top edge of the line the specified distance from the top edge of the page. For example, to place a horizontal line 2.15 inches from the top margin, select *Margin* in the From option, then key 2.15 in the Vertical option.

Use the Horizontal option to enter the specific distance between the left edge of the line (or object) and the left edge of the page, margin, or column. Use the Vertical option to enter the specific distance between the top edge of the line and the page, margin, or paragraph.

If surrounding text is edited, the position of a horizontal or vertical line may need to be readjusted so that it maintains its appropriate position in relationship to the text.

To have more precise control over the line's location on the page, you can also change the location of a line at the Format AutoShape dialog box. With the Position tab selected, you can specify the distance you want the object positioned horizontally from the left margin, the left edge of the page, or the left edge of the column. You can also specify the vertical distance for the object relative to the top margin, the top edge of the page, or the top of the paragraph to which it is anchored. Using any of these methods places a line at a specific location on the page.

Anchoring Horizontal and Vertical Lines

All objects, including lines, are automatically anchored or attached to the paragraph closest to the object. With the object selected and nonprinting symbols displayed, an anchor symbol will display by the paragraph to which the object is anchored. By default, an object will move up or down the page if you move the paragraph to which the object is anchored. If you do not want the object to move with its anchored paragraph, select the object, then access the AutoShape dialog box. Select the Position tab, then remove the check mark from the Move object with text check box. If you want to always keep the object on the same page as its anchor paragraph, you must lock the anchor. To do this, select the object, then access the Format AutoShape dialog box. Select the Position tab, then click the Lock anchor check box to insert a check mark. If you want an object to remain stationary at a specific location on a page irregardless of the text that surrounds it, access the Position tab in the AutoShape dialog box. In the Horizontal text box in the Position section, enter the distance that the object is to be located from the left edge of the page, then select Page in the From option. In the Vertical text box, enter the distance that the object is to be located from the top edge of the page, then select Page in the corresponding From option.

Removing Horizontal or Vertical Lines

To remove a line created with the Drawing toolbar, select the line, than press the Delete key.

Customizing Horizontal and Vertical Lines

In typesetting, the thickness of a line, called its *weight*, is measured in points. Word defaults to a line thickness of ¾ of a point. To change the style or weight of a line, select the line first. You can then select different styles and weights of solid lines from the Line Style palette, shown in figure 3.7, that displays when you click the Line Style button (the fourteenth button from the left) on the Drawing toolbar. You can choose various styles of dashed lines from the Dash Style palette by clicking the Dash Style button on the Drawing toolbar (the fifteenth button from the left). In addition, you can create a variety of arrow lines that begin and/or end with arrows, circles, or diamond shapes, as shown in figure 3.8, by clicking the Arrow Style button (the sixteenth button from the left).

Weight
Describes the thickness of a line.

figure 3.7

Line Style Options

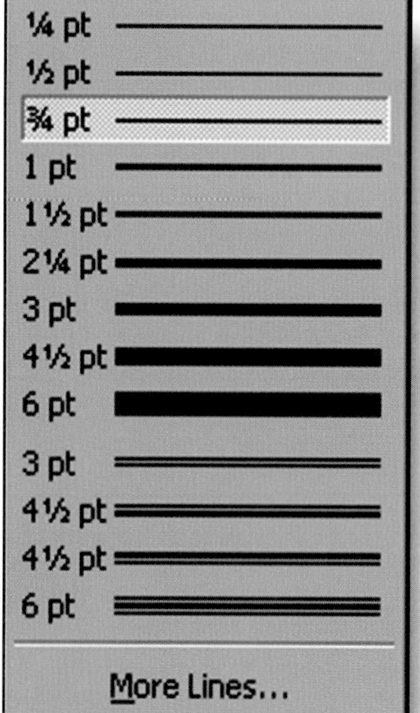

figure 3.8

Arrow Style Options

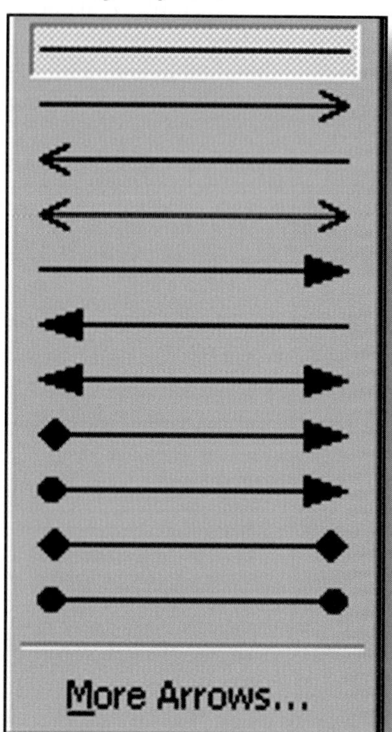

To have more control over the appearance of your lines (solid, dashed, or arrow), you can select More Lines from the Line Style palette or More Arrows from the Arrow Style palette to display the Format AutoShape dialog box. You may also access the Format AutoShape dialog box by double-clicking on the line you want to edit, or select the line first, then click Format, AutoShape. From this dialog box with the Colors and Lines tab chosen, as illustrated in figure 3.9, you can enter a point measurement to determine the weight (thickness) of a horizontal or vertical ruled line (solid, dashed, or arrow). Each time you click the up or down arrows in the Weight text box, Word will either increase or decrease the existing point measurement by 0.25 of a point. If that does not produce the desired thickness, you can key in a specific measurement. It is not necessary to key *pt* when keying a weight measurement. Figure 3.10 shows several styles of horizontal ruled lines at varying point sizes (weights). Every time you click the Line or Arrow button on the Drawing toolbar to draw a new line, Word reverts back to the default of a ¾-point solid line. For example, if you just drew a 3-point double line, the next line drawn will be a ¾-point single line. To draw several lines of the same style and weight, double-click the Line or Arrow button first, as mentioned above.

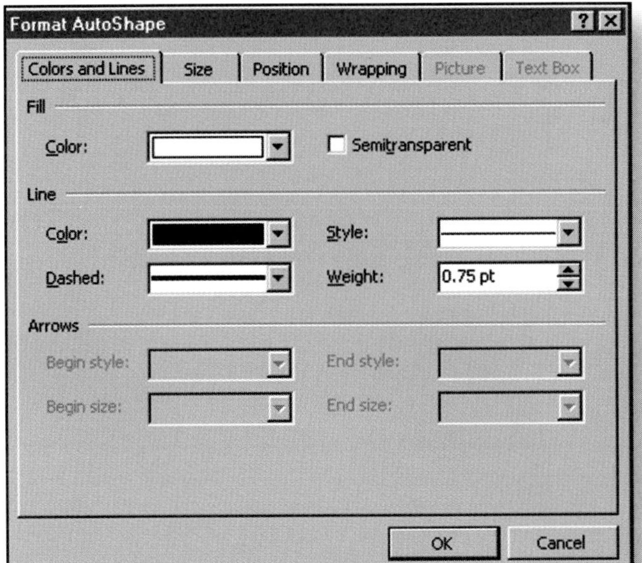

figure 3.9

Format AutoShape Dialog Box

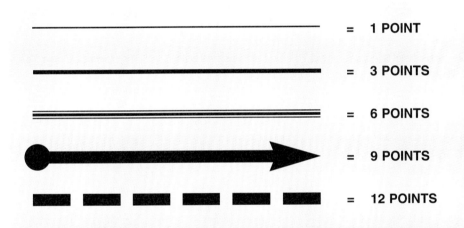

= 1 POINT

= 3 POINTS

= 6 POINTS

= 9 POINTS

= 12 POINTS

figure 3.10

Varying Weights and Styles of Lines

To change the color of a horizontal or vertical line created with the Line button or the Arrow button, select the line first, then click the arrow to the right of the Line Color button (the twelfth button from the left) on the Drawing toolbar to display the Line Color palette, shown in figure 3.11. Your most recent line color choice is automatically assigned to the line color button and remains displayed on the button until you choose a different color. To access other line color options, click More Line Colors displayed in the Line Color palette. This option enables you to select from an enlarged sampling of colors or to create your own custom colors. In addition, you can select Patterned Lines from the Line Color palette to assign a patterned design to your line such as dots, stripes, cross-hatching, checkerboard, etc. You can also change the color of the line by accessing the AutoShape dialog box. To do this, double-click the line to be changed or click Format, then AutoShape. Select the Colors and Lines tab in the Format AutoShape dialog box, then change the Color option in the Line section.

Line Color

figure 3.11

Line Color Palette

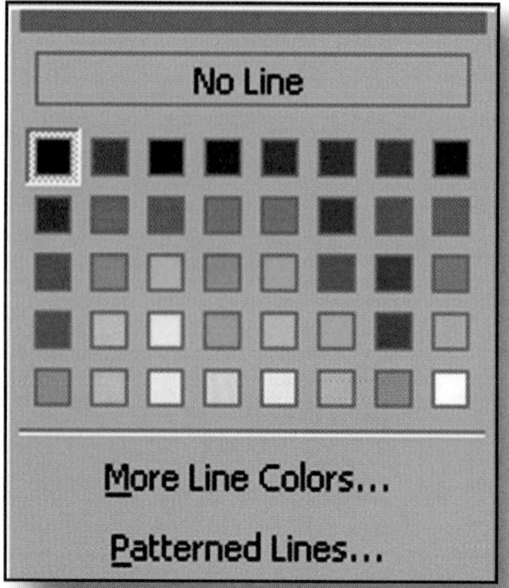

Creating Horizontal Lines Using the Borders Toolbar

Word's Borders feature can be used to add horizontal or vertical lines in headers and/or footers, as well as to any other text. Every paragraph you create in Word contains an invisible frame. (Remember that a paragraph may contain text or it may only consist of a hard return.) A border can be added to the invisible frame that exists around a paragraph. In addition, a border can be added to specific sides of a paragraph. Consequently, you can add a border above and/or below a paragraph to create a horizontal line, or you can add a border to the left and/or right sides of a paragraph to create a vertical line. A ruled line created with the borders feature stays with the paragraph that was current when the feature was applied.

Border

To create a border on the top or sides of your paragraph, you may use the Border button (third button from the right) on the Formatting toolbar. The Border button icon changes according to the most recent border position selected. To change the position of the border, click the arrow to the right of the Border button, then select the desired border location. Select the Top Border button to create a horizontal line above the current paragraph, or select the Bottom Border button to insert a horizontal line below the current paragraph. Select the Left Border button to insert a vertical line on the left side of the current paragraph, or select the Right Border button to insert a vertical line on the right side of the current paragraph. For example, you can add a line below text in a header or add a line above text in a footer. This line acts as a graphic element that separates the header/footer text from the rest of the text and adds visual appeal to the document.

You can further customize lines created with the Border button by choosing Format, then Borders and Shading. With the Borders tab selected at the Borders and Shading dialog box shown in figure 3.12, additional options exist to change the border settings, the border line style, the border line color, the border line width, the border location, and the distance between any border and text. The Style option contains a variety of choices for changing the style of a border line. You can make the border line single, dotted, dashed, double, triple, wavy, striped, or variegated. The Color option lets you change the color of the border line, while the Width option allows you to change the thickness of the line style you have chosen. You may even select different line styles for specific sides of the border by choosing the Custom option in the Settings section.

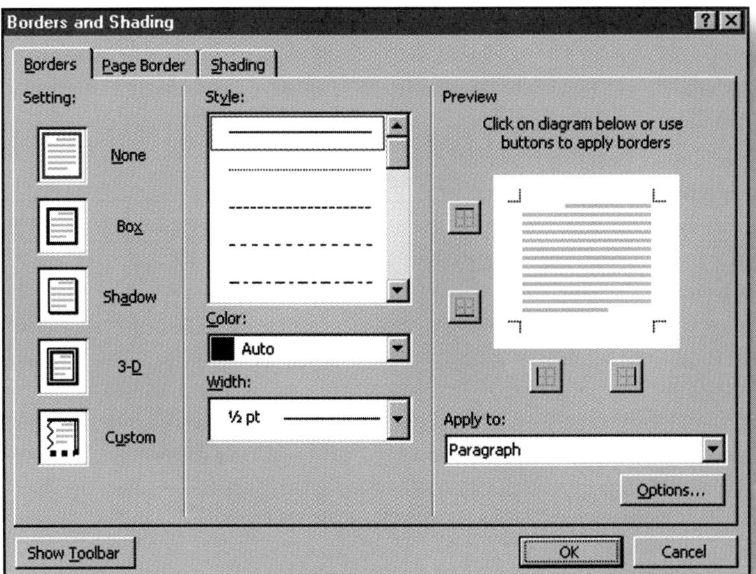

figure 3.12

Borders and Shading Dialog Box

The length of a horizontal line created with the Borders feature can only be adjusted by changing the width of the left and/or right paragraph indents. To do this, position the insertion point in the paragraph that contains the border, then drag the left and/or right margin indent on the Ruler Bar to the left or right until the line is the desired length. The length of a vertical line created with the Border feature is dictated by the length of the paragraph. Even though you can create a variety of customized horizontal and vertical lines with the Borders feature, you have much more flexibility when creating lines with the Drawing toolbar. The Draw program has the ability to create both custom horizontal and vertical lines at any location on a page, whereas lines created with the Borders features may only be placed above, below, to the left, or to the right of a paragraph.

Placing Text at Specific Locations on a Page Using Text Boxes

When creating desktop-published documents, there is often a need to place design elements at specific locations on a page. The Enter key and the space bar are ways of placing the insertion point on the page, but they may not give you the exact location desired. For example, pressing the Enter key one time after a line of text or a design element may not allow enough vertical white space, but pressing Enter two times may allow too much white space. Adjustments to the spacing before and after a paragraph (or hard return) can be made more specifically at the Paragraph dialog box; however, paragraph spacing adjustments affect vertical spacing of text only. The space bar and the tab function in Word can place text in specific locations horizontally across the page, but have no effect on vertical placement. In addition, the tab function works best with text as opposed to graphic elements.

As mentioned briefly in chapter 2, Word has a great formatting feature, known as a *text box*, that enables you to place design elements, both text and graphics, at precise horizontal and vertical locations on a page. When text and/or graphics are enclosed in a text box, you can drag the text box to any position on the page using the mouse, or you can specify an exact location at the Format Text Box dialog box. This feature is extremely useful in desktop publishing because it lets you keep text and graphics together, makes text flow

DTP POINTERS
Use the text box feature to place design elements at specific locations on the page.

around other text or graphics, allows you to layer text and/or graphics, enables you to align design elements on a page, allows just the right amount of white space around elements, and helps fit text and other design elements into a specific amount of space (called copy fitting) on a page.

A text box may seem similar to a frame in that they are both used as containers for text and/or graphics. Frames were used extensively in previous versions of Word but have now been replaced, for the most part, with the use of text boxes in Word 97. Almost anything that can be inserted into a Word document, such as text, tables, worksheets, pictures, or other objects, can be placed into a text box. (Exceptions include a page break, column break, section break, or text formatted into columns.) A text box can also be inserted into a document as a placeholder for a photograph or illustration to be inserted at a later date. Text boxes offer many advantages when designing documents. A text box is created in the drawing layer and is considered a drawing object. Therefore, a text box (whether it contains text or a picture) can be placed above or below the main text (created in the text layer) in a Word document. As mentioned in chapter 2, a watermark can be created using a text box in this manner. Text can be wrapped around a text box in a variety of ways, text boxes can be flipped and rotated, the direction of the text can be changed, and text boxes can also be linked (discussed in chapter 11). Additionally, text boxes can be formatted by using options from the Drawing toolbar, such as applying 3-D effects, shadows, border styles and colors, fills, and backgrounds. Text boxes can also be formatted by accessing the Format Text Box dialog box. A text box does not automatically expand to the amount or size of text, table, picture, or object that is being inserted. For example, if you key more text than can fit in the text box, only the part of the text that fits within the text box size will be visible. Text that has been keyed in the text box will not be lost even if it is not visible; simply adjust the size of the text box.

DTP POINTERS
A text box operates in the drawing layer and can be layered, flipped, or rotated.

Inserting a Text Box

Text Box

You can insert a text box by using the Insert, Text Box command from the Insert menu or by using the Text Box button on the Drawing toolbar. Either method will change the arrow pointer to crosshairs and automatically change the view to Page Layout View. Position the crosshairs where you want the top left corner of the text box to appear, hold down the left mouse button, drag the outline of the text box to the location where you want the lower right corner of the text box to appear, then release the mouse button. After the mouse button is released, an empty box with a hatched border will appear as displayed in figure 3.13. As an alternative to drawing your own text box, Word provides an easy way to insert a one-inch square text box. To do this, simply position the crosshairs and click the left mouse button one time.

Inserting Text Box Contents

As mentioned above, almost anything that can be inserted into a Word document may be placed into a text box. After a text box has been inserted, the insertion point is automatically positioned within the text box so that you can enter text, insert a picture, insert an Excel worksheet, etc. To edit text in a text box, simply position the I-beam within the text box at the desired location and click once. You can also insert existing text into a text box. If you have already keyed some text and then decide to place the text in a text box, simply select the desired text and then click the Text Box button on the Drawing toolbar.

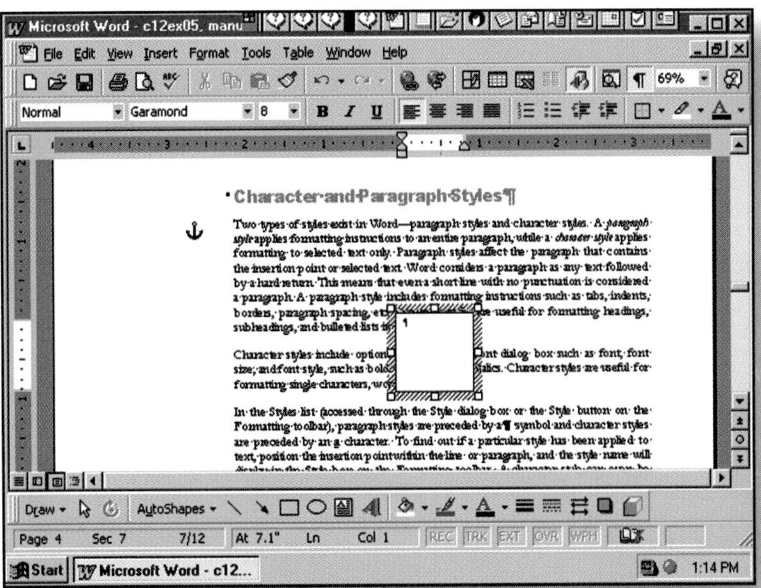

figure 3.13

An Empty Text Box Inserted into a Document

Setting Internal Margins in a Text Box

By default, a text box has left and right internal margins of 0.1 of an inch, and top and bottom internal margins of 0.05 of an inch. These margins can be adjusted to increase or decrease the distance between the contents of the text box and the text box borders. To do this, select the desired text box, click Format, Text Box, or double-click the text box border, and then select the Text Box tab. At the Text Box tab, as shown in figure 3.14, change the left, right, top, and bottom internal margins as desired.

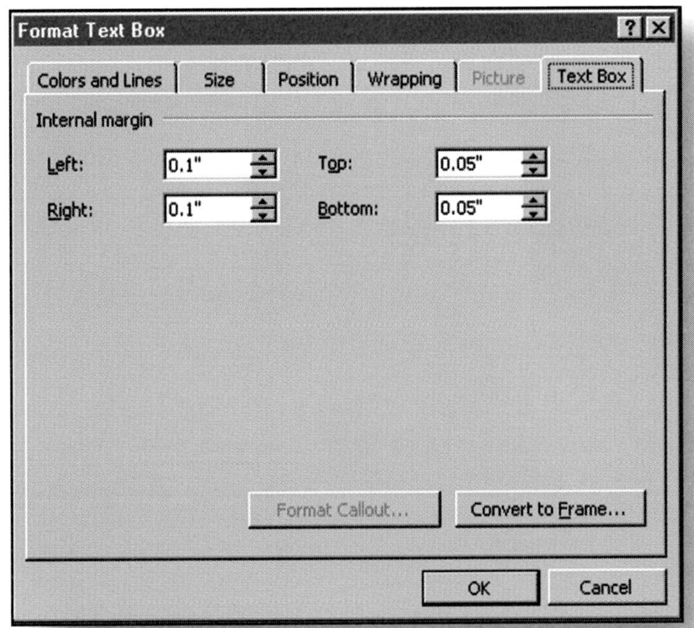

figure 3.14

Text Box Tab Displayed from the Format Text Box Dialog Box

Sizing a Text Box

The size and position of a text box can be changed using the mouse or options in the Format Text Box dialog box. With either method, you must first select the text box. To do this, position the I-beam pointer within the text box, then click the left mouse button. This selects the text box and adds sizing handles (white squares) to the text box borders as illustrated in figure 3.13.

Using the Mouse

Once the text box has been selected, you can use the mouse in combination with the sizing handles to change the size of the text box. To make a text box wider or thinner, position the arrow pointer on the middle sizing handle at the left or right side of the text box until it turns into a double-headed arrow pointing left and right. Hold down the left mouse button, drag the double-headed arrow to the left or right until the text box is the desired size, then release the mouse button. Complete similar steps using the middle sizing handles at the top or bottom of the text box to make the text box taller or shorter. To maintain the proportions of the existing text box dimensions, change both the width and the height at the same time with the corner sizing handles.

If you use the sizing handles to change the size of a text box that contains a picture, the size of the picture does not change. However, if you select the picture first and then size the picture with its own sizing handles, the size of the text box will automatically adjust to the size of the picture.

Using Options in the Format Text Box Dialog Box

If you want to precisely size a text box, use options from the Size tab of the Format Text Box dialog box shown in figure 3.15. To display this dialog box, select the text box to be sized, choose Format, Text Box, and then select the Size tab. This dialog box can also be accessed by double-clicking the text box border or by right-clicking the text border, then selecting Format Text Box from the shortcut menu.

The Size tab of the Format Text Box dialog box offers two ways to change the size of a text box. In the Size and rotate section, you can enter specific measurements for the width and height of the text box. In the Scale section, you can enter width and height measurements as a percentage of the original size of the text box. If you want to change the height and width settings in relation to each other, select the Lock aspect ratio option in the Scale section.

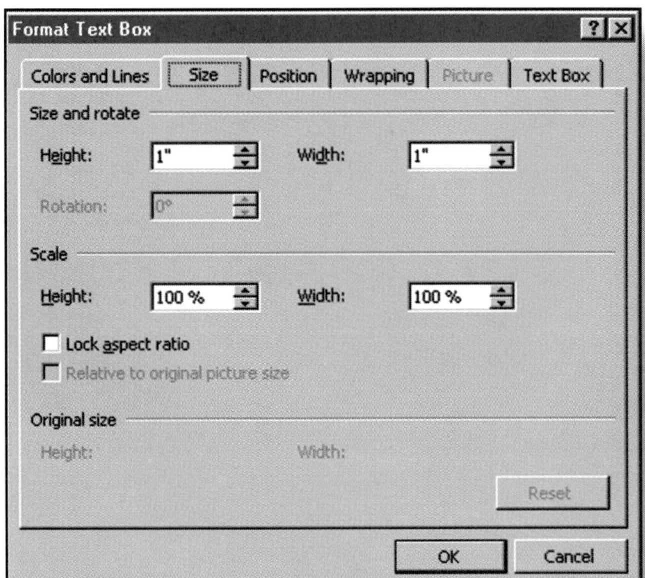

figure 3.15

Size Tab Displayed from the Format Text Box Dialog Box

Positioning a Text Box at a Specific Location on the Page

Using the Mouse

One of the biggest advantages to using a text box is the ability to easily position the text box anywhere on the page in a document. To position a text box using the mouse, place the I-beam pointer on any side of the text box until it turns into an arrow pointer with a four-headed arrow attached. Hold down the left mouse button, drag the outline of the text box to the desired location, then release the mouse button.

When positioning a text box on a page, changing Zoom to Whole Page is helpful so that you can see the entire page on the screen. If you want to move a text box to a different page in a multipage document, choose Zoom from the View menu, and then change the Many pages option (as discussed in chapter 1) to display the desired configuration of pages. Select the text box, position it, then return the view back to your preferred document view.

DTP POINTERS
Change the display to whole page when repositioning a text box.

Using Options from the Format Text Box Dialog Box

To have more precise control over the location of a text box on the page, use options from the Position tab in the Format Text Box dialog box as shown in figure 3.16. With the Position tab selected, you can specify the distance you want the text box (or object) positioned horizontally from the left margin, the left edge of the page, or the left edge of the column. You can also specify the vertical distance for the text box (or object) relative to the top margin, the top edge of the page, or the top of the paragraph to which it is anchored. The options in the Position tab of the Format Text Box dialog box are the same as those in the Position tab of the Format AutoShape dialog box as discussed earlier in this chapter in the section on Positioning Horizontal and Vertical Lines. As with positioning horizontal and vertical lines, remember to set the horizontal or vertical "from" options first, then set the horizontal or vertical measurement when positioning a text box.

figure 3.16

Position Tab Displayed from the Format Text Box Dialog Box

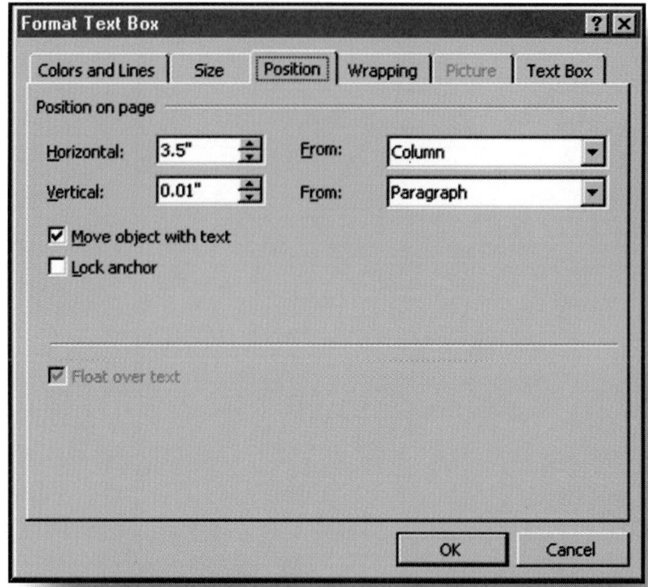

Anchoring a Text Box

Anchor
A connection between a text box and the nearest paragraph that causes the text box to move with the paragraph.

By default, a text box is *anchored* to the nearest paragraph. When a text box is inserted in a document, an anchor symbol displays to the left of the paragraph to which the text box is anchored, as shown in figure 3.13. If a text box is repositioned, the anchor moves to the paragraph closest to the text box. To view this anchor, click the Show/Hide ¶ button on the Standard toolbar to turn on the display of nonprinting characters, and then select the text box.

A text box always appears on the same page as the paragraph to which it is anchored. By default, the Move object with text option is selected in the Position tab of the Format Text Box dialog box. With this option selected, the text box moves with the paragraph to which it is anchored. If you want a text box to stay in a specific spot and not move with the paragraph to which it is anchored, select the text box, access the Format Text Box dialog box, select the Position tab, then remove the check mark from the Move object with text option.

The anchor associated with a text box can be moved to another paragraph without moving the text box itself. Consequently, a text box can be anchored to a paragraph that is not the nearest paragraph to the text box. To move an anchor, make sure the Page Layout viewing mode and the display of nonprinting characters is turned on, then select the text box. Position the I-beam pointer on the anchor icon until the pointer turns into an arrow with a four-headed arrow attached. Hold down the left mouse button, drag the anchor icon to the desired paragraph, then release the left mouse button. When you move an anchor icon, the text box stays in the existing location on the page. However, if the anchor is dragged to another page, the text box will move to that page. Furthermore, if the paragraph containing the anchor is moved to another page, the text box will move also.

To keep a text box on the same page as the text to which it is anchored, select the text box, then choose the Lock anchor option in the Position tab of the Format Text Box dialog box. With this option selected, the text box will always stay on the current page when you drag the text box to change its position. For example, if you lock the anchor associated with a text box on page 9 of a document, you can drag the text box to any location on the same page, but the locked anchor will prevent you from dragging the text box to a different page.

Wrapping Text Around a Text Box

By default, text in a document does not automatically wrap around a text box as shown in figure 3.13. If you want text to wrap around a text box, first select the text box, then display the Format Text Box dialog box, and then click the Wrapping tab. Several wrapping options are available as illustrated in figure 3.17. The Wrapping style section offers the following selections:

- **Square:** Text can wrap around all four sides of the text box depending on the selection made in the Wrap to section.
- **Tight:** Text wraps around the shape of an object rather than the box holding the object. This option is more apparent when applied to a shape other than a square or rectangle. With a text box selected, the Square and Tight options produce the same result.
- **Through:** Text wraps around the shape of an object and through any open areas of the object box. This does not produce any changes when applied to a text box.
- **None:** By default, the text box floats above the text layer and obscures some of the text.
- **Top & bottom:** Text wraps above and below the text box but not on the sides.

The Wrap to section, operating in conjunction with the Wrapping style section, offers the following selections:

- **Both sides:** Text wraps on both sides of the text box.
- **Left:** Text wraps along the left side of the text box but not on the right side.
- **Right:** Text wraps along the right side of the text box but not on the left side.
- **Largest side:** Text wraps along the largest side of the object. This does not produce any changes when applied to a text box.

The Wrapping tab also provides a third section, labeled Distance from text. In this section, you can set the distance between the edges of the text box and the surrounding text. The choice made in the Wrapping style section determines which measurements may be changed.

figure 3.17

Wrapping Tab Displayed from the Format Text Box Dialog Box

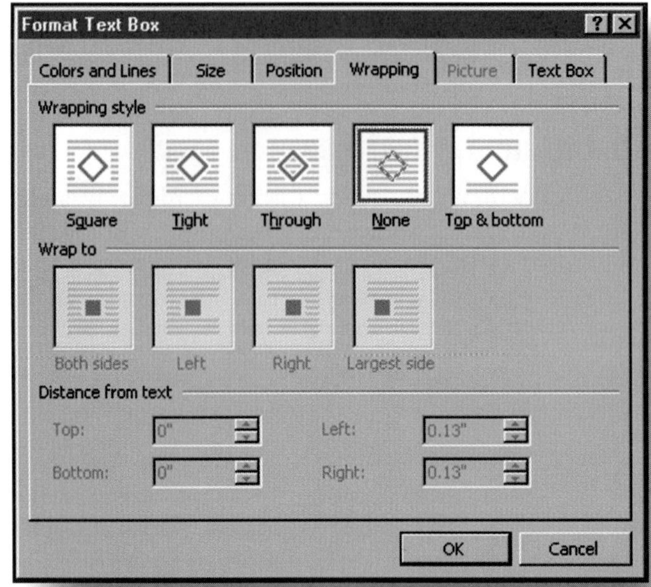

Removing a Text Box

To remove a text box, position the I-beam pointer on one of the text box borders until it turns into an arrow with a four-headed arrow attached, then click once. The text box border will now display as a series of closely spaced dots as opposed to a diagonally slashed border. Press the Delete key. The text box and its contents are then removed from the document.

Customizing a Text Box

By default, a text box contains a black single-line border around all sides and white background fill. However, a border can be added or removed around a text box at any time. In addition, a text box can be customized in a variety of ways, including changing style and color of the border and changing the background fill color.

Changing the Fill

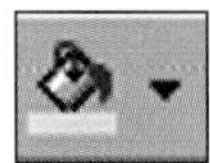

Fill Color

You can fill a text box or any drawing object with solid or gradient (shaded) colors, a pattern, a texture, or a picture. To change the color of the background fill, select the desired text box, then check the color of the stripe on the Fill Color button on the Drawing toolbar. If the stripe is the fill color you want, simply click the Fill Color button. To select a different fill color, click the arrow to the right of the Fill Color button on the Drawing toolbar to display the Fill Color Palette shown in figure 3.18. You can also get the same results by selecting the Colors and Lines tab in the Format Text Box dialog box, and clicking the Fill Color list box. Select the desired color from the color palette or choose More Fill Colors to display the Colors dialog box. With the Standard tab selected in the Colors dialog box, as illustrated in figure 3.19, click the desired color spot from the extended color selection. To make the color somewhat transparent, click the Semitransparent check box. To create your own colors, select the Custom tab at the Colors dialog box, as shown in figure

3.19. Click anywhere in the large rectangle in the Colors section to select a color mix. If desired, adjust the luminosity (the amount of black or white added to the color) of the selected color by clicking or dragging anywhere in the luminosity bar (to the right of the large rectangle). To further refine your color choice, you can adjust the hue (the color itself), the saturation (intensity), the luminance (brightness), and/or the amount of red, green, and blue in each color. Word saves the custom color you select in the Standard tab or the Custom tab and places it in its own color block in the fill color palette in a new row above the More Fill Colors command. A color block is added to this row every time you select a new color from the Colors dialog box. The fill color palette in Figure 3.18 shows a new row above the More Fill colors command that contains four custom colors.

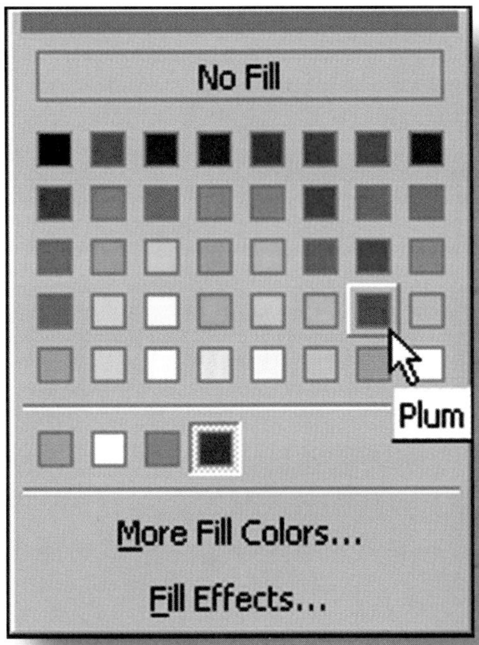

figure 3.18

Fill Color Palette

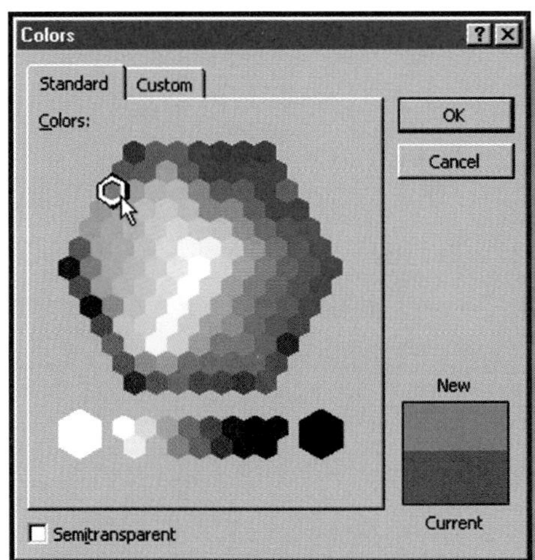

figure 3.19

Standard and Custom Tabs Displayed from the Colors Dialog Box

Instead of using a solid color fill, click the arrow to the right of the Fill Color button on the Drawing toolbar, then click Fill Effects for a gradient, textured, or patterned fill. You can also get the same results by selecting the Colors and Lines tab in the Format Text Box dialog box, clicking the Fill Color list box, and then clicking Fill Effects.

The Gradient tab displayed in figure 3.20 provides a variety of gradient shading styles. In Word, a gradient fill uses a single color that fades gradually to another color. In the Colors section of the Gradient tab, select One color to produce a single color gradient that gradually fades to black or white. When you click the One color option, a Color 1 list box appears that allows you to choose a specific color for your gradient. A Dark/Light slider also appears that lets you choose whether the color fades to black or white and also allows you to adjust the intensity of the color. Use the Two colors option to produce gradient shading that gradually fades from one color to another color. When you click the Two colors option, Color 1 and Color 2 list boxes appear so that you can select the two colors for the gradient fill. Once you have made your color(s) selection, you can choose from a variety of gradient styles in the Shading styles section. In the Variants section, you can then select from different variations of the selected shading style. Examples of different gradient color and shading styles are displayed in figure 3.21. As an example, to create the gradient fill displayed in the fourth box from the left in figure 3.21, select Two colors in the Colors section, then select black as Color 1 and turquoise as Color 2. Choose From center in the Shading styles section, then select the first box on the left in the Variants section.

The Colors section of the Fill Effects dialog box contains another setting labeled Preset colors. Use this option to select from a list of predesigned gradient fills. Figure 3.21 shows an example of the preset colors gradient called Horizon.

figure 3.20

Gradient Tab Displayed from the Fill Effects Dialog Box

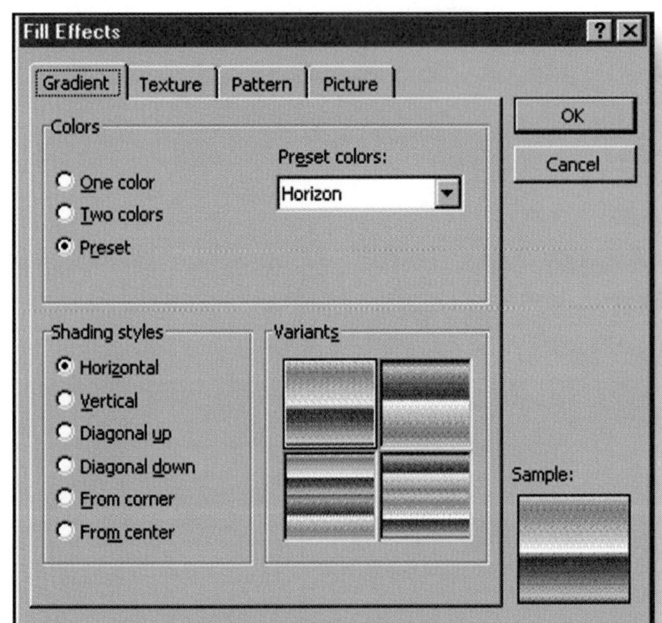

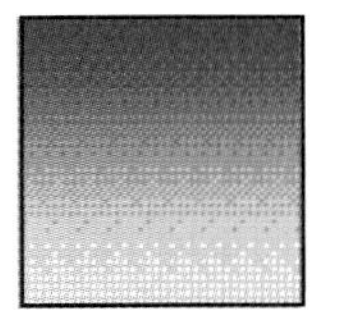

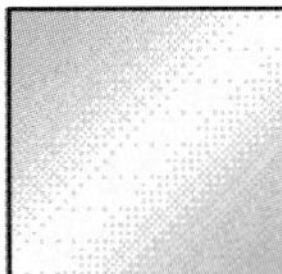

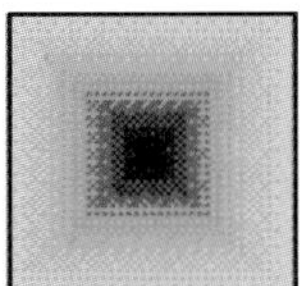

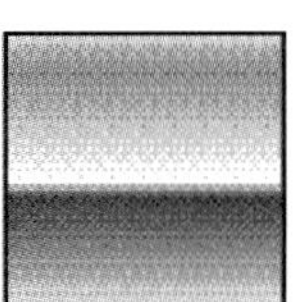

figure 3.21

Examples of Gradient Color and Shading Styles

The Texture tab in the Fill Effects dialog box, shown in figure 3.22, offers twenty-four different textured backgrounds from which to choose. You may also select Other Texture to open a different file. For instance, you can use one of the wallpaper files located in your Windows 95 folder or a background file located in the Clipart folder (most likely the path is Program Files\Microsoft Office\Clipart) as a textured background. Files such as a Windows Bitmap (a .bmp file) or a Windows Metafile (a .wmf file) can be used as a textured fill. (See chapter 11 for further discussion of graphic file formats.) Every time you open a different file through the Other Texture command, the resulting new texture will display in its own block as the last texture selection in the Texture section.

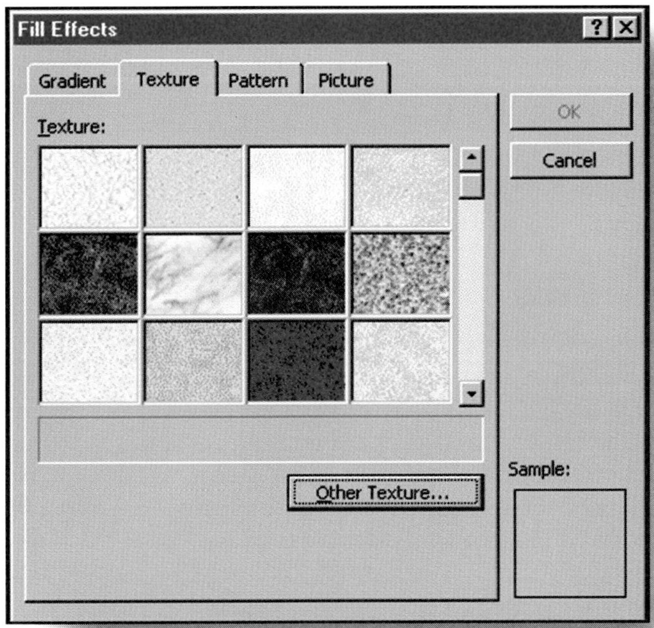

figure 3.22

Texture Tab Displayed from the Fill Effects Dialog Box

The Pattern tab in the Fill Effects dialog box, shown in figure 3.23, provides 48 patterns that can be used as fill for a text box. To use this feature, click the desired pattern block in the Pattern section, then select colors for the pattern foreground and background. Click the Foreground list box to select a color for the dots, dashes, lines, waves, etc., of the pattern. Click the Background list box to select a color for the spaces between the dots, dashes, lines, waves, etc.

figure 3.23

Pattern Tab Displayed from the Fill Effects Dialog Box

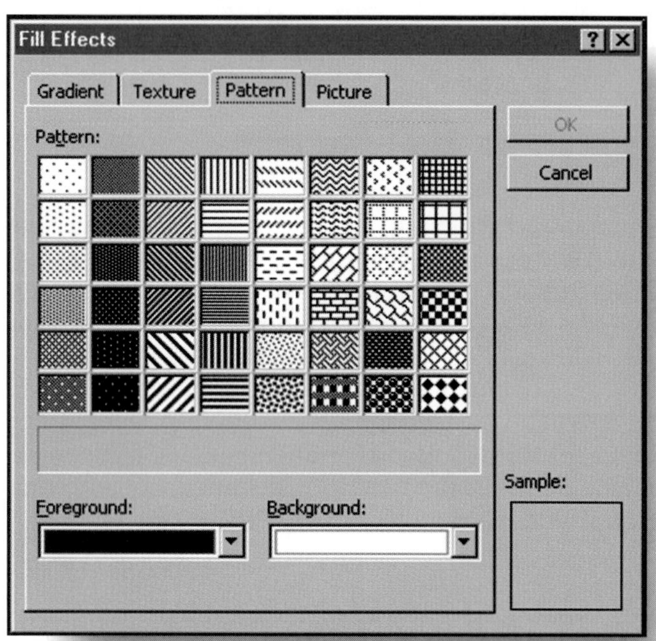

The Picture tab of the Fill Effects dialog box lets you select a picture as the fill for a text box. Choose Select Picture to access the Select Picture dialog box, change the active folder to the location of the desired picture files, and then select the picture file you want to use as fill.

Changing the Border

DTP POINTERS
Customize borders by changing the line style, thickness, color, and location.

You can change or format a text box border the same way you can change or format a line as discussed earlier in this chapter. To add, remove, or change the color of a text box border, select the text box, then click the Line Color arrow on the Drawing toolbar to display the line color palette. Select a color from the line color palette or select the More Line Colors command to pick from an extended selection of standard colors or to create your own custom colors. If you want to add a pattern to the border, choose Patterned Lines from the line color palette.

Line Style

Dash Style

To change the style and thickness of text box borders, select the text box, then click the Line Style button on the Drawing toolbar to display the line style palette. Select the desired line style and thickness. To further refine the line style and weight of your text box border, select More Lines to display the Colors and Lines tab of the Format Text Box dialog box. You may also choose from a selection of dashed lines by clicking the Dash Style button on the Drawing toolbar.

Shadow box effects can be added to text box borders by clicking the Shadow button on the Drawing toolbar. Select a shadow design from the shadow palette that displays. Click the Shadow Settings command to display the Shadow Settings toolbar. Use the four Nudge Shadow buttons to move the shadow in small increments either closer to the shape or farther away. Use the Shadow Color button to change the color of the shadow, and use the Shadow On/Off button to add or remove the shadow effect.

Shadow

In exercise 3, you will create a letterhead using a text box that is inserted in the header and footer layer in the left margin space. Inserting it in this layer is a safeguard against users who might inadvertently make a change in the letterhead. Placing the letterhead in the header and footer layer will result in the letterhead appearing on all subsequent pages which is not appropriate for a multipage letter. To eliminate the letterhead on subsequent pages, click the Page Setup button on the Header and Footer toolbar, then click the Layout tab in the Page Setup dialog box. In the Headers and Footers section, click the Different first page check box to insert a check mark. This option tells Word that this header is to be used for the first page only. Subsequent pages may have a different header if desired.

exercise 3

Creating a Letterhead Using a Customized Text Box and Customized Horizontal Line

1. At a clear document screen, create the letterhead along the side of the page shown in figure 3.24 by completing the following steps:
   a. Change the left margin to 2.5 inches and the right margin to 1 inch.
   b. Insert a text box for the company letterhead by completing the following steps:
      (1) Click View, then Header and Footer to display the Header pane. (The letterhead text box is going to be inserted in the header and footer layer. This way you can prevent other users from inadvertently changing the letterhead.)
      (2) Click the Zoom button on the Standard toolbar, then select Whole Page.
      (3) Click the Drawing button on the Standard toolbar to display the Drawing toolbar; or position the arrow pointer anywhere within the Standard toolbar, click the right mouse button once, then select *Drawing* from the drop-down menu.
      (4) Click the Text Box button on the Drawing toolbar, then position the crosshairs in the upper left corner of the page and click and drag to draw a text box in the left margin approximately the same size as that shown in figure 3.24. (The text box will be specifically sized and positioned in the next few steps.)
   c. Size and position the text box by completing the following steps:
      (1) Position the I-beam pointer on the text box border so that it displays as an arrow with a four-headed arrow attached, then double-click to display the Format Text Box dialog box.
      (2) At the Format Text Box dialog box, select the Size tab, then change the height of the text box to 10 inches and the width to 1.8 inches.
      (3) Select the Position tab, then change the horizontal From option to Page and the Horizontal option to 0.3 inches. Change the vertical From option to Page and the Vertical option to 0.5 inches.
   d. Remove the text box borders and insert the textured fill by completing the following steps:
      (1) With the Format Text Box dialog box still displayed, click the Colors and Lines tab.

(2) In the Fill section, click the Color list box, click Fill Effects, then click the Texture tab in the Fill Effects dialog box.
(3) In the Texture section, click the second texture block from the left in the first row. The texture name, *Recycled paper*, will display below the texture selections.
(4) Click OK or press Enter to close the Fill Effects dialog box
(5) In the Line section, click the Color list box, then click No Line.
(6) Click OK again to close the Format Text Box dialog box.

e. Insert and format the text box contents by completing the following steps:
(1) Click the Zoom button on the Standard toolbar, then select *75%*.
(2) Click once inside the text box, then press Enter two times.
(3) Key the following text, pressing Enter the number of times indicated:

Desktop (press Enter)
Design (press Enter twice)
"Where Concepts Become a Reality" (press Enter 37 times)
568 Pine Street (press Enter)
St. Louis, MO 63131 (press Enter)
(314) 555-8755 (press Enter)
Fax: (314) 555-8758 (Press Enter)
E-mail: www.dtp.com

(4) Select all the text just entered and change the justification to center, then change the font to Arial and the color to Teal.
(5) Select *Desktop Design*, then change the font size to 26-point, then apply bold.
(6) Select the slogan *"Where Concepts Become a Reality,"* then change the font to 12-point Times New Roman Bold Italic.
(7) Select the address, phone number, fax number, and E-mail address, then change the font size to 10-point.
(8) Make sure the address, phone and fax numbers, and the E-mail address are positioned similarly to the example in figure 3.24. Adjust by inserting or deleting hard returns if necessary.

f. Insert the horizontal line by completing the following steps:
(1) Click the Line button on the Drawing toolbar, then position the crosshairs under *Design*.
(2) Hold down the Shift key, then click and drag the crosshairs to the right to create a straight horizontal line the approximate length of the horizontal line shown in figure 3.24.

g. Size and position the horizontal line by completing the following steps:
(1) Position the I-beam pointer on the line until it displays as an arrow with a four-headed arrow attached.
(2) Double-click the line to display the Format AutoShape dialog box, then click the Size tab.
(3) In the Size and rotate section, change the Width to 1.6 inches.
(4) Select the Position tab, then change the horizontal From option to Page and the Horizontal option to 0.41 inches. Change the vertical From option to Page and the Vertical option to 1.9 inches.

h. Change the color and weight of the horizontal line by completing the following steps:
(1) With the Format AutoShape dialog box still displayed, click the Colors and Lines tab.

(2) In the Line section, click the Color list box, then click More colors.
(3) At the Colors dialog box, click the Standard tab.
(4) From the Standard tab color selections, select the dark brown/burgundy color on the right side in the outer row, third color up from the bottom right corner. (If you have trouble finding this color, select a similar color.)
(5) Click OK to close the Colors dialog box.
(6) In the Line section of the Colors and Lines tab, change the line Weight option to 4.5 pt.
(7) Click OK or press Enter.

i. Click Close on the Header and Footer toolbar. (Due to the wide left margin setting, the insertion point is located an appropriate distance to the right of the text box in the text layer so that letter text may be entered.)
j. Use Print Preview to view the entire document.

2. Save the letterhead and name it c03ex03, ddltrhead.
3. Print and then close c0e3x03, ddltrhead.

figure 3.24

Desktop
Design

*"Where Concepts
Become a Reality"*

568 Pine Street
St. Louis, MO 63131
(314) 555-8755
Fax: (314) 555-8758
E-mail: www.dtp.com

Review the letterhead created in exercise 3. What is the focus? Is the design symmetrical or asymmetrical? How is balance achieved on the page? Are the type sizes in proportion to each other? Does the type size indicate a logical order of importance? How is directional flow established? What elements provide contrast? If color was used, was it used effectively? Can you identify any consistent elements? Are any elements out of alignment? Continually asking yourself these kinds of questions will help develop your sense of design and layout.

Using The Template Feature to Produce Individualized Documents

DTP POINTERS
Templates can provide the framework for creating customized documents.

Word's Template feature can make your task of producing individualized documents easier. As briefly discussed in chapter 2, a document created from a template can be customized once it is displayed in the document window, a new template can be created based on an existing template, the template itself can be modified permanently, an existing Word document can be converted to a template, or a new template can be made from scratch. For example, if you like the design of the *Contemporary Letter* template but would like to change the location of the world graphic and change the font for the letterhead and body text, you have three choices—the document can be revised when it is displayed in the editing window, a new template based on the *Contemporary Letter* template can be created, or the original *Contemporary Letter* template can be permanently modified.

If you choose to revise the document created by the template, you would select the *Contemporary Letter* template, replace the text markers with the appropriate information for your letter, and then make the graphic location and font changes when the document is displayed in the document window. You would then save and name the document as normal. The changes you make only affect the current document on the screen. No changes will be made to the original *Contemporary Letter* template. It will still be available for you to use over and over again.

Your second alternative, creating a new template based on the *Contemporary Letter* template, keeps the original template intact in addition to creating a new modified template for your future use. This process is accomplished by opening the original template file, making the desired changes, then saving the template to the default template folder with a new name. To do this, you would complete the following steps:

1. Click File, New, then select the Letters & Faxes tab.
2. Click the Contemporary Letter.dot icon, then click Template in the Create New section of the New dialog box.
3. Click OK or press Enter.
4. With the *Contemporary Letter* template displayed on the screen, use any of Word's features to make the desired changes.
5. Click File, then Save to display the Save As dialog box. Word automatically switches to the default templates folder (most likely this folder will be called Templates).
6. With the default template folder displayed as the folder in the Save in: list box, change to the appropriate folder in which you want to save your template (for example, the *Letters & Faxes* folder), then key a new name in the File name text box. Keying an extension as part of the filename is not necessary. Word automatically adds a *.dot* extension to a template.
7. Click Save. Your new template will now be displayed in the appropriate tab when you access the New dialog box.

As a result of following this procedure, a new template now exists in your template folder that resembles the *Contemporary Letter* template. To use the new template, choose File, then New. Select the appropriate tab, such as Letters & Faxes, and the new template you just created is listed with the other available templates. This new template has all the characteristics of the original template except for the changes that were made. This method will not change the original *Contemporary Letter* template. Both templates are available to use as often as you like. This approach is preferable to making permanent changes to any of Word's original templates.

To modify an original template permanently, follow the same steps as above; however, name the edited template with the same name as the original template. For instance, to edit the *Contemporary Letter.dot*, follow steps 1 through 7 on the previous page, but name the changed template *Contemporary Letter.dot* instead of giving the file a new name. The original *Contemporary Letter* template is now altered and will reflect these changes every time you access it. CAUTION: Avoid modifying the templates provided by Word. This approach is not recommended since many of the Word templates might be difficult to recreate.

DTP POINTERS
Avoid editing Word's predesigned templates.

A template can also be created from any existing Word document. If you have documents that you have already created, you can easily make any one of them into a Word template. To do this, you would complete the following steps:

1. With the document you want to change into a template displayed on your screen, delete any unnecessary text, graphics, and/or formatting. Leave only the text, graphics, and formatting instructions that you want available every time you use the template. Consider including some placeholder text such as *[Insert date here]*.
2. Choose File, then Save As.
3. At the Save As dialog box, change the Save as type: option to *Document Template (*.dot)*.
4. With the default templates folder displayed in the Save in: list box, change to the appropriate template folder in which you want to save the template.
5. Replace any existing name in the File name text box with a name for your new template. Word automatically adds a *.dot* extension to the template.
6. Choose Save to save the new template. This new template will now be listed in the appropriate tab when you access the New dialog box.

Since the existing templates that come with the Word program cannot satisfy all needs, creating a template from scratch is possible. At a clear editing window, create the desired document and then follow the steps above to save it as a template.

A letterhead would benefit from being converted into a template. Since your letterhead helps to establish an identity for your organization, it will probably stay the same for quite a long period of time. Converting your letterhead into a template ensures that your letterhead is always available in its original form. If the letterhead is mistakenly rearranged while keying the letter content, the original template can be opened again to start anew. For more efficiency, you can even include styles, AutoText entries, field codes, macros, and more in your template letterhead. (See the Word Reference Manual for including these items in your template.)

exercise 4

Creating a Template from an Existing Word Document

1. Convert the Desktop Design letterhead created in exercise 3 into a template by completing the following steps:
   a. Open c03ex03, ddltrhead.doc.
   b. Choose File, then Save As.
   c. In the Save As dialog box, change the Save as type: option at the bottom of the dialog box to *Document Template (*dot).*
   d. With the default template folder name displayed in the Save in: list box, double-click the *Letters & Faxes* folder. (If you are working on a network, consult your instructor about any problems associated with saving files as templates.)
   e. Replace the existing filename in the File name text box with **(your last name), letterhead.** Word automatically adds a *.dot* extension to the template. (Ordinarily, a filename like *Company letterhead.dot* might be more appropriate; however, in a classroom situation, students would be replacing each other's templates in the *Letters & Faxes* folder if each student did not use a unique filename.)
   f. Choose Save to save the new template.
2. Close the document. (Ask your instructor about deleting this template from the template folder after completing this chapter.)

Refining Letter and Word Spacing

Certain refinements such as kerning and tracking make your letterhead or any other document look more professional.

Kerning Character Pairs

Kerning
Decreasing or increasing white space between specific character pairs.

The process of decreasing or increasing the white space between specific character pairs is called *kerning*. Kerning is used only on headlines and other blocks of large type. Generally, the horizontal spacing of typefaces is designed to optimize body text sizes (9- to 13-point). At larger sizes, the same relative horizontal space appears "loose," especially when uppercase and lowercase letters are combined. Kerning visually equalizes the space between characters and is especially important at large point sizes (14-point and larger).

Figure 3.25 illustrates character pair kerning set in 18-point Times New Roman Bold. As you can see, kerning results in very minor but visually important adjustments.

figure 3.25

Character Pair Kerning

WA (kerned)	**Ta (kerned)**
WA (not kerned)	**Ta (not kerned)**
Ty (kerned)	**Vi (kerned)**
Ty (not kerned)	**Vi (not kerned)**

Kerning can be accomplished automatically or manually in Word by selecting the Character Spacing tab at the Font dialog box as displayed in figure 3.26. If the automatic kerning feature is turned on, Word adjusts the space between specific letter pairs, depending on the font design, above a specific point size. For example, some common character pairs that may be automatically kerned are *Ta, To, Ty, Vi,* and *WA*. The amount of kerning for specific character pairs is defined in a kerning table, which is part of the printer definition. The printer definition is a preprogrammed set of instructions that tells the printer how to perform various features. Word contains printer definitions for hundreds of printers. When a printer is selected during the installation of Word, a file containing the particular printer definition is copied to the folder specified for printer files. Word has defined kerning tables for True Type and Adobe Type Manager fonts only. You may want to print some of the character pairs listed in figure 3.25 as kerned and not kerned in large point sizes (14-point and larger) to see if your printer definition supports kerning. To turn on the automatic kerning feature, you would complete the following steps:

DTP POINTERS
Kern when the type size exceeds 14 points.

1. If the text to be kerned has not been keyed yet, go to the next step. If the text to be kerned already exists, select the text first.
2. Click Format, then Font, and then select the Character Spacing tab.
3. Click the check box to the left of the Kerning for fonts option to insert a check mark.
4. In the Points and above text box, use the up and down arrows to specify the minimum point size for kerning to take effect; or key the desired point size.
5. Click OK.

The best way to incorporate kerning into entire documents is to modify the Normal style to include automatic kerning. Styles will be discussed in greater detail in chapter 6.

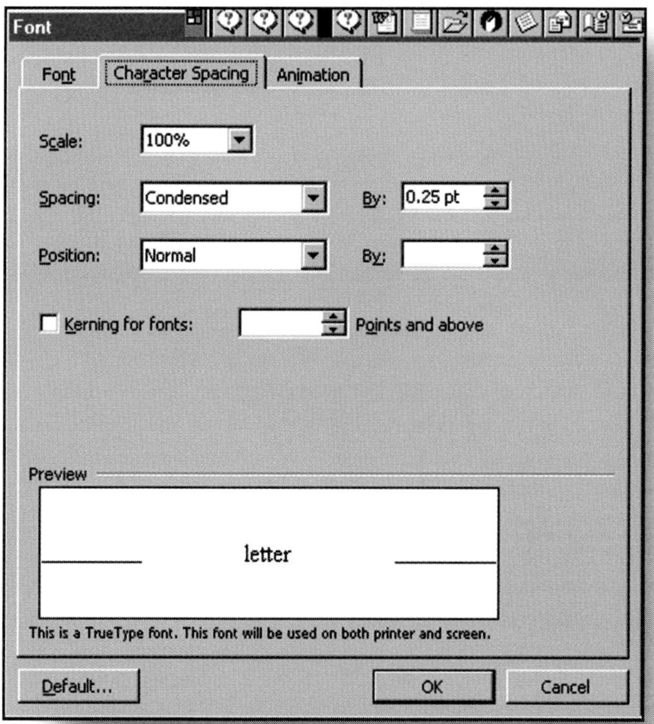

figure 3.26

Character Spacing Tab Displayed from the Font Dialog Box

If you choose to manually kern letters, you make the decision as to which letters to kern. Manual kerning is especially helpful if you need to increase or decrease space between letters to improve legibility or to create a special effect. Manual kerning can provide very accurate results; however, it can be very tedious. To manually kern a specific pair of letters, you would complete the following steps:

1. Select the pair of characters you want to kern.
2. Choose Format, then Font, and then select the Character Spacing tab.
3. Click the Spacing list box, then select Expanded (if you want to increase the spacing between the selected character pair) or Condensed (if you want to decrease the spacing).
4. In the By: list box, click the up or down arrows to specify the amount of space the selected character pair is to be increased or decreased.
5. Click OK.

Tracking Text

Tracking
Equally reducing or increasing the horizontal space between all characters in a block.

In typesetting, equally reducing or increasing the horizontal space between all characters in a block of text is called *tracking*. Tracking affects all characters, while kerning affects only specific character pairs. The purpose of tracking is the same as kerning: to produce more attractive, easy-to-read type. In addition, you can use tracking to create unusual spacing for a specific design effect.

Like kerning, tracking adjustments in Word are also made at the Font dialog box with the Character Spacing tab selected, as shown in figure 3.26. At this dialog box, you can reduce or increase spacing between characters. Figure 3.27 specifies what occurs with each option.

figure 3.27

Character Spacing Options

Normal	The default setting chosen by the program or the printer as the best spacing between words and letters.
Condensed	Condenses the spacing between all characters in a block of text by subtracting the amount of space specified in the By: box from the current letter spacing.
Expanded	Expands the spacing between all characters in a block of text by adding the amount of space specified in the By: box to the current letter spacing.

In Word, condensing or expanding character spacing affects all spacing in a block of text, including the spaces between words. Generally, in typesetting, if the character spacing is adjusted, then the space between words is also adjusted. However, the amount of space specified between characters and the amount of space specified between words does not have to be the same. The headings shown in figure 3.28 are set in 24-point Garamond Bold. The first heading is set at the default character spacing of Normal. The character spacing for the text in the second heading was condensed by 1 point and the space between each word was condensed by 0.5 points.

figure 3.28

Tracking Example

DESKTOP PUBLISHING IN THE 90s
DESKTOP PUBLISHING IN THE 90s

Tracking (reducing character spacing) is usually done on headings and subheadings. While reducing character spacing on body text allows more text in the same amount of space, the text appears more dense and can be more difficult to read. On the other hand, reducing the character spacing of italicized text can give it the appearance of script, as illustrated in figure 3.29.

figure 3.29

Tracking Example

The text in this paragraph is set in 11-point Book Antiqua Italic. The character spacing is set at the default of ***Normal.***

The text in this paragraph is also set in 11-point Book Antiqua Italic; however, the character spacing is ***Condensed By: 0.5 pt.***

In typesetting, headings and subheadings are almost always tracked and then kerned. In exercise 5, you will create a letterhead that requires kerning and tracking to achieve the desired effect.

DTP POINTERS
Kern and track headings and subheadings.

exercise 5

Kerning and Tracking Text in a Letterhead

1. At a clear document screen, kern and track the text in the Johnson letterhead shown in figure 3.30 by completing the following steps:
   a. Change the top margin to 0.5 inches, the left and right margins to 1 inch, and the bottom margin to 0.5 inches. (If your printer does not allow a 0.5-inch bottom margin, accept whatever margin Word determines.)
   b. Insert a text box for the company letterhead in the header and footer layer by completing the following steps:
      (1) Click View, then Header and Footer to display the Header pane.
      (2) Click the Zoom button on the Standard toolbar, then select Page Width.
      (3) Click the Drawing button on the Standard toolbar to display the Drawing toolbar.
      (4) Click the Text Box button on the Drawing toolbar, then position the crosshairs in the upper left corner of the header pane and click and drag down and to the right to draw a text box approximately 1 inch high and 2.5 inches wide. The text

box will extend below the header pane. (The text box will be specifically sized and positioned in the next few steps.)

c. Size and position the text box by completing the following steps:
   (1) Position the I-beam pointer on the text box border so that it displays as an arrow with a four-headed arrow attached, then double-click to display the Format Text Box dialog box.
   (2) At the Format Text Box dialog box, select the Size tab, then change the height of the text box to 1.1 inches and the width to 2.5 inches.
   (3) Select the Position tab, then change the horizontal From option to Page and the Horizontal option to 0.85 inches. Make sure the vertical From option displays Paragraph, then change the Vertical position to 0 inches.
   (4) Click OK or press Enter.

d. Insert the text box contents by completing the following steps:
   (1) Click once inside the text box, then key the following text. To insert the diamond-shaped bullet, choose Insert and Symbol, select the Symbols tab, change Font to Monotype Sorts, and insert the diamond symbol in the fourth row, second symbol from the left.

   JOHNSON (press Enter)
   FURNITURE COMPANY (press Enter)
   Providing comfort ◆ since 1930

   (2) Select all of the text just entered and change the font to Arial Rounded MT Bold and change the color to Violet.
   (3) Select *JOHNSON*, then change the font size to 30 points.
   (4) Select *FURNITURE COMPANY*, then change the font size to 14 points.
   (5) Select *Providing comfort ◆ since 1930*, then change the font size to 10 points and apply italics.
   (6) Select the diamond shape symbol, change the font color to Dark Blue, then remove italic formatting.

e. Kern *JOHNSON* by completing the following steps:
   (1) Select *JOHNSON*.
   (2) Click Format, Font, then click the Character Spacing tab.
   (3) Click the Kerning for fonts check box to insert a check mark. Make sure that the Points and above box displays 30.
   (4) Click OK or press Enter.

f. Kern and track *FURNITURE COMPANY* by completing the following steps:
   (1) Select *FURNITURE COMPANY*.
   (2) Display the Font dialog box with the Character Spacing tab selected.
   (3) Click the Kerning for fonts check box to insert a check mark. Make sure that the Points and above box displays 14.
   (4) In the Spacing list box, change the letter spacing to Condensed.
   (5) In the By: box, change the point specification to 0.5 pt.
   (6) Click OK or press Enter.
   (7) Insert a single space before *FURNITURE COMPANY* to provide a more pleasing alignment in relation to *JOHNSON*.

g. Track *Providing comfort ◆ since 1930* by completing the following steps:
    (1) Select *Providing comfort ◆ since 1930*.
    (2) Display the Font dialog box with the Character Spacing tab selected.
    (3) In the Spacing list box, change the letter spacing to Condensed.
    (4) In the By: box, change the point specification to 0.2 pt.
    (5) Click OK or press Enter.
    (6) Insert a single space before *Providing comfort...* to provide a more equal alignment in relation to the horizontal line.

h. Adjust the spacing after *FURNITURE COMPANY* to allow room for the horizontal line by completing the following steps:
    (1) Position the insertion point anywhere within *FURNITURE COMPANY*.
    (2) Click Format, Paragraph, then click the Indents and Spacing tab.
    (3) In the Spacing section, change the spacing after the paragraph to 6 pt.

i. Insert the horizontal line under *FURNITURE COMPANY* by completing the following steps:
    (1) Click the Line button on the Drawing toolbar, then position the crosshairs at the beginning of the space between the lines containing *FURNITURE COMPANY* and *Providing comfort ◆ since 1930*.
    (2) Hold down the Shift key and the left mouse button, then drag the mouse across to draw a line the approximate size of the line in figure 3.30. (The line will be sized and positioned more accurately in the following steps.)

j. Customize the horizontal line by completing the following steps:
    (1) With the line still selected, click Format, AutoShape (or position the I-beam pointer on the line until it displays as a four-headed arrow, then double-click the left mouse button).
    (2) At the Format AutoShape dialog box, select the Colors and Lines tab.
    (3) In the Line section, click the Color list box and change the color to Dark Blue, then change the Weight option to 2.5 pt.
    (4) In the Arrows section, click the Begin style list box, then select the line that begins with a diamond shape. Click the Begin size list box, then select the first choice on the left in the first row.
    (5) Make corresponding selections in the End style and End size list boxes.
    (6) Click the Size tab and change the Width of the line to 2.1 inches.
    (7) Click the Position tab and change the horizontal From option to Page and the Horizontal option to 0.98 inches. Change the vertical From option to Page and the Vertical position to 1.29 inches.
    (8) Click OK or press Enter.

k. To remove the border around the text box, select the text box, click the arrow to the right of the Line button on the Drawing toolbar, then click No Line.

l. Create the footer containing the company address and phone and fax numbers by completing the following steps:
    (1) Click the Switch Between Header and Footer button on the Header and Footer toolbar.
    (2) Click the Page Setup button on the Header and Footer toolbar, then select the Margins tab. In the From Edge section, change the Footer box measurement to 0.7 inches, then click OK. (This change ensures that the footer will not fall in a printer's unprintable zone.)

(3) With the insertion point positioned in the footer pane, key the following address and phone and fax numbers, as shown in figure 3.30, according to the following specifications:
   (a) Change the justification to Center.
   (b) Change the font to 11-point Arial Rounded MT Bold Italic and the color to Violet.
   (c) Use the diamond shape from the Monotype Sorts font as indicated in step 1d(1).
   (d) Space once before and after each diamond-shaped bullet.
   (e) Select each bullet, remove italics formatting, and then change the font color to Dark Blue.

4302 Garden Avenue
Salem, Oregon 97326
(509) 555-3200
Fax: (509) 555-3201

m. Create the customized horizontal line in the footer by completing the following steps:
   (1) Click the Line button on the Drawing toolbar, then position the crosshairs above the address line. Hold down the Shift key and the left mouse button, then drag the mouse across to draw a line the approximate size of the footer line in figure 3.30. (The line will be sized and positioned more accurately in the following steps.)
   (2) Customize the horizontal line as in steps 1j(1-5), then complete the following steps:
      (a) Click the Size tab and change the Width to 6.5 inches.
      (b) Click the Position tab and change the horizontal From option to Margin and the Horizontal option to 0 inches. Change the vertical From option to Page and the Vertical option to 10.05 inches.
      (c) Click OK or press Enter.
   (3) Click Close on the Header and Footer toolbar.

n. Use Print Preview to view your document.

2. Save the document and name it c03ex05, Johnson ltrhead.
3. Print and then close c03ex05, Johnson ltrhead.

4302 Garden Avenue ◆ Salem, Oregon 97326 ◆ (509) 555-3200 ◆ Fax: (509) 555-3201

figure 3.30

Using WordArt for Interesting Text Effects

You can create compelling text effects using WordArt as illustrated in figure 3.31. WordArt can distort or modify text to create a variety of shapes. This is useful for creating company logos and headings and can be easily incorporated into a company letterhead. It is also especially useful for headlines in flyers and announcements. The available shapes can exaggerate the text to create an interesting focal point. Using WordArt in a letterhead is one way to project a particular image and to establish an identity with your target audience.

To create a WordArt object, click the Insert WordArt button on the Drawing toolbar or click Insert, point to Picture, then click WordArt. Select the template style you want at the WordArt Gallery dialog box, shown in figure 3.32, and then type your text in the Edit WordArt text dialog box as shown in figure 3.33.

Insert WordArt

The WordArt toolbar appears automatically whenever you select a WordArt object. Figure 3.34 illustrates the WordArt toolbar. The WordArt toolbar enables you to change fonts, font styles, alignment, color, color effects, size, position, wrapping style, rotation, vertical text position, letter height, and character spacing (kerning and tracking).

figure 3.31

Examples of WordArt Objects

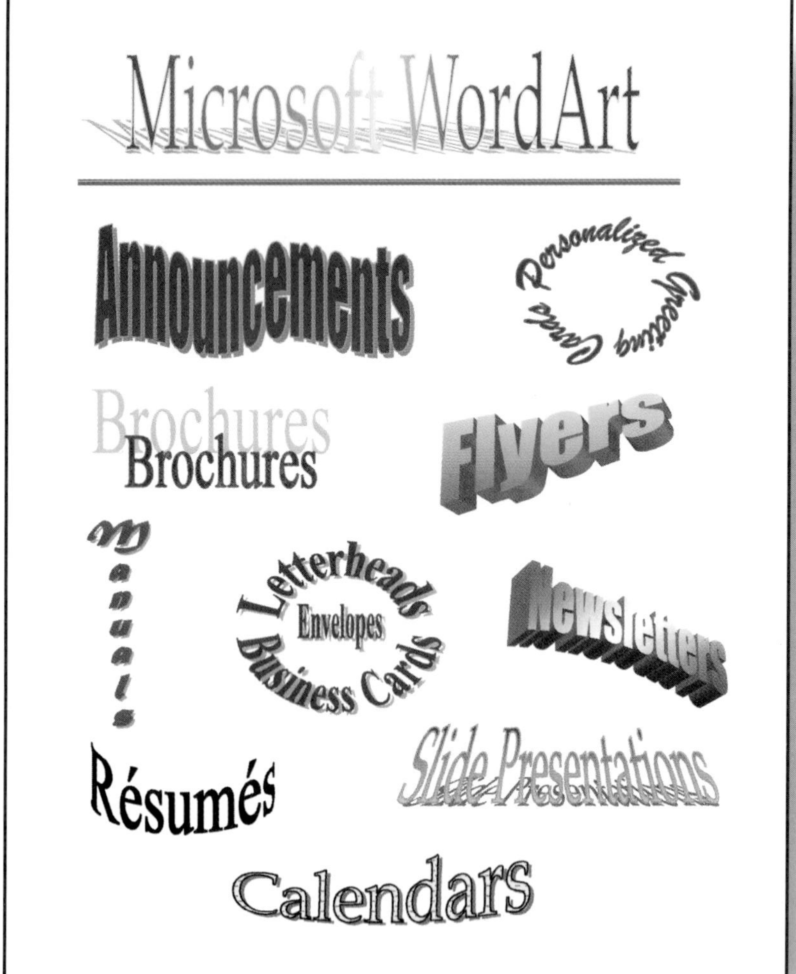

figure 3.32

WordArt Gallery Dialog Box

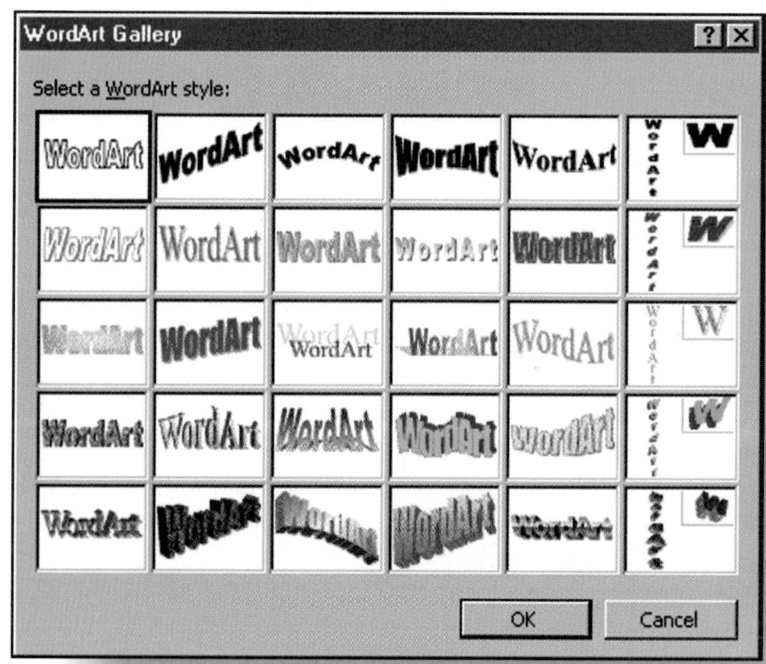

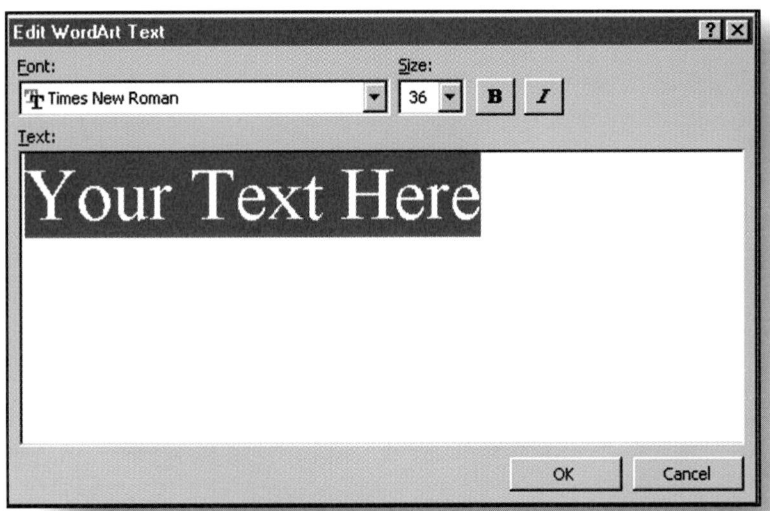

figure 3.33

Edit WordArt Text Dialog Box

figure 3.34

WordArt Toolbar

If you decide you want a different shape for your WordArt object, click the WordArt Shape button (fifth button from the left) on the WordArt toolbar. The WordArt Shape button opens up a palette of approximately forty shapes as shown in figure 3.35. Some shapes produce different results depending on how many lines of text and spaces you key into the text entry box in WordArt. When you are deciding on which shape to use, experiment with several to find the right effect. You may want to experiment with various fonts, font sizes, colors, and color effects to find the right combination for your text.

WordArt Shape

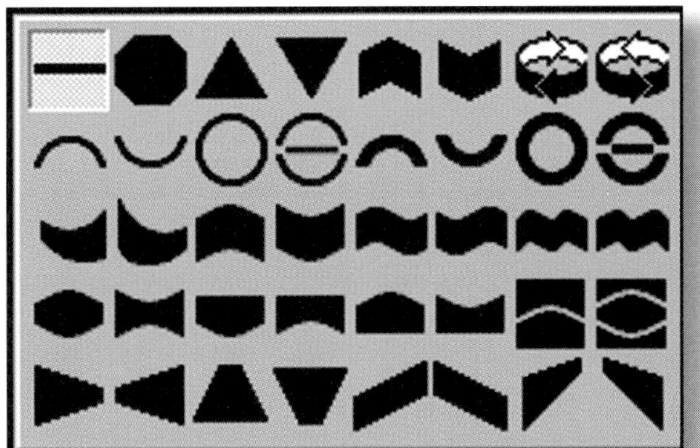

figure 3.35

WordArt Shapes

Format WordArt

You can size, crop, move, copy, or add a border to a WordArt object by using the same techniques you use to customize any other drawing object, such as a text box, a line, or a picture. The Format WordArt button on the WordArt toolbar opens the Format WordArt dialog box where you can change the fill color of the letters or add gradient, texture, pattern or picture fill. You can change the color, style, and weight of the letter borders depending on the options selected. Additionally, you can change the height, width, and rotation of the object depending on the options you select at the Format WordArt dialog box.

exercise 6

Creating a Letterhead Using WordArt and Text Boxes

1. At a clear document screen, create the letterhead shown in figure 3.36 by completing the following steps:
   a. Change the top margin to 0.7 inches and the left and right margins to 1 inch.
   b. Create the WordArt company logo by completing the following steps:
      (1) Display the Drawing toolbar by clicking the Drawing button on the Standard toolbar.
      (2) Click the Insert WordArt button on the Drawing toolbar.
      (3) At the WordArt Gallery dialog box in the Select a WordArt style section, click the second style from the left in the second row.
      (4) Click OK or press Enter.
      (5) At the Edit WordArt Text dialog box with *Your Text Here* selected, key the following pressing Enter as indicated:

         Carlucci (press Enter)
         & (press Enter)
         Associates

      (6) Click the Bold button near the top of the dialog box.
      (7) Click OK.
      (8) With the WordArt object selected in your document, click the WordArt Shape button on the WordArt toolbar.
      (9) Select the fourth shape from the left in the second row, labeled as *Button (Curve)*.
   c. Size and position the WordArt object by completing the following steps:
      (1) With the WordArt object still selected, click the Format WordArt button on the WordArt toolbar.
      (2) At the Format WordArt dialog box, click the Size tab, then change the height to 1.2 inches and the width to 1.3 inches.
      (3) Select the Position tab, change the horizontal From option to Page, then change the Horizontal option to 0.8 inches. Change the vertical From option to Margin, then change the Vertical option to 0 inches.
   d. Change the color of the WordArt text by completing the following steps:
      (1) With the Format WordArt dialog box still displayed, click the Colors and Lines tab.
      (2) In the Fill section, click the Color list box, then select the fourth color block from the left in the second row (Green).
      (3) Click OK or press Enter.

e. Insert the horizontal line by completing the following steps:
   (1) Click the Line button on the Drawing toolbar, then position the crosshairs to the right and center of the WordArt object.
   (2) Hold down the Shift key, then click and drag the mouse to the right to create a line approximately the same length as the line in figure 3.36.

f. Size and position the horizontal line by completing the following steps:
   (1) Double-click the line to display the Format AutoShape dialog box.
   (2) Click the Size tab, then change the width of the line to 5.3 inches.
   (3) Click the Position tab, change the horizontal From option to Page and the Horizontal option to 2.5 inches. Change the vertical From option to Page and the Vertical option to 1.2 inches.

g. Change the color and weight of the line by completing the following steps:
   (1) With the Format AutoShape dialog box still displayed, click the Colors and Lines tab.
   (2) In the Line section, click the Color list box, then select More Colors.
   (3) At the Colors dialog box, make sure the Standard tab is selected, then click the fourth gray color spot from the left in the bottom row of the white, gray, and black color selections. Click OK.
   (4) Change the Weight of the line to 2.5 pt.
   (5) Click OK or press Enter.

h. Insert the text box containing *Marketing Specialists* by completing the following steps:
   (1) Click the Text Box button on the Drawing toolbar, then position the crosshairs in the upper right corner above the line.
   (2) Click and drag to draw a text box approximately ½ inch by 2½ inches.

i. Change the fill and line color, then size and position the text box by completing the following steps:
   (1) With the text box still selected, double-click one of the text box borders (or click Format, then Text Box) to display the Format Text Box dialog box:
   (2) Click the Colors and Lines tab. In the Fill section, click the arrow to the right of the Color list box, then select No Fill. In the Line section, click the arrow to the right of the Color list box, then select No Line.
   (3) Click the Size tab, then change the height to 0.3 inches and the width to 2.58 inches.
   (4) Click the Position tab, change the horizontal From option to Page and the Horizontal option to 5.3 inches. Change the vertical From option to Page and the Vertical option to 0.8 inches.
   (5) Click OK or press Enter.

j. Insert and format the text box contents by completing the following steps:
   (1) Click once inside the text box to position the insertion point.
   (2) Key **Marketing Specialists**.
   (3) Select the text just entered, change the alignment to right, then change the font to 15-point Moderne, Bold Italic. Change the color to Green and then select Emboss and Small caps from the Effects section.

k. Insert the text box containing the address and phone and fax numbers in the approximate location as shown in figure 3.36 by following steps similar to 1h(1-2) above.

l. Change the fill and line color, then size and position the text box by following steps similar to 1i(1-5) above with the following changes:
   (1) Change the height of the text box to 0.8 inches and the width to 2.5 inches.
   (2) Change the horizontal position of the text box to 5.4 inches from the edge of the page and the vertical position to 1.2 inches from the top of the page. (Remember to change the "From" options first.)

m. Insert and format the text box contents by completing the following steps:
   (1) Click once inside the text box to position the insertion point.
   (2) Key the following text pressing Enter where indicated:

      2021 Washington Street (press Enter)
      Providence, Rhode Island 02890 (press Enter)
      Phone: (401) 555-3595 (press Enter)
      Fax: (401) 555-3593

   (3) Select the text just entered, change the justification to right, then change the font to 10-point Moderne, Bold, and the color to Green.

n. Create the slogan at the bottom of the page by completing the following steps:
   (1) Click View, Header and Footer, then click the Switch Between Header and Footer button on the Header and Footer toolbar.
   (2) In the Footer pane, insert a text box the approximate size of the text box shown in figure 3.36.
   (3) Remove the text box borders.
   (4) Change the fill color to 25%-Gray (the last color block on the right in the fourth row of the line color palette).
   (5) Change the height of the text box to 0.3 inches and the width to 5 inches.
   (6) Change the horizontal position of the text box to 1.6 inches from the edge of the page and the vertical position to 10 inches from the top of the page. (Remember to change the "From" options first.)
   (7) Insert and format the text box contents by completing the following steps:
      (a) Click once inside the text box to position the insertion point.
      (b) Key **Over 25 years' experience in developing successful marketing plans.**
      (c) Select the text just entered, change the font to 11-point Times New Roman, Bold Italic, and the color to Green.
      (d) Change the paragraph alignment to center.
      (e) Click Close on the Header and Footer toolbar.
   (8) Use Print Preview to view the whole document. Make sure the footer displays correctly. A printer's unprintable zone may cause the footer to be cut off when printing. If the footer appears cut off, change the distance from the bottom edge of the paper to the bottom edge of the footer by completing the following steps:
      (a) Click the Page Setup button on the Header and Footer toolbar, then select the Margins tab.
      (b) In the From edge section, change the Footer distance to 0.8 inches.
      (c) Click OK or press Enter.

2. Save the letterhead and name it c03ex06, Carlucci ltrhead. (This letterhead could be saved as a template also.)
3. Print and then close c03ex06, Carlucci ltrhead.

3.36

MARKETING SPECIALISTS

2021 Washington Street
Providence, Rhode Island 02890
Phone: (401) 555-3595
Fax: (401) 555-3593

Over 25 years' experience in developing successful marketing plans.

Creating Envelopes

Let your company's letterhead be the starting point for the design of your other business documents. An envelope designed in coordination with a letterhead is another way of establishing your identity with your target audience. Using some of the same design elements in the envelope as in the letterhead contributes to continuity and consistency among your documents. These same elements can be carried over into memos, faxes, business cards, invoices, and brochures.

DTP POINTERS
Use your company's letterhead as the starting point for the design of your other business documents.

Creating the Content

As in a letterhead, there is certain information that must be included on the front of an envelope. Include all necessary information so your correspondence reaches its intended destination, such as the following:

Return Address:

- Logo
- Name
- Address
- Mailing address if different
- Optional: Company motto or slogan
- Optional: Telephone (include area code) and fax number

Recipient's Address:

- Name
- Title (only if you really know it)
- Company name
- Street address
- City, State, ZIP (check a ZIP Code directory if necessary)

Designing Your Own Envelope

DTP POINTERS
Consider the actual size of your design area.

If you decide to design your own envelope, consider the size of the envelope to be used. Any design elements will most likely be located on the left side of the envelope, concentrated in the upper left corner. Hence, your design area is much smaller than that of a letterhead.

When planning your design, remember that the envelope design does not have to be an exact replica of the letterhead. Select enough common elements for your design so a link is established in the viewer's eyes between the two documents. For example, using the same typeface and type styles in a smaller type size and repeating a graphic element on a smaller scale may be just enough to establish that link. Size the fonts used on the envelope so they are in proportion to those used in the letterhead. Restrain from making the design too large or overpowering. The design should not interfere in any way with the recipient's name and address. Be conscious of the fact that the post office sorting equipment reads an envelope both from left to right and bottom to top at the same time. The "reader" is searching for an address and will respond first to the darkest item that includes numbers. Therefore, if you position the return address in the upper left corner of the envelope, the reader will first encounter the delivery address before it finds the return address. Check with your local post office for any mailing restrictions on placing text or design elements on the front of an envelope.

Using Word's Envelope Feature

Word has a very convenient Envelope feature that makes creating professional-looking envelopes easy and inexpensive. The Envelope feature lets you insert the return address, the delivery address, a United States Postal Service Postnet Bar Code, and Facing Identification Marks (FIM). FIMs are used in the United States on courtesy reply mail to identify the front of the envelope during presorting. Additional Envelope options allow the user to change fonts for the delivery and return addresses, adjust the placement of the return or delivery addresses on the envelope, print the envelope, or add the envelope to the document currently displayed in the editing window. The envelope size defaults to a $4^1/8$-inch by $9^1/2$-inch, size 10 business envelope, but the envelope size definition can be changed, or you can create your own custom-size envelope definition. Names and addresses for both the return and delivery addresses can be stored in Word's Address Book feature for later use.

If you have a letter currently displayed in the editing window when accessing the Envelope feature, the inside address from the letter is automatically inserted in the Delivery Address section of the Envelopes and Labels dialog box. In addition, an address may automatically display in the Return Address section. A return address will automatically display if an address has been entered in User Information. To access User Information, choose Tools, then Options. At the Options dialog box, select the User Information tab. Any address that displays in the Mailing Address section in the User Information tab will automatically appear in the Return Address section of the Envelopes and Labels dialog box. Entering an address at this dialog box is useful if the return address will remain the same for the majority of your correspondence. You can change a return address at the Options dialog box with the User Information tab selected or in the Envelopes and Labels dialog box.

After the delivery address and the return address have been filled in, the envelope can either be printed or added to the current active document. If Add to Document is chosen, Word adds the envelope to the beginning of the current active document. The program numbers the envelope as page 0. If you add the envelope to a blank document and then save the envelope, a blank page will be saved with your envelope and ejected from the printer when printing the envelope.

Word determines the feed method for envelopes and the feed form that is best suited to your printer as shown in the Feed section of the Envelopes and Labels dialog box (with the Envelopes tab selected). If this method does not work for your printer, choose the correct feed method and feed form at the Envelope Options dialog box with the Printing Options tab selected. Feed methods are visually displayed at this dialog box. You can also determine if the envelope is fed into the printer face up or face down.

In addition to including text in a return address, a clip art image, a company logo, a graphic created using Word's drawing tools, or an image created using WordArt can also be included. To use the Envelope feature and to include your own design for the envelope, key the delivery address and the return address (depending on how the return address is to be incorporated with the design), add the envelope to the document, and then create the design. Or you may add a blank envelope to a document and then add your design and return address to the blank envelope. If you are taking the time to design an envelope, convert it to a template as in the following exercise, so you can use it over and over again.

exercise 7

Designing and Creating an Envelope Template Using the Envelope Feature

1. At a clear document screen, create an envelope design, as shown in figure 3.37, to coordinate with the *Desktop Design* letterhead created in exercise 3, then convert the envelope to a template by completing the following steps:
   a. Click Tools, then Envelopes and Labels.
   b. At the Envelopes and Labels dialog box, select the Envelopes tab.

c. If any text appears in the Delivery Address text box, select and delete it.
d. If a default address appears in the Return Address text box, click the Omit check box to insert a check mark.
e. Make sure a business size envelope appears in the Preview box, then click Add to Document to insert a blank envelope form in your document. The screen will display with the insertion point in the return address position. The page number in the status line will display as *Page 0*. A blank page will also be included following the envelope because the envelope was added to a clear document screen.
f. With the insertion point in the upper left corner, change the left margin to 0.3 inches. If Word prompts you that your printer will not accept this measurement, choose Fix to accept the minimum margin setting as determined by Word.
g. Insert a text box for the return address design by completing the following steps:
    (1) Click the Zoom button on the Standard toolbar, then select Page Width.
    (2) Click the Drawing button on the Standard toolbar to display the Drawing toolbar.
    (3) Click the Text Box button on the Drawing toolbar, then position the crosshairs in the upper left corner of the envelope, and click and drag to draw a text box in the left margin approximately the same size as that shown in figure 3.37. (The text box will be specifically sized and positioned in the next few steps.)
h. Size and position the text box by completing the following steps:
    (1) Position the I-beam on the text box border so that it displays as an arrow with a four-headed arrow attached, then double-click to display the Format Text Box dialog box (or click Format, then Text Box).
    (2) At the Format Text Box dialog box, select the Size tab, then change the Height of the text box to 3.3 inches and the Width to 1.5 inches.
    (3) Select the Position tab, then change the horizontal From option to Margin and the Horizontal option to 0.0 inches. Change the vertical From option to Page and the Vertical option to 0.4 inches.
i. Insert the textured fill and then remove the text box borders by completing the following steps:
    (1) With the Format Text Box dialog box still displayed, click the Colors and Lines tab.
    (2) In the Fill section, click the Color list box, click Fill Effects, then click the Texture tab in the Fill Effects dialog box.
    (3) In the Texture section, click the second texture block from the left in the first row. The texture name, *Recycled paper*, will display below the texture selections.
    (4) Click OK or press Enter to close the Fill Effects dialog box.
    (5) In the Line section, click the Color list box, then click No Line.
    (6) Click OK to close the Format Text Box dialog box.
j. Insert and format the text box contents by completing the following steps:
    (1) Click once inside the text box to position the insertion point.
    (2) Key the following text, pressing Enter the number of times indicated:

Desktop (press Enter)
Design (press Enter)
568 Pine Street (press Enter)
St. Louis, MO 63131 (press Enter 10 times)
"Where Concepts Become a Reality"

(3) Select all the text just entered, change the justification to center, then change the font to Arial and the color to Teal. (Hint: Press Ctrl + A or click Edit, then Select All to select all the text in the text box.) Do not be concerned if part of the slogan is not visible at this point.
(4) Select *Desktop Design*, then change the font size to 16 points and apply bold.
(5) Select the address, city, state, and Zip Code and change the font size to 10 points.
(6) Select *"Where Concepts Become a Reality"* and change the font to 10-point Times New Roman, Bold Italic.
(7) Make sure the slogan is positioned similarly to the example in figure 3.37. Adjust by inserting or deleting hard returns if necessary.

k. Insert the horizontal line by completing the following steps:
(1) To adjust the spacing between *Design* and the street address to accommodate the horizontal line, position the insertion point anywhere within the line containing *Design*. Click Format, Paragraph, then select the Indents and Spacing tab. In the Spacing section, change the spacing after the paragraph to 8 points. Click OK or press Enter.
(2) Click the Line button on the Drawing toolbar, then position the crosshairs under *Design*.
(3) Hold down the Shift key, then click and drag the crosshairs to the right to create a straight horizontal line the approximate length of the horizontal line shown in figure 3.37.

l. Size and position the horizontal line by completing the following steps:
(1) Position the I-beam on the line until it displays as an arrow with a four-headed arrow attached.
(2) Double-click the line to display the Format AutoShape dialog box, then click the Size tab.
(3) In the Size and rotate section, change the Width to 1.3 inches.
(4) Select the Position tab, then change the horizontal From option to Page and the Horizontal option to 0.43 inches. Change the vertical From option to Page and the Vertical option to 1.01 inches.

m. Change the color and weight of the horizontal line by completing the following steps:
(1) With the Format AutoShape dialog box still displayed, click the Colors and Lines tab.
(2) In the Line section, click the Color list box, then click More Colors.
(3) At the Colors dialog box, click the Standard tab.
(4) From the Standard tab color selections, select the dark brown/burgundy color on the right side in the outer row, third color up from the bottom right corner. (If you have trouble finding this color, simply select a similar color.)
(5) Click OK or press Enter to close the Colors dialog box.
(6) In the Line section, change the Weight option to 3 pt.
(7) Click OK or press Enter to close the Format AutoShape dialog box.

n. Add placeholder text to indicate placement of the delivery address by completing the following steps:
(1) Click the Show/Hide ¶ button on the Standard toolbar to turn on the display of nonprinting characters. Click the paragraph symbol located in the delivery address area to display a text box reserved for the delivery address. (This text box exists when an envelope is produced using the Envelopes and Label feature.)
(2) Key **[Type delivery address here]**.

o. Use Print Preview to view the entire envelope.

2. Save your envelope as a template by completing the following steps:
   a. Choose File, then Save As, and change the Save as type: option to *Document Templates (*.dot)*. (The default templates folder name should appear in the Save in: list box.)
   b. Double-click the *Letters & Faxes* folder to make it active.
   c. In the File name text box, name the template **(your last name), ddenvelope**.
   d. Click Save.
   e. Close the envelope template.
3. Open a copy of your envelope template and insert a delivery address by completing the following steps:
   a. Choose File, New, and then select the Letters & Faxes tab.
   b. Double-click on *(your last name), ddenvelope.dot*; or select the envelope template and click OK.
   c. With the envelope template document displayed on the screen, select *[Type delivery address here]* and key the following address:

      Mr. Vincent Martinez
      Carter Corporation
      1232 North Randolph Street
      Chicago, IL 60631

4. Save and name the document c03ex07, ddenvelope.
5. Print the page containing the envelope and then close c03ex07, ddenevlope.

figure 3.37

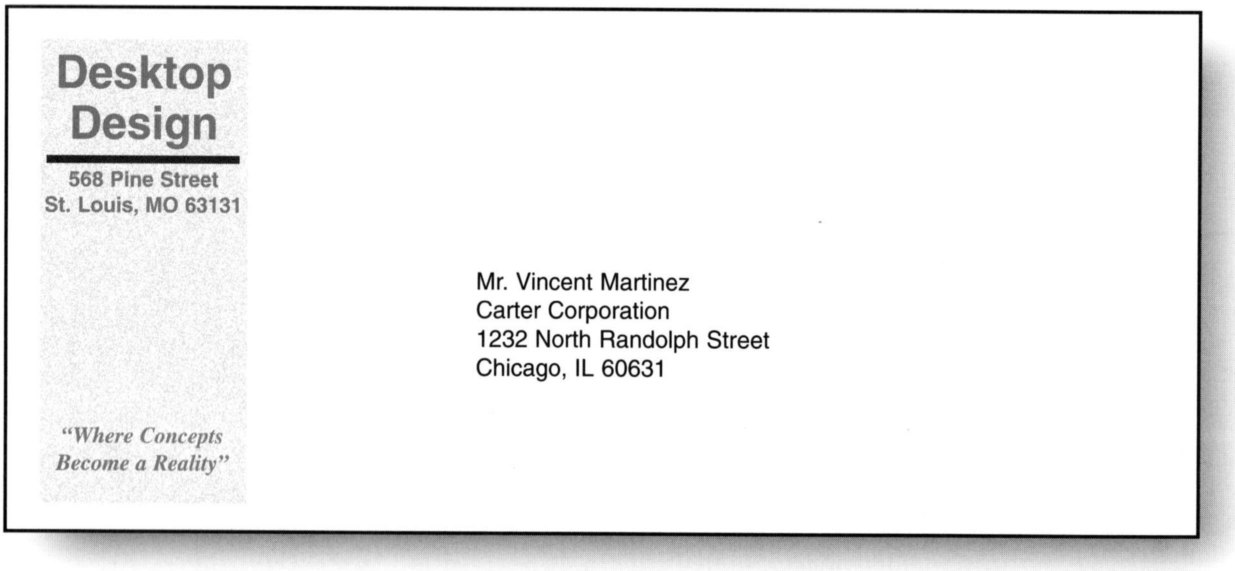

Desktop
Design

568 Pine Street
St. Louis, MO 63131

"Where Concepts Become a Reality"

Mr. Vincent Martinez
Carter Corporation
1232 North Randolph Street
Chicago, IL 60631

Using AutoText to Store and Reuse Text and Graphics

AutoText allows you to quickly and easily store and reuse commonly used text and/or graphics, including any associated formatting, and to insert them into documents whenever you need them. By default, AutoText entries are saved as part of the *Normal* template and, therefore, are always available for future use. You can limit AutoText entries to specific templates, if desired. The AutoText feature is useful for items such as addresses, a company logo, lists, standard text, a closing to a letter, or any other text that you use on a frequent basis or that you don't want to recreate every time you need them.

DTP POINTERS
Use the AutoText feature to store commonly used text and/or graphics.

In exercise 8, you will create a business card, save the business card as an AutoText entry, then use the AutoText entry to create a full sheet of business cards.

Creating an AutoText Entry

To create an AutoText entry, key the desired text, apply any formatting, and/or insert any graphics or objects. Select the text and/or graphics you want to store as an AutoText entry. Click Insert, point to AutoText, then click New. At the Create AutoText dialog box, either accept the default name assigned to the AutoText entry or key a new name. Try to name the AutoText entry something that is short but indicative of the entry contents. If you plan to create, insert, or edit several AutoText entries, display the AutoText toolbar to save you some time. To display the AutoText toolbar, position the arrow pointer anywhere within a toolbar that is currently displayed on the screen, then right-click. Select *AutoText* from the toolbar drop-down list. After selecting the desired text and/or graphics, click New on the AutoText toolbar to access the Create AutoText dialog box.

When you save selected text as an Auto Text entry, the formatting applied to the text is also saved. If you are saving a paragraph or paragraphs of text that have paragraph formatting applied, make sure you include the paragraph mark with the selected text. To make sure the paragraph mark is included, turn on the display of nonprinting characters before selecting the text.

Inserting an AutoText Entry

An AutoText entry can be inserted by using the AutoCorrect dialog box or by using a shortcut method. To insert an entry using the AutoCorrect dialog box, choose Insert, point to AutoText, then click AutoText. At the AutoCorrect dialog box, click the name of the AutoText entry in the list box, then click Insert. If you cannot remember the name of a desired entry at the AutoCorrect dialog box, click each entry in the list box and view the contents in the Preview box. You can also quickly display the AutoCorrect dialog box by clicking the AutoText button on the AutoText toolbar.

Word also includes many built-in AutoText entries. When you click Insert, then point to AutoText, a drop-down menu displays several categories of AutoText entries. These categories are also displayed when you click All Entries on the AutoText toolbar. Point to an appropriate category to see the AutoText entries that Word offers for that category. For example, if you are creating a business letter, click the *Salutation* category to display a selection of different salutations from which to choose, as shown in figure 3.38 Word even adds salutations you may have used in the past to the selection.

figure 3.38

Sample Built-In AutoText Entries

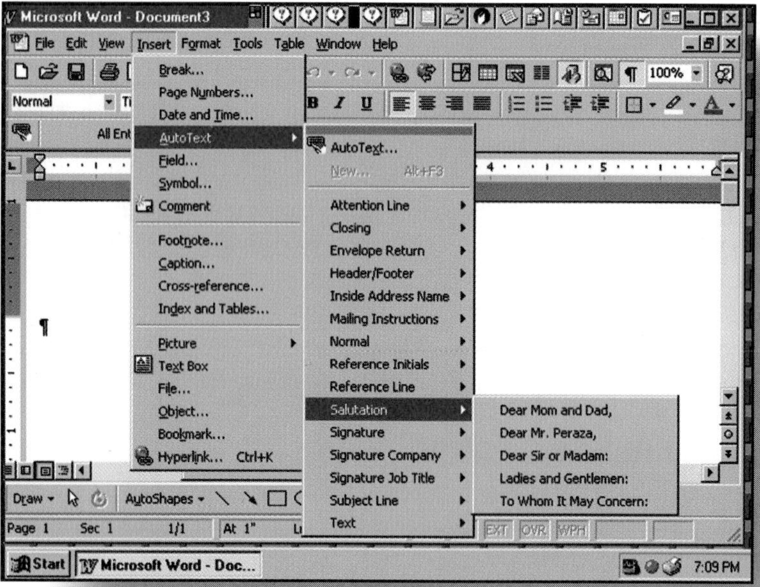

An AutoText entry can be inserted into a document by using two different shortcut methods. To use the first shortcut method, key the name given to the AutoText entry, then press the shortcut key F3. The AutoText entry will immediately appear in your document at the location of the insertion point.

To use the second shortcut method, you must first change a setting in the AutoCorrect dialog box. To do this, click Insert, point to AutoText, then click AutoText to display the AutoCorrect dialog box. In the AutoText tab, click the check box to the left of Show Auto Complete tip for AutoText and dates to insert a check mark, then click OK. Once this feature is activated, it remains active during all future working sessions unless you deactivate the feature by removing the check mark. The second shortcut method comes into play when you begin to key a name given an AutoText entry. After you have keyed the first four letters of an AutoText entry name, Word suggests the complete word or phrase in a small box displayed above the current line of typing. When the suggestion appears, press Enter or F3 to accept Word's suggestion or keep typing to ignore the suggestion. If your AutoText entry is a picture, Word does not offer any suggestion.

Editing an AutoText Entry

An AutoText entry can be edited by inserting the entry in a document, making any necessary changes, then saving it again with the same AutoText entry name. When Word asks if you want to redefine the AutoText entry, choose Yes.

Deleting an AutoText Entry

An AutoText entry can be removed from the AutoCorrect dialog box. To do this, display the AutoText tab in the AutoCorrect dialog box, select the entry name from the AutoText entry list box, then click the Delete button. In a classroom lab setting, check with your instructor about deleting AutoText entries after you are finished with them. Deleting them would allow other students the opportunity to create their own entries with the same names.

Creating Business Cards

Business cards eliminate the unprofessional and sometimes awkward scribbling of your name, address, and telephone number on whatever piece of paper you can find. A business card represents you and your company and projects an organized, professional image. A business card is one of your best marketing opportunities.

A business card usually includes your name, title, company name, address, E-mail address, telephone number, and fax number. You can also include a one-sentence description of your business, philosophy, or slogan. To further establish your identity and to stay consistent with your other business documents such as letterheads, envelopes, etc., include the same company logo or symbol in reduced size. Also, continue to use the same typefaces and colors used in your other business documents. Most business cards are created with sans serif typefaces because the characters are easier to read. The type sizes vary from 12 to 14 points for key words and 8 to 10 points for telephone and fax numbers. Vary the appearance by using bold, italics, or small caps.

DTP POINTERS
Using coordinating design elements in your business documents establishes identity and consistency.

Business cards should be printed on high-quality cover stock paper. Specially designed full-color papers and forms for creating business cards more easily and professionally are available at office supply stores and paper companies. Printing your own business cards saves you the expense of having to place a large minimum order with an outside printer. This is especially helpful to a new small business. You may decide to design your own card and then take it to a professional printer to be printed in larger quantities.

Using Word's Labels Feature to Create Business Cards

Although Word does not include a template for creating business cards, you can use Word's business card label definition when designing and creating your own business cards. To automatically create a full sheet of business cards with the same information on each card, you would complete the following steps:

1. Click Tools, then Envelopes and Labels.
2. At the Envelopes and Labels dialog box, select the Labels tab.
3. Key the information and/or insert any AutoText entry (using the F3 shortcut method) you want to appear on the business cards/labels in the Address text box.
4. Click Options.
5. At the Label Options dialog box, select *Avery Standard* in the Label products list box, then choose *5371-Business Card* or *8371-Business Card* from the Product number list box.
6. Click OK or press Enter.
7. At the Envelopes and Labels dialog box, make sure Full page of the same label is selected, then choose New Document.

There is no difference between the two business card label definitions mentioned in step 5 above. The difference occurs in the actual product when you purchase these brand-name items at an office supply store—the *5371* is made to be used in a laser printer and the *8371* is made to be used in an ink jet printer.

When you select a label, information about that label is displayed in the Label information section of the Label Options dialog box, including the type, height, width, and page size. (In this case, each business card will be 3½ inches by 2 inches. The sheet containing the business cards will be 8½ inches by 11 inches.) To further customize your business card label selection, choose Details from the Label Options dialog box. The Business Card 5371 (or 8371) information dialog box appears. The Preview box displays a label with the margins, pitch measurements, and height and width indicated. At this dialog box, you can customize the top and side margins, vertical pitch (the distance from the top of one label to the top of the next label), horizontal pitch (the distance from the left edge of one label to the left edge of the adjacent label), the label height and width, and the number of labels across and down the label page.

When you change any of the predefined settings of a label listed in the Product number list box, you are actually creating a new label definition. Since these labels are actually cells in a table on an 8½-inch by 11-inch page, margin setting changes affect the whole page. If you change the margin settings in a label, you are really changing where the cell begins in relation to the edge of the paper. You are not changing the margins within each label or cell—that is, the area between the edge of the label and the beginning of the address. In this instance, the label definition will produce 10 business cards—two columns of labels with five rows in each column.

As an alternative method for creating your business cards, you can leave the Address text box empty, then choose New Document and a full page of blank label forms will be displayed at the document screen. You can then create the first business card/label at the document screen and copy it to the rest of the label forms.

You will create 10 business cards in exercise 8 using the Avery 5371 Business Card label definition. You will first use the Labels feature to create a business card that will be saved as an Auto Text entry. To actually create the 10 business cards, you will access the Envelopes and Labels dialog box, insert the AutoText entry in the Address list box, and create a full sheet of business cards. Because several objects (text boxes and a line) are used to construct the business card, you will use Word's object grouping feature to treat the multiple objects as a single object.

Consider using the business card label definition to create membership cards, name tags, coupons, place holders, or friendly reminders.

exercise 8

Creating a Business Card Using Word's Envelopes and Labels Feature and AutoText

1. At a clear document screen, create the AutoText entry to be used to produce the business cards shown in figure 3.39 by completing the following steps:
   a. Insert a blank sheet of labels by completing the following steps:
      (1) Click Tools, then Envelopes and Labels. Select the Labels tab, then click Options.
      (2) At the Label Options dialog box, select *Avery Standard* in the Label products list box, then choose *5371-Business Card* from the Product number list box.
      (3) Click OK or press Enter.
      (4) At the Envelopes and Labels dialog box, delete any text that may appear in the Address list box.
      (5) At the same dialog box, make sure Full page of the same label is selected, then click New Document.

(6) Display the table gridlines that define the label page by clicking Table, and then Show Gridlines.

b. Insert the text box containing the company name, slogan, and address by completing the following steps:
   (1) Click the Zoom arrow on the Standard toolbar and change the display to Page Width.
   (2) Click the Drawing button on the Standard toolbar to display the Drawing toolbar.
   (3) Click the Text Box button on the Drawing toolbar, then position the crosshairs in the upper left corner of the first label (or cell), and click and drag to draw a text box in the left margin approximately the same size as that shown in figure 3.39. (The text box will be specifically sized and positioned in the next few steps.)

c. Size and position the text box by completing the following steps:
   (1) Position the I-beam pointer on the text box border so that it displays as an arrow with a four-headed arrow attached, then double-click to display the Format Text Box dialog box (or click Format, then Text Box).
   (2) At the Format Text Box dialog box, select the Size tab, then change the Height of the text box to 1.7 inches and the Width to 1.35 inches.
   (3) Select the Position tab, make sure the horizontal From option displays Column, then change the Horizontal option to 0.2 inches. Make sure the vertical From option displays Paragraph, then change the Vertical option to 0.18 inches.

d. Insert the textured fill and remove the text box borders by completing the following steps:
   (1) With the Format Text Box dialog box still displayed, click the Colors and Lines tab.
   (2) In the Fill section, click the Color list box, click Fill Effects, then click the Texture tab in the Fill Effects dialog box.
   (3) In the Texture section, click the second texture block from the left in the first row. The texture name, *Recycled paper*, will display below the texture selections.
   (4) Click OK or press Enter to close the Fill Effects dialog box.
   (5) In the Line section, click the Color list box, then click No Line.
   (6) Click OK to close the Format Text Box dialog box.

e. Insert and format the text box contents by completing the following steps:
   (1) Click once inside the text box to position the insertion point.
   (2) Change the justification to center, then change the Font to Arial and the color to Teal.
   (3) Key the following text pressing Enter as indicated. (The zip code will only be partially visible at this point.)

      Desktop (press Enter)
      Design (press Enter)
      "Where Concepts Become a Reality" (press Enter)
      568 Pine Street (press Enter)
      St. Louis, MO 63131

   (4) Select *Desktop Design*, then change the font size to 16 points and apply bold.
   (5) Select *"Where Concepts Become a Reality"* and change the font to 9-point Times New Roman, Bold Italic.
   (6) Select the address, city, state, and Zip Code and change the font size to 9 points.
   (7) Position the insertion point to the left of *568 Pine Street*, then press Enter as many times as necessary to place the address in a similar position to the address shown in figure 3.39.

f. Insert the horizontal line by completing the following steps:
   (1) To adjust the spacing between *Design* and the slogan to accommodate the horizontal line, position the insertion point anywhere within the line containing

Design. Click Format, Paragraph, then select the Indents and Spacing tab. In the Spacing section, change the spacing after the paragraph to 8 points. Click OK or press Enter.

(2) Click the Line button on the Drawing toolbar, then position the crosshairs under *Design*.

(3) Hold down the Shift key, then click and drag the crosshairs to the right to create a straight horizontal line the approximate length of the horizontal line shown in figure 3.39.

g. Size and position the horizontal line by completing the following steps:

(1) Position the I-beam pointer on the line until it displays as an arrow with a four-headed arrow attached.

(2) Double-click the line to display the Format AutoShape dialog box, then click the Size tab.

(3) In the Size and rotate section, change the Width to 1.1 inches.

(4) Select the Position tab, make sure the horizontal From option displays Column, then change the Horizontal option to 0.32 of an inch. Make sure the vertical From option displays Paragraph, then change the Vertical option to 0.8 of an inch.

h. Change the color and weight of the horizontal line by completing the following steps:

(1) With the Format AutoShape dialog box still displayed, click the Colors and Lines tab.

(2) In the Line section, click the Color list box, then click More Colors.

(3) At the Colors dialog box, click the Standard tab.

(4) From the Standard tab color selections, select the dark brown/burgundy color on the right side in the outer row, third color up from the bottom right corner. (If you have trouble finding this color, simply select a similar color.)

(5) Click OK or press Enter to close the Colors dialog box.

(6) In the Line section, change the Weight option to 3 pt.

(7) Click OK or press Enter to close the Format AutoShape dialog box.

i. Insert, size, and position a text box for the business person's name and title by completing the following steps:

(1) Insert a text box following steps similar to 1b(1-3). Draw a text box approximately 1½ inches by ½ inch in a location similar to the placement of the name and title shown in figure 3.39.

(2) To size the text box more precisely, follow steps similar to steps 1c(1-2) and change the height to 0.5 inches and the width to 1.6 inches.

(3) To position the text box, follow steps similar to steps 1c(1-3) and change the horizontal position to 1.75 inches from the column and the vertical position to 0.4 inches from the paragraph. (Remember to set the "From" options first.)

j. Follow steps 1d(2-5) above to remove the text box borders.

k. Insert and format the name and title in the text box by completing the following steps:

(1) Click once inside the text box to position the insertion point.

(2) Change the alignment to center, then change the font to Arial and the color to Teal.

(3) Key the following text pressing Enter as indicated. The last line of text may not be completely visible in the text box; the font size will be changed in step (5).

Linda Urban (press Enter)
Publications Designer

(4) Select *Linda Urban*, make sure the font size is set to 12 points, then apply bold and italic formatting.
(5) Select *Publications Designer*, then change the font size to 10 points and apply italic formatting. (Hint: Position the insertion point to the left of *Publications*, hold down the Shift key, then press Ctrl + End to select the remaining text that is not visible in the text box.)

l. Insert, size, and position a text box for the phone and fax numbers and the E-mail address by completing the following steps:
(1) Insert a text box by following steps similar to 1b(1-3). Draw a text box approximately 1½ inches by ½ inch in a location similar to the placement of the phone and fax numbers and the E-mail address shown in figure 3.39.
(2) To size the text box, follow steps similar to steps 1c(1-2) and change the height to 0.5 inches and the width to 1.6 inches.
(3) To position the text box, follow steps similar to steps 1c(1-3) and change the horizontal position to 1.75 inches from the column and the vertical position to 1.4 inches from the paragraph. (Remember to set the "From" options first.)

m. Follow step 1d(1-5) above to remove the text box borders.

n. Insert and format the phone and fax numbers and the E-mail address by completing the following steps:
(1) Click once inside the text box to position the insertion point.
(2) Change the alignment to center, then change the font to 8-point Arial Bold and the color to Teal.
(3) Key the following text pressing Enter as indicated.

Phone: (314) 555-8755 (press Enter)
Fax: (314) 555-8758 (press Enter)
E-mail: urban@dtp.com

o. To save the business card as an AutoText entry, the objects (the text boxes and the horizontal line) in the business card must be grouped together so they may be treated as one unit. Group the objects by completing the following steps:
(1) Select the text box that contains the company name.
(2) Hold down the Shift key, then select the horizontal line. (The text box should still be selected.)
(3) Hold down the Shift key again, then select the two remaining text boxes. (All objects should be selected.)
(4) Click Draw on the Drawing toolbar, then click Group. (Sizing handles should display on all four sides of the business card.)

p. To complete the process of preparing the business card to be saved as an AutoText entry so that it can be correctly and easily used with the Labels feature, the business card must be copied to the adjacent label on the right. To copy the first label, complete the following steps:
(1) Position the I-beam pointer in the business card until it displays as an arrow with a four-headed arrow attached. (Hint: Move the insertion point close to any of the invisible text box borders to find the four-headed arrow.)
(2) Click once to select the business card.
(3) With the four-headed arrow displayed, hold down the Ctrl key, then click and drag the selected object (you will only see the outlines of the text boxes being dragged) and position it in a similar position in the adjacent label on the right, let go of the mouse and then the Ctrl key.

q. Check the position of the second business card by completing the following steps:
   (1) Follow steps 1p(1-2) to select the second business card.
   (2) Click Format, then Object, and then select the Position tab.
   (3) Make sure the horizontal position of the object is 3.7 inches from the column and the vertical position is 0.18 inches from the paragraph.
   (4) Click OK or press Enter.

r. Group the two business cards so they will be treated as one unit by completing the following steps:
   (1) Select the first business card.
   (2) Hold down the Shift key, then select the second business card.
   (3) Click Draw on the Drawing toolbar, then click Group. (Sizing handles will now display around both objects.)

s. Save the selected object (the two business cards) as an Auto Text entry by completing the following steps:
   (1) With the two business cards selected as one unit, click Insert, point to AutoText, then click New.
   (2) At the Create AutoText dialog box, key **business card**.
   (3) Click OK or press Enter.
   (4) Close the document and do not save the changes. (Remember, the text has already been saved as an AutoText entry. It does not need to be saved as a separate document.)

t. Create a full sheet of business cards by completing the following steps:
   (1) Click Tools, then Envelopes and Labels. Select the Labels tab, then click Options.
   (2) At the Label Options dialog box, select *Avery Standard* in the Label products list box, then choose *5371-Business Card* from the Product number list box.
   (3) Click OK or press Enter.
   (4) At the Envelopes and Labels dialog box, delete any text that may appear in the Address list box, key **business card**, and then press F3.
   (5) At the same dialog box, make sure Full page of the same label is selected, then click New Document. (It may take a few seconds before the full sheet of business cards displays on your screen.)
   (6) Use Print Preview to make sure your document will print correctly. Depending on your printer's unprintable zone and the margins set in the business card's label definition, the printing on the bottom row of the business cards may be cut off. One easy way to avoid this is to fool your printer into thinking your document is going to be printed on a longer piece of paper. To do this, complete the following steps:
      (a) Click File, Page Setup, then select the Paper Size tab.
      (b) In the Paper Size list box, select Legal, then click OK.

2. Save the document with the name c03ex08, business card.
3. Print and then close c03ex08, business card. Printing the business cards on a sheet of business cards made especially for your type of printer is preferable. If you print the business cards on plain paper, you may want to print the table grid lines as shown in figure 3.39. To print the grid lines, complete the following steps:
   a. Click Table, then Select Table.
   b. Click Format, Borders and Shading, then select the Borders tab.
   c. In the Settings section, click All.
   d. In the Style list box, click the second line choice (the fine dotted line) from the top.
   e. Click OK.

figure 3.39

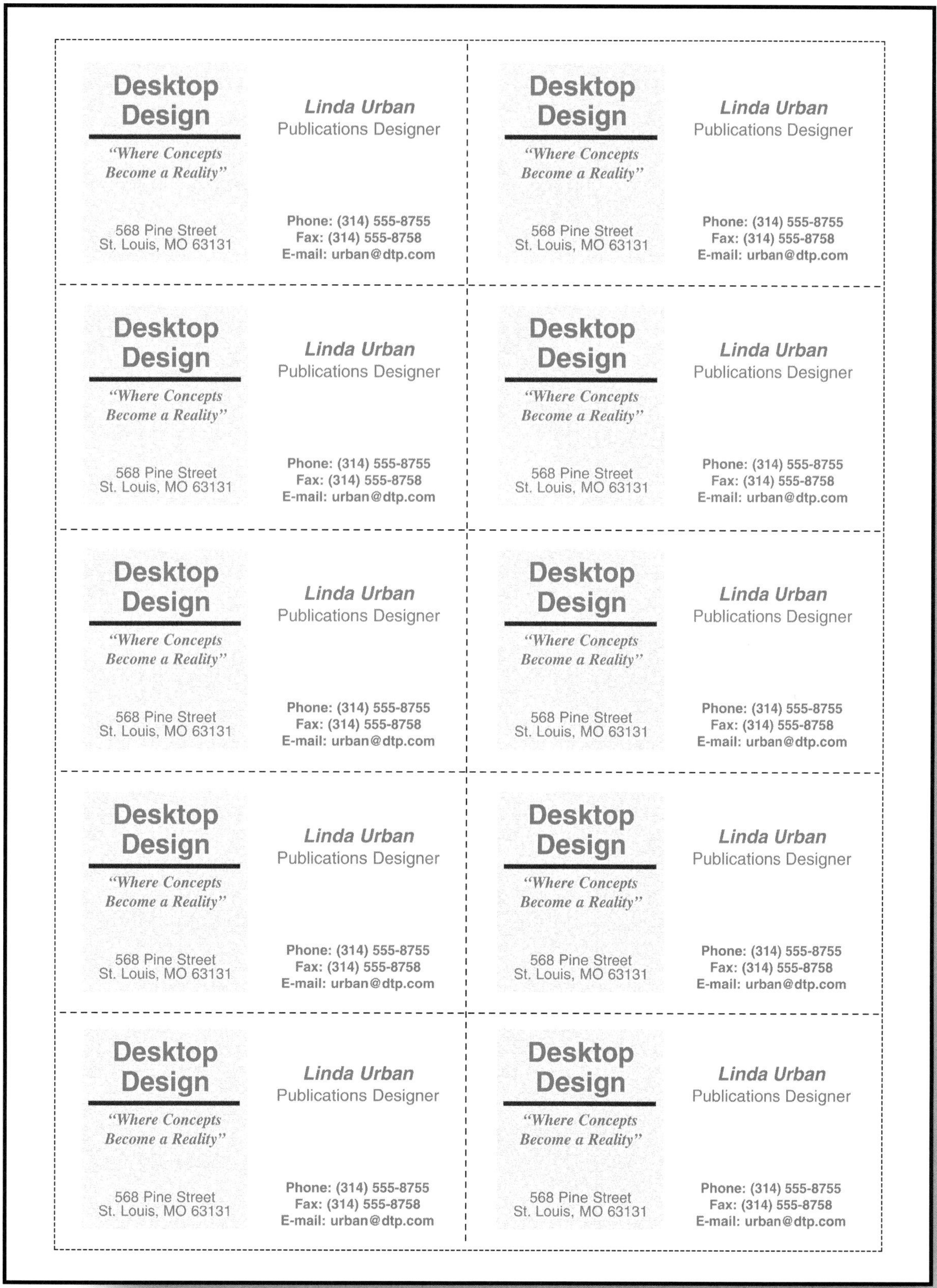

Desktop Design
"Where Concepts Become a Reality"
568 Pine Street
St. Louis, MO 63131

Linda Urban
Publications Designer

Phone: (314) 555-8755
Fax: (314) 555-8758
E-mail: urban@dtp.com

Desktop Design
"Where Concepts Become a Reality"
568 Pine Street
St. Louis, MO 63131

Linda Urban
Publications Designer

Phone: (314) 555-8755
Fax: (314) 555-8758
E-mail: urban@dtp.com

Desktop Design
"Where Concepts Become a Reality"
568 Pine Street
St. Louis, MO 63131

Linda Urban
Publications Designer

Phone: (314) 555-8755
Fax: (314) 555-8758
E-mail: urban@dtp.com

Desktop Design
"Where Concepts Become a Reality"
568 Pine Street
St. Louis, MO 63131

Linda Urban
Publications Designer

Phone: (314) 555-8755
Fax: (314) 555-8758
E-mail: urban@dtp.com

Desktop Design
"Where Concepts Become a Reality"
568 Pine Street
St. Louis, MO 63131

Linda Urban
Publications Designer

Phone: (314) 555-8755
Fax: (314) 555-8758
E-mail: urban@dtp.com

Desktop Design
"Where Concepts Become a Reality"
568 Pine Street
St. Louis, MO 63131

Linda Urban
Publications Designer

Phone: (314) 555-8755
Fax: (314) 555-8758
E-mail: urban@dtp.com

Desktop Design
"Where Concepts Become a Reality"
568 Pine Street
St. Louis, MO 63131

Linda Urban
Publications Designer

Phone: (314) 555-8755
Fax: (314) 555-8758
E-mail: urban@dtp.com

Desktop Design
"Where Concepts Become a Reality"
568 Pine Street
St. Louis, MO 63131

Linda Urban
Publications Designer

Phone: (314) 555-8755
Fax: (314) 555-8758
E-mail: urban@dtp.com

Desktop Design
"Where Concepts Become a Reality"
568 Pine Street
St. Louis, MO 63131

Linda Urban
Publications Designer

Phone: (314) 555-8755
Fax: (314) 555-8758
E-mail: urban@dtp.com

Desktop Design
"Where Concepts Become a Reality"
568 Pine Street
St. Louis, MO 63131

Linda Urban
Publications Designer

Phone: (314) 555-8755
Fax: (314) 555-8758
E-mail: urban@dtp.com

chapter summary

- A letterhead contains a specific design and layout that helps establish an organization's identity with a target audience. Designing your own letterhead can be a less costly alternative to having it designed and produced through a professional printer.
- A number of letter templates are available, including Contemporary, Elegant, and Professional. A Letter Wizard is also available that guides you through the creation of a business letter.
- Template documents may contain several styles that automatically format a specific section of text.
- Ruled lines act as boundaries to the surrounding text. Ruled lines can be used in a document to create a focal point, draw the eye across or down the page, separate columns and sections, or add visual appeal. The thickness of a line is measured in points.
- Design elements can be placed at exact horizontal and/or vertical locations on the page by using the text box feature. Paragraph spacing can also be used to vertically position elements on the page.
- An existing template document can be customized once it is displayed at the document screen. Any changes made only affect the document displayed on the screen, leaving the template available in its original format.
- A template can be edited permanently. If changes are made and the template is saved with the same name, the template will reflect those changes every time it is used.
- A new template can be created that is based on an existing template. The new template will have all the characteristics of the original template except for any changes made. A new template can also be created from an existing Word document or from scratch.
- Kerning is the process of decreasing or increasing the white space between specific character pairs and is used on headlines and other blocks of large type.
- Tracking is the equal reduction or enlargement of the horizontal space between all characters in a block of text.
- WordArt can be used to distort or modify text to create a variety of interesting shapes. Use WordArt to create company logos, letterheads, headlines, and headings in flyers and announcements.
- When creating a design for an envelope, select enough common elements so a link is established in the viewer's eyes between the letterhead and the envelope.
- Use the AutoText feature to save and insert frequently used text and/or graphics.
- Business cards are another way to establish identity among a target audience. Establish an identifying connection between a business card and a letterhead by repeating some of the design elements from the letterhead.

commands review

	Mouse/Keyboard
New dialog box to access a template	File, New, select desired tab
Letter Wizard	File, New, Letters & Faxes tab
User Information	Tool, Options, User Information tab
Change font	Format, Font; or click the Font list box, Font Size list box, and/or character formatting buttons on the Formatting toolbar
Display Drawing toolbar	Click Drawing button on Standard toolbar; or right-click Standard toolbar, select Drawing; or View, Toolbars, then click Drawing
Format AutoShape dialog box	Select object, click Format, then AutoShape; or double-click the object
Border a paragraph	Position insertion point, click Border button or arrow on Formatting toolbar; or click Format, Borders and Shading, and Borders tab
Create Header/Footer	View, Header and Footer, click Switch Between Header and Footer to display Footer pane
Insert a text box	Click Text Box button on Drawing toolbar, position crosshairs, click and drag to draw box
Format Text Box dialog box	Select text box, click Format, then Text Box; or double-click the text box border
Kerning (character spacing between specific pairs of characters)	Format, Font, Character Spacing tab, Kerning for fonts, enter Points and above
Tracking (character/letter spacing)	Format, Font, Character Spacing tab, Spacing, enter point By: amount in point increments
Create a WordArt object	Click the WordArt button on the Drawing toolbar; or click Insert, point to Picture, then click WordArt
Envelopes and Labels dialog box	Tools, Envelopes and Labels, select Envelopes or Labels tab
Symbol dialog box	Insert, Symbol
Create AutoText entry	Click Insert, point to AutoText, then click New
Insert an AutoText entry	Key AutoText entry name, then press F3; or click Insert, point to AutoText, then click AutoText

check your understanding

Terms: In the space provided at the left, indicate the correct term.

_______ 1. This feature guides you through the steps for creating a business letter using any of the available letter templates.

_______ 2. This term refers to the decreasing or increasing of white space between specific character pairs.

_______ 3. In typesetting, the thickness of a line is called its weight and is measured in this.

_______ 4. A customized horizontal or vertical ruled line can be created using this feature.

_______ 5. This term refers to the equal reduction or enlargement of the horizontal space between all characters in a block of text.

_______ 6. When saving a document as a template into the template folder, Word automatically adds this extension.

_______ 7. Turn on kerning for specific point sizes and above at this dialog box.

_______ 8. This feature allows you to store commonly used text and/or graphics along with their formatting.

_______ 9. Use this type of paper size definition when designing and creating your own business cards.

Concepts: Answer the following questions in the space provided.

1. What is the purpose of a letterhead?

2. What information might be contained in a letterhead?

3. Define the User Information feature. What other Word features does it affect?

4. When creating your own letterhead, design concepts presented in chapter 1 such as focus, balance, and proportion should be considered. What are some other design concepts that should be considered?

5. Name two methods of creating lines in Word. Explain advantages or disadvantages of using one method over the other.

6. Explain the various ways a text box may be customized.

skill assessments

Assessment 1

1. You have decided to open your own restaurant. Design a letterhead for your business that will be used for a mailing to introduce your business to the community. Include the following information:

Company Name:	**You decide on the name depending on the picture/graphic that you incorporate into your design.**
Name of Owner:	**Use your own name and include *Owner* or *Proprietor* as your title.**
Slogan:	**You decide on a slogan.**
Address:	**250 San Miguel Boulevard Mission Viejo, CA 92691**
Phone:	**(714) 555-8191**
Fax:	**(714) 555-8196**

2. Create a thumbnail sketch(es) of your proposed letterhead incorporating the following elements:
   a. Create an asymmetrical design.
   b. Incorporate appropriate and proportional typeface, type size, and type style selections.
   c. Turn on kerning and use tracking (condensing or expanding character spacing) if necessary or for a desired effect.
   d. Include ruled lines using either the Draw feature or the Borders feature; you decide on the placement, thickness, color, etc.
   e. Include one of the following pictures/graphics: *Coffee.wmf, Dinner1.wmf, Dinner2.wmf, Drink.wmf, Server.wmf,* or *Wine.wmf* included on your student data disk or create a WordArt object as part of your design.
   f. Use special characters if appropriate.
   g. Incorporate some color if a color printer is available.
3. Save the document and name it c03sa01, restaurant ltrhd.
4. Print and then close c03sa01, restaurant ltrhd.
5. As a self-check for your design, print a copy of *document analysis guide.doc* from your student data disk and answer the questions on the form. Name the exercise c03sa01, restaurant ltrhd.
6. Attach the *Document Analysis Guide* to the hard copy of the letterhead.

Assessment 2

1. Design an envelope to be used with the letterhead created in assessment 1. Include some consistent elements that demonstrate continuity from the letterhead to the envelope. Include the following specifications:
   a. Create a thumbnail sketch(es) of your proposed envelope design.

b. At a clear editing window, use the automatic envelope feature and add the envelope to the blank document.
c. Use the same typeface(s) as in your letterhead. Pay attention to size and proportion.
d. Turn on automatic kerning and adjust character spacing if necessary.
e. Use the same colors in the envelope as in your letterhead.
2. Save your envelope as a template and name it (your name) restaurant env.
3. Close (your name) restaurant env.
4. Access your envelope template, then insert your own name and address in the delivery address area.
5. Save the document and name it c03sa02, restaurant env.
6. Print and then close c03sa02, restaurant env.

Assessment 3

1. Create a page of business cards to coordinate with the letterhead and envelope created in assessments 1 and 2. Even though a business card does not have to be an exact replica of your letterhead, include some consistent identifying elements that link the two documents together. Include the following specifications when creating the business cards:
   a. Create a thumbnail sketch(es) of your proposed business card design and layout.
   b. Use the Labels feature and the Avery 5371 (or 8371) business card label definition.
   c. Use the same typeface(s) used in your letterhead. You decide on size and proportion.
   d. Kern and track if necessary.
   e. If you used color in your letterhead, use it here also.
   f. Create an AutoText entry that will work easily in the Envelope and Labels feature. If you are having difficulty incorporating the AutoText entry into the label/business card, you may have to add a blank sheet of label forms to a clear document screen, create the business card in the first label form, and then copy it to the rest of the labels.
2. Save and name the business cards as c03sa03, restaurant buscard.
3. Print and then close c03sa03, restaurant buscard.

creative activity

Find an example of a letterhead from a business, school, volunteer organization, etc. Redesign the letterhead using the desktop publishing concepts learned so far. On a separate sheet, key the changes you made and explain why you made those changes. Evaluate your letterhead using the Document Analysis Guide, (*document analysis guide.doc*) located on your student data disk. Name the revised letterhead c03ca01. Submit a thumbnail sketch, the original letterhead (or a copy), the revised letterhead, and the Document Analysis Guide.

4 Creating Personal Documents

PERFORMANCE OBJECTIVE

Upon successful completion of chapter 4, you will be able to create résumés, calendars, personal address labels, and certificates.

Desktop Publishing Concepts

Templates	Kerning	Balance
Rules	Consistency	Gradient
Character spacing	Contrast	Color
Em and en dashes	Planning	Bullets

Word Features Used

Résumé template	Watermark	Form fields
Résumé Wizard	Tables	Text fields
Text boxes	Format Painter	Image Control
Pictures	Send Behind Text	More Contrast
Labels	Fill effects	Less Contrast
Calendar Wizard	Drawing toolbar	More Brightness
Cut and paste	Page border	Less Brightness
AutoShapes	Group	

In this chapter, you will produce personal documents using Word's templates and wizards, and create and format your own personal documents. You will use other Word features such as tables, text boxes, labels, and more to produce résumés, calendars, address labels, and certificates. In addition, you will apply basic desktop publishing concepts of planning document content, maintaining consistency, and achieving balance through the use of pictures, borders, and column placement.

Creating a Résumé

A résumé is a summary of your qualifications, skills, and experiences. The main purpose of a résumé is to convince a prospective employer to grant you an interview and, ultimately, employment. Before creating your résumé, consider researching the prospective company and tailoring your résumé to what the company is seeking. Different types of business people respond differently to the same résumé. The kind of résumé that might catch an advertising executive's eye might not appeal to the personnel director of a bank.

Planning a Résumé

As you learned in chapter 1, plan your document (résumé) with a goal in mind. Take time to identify your objectives, employment experiences, qualifications, and skills. Then decide how to design your résumé to highlight the qualifications you want to emphasize. With this information in mind, categorize your qualifications by creating appropriate section headings for your résumé. Arrange the headings in the order important to you and to the job you are seeking. The order of these headings is important, because it will benefit you to showcase your best qualifications. You should refer to an up-to-date reference manual for additional information on résumés and sample résumés.

Composing your résumé in clear, concise language is important. Many sources suggest that you limit your résumé to one page. However, you might need more than a page depending on the extent of your work experience and the job you are seeking.

The information you provide about your business experience is usually presented in reverse chronological order (most current first and then working backward). This approach is useful in demonstrating your employment growth.

Most résumés are prepared in a traditional format with the section headings keyed at the left margin and pertinent information keyed to the right of the headings. This is easily accomplished with the use of side-by-side columns created in tables or a wide left margin with the headings back-tabbed into the left margin.

Word provides three résumé templates and one résumé wizard, each serving as partially completed forms or frameworks for your résumé. You will be creating résumés in the upcoming exercises using these templates, the template wizard, rotated text, and tables.

Designing a Résumé

If you are not using one of Word's templates, keep in mind that, typically, résumés are conservative in design. The design of your résumé depends on the type of employment you are considering and the image you want to portray. Think about focus, balance, and consistency in designing your résumé, as you would consider these concepts in preparing all documents. You are the focus of this résumé! So the heading with your name, address, and telephone number should be emphasized in a larger font with bold, small caps, or italics used to add visual interest.

DTP POINTERS
Limit the use of all caps in résumés.

Many résumés use the italics version of a serif typeface in a larger type size for headings. Using the italics version can soften the effect between the headings and the body text. Avoid using all caps in the section headings—you may want to use small caps in place of all caps. Also, do not use underlining to emphasize—underlining is a dated practice.

DTP POINTERS
Do not use underlining.

Your choice of typefaces and type sizes will lend consistency to your document. All of the section headings should use the same typeface and type size. Remember to turn on kerning if the point size exceeds 14 points. A general rule is to limit your use of typefaces to two to three per document. In a résumé, two typefaces are sufficient. Consider using these typefaces for body text: Times New Roman, Garamond, Century Schoolbook, or Book Antiqua. For headings, you can choose any of these suggestions: Arial, Century Gothic, Impact, or Britannic Bold. Times New Roman or other serif typefaces can also be used in résumé headings.

DTP POINTERS
Use kerning when type size exceeds 14 points.

DTP POINTERS
Use no more than two or three typefaces.

You can vary the design of your résumé by using rules (borderlines) between the different sections. White space, section titles, and rules can be added to a résumé to assist in organizing information, to aid in directional flow, and to create balance. The placement of headings on the left side of a résumé with sufficient amount of white space balances a heavier right side that includes more text. Also, use bullets to create attractive lists. Bullets are good tools for organizing facts and they give the reader rest from text-intensive copy.

The main purpose of a résumé is to convince a prospective employer to hire you. This is serious business and your résumé should be conservative, neat, organized, concise, and truthful. If you are interested in varying the design so your résumé stands out from the crowd, carefully incorporate some creativity. One approach that adds a unique touch is to rotate the heading of your résumé.

Choosing and Placing Section Headings

Begin your résumé by deciding which section headings are appropriate and in which order they should appear. Most résumés include these essential parts:

- Heading—Name, Address, Telephone Number, Fax Number, E-mail Address
- Career Objective
- Work Experience
- Education
- Special Skills or Achievements
- Interests
- References

Carefully plan your career objective and position this statement at the beginning of your résumé. Typically, the career objective is composed of one or two statements about the kind of job you want and what you can contribute to the company interviewing you. The career objective gives the résumé a sense of direction. Do not make your goal statement so vague that it is meaningless.

Your work experience history usually follows the career objective. In the work experience section, list your responsibilities, contributions, and special achievements. Many companies give the most weight to relevant job experiences. This is a crucial section of your résumé. This is where you want to sell yourself by emphasizing your strengths in dealing with people, problem-solving skills, goal-setting abilities, and more. With your current position, use present tense verbs; with your past employment, use the past tense of verbs. Include action words, such as *achieved, advised, appraised, compiled, conducted, designed, directed, established, executed, implemented, organized, promoted, supervised, etc.*

Educational history is usually listed next on the résumé, although the exact location may vary depending on the length of your professional experience and the strength of your educational achievements. If you recently completed school and have very little work experience, your education is probably your best achievement and should be listed before job experience. As you gain work experience, your education may be less important to a prospective employer.

The next essential heading may be special skills, achievements, or interests. This area could include your membership in any professional organizations, community, or volunteer organizations.

A current trend in writing résumés is to eliminate the last category—references. If you decide to include references, you must ask permission to use someone's name as a reference before making that information available. Another choice is to simply state, "References will be furnished upon request."

When printing a professional-looking résumé, use conservative colors for the paper such as light gray, white, or cream. A good quality bond paper is also recommended. Print your résumé using a laser printer or high-resolution quality ink jet printer. Avoid using a dot matrix printer.

Preparing Faxed or Scanned Résumés

The use of faxes, E-mail, scanners, and the Internet has made an impact on the way individuals find jobs and the way employers screen applicants. To ensure that your résumé scans or faxes well, you should avoid some of the graphical techniques you may have used in your conventional résumé. For instance, use typefaces that give you distinct and separate lettering such as Arial or Century Gothic. Avoid using italics, underlining, shading, boxes, or fancy typefaces. With faxing and scanning, simplicity works best.

The Résumé Wizard includes prompts to help you send your résumé and cover letter to someone by E-mail or fax. To send items by E-mail or fax, your computer must support these services.

Choosing a Résumé Template

Word's predefined résumé templates contain text, formatting, borderlines, bullets, and styles. The résumé templates vary slightly in design and layout. The differences are primarily in typefaces, type sizes, appearance attributes (bold and italics), and rules.

DTP POINTERS
Consistency is important in designing documents that are meant to be used together.

Word includes three résumé templates from the same template family discussed earlier—Contemporary, Elegant, and Professional. If you use the Professional Résumé template, use the Professional Letter template to create a cover letter. Consistency is important in designing documents that are used together. Take the time to view each version illustrated in figure 4.1 and note the subtle variations in each.

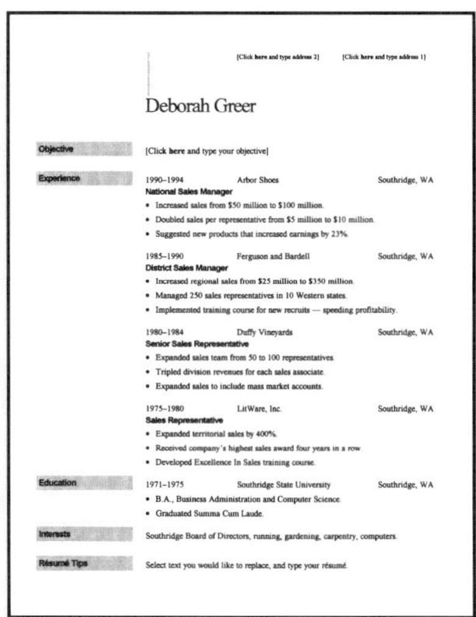

[Click here and type address 2] [Click here and type address 1]

Deborah Greer

Objective [Click here and type your objective]

Experience 1990–1994 Arbor Shoes Southridge, WA
National Sales Manager
• Increased sales from $50 million to $100 million.
• Doubled sales per representative from $5 million to $10 million.
• Suggested new products that increased earnings by 23%.

1985–1990 Ferguson and Bardell Southridge, WA
District Sales Manager
• Increased regional sales from $25 million to $350 million.
• Managed 250 sales representatives in 10 Western states.
• Implemented training course for new recruits — speeding profitability.

1980–1984 Duffy Vineyards Southridge, WA
Senior Sales Representative
• Expanded sales team from 50 to 100 representatives.
• Tripled division revenues for each sales associate.
• Expanded sales to include mass market accounts.

1975–1980 LitWare, Inc. Southridge, WA
Sales Representative
• Expanded territorial sales by 400%.
• Received company's highest sales award four years in a row.
• Developed Excellence In Sales training course.

Education 1971–1975 Southridge State University Southridge, WA
• B.A., Business Administration and Computer Science.
• Graduated Summa Cum Laude.

Interests Southridge Board of Directors, running, gardening, carpentry, computers.

Résumé Tips Select text you would like to replace, and type your résumé.

CONTEMPORARY

RICH ANDREWS

OBJECTIVE
[Click here and type objective]

EXPERIENCE
1990–1994 Arbor Shoe Southridge, SC
National Sales Manager
• Increased sales from $50 million to $100 million.
• Doubled sales per representative from $5 million to $10 million.
• Suggested new products that increased earnings by 23%.

1985–1990 Ferguson and Bardell Southridge, SC
District Sales Manager
• Increased regional sales from $25 million to $350 million.
• Managed 250 sales representatives in 10 Western states.
• Implemented training course for new recruits — speeding profitability.

1980–1984 Duffy Vineyards Southridge, SC
Senior Sales Representative
• Expanded sales team from 50 to 100 representatives.
• Tripled division revenues for each sales associate.
• Expanded sales to include mass market accounts.

EDUCATION
1971–1975 Southridge State University Southridge, SC
• B.A., Business Administration and Computer Science.
• Graduated Summa Cum Laude.

INTERESTS
Southridge Board of Directors, running, gardening, carpentry, computers.

RÉSUMÉ TIPS
Select text you would like to replace, and type your résumé.

12345 MAIN STREET • ANY CITY, STATE 12345-6789 • PHONE (123) 456-7890
123 ANY STREET • ANY CITY, STATE 12345 • PHONE (123) 456-7890

ELEGANT

figure 4.1

Résumé Template Types

[Click here and type address 1] [Click here and type address 2]

Max Benson

Objective [Click here and type objective]

Experience 1990–1994 Arbor Shoe Southridge, SC
National Sales Manager
• Increased sales from $50 million to $100 million.
• Doubled sales per representative from $5 million to $10 million.
• Suggested new products that increased earnings by 23%.

1985–1990 Ferguson and Bardell Southridge, SC
District Sales Manager
• Increased regional sales from $25 million to $350 million.
• Managed 250 sales representatives in 10 Western states.
• Implemented training course for new recruits — speeding profitability.

1980–1984 Duffy Vineyards Southridge, SC
Senior Sales Representative
• Expanded sales team from 50 to 100 representatives.
• Tripled division revenues for each sales associate.
• Expanded sales to include mass market accounts.

1975–1980 LitWare, Inc. Southridge, SC
Sales Representative
• Expanded territorial sales by 400%.
• Received company's highest sales award four years in a row.
• Developed Excellence In Sales training course.

Education 1971–1975 Southridge State University Southridge, SC
• B.A., Business Administration and Computer Science.
• Graduated Summa Cum Laude.

Interests SR Board of Directors, running, gardening, carpentry, computers.

Résumé Tips Select the text you would like to replace, and type your résumé.

PROFESSIONAL

The Contemporary design is straightforward and uses clean lines. The section titles are set in Arial typeface; the text is set in Times New Roman. The gray vertical line located at the top of the résumé points to the name on the résumé and promotes a downward directional flow. The shaded boxes used in the section titles maintain consistency through percent of shading and text formatting. Styles are very important in each of the templates since they reduce time and effort in formatting the résumés. These styles are used consistently in all the résumé templates—Objective, Section Title, Company Name, Job Title, Institution, and Achievement styles. In addition, an asymmetrical design is consistent among the résumé templates.

The Elegant template design is a compromise between the Contemporary and Professional templates. Garamond was selected for the document typeface. Rules help to organize the text and aid directional flow. Again, styles play an important role in formatting the entire template. Using expanded character spacing emphasizes the name. The expanded information at the bottom of the résumé balances the name at the top of the page.

The design and layout of all of the elements in the Professional Résumé template are basic and predictable. Two sans serif typefaces, Arial Black and Arial, are used throughout the entire résumé. The "no frills" approach to the formatting of this résumé is shown through the lack of shaded boxes or lines around the section titles, the simple and plain formatting of the name, and the use of square bullets that complement the blocked look of the Arial typeface.

Accessing a Résumé Template or Wizard

To access a résumé template, click File, then New. At the New dialog box, select the Other Documents tab. Select one of three résumé templates or the Résumé Wizard that displays. Double-click the résumé icon that corresponds with the style you want to use or click the icon once and press Enter or click OK. Key your résumé information and then save it when completed. You can save the résumé as a document or as a template.

Using the Résumé Wizard

The Résumé Wizard helps you organize your skills, education, and experience to highlight your best qualities for the position you are seeking. The wizard offers built-in headings that you can place in any order, along with an option to add your own. The wizard also helps you create a cover letter.

To start the Résumé Wizard, click New at the File menu, then select the Other Documents tab and double-click the Résumé Wizard icon. When you click Finish at the last wizard screen, your new résumé displays and the Office Assistant appears as shown in figure 4.2.

The Office Assistant provides additional formatting options, such as to change the style of your résumé, to shrink the résumé to fit on a page, to add a cover letter, or to send your résumé to someone through fax or E-mail (if your computer supports these systems). However, before choosing one of these options, complete your résumé by replacing the placeholder text with your personal information. To access the assistant at any time while using the Résumé Wizard, click the Office Assistant button located at the bottom of the wizard screen.

Office Assistant

Résumé Wizard with Office Assistant Displayed

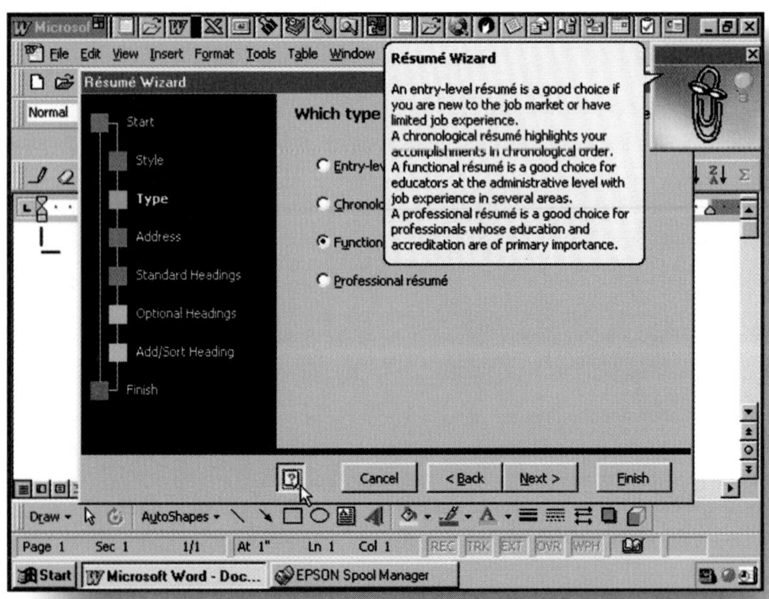

Customizing Résumés

As discussed earlier in chapter 2, Word's templates include placeholder (sample) text that shows what the finished document will look like. Select the placeholder text and replace it with your personal information. Avoid deleting the paragraph symbol at the end of the sample text; formatting codes in the styles are embedded in the paragraph symbols. Placeholder text also offers helpful tips on using the template.

Word templates also contain "click **here** and type" features that make creating a résumé easier. For instance, to include an objective in a résumé based on a template, position the arrow pointer on "**here**", click once, then key your objective statement.

As previously mentioned, Word résumé templates include many styles. Styles are useful because they apply a whole group of formats in one step. If you decide to edit a style, all the changes you make will automatically apply to all occurrences of that style in your document. With the Style command from the Format menu or the Style box on the Formatting toolbar, you can apply the styles that come with Word, alter the styles, or create your own styles. In the next exercise, you will apply preexisting styles to text. More information on creating styles will be presented in a later chapter.

Applying Desktop Publishing Guidelines to a Résumé

When creating a résumé, remember to use typographical symbols for en and em dashes. An *en dash* is used in place of a hyphen indicating a duration or range, such as 1991–1993. Use an *em dash* to indicate a change of thought or where a period is too strong and a comma is too weak.

When using bullets to list items in a résumé, be consistent with ending punctuation. If the bulleted items consist of phrases, do not key a period at the end of the phrase. However, if the bulleted items are stated as complete sentences, key a period at the end of each sentence. Consistency is important, so try not to mix phrases and complete sentences together as bulleted items. Reword the items if necessary to maintain consistency.

DTP POINTERS
Use an en dash to indicate a duration or range.

DTP POINTERS
Use an em dash to indicate a change of thought.

DTP POINTERS
Use consistent ending punctuation in lists in a résumé.

exercise 1

Creating a Résumé Using the Résumé Wizard

1. Create the résumé shown in figure 4.3 by completing the following steps:
   - **a.** Click File, then New.
   - **b.** At the New dialog box, select the Other Documents tab.
   - **c.** Make sure Document is selected in the Create New section, then double-click the Résumé Wizard icon.
   - **d.** At the Start screen, click Next.
   - **e.** At the Style screen, select Professional, then click Next>.
   - **f.** At the Type screen, select Professional résumé, then click Next>. (Click the Office Assistant button at the bottom of each of the wizard screens any time you need help or advice.)
   - **g.** At the Address screen, key the following text, then click Next>:

Name: Your Name
Address: **531 Pineland Avenue**
Manchester, MO 63011
Phone: **(314) 555-5946**
Fax: **(314) 555-9050**
E-mail: yname@msn.com

h. At the Standard Headings screen, click inside the following check boxes to include these headings, then click Next>:

Education
Professional experience

i. At the Optional Headings screen, click inside the following check boxes to include these headings, then click Next>:

Objective
Interests and activities
Volunteer experience
Awards received

j. At the Add/Sort Heading screen, click the Move Up or Move Down buttons to display the headings in the following order, then click Next>:

Objective
Professional experience
Education
Awards received
Interests and activities
Volunteer experience

k. At the Finish screen, click Finish.
l. Ignore the Office Assistant until the optional step at the end of exercise 1. (Click the Office Assistant's title bar and drag the box to another location if it interferes with completing the résumé.)
m. Click the Show/Hide ¶ button on the Standard toolbar to display spaces, tabs, and paragraph symbols in the document. This will be helpful in deleting and replacing text.
n. Select *Your Name* and key your own name.
o. Click *Type Objective Here* and key the following:

To work in an Accounting/Business position that offers opportunities for advancement.

p. Select *19xx–19xx*, then key **1994–Present**. (Insert an en dash by clicking Insert, Symbol, Special Characters tab, En dash, Insert, and then Close.) Click each placeholder in the Professional experience section and key the following text:

Patterson Company
Manchester, MO
Accountant
Responsible for accounts receivable.
Responsible for all basic accounting functions: coding and distribution of invoices, classifying transactions, and processing orders.
Responsible for preparation of tax forms.

q. Press Enter, then press Backspace (to delete the bullet).
r. Key the following text along with Ctrl + Tab where indicated: (This template was created in a table format—Ctrl + Tab inserts a tab into a cell.)
   (1) Key **1993**, press Ctrl + Tab, key **Case Foods, Inc.**, press Ctrl +Tab, key **Springfield, MO**, then press Enter.
   (2) Key **Accounting Clerk—Cooperative Education** (insert an em dash), then press Enter.
   (3) Key **Entered data entry into computer system.** Press Enter.
   (4) Key **Prepared product orders for regional representatives.** Press Enter.
s. Select the line beginning with *1993* and ending with *Springfield, MO*. With the line selected, click the down arrow to the right of the Style button (first button from the left) on the Formatting toolbar and select the *Company Name* style from the drop-down list. (The line formatting should resemble the formatting in the first line of the Professional experience section.)
t. Select the line beginning with *Accounting Clerk...*, and apply the *Job Title* style.
u. Select the lines beginning with *Entered...* and *Prepared ...* and apply the *Achievement* style. If a prompt displays, select *Reapply the formatting of the style to the selections?* Click OK or press Enter.
v. Key the remaining text in figure 4.3. Insert Ctrl + Tab and apply styles when needed.

2. Save the document with the name c04ex01, résumé.
3. Print and then close c04ex01, résumé.

Optional: Click the *Send to someone* option at the Office Assistant dialog box that displays when you finish the Résumé Wizard. If your classroom is connected to fax or E-mail, send your résumé to one of your classmates as an attachment to an E-mail message or as a fax by following the options through the Office Assistant. Ask your classmate to fax or E-mail an acceptance of the résumé along with a message offering an interview.

531 Pineland Avenue
Manchester, MO 63011

Phone (314) 555-5946
Fax (314) 555-9050
E-mail yname@msn.com

Your Name

Objective

To work in an Accounting/Business position that offers opportunities for advancement.

Professional experience

1994–Present Patterson Company Manchester, MO
Accountant

- Responsible for accounts receivable.
- Responsible for all basic accounting functions: coding and distribution of invoices, classifying transactions, and processing orders.
- Responsible for preparation of tax forms.

1993 Case Foods, Inc. Springfield, MO
Accounting Clerk—Cooperative Education

- Entered data into computer system.
- Prepared product orders for regional representatives.

1992 Morris Insurance Company St. Louis, MO
Accounting Clerk—College Summer Internship

- Processed billing and receiving payments from multistate area.
- Revised and updated accounts.
- Assisted in telephone survey.

Education

1991–1993 Hadley University Springfield, MO
Bachelor of Science Degree

- Major in Accounting
- Minor in Computer Science

1989–1991 Westlake Community College Manchester, MO
Associate Degree

- Major in Accounting.
- Minor in Computer Information Systems.

Awards received

Phi Kappa Phi Honor Society and National Honor Society

Interests and activities

Hadley University Student Government Representative and Junior Varsity and Varsity Tennis Team.

Volunteer experience

Habitat for Humanity, Tax Returns for Seniors program, and Manchester Youth Camp Counselor.

Designing Your Own Résumé

As mentioned earlier in this chapter, most résumés are conservative in layout and design. In exercise 2, you will be creating a résumé that will probably stand out from the crowd. The heading text is rotated and formatted to attract a prospective employer's eye.

Formatting Text Boxes

There are two ways that you can affect the appearance of text within a text box: by changing the internal margins (the distance between the text and the edges of the text box), and by rotating the text as shown in the heading of the résumé in figure 4.5. As mentioned in chapter 3, you can change the internal margins of a text box by accessing the Format Text Box dialog box, and then clicking the Text Box tab.

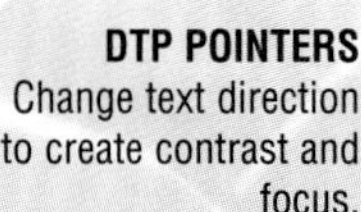

DTP POINTERS
Change text direction to create contrast and focus.

Text within a text box can be rotated clockwise or counter-clockwise by 90-degree increments, as shown in figure 4.4. To rotate text inside a text box, select the text box. Display the Text Box toolbar and then click the Change Text Direction button on the toolbar, or complete the following steps:

Change Text Direction

1. Select the text box.
2. Click Format, Text Direction to display the Text Direction dialog box.
3. In the Orientation section, click the desired orientation.
4. Click OK or press Enter.

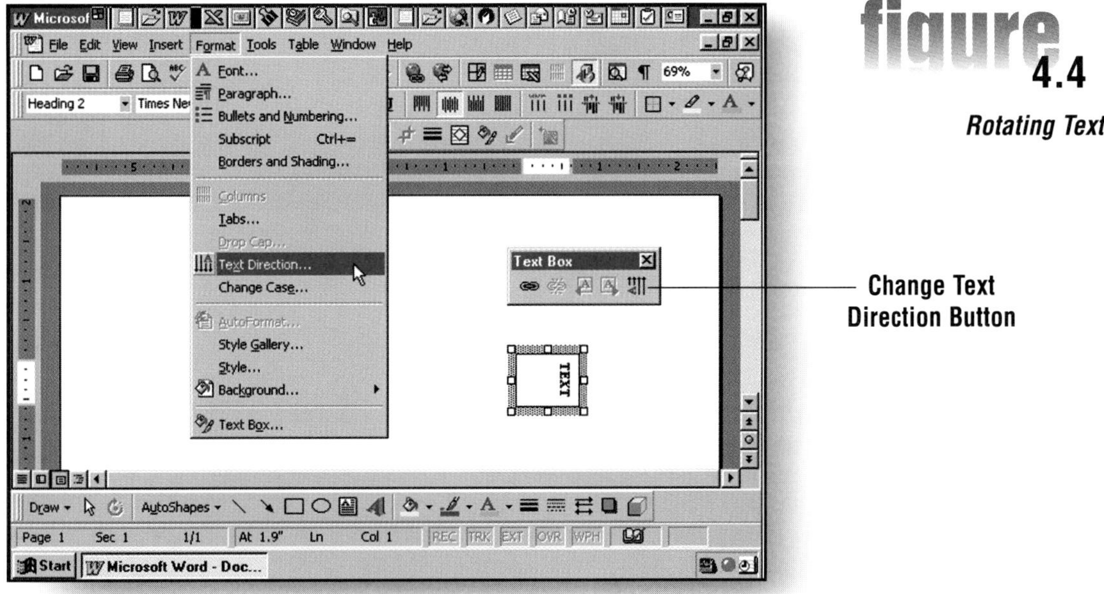

figure 4.4

Rotating Text

Applying Fill Effects to Text Boxes

As mentioned in detail in chapter 3, you can apply special fill effects to a selected text box by clicking the down arrow next to the Fill Color button on the Drawing toolbar and then clicking Fill Effects. The Fill Effects dialog box includes several special patterns and textures. You can create *gradient* fills, with one or two colors, use special textures such as wood and granite, and fill objects with pictures.

Gradient
A gradual varying of color.

Using Format Painter in a Résumé

You will be using a Word feature called Format Painter to copy or "paint" formatting codes from one section heading to the rest of the section headings in a résumé. To use the Format Painter, you would complete the following steps:

1. Position the insertion point on the text that has the formatting you want to copy.
2. Click the Format Painter button on the Standard toolbar (tenth button from the left—it looks like a paintbrush). Double-click if you want to format more than one occurrence.
3. Select the text to which you want the format applied using the mouse. (The I-beam pointer displays with a paintbrush attached.) When you release the mouse button, the text will take on the new formatting.
4. Click the Format Painter button again to turn the feature off, if you double-clicked the Format Painter button to format more than one occurrence.

Format Painter

The keyboard can also be used to apply formatting to text. To do this, select the text containing the formatting to be applied to other text, then press Ctrl + Shift + C. Select the text to which you want to apply the formatting, then press Ctrl + Shift + V.

To remove all character formatting, select the text that has the formatting you want to remove, then press Ctrl + space bar.

exercise 2

Creating a Résumé with Rotated Text

1. At a clear document screen, create a résumé with rotated text as shown in figure 4.5 by completing the following steps:
   a. Change the top and bottom margins to 0.75 inches. Change the left and right margins to 0.50 inches. (If the prompt *One or more of the margins are set outside the printable zone...* appears, click the Fix button and then click OK.)
   b. Create the rotated text by completing the following steps:
      (1) Click View, then Zoom and change the Zoom to Whole page.
      (2) Display the Drawing toolbar.
      (3) Click the Text Box button on the Drawing toolbar and draw a text box approximately 9.25 inches in Height and 1.5 inches in Width at the left margin. (Verify these settings by clicking Format, then Text Box, selecting the Size tab, then keying the correct settings if needed.)
      (4) At the Format Text Box dialog box, select the Position tab.
      (5) At the Position on page section, key **0.1** inches in the Horizontal text box and select Margin in the From list box.
      (6) Key **0.1** inches in the Vertical text box and select Margin in the From list box.
      (7) Click the Lock anchor check box to turn this option on. (Make sure the Move object with text option is deselected.)
      (8) Select the Wrapping tab.
      (9) Make sure None is selected.
      (10) Click OK or press Enter.
      (11) Position the insertion point inside the text box.

(12) Click the Center align button on the Formatting toolbar.
(13) Change the Zoom to 50 percent.
(14) With the text box selected, click Format, then Text Direction.
(15) At the Text Direction – Text Box dialog box, select the first vertical box from the left in the Orientation section.
(16) Click OK or press Enter.
(17) With the text box still selected, click the down arrow to the right of the Line Color button on the Drawing toolbar, then select No Line.
(18) Key **Nancy Weber**, then press Enter.
(19) Key **204 Shanahan Court, Wheaton, IL 60153**, then press Enter.
(20) Key **(630) 555-8960**.
(21) Select *Nancy Weber* and change the font to 36-point Garamond Bold in Small caps with Shadow.
(22) Select *204 Shanahan Court...*and *(630) 555-8960* and change the font to 20-point Garamond Bold.

c. Add a gradient fill to the text box by completing the following steps:
   (1) Select the text box.
   (2) Click the down arrow to the right of the Fill Color button on the Drawing toolbar and select Fill Effects.
   (3) Select the Gradient tab.
   (4) Select One color in the Colors section.
   (5) At the Color 1: list box, select the light gray color in the fourth row and the last column.
   (6) Click the scroll box in the slider and drag it to Light.
   (7) Select Diagonal up in the Shading Styles section.
   (8) Select the first Variants box.
   (9) Click OK or press Enter.
d. Deselect the text box and position the insertion point in the upper left corner.
e. Click Format, then Paragraph.
f. Change the Left Indentation setting to 2 inches. Click OK or press Enter.
g. Key **Professional Objective**, then press Enter.
h. Key **Provide word processing software installation and support for small- to medium-sized businesses.**, then press Enter twice. (Use a regular hyphen.)
i. Select *Professional Objective* and change the font to 18-point Garamond Bold Italics (or a similar font) and turn on Small caps.
j. Position the insertion point at the beginning of the line *Provide word processing...*, then click Format, then Paragraph. Make the following changes:
   (1) At the Paragraph dialog box, select the Indents and Spacing tab.
   (2) Change the Left Indentation setting to 2.25 inches.
   (3) Change the Spacing Before to 6 pt.
   (4) At the Line Spacing box, select *At Least* and change the At setting to 11 points.
   (5) Click OK or press Enter.
   (6) Press Ctrl + End.
k. At the Insert File dialog box, select the drive where your student data files are located. Double-click the file *para01.doc*.
l. Key **Education**, then press Enter.
m. Insert *para02.doc* from your student data disk.
n. Key **Interests and Activities**, then press Enter.
o. Insert *para03.doc* from your student data disk.

p. Key **References**, then press Enter.
q. Insert *para04.doc* from your student data disk.

2. Use the Format Painter to format the section titles by completing the following steps:
   a. Position the insertion point anywhere on the already formatted section title *Professional Objective.*
   b. Double-click the Format Painter button on the Standard toolbar. (The I-beam pointer will display with a paintbrush attached.)
   c. Select each remaining section title one at a time using the mouse. (This applies the formatting.)
   d. Click once on the Format Painter button to turn off the feature.
3. Save the résumé and name it c04ex02, rotated.
4. Print and then close c04ex02, rotated.

NANCY WEBER
204 Shanahan Court, Wheaton, IL 60153
(708) 555-8960

PROFESSIONAL OBJECTIVE

Provide word processing software installation and support for small- to medium-sized businesses.

WORK EXPERIENCE

Bayman Computer Consultants, Downers Grove, IL
Computer Systems Consultant, August 1993–Present
- Provides word processing software installation, implementation, and technical support for various firms in Illinois, Indiana, and Michigan.

Computer Solutions, Naperville, IL
Office Manager, November 1990–June 1993
- Supervised and trained office staff in Microsoft Office Professional.
- Established and supervised production of office procedures manual.
- Created and implemented automated accounts payable system.

College of DuPage, Glen Ellyn, IL
Part-time instructor in Office Careers Department, September 1992–Present
- Taught Microsoft Word for Windows 6.0, Microsoft Word for Windows 95, and PowerPoint for Windows 95.

EDUCATION

North Central College, Naperville, IL
1993–Present
Courses include Mastering the Internet, Windows 95, and Desktop Publishing using Microsoft Word for Windows 95.

College of DuPage, Glen Ellyn, IL
1991-1992
Courses include Word 6.0 and Graphic Design.

Western Michigan University, Kalamazoo, MI
Master's Degree in Business Administration—August 1990
Bachelor's Degree in Business Education—December 1989
Pi Omega Pi Honorary
President's Honor Roll

INTERESTS AND ACTIVITIES

Chicago Area Business Education Association
National Secretaries Association

REFERENCES

References available upon request.

Creating a Résumé Using Side-by-Side Columns

In Word you can create two types of columns: newspaper columns (also called snaking columns) and side-by-side columns (also referred to as parallel columns). Newspaper columns are frequently used for text in newspapers, newsletters, and magazines, and are created by clicking Format, then Columns or by clicking the Columns button on the Standard toolbar.

Side-by-side columns group text horizontally across the page in rows and are commonly used in an agenda, résumé, itinerary, script, or address list. Side-by-side columns are created by inserting a table into a document using either the Insert Table button on the Standard toolbar (seventh button from the right) or the Table option from the menu bar.

Insert Table

To create a résumé using the table feature, you may want two columns and possibly six rows. The number of rows will depend on the number of section titles needed in your résumé. To learn how to create a résumé using a table, complete exercise 3.

Removing Hyperlink Formatting

E-mail addresses are frequently used in résumés as well as many other business documents. When you key the address in a document, Word automatically converts the E-mail address to a hyperlink. To prevent the E-mail address from displaying in a document as a hyperlink, which usually appears in blue and is underlined, press the space bar once after keying the address, then press the backspace key once to delete the hyperlink formatting. You can also delete the hyperlink formatting by using an arrow key to position the insertion point on the hyperlink, then clicking Insert, then Hyperlink, then Remove Link at the Insert Hyperlink dialog box. Alternatively, you can right-click on the hyperlinked address, point to Hyperlink, click Edit Hyperlink, then click Remove Link.

exercise 3

Creating a Résumé in a Table

1. At a clear document window, create the résumé shown in figure 4.6 using a table by completing the following steps:
   a. Change the top, bottom, left, and right margins to 0.75 inches.
   b. Turn on kerning at 14 points and above using Format, Font, then Character Spacing.
   c. Create and format a table by completing the following steps:
      (1) Position the arrow pointer on the Insert Table button on the Standard toolbar, hold down the left mouse button, drag down and to the right until two columns and eight rows are selected in the grid (and *8 x 2 Table* displays below the grid), then release the mouse button.
      (2) Change the width of the two columns by completing the following steps:
         (a) Click Table, then Cell Height and Width.
         (b) At the Cell Height and Width dialog box, select the Column tab.
         (c) Change the Width of column 1 to 2.25 inches.
         (d) Change the Space between columns to 0.25 inches.
         (e) Click the Next Column button, then change the Width of column 2 to 5 inches.
         (f) Click OK or press Enter.

d. Position the insertion point in the first cell, then insert the round bullet symbol as shown in figure 4.6 by completing the following steps:
   (1) Click Insert, then Symbol.
   (2) At the Symbol dialog box, select the Symbols tab.
   (3) In the Font text box, select *Wingdings* from the drop-down list.
   (4) Click the round bullet symbol located in the fifth row and the sixteenth column from the right.
   (5) Click Insert three times, then click Close.
   (6) Insert a blank space between each symbol.
   (7) Press Tab.

e. Click the Align Right button (ninth button from the right) on the Formatting toolbar, key **Diane Anderson**, and then press Tab twice.

f. Click the Align Right button on the Formatting toolbar, key **1414 Cleveland Avenue • St. Joseph • MI 49605** (use the same symbol as in step 1d), then press Tab twice. (*Hint:* Copy the bullet symbol using the copy and paste commands.)

g. Click the Align Right button, key **(616) 555-4476 • Fax (616) 555-7032 • E-mail anders@msn.com**, press the space bar once, (remove the hyperlinked formatting by backspacing once after keying the E-mail address), then press Enter three times.

h. Position the insertion point in the selection bar in front of the first row, then click to select the first row.

i. Change the font to 36-point Footlight MT Light Bold with Shadow, then click inside any cell to deselect the first row.

j. Select *Diane Anderson* and change the character spacing by completing the following steps:
   (1) Click Format, then Font.
   (2) At the Font dialog box, select the Character Spacing tab.
   (3) Click the down arrow to the right of the Spacing list box and select *Expanded* from the drop-down list.
   (4) Key **3** in the By text box.
   (5) Click OK or press Enter.

k. Select *1414 Cleveland...*, then change the font to 12-point Footlight MT Light.

l. While still selected, display the Font dialog box with the Character Spacing tab selected. Click the down arrow to the right of the Position list box, select *Lowered*, then key **16** in the By text box. Click OK or press Enter.

m. Select *(616) 555-4476...*, change the font to 12-point Footlight MT Light, then press Tab.

n. Key **Career Objective**, then press Tab.

o. Insert *para05.doc* located on your student data disk, then press Tab.

p. Key **Experience**, and then press Tab.

q. Insert *para06.doc* located on your student data disk, then press Tab.

r. Key **Education**, then press Tab.

s. Insert *para07.doc* located on your student data disk, then press Tab.

t. Key **Interests**, then press Tab.

u. Insert *para08.doc* located on your student data disk, then press Tab.

v. Key **References**, then press Tab.

w. Key **References available upon request.**, then press Tab twice.

x. Click the Align Right button on the Formatting toolbar, then insert three symbols like the ones created at the beginning of the résumé (the symbol should still be located on the clipboard). Insert a blank space between each symbol.

y. Select the three symbols in step 1x, then change the Font to 36-point Footlight MT Light Bold with Shadow.

z. Select the first section title, *Career Objective,* then change the font to 16-point Footlight MT Light Bold. Format the remaining section titles by completing the following steps:
   (1) Position the insertion point on any character in the title *Career Objective*.
   (2) Double-click the Format Painter button on the Standard toolbar.
   (3) Click and drag the Format Painter on each of the remaining section titles.
   (4) Click once on the Format Painter button to turn off this feature.

2. Save the résumé and name it c04ex03, table.
3. Print and then close c04ex03, table.

Optional: Create *c04ex02, rotated* in a table format. (Text inside a cell can be rotated—use the Tables and Borders toolbar.)

• • • **Diane Anderson**

1414 Cleveland Avenue • St. Joseph • MI 49605
(616) 555-4476 • Fax (616) 555-7032 • E-mail anders@msn.com

Career Objective

Seeking an executive assistant position utilizing my knowledge and experience in word processing, desktop publishing, and office management.

Experience

McMann Printing Company, St. Joseph, MI
1988–Present
Executive Secretary
Responsibilities and duties include:

- Manage correspondence and all travel arrangements and accommodations for executives.
- Compile and graph financial data for weekly management meetings.
- Prepare desktop slide presentations, forms, graphs, etc.
- Compose, format, and distribute monthly newsletter.
- Instruct various personnel in Microsoft Word 7.0 and desktop publishing.

Case, Newman, and Company, CPA, South Bend, IN
1978–1987
Office Supervisor
Responsibilities and duties included:

- Prepared monthly and quarterly financial reports.
- Performed word processing, filing, and general office duties; set appointments.
- Coordinated company meetings and social functions.
- Designed and created seminar pamphlets, flyers, invitations, evaluation forms, and transparencies.
- Created office and staff procedures manual.

Education

Indiana Vocational & Technical Institute, South Bend, IN
Associate Degree in Secretarial Science—August 1987
Lake Michigan Community College, Benton Harbor, MI
Word Processing Certificate—March 1993

Interests

Office Careers Advisory Committee, Lake Michigan College
National Secretaries Association, Lake Michigan Chapter
St. Joseph Chamber of Commerce, Secretary

References

References available upon request.

• • •

Creating a Personal Calendar

A calendar can be one of the most basic tools of organization in your household. No desk at home or at work is complete without a calendar to schedule appointments, plan activities, and serve as a reminder of important dates and events.

A calendar can also be used as a marketing tool in promoting a service, product, or program. For example, a schedule of upcoming events may be keyed on a calendar to serve as a reminder to all the volunteers working for a charitable organization, or the calendar could be sent to possible donors to serve as a daily reminder of the organization.

You will create and customize your own calendars using Word's Calendar Wizard. If you want to create your own calendar from scratch without the help of the Calendar Wizard, you may want to start by creating a table using Word's Table feature.

The Calendar Wizard is not available through a typical or custom installation. Calendar Wizard is included on the Microsoft Office 97 or Word 97 ValuPack CD-ROM or by down-loading the wizard from the Microsoft Web site as explained in chapter 1.

If you installed Microsoft Office 97 or the standalone Word 97 as an update to Microsoft Office for Windows 95 or Word for Windows 95, you may also find the Calendar Wizard in the Office 95 Templates tab of the New dialog box.

Using the Calendar Wizard

The Calendar Wizard helps you create monthly calendars. Three basic styles of calendars are available: Boxes and borders, Banner, and Jazzy. See figure 4.7 for an illustration of the different styles. In addition, other customizing options in the wizard include: Portrait or Landscape orientation, placeholder for a picture, and starting and ending months.

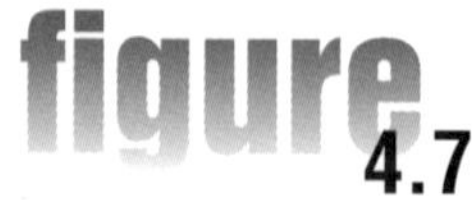

Calendar Wizard Template Types

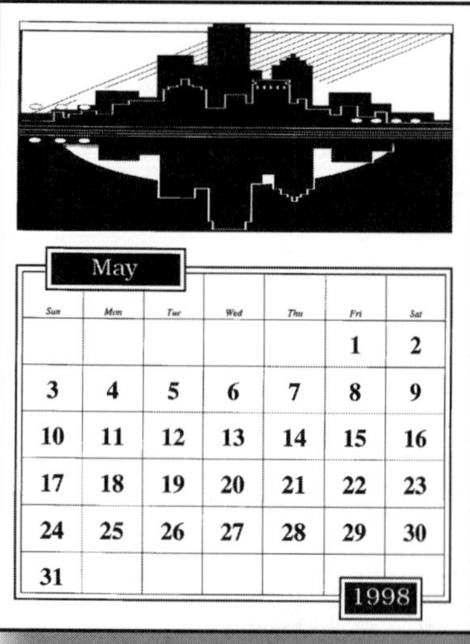

BOXES AND BORDERS

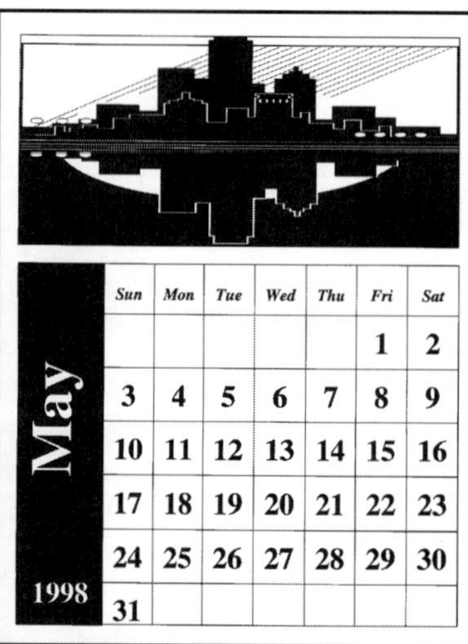

BANNER

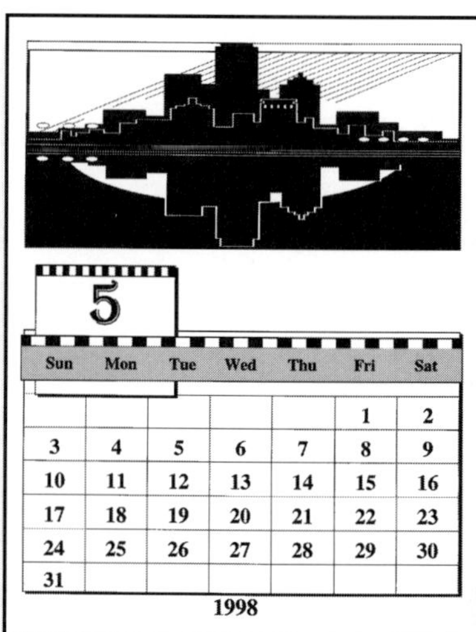

JAZZY

To access the Calendar Wizard, click File, then New. Select the Other Documents tab (or the General tab if you downloaded the Calendar Wizard from the Web), then double-click the Calendar Wizard icon. Proceed with making choices from the prompts built into the template. Continue clicking the Next> button to advance to the next screen. Click Finish when the calendar is complete.

Customizing a Calendar

To avoid having a calendar that looks like everyone else's, consider the following suggestions for personalizing your calendar: select an appropriate picture, add text near important dates, add a watermark, add an AutoShape form, scan a photograph, add a favorite quote, or print on color or preprinted papers.

Adding, Removing, or Replacing a Picture in a Calendar

If you choose to add a picture to your calendar in the Calendar Wizard, the default picture is a city landscape (*Cityscpe.wmf*). This picture is inserted into a placeholder, so you can easily replace it with a different image. After using the Calendar Wizard, select the existing picture, then press Delete. To replace the image, click Insert, then Picture, or Insert, then Object, depending on the source of your graphic.

Entering Information into a Calendar

To enter information, click where you want to insert the text, then start typing. To move between different dates in the calendar, press Tab to move forward and press Shift + Tab to move to the previous date. Remember that the calendar template is formatted in a table. Click the Center align button on the Formatting toolbar to center text within a cell. Select rows or columns and apply different styles if you are not satisfied with the default ones, or customize the styles to fit your specific needs.

Understanding how the template is formatted in Word can be helpful. Turning on the Show/Hide ¶ button on the Standard toolbar will provide helpful formatting information. The Show/Hide ¶ button is the second button from the right on the Standard toolbar and it displays symbols indicating where text was spaced, indented, tabbed, or placed in paragraphs.

If the bottom line of your document does not print, you may have to make adjustments to your document to compensate for the unprintable zone of your particular printer. For instance, if the bottom line of the calendar created in exercise 4 does not print properly, increase or decrease the top and/or bottom margins, or use a smaller font size, or rewrite some of the text. If the margins cannot be changed, experiment with moving the text up or reducing the length of the document. See the steps listed at the end of exercise 4 for suggestions and adjustments.

Adding a Shape to a Calendar

You can automatically create a variety of shapes by using the AutoShapes tools on the Drawing toolbar. The AutoShapes menu contains several categories of shapes. In addition to lines, there are basic shapes, block arrows, flowchart elements, stars and banners, and callouts. One of the star shapes (16-Point Star) was selected in exercise 4 to show emphasis and draw attention to an important fact, as shown in figure 4.8. In addition, yellow fill was added for impact. Text was added to the shape by selecting the star shape, right-clicking the mouse, and then clicking the Add Text option as shown in figure 4.9.

To draw an AutoShape, click AutoShapes on the Drawing toolbar, point to a category, and then click the shape you want. Click in the document to add the shape at its default size, or drag it to the size you want. Notice in figure 4.10 the yellow adjustment handle in the AutoShape form. Many AutoShapes have adjustment handles you can drag to adjust a unique aspect of the shape.

figure 4.8

Adding an AutoShape to a Calendar

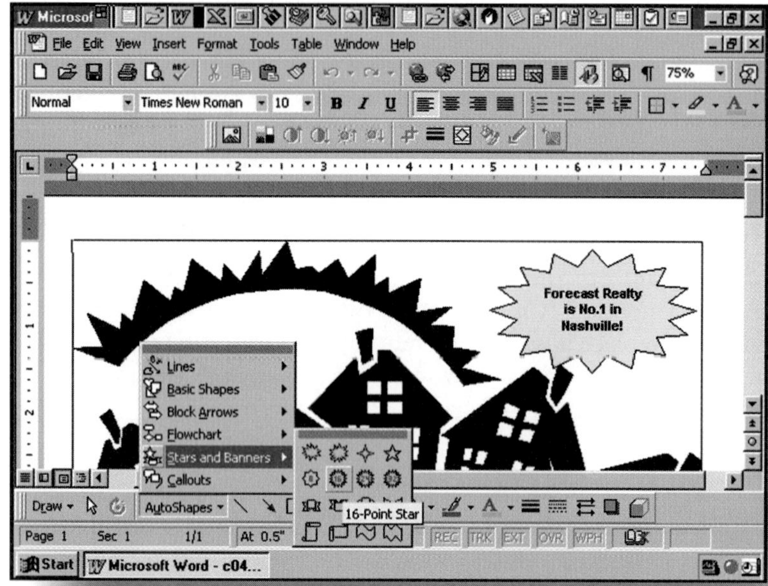

figure 4.9

Adding Text to an AutoShape Form

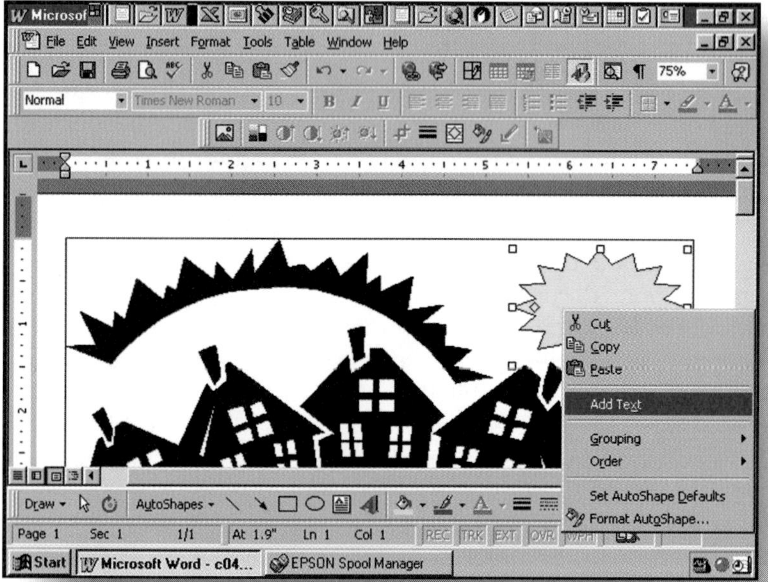

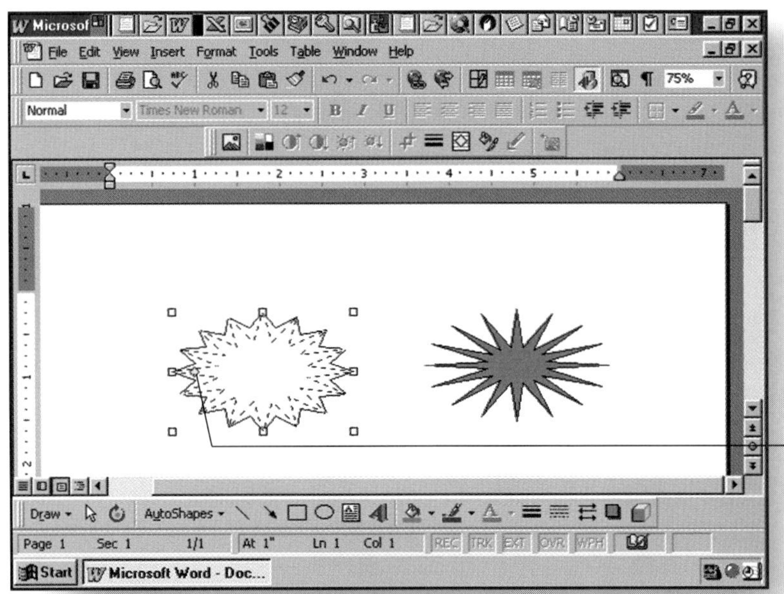

figure 4.10

Dragging an Adjustment Handle to Reshape an AutoShape Form

exercise 4

Customizing a Calendar

1. Create the calendar in figure 4.11 using the Calendar Wizard by completing the following steps:
   a. Click File, then New.
   b. At the New dialog box, select the Other Documents tab or the General tab, depending on the wizard's source.
   c. Double-click the Calendar Wizard icon.
   d. At the Start screen, click Next>.
   e. At the Style screen, select the Banner style, then click Next>.
   f. At the Direction & Picture screen, select Portrait, then select Yes to leave room for a picture. Click Next>.
   g. At the Date Range screen, select *February* and *1998* in the Start Month, End Month, and Year list boxes. Then, click Next>.
   h. At the Finish screen, click Finish.
   i. If the Office Assistant appears, click the *Add, remove, or replace picture* option. Read the Office Assistant's advice, then click OK.
   j. Click the *Enter information into the calendar* option. Read the Office Assistant's advice, then click OK.
   k. Click the Cancel button to remove the Office Assistant.
2. Replace the picture in the calendar by completing the following steps:
   a. Display the Drawing toolbar.
   b. At the document window, select and then delete the placeholder picture (*Cityscpe.wmf*). (You will know the picture has been selected when eight black sizing handles display inside the border of the picture. Be careful not to select the frame instead of the picture. The frame should remain once the picture has been deleted. If you accidentally remove the frame, you can undo the deletion by clicking the Undo button on the Standard toolbar.)

c. With the insertion point positioned inside the frame, click Insert, point to Picture, click From File, then double-click *Houses.wmf* located on your student data disk.

3. Insert text near calendar dates by completing the following steps:
   a. Select all of the rows in the calendar (table) except for the first row, which contains the days of the week. (Include the blank cells, too.)
   b. Click the down arrow to the right of the Style button on the Formatting toolbar, then select *Normal (10 pt)* from the list. (The calendar dates will display in 10 points allowing space in the cells to add text.)
   c. Click the Center align button on the Formatting toolbar.
   d. Deselect the rows by clicking anywhere in the calendar.
   e. Position the insertion point to the right of February 2, then press Enter.
   f. Click Insert, then Symbol.
   g. Select the Symbols tab and change the Font to Wingdings.
   h. Click the telephone symbol in the first row and the ninth column.
   i. Click Insert, then Close.
   j. Press Enter.
   k. Key **Call for a free appraisal.**
   l. Select the telephone symbol and change the font size to 14 points.
   m. Position the insertion point to the right of February 12, then press Enter twice.
   n. Key **Abraham Lincoln's Birthday**.
   o. Position the insertion point to the right of February 14, then press Enter.
   p. Insert the heart symbol located in the fifth row and the eighth column from the right in the Monotype Sorts Font list box.
   q. Press Enter.
   r. Click the down arrow to the right of the Font Color button on the Standard toolbar and select *Red*, then key **Valentine's Day**.
   s. Select the heart symbol and change the font color to red and the font size to 14 points.
   t. Key **President's Day** on February 19.
   u. Key **George Washington's Birthday** on February 22 (change the font size to 9 points).
   v. Key **Join our tour of homes at 10:00 a.m.** on February 27.
4. Key the text at the bottom of the calendar in figure 4.11 by completing the following steps:
   a. Select the last two rows of blank cells, click Table, then Merge Cells.
   b. Deselect the cell, then press Enter.
   c. Turn kerning on at 14 points.
   d. Key **Forecast Realty**, then press Enter.
   e. Key **Predicting a Successful Move for You...**, then press Enter.
   f. Key **450 South Ashton Avenue ❖ Nashville ❖ TN 37201-5401**, then press Enter. (The ❖ symbol is located in the fourth row and third column of the Monotype Sorts Font list box.)
   g. Key **(901) 555-1000 ❖ Fax (901) 555-6752 ❖ E-mail Forecst@msn.com**, then press Enter.
   h. Position the insertion point on the hyperlink, then clicking Insert, then Hyperlink, and then Remove Link at the Insert Hyperlink dialog box. (The E-mail address should remain, but the hyperlink (blue text and underline) should be removed.)
   i. Select *Forecast Realty* and change the font to 22-point Braggadocio in Green with the Emboss and Small caps effects and expand the Character Spacing by 5 points.

j. Select *Predicting...* and change the font to 16-point Brush Script MT.
k. Select the last two lines, *450 South Ashton...* and *(901) 555-1000...*, and change the font to 12-point Times New Roman.
l. Position the insertion point in front of the *4* in *450 South Ashton...*and change the paragraph spacing Before to 6 pt.
m. Select the text box containing the year *1998*.
n. Click Format, Borders and Shading, then select the Shading tab.
o. Select Green in the seventh row and third column of the Fill color palette.

5. Create the AutoShape form at the top of the calendar by completing the following steps:
    a. Click the AutoShapes button on the Drawing toolbar, point to Stars and Banners, and then click the second shape in the second row (16-Point Star).
    b. Drag the crosshairs to the upper right corner of the calendar and draw a shape in a size similar to the one in figure 4.11, then release the left mouse button.
    c. Select the shape, click the down arrow to the right of the Fill Color button on the Drawing toolbar and select Yellow.
    d. Select the shape, right-click the mouse, and then select Add Text.
    e. Click the Center align button on the Formatting toolbar.
    f. Change the font to 11-point Arial Bold, then key **Forecast Realty is No. 1 in Nashville!**. (You may need to change the font size and position to fit the text inside your shape or change the size of the shape.)
6. Save the document and name it c04ex04, realty.
7. Print and then close c04ex04, realty.

If the bottom line of the calendar does not print, you may need to adjust the length of the calendar so the bottom line will not be positioned within the unprintable zone defined by your printer. First try to fool your printer into thinking the document is going to be printed on a longer piece of paper by completing the following steps:

1. Click File, Page Setup, then select the Paper Size tab.
2. In the Paper size list box, select Legal, then click OK.

If this procedure does not work, experiment with the following adjustments to find one that works for you:

1. Change the bottom margin to 0.70 inches, then print. If the bottom border still does not print, go to step 2.
2. Click to select *1998* in the reversed text box located on the left side of the calendar.
3. With the sizing handles displayed, click the bottom-middle sizing handle. When the mouse pointer becomes a double-pointed arrow, drag the bottom border up slightly.
4. Click the Line button on the Drawing toolbar and, while holding down the Shift key, drag a straight line at the bottom of the calendar, then print.

figure 4.11

February 1998

Sun	Mon	Tue	Wed	Thu	Fri	Sat
1	2 ☎ Call for a free appraisal	3	4	5	6	7
8	9	10	11	12 Abraham Lincoln's Birthday	13	14 ❤ Valentine's Day
15	16	17	18	19 President's Day	20	21
22 George Washington's Birthday	23	24	25	26	27 Join our tour of homes at 10:00 a.m.	28

FORECAST REALTY

Predicting a Successful Move for You...

450 South Ashton Avenue ❖ Nashville ❖ TN 37201-5401
(901) 555-1000 ❖ Fax (901) 555-6752 ❖ E-mail Forecst@msn.com

Customizing a Calendar by Adding a Watermark

A calendar is a perfect document in which to use a watermark. The watermark adds visual interest to a calendar. It can also be used to promote a theme or identity for a person or an organization. Two important considerations when using a watermark in a calendar, or any other document, are that the shading of the picture or object can be lightened to improve the readability of the text, and that the picture or text you select should relate to the subject of the document.

DTP POINTERS
Reduce watermark shading to improve text readability.

exercise 5

Adding a Watermark to a Calendar

1. Create a calendar as shown in figure 4.12 by completing the following steps:
   a. Click File, then New.
   b. At the New dialog box, select the Other Documents tab or General tab, depending on the wizard's source.
   c. Double-click the Calendar Wizard icon.
   d. At the Start screen, click Next>.
   e. At the Style screen, select the Boxes and borders style, then click Next>.
   f. At the Direction & Picture screen, select Landscape, then select No to leave room for a picture. Click Next>.
   g. At the Date Range screen, select *June* and *1998* in the Start Month, End Month, and Year list boxes. Then, click Next>.
   h. At the Finish screen, click Finish.
   i. If the Office Assistant appears, click the *Add, remove, or replace picture* option. Read the Office Assistant's advice, then click OK.
   j. Click the *Enter information into the calendar* option. Read the Office Assistant's advice, then click OK.
   k. Click the Cancel button to remove the Office Assistant.
2. Create the text in the calendar by completing the following steps:
   a. Display the Drawing toolbar and the Picture toolbar.
   b. Position the insertion point in the text box containing *June*, then click Format, Borders and Shading.
   c. Select the Shading tab.
   d. Select Green in the seventh row and the third column of the Fill color palette, then click OK or press Enter. (The Patterns Style text box should display Clear.)
   e. Position the insertion point in the text box containing *1998* and change the fill color to Green following steps similar to 2a through 2d.
   f. Change the Zoom to Page width.
   g. Select the last row of cells in the calendar, then click Table, and Merge Cells.
   h. With the insertion point positioned inside the last row, make sure Center alignment has been selected for this area.
   i. Change the font to 36-point Times New Roman Bold with Shadow.
   j. Key **South Bend Park District**, then press Enter.
   k. Click the Center align button on the Formatting toolbar.
   l. Change the font to 22-point Times New Roman Bold in Green.
   m. Key **Summer '98 Tennis Schedule (Team A)**.

n. Position the insertion point inside the cell for June 8 and make sure Center alignment has been selected.
o. Change the font to 11-point Times New Roman Regular, then press Enter.
p. Change Zoom to a higher percentage if needed.
q. Key **Team Tryouts** (press Enter) **9 – 11 a.m.**. (Use an en dash between the times.)
r. Key the rest of the text in the cells as shown in figure 4.12. (Press tab to move forward to the next cell and Shift + Tab to move to a previous cell.)

3. Create the watermark in figure 4.12 by completing the following steps:
   a. Click View, then Zoom, and then change the zoom to Whole Page.
   b. Click View, then Header and Footer.
   c. At the Header and Footer screen, click Insert, point to Picture, click From File, and then double-click *tennis4.cgm* located on your student data disk. (If this file does not transfer properly, select a similar picture from the Popular folder, Clip Gallery [Sports & Leisure category], Microsoft Office 97 or Word 97 CD-ROM, or from Free Stuff at the Microsoft Web Site.)
   d. Select the picture, then drag a corner sizing handle outward to increase the size of the picture proportionately. (Drag a corner sizing handle inward to decrease the size.)
   e. With the picture still selected, drag it to the middle of the calendar as shown in figure 4.12.
   f. Click the Image Control button on the Picture toolbar.
   g. Click Watermark at the Image Control menu.
   h. Click the Less Brightness button twice (sixth button from the left) on the Picture toolbar. (The Less Brightness button removes light from all areas of the picture, making it darker.)
   i. Click the Close button.
4. Save the document and name it c04ex05, tennis.
5. Print and then close c04ex05, tennis. (If a prompt appears stating that one of the sections is in the unprintable zone, change the left and right margins to 0.6 inches and try to print again. Continue to change the margins to correct this problem.)

figure 4.12

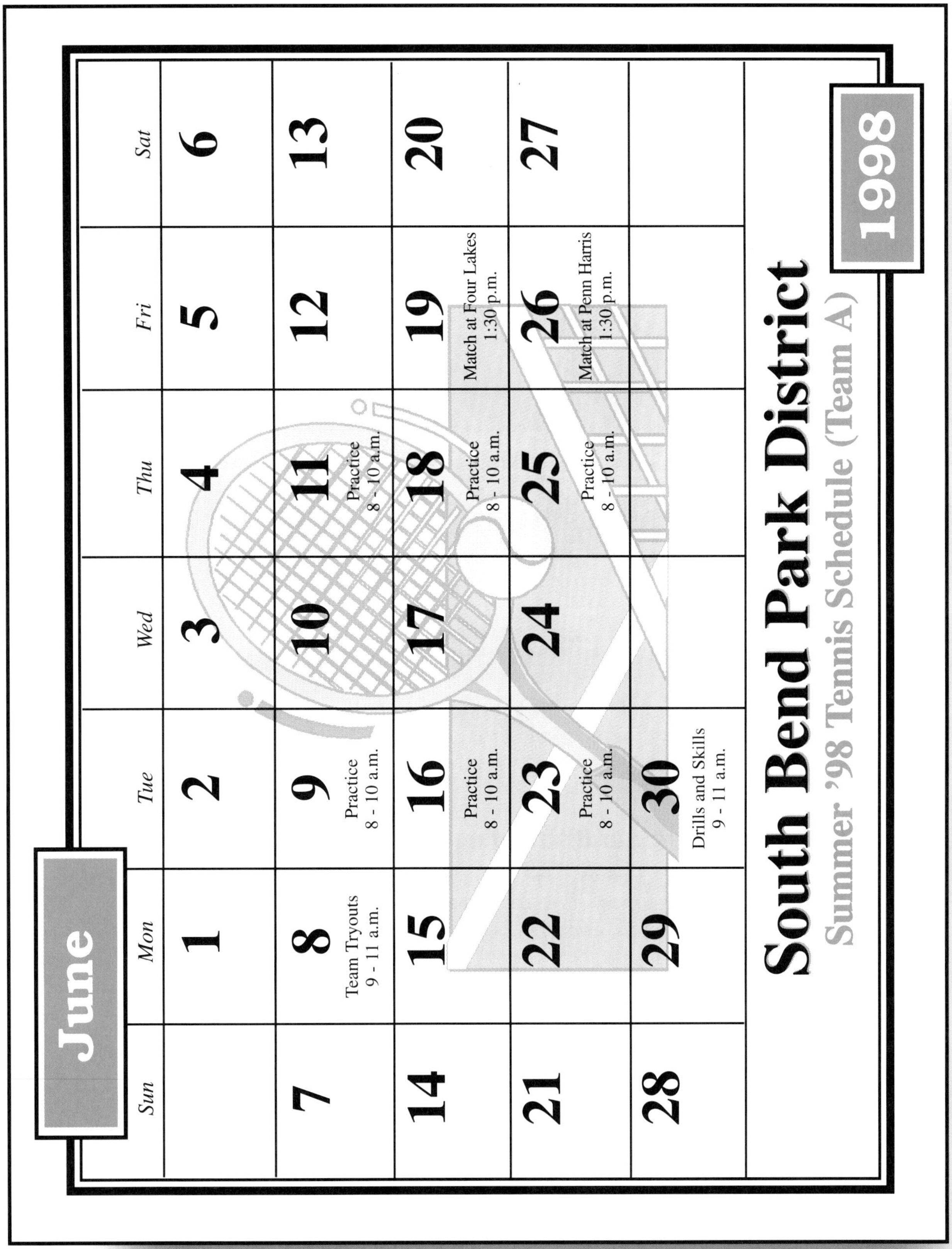

June **1998**

Sun	Mon	Tue	Wed	Thu	Fri	Sat
	1	**2**	**3**	**4**	**5**	**6**
7	**8** Team Tryouts 9 - 11 a.m.	**9** Practice 8 - 10 a.m.	**10**	**11** Practice 8 - 10 a.m.	**12**	**13**
14	**15**	**16** Practice 8 - 10 a.m.	**17**	**18** Practice 8 - 10 a.m.	**19** Match at Four Lakes 1:30 p.m.	**20**
21	**22**	**23** Practice 8 - 10 a.m.	**24**	**25** Practice 8 - 10 a.m.	**26** Match at Penn Harris 1:30 p.m.	**27**
28	**29**	**30** Drills and Skills 9 - 11 a.m.				

South Bend Park District

Summer '98 Tennis Schedule (Team A)

Arranging Drawing Objects to Enhance a Calendar

See figure 4.13 for additional suggestions for enhancing a calendar. A brief explanation of each feature follows figure 4.13. More information can be found by clicking Help, then Contents and Index, selecting the Index tab, keying **aligning**, then selecting *drawing objects*, and then clicking Display. More information is available in chapter 5.

figure 4.13

Arranging Drawing Objects in a Calendar (From Help)

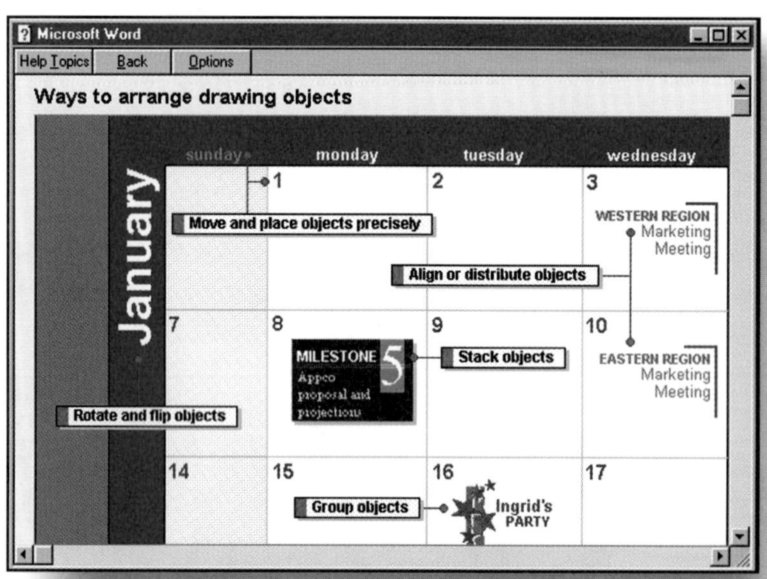

Moving and Placing Objects Precisely

To move a drawing object, click the object, then drag it when the mouse pointer becomes a four-headed arrow, or use the arrow keys on the keyboard. To use the keyboard to move an object, click the object, then hold down the Ctrl key as you press the arrow key on the keyboard that corresponds to the direction you want to move the object.

Aligning or Distributing Objects

Draw ▾

Draw

You can align two or more drawing objects relative to each other by their left, right, top, or bottom edges or by their centers (vertically) or middles (horizontally). To align objects, click the Draw button on the Drawing toolbar, point to Align or Distribute, then select one of the options listed, such as Align Left, Align Center, etc.

Stacking Objects

When you draw an object on top of another, you create an overlapping stack. Objects automatically stack in individual layers as you add them to a document. You see the stacking order when objects overlap—the top object covers a portion of objects beneath it.

You can overlap as many drawing objects as you want and then rearrange them in the stack by clicking the Draw button on the Drawing toolbar, pointing to Order, then selecting on one of the options listed, such as Bring to Front, Send to Back, etc. If you lose an object in a stack, you can press Tab to cycle forward or Shift + Tab to cycle backward through the objects until it is selected.

Grouping Objects

Grouping objects combines the objects as a single unit. To group drawing objects, hold the Shift key as you click each object, click the Draw button on the Drawing toolbar, and then click Group. Alternatively, you can click the right mouse button, point to Grouping, and then click Group. When objects have been grouped, sizing handles should appear around the new unit, as shown in figure 4.14, and not around each individual object.

Grouping
Combining objects as a single unit.

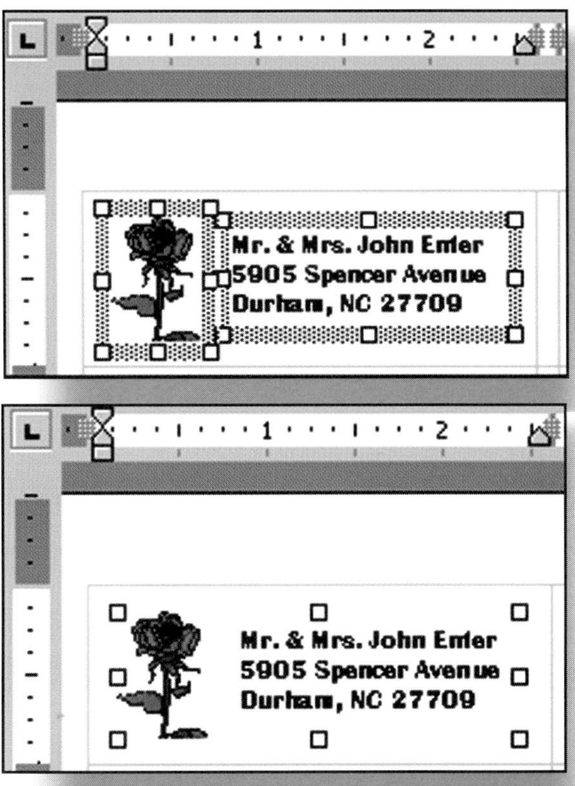

figure 4.14

Grouping Text Boxes

Rotating and Flipping Objects

To rotate or flip objects, select the object or grouped objects, then click the Draw button on the Drawing toolbar, point to Rotate or Flip, then click the option you want. You can also use the Free Rotate button on the Drawing toolbar.

Creating Personal Return Address Labels

Return address labels are convenient and cost efficient to use at home as well as at the office. Whether paying a huge stack of bills, addressing holiday cards, or volunteering to mail a hundred PTA newsletters, the convenience of having preprinted return labels is worth the little time it takes to create them. Instead of purchasing personalized return labels through a stationery store or printing company, you can create your own return labels using Word's label feature. Word includes a variety of predefined label definitions that coordinate with labels that can be purchased at office supply stores.

When purchasing labels, be careful to select the appropriate labels for your designated printer. Labels are available in sheets for laser and ink jet printers and tractor-feed forms for dot matrix printers. Carefully follow the directions given with your printer to insert the forms properly into the printer.

Return labels can be created using two different methods—creating labels individually and copying them using the label feature or creating labels using a data source and the merge feature. In exercise 6, you will be creating labels using a label definition and inserting a picture. Merge will be used in a later chapter.

Using the Label Feature

To create the personalized labels in figure 4.15, select a standard label definition in Word's Envelopes and Labels feature. At the Labels and Envelopes dialog box with the Labels tab selected, click the New Document button, which will take you to a document screen displaying gridlines of the labels you have selected. If the gridlines do not display, click Table, then Show Gridlines. (Remember that labels are actually cells in a table. You must use commands that are recognized in a table such as pressing Tab to advance forward to the next cell and Shift + Tab to move to a previous cell.)

The gridlines provide visual boundaries that will help you in creating and positioning text boxes as containers for a picture and the address text. The text boxes will be grouped and then copied to the remaining labels in the first row. After selecting the first row of personalized labels, you will use the copy and paste commands to create an entire sheet of labels. To learn how to create personalized labels, complete exercise 6.

exercise 6

Personal Return Address Labels with a Graphic

1. At a clear document window, create the return address labels in figure 4.15 by completing the following steps:
   a. Display the Drawing toolbar.
   b. Click Tools, then Envelopes and Labels.
   c. Select the Labels tab.
   d. Click the Options button.
   e. At the Label Options dialog box, select *5160 Address* in the Product number list box. (Make sure the Printer information is correct for your specific printer.)
   f. Click OK or press Enter.
   g. At the Envelopes and Labels dialog box, click the New Document button.
   h. If gridlines of the labels (cells) do not display, click Table, then Show Gridlines.
   i. Position the insertion point inside the first label (cell), click the Text Box button on the Drawing toolbar.
   j. Drag the crosshairs into the first label and create a text box approximately 0.75 inches in height and 0.5 inches in width. (Verify these settings by clicking Format, then Text Box. Select the Size tab and key **0.75** inches in the Height text box and **0.50** inches in the Width text box.)
   k. Select the Wrapping tab, make sure None displays in the Wrapping style section.
   l. Click OK or press Enter.
   m. With the insertion point positioned in the text box, click Insert, point to Picture, and then click From File.
   n. At the Insert Picture dialog box, make sure *Popular* displays in the Look in: list box,

then select *Flower.wmf* in the Name list box. (The entire path to the picture is *Program Files|Microsoft Office|Clipart|Popular|Flower.wmf*.)

o. Click Insert.

p. To remove the border around the text box, click the down arrow to the right of the Line Color button on the Drawing toolbar and select No Line.

q. Click the Text Box button on the Drawing toolbar.

r. Drag the crosshairs into the first label and to the right of the text box containing the picture.

s. Create the text box to measure approximately 0.65 inches in height and 1.5 inches in width. (Verify the settings at the Format Text Box dialog box.)

t. At the Format Text Box dialog box, select the Text Box tab and change the internal margins to **0** in each of the margin text boxes.

u. Select the Wrapping tab, then click None in the Wrapping style section.

v. Click OK or press Enter.

w. With the insertion point positioned inside the text box, change the font to 10-point Britannic Bold.

x. Key **Mr. & Mrs. John Enter** (press Enter) **5905 Spencer Avenue** (press Enter) **Durham, NC 27709**.

y. Remove the border around the text box.

2. Group the two text boxes by completing the following steps:
   a. Click the text box containing the picture, hold down the Shift key, and click the text box containing the address.
   b. Click the Draw button on the Drawing toolbar.
   c. Click Group. (Sizing handles should display around the new unit.)
   d. If the grouped text box displays above the cell, click Format, then Object, then select the Wrapping tab, and then click None in the Wrapping style section.
3. Copy the grouped text box to the second and third labels in the first row by completing the following steps:
   a. Click the grouped text box, hold down the Ctrl key, and drag a copy of the box to the second label.
   b. The arrow pointer should display with a + symbol to indicate a copy.
   c. Release the mouse and a copy should display in the second label.
   d. Drag and drop another copy of the grouped text box into the third label.
4. Copy the first row of labels by completing the following steps:
   a. Position the insertion point in the first cell (label) in the first row of labels, click Table, then Select Row.
   b. Click Edit, then Copy.
   c. Position the insertion point in the first label in the second row, click Edit, then Paste Rows.
   d. Press the F4 key (the Repeat key repeats the last command).
   e. Continue pressing the F4 key to copy the picture and address text to the remaining labels on the page.
   f. When you have one complete page of labels, select any blank labels that may display on another page, then click Table, then Delete Rows.
5. Use Print Preview to make sure your document will print correctly. If the bottom line does not display, select the Legal size paper definition at Page Setup.
6. Save the document and name it c04ex06, labels.
7. Print and then close c04ex06, labels.

figure 4.15

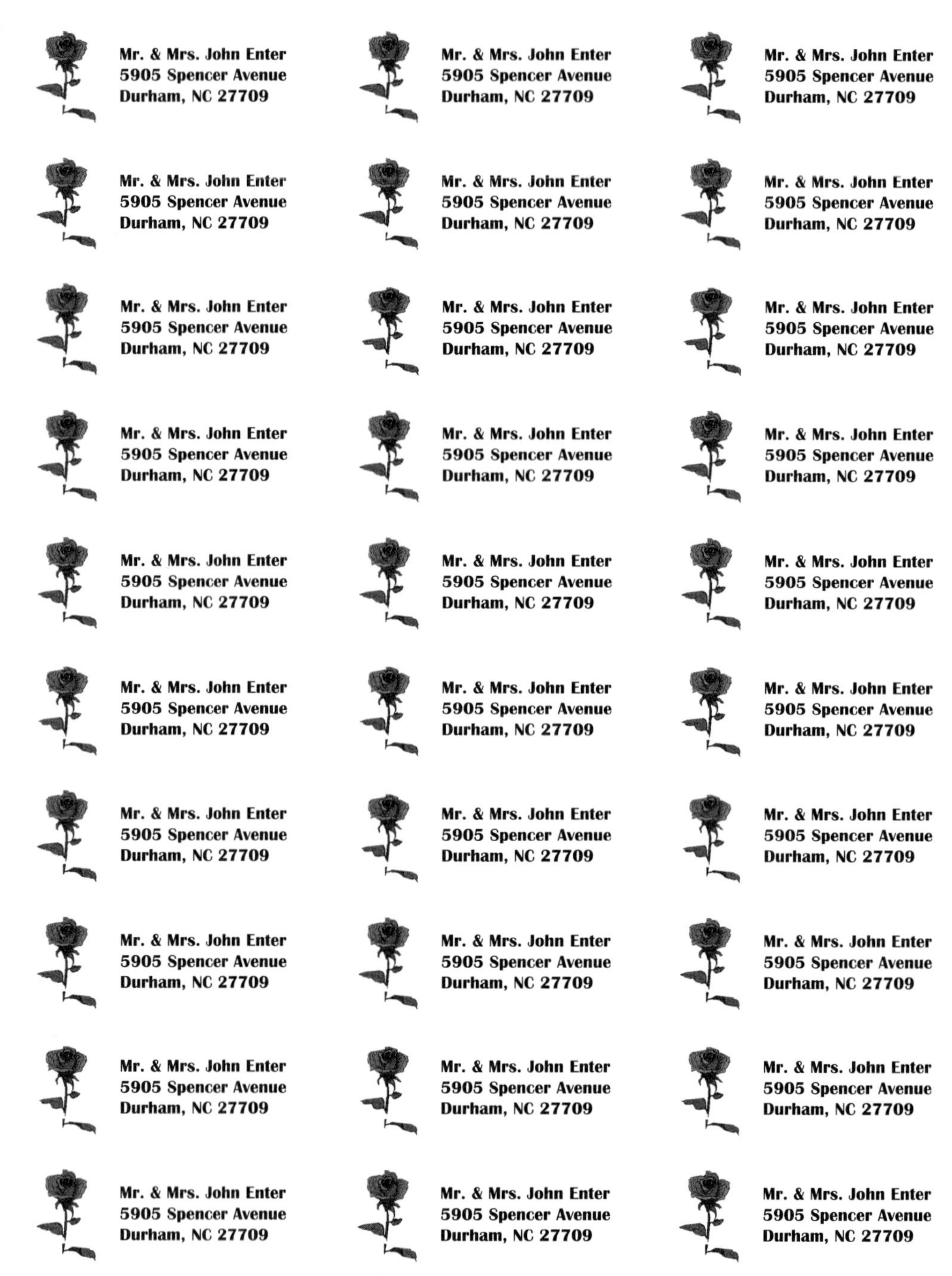

Mr. & Mrs. John Enter
5905 Spencer Avenue
Durham, NC 27709
Mr. & Mrs. John Enter
5905 Spencer Avenue
Durham, NC 27709
Mr. & Mrs. John Enter
5905 Spencer Avenue
Durham, NC 27709
Mr. & Mrs. John Enter
5905 Spencer Avenue
Durham, NC 27709
Mr. & Mrs. John Enter
5905 Spencer Avenue
Durham, NC 27709
Mr. & Mrs. John Enter
5905 Spencer Avenue
Durham, NC 27709
Mr. & Mrs. John Enter
5905 Spencer Avenue
Durham, NC 27709
Mr. & Mrs. John Enter
5905 Spencer Avenue
Durham, NC 27709
Mr. & Mrs. John Enter
5905 Spencer Avenue
Durham, NC 27709
Mr. & Mrs. John Enter
5905 Spencer Avenue
Durham, NC 27709
Mr. & Mrs. John Enter
5905 Spencer Avenue
Durham, NC 27709
Mr. & Mrs. John Enter
5905 Spencer Avenue
Durham, NC 27709
Mr. & Mrs. John Enter
5905 Spencer Avenue
Durham, NC 27709
Mr. & Mrs. John Enter
5905 Spencer Avenue
Durham, NC 27709
Mr. & Mrs. John Enter
5905 Spencer Avenue
Durham, NC 27709
Mr. & Mrs. John Enter
5905 Spencer Avenue
Durham, NC 27709
Mr. & Mrs. John Enter
5905 Spencer Avenue
Durham, NC 27709
Mr. & Mrs. John Enter
5905 Spencer Avenue
Durham, NC 27709
Mr. & Mrs. John Enter
5905 Spencer Avenue
Durham, NC 27709
Mr. & Mrs. John Enter
5905 Spencer Avenue
Durham, NC 27709
Mr. & Mrs. John Enter
5905 Spencer Avenue
Durham, NC 27709
Mr. & Mrs. John Enter
5905 Spencer Avenue
Durham, NC 27709
Mr. & Mrs. John Enter
5905 Spencer Avenue
Durham, NC 27709
Mr. & Mrs. John Enter
5905 Spencer Avenue
Durham, NC 27709
Mr. & Mrs. John Enter
5905 Spencer Avenue
Durham, NC 27709
Mr. & Mrs. John Enter
5905 Spencer Avenue
Durham, NC 27709
Mr. & Mrs. John Enter
5905 Spencer Avenue
Durham, NC 27709
Mr. & Mrs. John Enter
5905 Spencer Avenue
Durham, NC 27709
Mr. & Mrs. John Enter
5905 Spencer Avenue
Durham, NC 27709
Mr. & Mrs. John Enter
5905 Spencer Avenue
Durham, NC 27709

Creating a Certificate

Certificates are generally used to show recognition and promote excellence. Some other suggested uses for certificates include: diplomas, coupons, warranties, special event awards, program completion awards, and special-offer documents.

When printing your certificate, consider using an appropriate choice of high-quality bond paper or parchment paper in conservative colors, such as natural, cream, off-white, light gray, or any light marbleized color. In addition, consider using preprinted borders, ribbons, seals, and jackets, which are generally available through many mail-order catalogs and office supply stores.

Creating an Award Template

In earlier versions of Word, an Award Wizard was included in the Template folder. However, Word 97 does not include this template, so you will create your own award template in the next exercise. If you installed Word 97 as an upgrade, you may have the Award Wizard in the Office 95 Templates folder located in the New dialog box.

In exercise 7, you will create a distinctive, professional-looking certificate using a page border, various fonts, font effects, lines, and a watermark. In addition, you will add text fields (in which users type information), and save the certificate as a template. Finally, you will access your template, key text in place of the text fields, save the certificate as a document, and then print it.

Adding a Page Border

Word provides page borders that range from simple to highly ornate. When planning the layout and design of your certificate, choose a border that best complements the content and purpose of your certificate.

You can add a picture border (such as a row of ice cream cones) to any or all sides of each page in a document. To see the different kinds of page borders available, click Format, Borders and Shading, then select the Page Border tab. You can use one of the standard line borders and select different colors and widths, or click the down arrow to the right of the Art list box and choose more elaborate designs, as shown in figure 4.16.

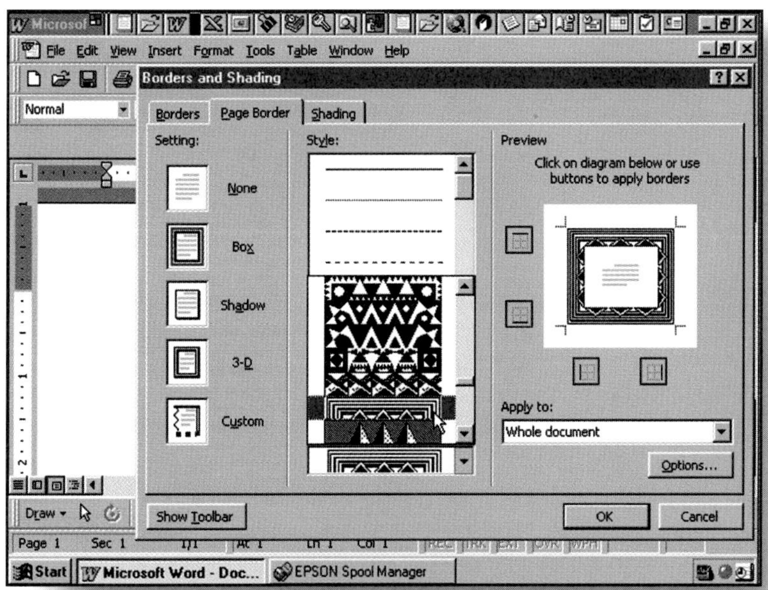

figure 4.16

Selecting a Page Border

Changing Page Border Margins

Unprintable Zone
Area on a page where text will not print.

Most printers cannot print to the edge of a page, especially at the bottom of the page. The minimum amount of space needed between the margin and the edge of the page varies by printer. This area, where text will not print, is known as the *unprintable zone*. You may find that occasionally the bottom border (in portrait orientation) or the side border (in landscape orientation) may fall within this unprintable zone and not print completely. In this case, you may need to try to increase the margins of the document or adjust the page border margins. Experiment with one of the following methods for moving the border farther away from the unprintable zone:

1. Try adjusting the page border margins by clicking Format, Borders and Shading, selecting the Page Border tab, and then clicking Options. Key settings in the Margin section, then view your document in Print Preview.
2. If the page border remains unchanged, click the down-pointing arrow to the right of the Measure from list box in the Borders and Shading Options dialog box, and select *Text* as shown in figure 4.17. Then change your document margins at the Page Setup dialog box or on the horizontal and vertical rulers.

Borders and Shading Options Dialog Box

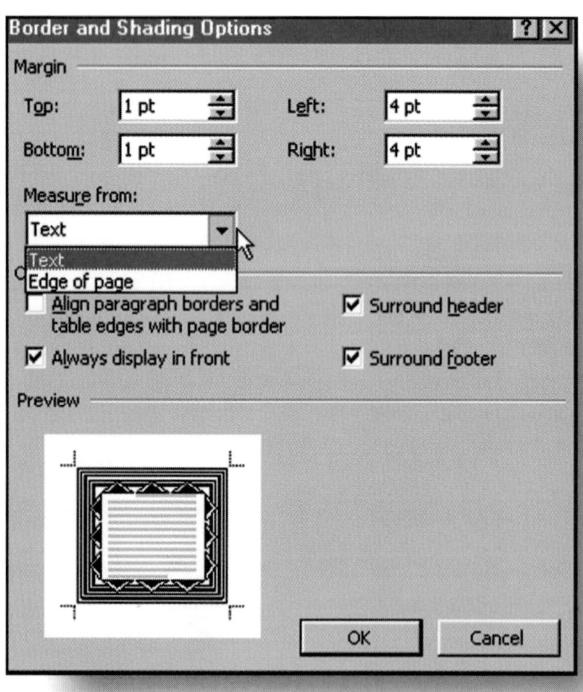

Form
A protected document that includes form fields.

Form Fields
Locations in a document where text is entered; a check box is turned on or off; or a drop-down line is accessed.

Inserting Text Fields

Whether creating a client survey form for your company's marketing and research department, or creating an award certificate for volunteers at your local hospital, using form fields in your templates saves time and effort. In Word, a *form* is a protected document that includes fields where information is entered. A form document contains *form fields* that are locations in the document where one of three things is performed: text is entered (text field), a check box is turned on or off, or information is selected from a drop-down list. Basically three steps are completed in creating a form document:

1. Design the structure and enter the text that will appear in your document or template.
2. Insert form fields prompting the user to insert information at the keyboard.
3. Save the document as a protected document (or template).

In exercise 7, you will use the Forms toolbar, as shown in figure 4.18 and insert very basic text fields into your template. For creating more advanced form fields, refer to Word's documentation. To learn how to insert text fields into a template, complete exercise 7.

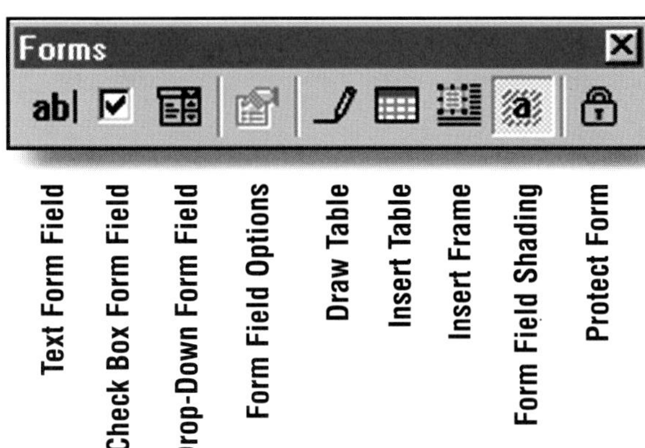

figure 4.18

Forms Toolbar

exercise 7

Creating an Award Certificate

1. Create the certificate in figure 4.19 by completing the following steps:
   a. Click File, then New.
   b. At the New dialog box with the General tab selected, make sure *Blank Document* is selected in the list box.
   c. Click Template in the Create New section located at the bottom right corner of the dialog box.
   d. Click OK or press Enter.
   e. Display the Drawing toolbar and Picture toolbar.
   f. Set all document margins at 1.25 inches and select Landscape orientation.
   g. Create the page border in figure 4.19 by completing the following steps:
      (1) Click Format, then Borders and Shading.
      (2) Select the Page Border tab.
      (3) Click the down arrow to the right of the Art list box and select the border displayed in figures 4.16 and 4.19.
      (4) Key **31 pt** in the Width text box.
      (5) Click the Options button.
      (6) Click the down arrow to the right of the Measure from list box and select *Text*.
      (7) Key **4 pt** in each of the four margin text boxes.
      (8) Click OK or press Enter.
      (9) Click OK or press Enter again.

h. With the insertion point positioned inside the page border, insert *award.doc* from your student data disk.
i. Select the entire document by pressing Ctrl + A and turn on kerning at 14 points.
j. Select the following text and apply the listed formatting:

Community Service Award	42-point Matura MT Script Capitals with Shadow.
Awarded to	14-point Arial Bold Italic
XXX	24-point Britannic Bold
As an expression...	12-point Arial
Your commitment of time...	12-point Arial
Presented by	14-point Arial Bold Italic
Edward Hospital...	22-point Britannic Bold in Small caps with Spacing Expanded by 1.5 points.
YYY	14-point Arial Bold Italic
Stephen, Ameeta, Joseph, Laurel...	12-point Arial

k. Change the Zoom to Page width.
l. Draw the signature lines in the award by completing the following steps:
   (1) Click the Line Color button on the Drawing toolbar and make sure that Black has been selected in the first row and first column of the palette.
   (2) Click the Line button (fifth button from the left) on the Drawing toolbar.
   (3) Position the crosshairs above *Stephen P. Becker, M.D.*
   (4) Hold down the Shift key and drag the crosshairs to create a ¾-inch single line that is approximately 3.25 inches in length, then release the left mouse button. (Verify the length at the Format AutoShape dialog box.)
   (5) Select the line, then drag and drop a copy of the line above each of the names. (Be sure to hold down the Ctrl key as you drag a copy above another name.)
m. Align the four lines by completing the following steps:
   (1) Select the line above Stephen P. Becker, M.D., hold down the Shift key and select the line above Joseph M. Kaminsky, M.D.
   (2) Click the Draw button on the Drawing toolbar, point to Align or Distribute, and then click Align Left.
   (3) Align the remaining lines by following steps similar to m(1) and m(2); however, click Align Right.
   (4) Align the lines horizontally by following steps similar to m(1) and m(2).
n. Create two text fields to replace *XXX* and *YYY* in the document by completing the following steps:
   (1) Display the Forms toolbar.
   (2) Select *XXX*, then click the Text Form Field button (first button from the left) on the Forms toolbar.
   (3) Click the Form Fields Options button (fourth button from the left) on the Forms toolbar.
   (4) Key **Insert recipient's name** in the Default text: text box.
   (5) Click the down arrow to the right of the Text format list box and select *Title case*.
   (6) Click OK or press Enter.
   (7) Select *YYY* and follow steps similar to steps n(1) through n(3), then key **Insert a date in February** in the text field.

(8) Close the Forms toolbar. (Click the X in the upper right corner.)

o. Create the heart watermark in figure 4.19 by completing the following steps:
   (1) Click the Text Box button on the Drawing toolbar.
   (2) Drag the crosshairs into the middle of the certificate and create a box approximately 4 inches in Height by 4.5 inches in Width. (See figure 4.19 for an approximate location.)
   (3) Select the text box, then click Format, then Text Box. Select the Wrapping tab, make sure None is selected in the Wrapping style section. Choose OK or press Enter.
   (4) Position the insertion point inside the text box and insert *Heart.wmf* located on your student data disk.
   (5) Select the picture. (Black sizing handles should display around the image.)
   (6) Click the Image Control button on the Picture toolbar and select Watermark.
   (7) Click the Less Brightness button on the Picture toolbar four times.
   (8) Click the More Contrast button on the Picture toolbar twice.
   (9) Select the text box containing the picture. (Hollow sizing handles should display around the border of the box.)
   (10) Click the down arrow to the right of the Line Color button on the Drawing toolbar and select No Line.
   (11) Click the Draw button on the Drawing toolbar, point to Order, and then select Send Behind Text.

p. Save the template with Save As and name it XXXAward.dot. Use your initials in place of XXX. (Check with your instructor to see if this document should be saved as a template to the hard drive or saved as a document to your data disk.) The template document will be saved in the Templates\Other Documents folder.

q. Close the template.

r. Click File, then New.

s. Double-click the *XXXAward.dot* template. (Make sure Document is selected in the Create New section.)

t. Click the first text field and key **Joan Polak**. Click the next text field and key **February 19, 1999**.

2. Save the document and name it c04ex07, award.
3. Print and then close c04ex07, award.

figure 4.19

Community Service Award

Awarded to

Joan Polak

As an expression of your volunteer efforts for National Healthy Heart Month.
Your commitment of time, energy, and dedicated service is greatly appreciated.

Presented by

EDWARD HOSPITAL CARDIOVASCULAR INSTITUTE

Februrary 19, 1999

Stephen P. Becker, M.D.

Ameeta Singh, M.D.

Joseph M. Kaminsky, M.D.

Laurel K. Zapata, R.N.

chapter summary

- Most current résumés use these essential parts: Heading, Career Objective, Work Experience, Education, Special Skills, Interests, and References.
- Em and en dashes are used in place of keyboard hyphens and dashes.
- The Change Text Direction button on the Text Box toolbar can be used to rotate a heading in a résumé.
- The Office Assistant provides an option to send your résumé via E-mail or fax when using the Résumé Wizard.
- Fill effects are added to documents for impact and focus.
- Use the Format Painter to copy formatting from one area of text to another.
- Side-by-side columns (tables) can be used to create résumés.
- Word provides a Calendar Wizard that guides you through the steps of creating monthly calendars in either portrait (narrow) or landscape (wide) orientation.
- Watermarks, pictures, special characters, shading, and text can be added to a calendar to enhance its appearance and add to its effectiveness. Reducing the shading of a watermark in a calendar improves the readability of the calendar text.
- AutoShape forms are added to documents to emphasize important facts. Text and fill can be added to an AutoShape form.
- Many AutoShape forms have adjustment handles you can drag to adjust a unique aspect of the shape.
- Adjustments may be necessary in the size and position of document elements to compensate for the unprintable zone of a particular printer.
- Selecting a predefined label definition at the Envelopes and Labels dialog box creates address labels.
- You can move objects precisely by holding down the Ctrl key as you press an arrow key on the keyboard.
- Objects automatically stack in individual layers as you add them to a document. You see the stacking order when objects overlap—the top object covers a portion of the objects beneath it.
- Grouping objects combines the objects into a single unit.
- Aligning objects positions objects in relation to each other or to a specific setting on a page.
- Use the F4 key to repeat a previous command.
- A page border can be added to any or all sides of a page.
- Form fields are added to documents or templates to allow the user to efficiently insert variable information.

commands review

	Mouse/Keyboard
Résumé Templates and Wizard	File, New, Other Documents tab
Rules (Borderlines)	Border button on Formatting toolbar; or Format, Borders and Shading, Borders tab
Format Painter	Format Painter button on Standard toolbar
Side-by-Side Columns	Tables, Insert Table; or Insert Table button on the Standard toolbar
Picture	Insert, Picture, Clip Art or From File
Text Box	Text Box button on Drawing toolbar
Watermark	View, Header and Footer. At the Header and Footer pane, create a text box, insert picture, click Image Control on the Picture toolbar, then select Watermark. Close Header and Footer pane. Or, create text box, insert picture, click Draw on Drawing toolbar, Order, then Send Behind Text. (You do not have to insert picture into a text box—the text box helps control the picture size and location.)
Labels	Tools, Envelopes and Labels
Page Border	Format, Borders and Shading, Page Border tab
Form Fields	View, Toolbars, Forms toolbar

check your understanding

True/False: Circle the letter T if the statement is true; circle the letter F if the statement is false.

T F **1.** Résumés can be sent via E-mail or fax through an option in the Calendar Wizard.

T F **2.** References must always be listed in a résumé.

T F **3.** All bulleted items in a list should be punctuated with a period.

T F **4.** Text can be rotated in a text box or cell in a table.

T F **5.** The Format Painter changes the intensity of color in a picture.

T F **6.** A text field is a form field where the user is prompted to enter text.

T F **7.** A watermark image can be inserted into a calendar through a built-in prompt within the Calendar Wizard.

T F **8.** To reduce the shading of a watermark, click the More Contrast, Less Contrast, More Brightness, or Less Brightness buttons on the Drawing toolbar.

T F **9.** To add a picture to a return address label, position the picture inside a label by framing it.

T F **10.** Objects and text can be grouped into a single unit.

Concepts: Answer the following questions in the space provided.

1. What is the main purpose of a résumé?

2. What essential parts are contained in most current résumés?

3. What are the two page orientations used in the Calendar Wizard?

4. What are the three descriptive types of résumé templates?

5. Why would you add a watermark to a document? What are two important considerations to keep in mind when using a watermark in a document?

skill assessments

Assessment 1

1. At a clear document screen, create your own résumé using any one of the three techniques discussed in this chapter. You can use one of Word's résumé templates or wizard or you can create a résumé using a rotated text box or side-by-side columns. Prepare your career objective with a particular job in mind, or look in your local newspaper for employment ads and tailor your résumé toward one job description that interests you. Arrange the sections of your résumé according to your particular qualifications.
2. Save your completed résumé and name it c04sa01, résumé.
3. Print and then close c04sa01, résumé.

Optional: Click Contents and Index at the Help menu, select the Index tab, key **Getting Results – Résumé**, and then click the Display button. (*Getting Results* is a component installed with a typical installation of Microsoft Office 97. *Getting Results* may not be available if you installed standalone Word.) If *Getting Results* is not available to you, click Contents and Index at the Help menu, select the Index tab, then key **résumés, creating**. Read the information presented and experiment with a feature that is new to you. (Example: Importing a list of contacts into Outlook!)

Assessment 2

Assume you are a parent volunteer for the all sports awards banquet at Kennedy Junior High. Create a generic certificate that can be used for any sports category. Create the certificate based on the following specifications:

1. Create an award using your own design and layout ideas. The award in figure 4.20 is a sample award. (Create a thumbnail sketch first!)
2. Key the text from the sample award in figure 4.20 and add appropriate enhancements.
3. Add a page border to the certificate.
4. Insert a picture or watermark. Two sports pictures are included on your student data disk (*awardwin.cgm* and *sports.wmf*); however, additional pictures are available in the Popular folder, Microsoft Clip Gallery 3.0, Free Stuff on the Web, and in the ValuPack folder on your program CD-ROM.
5. Insert at least two text fields.
6. Save the completed certificate and name it c04sa02, sports.
7. Print and then close c04sa02, sports.

Optional: Save c04sa02, sports as a template.

Assessment 3

1. Use the Calendar Wizard to create a calendar similar to the one shown in figure 4.21 with the following specifications:
   a. Use the Calendar Wizard to create a calendar for September 1998.
   b. Select a calendar style and page orientation.
   c. Insert *Computer.wmf* or any other appropriate image as a picture or watermark.
   d. Insert calendar text at the designated dates.
   e. Key the company name, address, phone/fax numbers and E-mail address at the bottom of the calendar.
   f. Make sure all the lines around the calendar print by viewing the document at Print Preview before printing. (If any of the vertical or horizontal lines do not display, make any necessary adjustments for the nonprintable zone of your particular printer. Experiment to find the appropriate settings.)
2. Save the calendar and name it c04sa03, calendar.
3. Print and then close c04sa03, calendar.

figure 4.20

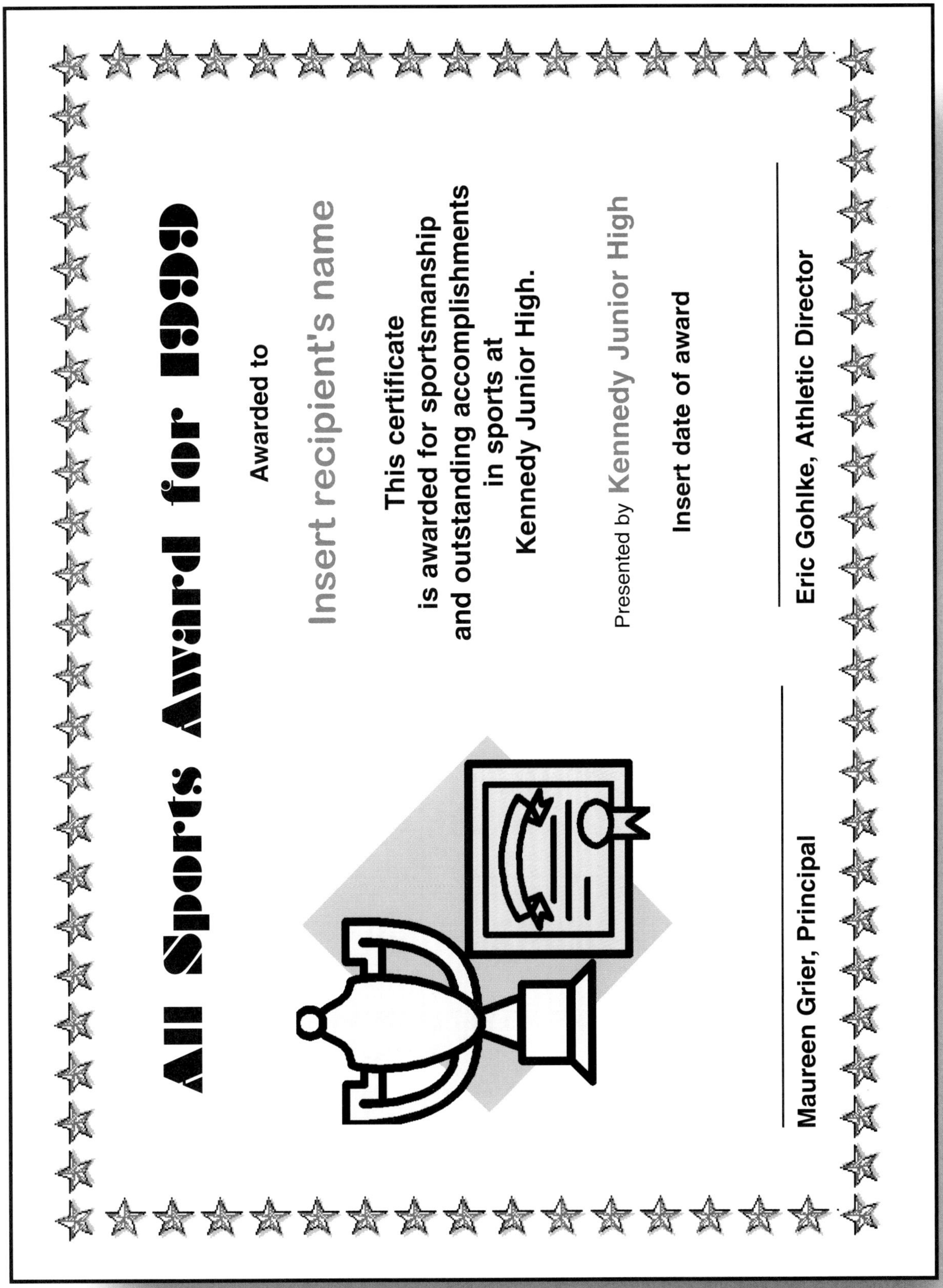

All Sports Award for 1999

Awarded to

Insert recipient's name

This certificate
is awarded for sportsmanship
and outstanding accomplishments
in sports at
Kennedy Junior High.

Presented by Kennedy Junior High

Insert date of award

Maureen Grier, Principal

Eric Gohlke, Athletic Director

figure 4.21

September 1998

Sun	Mon	Tue	Wed	Thu	Fri	Sat
		1 Staff Meeting 8:30 a.m. Conference Rm.	**2**	**3**	**4** Board Meeting 9:00 a.m. Conference Rm.	**5**
6	**7**	**8**	**9** Regional Directors Meeting 8:00 a.m. Corporate Office	**10**	**11** Employee Award Dinner 7:00 p.m. Radcliffe Inn	**12**
13	**14** Staff Meeting 8:30 a.m. Conference Rm.	**15**	**16**	**17** Word 97 Training Session 1 Rm. 240 9 a.m. – 3 p.m.	**18**	**19**
20	**21**	**22**	**23**	**24**	**25** Area Sales Meeting 2:00 p.m. Conference Rm.	**26**
27	**28**	**29**	**30**			

TAYLOR INFORMATION MANAGEMENT SERVICES
5789 South Meridian Street
Indianapolis, IN 46606
Phone: (317) 555-7903 Fax: (317) 555-7901 *E-mail: Taylor@msn.com*

Assessment 4

1. Create a sheet of personal return address labels using your name and address. Include a picture of your choice. Use the Avery Standard 5160-Address label definition. Size the picture and address to fit into the label dimensions of 1 inch in height and 2.63 inches in width.
2. Save the address labels as c04sa04, labels.
3. Print and then close c04sa04, labels.

creative activity

1. Find an example of a calendar, certificate, award, or any other type of personal document.
2. Recreate the example improving it with appropriate font selections and enhancements, a picture, watermark, page border, or special characters. Be sure to apply appropriate desktop design concepts to the layout of your document.
3. Save your document as c04ca01, redo and then print and close c04ca01, redo.
4. Attach the original document to your recreated document, then turn both of them into your instructor. The instructor should then randomly pass the completed documents around the classroom and ask each student to write a short evaluation on the back of each document—each student should sign their evaluation with the name of a their favorite movie star, sports figure, hero, etc. (Students may refer to a copy of the Document Analysis Guide or the Document Evaluation Checklist for pointers.)
5. Read your document evaluations and make any suggested changes.
6. Resubmit your documents to your instructor.

Unit one

PERFORMANCE ASSESSMENTS

Assessment one

1. Use the Professional Memo template to create the memo shown in figure U1.1 and include the following specifications:
   a. Key **Alpine Ski Company** in the shaded box in the upper right corner of the memo. Change the shading color in the box to Dark Blue.
   b. Key the heading text and body text as shown in figure U1.1. The letters with accents can be found in the (normal text) Font.
   c. Key your reference initials below the last paragraph and include the document name **u01pa01, memo**.
   d. Select the heading, *Memo*, then change the font color to Dark Blue.
   e. Select the three Canadian locations, Lac-Frontière, Quebec, etc., then apply bullets. To do this, display the Bullets and Numbering dialog box (Format, then Bullets and Numbering). At the Bullets and Numbering dialog box, click the Customize button. At the Customize Bulleted List dialog box, click the Bullet button. At the Symbol dialog box, select the Wingdings Font, and then select the bullet in the seventh row and seventeenth column. Click OK to close the Symbol dialog box. At the Customize Bulleted List dialog box, click the Font button. Click the down arrow to the right of the Color list box, then select Dark Blue. You decide the amount of space before and after each bullet to create the memo similar to figure U1.1.
   f. Create the graphic image to the right of the memo heading text by inserting *Winter.wmf* located on your student data disk. Remove the border around the image.
   g. Delete the footer containing the page number by completing the following steps:
      (1) Choose View, then Header and Footer; or double-click the footer in the document window.
      (2) At the header pane, click the Switch Between Header and Footer button.
      (3) At the first page footer pane, select the bullet symbol and *Page 1*, then press Delete.
      (4) Click the Close button on the Header and Footer toolbar.
2. Save the memo and name it u01pa01, memo.
3. Print and then close u01pa01, memo.

Optional: Open the memo (u01pa01, memo) as completed in assessment 1. Choose a different bullet for the bulleted items. Create a watermark in the memo using a special character or picture of your choice.

Alpine Ski Company

Memo

To: Maggie Rivière, Vice President

From: (your name)

CC: Martin Schoenfeld, Senior Vice President

Date: (current date)

Re: Company Expansion

The board of directors has agreed to consider expanding the company into Canada and/or Europe. The following locations in Canada are being considered:

- Lac-Frontière, Quebec
- Pointe-à-la-Frégate, Quebec
- St. Benoît, Quebec

Several of the board members feel that Canada should be our first choice. They are, however, not ruling out Europe. The following locations in Europe are being considered:

- Mühldorf, Germany
- Alençon, France
- Zürich, Switzerland

A site selection committee is being formed to assess the viability of each site. I would like you to be a member of this committee. Members will be asked to visit a specific site to gather information. I would like you to fly to Pointe-à-la-Frégate, Quebec, next week to gather information on land prices, availability of workers, educational facilities, and the general economic situation. Please let me know as soon as possible if you will be available to visit Pointe-à-la-Frégate.

xx:u01pa01, memo

Figure U1.1 • Assessment 1

Assessment two

1. At a clear document screen, use the Letter Wizard to create a single business letter as shown in figure U1.2 with the following specifications:
   a. Include the current date.
   b. Select Contemporary and full block as the letter style.
   c. Send the letter to:

      Mr. Daniel Harrigan
      Harrigan Construction Company
      413 Pinecrest Road
      Scarborough, ME 04104

   d. Include a formal salutation.
   e. Include your name as the sender and key the following as the return address:

      Portland Lock & Key Service
      370 Brighton Avenue
      Portland, ME 04102
      Phone: (207) 555-3777
      Fax: (207) 555-3780

   f. Select *Yours truly,* as the complimentary closing.
   g. Include **Account Representative** as your job title.
   h. Use your initials as the writer/typist initials.
   i. Just display the letter without making an envelope or mailing label.
   j. With the letter displayed on the screen, position the insertion point to the left of the date, then press Enter four or five times.
   k. Insert the company name on top of the gray shaded rectangle by completing the following steps:
      (1) Click View, then Header and Footer.
      (2) Position the mouse in the shaded rectangle until it displays as an arrow with a four-headed arrow attached, then right-click one time.
      (3) Click Add Text.
      (4) Change the font to 30-point Garamond Bold, then key **Portland Lock & Key Service**.
   l. Customize the rectangle (AutoShape) according to the following specifications:
      (1) Using the bottom center sizing handle, change the size of the rectangle (AutoShape) as necessary and appropriate to accommodate the company name.
      (2) Change the fill color of the rectangle to semitransparent yellow.
      (3) Close the header/footer view.

m. Change the font of the company return address, phone, and fax number to 10-point Garamond. Extend the bottom border of the frame to see all of the text.
n. Position the insertion point below the salutation, select the placeholder letter body text, then key the letter body text shown in figure U1.2.
o. Position the insertion point to the left of the date. Select from the date through the end of the text, then change the font to 12-point Garamond.
p. Replace the globe picture with a picture of a lock and key by completing the following steps:
   (1) In the Header and Footer layer, select the globe graphic image, then press delete.
   (2) Click Insert, point to Picture, then click From File. At the Insert Picture dialog box, double-click the *Popular* folder. Double-click *Lock.wmf.*
   (3) Click once to select the picture. Click Format, then Picture, and then customize the picture at the Picture dialog box as follows:
      (a) Select the Size tab, then change the height of the picture to 0.84 inches and the width to 1.5 inches.
      (b) Select the Position tab, then change the horizontal position of the picture to 0.5 inches from the edge of the page and the vertical position to 4.4 inches from the top of the page. (Remember to change the "From" options first.)
      (c) Select the Wrapping tab, then change the wrapping style to None.
      (d) Select the Picture tab, change the color to Watermark, the brightness option to 75%, and the contrast option to 20% in the Image Control section.
      (e) Click OK or press Enter.
q. Switch to the footer pane and change the color of the rectangle (AutoShape) to the same yellow color used in the previous rectangle.
r. Insert and appropriately position a slogan in the yellow-shaded rectangle at the bottom of the page by completing the following steps:
   (1) Make sure the rectangle (AutoShape) is selected.
   (2) With the rectangle selected, right-click, then select Add Text.
   (3) At the Paragraph dialog box, change the line spacing to exactly 12 points, then press Enter.
   (4) Change the font to 14-point Garamond, Bold Italic, then key **24-Hour Emergency Service**.

2. Save the completed letter and name it u01pa02, lock letter.
3. Print and then close u01pa02, lock letter.

Optional: Open u01pa02, lock letter and rewrite the letter in a more firm tone of voice. Include information that the account is more than four months past due and payment is due immediately. After rewriting the letter, save it as u01pa02, optional. Print and then close u01pa02, optional.

Portland Lock & Key Service
370 Brighton Avenue
Portland, ME 04102
Phone: (207) 555-3777
Fax: (207) 555-3780

Portland Lock & Key Service

(Current date)

Mr. Daniel Harrigan
Harrigan Construction Company
413 Pinecrest Road
Scarborough, ME 04104

Dear Mr. Harrigan:

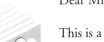

This is a reminder about invoice number 1546 for $527.39, which is now over 30 days past due. If there is a problem with this invoice, please call me at once so we can correct it.

Thank you for your business and for your prompt attention to this matter.

Yours truly,

(Your name)
Account Representative

(Your initials)

24-Hour Emergency Service

Figure U1.2 • Assessment 2

Assessment three

1. You work for a company named Design 2000 that specializes in ergonomically designed offices. Your company works hard to create designs that provide maximum worker comfort. Create a letterhead and envelope for Design 2000. Include the following information in your letterhead design:

Slogan	=	(Make up a slogan for your company.)
Address	=	300 Sun Drive
	=	Tucson, AZ 96322
Phone	=	(304) 555-2344
Fax	=	(304) 555-2345

2. Include the following in the letterhead and envelope design:
   a. Create a thumbnail sketch or sketches of your proposed letterhead and envelope design and layout.
   b. Create an asymmetrical design.
   c. Incorporate appropriate and proportional typeface, type size, and type style. Consider using the WordArt feature.
   d. Turn on kerning for fonts 14 points and above.
   e. Use tracking (condensing or expanding character spacing) if necessary.
   f. Use one or more horizontal or vertical ruled lines in any length or thickness that fits into your design.
   g. You may use special characters or a graphic image if appropriate.
   h. Use some color if a color printer is available.
   i. Save the letterhead and name it u01pa03, letterhead.
   j. With the letterhead still displayed on the screen, create a coordinating envelope by completing the following steps:
      (1) Display the Envelopes and Labels dialog box with the Envelopes tab selected.
      (2) Delete any text in the Delivery Address and Return Address text boxes.
      (3) Display the Envelope Options dialog box (with the Envelope Options tab selected) and make sure the Envelope size list box displays *Size 10 (4¹/₈ x 9 ½ in)*.
      (4) Add the envelope to your document (your letterhead) and create a return address for Design 2000 that incorporates some of the same design elements as your letterhead. You decide what information from your letterhead will also be included in the envelope return address.
3. Save the document containing the envelope and name it u01pa03, ltr&env.
4. Print and then close u01pa03, ltr&env.

Optional: Print *document analysis guide.doc* located on your student data disk and use it to evaluate your finished document.

Assessment four

1. At a clear document screen, create the résumé in figure U1.3 following the handwritten specifications.
2. Insert *para09, para10,* and *para11* located on your student data disk following each appropriate heading.
3. Save the résumé and name it u01pa04, résumé.
4. Print and then close u01pa04, résumé.

Optional: Assume you are a personnel director and the résumé prepared in u01pa04 has landed on your desk for review. Write a critique of this résumé by considering the following points:

- Appropriate layout and design?
- Consistency in headings and bulleted items?
- Headings in proper order?
- Appropriate choice of fonts, type sizes, and type styles?
- Career Objective—clear? vague? restrictive?
- Proper punctuation?
- Job Experience—clear? specific? descriptive?
- Education—thorough? too lengthy? appropriate?
- References—more information needed? delete?

When your critique is complete, label the assignment as u01pa04x, optional.

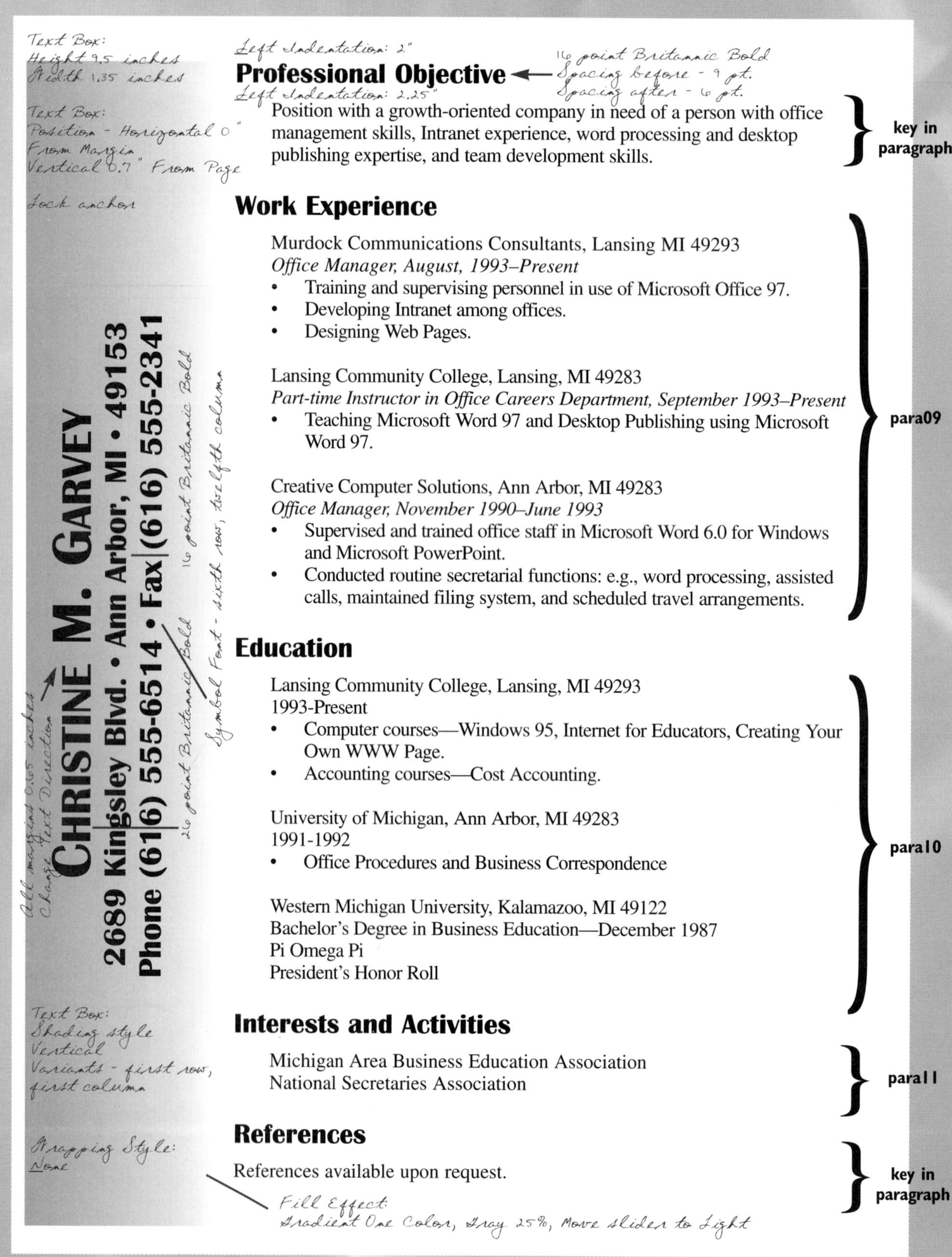

Text Box:
Height 9.5 inches
Width 1.35 inches
Text Box:
Position - Horizontal 0" From Margin
Vertical 0.7" From Page
Lock anchor
Left Indentation: 2"
Professional Objective
16 point Britannic Bold
Spacing before - 9 pt.
Spacing after - 6 pt.
Left Indentation: 2.25"
Position with a growth-oriented company in need of a person with office management skills, Intranet experience, word processing and desktop publishing expertise, and team development skills.
key in paragraph
Work Experience
Murdock Communications Consultants, Lansing MI 49293
Office Manager, August, 1993–Present
• Training and supervising personnel in use of Microsoft Office 97.
• Developing Intranet among offices.
• Designing Web Pages.
Lansing Community College, Lansing, MI 49283
Part-time Instructor in Office Careers Department, September 1993–Present
• Teaching Microsoft Word 97 and Desktop Publishing using Microsoft Word 97.
Creative Computer Solutions, Ann Arbor, MI 49283
Office Manager, November 1990–June 1993
• Supervised and trained office staff in Microsoft Word 6.0 for Windows and Microsoft PowerPoint.
• Conducted routine secretarial functions: e.g., word processing, assisted calls, maintained filing system, and scheduled travel arrangements.
para09
Education
Lansing Community College, Lansing, MI 49293
1993-Present
• Computer courses—Windows 95, Internet for Educators, Creating Your Own WWW Page.
• Accounting courses—Cost Accounting.
University of Michigan, Ann Arbor, MI 49283
1991-1992
• Office Procedures and Business Correspondence
Western Michigan University, Kalamazoo, MI 49122
Bachelor's Degree in Business Education—December 1987
Pi Omega Pi
President's Honor Roll
para10
Interests and Activities
Michigan Area Business Education Association
National Secretaries Association
para11
References
References available upon request.
key in paragraph
CHRISTINE M. GARVEY
2689 Kingsley Blvd. • Ann Arbor, MI • 49153
Phone (616) 555-6514 • Fax (616) 555-2341
All margins 0.05 inches
Change Text Direction
26 point Britannic Bold
16 point Britannic Bold
Symbol Font - sixth row, twelfth column
Text Box:
Shading style
Vertical
Variants - first row, first column
Wrapping Style:
None
Fill Effect:
Gradient One Color, Gray 25%, Move slider to Light

Figure U1.3 • Assessment 4

Assessment five

1. Use the Calendar Wizard to create a calendar similar to the sample solution in figure U1.4 for your employer, Harbor Realty. The calendar should include office-related events and client appointments for May 1998. Your employer is extremely busy, with a full client load and a real estate class to teach at your local community college. Perhaps your calendar will help your employer stay organized and informed.
   a. Select the Calendar Wizard and choose the Jazzy style in portrait orientation.
   b. Create the calendar for May 1998.
   c. Choose an appropriate typeface and type size for the text that will be inserted into the calendar. Apply color to the text if appropriate.
   d. For added interest, include a picture or watermark that relates to the real estate theme. Access the Office Assistant for advice on inserting pictures. Include a "catchy" slogan that correlates to the picture and the real estate theme. If you create a watermark, be sure to reduce the shading to increase the readability of the text.
   e. Include the real estate agency's name, address, telephone number, and fax number somewhere on the calendar. Use the following information:

      Harbor Realty, 34 Saybrooke Lane, Chatham, MA 03270, Telephone: (508) 555-9402, Fax: (508) 555-5900, E-mail: HarborR@msn.com.

   f. Include the following information in the calendar along with any special characters or pictures that you may want to add. (*Hint:* Select the calendar cells and change the font to 20-point Times New Roman and change the paragraph spacing from 6 points Before to 0 points.) The *Coffee.wmf* and *Golf.wmf* pictures are located on your student data disk. The *Flower.wmf, Ribbon.wmf, Sailboat.wmf,* and *Key.wmf* pictures are available in the Popular folder. The airplane symbol is located in the Wingdings character set. You may want to Center align the text within each cell.

May 1	**9:00 a.m. Real Estate Class**
May 4	**8:00 a.m. Staff Meeting**
May 6	**Office Golf Outing**
May 8	**9:00 a.m. Real Estate Class**
May 10	**Mother's Day**
May 14	**7:00 p.m. Award Dinner**
May 15	**9:00 a.m. Real Estate Class**
May 18	**Seminar in San Diego**
May 22	**9:00 a.m. Real Estate Class**
May 25	**Memorial Day**
May 29	**2:00 p.m. Open House**

2. Save the calendar and name it u01pa05, calendar.
3. Print and then close u01pa05, calendar.

HARBOR REALTY

34 Saybrooke Lane
Chatham, MA 03270
Telephone: (508) 555-9402
Fax: (508) 555-5900
E-mail: HarborR@msn.com

Sun	Mon	Tue	Wed	Thu	Fri	Sat
					1 9:00 a.m. Real Estate Class	2
3	4 8:00 a.m. Staff Meeting	5	6 Office Golf Outing	7	8 9:00 a.m. Real Estate Class	9
10 Mother's Day	11	12	13	14 7:00 p.m. Award Dinner	15 9:00 a.m. Real Estate Class	16
17	18 Seminar in San Diego	19	20	21	22 9:00 a.m. Real Estate Class	23
24	25 Memorial Day	26	27	28	29 2:00 p.m. Open House	30
31	HARBOR REALTY *A Leader on the East Coast!*					

1998

Figure U1.4 • Assessment 4

Unit two

PREPARING PROMOTIONAL DOCUMENTS, WEB PAGES, AND POWERPOINT PRESENTATIONS

In this unit, you will learn to plan, design, and create promotional documents including flyers, brochures, and greeting cards, along with Web pages and PowerPoint presentations.

scans

The Secretary's Commission on Achieving Necessary Skills

DECISION MAKING

TECHNOLOGY

PROBLEM SOLVING

COMMUNICATIONS

chapterFIVE

5 Creating Promotional Documents

PERFORMANCE OBJECTIVE

Upon successful completion of chapter 5, you will be able to produce promotional documents such as flyers and announcements using Word's Tables and Borders toolbar, Picture toolbar, Drawing toolbar, Microsoft Word Picture editor, and WordArt along with text boxes, pictures, lines, AutoShapes, 3-D boxes, shadow boxes, and borders.

Desktop Publishing Concepts

Indentifying purpose	Directional flow	Kerning
Focus	Consistency	Proportion
Balance	Graphic images	Contrast
Design and layout	Leading	Logo
Thumbnail sketch	White space	

Word Features Used

Pictures	Text boxes	Scale
WordArt	Drawing objects	Group
Tables	Ungroup	Regroup
Rotating text	AutoShapes	Align or distribute
Character spacing	Lines	Fill color
Fill effects	Line color	Drawing toolbar
Microsoft Word picture	Crop	Picture toolbar

In this chapter, you will produce flyers and announcements for advertising products, services, events, classes, and more using your own design and layout ideas with the help of Word features. First, you will review basic desktop publishing concepts for planning and designing promotional documents. Then, you will incorporate fonts, graphics, borders, and objects into your documents to increase their appeal. Finally, more complex and powerful features such as WordArt, Microsoft Word Picture, and the tools on the Drawing toolbar will be introduced to further enhance the appeal of your publications. Information, suggestions, and examples are provided in this chapter to stimulate your interest and creativity so you will be able to produce effective promotional documents.

Planning and Designing Promotional Documents

As you learned in chapter 1, planning your document is a basic desktop publishing concept that applies to flyers and announcements as well as to other publications. Clearly define your purpose and assess your target audience. Besides assessing your needs and your approach, consider your budget as well. Flyers and announcements are generally considered one of the least expensive means of advertising.

Start thinking about what elements are needed to produce a document that gets results. A successful document attracts the reader's attention and keeps it. In designing your document, consider how you can attract the reader's eye: by using eye-catching headlines, displaying graphics that create impact, or using color for emphasis or attention.

Using a Table for Layout

DTP POINTERS
Prepare a thumbnail sketch.

Use a thumbnail sketch as a tool to guide you in creating a visually pleasing and effective document. In addition, you may draw a table to block off areas of the page to reflect the layout you have sketched in your thumbnail. Figure 5.1 shows how a table can serve as a framework for a flyer. Tables provide an efficient means for aligning text and objects using options on the Tables and Borders toolbar such as Align Top, Center Vertically, Align Bottom, and Change Text Direction as shown in figure 5.2. You will learn how to create a flyer in a table in exercise 1.

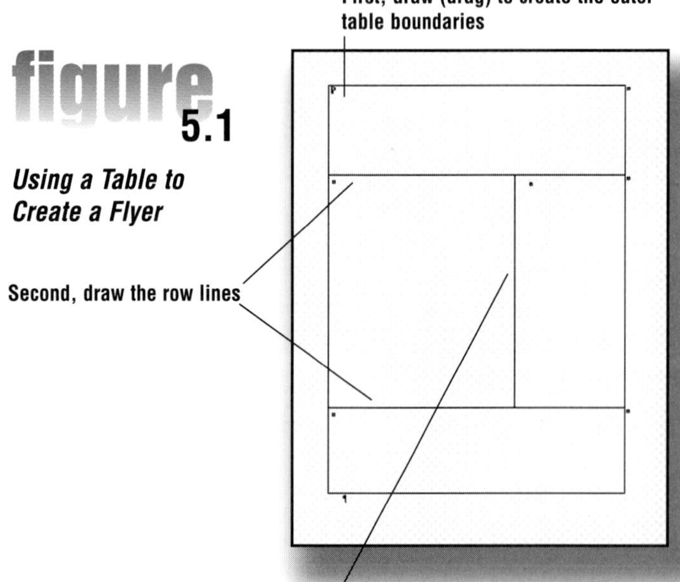

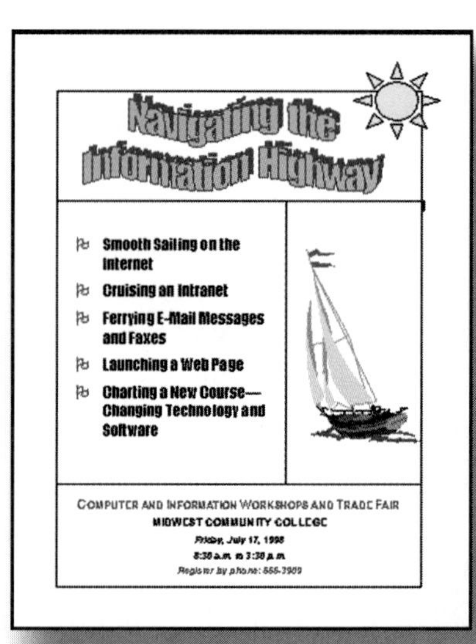

figure 5.1

Using a Table to Create a Flyer

To create a table for the flyer in figure 5.1, you would complete the following steps:

1. Change the Zoom to 50% and make sure the ruler is displayed.
2. Click the Tables and Borders button (ninth button from the right) on the Standard toolbar.
3. Click the Draw Table button (first button from the left) on the Tables and Borders toolbar. (The arrow pointer will display as a pen—see figure 5.2 for the Tables and Borders toolbar.)
4. Position the pen in the upper-left corner, and then drag to create a table.
5. Draw lines by clicking and dragging.
6. To erase lines, click the Eraser button (second button from the left) on the Tables and Borders toolbar—see figure 5.2. Drag the eraser along the line you want to erase. Remember to turn the Eraser off when you are done.
7. If you do not want borders on your table, click the down arrow on the Borders button on the Tables and Borders toolbar (see figure 5.2), then click the No Border button.
8. If you want to change the cell width or length, drag the boundary you want to change. (Position the insertion point on the boundary line you want to change; when the insertion point displays as either two vertical or horizontal lines with up/down or left/right pointing arrows, drag the line to a new location.)

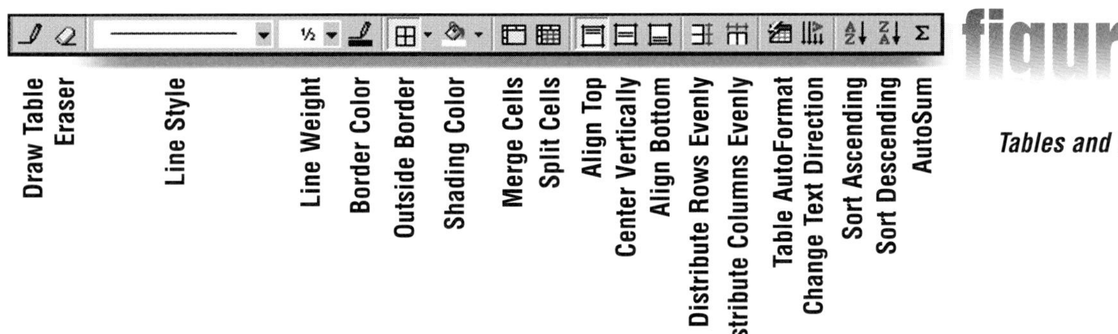

figure 5.2

Tables and Borders Toolbar

Using Text for Focus

Flyers and announcements provide enormous opportunities for creative freedom within the parameters of design concepts. To grab attention, consider using BIG graphics, uncommon typefaces, and plenty of white space. Figure 5.3 illustrates a flyer that attracts attention through the use of varying fonts and font attributes.

DTP POINTERS
White space creates a clean page that is easy to read.

Once you have finished a document, look at the document from a distance to make sure that the important information is dominant.

5.3

Sample Flyer (All Text)

COME SEE THE NEW LOOK AT NORTH BROOK

Friday through Sunday,
November 20-22

especially for

Kids

Arts & Crafts

Show

Beginning November 20—See Santa Claus and ride the Elves' train, still only 50¢ a ride.

Sunday, November 22—Receive a free "especially for kids" chocolate rose 12 p.m.-3 p.m.

THE PLACE FOR YOU

NORTH BROOK

Choosing Fonts for Headlines

DTP POINTERS
With text-intensive material vary type sizes and styles. Use varying shades of black and white as well as color.

Text-intensive material is usually not appropriate for flyers or announcements unless you vary the typefaces, type sizes, and type styles as shown in figure 5.3, otherwise your reader probably will not take the time to read it. In designing this type of publication, careful selection of fonts and type sizes is important. Select typefaces that match the tone of the document and type sizes that stress important information. For instance, avoid choosing a typeface that is characteristically formal, such as Brush Script MT, if you are creating a flyer advertising a garage sale. For a strong headline you might want to use Braggadocio, Impact, or Arial MT Black, all of which demand attention. For a casual appearance, consider using Century Gothic, Arial, or Kino MT.

A headline should be a dominant visual element, set significantly larger than the words that follow. Standard headlines are usually 36 to 48 points in size. However, depending on your document, the headline may even exceed 72 points.

Besides increasing the point size for headlines, you may want to change the shading and/or color of the font. Depending on your needs, you may choose a large, thick typeface and change the shading to a desired percentage of black, or select a color from the font color palette. Changes to font colors are made at the Font dialog box or by clicking the down arrow on the Font Color buttons located on the Formatting or Drawing toolbars. Existing text in a document must first be selected.

Figure 5.4 provides examples of different typefaces and colors. Notice that all of the examples are keyed in the same type size, but the amount of horizontal space they occupy varies greatly.

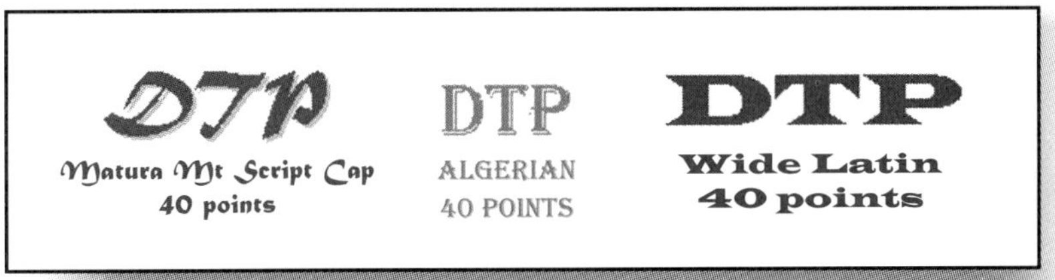

DTP
Matura Mt Script Cap
40 points

DTP
ALGERIAN
40 POINTS

DTP
Wide Latin
40 points

figure 5.4

Type Variations and Color Choices

Using WordArt for Headlines

Consider the impact that text can have, as shown in figure 5.5. The name of the font used in this example is *Impact* and when used with a WordArt shape in a green color, you can imagine the impact this heading will have—a big savings in dollars! Wise use of text in publications can have a forceful effect on how the message is communicated. A flyer with a large, colorful headline is an eye-catching way to announce an event or advertise a product or service.

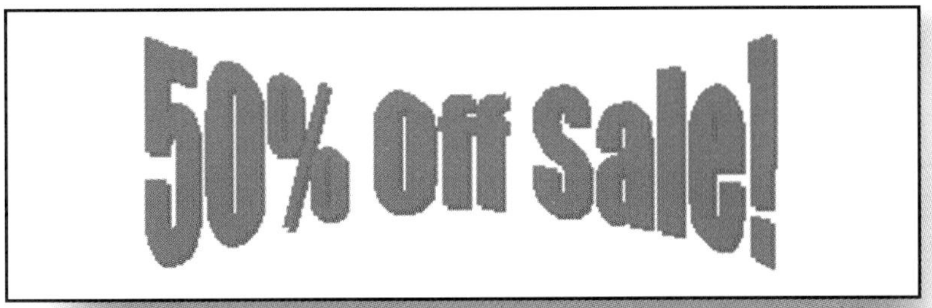

50% Off Sale!

figure 5.5

WordArt for Emphasis

WordArt changes ordinary text into graphic objects, and since WordArt is based on text, fonts are very important in creating interesting text designs. The fonts that are available in WordArt applications include Windows fonts, Word program fonts, printer fonts, and any other soft fonts you may have added to your computer.

Using Graphics for Emphasis

Graphics can add excitement and generate enthusiasm for a publication. A well-placed graphic can transform a plain document into a compelling visual document. However, it is effective only if the image relates to the subject of the document. Graphics can be the key to attracting the attention of your audience.

DTP POINTERS
Choose images that relate to the message.

Before selecting a graphic, decide what your theme or text will be. If you are deciding between many graphics, select the simplest. A simple graphic demands more attention and has more impact. Too many graphics can cause clutter and confusion. Also, use a generous amount of white space. Use a graphic to aid in directional flow. Use a thumbnail sketch as a tool to help you make decisions on position, size, and design.

DTP POINTERS
Leave plenty of white space.

Also consider using clip art as a basis for your own creations. Combine clip art images with other clip art images, then crop, size, or color different areas of the image to create a unique look. Alternatively, you can include photographs in your flyers or announcements.

DTP POINTERS
Do not overuse clip art; use one main visual element per page.

Keep in mind that if you have access to the Internet, you can add to your clip art, photographs, videos, and sound clips collection by downloading images and clips from Microsoft. You can easily download these images by first accessing the Internet through your Internet Service Provider, then opening Word 97. While in Word 97, click Help, point to Microsoft on the Web, then click Free Stuff, as shown in figure 5.6.

Alternatively, you can access Free Stuff by clicking Insert, pointing to Picture, then clicking Clip Art. Complete the following steps to download files from the Web:

1. Click Insert, Picture, Clip Art to display Microsoft Clip Gallery.
2. Click the Connect to Web for Additional Clips button, which looks like a globe, at the bottom right of the dialog box—see figure 5.7. Then click OK. (Access to the Internet is necessary.)
3. Click Accept when the Microsoft Clip Gallery Live screen appears.
4. Click the buttons that correspond to the types of clips you want to download.
5. Define your research criteria by clicking Browse and selecting a clip art category, or click Search and enter keywords.
6. Click Go to perform the search. Results will display on the screen.
7. To download an image, click the file name under the preview picture.
8. Click Open it to install the image in the Microsoft Clip Gallery. Or, click Save It to Disk to copy the file to your disk (enter a name and path).
9. Exit your browser.

Free Stuff on the Web

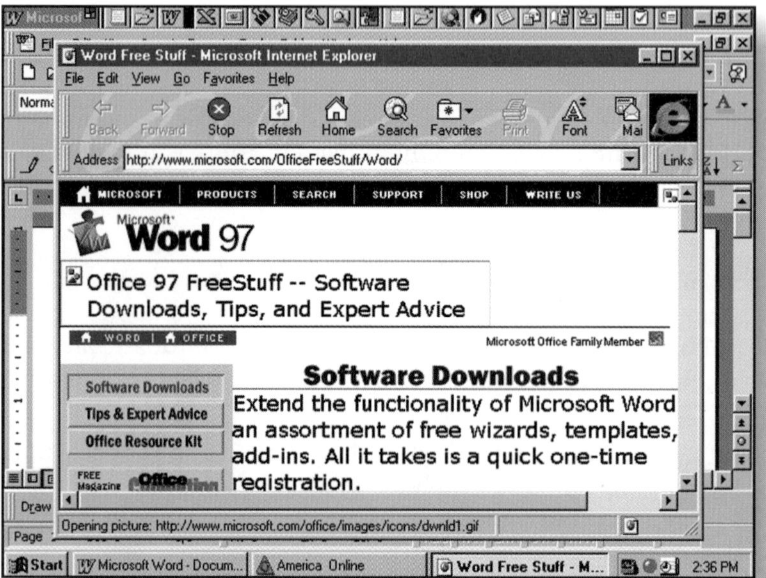

figure 5.7

Connect to Web for Additional Clips Button

Using Color in Promotional Documents

Color is a powerful tool in communicating information. Color elicits feelings, emphasizes important text, attracts attention, organizes data, and/or creates a pattern in a document. Color focuses a reader's attention, but use color sparingly or it will lose its power. The colors you choose should reflect the nature of the business you represent. Someone in an artistic line of work may use bolder, splashier colors than someone creating documents for a business dealing with finance. Additionally, men and women often respond differently to the same color. Always identify your target audience in planning your documents and think about the impact color will have on your audience.

DTP POINTERS
Use color consistently within a document.

Choose one or two colors for a document and stick with them to give your page a unified look. Use "spot color" in your document by using color only in specific areas of the page. Also, pick up a color from your graphic in your text.

DTP POINTERS
Use spot color to attract the reader's eye.

Many of the Word graphic images included in this program are created in color. In Word, everything you key onto a page can be printed in color. You can choose from millions of different colors depending on your monitor and color printer. You have the capability to alter graphic images and the distribution of their colors through Microsoft Word Picture, the Picture or Object dialog boxes, and tools on the Picture toolbar.

Many flyers and announcements are prepared on personal computers and printed on either white or color paper and duplicated on a copy machine to help keep costs down. A color printer or color copier adds to the cost but can help the appeal of the document. If you are using a color printer, limit the color to small areas so it attracts attention but does not create visual confusion.

DTP POINTERS
Color can create a mood.

As an inexpensive alternative to printing in color, use color paper or specialty papers to help get your message across. Specialty papers are predesigned papers used for brochures, letterheads, postcards, business cards, certificates, etc., and can be purchased through most office supply stores or catalog paper supply companies such as *Paper Direct* and *Quill*. Be sure to choose a color that complements your message. Choose colors that match the theme of your document—orange for Halloween, green for spring, yellow for summer, or blue for water and sky.

Understanding Desktop Publishing Color Terms

When working in desktop publishing and using Word 97 you may encounter terms used to explain color. Here is a list of color terms along with definitions:

- *Balance* is the amount of light and dark in a picture.
- *Brightness* or *value* is the amount of light in a color.
- *Contrast* is the amount of gray in a color.
- *Color Wheel* is a device used to illustrate color relationships.
- *Complementary Colors* are colors directly opposite each other on the color wheel, such as red and green, which are among the most popular color schemes.
- *CYMK* is an acronym for cyan, yellow, magenta, and black. A color printer combines these colors to create different colors.
- *Dither* is similar to halftone. It is a method of combining several different-colored pixels to create new colors.
- *Gradient* is a gradual varying of color.
- *Grayscale* is a range of shades from black to white.
- *Halftone* is a process of taking basic color dots and combining them to produce many other colors. Your print driver can use halftoning to produce more shades of color.
- *Hue* is a variation of a color, such as green-blue.
- *Pixel* is each dot in a picture or graphic.
- *Resolution* is the number of dots that make up an image on a screen or printer—the higher the resolution, the higher the quality of the print.
- *Reverse* is a black background and white foreground or white type against a colored background.
- *RGB* is an acronym for red, green, and blue. Each pixel on your color monitor is made up of these three colors.
- *Saturation* is the purity of a color. A color is completely pure, or saturated, when it is not diluted with white. Red, for example, has a high saturation.

exercise 1

Creating a Flyer Using a Table

1. At a clear document screen, create the flyer in figure 5.8 by completing the following steps: (You will create a table similar to figure 5.1.)
   a. Change all the margins to 0.75 inches.
   b. Change the Zoom to Whole page.
   c. Click the Tables and Borders button (ninth button from the right) on the Standard toolbar.
   d. Click the Draw Table button (first button from the left) on the Tables and Borders toolbar. The arrow pointer will display as a pen.
   e. Position the pen in the upper-left corner, then drag to create the outer boundary lines of a table approximately 1 inch from all edges of the page. The size should be similar to figure 5.8. (Use your horizontal and vertical ruler bars to guide you.)
   f. Position the pen approximately 2 inches below the top boundary line of the table, then draw a horizontal line by clicking and dragging.

g. Position the pen approximately 2 inches above the bottom boundary line of the table, then draw another horizontal line by clicking and dragging.
h. Position the pen approximately 2½ inches from the right boundary line, then draw a vertical line by clicking and dragging.
i. Click the Draw Table button to turn this feature off.
j. Change the Zoom to Page width.

2. Insert the flyer text by completing the following steps:
   a. Position the insertion point inside the first cell, then insert *navigating.doc* located on your student data disk. Select the WordArt text and drag it to the center of the cell. (You will create text in WordArt in a later exercise.)
   b. Position the insertion point inside the first cell of the second row of the table and insert *sailing.doc* located on your student data disk. Click the Center Vertically button (ninth button from the right) on the Tables and Borders toolbar.
   c. Position the insertion point inside the second cell in the second row of the table and insert the sailboat picture in figure 5.8 by completing the following steps:
      (1) Click Insert, point to Picture, and then click From File.
      (2) At the Insert Picture dialog box, make sure the *Clipart* folder displays in the Look in: list box, then double-click the *Popular* folder.
      (3) Double-click *Sailboat.wmf* from the list box. (You can view the picture at the Insert Picture dialog box by clicking the Preview button that is the eighth button to the right of the Look in: list box.)
      (4) Click the Center Vertically button on the Tables and Borders toolbar.
   d. Position the insertion point inside the cell in the third row of the table, then insert *midwest.doc* located on your student data disk.
   e. Click the Center Vertically button on the Tables and Borders toolbar.
   f. Select the text in step 2d, then click the Center align button on the Standard toolbar.
3. Create the AutoShape form in figure 5.8 by completing the following steps:
   a. Display the Drawing toolbar.
   b. Click the down arrow to the right of the AutoShapes button on the Drawing toolbar, point to Basic Shapes, and then click the sun shape in the sixth row.
   c. Drag the crosshairs to the top of the table and draw the sun shape similar in size to the one in figure 5.8. (The shape may display above the cell and it may force the WordArt text to move above the cell also. This situation will be corrected in the next step.)
   d. Click to select the sun shape, then click Format, and then AutoShape. At the Format AutoShape dialog box, select the Wrapping tab, then select None in the Wrapping style section. Click OK or press Enter.
   e. With the sun shape selected, click the arrow on the Fill Color button on the Drawing toolbar and click Yellow in the fourth row and the third column.
4. View your flyer at Print Preview. Drag any boundary line in the table if the cells are not sized and located as in figure 5.8. (When you click on a line in a table, the arrow pointer should display as two vertical bars with two arrows pointing to the left and right; drag to move the line, then release the left mouse button when you are satisfied with the position.) If the flyer displays too high or low on the page, change the top and/or bottom margins to help center the flyer vertically on the page.
5. With the insertion point positioned inside the table, click Table, then Select Table. Click the down arrow to the right of the Borders button (sixth button from the left) on the Tables and Borders toolbar, then select the No Border button.
6. Save the document and name it c05ex01, sailing.
7. Print and then close c05ex01, sailing.

figure 5.8

- Smooth Sailing on the Internet
- Cruising an Intranet
- Ferrying E-Mail Messages and Faxes
- Launching a Web Page
- Charting a New Course—Changing Technology and Software

COMPUTER AND INFORMATION WORKSHOPS AND TRADE FAIR

MIDWEST COMMUNITY COLLEGE

Friday, July 17, 1998

8:30 a.m. to 3:30 p.m.

Register by phone: 555-3909

Adding Lines, Borders, and Special Effects to Text, Objects, and Pictures

As discussed in chapter 3, ruled lines can be used in a document to create a focal point, draw the eye across or down the page, separate columns and sections, or add visual appeal. Rules are generally thought of as single vertical, horizontal, or slanted lines in various line styles. Borders are generally used to frame text or an image with more than one side. Shading can be added to the background of a table, a paragraph, selected text, or as fill in a drawing object. Examples of lines, borders, shading, shadow, and 3-D effects are displayed in figure 5.9.

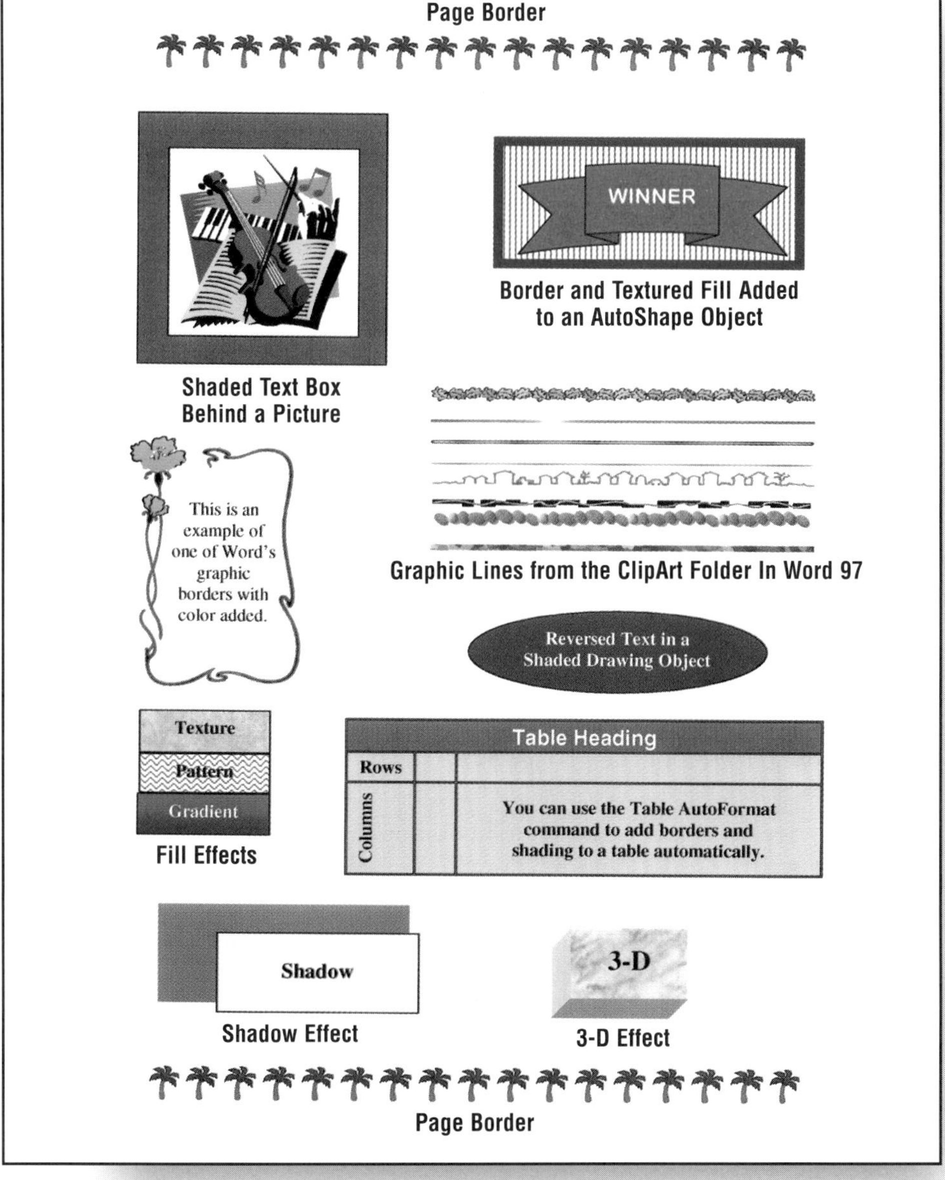

figure 5.9

Examples of Lines, Borders, and Shading

Adding Lines and Borders

Borders, like ruled lines, can be used to customize text, create interest, and attract attention to a headline in an announcement or flyer. You can add a border to any or all sides of a table, a paragraph, or selected text in a document. You can also add a border or an art border (such as a row of trees) to any or all sides of each page or section in a document. You can also add borders to text boxes, pictures, and imported pictures. When you draw an object, it automatically displays with a border around it—a thin line that defines its shape.

Line

Rectangle

Rules and/or borders can be drawn using the Line button or the Rectangle button on the Drawing toolbar, clicking the Border button on the Tables and Borders toolbar or the Formatting toolbar, or using the Borders and Shading dialog box from the Format menu. However, be sure to note the default color and size before using one of these features.

In addition, graphic borders are available in Word and accessed as any other clip art (available in the Clip Gallery, Frames and Borders category—additional borders are available on the program CD-ROM). Rules can even be created using a series of special symbols, as shown in figure 5.10.

figure 5.10

Using Symbols to Create a Ruled Line

DTP POINTERS
Bold text in shaded boxes to increase readability.

To add a line or border to selected paragraphs or text, position the insertion point where you want the line or border to appear, click Format, then Borders and Shading to display the Borders and Shading dialog box, as shown in figure 5.11. Next, select the Borders tab, then select one of the following: None, Box, Shadow, 3-D, or Custom in the Setting section. Select a line style from the Style list box and select a color from the Color list box. Finally, click in the preview box where you want the line or border to appear, or click a corresponding button in the preview box.

When a border is added to a paragraph(s) of text, the border expands as text is inserted. If a paragraph contains a border and you want to remove it, click None at the Borders and Shading dialog box.

To change the thickness of lines or borders, use the Line Style and Line Weight buttons on the Tables and Border toolbar or click the Line Style button on the Drawing toolbar. Use the Dash Style button to make borders dashed or dotted, and use the Line Color button to add color to borders and remove borders entirely.

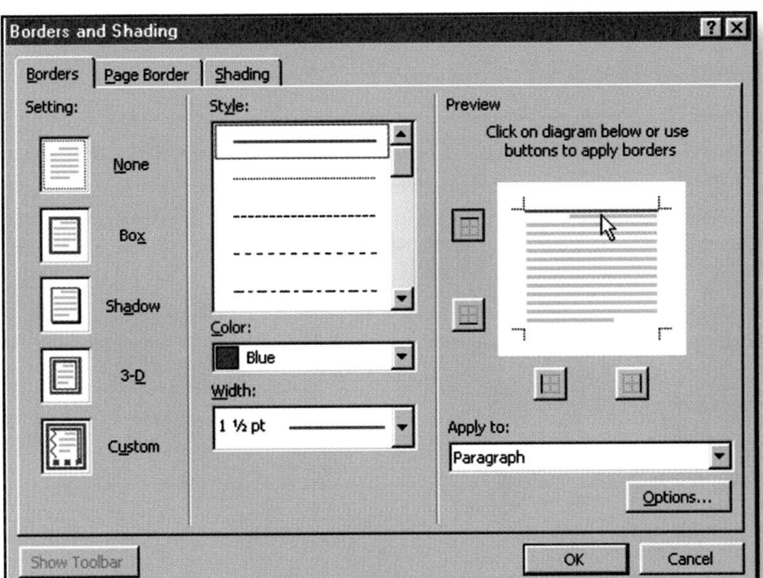

figure 5.11

Borders and Shading Dialog Box

Adding Lines and Borders to Tables

All tables by default have a ½ pt. black, single solid-line border that prints. To add a line or customized border to a table, display the Tables and Borders toolbar as shown in figure 5.2. Select the cells where you want the line or border to appear, then click any one or more of the following buttons to customize the line or border: Line Style, Line Weight, Border Color, and/or the Border button. If you prefer drawing the line or border, use the Draw Table button. Alternatively, you can use the Table AutoFormat command to add borders and shading to a table automatically.

To add a border to a table, click anywhere in the table. To add borders to specific cells, select only those cells, including the end-of-cell mark.

Adding a Page Border

As mentioned earlier, Word provides page borders that range from simple to highly ornate. Choose the art border that best compliments the content of your document. Refer to chapter 4 for additional information about using the Page Border option in the Borders and Shading dialog box.

Adding Shading to Design Elements

You can add shading to the background of a table, a paragraph, or selected text. Shading added to drawing objects—including a text box or an AutoShape—is called a *fill*. You can fill drawing objects with solid or gradient (shaded) colors, a pattern, a texture, or a picture.

Fill
Shading added to drawing objects.

Color can be effective in promotional documents by organizing information, creating focus and emphasis, producing contrast, and providing balance among other design elements. The reversed text in figure 5.9 creates a high degree of contrast.

DTP POINTERS
Use contrast to add interest and impact.

Adding Special Effects—Shadow and 3-D—to Lines and Drawing Objects

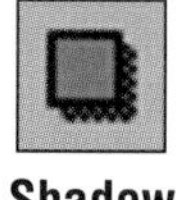

Shadow

You can add depth to lines and drawing objects by using the Shadow button (second button from the right) on the Drawing toolbar. To make adjustments to the shadow position, click Shadow Settings, and then click the appropriate buttons on the Shadow Settings toolbar, as shown in figure 5.12. You can add either a shadow or a 3-D effect to a drawing object, but not both.

figure 5.12

Shadow Palette and Shadow Settings Toolbar

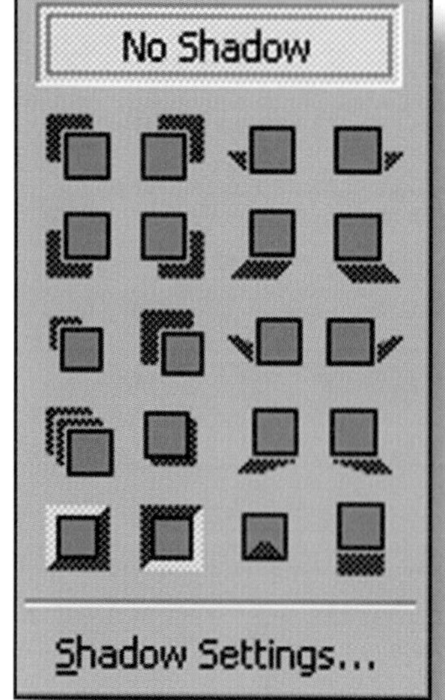

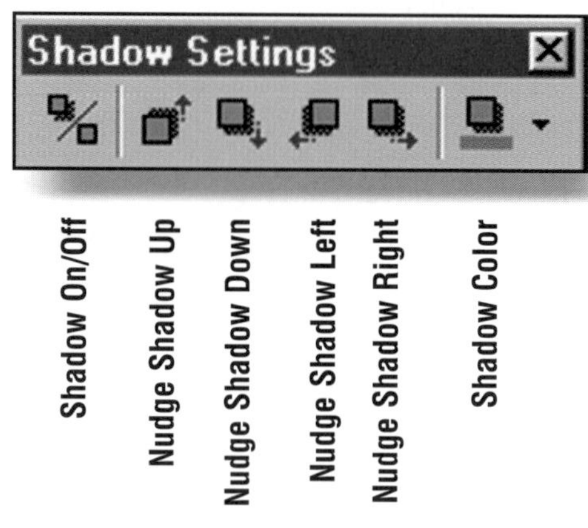

3-D

You can add a 3-D effect to lines, AutoShapes, and other drawing objects by clicking the 3-D button (last button) on the Drawing toolbar. You can modify any of the settings by clicking the 3-D Settings button, then clicking options to change its color, angle, direction, etc., at the 3-D Settings toolbar shown in figure 5.13. Experiment with these settings—you will be amazed by the possibilities these options provide. Figure 2.18 in chapter 2 was created by applying 3-D effects to text boxes.

figure 5.13

3-D Effects and 3-D Settings Toolbar

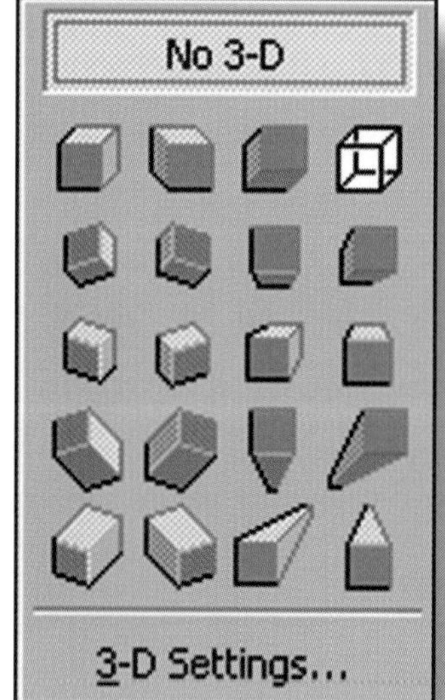

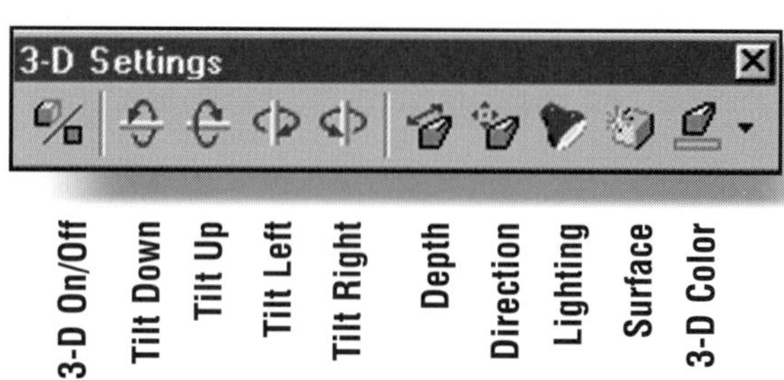

Creating Announcements

Announcements communicate or inform an audience of upcoming events. They may promote interest in events, but do not necessarily promote a product or service. For instance, you may have received an announcement for course offerings at your local community college or an announcement of an upcoming community event, sporting event, concert, race, contest, raffle, or a new store opening. Announcements, like flyers, are an inexpensive means of advertising.

Creating a Logo

In exercise 2, you will create a *logo*, which is a unique design that may be made up of combinations of letters, words, shapes, symbols, AutoShapes, WordArt objects, other drawing objects, or graphics. A logo may serve as an emblem for an organization or for a product.

Logo
A unique design that serves as an emblem for an organization or for a product.

For convenience in retrieving, a logo can be saved as an AutoText entry. AutoText entries can include frequently used phrases, pictures, graphic letterheads, graphics of digitized signatures, logos, or symbols. If you frequently use a logo in your documents, you may want to save the logo as an AutoText entry.

The logos in figure 5.14 were created using AutoShape forms, Word pictures, and WordArt to configure text. The *Float over text* option, located in the Insert Picture dialog box, was deselected to place the picture used in the McGuire logo inline where it was treated as regular text. By default, this option is selected causing an object to exist in the drawing layer, where you can position it in front of or behind text and other objects by using commands on the Draw menu. Also, you should select each design element in your logo, and group all of the elements as one unit.

The *Cajun Delights* logo and the picture in the *Lighthouse Inn* logo are Word 97 sample logos (C:\Msoffice\Office\Samples\Cajlogo.gif and Nwlogo.gif). WordArt was added to the Lighthouse logo. The *.gif* extension is a graphic file extension that stands for Graphics Interchange Format. This graphic format is frequently used on the Web. You cannot edit a *.gif* file in Word unless you save it as a Word document. If you selected a Typical Installation, you might not have the graphic filter necessary to read this file. If you selected a Custom Installation, the necessary graphic filters should be available. Read the contents of the Files of type list in the Insert Picture dialog box to see if the *.gif* or other file formats are available and compatible.

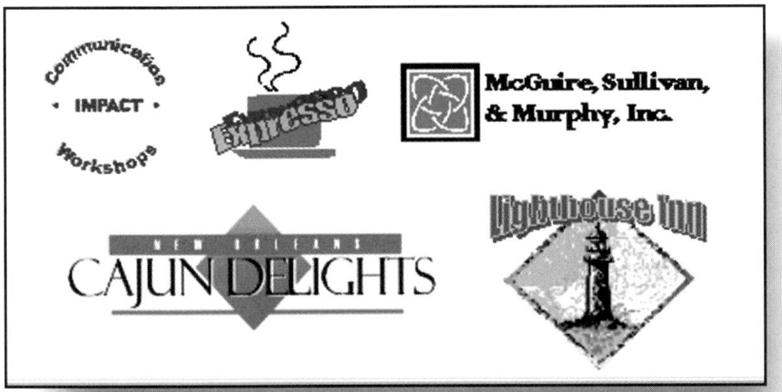

figure 5.14
Logo Examples

exercise 2

Creating a Seminar Announcement Using a Logo, Graphic Image, and Border

1. At a clear document screen, create the seminar announcement in figure 5.15 by completing the following steps:
   a. Click the Show/Hide ¶ button on the Standard toolbar to turn this feature on.
   b. Turn on kerning at 14 points and above.
   c. Display the Picture toolbar and Drawing toolbar.
   d. Click the Insert Picture button on the Picture toolbar.
   e. At the Insert Picture dialog box, make sure the location of your student data disk displays in the Look in: list box.
   f. Clear the check box to the left of the Float over text option located below the Advanced button. (This option places the object inline, in the current paragraph, where the object behaves like regular text.)
   g. Double-click *Celtic.wmf* located on your student data disk. (This graphic will become part of the company logo.)
   h. Click the Text Box button on the Drawing toolbar, drag the crosshairs to the right of the *Celtic* picture, and then create a text box approximately 0.65 inches in Height and 2.25 inches in Width. (Verify this setting by clicking Format, then Text Box, then select the Size tab.)
   i. Make sure None is selected as the Text Wrapping style for the text box.
   j. Position the insertion point inside the text box, then change the font to 18-point Colonna MT and key **McGuire, Sullivan**, press Enter, then key **& Murphy, Inc.**
   k. Select the text box, then click the down arrow to the right of the Line Color button on the Drawing toolbar and select No Line.
   l. Deselect the text box, then position the insertion point before the paragraph mark to the right of the graphic, and then press Enter four times.
   m. Click the Center align button on the Standard toolbar.
   n. Click Insert, Symbol, and then select *Monotype Sorts* at the Font drop-down list. Click the check mark symbol in the first row and the eighth column from the right. Click Insert, then Close.
   o. Key **Check Your Calendar and Reserve a Date!**, then press Enter five times. Select *Check Your Calendar...* and change the font to 22-point Footlight MT Light Bold Italic in Small caps. Press Ctrl + End.
   p. Key **1998 SUMMER EVENTS** in all caps, then press Enter five times. Select *1998 SUMMER EVENTS* and change the font to 20-point Footlight MT Light Bold and the Character Spacing to Expanded By 3.5 pts.
   q. Create a shaded box around *1998 SUMMER EVENTS* as shown in figure 5.15 by completing the following steps:
      (1) Select *1998 SUMMER EVENTS* along with one paragraph symbol above and below the line.
      (2) Click Format, then Borders and Shading.
      (3) Select the Borders tab and make sure None is selected.
      (4) Select the Shading tab. At the Fill color palette, select White in the first row and second column.
      (5) Click the down arrow to the right of Style in the Patterns section and select *25%*.
      (6) Click the down arrow to the right of the Color list box and select Green.

(7) Make sure that Apply to Paragraph has been selected.
(8) Click OK or press Enter, then press Ctrl + End.

r. Key **MSM Investment Seminars**, then press Enter three times. Select *MSM Investment Seminars* and change the font to 26-point Colonna MT Bold. Press Ctrl + End.

s. Change the font to 18-point Footlight MT Light, then insert the bullets in figure 5.15 by completing the following steps:
   (1) Click the Align Left button on the Standard toolbar.
   (2) Click Format, then Bullets and Numbering.
   (3) At the Bullets and Numbering dialog box, select the Bulleted tab, and then click on any bullet displayed. Click the Customize button.
   (4) Click the Bullet button, then select *Monotype Sorts* from the Font list. Click the diamond bullet in the fourth row and the second column from the left. Click OK or press Enter. In the Bullet position section, change the Indent at setting to 1.75 inches. In the Text position section, change the Indent at setting to 2.25 inches. Click OK or press Enter.
   (5) Key the following: **Friday, June 5**, press Enter; **Friday, June 12**, press Enter; **Friday, June 19**; then press Enter twice.

t. Change the font to 16-point Footlight MT Light Italic, then key **Followed by...**, then press Enter twice.

u. Click the Center align button on the Standard toolbar. Then, change the font to 18-point Footlight MT Light Bold (turn off italic) and change the font color to Green by clicking the down arrow to the right of the Font Color button on the Formatting toolbar and selecting Green from the color palette.

v. Key **Dinner and a performance of**, press Enter, key **the musical "Show Boat"**, then press Enter twice.

w. Click the Center align button on the Standard toolbar. Change the font to 12-point Footlight MT Light (turn off bold) and change the font color to Black, then key **Seminars are being held in our Chicago office on the dates listed above. Seminar attendees, along with their spouse or one guest, will be invited to join us for dinner and a performance of "Show Boat."** Press Enter three times.

x. Change the font to 12-point Footlight MT Light Italic, then key **More details and registration information will be forthcoming.**

y. Position the insertion point on the paragraph symbol below *Dinner and a performance of...* and insert the *Divider.wmf* picture located on your student data disk. Delete the paragraph symbol below the divider graphic. Click to select the divider and drag it to the center, then increase the size of the divider similar to figure 5.15 by clicking and dragging a corner-sizing handle. (If you hold down the Ctrl key as you drag a corner-sizing handle, the image remains centered.)

z. Create the page border in figure 5.15 by completing the following steps:
   (1) Click Format, then Borders and Shading, and then select the Page Border tab.
   (2) Click the down arrow to the right of the Art list box and select the border shown in figure 5.16. (The border will display in black.)
   (3) Change the Color to Green, then change the Width to 18 pt.
   (4) Click the Options button.
   (5) At the Border and Shading Options dialog box, change all the margin settings to 10 pt.
   (6) Click the down arrow to the right of the Measure from list box and select *Text*.
   (7) Make sure the Align paragraph border and table edges with page border option is deselected. The rest of the options should be selected. Click OK or press Enter.
   (8) Click OK or press Enter again.

2. View the document in Print Preview.
3. Save the document as c05ex02, flyer.
4. Print and then close c05ex02, flyer.

figure 5.15

McGuire, Sullivan, & Murphy, Inc.

✓*Check Your Calendar and Reserve a Date!*

1998 SUMMER EVENTS

MSM Investment Seminars

- Friday, June 5
- Friday, June 12
- Friday, June 19

Followed by...

Dinner and a performance of the musical "Show Boat"

Seminars are being held in our Chicago office on the dates listed above. Seminar attendees, along with their spouse or one guest, will be invited to join us for dinner and a performance of "Show Boat."

More details and registration information will be forthcoming.

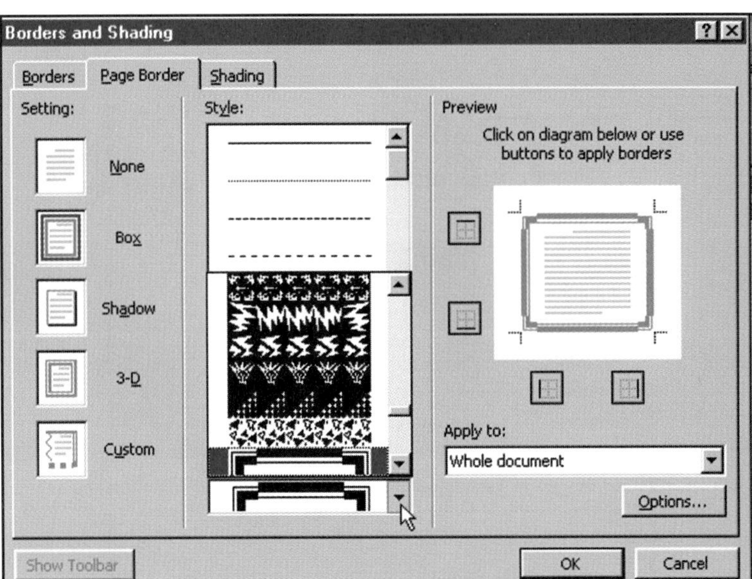

figure 5.16

Page Border for c05ex02, flyer

Creating Flyers

Flyers are generally used to advertise a product or service that is available for a limited amount of time. Frequently, you may find flyers stuffed in a grocery bag; attached to a mailbox, door handle, or windshield; placed in a bin near an entrance; or placed on a countertop for prospective customers to carry away. Examples of businesses that use flyers for advertising services include: lawn maintenance companies, babysitters, window washers, cleaning services, realtors, dentists, doctors, lawyers, and more. As you can see, this form of advertising is used by just about anyone.

Typically, flyers are one of the least expensive forms of advertising. The basic goal of a flyer is to communicate a message at a glance, so the message should be brief and to the point. For the flyer to be effective, the basic layout and design should be free of clutter—without too much text or too many graphics. Have the information arranged so it is easy to understand.

As you learned in chapter 1, use white space generously to set off an image or text. Also, consider directional flow in placing elements on a page. The left corner is usually read first. Consider your audience when choosing type sizes. The older your audience, the larger the print might need to be. Most important, always prepare a thumbnail sketch, which is like thinking on paper, before beginning a project.

DTP POINTERS
The upper left corner is usually read first.

DTP POINTERS
Consider your audience when choosing type size.

Creating a Flyer Using a Graphic Border

In exercise 3, you will create a flyer using a Word graphic border and insert text inside the border. Compare figure 5.17 to figure 5.18. Which flyer attracts your attention and pulls you in to read the text? Of course, figure 5.18 communicates more effectively because of the relevant graphic border and the varied typefaces, type styles, and type sizes. How many typefaces can you find in this document? (There are only two typefaces used in this flyer—Brush Script MT and Book Antiqua.)

A graphic border is inserted into a document like any other picture. Click Insert, then Picture. Size and position a graphic border using the sizing handles or use the options in the Format Picture dialog box.

figure 5.17

Flyer Before

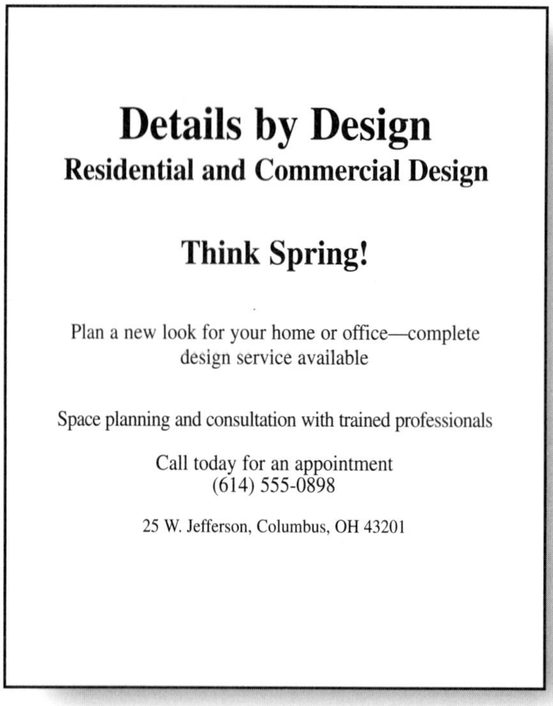

Details by Design
Residential and Commercial Design
Think Spring!
Plan a new look for your home or office—complete design service available
Space planning and consultation with trained professionals
Call today for an appointment
(614) 555-0898
25 W. Jefferson, Columbus, OH 43201

figure 5.18

Flyer After

Details by Design
Residential and Commercial Design
Think Spring!
Plan a new look for your home or office—complete design service available
Space planning and consultation with trained professionals
Call today for an appointment
(614) 555-0898
25 W. Jefferson • Columbus, OH • 43201

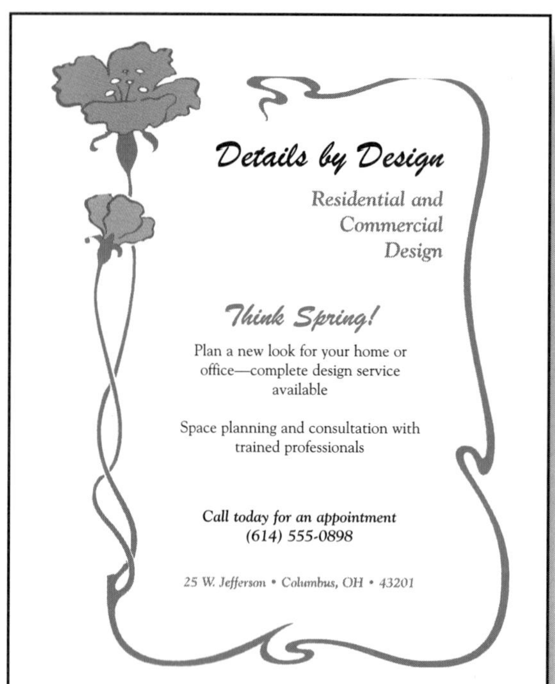

Using Microsoft Word Picture to Edit Pictures

Microsoft Word Picture is a graphic editor available within Word. If you do not have the original program where your graphic was created loaded on your computer, Word will place the image in a Microsoft Word Picture window where you can edit it.

Word recognizes a wide variety of picture formats dependent on the graphic filters installed with your program. Basically, there are two types of picture—*bitmaps*, that cannot be ungrouped, and *metafiles* that can be ungrouped, converted to drawing objects, and then edited by using tools on the Drawing toolbar. Pictures created in bitmaps are made from a series of small dots that form shapes and lines. Many scanned pictures are bitmapped. Bitmaps can not be converted to drawing objects, but they can be scaled, cropped, and recolored by using tools on the Picture toolbar. Most clip art is saved in metafile format (files named with a .wmf extension). Metafiles can be edited in Microsoft Word Picture; bitmap files cannot. However, bitmaps can be edited in Microsoft Paint, Microsoft Photo Editor, or the program in which they were created.

Bitmaps
Pictures made up of small dots that form shapes and lines.

Metafiles
Graphic files that allow images to be ungrouped and edited in Microsoft Word Picture.

You can invoke the graphic editor by double-clicking the image at your document window. However, occasionally, you may be returned to the Clip Gallery if you double-click on a particular image. In this case, first ungroup the image by clicking the D<u>r</u>aw button on the Drawing toolbar, clicking <u>U</u>ngroup at the Draw menu, clicking outside the image, then finally double-clicking the image again. (Ungrouping the image by using tools on the Drawing toolbar converts the image into an object that can be edited at Microsoft Word Picture.) You may also ungroup an image by clicking the image to select it, then right-clicking the mouse to access a shortcut menu where the Group option appears, then left-clicking the mouse to select the Group option.

An ungrouped object in the Microsoft Word Picture's special editing screen is shown in figure 5.19. While at the editing screen, an image can be grouped as one unit, ungrouped into separate components, rotated, recolored, scaled, realigned, redesigned, and cropped. Figure 5.19 shows an image recolored in Microsoft Word Picture using tools on the Drawing toolbar. You can also edit a picture by using the Format Picture or Format Object dialog boxes accessed through the F<u>o</u>rmat menu. More than one component of an image can be selected and altered at the same time by holding down the Shift key while clicking to select each component.

To exit this screen and return to your document screen, click <u>F</u>ile, then <u>C</u>lose to Return to Document X.

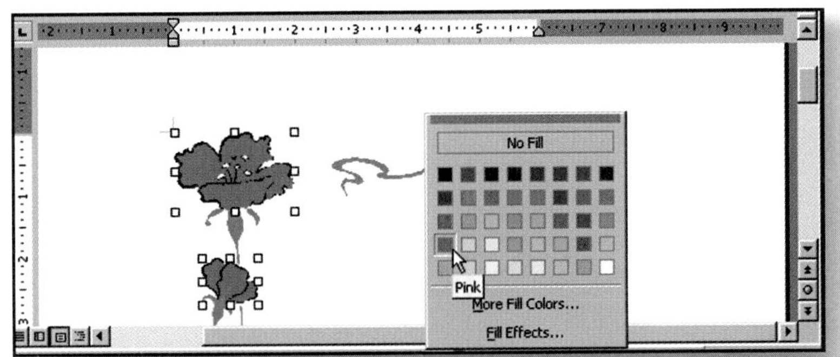

figure 5.19

Recoloring a Picture in Microsoft Word Picture

exercise 3

Creating a Flyer Using a Graphic Border

1. At a clear document screen, create the flyer in figure 5.20 by completing the following steps:
   a. Display the Drawing toolbar and Picture toolbar.
   b. Make sure the default font is 12-point Times New Roman.
   c. Turn on kerning at 14 points and above.
   d. Insert the picture *Nouvflwr.wmf* located on your student data disk.
   e. Click to select the picture, then change the size of the picture by completing the following steps:
      (1) Click the Format Picture button (third button from right) on the Picture toolbar.
      (2) At the Picture dialog box, select the Size tab.
      (3) Change the Height to 8.5 inches, then click inside the Width text box and a setting of approximately 5.97 inches should display.
      (4) Select the Position tab, then clear the Float over text option (click inside the check box to remove the check mark from the option).
      (5) Click OK or press Enter.
   f. Add color to the border by completing the following steps:
      (1) Double-click the picture to access Microsoft Word Picture.
      (2) Change the Zoom to Page width.
      (3) Click to select the large flower, then hold down the Shift key and click the small flower shown in figure 5.19.
      (4) Click the down arrow to the right of the Fill Color button on the Drawing toolbar and select Violet in the third row and the seventh column.
      (5) Hold down the Shift key as you click to select all the parts of the stems (may involve several selections), then click the down arrow to the right of the Fill Color button and select Green in the second row and the fourth column. Also, make sure the Line Color is Green.
      (6) Click File, then Close to Return to Document# or click the Close Picture button at the Edit Picture dialog box.
   g. Change the Zoom to 50%.
   h. Create a text box inside the graphic border by completing the following steps:
      (1) Click the Text Box button on the Drawing toolbar.
      (2) Drag the crosshairs inside the graphic border, then create a box about 0.25 inch from all sides of the graphic border.
      (3) Click Format, then Text Box, and make sure None is selected at the Wrapping tab.
      (4) Select the Colors and Lines tab, click the down arrow to the right of the Color list box in the Line section, and select No Line.
      (5) Click OK or press Enter.
   i. Position the insertion point inside the text box, then key the following text in 12-point Times New Roman (change the Zoom to 75%):
      Details by Design, press Enter.

Residential and, press Enter.
Commercial, press Enter
Design, press Enter five times.
Think Spring!, press Enter twice.
Plan a new look for your home or office—complete design service available., press Enter twice. (Use an em dash.)
Space planning and consultation with trained professionals., press Enter five times.
Call today for an appointment, press Enter.
(614) 555-0898, press Enter twice.
25 W. Jefferson • Columbus, OH • 43201 (create the bullet symbol by pressing the Num Lock key on the keypad to turn it on, holding down the Alt key, keying 0149 on the keypad, then turning off the Num Lock key).

j. Select *Details by Design*, then change the font to 36-point Brush Script MT with Shadow. Click the Align Right button on the Standard toolbar.
k. Select *Residential and Commercial Design*, then change the font to 16-point Book Antiqua Bold Italic and the font Color to Gray-50%. Click the Align Right button on the Formatting toolbar.
l. Position the insertion point before *Think Spring!* and press Ctrl + Shift + End to select to the end of the document, then click the Center align button on the Standard toolbar.
m. Select *Think Spring!*, then change the font to 28-point Brush Script MT in Green.
n. Select the next two paragraphs, then change the font to 14-point Book Antiqua.
o. Select *Call today for an appointment (614) 555-0898*, then change the font to 14-point Book Antiqua Bold Italic.
p. Select *25 W. Jefferson • Columbus, OH • 43201*, then change the font to 12-point Book Antiqua Bold Italic in Gray-50%.
q. Resize the text box if necessary.

2. View the document at Print Preview.
3. Save the document and name it c05ex03, border.
4. Print and then close c05ex03, border.

Details by Design

Residential and
Commercial
Design

Think Spring!

Plan a new look for your home or office—complete design service available.

Space planning and consultation with trained professionals.

Call today for an appointment
(614) 555-0898

25 W. Jefferson • Columbus, OH • 43201

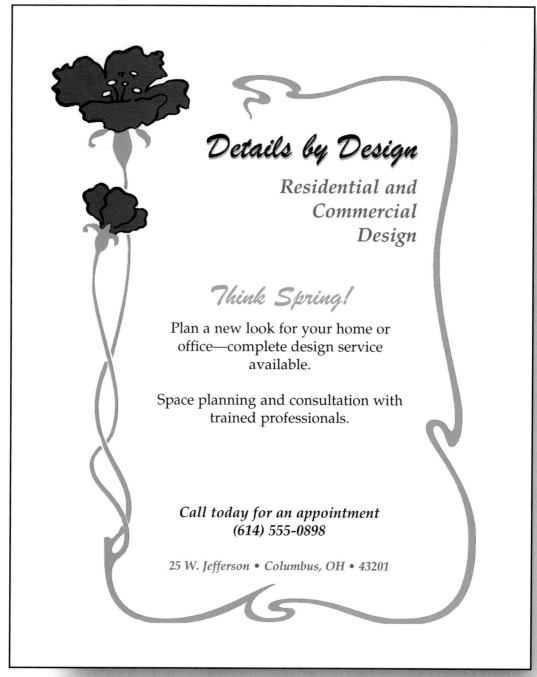

Customizing Pictures Using the Picture Toolbar

When you select a picture that you have inserted into a document, the Picture toolbar will appear with tools you can use to crop the picture, add a border to it, or adjust its brightness and contrast, as shown in figure 5.21. If the Picture toolbar does not appear, right-click the picture, and then click Show Picture Toolbar on the shortcut menu.

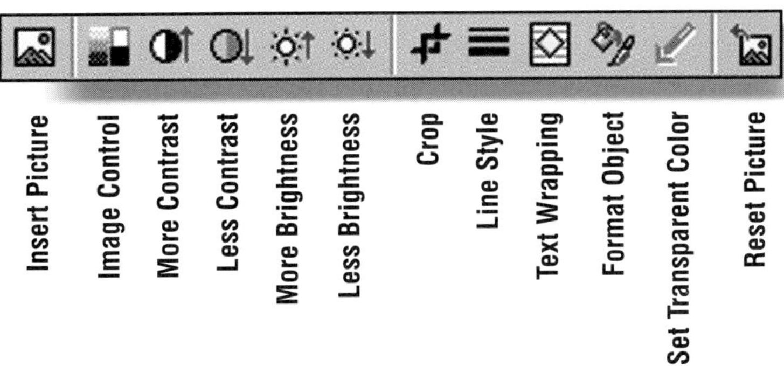

figure 5.21

Picture Toolbar

Using the Insert Picture Button

To quickly insert a picture into your document, display the Picture toolbar, then click the Insert Picture button (first button) on the Picture toolbar.

Insert Picture

Using the Image Control Button

Image Control

The Image Control button provides an option to change the color of an image into varying shades of gray, an option that converts a picture to black and white, and an option to lighten an image that can be layered behind text (watermark). The Image Control button options are illustrated in figure 5.22.

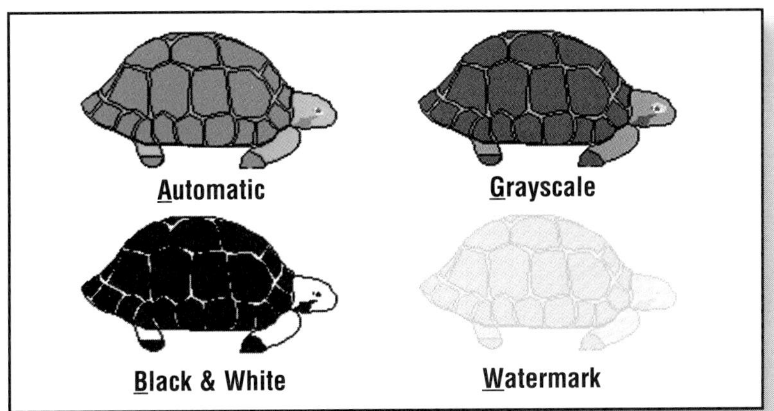

figure 5.22

Image Control Options

More Contrast

Using the Contrast and Brightness Buttons

The contrast and brightness options on the Picture toolbar are illustrated in figure 5.23. The Brightness option darkens or brightens a picture. Less contrast means a grayer picture; greater contrast means more black and white.

Less Contrast

Another way to adjust a picture's color, brightness, and contrast is through the Format Picture or Format Object dialog boxes. These options are found in the Image Control section of the Picture or Object tab as slider or percentage settings. Using these commands has the same effect as using the tools on the Picture toolbar.

More Brightness

Less Brightness

figure 5.23

Contrast and Brightness Settings

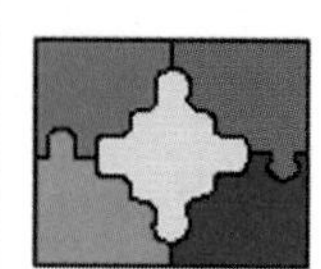
More Contrast

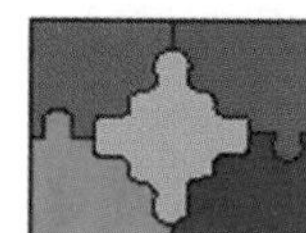
Less Contrast

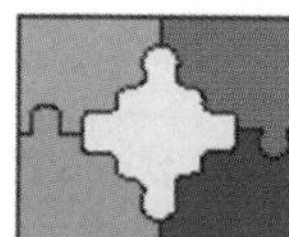
More Brightness

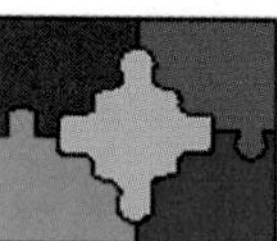
Less Brightness

Using the Crop Button

Crop
To trim vertical and horizontal edges off a picture.

To *crop* is to trim vertical and horizontal edges off of a picture as shown in figure 5.24. You can crop by using the cropping tool (seventh button from the left) on the Picture toolbar or holding down the Shift key as you drag a sizing handle. Photos are usually cropped to focus attention on a particular area of a picture (for instance, a person's face).

Crop

To use the cropping tool, select your image first, then click the Crop button on the Picture toolbar. Position the cropping tool, which displays as two overlapping right angles, on one of the sizing handles and drag. The corner handles enable you to crop from two sides. The center handles cut away part of the picture. As you drag the sizing handles, you see a dotted-line box that represents the picture's new size and shape. The picture adjusts to the size and shape of the box when you release the mouse button.

You can also crop pictures using the Format Picture dialog box. First select the image, then click Format, and then Picture. Select the Picture tab, then key specific increments in the Crop from text boxes. Click the Reset button to return to the original picture.

figure 5.24

Scaling and Cropping a Picture

Original Picture

Scaled Picture

Cropped Picture

Scaling or Resizing a Picture or Object

Scale
To increase or decrease the size of an image proportionally or nonproportionally.

To *scale* a picture or object is to increase or decrease the size of an image proportionally or nonproportionally, as shown in figure 5.24. To resize a picture or object, move the mouse over a sizing handle until it turns into a two-headed arrow. Drag a corner-sizing handle to scale a picture proportionally or drag a side handle to scale a picture nonproportionally.

In addition, you can scale or size a picture by selecting the picture, then clicking Format, Object, Size or Format, Picture, Size; or by clicking the right mouse and selecting Format Object or Format Picture. If you want your picture to be a specific size, key increments in the Height and Width boxes in the Size and Rotate group. If you want to scale your picture by percentages, use the Scale group, and enter percentages in the Height and Width boxes. To scale proportionally, select the Lock aspect ratio option. To scale in relation to the original size, select the Relative to original picture size option.

Using the Line Style Button

Line Style

You can add a border around a picture by clicking the Line Style button on the Picture toolbar. When you click the Line Style button, you can select any line style from the drop-down list or from the Format Picture dialog box that displays if you click the More Lines option at the bottom of the list. At the Format Picture dialog box you can add line color.

Using the Text Wrapping Button

Text Wrapping

You can place a picture anywhere in a document, even in a margin, and wrap text around it in many different ways. You can shape the text around the picture by editing the wrapping points. In addition, you can specify the amount of space between the picture and the text.

To wrap text around a picture, select the picture, then click the Text Wrapping button on the Picture toolbar. Select the Wrapping tab, then select the style of wrap that fits your needs. For example, the Square option wraps text around all four sides, the Tight option wraps text so that it conforms to the shape of the picture. Select None to remove text wrapping.

You can edit wrapping points on a picture to text wrap exactly where you want it. To edit wrapping points, select the picture, then click the Text Wrapping button on the Picture toolbar. Click Edit Wrap Points, then drag any one of the wrapping points that display around the picture. For an example of a document displaying editing points, see figure 5.25. The special pointer that displays as a small four-sided star lets you know you are in position to drag a wrapping point.

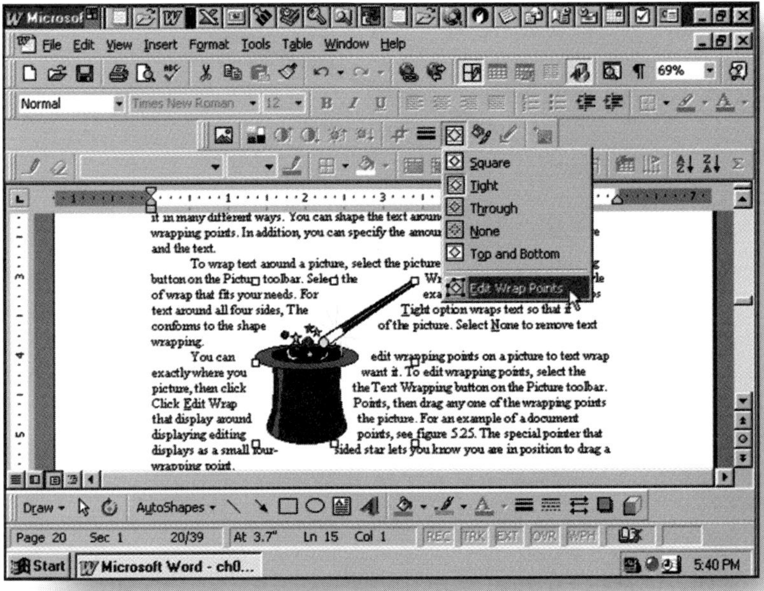

figure 5.25 *Using Wrapping Points*

Using the Format Object Button

Format Object

To quickly access the Format Object (or Format WordArt, Picture, or AutoShape) dialog boxes and all the options available within these dialog boxes, click the Format Object button (third button from the right) on the Picture toolbar. If you edit a picture with Microsoft Word Picture, Word converts the picture to an object.

Using the Transparent Color Button

Set Transparent Color

The Set Transparent Color button on the Picture toolbar offers a tool that can be used to alter colors in bitmap pictures. As discussed earlier, you cannot alter fill colors in bitmap pictures using Microsoft Word Picture or the Drawing tools. However, you can layer a transparent bitmap picture over a block of color to change the picture to the color of the block by using the Set Transparent Color button on the Picture toolbar, as shown in figure 5.26.

Transparent color can also be applied to a picture at the Colors and Lines tab of the Format Picture (Object) dialog box. In the Fill group, select a fill color, then click the Semi-Transparent option to lighten the shade of the color you have chosen.

figure 5.26

Using the Set Transparent Color Button

Using the Reset Button

Reset Picture

The Reset Picture button returns the picture to its original configuration.

Using WordArt in Announcements and Flyers

WordArt can distort or modify text to create a variety of shapes. This is useful for creating company logos and headings. It is especially useful for headlines in flyers and announcements. The shapes can exaggerate the text to draw in an audience. Many flyers that advertise sales use this feature to emphasize a discount and persuade an audience to act on this message.

Insert WordArt

You can create compelling text effects for your flyers by clicking the Insert WordArt button on the Drawing toolbar or by clicking Insert, pointing to Picture, then clicking WordArt. Select the template style you want at the WordArt Gallery dialog box, then key your text in the Edit WordArt Text dialog box.

The WordArt toolbar appears automatically whenever you select a WordArt object. Figure 5.27 displays the WordArt toolbar. WordArt objects are actually drawing objects and are not treated as text. You can use tools on the WordArt and Drawing toolbars to change a WordArt object in the same way you change a drawing object. For example—you can change its fill, line style, shadow, or 3-D effect. Experiment with the 3-D effect and shadows on headings for your flyers or announcements—the results can be unique and attention getting.

Refer to chapter 3 for additional information about WordArt.

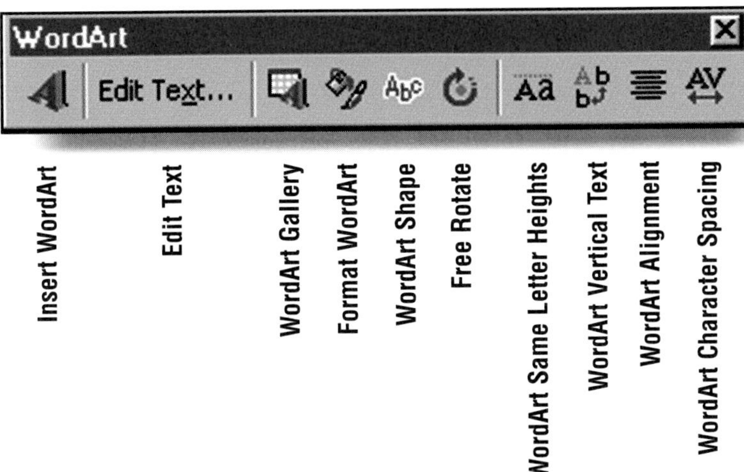

WordArt Toolbar

exercise 4

Creating a Flyer Using WordArt

1. At a clear document screen, create the flyer in figure 5.28 by completing the following steps:
   a. Open *jazz.doc* located on your student data disk.
   b. Save the document with Save As and name it c05ex04, jazz
   c. Display the Picture toolbar and Drawing toolbar.
   d. Make sure the default font is 12-point Times New Roman.
   e. Turn on kerning at 14 points and above.
   f. Create the heading, *Jazz Festival 1998* as shown in figure 5.28 by completing the following steps:
      (1) Position the insertion point on the paragraph symbol above the jazz graphic. Click the Insert WordArt button on the Drawing toolbar; display the WordArt toolbar; or click Insert, point to Picture, then click WordArt.
      (2) At the WordArt Gallery, select the style in the fourth row and the third column. Click OK or press Enter.
      (3) At the Edit WordArt Text dialog box, key **Jazz Festival 1998**, then change the Font to 48-point Wide Latin. Click OK or press Enter.
      (4) Click the Format WordArt button (fourth button from the left) on the WordArt toolbar, then select the Colors and Lines tab.
      (5) Click the down arrow to the right of the Color list box in the Fill section, then click the More Colors...button.
      (6) Select the Standard tab, then click the fourth purple pentagon from the top on the right side of the large color pentagon—see figure 5.29. Click OK or press Enter.(The new color will display below the color palette.)
      (7) Click the down arrow to the right of the Color list box again, then click the Fill Effects button. Select the Gradient tab.

(8) Make sure One color is selected in the Colors section and that purple displays in the Color 1 list box. Click Horizontal in the Shading styles section and click the second box in the first row of the Variants section. Click OK or press Enter.

(9) At the Colors and Lines tab, make sure the Line Color is Black. Click OK or press Enter.

(10) Click the Shadow button (second button from the right) on the Drawing toolbar, then click the Shadow Settings... button.

(11) Click the down arrow on the Shadow Color button (first button from the right) on the Shadow Settings toolbar and select Light Orange in the third row and the second column. Click the Close button (X) in the upper right corner of the Shadow Settings toolbar.

(12) If necessary, click and drag the heading to a position similar to figure 5.28. Also, resize the heading if needed.

g. Select the jazz picture, then scale the image by completing the following steps:

(1) Click the Format Picture button (third button from the right) on the Picture toolbar, then select the Size tab. (Make sure Lock aspect ratio and Relative to original picture are selected.)

(2) In the Scale section, change the percentages in the Height and Width text boxes to 120 percent. Click OK or press Enter.

(3) Drag the picture to the horizontal center of the page, then deselect the picture.

h. Create the heading below the jazz picture by completing the following steps:

(1) Click the WordArt button on the Drawing toolbar.

(2) At the WordArt Gallery, select the third style in the first row. Click OK or press Enter.

(3) Key **A Summer Event by the Lake**, then change the Font to 32-point Times New Roman. Click OK or press Enter.

(4) Click the WordArt Shape button (fifth button from the left) on the WordArt toolbar and select the fourth shape in the fourth row (Deflate Bottom).

(5) Click and drag the top-middle sizing handle slightly upward to increase the height of the heading. Drag the heading to a position similar to figure 5.28.

(6) Click the Format WordArt button (fourth button from the left) on the WordArt toolbar, select the Colors and Lines tab, then change the Fill Color to the same purple as in step f(6). The Line Color should remain Black. Click OK or press Enter.

(7) Click the Shadow button on the Drawing toolbar and select the fourth shadow style in the third row (Shadow Style 12).

(8) Click the Shadow button again, then click the Shadow Settings button.

(9) At the Shadow Settings toolbar, click the Shadow Color button, then select the Light Orange used in step f(11). Close the Shadow Settings toolbar.

i. Create the AutoShapes in figure 5.28 by completing the following steps:

(1) Click the AutoShapes button on the Drawing toolbar, point to Stars and Banners, and then click the second shape in the first row (Explosion 2).

(2) Drag the crosshairs to the left of the flyer text and draw a shape similar to figure 5.28.

(3) With the shape selected, click the down arrow to the right of the Fill Color button on the Drawing toolbar, then click Light Orange in the third row and second column.

(4) Make sure the Line Color is Black; otherwise, click the down arrow on the Line Color button.

(5) Click the Shadow button on the Drawing toolbar, then click the first style in the second row (Shadow Style 5).

(6) Click the WordArt button the Drawing toolbar, then select the style in the first row and the second column. Click OK or press Enter.

(7) At the Edit WordArt Text dialog box, key **Featuring**, then change the Font to 28-point Arial. Click OK or press Enter.

(8) Drag to position the WordArt text over the AutoShape as shown in figure 5.28. (You may need to resize the AutoShape.)

j. Create the AutoShape located to the right of the flyer in figure 5.28 by following steps similar to i(1) through i(8). Right click the AutoShape form and click Add Text, then key **Free** in 18-point Arial Bold. Experiment with rotating the shape—select the shape, click the Free Rotate button (third button from the left) on the Drawing toolbar, then position your insertion point over one of the green dots displaying in each corner. Drag the shape clockwise or counterclockwise to find a position that looks appropriate. (*Hint:* You may need to add space Before or After to vertically position the text correctly inside the AutoShape.)

2. View the flyer in Print Preview.
3. If necessary, drag to position any design elements similar to figure 5.28.
4. Save the document again with the same name, c05ex04, jazz.
5. Print and then close c05ex04, jazz.

Optional: Recreate the jazz flyer using the same text and graphic image, but use an asymmetrical design and layout. Consider using different lines and shapes to configure your headings and also using lines or symbols to help create a different directional flow. Name this exercise c05ex04x, jazz.

figure 5.28

Jazz Festival 1998

A Summer Event by the Lake

July 11-19, 1998

Grant Park
Michigan Avenue
Chicago

Blue Grass Jazz
Jazz Express
Duke Mitchell Duo
Jazzettes
Low Country Jazz
and more...

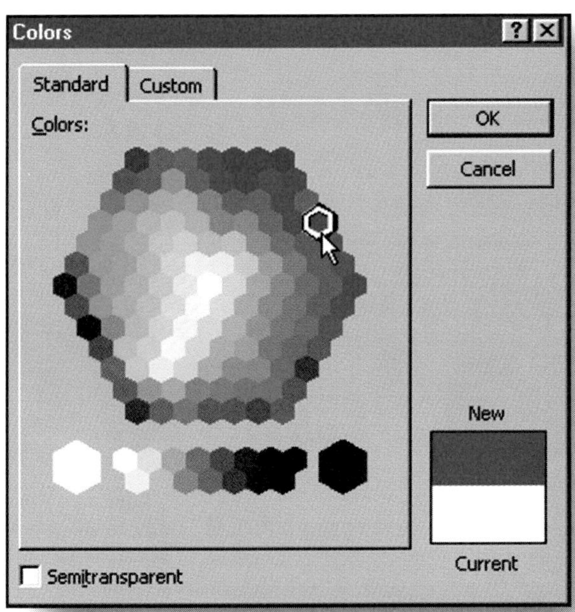

figure 5.29

Selecting a Shade of Purple

Using the Drawing Toolbar

The Drawing toolbar in figure 5.30 provides tools you can use to draw, manipulate, and format all kinds of drawing objects. A brief explanation of each tool is given in the next section. Additional information may be accessed from the Help menu.

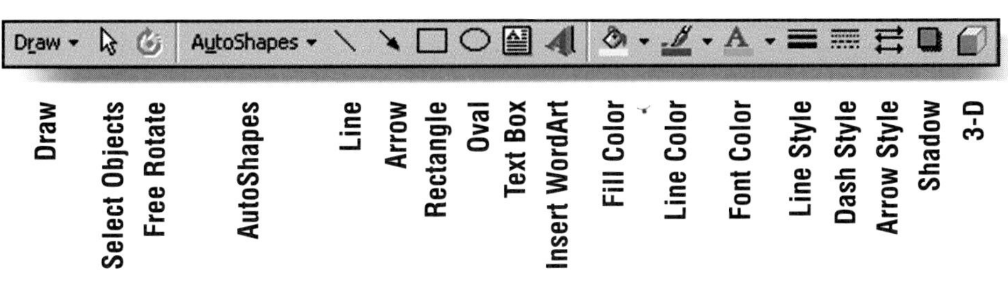

figure 5.30

Drawing Toolbar

Using the Draw Button

The Draw menu has many shape adjustment commands including grouping, ordering, using a grid, nudging, aligning, distributing, rotating, flipping, editing points, changing shape, and setting AutoShape defaults.

Group
Combining several components into one unit.

Using the Grouping and Ungrouping Commands

When you *group* pictures or objects, they function as a single unit. *Ungrouping* a group releases the individual components from a whole unit. Often you ungroup clip art to alter colors in separate parts of the image or to move separate parts. *Regrouping* an object or picture from a previous grouping returns the image to where it was before choosing the regrouping command. See figure 5.31 for examples of grouping and ungrouping.

Ungroup
Releasing individual components from a whole unit.

Regroup
Returning the object or picture to the previous grouping.

figure 5.31

Grouping and Ungrouping an Object

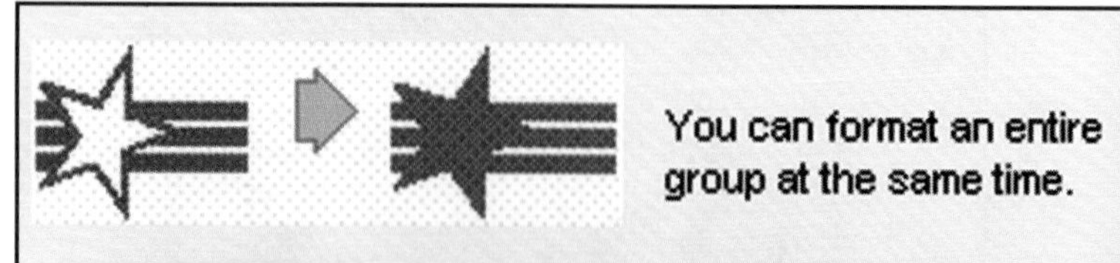

You can format an entire group at the same time.

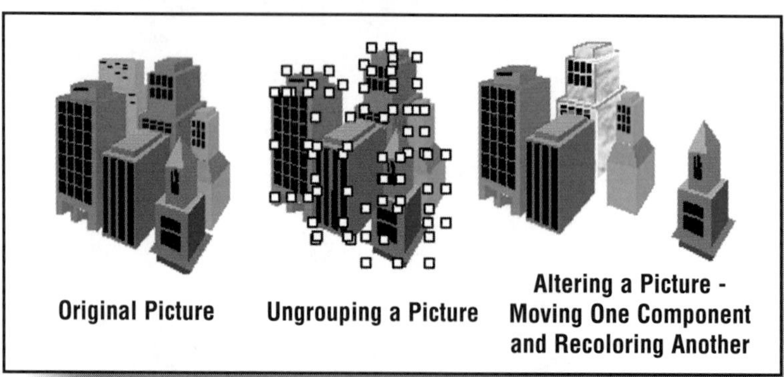

Altering a Picture - Moving One Component and Recoloring Another

Changing the Order of Pictures and Objects

When you create an object on top of another object, you create an overlapping stack. You can rearrange the stacked objects by using the Order command on the Draw menu. You can also stack groups and then change their stacking order. Figure 5.32 illustrates examples of the Order command.

Using the Order Command

Bring to Front places a selected object in front of others.

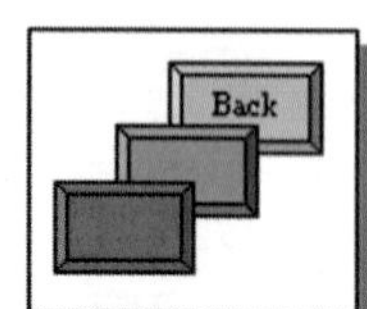

Send to Back places a selected object behind others.

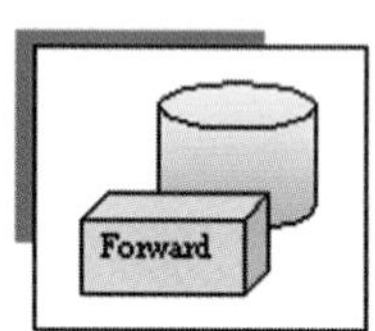

Bring Forward brings forward a single object or picture.

Send Backward sends a single picture or object backward.

Bring in Front of Text brings a picture in front of text.

Send Behind Text sends a picture behind text.

Using the Grid Option

The drawing grid is an invisible grid of lines that aligns drawing objects and draws straight lines. It acts as a magnet attracting your crosshairs as you draw lines at certain increments. At the Snap to Grid dialog box, you can change the spacing between the horizontal and vertical lines that make up the grid lines.

You can specify an exact location in your document where you want the Snap to Grid feature to be used by keying an increment in the Horizontal origin and/or Vertical origin text boxes in the Snap to Grid dialog box.

The Snap to shapes option automatically aligns objects with gridlines that go through the vertical and horizontal edges of AutoShapes.

Using the Nudge Option

To *nudge* an object is to move it in small increments. Select the object you want to nudge, click Draw, point to Nudge, and then click the direction you want to nudge the object. You can also nudge an object by selecting it and pressing the arrow keys. Press Ctrl and the arrow keys to nudge an object in one-pixel increments.

Nudge
To move something in small increments.

Using the Align or Distribute Command

You can align two or more drawing objects relative to each other by their left, right, top, or bottom edges, or by their centers (vertically) or middles (horizontally). By default, drawing objects align in relation to each other. However, you can select an option to align objects relative to the entire page. You can also use the Align or Distribute command to arrange objects equal distances from each other. To align several objects, select each while holding down the Shift key, click Draw, point to Align or Distribute, and then select a type of alignment. Figure 5.33 illustrates before and after results of aligning and distributing objects, as well as how to select and align objects using the Align command.

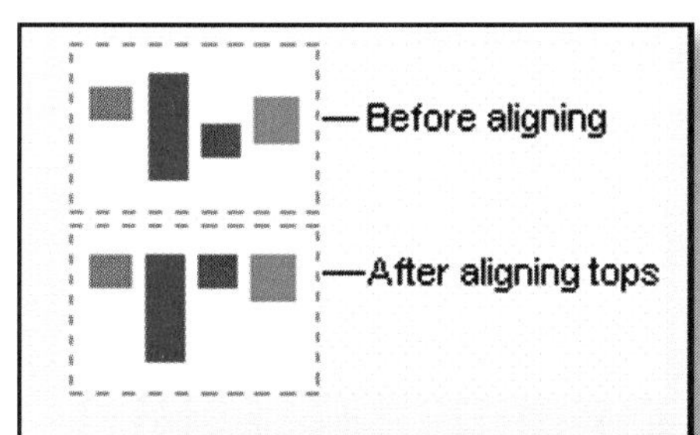

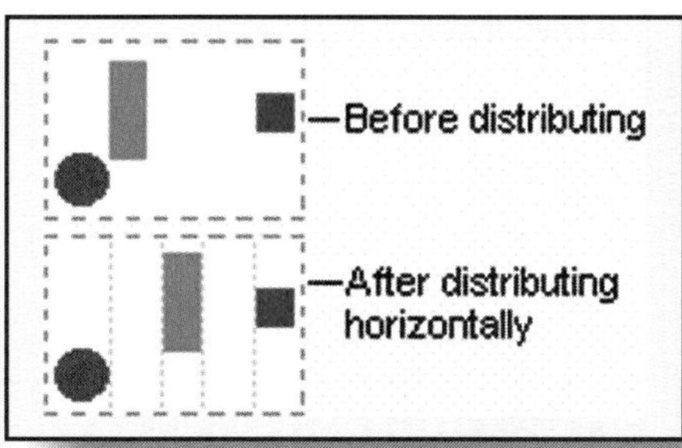

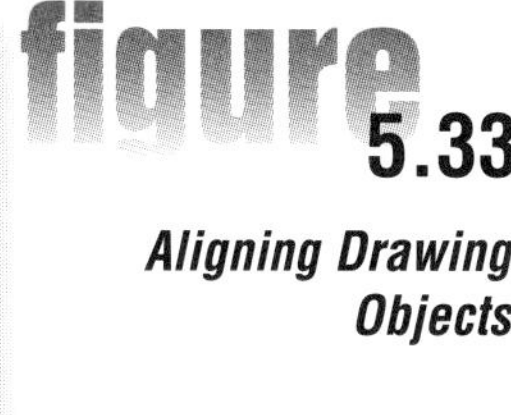

Aligning Drawing Objects

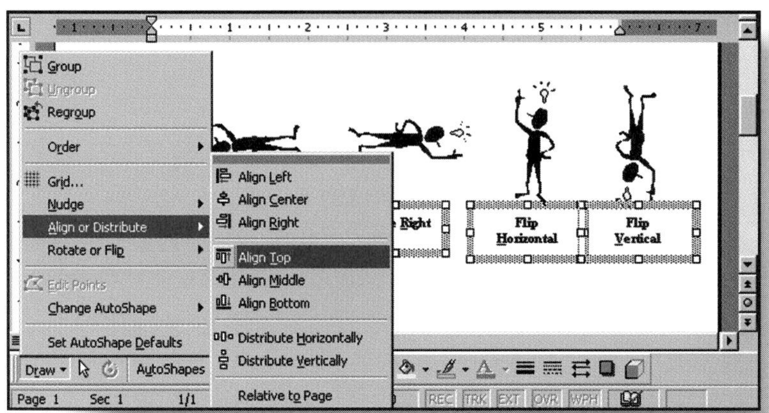

Using the Rotate or Flip Commands

You can rotate a drawing object or group of drawing objects 90 degrees to the left or right, or you can flip a drawing object or group of drawing objects horizontally or vertically. Select the object, click Draw, point to Rotate or Flip, then click the option you want to use. You can also click the Free Rotate tool on the Drawing toolbar.

If you want to rotate or flip a clip art image, select the image first, click Draw, and then click Ungroup. Next, click outside the image, then click to select the image again (you may need to click Regroup if the image is ungrouped into small segments). You may then click the Free Rotate button on the Drawing toolbar or use the Rotate or Flip commands from the Draw menu, as shown in figure 5.34. Ungrouping and regrouping the image converts the clip art image into an object, which can be edited using the Drawing tools.

5.34

Rotating and Flipping Pictures

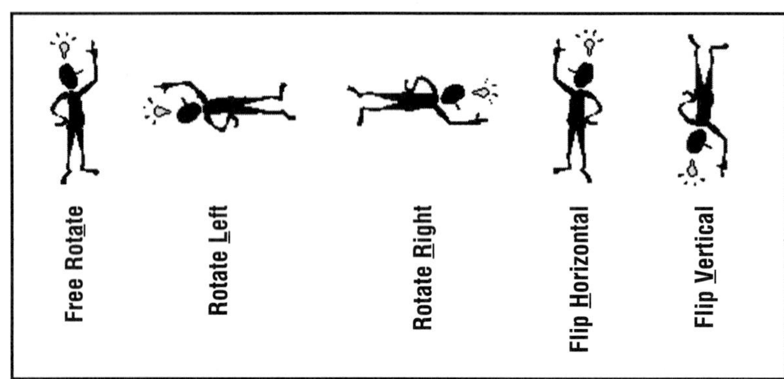

Using Editing Points

The Edit Points command on the Draw menu plots the points of your freehand drawing to enable you to modify it. You can point to any one of the editing points and drag it to a new location, altering the shape of your drawing. The drawing in figure 5.35 was created using the Scribble tool from the AutoShapes menu. Notice the editing points displayed in this figure. Envision how easily you could change the shape of this form.

5.35

Creating a Freehand Shape and Using Editing Points

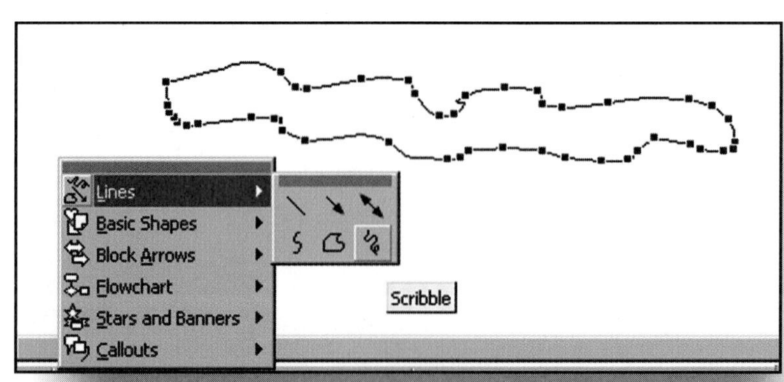

Using the Change AutoShapes Command

When you draw an AutoShape object in your document, then decide you want to use a different shape, select the object, click Draw, point to Change AutoShape, and then select a different AutoShape. The new shape will automatically replace the old one.

Using the Select Objects Button

Select Objects

The Select Objects button provides an option to draw a selection box around a picture or object, or a group of pictures or objects, as shown in figure 5.36. When editing separate components of a picture, click the Select Objects button on the Drawing toolbar, then draw a box around the component you want to change. Once you have drawn the box, release the left mouse button and sizing handles will display around the selected component. Then, drag to move the component, or recolor using the Format dialog box or the Drawing toolbar.

The Select Objects command is also helpful in selecting text, objects, or pictures that are positioned in different layers of the document. To select the picture, position the Select Objects pointer over the picture and click to select it, then click the Select Objects button to deselect it when you are finished.

Additionally, you can also select several objects by holding down the Shift key as you select each object.

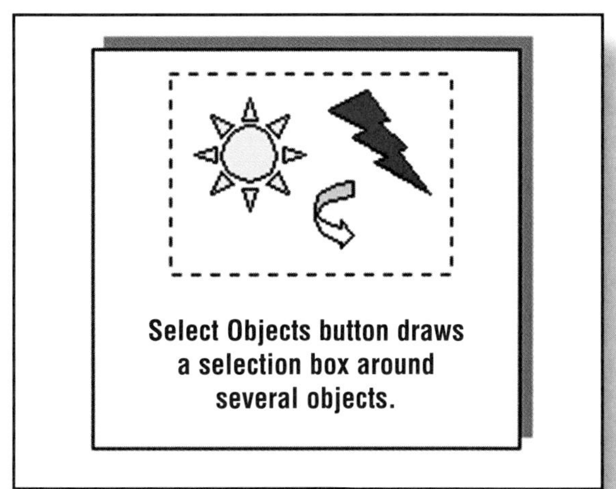

Select Objects button draws a selection box around several objects.

Select Objects Button

Using the Free Rotate Button

Free Rotate

You can rotate drawing objects to any degree by using the Free Rotate tool on the Drawing toolbar. Select the object or picture you want to rotate, click the Free Rotate button, then position the Free Rotate tool (circular arrow) over one of the green dots (rotation handles) that will display around the image, drag it in a desired direction, then release the left mouse button. See figure 5.37 for a rotated object. (If the Free Rotate button is grayed and inaccessible, ungroup your picture first, group it again, and then try using the Free Rotate tool.)

Using the Free Rotate Button

Using the AutoShapes Button

AutoShapes

The AutoShapes button opens a menu of shapes in six categories. These six categories open up palettes that enable you to select objects. Each of the categories offers a variety of shapes to work with to create visual impact. The AutoShapes palettes can be removed from the menu and placed in the document screen for easy access, as shown in figure 5.38 by dragging the title bar at the top of the menu.

AutoShapes Palettes

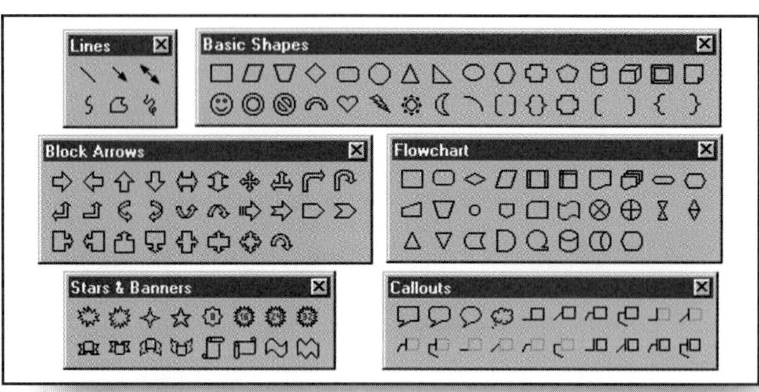

Using the Line, Arrow, Rectangle, and Oval Buttons

You can draw straight lines as well as vertical, horizontal, or lines at 15-, 30-, 45-, 60-, 75-, or 90-degree angles if you hold down the Shift key as you draw. Use the Arrow button to draw lines with arrowheads. The Shift key will cause the same effects as the Line button. If you hold down the Shift key as you draw a Rectangle shape, you will create a square. If you hold down the Shift key as you draw an Oval shape, you will create an ellipse or a circle.

Using the Text Box Button

Text Box

Use the Text Box button to create a container for text, pictures, or objects. You can double-click a text box to quickly display the Format Text Box dialog box. Using the dialog box is an efficient way to make several formatting changes at once. Refer to chapter 3 for additional information and figures concerning text boxes.

Using the Insert WordArt Button

Insert WordArt

WordArt creates text with special effects. You can pour text into a shape, flip or stretch letters, condense or expand letter spacing, rotate or angle words, or add shading, colors, borders, or shadows to text. Refer to chapter 3 for additional information and samples. See figure 5.39 for examples of WordArt.

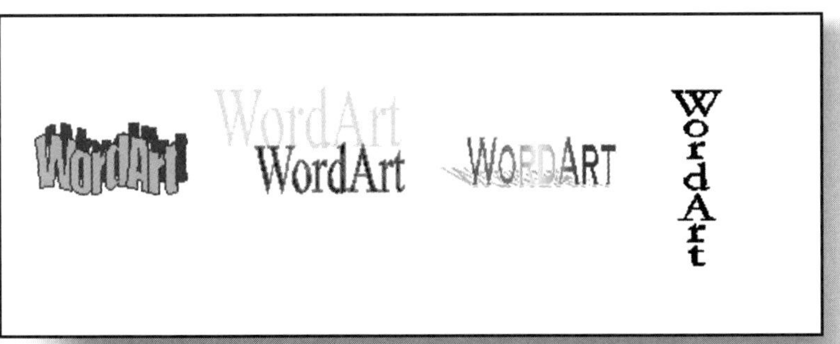

figure 5.39

Examples of WordArt

Using the Fill Color Button

Fill Color

The Fill Color option fills a selected object with color, or sets the default fill color if no object has been selected. You can select any color that is shown in the color palette that displays when you click the down arrow to the right of the Fill Color button on the Drawing toolbar. In addition, you can select from a larger palette of colors by clicking the More Fill Colors button or create a custom color at the Custom tab. Clicking the Fill Effects button provides palettes of various gradients, textures, patterns, or pictures as shown in figure 5.40.

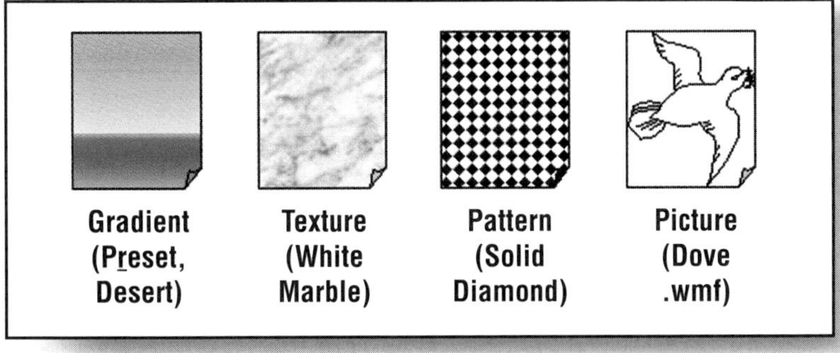

figure 5.40

Examples of Fill Effects

Using the Line Color, Font Color, Line Style, Dash Style, and Arrow Style Buttons

The Line Color button colors a selected line (or a line selected around a shape), or sets the default line color if no line is selected. The Font Color button colors the text for selected objects or sets the default if no font color is selected. The Line Style button changes the line width or sets the default if one has not been selected. The Dash Style button provides various types of dashes that can be used on different line styles and arrow styles. See figure 5.41 for examples created from each of these buttons.

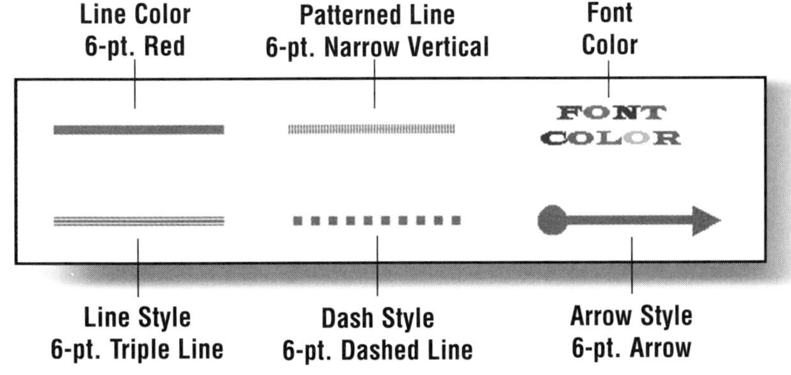

figure 5.41

Examples of Line Colors, Font Colors, Line Styles, Dash Styles, and Arrow Styles

Using the Shadow Button

Shadow

The Shadow button adds a shadow style to a selected object. The Shadow tool was described in greater detail earlier in the chapter. Refer to figure 5.12 for the Shadow palette and the Shadow Settings toolbar. See figure 5.42 for examples of different shadow styles. The effects of the Shadow button make the images seem to lift off the page.

Examples of Shadows

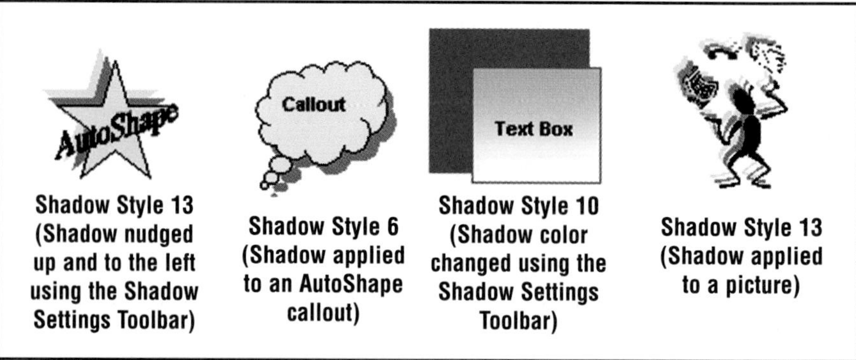

Using the 3-D Button

3-D

The 3-D button applies a three-dimension effect to a selected object or it sets the default if no object is selected. The 3-D Settings toolbar provides tools to make numerous adjustments to 3-D objects. You can tilt the shape up, down, left, or right to control its perspective. You can add depth, change the lighting source, or change the surface type to add additional effect. You can also change the color of the 3-D effect. See figure 5.43 for examples of enhanced 3-D objects.

Examples of 3-D Effects

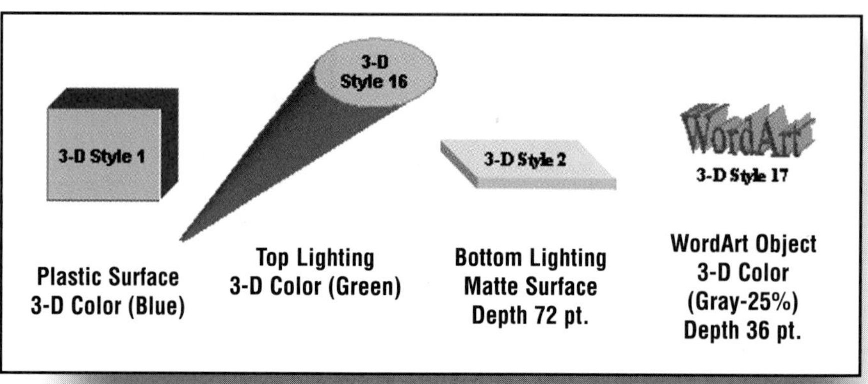

In exercise 5, you will create a flyer for the grand opening of a video store. You will open a partially completed document, then complete the document to make it an effective, attention-getting flyer. Dark red and bright yellow are two dominant colors in the graphic image. These colors are used throughout the flyer to establish a connection to the graphic and to attract attention at a glance. WordArt was used to configure *Grand Opening* in a shape that emphasizes grandness and excitement. You will create a map to provide detailed directions to the video store.

exercise 5

Creating a Flyer with a Map, Picture, WordArt, and AutoShapes

1. Create the video flyer shown in figure 5.44 by completing the following steps:
   a. Open *grand opening.doc* from your student data disk.
   b. Save the document with Save As and name it c05ex05, video.
   c. Display the Picture toolbar and Drawing toolbar.
   d. Click the Show/Hide ¶ button on the Standard toolbar to turn this feature on.
   e. Flip the movie picture located in the left corner of the flyer by completing the following steps:
      (1) Double-click the picture to enter Microsoft Word Picture.
      (2) At the Microsoft Word Picture screen, click to select the picture, then click the Draw button on the Drawing toolbar, point to Rotate or Flip, then click Flip Horizontal.
      (3) If the Rotate or Flip command is grayed and inaccessible to you, complete the following steps:
         (a) Click the Select Objects button on the Drawing toolbar. Position the crosshairs in the upper left corner of the image grid, hold down the left mouse button, drag the dashed box to the lower right corner of the image grid, and then release the mouse button. (When the mouse is released, the graphic may display in numerous segments.)
         (b) Click the Draw button on the Drawing toolbar, then click Group. (The graphic will display as one unit.)
         (c) Click the Draw button, point to the Rotate or Flip, then click Flip Horizontal.
      (4) Click File, then click Close & Return to c05ex05, video.doc.
   f. Select the heading, *Show It Again Video,* change the font to 28-point Braggadocio (or a similar font), then click the Center align button on the Formatting toolbar. Deselect the text box containing the heading. (The heading was created in a text box to make it easier to move and position the heading if necessary.)
   g. Create the stars in the upper right corner by completing the following steps:
      (1) Click the AutoShapes button on the Drawing toolbar, point to Stars and Banners, and then click the 5-Point Star located at the end of the first row.
      (2) Drag to draw and position the star similar to figure 5.44.
      (3) Select the star, click the down arrow to the right of the Fill Color button on the Drawing toolbar, and then click Yellow in the fourth row of the color palette.
      (4) Click the down arrow to the right of the Line Color button on the Drawing toolbar, then click Black in the first row.
      (5) With the star still selected, click the Shadow button on the Drawing toolbar, then click the third style in the first row (Shadow Style 3).
      (6) Create another star shape as shown in figure 5.44 by using Drag and drop editing by completing the following steps:
         (a) Make sure the Drag-and-drop editing option has been selected in the Tools menu (click Tool, Options, select the Edit tab, and click the Drag–and-drop text editing check box).
         (b) Right-click the star in step 1g(5) and continue holding down the right

mouse as you drag a copy of the star slightly below and to the left of the first star. Click Copy Here at the shortcut menu.

(c) With the second star selected, change the Fill Color to Dark Red in the first column of the second row of the Fill Color palette and change the Shadow to the third shadow style in the first row of the Shadow palette (Shadow Style 3).

(7) Group the two stars by clicking on one star, holding down the Shift while clicking on the second star, then clicking the Draw button on the Drawing toolbar, and then clicking Group.

(8) With the stars selected, click Format, then Object. Make sure None is selected at the Wrapping tab. Click OK or press Enter.

h. Create the callout in the picture by completing the following steps:

(1) Click AutoShapes on the Drawing toolbar, point to Callouts, and then click the Cloud Callout in the first row.

(2) Drag to draw and position the callout similar to figure 5.44.

(3) Position the insertion point inside the callout, change the font to 12-point Times New Roman Italic, and then key **"Please, pass the popcorn..."**.

i. Configure the heading, *Grand Opening*, in WordArt by completing the following steps:

(1) Position the insertion point on the fifth paragraph symbol below *Show It Again Video* (or approximately 3.7 inches from the top edge of the page).

(2) Click the Insert WordArt button on the Drawing toolbar, then select the WordArt style in the fourth column of the first row. Click OK or press Enter.

(3) At the Edit WordArt Text dialog box, key **Grand Opening**, then change the font to 72-point Impact. Click OK or press Enter.

(4) With the heading selected, click the down arrow to the right of the Fill Color button on the Drawing toolbar, then select Dark Red in the first column of the second row of the color palette. Then, change the Line Color to Dark Red.

(5) With the heading still selected, click the Shadow button on the Drawing toolbar. Select the first shadow style in the first row.

(6) Click the Shadow button again, then click the Shadow Settings button. Click the down arrow to the right of the Shadow Color button (last button) on the Shadow Settings toolbar, then click ***Gray-25%*** in the last column of the fourth row.

(7) Close the Shadow Settings toolbar.

(8) Drag the WordArt object to a position similar to figure 5.44.

j. Select the bulleted text and change the font to 26-point Britannic Bold (or a similar font).

k. Create the map in the bottom right corner of the flyer, as shown in figure 5.44, by completing the following steps:

(1) Click to select the text box positioned in the bottom right corner of the flyer, then click the Line Style button on the Drawing toolbar and select *2 1/4 pt.*

(2) Click the down arrow to the right of the Line Color button on the Drawing toolbar and select Dark Red in the first column of the second row. Deselect the text box.

(3) Click the Line button on the Drawing toolbar, hold down the Shift key, and then drag the crosshairs from the center of the top border downward to the

center of the bottom border as shown in figure 5.44. (Change the Line Color back to Black and the line style back to ¾ pt.)

(4) Click the Line button again and draw a diagonal line beginning in the upper left corner continuing to the bottom right corner as shown in figure 5.44.

(5) Click the Rectangle button on the Drawing toolbar, draw a small rectangle above the diagonal line, right-click the mouse, and then select Add Text from the shortcut menu. Change the font to 10-point Times New Roman, then key **Main**. Position the rectangle similar to figure 5.44, then click the Line Color button and select No Line.

(6) Click to select the box in step k (5), then hold down the Ctrl key as you drag a copy of the box to where *Ogden* is located in figure 5.44. Replace *Main* with **Ogden**.

(7) Drag another copy of the rectangular box and position it where the solid black box is located in figure 5.44, then select the box, remove *Ogden*, and change the Fill Color to Black.

(8) Click the AutoShapes button on the Drawing toolbar, point to Callouts, and then select the second callout in the second row (Line Callout 2). Drag to create the callout and position it as shown in figure 5.44. Position the insertion inside the callout, click the Center align button, then change the font to 10-point Times New Roman Bold. Key **Show It Again Video,** press Enter and remove the bold, then key **504 E. Ogden**. Add a Light Yellow fill color. (You may need to resize the callout to fit the words.)

(9) Create the arrow shape by clicking the AutoShapes button on the Drawing toolbar, pointing to Block Arrows, then clicking the arrow in the second column of the second row (Up-Down Arrow). Drag and draw the arrow inside the text box as shown in figure 5.44. Right-click the mouse, select Add Text, key **N** and **S**.

l. Group the map so that it can be moved easily within the flyer if repositioning is necessary. Click on each component of the map as you hold down the Shift key, click the Draw button, and then click Group from the Draw menu.

m. Change the Zoom to Whole Page.

n. Select the stars you created in step g (1) through g (7), then hold down the Ctrl key as you drag a copy of the stars to the bottom left corner of the flyer—see figure 5.44. With the stars still selected, click the Draw button, point to Rotate or Flip, then click Flip Vertical.

2. View the flyer in Print Preview and make sure all the design elements display as shown in figure 5.44. Select and drag any elements that are not properly positioned in the flyer.
3. Save the document again with the same name, c05ex05, video.
4. Print and then close c05ex05, video.

figure 5.44

Show It Again Video

Grand Opening

- **Rent two videos, get one FREE**
- **FREE popcorn—opening day**
- **Great selection**

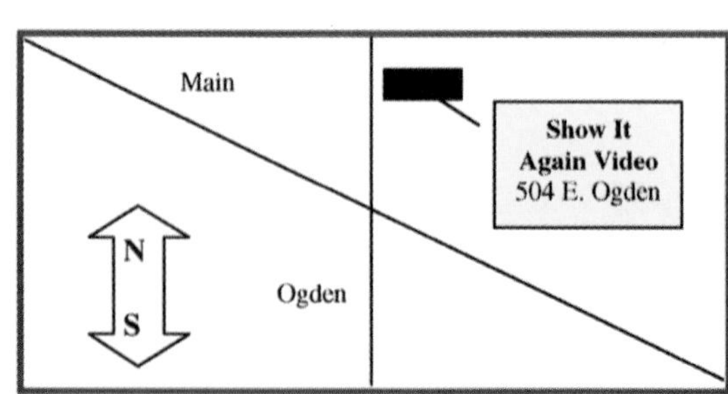

chapter summary

- Flyers and announcements are generally considered some of the least expensive means of advertising. Clearly define your purpose and assess your target audience before preparing a flyer or announcement. Flyers are generally used to advertise a product or service that is available for a limited amount of time. An announcement communicates or informs an audience of upcoming events.
- When creating headlines for flyers or announcements, select typefaces that match the tone of the document and type sizes that stress important information. A headline should be a dominant visual element, set significantly larger than the words that follow.
- Graphics added to a flyer or announcement can add excitement and generate enthusiasm for the publication. A simple graphic demands more attention and has more impact than a complex one.
- Use color in a publication to elicit a particular feeling, emphasize important text, attract attention, organize data, and/or create a pattern in a document. Limit the color to small areas so it attracts attention but does not create visual confusion.
- In planning a flyer or announcement, use a table to organize text, graphics, and other design elements on the page.
- Borders and lines can be used in documents to aid directional flow, add color, and organize text to produce professional-looking results.
- Clip art images can be altered and customized using tools on the Picture toolbar.
- Two basic graphic file formats include bitmap and metafile formats. Bitmapped pictures can not be ungrouped, while metafile pictures can be ungrouped, converted to drawing objects, and then edited by using tools on the Drawing toolbar. Pictures created in bitmaps are made from a series of small dots that form shapes and lines. Bitmaps cannot be converted to drawing objects, but they can be scaled, cropped, and recolored by using tools on the Picture toolbar.
- Metafiles can be edited in Word's graphic editor, Microsoft Word Picture.
- Use WordArt to distort or modify text to create a variety of shapes.
- Create your own shapes and images using Word's Drawing toolbar. You can draw shapes using AutoShapes or draw shapes freehand. Additional enhancements can be applied to your shapes using buttons on the Drawing toolbar.
- A text box can be used to position text, pictures, or objects above or below the text layer. A text box does not automatically resize for additional content.
- With buttons on the Drawing toolbar, you can add fill color, gradient, pattern, texture, and a picture to an enclosed object, change thickness and color of the line that draws the object, rotate, align, and change the position of the object.
- When objects overlap, use the Bring to Front and Send to Back buttons on the Drawing toolbar. You can also move an object in front or behind text and position an object in a stack.
- With the Group button on the Drawing toolbar, you can group two or more objects or sections of an object together as a single object. You can also ungroup objects or sections of an object using the Ungroup button.
- With the drawing grid turned on, an object is pulled into alignment with the nearest intersection of grid lines.
- Selected items can be aligned using the Align or Distribute command from the Draw menu.

commands review

	Mouse/Keyboard
Table	Click Table, Draw Table; click the Tables and Borders button on Standard toolbar; click View, Toolbars, Tables and Borders; right-click on toolbar, click Tables and Borders
WordArt	Click Insert, Picture, WordArt; click the Insert WordArt button on Drawing and WordArt toolbars
Microsoft Word Picture	Double-click picture in document window
Drawing Toolbar	Click Drawing button on Standard toolbar; right-click toolbar, click Drawing; or click View, Toolbars, Drawing
Picture Toolbar	Right-click on Standard toolbar, click Picture; or click View, Toolbars, Picture
AutoShapes	Click Insert, Pictures, AutoShapes; click the AutoShapes button on Drawing toolbar
Free Stuff	Click Help, Microsoft on the Web, Free Stuff; Click Insert, Picture, Clip Art, click Connect to Web for additional clips button

check your understanding

Terms: Match the terms with the correct definitions by writing the letter (or letters) of the term on the blank line in front of the correct definition.

- A Announcement
- B Flyer
- C Group
- D WordArt
- E Text box
- F Gradient
- G Nudge
- H Pixel
- I Ungroup
- J Drawing toolbar
- K Picture toolbar
- L Crop
- M Logo
- N Scale
- O Resolution
- P Contrast

_____ 1. With this Word feature, you can distort or modify text to create a variety of shapes.

_____ 2. A gradual varying of color.

_____ 3. To trim vertical and horizontal edges off a picture.

_____ 4. Selecting individual components from a whole unit.

_____ 5. Each dot in a picture or graphic.

_____ 6. To increase or decrease the size of an image.

_____ 7. The number of dots that make up an image on a screen or printer.

_____ 8. This type of document communicates or informs an audience of an upcoming event.

_____ 9. This toolbar includes buttons that are used to create shapes, rotate objects, add fill and effects, access WordArt, group and ungroup objects, align and distribute objects, add shadows, and apply 3-D effects.

_____ 10. A unique design that may be made up of combinations of letters, words, shapes, or graphics that serve as an emblem for an organization or a product.

_____ 11. This box positions text, pictures, or objects in the layer above or below the text layer.

_____ 12. To move an object in small increments.

True/False: Circle the letter T if the statement is true; circle the letter F if the statement is false.

T F 1. A complex graphic demands more attention and has more impact than a simple graphic.

T F 2. Generally, the upper right side of a document is read first.

T F 3. To display the Drawing toolbar, click Tools, then Draw.

T F 4. A grouped picture or object functions as a single unit.

T F 5. Bitmap pictures can be converted to drawing objects and customized using tools on the Drawing toolbar.

T F 6. Use the Select Objects tool to select an object positioned below the text layer.

T F 7. To draw a square shape using the Rectangle button on the Drawing toolbar, hold down the Ctrl key as you draw the shape.

T F 8. To reverse a selected object from top to bottom, click Flip Horizontal at the Rotate or Flip command.

T F 9. Once objects have been grouped, they cannot be ungrouped.

T F 10. If you rotate an AutoShape containing text, the shape rotates but the text does not.

T F 11. Hold down the Shift key and select each object you want to align using the Align or Distribute command from the Draw menu.

T F 12. Text automatically wraps around all sides of a text box.

skill assessments

Assessment 1

Create a flyer similar to figure 5.45 and include the following specifications:

1. Use your own layout and design ideas.
2. Use either portrait or landscape orientation.
3. Sketch a thumbnail of your document.
4. Use a table as the framework for your document.
5. Use WordArt for the heading.

6. Select an appropriate picture or watermark—size, scale, or crop if necessary. (The rose picture in the sample solution is *Flower.wmf.* The image of a single rose was ungrouped, copied using drag-and-drop editing, and rotated in Microsoft Word Picture.)
7. Use appropriate spot color.
8. Key the text from figure 5.45.
9. Select an appropriate page border.
10. Save the document as c05sa01, gardens.
11. Print c05sa01, gardens with the table borders displayed.
12. Remove the table borders, print c05sa01, gardens again, then close the document.
13. At a clear document window, open *document evaluation checklist.doc.*
14. Print one copy of the form.
15. Evaluate your flyer according to the guidelines on the form. Attach the form to the back of c05sa01, gardens.

figure 5.45

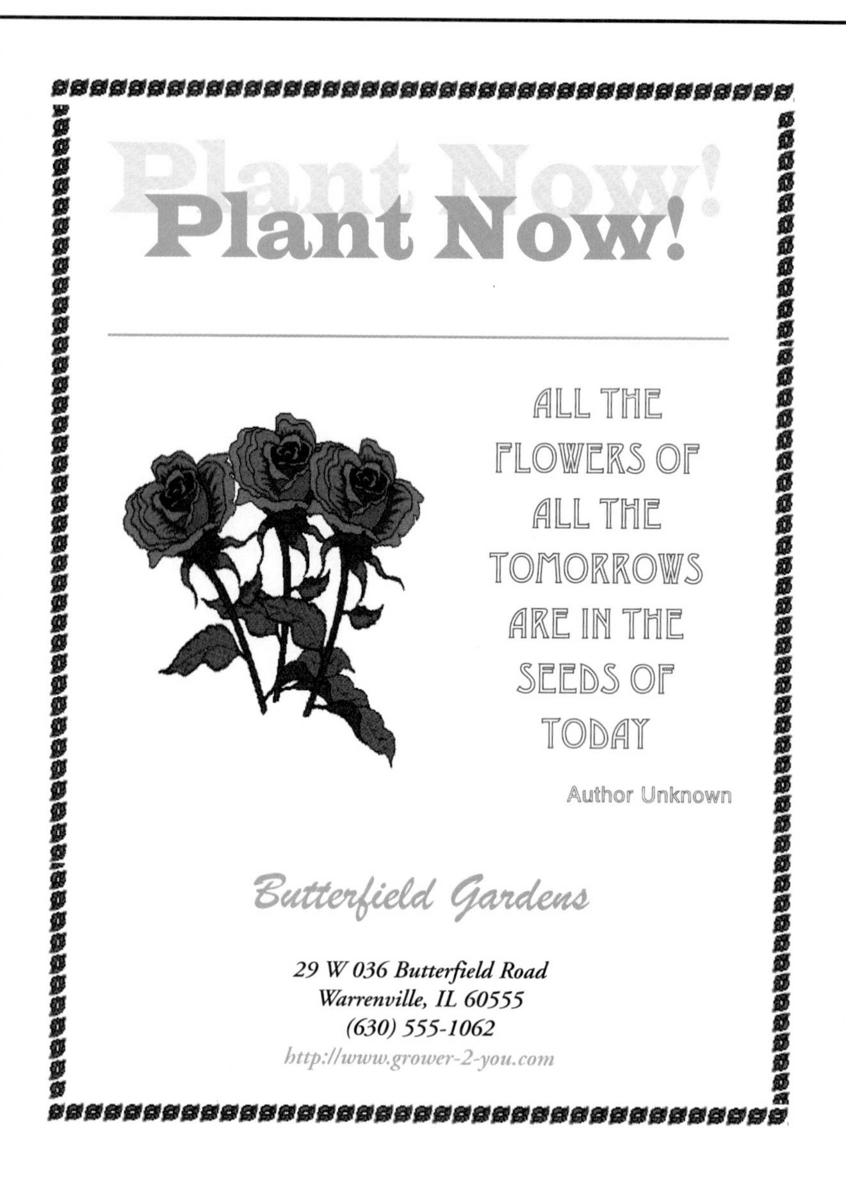

Assessment 2

You are volunteering in the office of your son's junior high school and are well-known for your desktop publishing skills. You have been asked to create a flyer advertising a writing workshop in April. (Figure 5.46 is a sample solution—use your own creative ideas for the layout and design of your document.)

1. Create a flyer and include these elements:
   a. The headline *Writing is for Everyone*.
   b. A line that reads *Parents and Students in Grades 7–9....*
   c. A line that reads *Make writing a family affair at a special workshop*.
   d. The following bulleted items in your choice of bullet style:

      Explore creative writing
      Attend dynamic sessions
      Participate in writing a short story
      Meet with the authors
      Celebrate learning
      Visit the library display
      Enjoy refreshments
      Shop at the Book Fair
      Win a door prize

   e. Location, date, and time of the workshop, which is *Spring Hill Junior High School, Friday, April 24, 1998, from 2 to 4 p.m.*
   f. The slogan *Milton School District...a great place to learn!*
2. Consider creating a thumbnail sketch to help you organize your ideas. Be creative. Use any desktop publishing features you have learned to produce an appealing flyer. (The watermark in the sample solution is a symbol located in the Wingdings font.)
3. Save the document and name it c05sa02, writing.
4. Print and then close c05sa02, writing.
5. At a clear document window, open *document evaluation checklist.doc*.
6. Print one copy of the form.
7. Evaluate your flyer according to the guidelines on the form. Attach the form to the back of c05sa02, writing.

figure 5.46

Sample Solution

Writing is for Everyone

PARENTS AND STUDENTS IN GRADES 7-9...

Make writing a family affair at a special workshop

- Explore creative writing
- Attend dynamic sessions
- Participate in writing a short story
- Meet with the authors
- Celebrate learning
- Visit the library display
- Enjoy refreshments
- Shop at the Book Fair
- Win a door prize

Spring Hill Junior High School
Friday, April 24, 1998
From 2 to 4 p.m.

MILTON SCHOOL DISTRICT...

a great place to learn!

Assessment 3

You are working in the Dallas office of Universal Packaging Company. Your company is well known for its involvement in environmental issues. On April 21, several Dallas businesses will offer free seminars, flyers, brochures, etc., in an effort to promote public awareness and involvement in Earth Day 1998. Complete the following task:

1. Create the document shown in figure 5.47 with the handwritten specifications.
2. Save the document and name it c05sa03, earth.
3. Print and then close c05sa03, earth.

figure 5.47

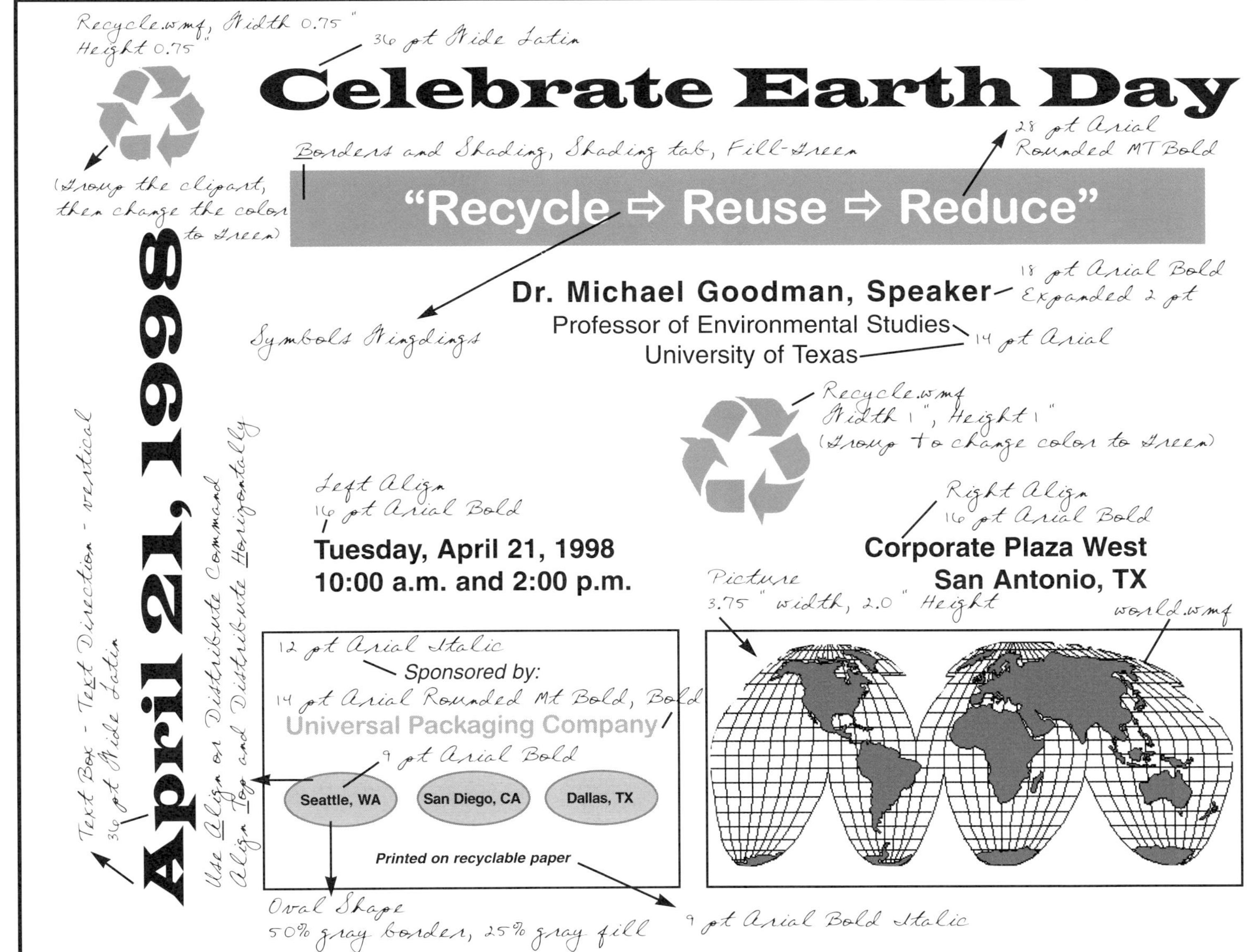
Recycle.wmf, Width 0.75"
Height 0.75"
36 pt Wide Latin
Celebrate Earth Day
(Group the clipart, then change the color to Green)
Borders and Shading, Shading tab, Fill-Green
28 pt Arial Rounded MT Bold
“Recycle ⇨ Reuse ⇨ Reduce”
18 pt Arial Bold Expanded 2 pt
Dr. Michael Goodman, Speaker
Symbols Wingdings
Professor of Environmental Studies
University of Texas
14 pt Arial
Recycle.wmf
Width 1", Height 1"
(Group to change color to Green)
Text Box - Text Direction - vertical
36 pt Wide Latin
April 21, 1998
Use Align or Distribute Command
Align Top and Distribute Horizontally
Left Align
16 pt Arial Bold
Tuesday, April 21, 1998
10:00 a.m. and 2:00 p.m.
Right Align
16 pt Arial Bold
Corporate Plaza West
San Antonio, TX
Picture
3.75" width, 2.0" Height
world.wmf
12 pt Arial Italic
Sponsored by:
14 pt Arial Rounded Mt Bold, Bold
Universal Packaging Company
9 pt Arial Bold
Seattle, WA
San Diego, CA
Dallas, TX
Printed on recyclable paper
Oval Shape
50% gray border, 25% gray fill
9 pt Arial Bold Italic

Assessment 4

You are employed at Smith & Barney, a regional accounting firm in Atlanta, GA. You have volunteered to coordinate the annual office golf outing. You scheduled the date at a local golf course and are now ready to create an announcement to send to all the employees. You need a reply from the employees interested in attending, so include a response form at the end of the announcement. Design an announcement using the following guidelines and text: (Figure 5.48 is a sample solution—use your own creative design ideas.)

1. Prepare a thumbnail sketch.
2. Use appropriate fonts—vary the size and style of each.
3. Use at least one special character.
4. Use a vertical or horizontal line, graphic border, or page border (optional).
5. Use an appropriate graphic image, WordArt object, or a watermark (text or graphic).
6. Use spot color.
7. Include the following information:
   - Date: June 26, 1998.
   - Reply needed by June 1, 1998.
   - Kendall Pointe Golf Course.
   - Tee-Off Times—Beginning at 9:00 a.m. (every 15 minutes).
   - Set up your own foursome or you will be assigned to a group.
   - Provide your handicap.
   - Indicate whether you are going to stay for dinner.
   - Dinner: 7:00 p.m. in the Kendall Pointe Clubhouse.
   - Sign up for Prize Raffle.
   - Prizes will be awarded for low gross score, low net, low front nine, low back nine, longest drive, and closest to the pin.
8. Save your document and name it c05sa04, golf.
9. Print and then close c05sa04, golf.

figure 5.48

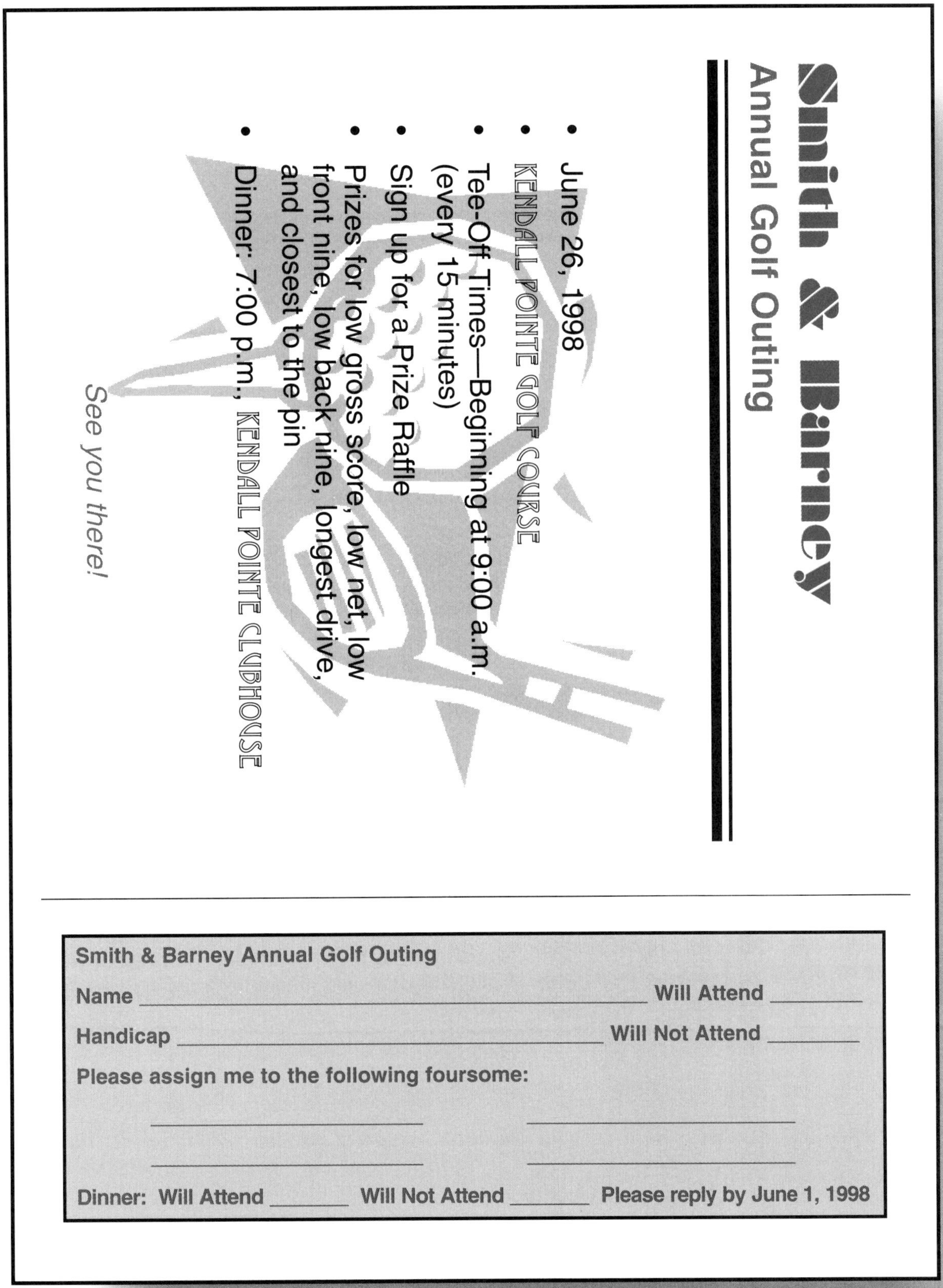

Smith & Barney

Annual Golf Outing

- June 26, 1998
- KENDALL POINTE GOLF COURSE
- Tee-Off Times—Beginning at 9:00 a.m. (every 15 minutes)
- Sign up for a Prize Raffle
- Prizes for low gross score, low net, low front nine, low back nine, longest drive, and closest to the pin
- Dinner: 7:00 p.m., KENDALL POINTE CLUBHOUSE

See you there!

Smith & Barney Annual Golf Outing

Name ______________________________ **Will Attend** ________

Handicap ___________________________ **Will Not Attend** ________

Please assign me to the following foursome:

________________________ ________________________

________________________ ________________________

Dinner: Will Attend _______ **Will Not Attend** _______ **Please reply by June 1, 1998**

creative activity

Activity 1

Collect three examples of flyers and/or announcements and evaluate them according to the guidelines presented in the document, *document evaluation checklist.doc*. Use any of the flyers and announcements that you started collecting in chapter 1. Include at least one example of a flyer or announcement that demonstrates: poor layout and design; no graphic or one that does not relate to the subject; poor use of fonts, sizes, and styles; and a message that is unclear. Complete the following steps:

1. Open *document evaluation checklist.doc*.
2. Print three copies of the form.
3. Complete and attach an evaluation form to each publication.
4. Recreate one of the flyers incorporating your own ideas and formatting. You do not have to reconstruct the poor example. However, the poor example will show the greatest amount of improvement.
5. A few possible suggestions for improving your document are to include: appropriate fonts, sizes, and styles; reverse; WordArt; special characters; color paper; color graphics, watermarks, and/or text; horizontal or vertical lines; borders, shadow, or 3-D effects, etc.
6. Create a thumbnail sketch first.
7. Format and key the document.
8. Save your document and name it c05ca01, example.
9. Print and then close c05ca01, example. Turn in the evaluation forms and examples along with c05ca01, example.

Activity 2

1. Use Word's Help feature to learn more about flyers. *Hint:* Click Contents and Index at the Help menu, select the Index tab, key **Getting Results – Flyer**, and then click the Display button. (*Getting Results* is a component included with a typical installation of Microsoft Office 97.) *Getting Results* may not be available if you installed standalone Word.
2. If *Getting Results* is available to you, select one of the topics listed, read the "how to" information, experiment with applying this information to a flyer, then present the information and demonstrate your findings to the class. (Ask you instructor if you may work with another classmate in a "team presentation.")

chapter SIX

Creating Brochures

PERFORMANCE OBJECTIVE

Upon successful completion of chapter 6, you will be able to create brochures using a variety of page layouts and design techniques.

Desktop Publishing Concepts

Determining size and type of paper	Screens
Types of brochure folds	Color
Dummy	Styles
Newspaper columns	Templates
Reverse text	Drop caps

Word Features Used

Paper size	Bullets and numbering	Indents
Margins	Picture	Styles
Columns	Brochure template	Drop caps
Drawing toolbar	Paragraph spacing	Tabs
Text boxes	Paragraph alignment	

In this chapter, you will be introduced to different methods for creating your own brochures. You will use the Columns feature and the Word brochure template to create brochures. Purpose, content, paper selection, brochure folds, page layout, design considerations, and desktop publishing concepts are also discussed.

Planning a Brochure

As mentioned in chapter 1, a very important step in initiating the desktop publishing process is to clearly identify the purpose of your communication.

Consequently, defining purpose is as important to the creation of a brochure as it is to the creation of any other publication.

Defining the Purpose

A brochure can inform, educate, promote, or sell. Identify the purpose in the following examples:

- A city agency mails brochures to the community explaining a local recycling program.
- A doctor displays brochures on childhood immunizations in the patient waiting room.
- A car salesperson hands out a brochure on a current model to a potential buyer.
- A new management consulting firm sends out brochures introducing its services.
- A professional organization mails brochures to its members about an upcoming convention.

If you found yourself thinking that some brochures have more than one purpose, you are correct. For example, the goal of a brochure on childhood immunizations may be to inform and educate, while the goal of a brochure on a new car model may be to inform and promote the sale of the product.

In addition, a brochure may be another means of establishing your organization's identity and image. Incorporating design elements from your other business documents into the design of your brochure reinforces your image and identity among your readers.

Determining the Content

Before creating the actual layout and design of your brochure, determine what the content will be. Try to look at the content from a reader's point of view. The content should include the following items:

- A clearly stated description of the topic, product, service, or organization
- A description of the people or company doing the informing, educating, promoting, or selling
- A description of how the reader will benefit from this information, product, service, or organization
- A clear indication of what action you want your audience to take after reading the brochure
- An easy way for readers to respond to the desired action, such as a fill-in form or detachable postcard

Determining the Size and Type of Paper

Brochures are usually printed on both sides of the page on an assortment of paper stocks. The paper stock may vary in size, weight, color, and texture, and it can also have defined folding lines.

Parallel Folds
All folds run in the same direction.

Brochures can be folded in a number of different ways. The manner in which a brochure is folded determines the order in which the panels are set on the page and read by the recipient. The most common brochure fold is called a *letter fold*. It is also known as a *trifold* or *three-panel brochure*. The letter fold and other common folds, as shown in figure 6.1, are referred to as *parallel folds*. All of the folds run in the same direction. *Right-angle folds* are created by pages that are folded at right angles to each other, such as the folds in a greeting card. Standard-size 8½-by-11-inch (landscape orientation) paper stock can easily accommodate a letter fold, accordion fold, and single fold. Standard legal-size paper, 8½-by-14 inches, can be used to create a brochure with a map fold or a gate fold. Different paper sizes can be used to create variations of these folds. In addition, folds do not always have to create equal panel sizes. Offsetting a fold can produce an interesting effect.

Right-Angle Folds
Folds created by pages folded at right angles to each other.

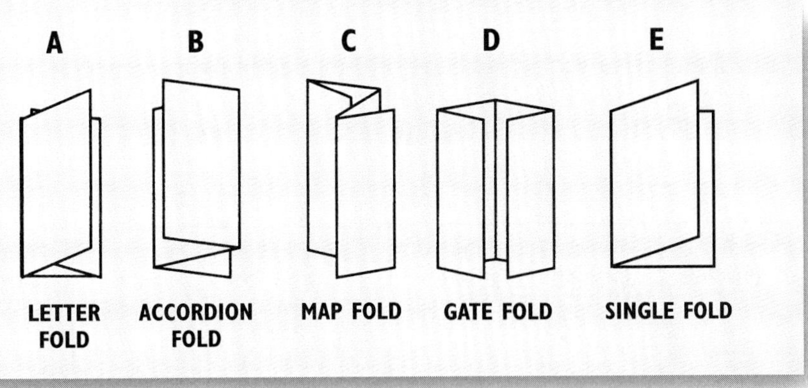

figure 6.1
Brochure Folds

The type of paper selected for a brochure affects the total production cost. When selecting the paper stock for a brochure, consider the following cost factors:

- Standard-size brochures, such as a three-panel brochure created from 8½-by-11-inch paper stock or a four-panel brochure created from 8½-by-14-inch paper stock, are easily enclosed in a #10 business envelope.
- Standard-size brochures designed as self-mailers satisfy postal regulations and are, therefore, less costly to mail.
- Nonstandard-size paper stock may be more expensive to purchase and to mail.
- Higher quality paper stocks are more expensive to purchase.
- Heavier weight papers are more costly to mail.
- Color paper is more costly than standard white, ivory, cream, or gray.
- Predesigned paper stock is more expensive than plain paper stock.

While cost is an important issue when choosing paper stock, also take into account how the brochure will be distributed, how often it will be handled, and the image you want to project. If you plan to design the brochure as a self-mailer, take a sample of the paper stock to the post office to see if it meets USPS mailing regulations. If you expect your target audience to keep your brochure for a period of time or to handle it often, plan to purchase a higher quality, heavier paper stock. By the same token, choose a paper within your budget that enhances the image you want to leave in the reader's mind.

If you intend to print the brochure yourself, run a sample of the paper you intend to use through your printer. Some papers are better suited for laser and ink jet printers than others. If you are unsure about what type of paper to purchase, take a master copy of your brochure to a printer for advice on the best type of paper for the situation. You can also take your brochure to a print shop and have it folded on their folding equipment.

Understanding a Basic Brochure Page Layout

Panels
Sections separated by folds in a brochure page layout.

A brochure page (defined by the dimensions of the paper stock) is divided into sections called *panels*. At least one fold separates each panel. Folds create distinct sections to place specific blocks of text. For example, a three-panel or letter-fold brochure layout actually has six panels available for text—three panels on one side of the paper and three more panels on the other side. The way a brochure is folded determines the order in which the panels are read by the recipient. The correct placement of text depends on understanding this order. As illustrated in figure 6.2, panels 1, 2, and 3 are located on the inside of the brochure, counting left to right. Panel 4 is the page you see when the cover is opened. Panel 5 is the back of the folded brochure, which may be used for mailing purposes, if desired. Panel 6 is the cover of the brochure. The main content of the brochure is focused in panels 1, 2, and 3.

figure 6.2

Letter-Fold Panel Layout

PANEL 1 (inside)	PANEL 2 (inside)	PANEL 3 (inside)

PANEL 4 (first flap viewed when cover is opened)	PANEL 5 (back/ mailing)	PANEL 6 (cover)

Dummy
A mock-up that is positioned, folded, trimmed, and/or labeled as the actual publication.

To avoid confusion about the brochure page layout and the panel reference numbers, create a mock-up or *dummy* of your brochure. A dummy is folded in the same manner as the actual brochure and is particularly useful since brochures can be folded in a number of different ways. A dummy can be as simple or as detailed as you would like. If you only need a visual guide to make sure you are placing the correct text in the correct panel, make a simple dummy using the default of three even columns and label each panel. If you need to visualize the placement of text within each panel, the margins, and the white space between columns, make a more detailed dummy that includes very specific margin settings, column width settings, and settings for the spacing between columns.

A brochure or a dummy can be created using Word's Columns, Table, or Text Box features. These features can be used to create brochures, programs, booklets, cards, tickets, bookmarks, and more. For example, for a standard-size three-panel brochure, the actual page size is 8½-by-11 inches positioned in a landscape orientation. The page is then divided into three columns using the Columns feature or into three columns and one row when using the Table feature. Or three text boxes could be sized and positioned on the page to represent three panels. Although each method has its advantages and disadvantages, the Columns feature requires the least adjustments. Consequently, having a solid understanding of the Columns feature is necessary to create a brochure, a dummy of your brochure, or to use the brochure template provided by Word.

Setting Brochure Margins

The left and right margins for a brochure page are usually considerably less than those for standard business documents. Many printers will only allow a minimum of a 0.5 inch left or right side margins (depending on the page orientation), since a certain amount of space is needed for the printer to grab the paper and eject it from the printer. If you set margins less than the minimum, Word prompts you with the following message: *One or more margins are set outside the printable area of the page. Choose the Fix button to increase the appropriate margins.* Click Fix to set the margins to the printer's minimum setting. Check the new margin setting in the Margins tab of the Page Setup dialog box. If landscape is the selected paper orientation, the right margin will be the only margin "fixed" by Word since that is the side of the paper the printer grabs to eject the paper from the printer. When creating a brochure, adjust the opposite side margin to match the margin adjusted by Word. For example, the printer used to create the brochure exercises in this chapter will only allow a minimum of 0.67 inches for the right margin with landscape chosen as the paper orientation. Hence, you are directed to set the left and right margins at 0.67 inches. Alternately, the printer imposes minimum margin settings when portrait is the selected paper orientation. The bottom margin setting is affected the most since it is the last side of the paper to come out of the paper.

If you choose to click Ignore as a response to Word's prompt about "fixing" the margins, the program will ignore the printer's minimum requirement and accept whatever margins you have set. However, the printer will not print anything in its defined unprintable area resulting in text that is cut off. Use Print Preview to view the results of setting margins less than the printer's minimum requirement.

Determining Column Widths

DTP POINTERS
Use unequal column widths in a brochure to accommodate appropriate placement of the text and folds.

The size of each panel in most brochures cannot be equal. If equal panel sizes are used, the margins on some of the panels will appear uneven and the brochure will not fold properly in relation to the text. In addition, the thickness of the paper stock used affects the amount of space taken up by the fold. To solve this problem, individually size the text columns, the space between columns, and the margins within each panel to accommodate the appropriate placement of the text and the folds. Additionally, the space between each column may vary, depending on the desired result. You will have to experiment somewhat and make adjustments to find the appropriate column width and the space between columns. Using panels 1, 2, and 3 of a letter-fold brochure as illustrated in figure 6.3 as an example, consider the following suggestions when setting column widths and the space between columns:

1. One way to determine the approximate width of each panel is to create a dummy on the paper stock being used and measure the width of each panel. The width obtained will be approximate since a ruler cannot measure tenths or hundredths of an inch, but it will be a good starting point.
2. Establish the left and right margins for the whole page. (See the section above on setting brochure margins.)

3. For panel 1, the left margin for the whole brochure page is also the left margin for the panel. Therefore, subtract the left margin setting from the total width of the panel. From the remaining amount, determine an appropriate column width for the text and an appropriate amount of white space on the right side of the panel.
4. For panel 2, use the whole panel width to establish an appropriate column width for the text and an appropriate amount of white space on the left and right sides of the panel.
5. For panel 3, the right margin for the whole brochure page is also the right margin for the panel. Therefore, subtract the right margin setting from the total width of the panel. From the remaining amount, determine an appropriate column width for the text and an appropriate amount of white space on the left side of the panel.
6. After establishing text column widths and the amount of white space in between for panels 1, 2, and 3, reverse the measurements for panels 4, 5, and 6. For example, panels 1 and 6 will be the same, panels 2 and 5 will be the same, and panels 3 and 4 will be the same. (You will need to insert a section break to vary the column formatting on the second page. See the section below on *Varying Column Formatting Within the Same Document*.)
7. Refer to figure 6.3 to see that the space between columns is actually divided by the fold, allowing white space on either side of the fold. When setting the space between columns in Word, you must realize that you are adding a specific amount of space to the right of the preceding column that must act as white space for two different panels. For example, the space between columns surrounding the first fold in figure 6.3 provides the white space for the right side of panel 1 and the left side of panel 2. Increasing the space between columns 1 and 2 will cause the text in panel 2 to be shifted to the right, whereas, decreasing the space between columns 1 and 2 will cause the text in panel 2 to shift to the left.

figure 6.3

Column Width Guide for a Letter-Fold Brochure

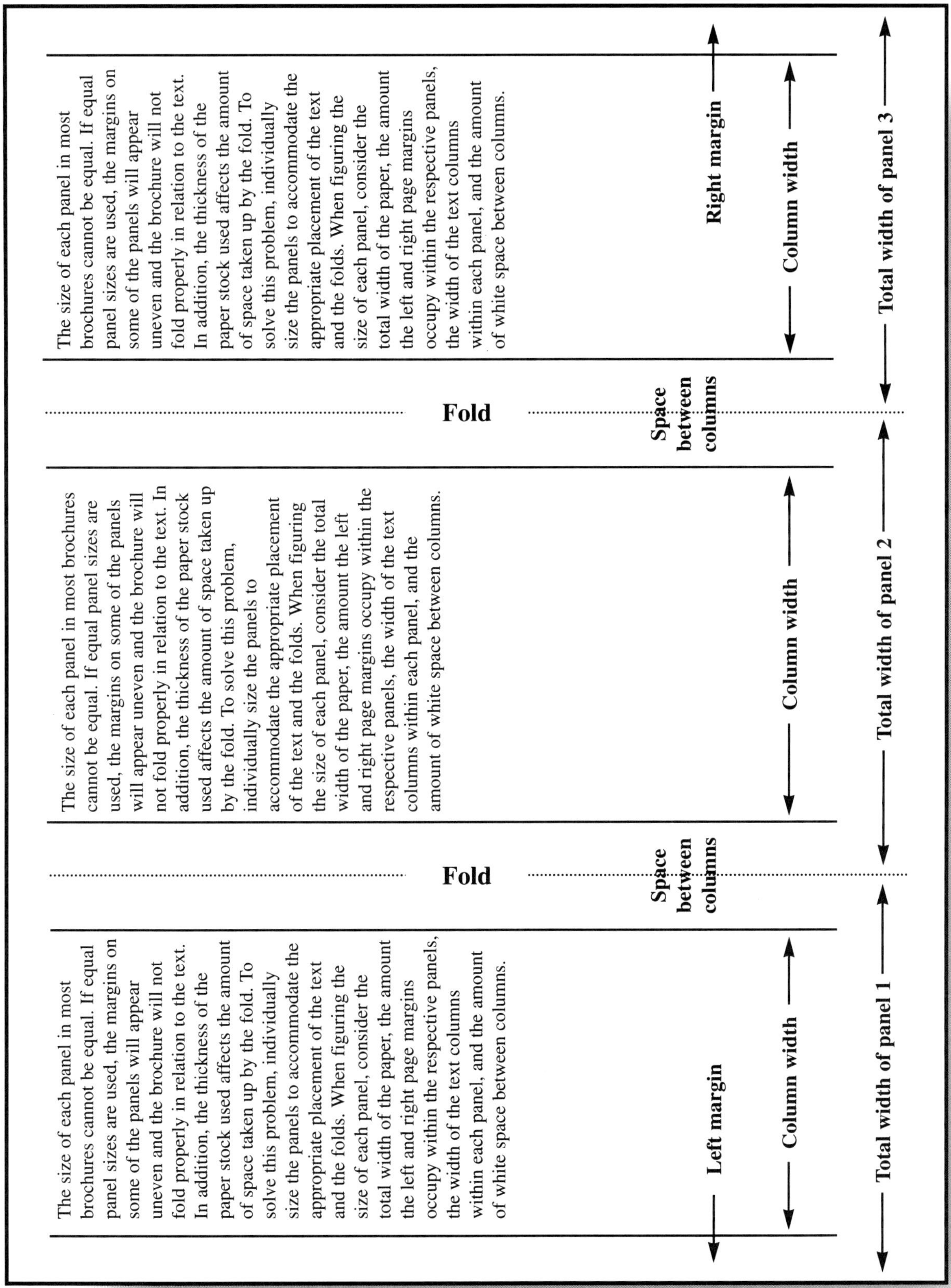

The size of each panel in most brochures cannot be equal. If equal panel sizes are used, the margins on some of the panels will appear uneven and the brochure will not fold properly in relation to the text. In addition, the thickness of the paper stock used affects the amount of space taken up by the fold. To solve this problem, individually size the panels to accommodate the appropriate placement of the text and the folds. When figuring the size of each panel, consider the total width of the paper, the amount the left and right page margins occupy within the respective panels, the width of the text columns within each panel, and the amount of white space between columns.

Fold

The size of each panel in most brochures cannot be equal. If equal panel sizes are used, the margins on some of the panels will appear uneven and the brochure will not fold properly in relation to the text. In addition, the thickness of the paper stock used affects the amount of space taken up by the fold. To solve this problem, individually size the panels to accommodate the appropriate placement of the text and the folds. When figuring the size of each panel, consider the total width of the paper, the amount the left and right page margins occupy within the respective panels, the width of the text columns within each panel, and the amount of white space between columns.

Fold

The size of each panel in most brochures cannot be equal. If equal panel sizes are used, the margins on some of the panels will appear uneven and the brochure will not fold properly in relation to the text. In addition, the thickness of the paper stock used affects the amount of space taken up by the fold. To solve this problem, individually size the panels to accommodate the appropriate placement of the text and the folds. When figuring the size of each panel, consider the total width of the paper, the amount the left and right page margins occupy within the respective panels, the width of the text columns within each panel, and the amount of white space between columns.

Left margin | **Space between columns** | **Space between columns** | **Right margin**

Column width | **Column width** | **Column width**

Total width of panel 1 | **Total width of panel 2** | **Total width of panel 3**

Understanding Newspaper Columns

Newspaper Columns
Text in this type of column flows up and down in the document.

The types of columns used to create a brochure are commonly referred to as *newspaper columns* or *snaking columns*. Newspaper columns are commonly used for text in newspapers, newsletters, brochures, and magazines. Text in these types of columns flows up and down in the document, as shown in figure 6.4. When the first column on the page is filled with text, the insertion point moves to the top of the next column on the same page. When the last column on the page is filled with text, the insertion point moves to the beginning of the first column on the next page.

figure 6.4
Newspaper Columns

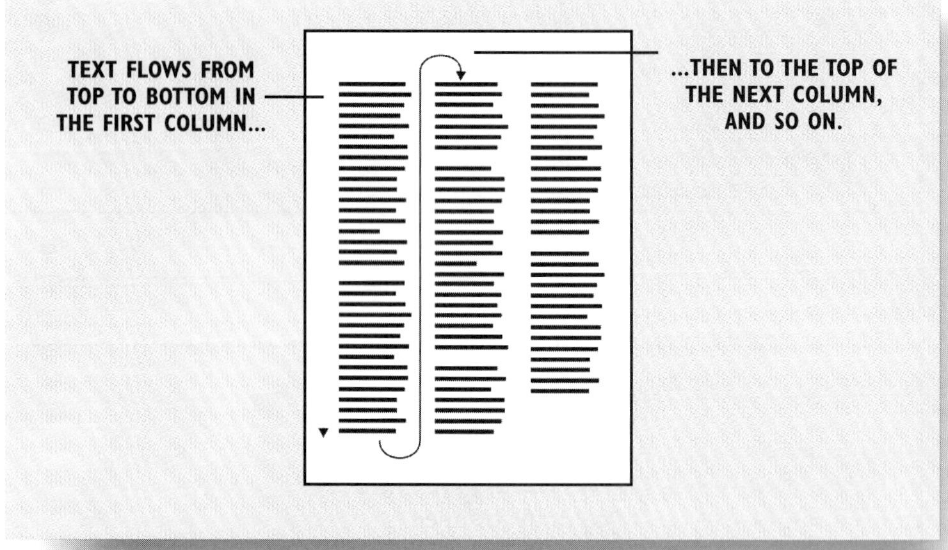

By default, all Word documents are automatically set up in a one-column format. However, a document can include as many columns as there is room for on the page. Word determines how many columns can be included on the page based on the page width, the margin settings, the size of the columns, and the spacing between columns. Column formatting can be assigned to a document before the text is keyed or it can be applied to existing text.

Creating Newspaper Columns of Equal Width

Columns

DTP POINTERS
Use Page Layout View to display columns side by side.

To easily create newspaper columns of equal width using the Columns button on the Standard toolbar, you would complete the following steps:

1. Position the arrow pointer on the Columns button.
2. Hold down the left mouse button, drag the mouse down and to the right highlighting the desired number of column displays, then release the mouse button.
3. The view will automatically change to the Page Layout View so you may view the columns side by side.

Even though only four column icons display, you can continue dragging toward the right to select a greater number of columns. Columns of equal width can also be created using the options at the Columns dialog box.

Creating Columns of Unequal Width

While the Columns button on the Standard toolbar is useful for creating columns of equal width, use the Columns dialog box to create columns of unequal width. To create columns with options at the Columns dialog box, you would complete the following steps:

DTP POINTERS
Be consistent when varying column widths within a document.

1. Choose Format, then Columns.
2. At the Columns dialog box, select One, Two, Three, Left, or Right in the Presets section; or key the desired number of columns in the Number of columns text box.
3. Click the Equal column width check box to disable this option.
4. In the Width and spacing section, find the column number(s) you want to change, then enter the desired column widths and spacing between columns in the corresponding Width and Spacing text boxes.
5. Choose OK or press Enter. Word automatically changes to Page Layout View so the column text is displayed side by side.

The first three choices of One, Two, or Three in the Presets section will result in columns of equal width. The Left and Right options will result in unequal columns of a predetermined width. If you choose the Left option, the right column of text will be twice as wide as the left column of text. Choose the Right option if you want the left column twice as wide. The options contain a preview box showing what the columns will look like.

By default, the Equal column width option contains a check mark. With this option selected, Word automatically determines column widths and the spacing between columns for the number of columns specified. This check mark must be removed in order to create columns of unequal width.

By default, columns are separated by 0.5 inches of space. The amount of space between equal or unequal column widths can be increased or decreased with the Spacing option in the Width and spacing section.

The dialog box only has room to display measurements for three columns. If you specify more than three columns, a vertical scroll bar displays to the left of the column numbers. To view other column measurements, click the down arrow at the bottom of the scroll bar.

Column widths and spacing can also be changed with the column markers on the horizontal ruler. To do this, you would complete the following steps:

1. Choose View, then Ruler to display the horizontal ruler.
2. Position the arrow pointer in the middle of the left or right margin column marker on the horizontal ruler until it turns into a double-headed arrow pointing left and right.
3. Hold down the left mouse button, drag the column marker to the left or right to make the column wider or narrower, then release the mouse button.

If the columns are of equal width, changing the width of one column changes the width of all columns. If the columns are of unequal width, changing the width of a column only changes that column.

Varying Column Formatting Within the Same Document

By default, any column formatting you select is applied to the whole document. If you want to create different numbers or styles of columns within the same document, the document must be divided into sections. For example, if a document contains a title, you may want the title to span the top of all the columns rather than be included within the column formatting. To span a title across the tops of columns, you would complete the following steps:

1. Key and format the title.
2. Position the insertion point at the left margin of the first line of text to be formatted into columns.
3. Display the Columns dialog box, select the desired number of columns, make any necessary column width and spacing changes, then change the Apply To option at the bottom of the Columns dialog box from *Whole document* to *This point forward*.

When the *This point forward* option is selected, a section break is automatically inserted in your document. Column formatting is then applied to text from the location of the insertion point to the end of the document or until other column formatting is encountered.

In addition to the method just described, you can manually insert the section break before accessing the Columns dialog box by choosing Insert, then Break. At the Break dialog box, choose Continuous, choose OK or press Enter, and then access the Columns dialog box.

If text that is formatted into columns is to be followed by text that is not formatted into columns, you must change the column format to one column and then select the *This point forward* option. An alternate approach is to insert a section break through the Break dialog box and then use the Columns button on the Standard toolbar to create one column.

Specific text in a document can also be formatted into columns by first selecting the text, then using the Columns button on the Standard toolbar or the options from the Columns dialog box.

If you want to remove column formatting, position the insertion point in the section containing columns and change the column format to one column either by using the Columns button on the Standard toolbar or the Columns dialog box.

Inserting a Column and/or Page Break

DTP POINTERS
Make sure all column breaks are in appropriate locations.

When formatting text into columns, Word automatically breaks the columns to fit the page. At times, a column may break in an undesirable location, or you may want a column to break in a different location. For example, a heading may appear at the bottom of the column, while the text that follows the heading begins at the top of the next column. You can insert a column break into a document to control where columns end and begin on the page. To insert a column break, position the insertion point where you want the new column to begin, then press Ctrl + Shift + Enter; or choose Insert, Break, Column Break, then choose OK or press Enter.

If you insert a column break in the last column on a page, the column begins on the next page. If you want any other column on the page to begin on the next page, insert a page break. To do this, press Ctrl + Enter or choose Insert, Break, Page Break.

If you want to "even out" or balance the text in columns, put a continuous section break at the end of the last column.

Moving the Insertion Point Within and Between Columns

To move the insertion point using the mouse in a document formatted into more than one column, position the I-beam pointer where desired, then click the left mouse button. If you are using the keyboard, the up and down arrow keys move the insertion point in the direction indicated. The left and right arrow keys move the insertion point in the direction indicated within the column and the insertion point follows the snaking pattern of newspaper columns—down one column and then to the top of the next column. Consequently, the mouse is most often the preferred method to move the insertion point in text formatted into columns.

To move the insertion point between columns using the keyboard, press Alt + up arrow to move the insertion point to the top of the previous column or Alt + down arrow to the top of the next column.

To familiarize you with the layout of panels in a letter-fold or three-panel brochure, you will create a simple dummy (three even columns labeled with each panel number) in the following exercise. Remember, you can always make a more detailed dummy if necessary.

exercise 1

Creating a Dummy of a Three-Panel Brochure Using Columns

1. At a clear document screen, create a dummy similar to the one illustrated in figure 6.2 by completing the following steps:
   a. Change to the Page Layout viewing mode.
   b. Change to landscape orientation and set left and right margins by completing the following steps:
      (1) Click File, then Page Setup.
      (2) At the Page Setup dialog box, click the Paper Size tab. Make sure the Paper Size list box displays *Letter* and then select Landscape in the Orientation section.
      (3) Click OK.
   c. Change to a three-column format by completing the following steps:
      (1) Click Format, then Columns.
      (2) At the Columns dialog box, change the Number of columns to 3; or select Three (equal columns) in the Presets section of the Columns dialog box.
      (3) Click OK to close the dialog box.
   d. Insert the panel labels by completing the following steps:
      (1) Change the paragraph alignment to Center.
      (2) Key **PANEL 1 (inside)** in the first panel (column 1).
      (3) Choose Insert, then Break.
      (4) At the Break dialog box, choose Column Break, then click OK.
      (5) Using figure 6.2 as a guide, repeat steps 2 through 4 until all six of the panels have been labeled.
   e. Print the three-panel brochure dummy by completing the following steps:
      (1) Position the insertion point on the first page by pressing Ctrl + Home.
      (2) Choose File, then Print.
      (3) At the Print dialog box, choose Current Page, then choose OK.

(4) Put the first printed page back in the printer so the second page can be printed on the back of the first page. (You may have to experiment with your printer to position the paper correctly.)
(5) Position the insertion point on the second page (panel 4, 5, or 6), then print the current page.
(6) Fold the dummy as you would for the real brochure and refer to the panel labels when creating the actual brochure to avoid confusion on the placement of text.

2. Save the dummy brochure and name it c06ex01, dummy.
3. Close c06ex01, dummy.

You can use a similar procedure to create a dummy using a table. Instead of creating three columns, insert a table with three columns and one row, label the panels, and then print as explained above.

A dummy can also be created with pencil and paper. Take a piece of the paper stock to be used and position it correctly (portrait or landscape). Fold the paper as the brochure will be folded, and label each panel as in figure 6.2.

You may create a paper size definition for paper stock that is different from the sizes available in the Paper Size drop-down list box. To do this, select Custom size from the Paper Size drop-down list. Insert the correct width and height of your paper stock in the corresponding text boxes and then choose portrait or landscape orientation. Depending on your printer's capabilities, you may be able to directly insert different standard sizes of paper and envelopes into your printer. For example, your printer may adjust to holding letter, legal, and executive-size paper, as well as two standard-size business envelopes. However, your printer may not be able to hold and feed odd or custom-size papers even though you can create a custom-size paper definition in Word. If that is the case, print the custom-size document on standard-size paper of the desired stock. The document will be printed within the parameters of the custom paper size definition. However, since it will be printed on standard-size paper, measure the desired size and trim the document to the correct size or have it printed and trimmed professionally.

Using Reverse Text as a Design Element

Reverse Text
White text set against a solid 100% black background.

Reverse text usually refers to white text set against a solid (100% black) background, as shown in the first example in figure 6.5. Setting headings, subheadings, or other significant blocks of text in reverse type can be a very effective design element. Reversing text is most effective with single words or short phrases set in a larger type size. Impact can also be achieved by screening (shading with lighter shades of gray or color) the background or lettering. Solid areas of black, white, and varying shades of gray on a page give the visual effect of color, allowing you to achieve a dramatic effect with the use of only one color. In addition, interesting effects can be achieved by reversing color text out of a solid, screened, gradient, or textured colored background. As illustrated in figure 6.5, different variations of reverse type can be created. Keep these examples in mind when you are trying to provide focus, balance, contrast, and directional flow in a document.

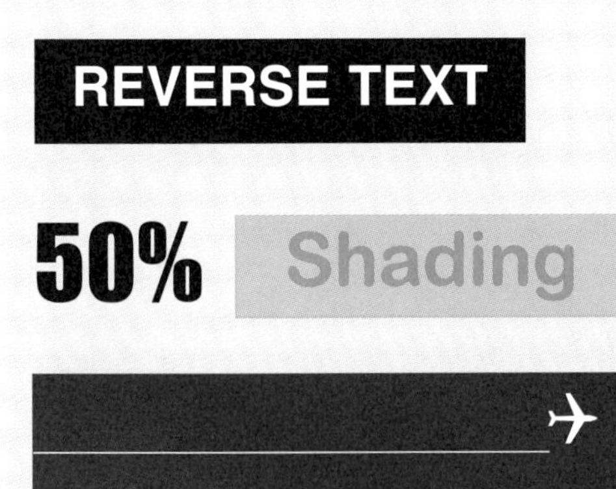

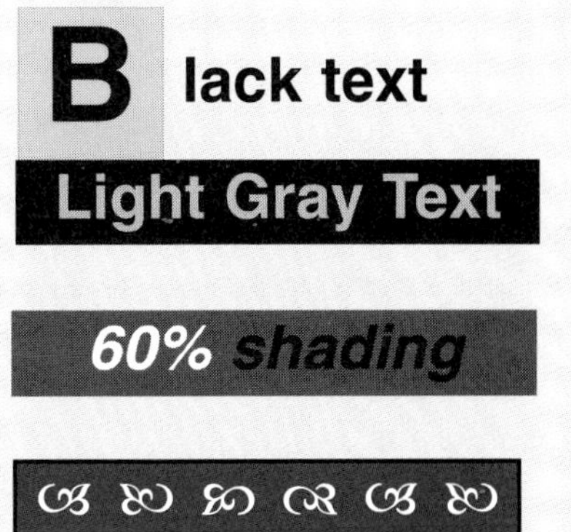

figure 6.5

Examples of Reverse Text

The most versatile method of creating reverse text is to use the text box feature. To create reverse text using a text box, you would complete the following steps:

1. Display the Drawing toolbar.
2. Click the Text Box button on the Drawing toolbar.
3. Position the crosshairs in the desired reverse text location, then click the left mouse button and drag the mouse to create a text box.
4. Key and format the text to be contained in the reverse text box, including the font color.
5. Size and position the text box if necessary.
6. Click the arrow to the right of the Fill button on the Drawing toolbar.
7. Select the desired fill color for the reverse text box from the fill color palette or choose More Fill Colors or Fill Effects.
8. Use the Line Color button on the Drawing toolbar if you want to add a border to the reverse text box.
9. Choose OK or press Enter when done.

Text Box

In exercises 2 and 3, you will have the opportunity to create a three-panel or letter-fold brochure using three uneven newspaper columns and other formatting features such as text boxes to create reverse text, color, and bulleted lists. A word of advice—**SAVE! SAVE! SAVE!** Creating even a simple brochure involves many steps. Save your document periodically as you are creating it to avoid any disasters—they happen to the best of us! Also, view your document frequently to assess the overall layout and design. Adjustments often need to be made that can affect other parts of the document not visible in the document window. In Word, click the arrow at the right of the Zoom Control button on the Standard toolbar (third button from the right). The Page Width and Full Page options are useful for viewing a brochure layout during the creation process.

DTP POINTERS
Desktop published documents involve many steps—SAVE as you work.

exercise 2

Creating Panels 1, 2, and 3 of a Three-Panel Brochure Using the Columns Feature and Reverse Text

1. Use the dummy created in exercise 1 to visually guide you in the correct placement of text (or create a new dummy following the directions in exercise 1).

2. At a clear document screen, create the first three panels of a brochure, as shown in figure 6.6, by completing the following steps:
   a. Change the margins and the paper size by completing the following steps:
      (1) Choose File, then Page Setup.
      (2) At the Page Setup dialog box, select the Paper Size tab.
      (3) Make sure *Letter* displays in the Paper size list box, then select Landscape in the Orientation section.
      (4) With the Page Setup dialog box still displayed, select the Margins tab. Change the top and bottom margins to 0.5 inches. Change the left and right margins to 0.67 inches. (The left and right margin settings were chosen because of the unprintable zone that exists within the printer that was used to create and print the brochure in figures 6.6 and 6.7. Use these settings for this exercise to work properly with the column widths given.)
      (5) Choose OK or press Enter to close the dialog box.
   b. Turn on automatic kerning for font sizes 14 points and above at the Character Spacing tab of the Font dialog box.
   c. Set up the three-column brochure page layout by completing the following steps:
      (1) Click Format, then Columns.
      (2) At the Columns dialog box, select Three in the Presets section or increase the number to 3 in the Number of columns option.
      (3) Remove the check mark in the Equal column width check box.
      (4) In the Width and spacing section, enter the following amounts in the Width and Spacing text boxes for the columns indicated:

Col #	Width	Spacing
1	2.64	0.7
2	3.00	0.7
3	2.62	

      (5) Click OK or press Enter.
   d. Insert the file containing the brochure text by completing the following steps:
      (1) Choose Insert, then File.
      (2) At the Insert File dialog box, double-click *ride safe four text.doc* (located on your student data disk) in the Look in: list box.
   e. Select the font for the whole document by completing the following steps:
      (1) Press Ctrl + Home to move the insertion point to the beginning of the document.
      (2) Choose Edit, then Select All, or press Ctrl + A.
      (3) Change the font to 12-point Arial Rounded MT Bold.
      (4) Deselect the text.
   f. Click the Zoom button on the Standard toolbar and change the view to 75% or Page Width.
   g. Click the Show/Hide ¶ button on the Standard toolbar to display nonprinting characters, such as paragraph symbols and spaces.
   h. Format the number *1* that displays at the top of the first panel (or column) of the brochure by completing the following steps:

(1) Select number *1* and the paragraph symbol that follows it.
(2) Change the font to 72-point Arial Rounded MT Bold and change the color of the font to red. (If you do not have a color printer, you may use either gray or white.)
(3) With the number and paragraph symbol still selected, click the Text Box button on the Drawing toolbar or click Insert, then Text Box.
(4) Select number *1* again and change the alignment to center.
(5) Double-click the text box border and make the following changes at the Format Text Box dialog box:
 (a) Select the Colors and Lines tab and change the fill color to black.
 (b) Select the Size tab, then change the height of the text box to 1.21 inches and the width to 1.15 inches.
 (c) Select the Position tab, make sure the horizontal From option displays Column and the Horizontal option displays 0 inches. Change the vertical From option to Page and the Vertical option to 0.5 inches. (Remember to change the "From" options first.)
 (d) Select the Wrapping tab and change the Wrapping style to Top & bottom.
 (e) Click OK or press Enter.

i. Format the lead-in text below the number by completing the following steps:
 (1) Position the insertion point to the left of *Before entering the street from your driveway or sidewalk:* and press Enter.
 (2) Select *Before entering the street from your driveway or sidewalk:*, change the font to 20-point Arial Rounded MT Bold Italic, and change the Effects to Small caps in the Font dialog box.

j. Create the red bulleted list by completing the following steps:
 (1) Position the insertion point to the left of *Stop.* and press Enter two times.
 (2) Select the text that starts with *Stop.* and ends with *Listen to be sure no traffic is approaching.* and change the font to 20-point Arial Rounded MT Bold.
 (3) With the text still selected, choose Format, then Bullets and Numbering.
 (4) At the Bullets and Numbering dialog box, select the Bulleted tab.
 (5) Click the first bullet option (first row, second column), then click Customize.
 (6) At the Customize Bulleted List dialog box, click the first box in the Bullet character section. (A round bullet should be displayed in this box. If not, click Bullet and select a round bullet from a font, such as Wingdings, at the Symbol dialog box.)
 (7) Click the Font button and change the Size to 32 points and change the Color to Red.
 (8) Click OK to close the Font dialog box, then click OK again to close the Customize Bulleted List dialog box.

k. Adjust the spacing between the bulleted items by completing the following steps:
 (1) With the bulleted list still selected, choose Format, then Paragraph.
 (2) At the Paragraph dialog box, select the Indents and Spacing tab.
 (3) Key **16 pt** in the After text box in the Spacing section.
 (4) Click OK or press Enter.

l. Format the text in panel 2 by completing the following steps:
 (1) If the number *2* is not positioned at the top of column two, position the insertion point to the left of *2*, then click Insert and Break. At the Break dialog box, click Column break.

(2) Format the number *2* that displays at the top of the second panel (or column) of the brochure by completing the following steps:
   (a) Select number *2* and the paragraph symbol that follows it.
   (b) Change the font to 72-point Arial Rounded MT Bold and change the color of the font to yellow. (If you do not have a color printer, you may use either gray or white.)
   (c) With the number and paragraph symbol still selected, click the Text Box button on the Drawing toolbar or click Insert, then Text Box.
   (d) The text box may move to the bottom of panel 2. The position of the text box will be corrected in steps to follow below.
   (e) Select number *2* again and change the alignment to center.
   (f) Double-click the text box border and follow steps 2h(5)(a-e) to format the text box.

(3) Format the lead-in text below the number *2* by completing the following steps:
   (a) Position the insertion point to the left of *At stop signs, stoplights, or other busy streets:* and press Enter.
   (b) Select *At stop signs, stoplights, or other busy streets:*, change the font to 20-point Arial Rounded MT Bold Italic, and change the Effects to Small caps in the Font dialog box.

(4) Create the yellow bulleted list by completing the following steps:
   (a) Position the insertion point to the left of *Stop.* and press Enter two times.
   (b) Select the text that starts with *Stop.* and ends *Listen and make sure the street is clear of traffic before crossing.* Change the font to 20-point Arial Rounded MT Bold.
   (c) With the text still selected, choose Format, then Bullets and Numbering.
   (d) At the Bullets and Numbering dialog box, select the Bulleted tab.
   (e) Click the first bullet option (first row, second column), then click Customize.
   (f) At the Customize Bulleted List dialog box, select the round red Bullet character (should display as the first choice in the Customize Bulleted List dialog box), then change the bullet color to yellow.
   (g) Click OK to close the Font dialog box, then click OK again to close the Customize Bulleted List dialog box.

(5) Follow steps 2k(1-4) to adjust the spacing between the bulleted items.

m. Format the text in panel 3 by completing the following steps:

(1) If the number *3* is not positioned at the top of column three, position the insertion point to the left of *3*, then click Insert and Break. At the Break dialog box, click Column break.

(2) Format the number *3* that displays at the top of the third panel (or column) of the brochure by completing the following steps:
   (a) Select number *3* and the paragraph symbol that follows it.
   (b) Change the font to 72-point Arial Rounded MT Bold and change the color of the font to Bright Green. (If you do not have a color printer, use either gray or white.)
   (c) With the number and paragraph symbol still selected, click the Text Box button on the Drawing toolbar or click Insert, then Text Box.
   (d) Select number *3* again and change the alignment to center.

(e) Double-click the text box border and follow steps 2h(5)(a-e) to format the text box.

(3) Format the lead-in text below the number *3* by completing the following steps:

(a) Position the insertion point to the left of *Before turning, changing lanes, or swerving to avoid an obstacle:* and press Enter.

(b) Select *Before turning, changing lanes, or swerving to avoid an obstacle:*, change the font to 20-point Arial Rounded MT Bold Italic, and change the Effects to Small caps in the Font dialog box.

(4) Create the green bulleted list by completing the following steps:

(a) Position the insertion point to the left of *Look back over your shoulder.* and press Enter two times.

(b) Select the text that starts with *Look back over your shoulder.* and ends with *Look again.* Change the font to 20-point Arial Rounded MT Bold.

(c) With the text still selected, choose Format, then Bullets and Numbering.

(d) At the Bullets and Numbering dialog box, select the Bulleted tab.

(e) Click the first bullet option (first row, second column), then click Customize.

(f) At the Customize Bulleted List dialog box, select the round yellow Bullet character (should display as the first choice in the Customize Bulleted List dialog box), then change the bullet color to Bright Green.

(g) Click OK to close the Font dialog box, then click OK again to close the Customize Bulleted List dialog box.

(5) Follow steps 2k(1-4) to adjust the spacing between the bulleted items.

n. Below the bulleted list, position the insertion point to the left of *4* and insert a column break.

3. Save the brochure and name it c06ex02, panels 1,2,3.
4. Print the first page of this exercise now or print after completing exercise 3.
5. Close c06ex02, panels 1,2,3.

figure 6.6

BEFORE ENTERING THE STREET FROM YOUR DRIVEWAY OR SIDEWALK:

- Stop.
- Look left.
- Look right.
- Look left again.
- Listen to be sure no traffic is approaching.

AT STOP SIGNS, STOPLIGHTS, OR OTHER BUSY STREETS:

- Stop.
- Look left.
- Look right.
- Look left again.
- Listen and make sure the street is clear of traffic before crossing.

BEFORE TURNING, CHANGING LANES, OR SWERVING TO AVOID AN OBSTACLE:

- Look back over your shoulder.
- Be sure the road is clear of traffic.
- Signal.
- Look again.

In exercise 3, you will complete the brochure started in exercise 2. As in the previous exercise, uneven columns will be used to form the panels on the reverse side of the brochure. Refer to your dummy to see that panel 4 is on the reverse side of panel 3, panel 5 is the reverse side of panel 2, and panel 6 is the reverse side of panel 1. Consequently, the specified width of each column will be reversed in order from the widths stated in panels 1, 2, and 3. As you progress through the exercise, remember to save your document every 10 to 15 minutes.

exercise 3

Creating Panels 4, 5, and 6 of a Three-Fold Brochure

1. At a clear document screen, open c06ex02, panels 1,2,3.doc.
2. Save the document with Save As and name it c06ex03, ride safe brochure.
3. Create panels 4, 5, and 6 of the Ride Safe brochure shown in figure 6.7 by completing the following steps:
   a. Set the column formatting for the outside panels of the brochure by completing the following steps:
      (1) Position the insertion point at the top of the second page of the brochure to the left of the number 4.
      (2) Click Format, then Columns.
      (3) At the Columns dialog box, make sure the number of columns is set to 3.
      (4) Make sure there is no check mark in the Equal column width check box.
      (5) In the Width and spacing section, enter the following amounts in the Width and Spacing text boxes for the columns indicated (remember: these settings are the opposite of panels 1, 2, and 3):

Col #	Width	Spacing
1	2.62	0.7
2	3.00	0.7
3	2.64	

      (6) Click the Apply to: list box and select *This point forward*. (This will automatically insert a section break in the document along with the new column formatting.)
      (7) Click OK or press Enter.
   b. Format the text in panel 4 by completing the following steps:
      (1) Position the insertion point to the left of the number 4 located at the top of panel 4.
      (2) Format the number 4 by following steps 2h(1-5) in exercise 2. Change the color of the number to Red.
      (3) Format the lead-in text, *Every time you go bicycling or in-line skating:*, located below the number 4 by repeating steps 2i(1-2) in exercise 2.
      (4) Create the bulleted list by following steps 2j(1-5) in exercise 2, then select the round yellow Bullet character (should display as the first choice in the Customize Bulleted List dialog box). Change the bullet color to Red.
      (5) Follow steps 2k(1-4) in exercise 2 to adjust the spacing between the bulleted items.
      (6) Position the insertion point to the left of *Ride Safe is committed to educating children. . .* and insert a column break.

c. Format the text in panel 5 by completing the following steps:
   (1) With the insertion point at the top of panel 5, press Enter.
   (2) Select the paragraph that begins with *Ride Safe is committed to educating children. . .* and make the following changes:
      (a) Change the paragraph alignment to Center.
      (b) Click Format, Borders and Shading, then select the Borders tab.
      (c) In the Setting section, click the Box option.
      (d) Change the Color to Red, then change the Width of the border to 1 pt.
      (e) Click OK or press Enter.
   (3) Position the insertion point to the left of *We want everyone to RIDE SAFE!* and press Enter eight times.
   (4) Select *We want everyone to RIDE SAFE!* and make the following changes:
      (a) Change the font size to 18 points, change the color to Bright Green, then apply bold and italics.
      (b) Change the paragraph alignment to Center.
   (5) Position the insertion point to the left of *Call us today. . .* and press Enter 12 times.
   (6) Select *Call us today at 1-800-555-RIDE* and make the following changes:
      (a) Change the font size to 20 points and change the font color to yellow.
      (b) Change the paragraph alignment to Center.
      (c) Click Format, Borders and Shading, then select the Shading tab. In the Fill section, select the black color block in the first row, first column. Click OK.
      (d) Position the insertion point after the word *at*, delete the space, and press Enter to force the phone number down to the next line.

d. *THE RIDE SAFE FOUR* title should be positioned at the top of panel 6. If not, insert a column break before the title.

e. Format the text and picture in panel 6 (the cover) by completing the following steps:
   (1) Select the company name, address, and phone number and insert and format a text box by completing the following steps: (It is easier if this text is positioned first before formatting the title. The stop sign image will be inserted last.)
      (a) Click the Text Box button on the Drawing toolbar or click Insert, then Text Box to insert a text box around the selected text.
      (b) Select the company name only and change the font size to 14 points.
      (c) Select the company name, address, and phone number and change the paragraph alignment to Center.
      (d) Double-click the text box border to display the Format Text Box dialog box.
      (e) Click the Colors and Lines tab, then change the line color to No Line.
      (f) Click the Size tab and change the height of the text box to 1 inch and the width to 2.2 inches.
      (g) Click the Position tab, then change the horizontal From option to Page and the Horizontal option to 8.2 inches. Change the vertical From option to Page, then change the Vertical option to 7.1 inches.
      (h) Click the Wrapping tab, then change the Wrapping style to Top & bottom.
      (i) Click OK or press Enter. The text box will move to the bottom of the panel.
   (2) Select the title *THE RIDE SAFE FOUR*, then insert and format a text box to contain the text by completing the following steps:

(a) Click the Text Box button on the Drawing toolbar or click Insert, then Text Box to insert a text box around the selected text.
(b) Select the title again, change the font to 36-point Arial Rounded MT Bold, and change the paragraph alignment to Center.
(c) Click and drag the bottom center sizing handle of the text box to display all of the text.
(d) Position the insertion point after *THE*, delete the space, and press Enter to force *RIDE* down to the next line.
(e) Delete the space after *RIDE* and then press Enter.
(f) Delete the space after *SAFE* and then press Enter.
(g) Select *RIDE* in the title and change the color to Red.
(h) Select *SAFE* in the title and change the color to Yellow.
(i) Select *FOUR* in the title and change the color to Green.
(j) Double-click the text box border to display the Format Text Box dialog box.
(k) Click the Colors and Lines tab, then change the line color to No Line.
(l) Click the Size tab and change the height of the text box to 2.41 inches and the width to 2 inches.
(m) Click the Position tab, then change the horizontal From option to Page and the Horizontal option to 8.3 inches. Change the vertical From option to Page, then change the Vertical option to 0.5 inches.
(n) Click the Wrapping tab, then change the Wrapping style to Top & bottom.
(o) Click OK or press Enter.

(3) Insert the picture of the stop sign by completing the following steps:
(a) Click once outside the title text box to position the insertion point to the left of the text box.
(b) Click Insert, point to Picture, then click From File.
(c) At the Insert Picture dialog box, double-click the *Popular* folder.
(d) Double-click *Stop.wmf* or click the filename once, then click Insert. The picture will be inserted on top of the title. The size and position will be adjusted in the next step.

(4) Size and position the stop sign by completing the following steps:
(a) Select the stop sign image.
(b) Click Format, then Picture to display the Format Picture dialog box.
(c) Click the Size tab and change the height of the text box to 2.4 inches and the width to 1.44 inches.
(d) Click the Position tab, then change the horizontal From option to Page and the Horizontal option to 8.62 inches. Change the vertical From option to Page, then change the Vertical option to 3.7 inches.
(e) Click OK or press Enter.

4. Save the brochure again with the same name (c06ex03, ride safe brochure).
5. Print both pages of the brochure using both sides of the paper. Refer to the directions for printing in exercise 1, if necessary.
6. Close c06ex03, ride safe brochure.

figure 6.7

EVERY TIME YOU GO BICYCLING OR IN-LINE SKATING:

- **Wear an ANSI, ASTM, or Snell certified helmet.**
- **Wear appropriate protective gear!**

Ride Safe is committed to educating children and their parents about bicycle safety and the importance of wearing helmets. In the last year, we've worked with over 1,200 PTAs/PTOs across the country to develop customized bicycle safety programs...and we'd like to work with you, too.

We want everyone to RIDE SAFE!

Call us today at 1-800-555-RIDE

THE RIDE SAFE FOUR

RIDE SAFE, INC.
P.O. Box 888
Warrenville, IL 60555
1-800-555-RIDE

Designing a Brochure

As with letterheads, envelopes, and business cards, designing your own brochure can be a cost-saving measure. It eliminates the cost of paying a professional designer and the cost of committing to a minimum order. In addition, if the information in your brochure needs to be updated, it can be easily changed. Although not as cost effective, you can design your own brochure, print a master copy, and then take it to a professional printer to be duplicated on high-quality paper.

For a brochure to be noticed, it must be well designed, easy to read, and have some element that sets it apart from the pack. As with all publications, consider your target audience and start drawing some thumbnail sketches. Consider the content of the brochure; any illustrations or graphics that might be a required part of your brochure, such as a logo or a picture of a product or service; or any colors that might be associated with your company, organization, or topic.

The front cover of a brochure sets the mood and tone for the whole brochure. The front cover title must attract attention and let the reader know what the brochure is about. The typeface selected for the title must reflect the image and tone intended. For example, Arial Rounded MT Bold was the typeface used in the brochure cover title in exercise 3. The rounded, slightly juvenile nature of this typeface reflects the target audience. The use of red, yellow, and green in the title, along with the wording and stoplight image, reinforces the traffic safety theme of this brochure. If the same title had been set in Times New Roman, the mood or tone would be much more businesslike and conservative. Which do you think would be more appealing to a target audience of school-aged bicyclists?

A great deal of information is often contained within the confines of a brochure. Using one typeface for the brochure title, headings, and subheadings and another typeface for the body copy can provide visual contrast in your brochure. Do not use more than two typefaces or the brochure will appear crowded, cluttered, and more difficult to read. To provide contrast within the brochure text, vary the style of the typeface rather than changing typefaces. Text can be set in all caps, small caps, shadow, outline, embossed, engraved, italics, reverse, bold, or color to achieve contrast. For example, Arial Rounded MT Bold was the only typeface used in the *Ride Safe Four* brochure shown in figures 6.6 and 6.7. The typeface was varied by using different type sizes, italics, small caps, all caps, and color.

DTP POINTERS
Vary the style of the typeface rather than changing typefaces.

While text set in color can be an effective contrasting element, use it sparingly. Use it for titles, headings, subheadings, and a small graphics element, if any. Remember to allow for white space between the headings and body copy and among separate sections of the body copy. For instance, in figure 6.6, extra white space exists between the lead-in statements and the bulleted lists in each panel, as well as within each bulleted list.

Several elements can be used to direct the reader's eyes through a brochure. Subheadings set in color or in reverse text can be useful directional tools. In figures 6.6 and 6.7, the numbers 1 through 4 are set in different colors on a solid black background (a variation of reverse text) to make them stand out. These numbered squares, which are actually text boxes with black fill, direct the reader to important points. A text box with a specific border can also be used to place items of importance. Horizontal and vertical ruled lines can be used as visual separators. A screen (a shaded area behind a block of text) can be used to emphasize and separate a block of text. Bullets or special characters can be used to aid directional flow. For example, in figures 6.6 and 6.7, the round bullets help to lead the reader's eyes down through the important points in each panel. Effective use of white space can be used to separate items on the page. White space makes the copy more appealing and easier to read.

Consistent elements are necessary to maintain continuity in a multipage brochure. Be consistent in the design and layout of your brochure. Generally, do not mix landscape and portrait orientations within the same brochure. Format each panel in the same basic manner so the reader knows what to expect. Be consistent in the font used for headings, subheadings, and body copy. For example, the lead-in text in each brochure panel in figures 6.6 and 6.7 is set in 20-point Arial Rounded MT Bold Italic, small caps. The bulleted items are also set in the same font without italics and small caps.

DTP POINTERS
Use bullets to organize text and improve directional flow.

Continuity can be maintained by emphasizing the same theme or style throughout the brochure. As you can see in figure 6.6 and 6.7, the stop sign image and the red, yellow, and green numbers and bullets reinforce the traffic safety theme of the brochure. Headers or footers can also make it easy to carry a theme or style throughout a document. In addition, consistent amounts of white space at the top and bottom of each panel and within each panel add to the continuity. When evaluating a brochure for continuity, open the brochure and view it the way your readers would. While the individual elements of each panel are important, viewing the design and layout as a whole unit is equally important. When you open a three-panel brochure, look at panels 1, 2, and 3 as a three-page spread. Does the design flow from one panel to the next? Do all three panels work together visually as a unit?

A visual, such as a clip art image, an illustration, a photograph, or a drawing, can be a powerful tool. While a visual may attract attention, it also delivers an immediate message. It can turn a reader away before the intended message has even been read. What message does the stop sign image in figure 6.7 convey to you? When selecting visuals, select only those visuals that best enhance the intended message of the brochure. Always find out about *copyright* restrictions before using any artwork. Often clip art software owners are allowed to use and publish the images contained in the software package; however, the clip art may not be resold in any manner. If you intend to use a drawing, clip art, scanned art, or photograph, find out the source and request permission from the copyright owner.

Copyright
Exclusive legal ownership of a literary, musical, or artistic work.

Formatting with Styles

Documents created with desktop publishing features generally require a great deal of formatting. Some documents, such as company newsletters or brochures, may be created on a regular basis. These documents should contain formatting that maintains consistency in their appearance from issue to issue. The formatting should also be consistent within each issue and within any document that uses a variety of headings, subheadings, and other design elements.

To maintain consistency within a document, such as a brochure, newsletter, or report, you may find yourself frequently repeating formatting instructions for specific sections of text. For example, to create the brochure in figures 6.6 and 6.7, the formatting instructions for the framed numbers, the font for the lead-in statements and the bulleted items, and the spacing between the bulleted items had to be repeated in each panel. You can save time and keystrokes by using Word's Style feature to store repetitive formatting.

A *style* is a group of defined formatting instructions, such as margin settings, paper size, font, paragraph spacing, and tab settings, that can be applied at one time to a whole document or to various parts of a document. Using styles is a quick and easy way to assure that your formatting is uniform throughout your document, while at the same time is quick and easy. For example, a style can be created for the bulleted text in figures 6.6 and 6.7 that contains bullet instructions and paragraph spacing instructions. Every time you are ready to format the text to be bulleted, you can quickly apply the specific style and save yourself the time of repeating the same keystrokes for each item. Because formatting instructions are contained within a style, a style can be edited, automatically updating any occurrence of that style within a document. For instance, if you applied a style for the bulleted text in all four panels of the brochure that specified an 18-point font size and then decided to change the font size to 16 points, all you would need to do is edit the formatting instructions in the style and then all of the bulleted text would be changed to 16 points at the same time.

Style
A group of defined formatting instructions that can be applied at one time to a whole document or to various parts of a document.

Understanding the Relationship Between Styles and Templates

As previously mentioned, a Word document, by default, is based on the *Normal.dot* template. The Normal template contains formatting instructions to set text in the default font (usually 10-point Times New Roman but this may vary depending on the printer you are using or if another font has been selected as the default font), to use left alignment and single spacing, and to turn on Widow/Orphan control. These formatting instructions are contained in a style called the *Normal style*. When you access a clear document window, *Normal* will display in the Style list box located at the left side of the Formatting toolbar. The *Normal* style is automatically applied to any text that is keyed unless you specify other formatting instructions. If you click the down arrow to the right of the Style list box at a clear document screen, you will see a total of five predesigned styles immediately available for your use, as shown in figure 6.8. The style names are listed along with the corresponding font selection and paragraph alignment for that style. In addition to these styles, Word provides a large selection of other predesigned styles. To view all the styles that come with Word in the Style list box on the Formatting toolbar, hold down the Shift key and then click the down arrow to the right of the Style list box.

Normal Style
A set of formatting instructions automatically applied to any text that is keyed unless other formatting instructions are specified.

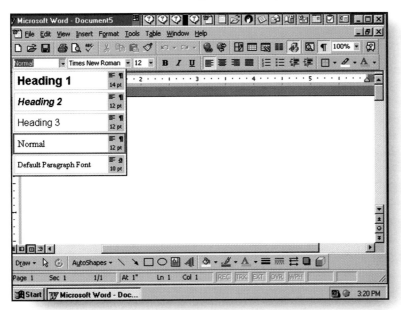

Style Drop-Down List

You can also view all available styles by choosing Format, and then Style. At the Style dialog box shown in figure 6.9, click the down arrow in the List box and choose All styles. Select any style name from the Styles list box and a description of the formatting instructions contained in that style will be displayed in the Description section of the Style dialog box. For example, if you select *Heading 7*, the description section displays the formatting instructions that are included in the *Heading 7* style. As displayed in figure 6.9, the *Heading 7* style includes all the formatting instructions contained in the *Normal* style in addition to a font selection of 10-point Arial and a paragraph spacing setting that will provide 12 points of spacing before and 3 points of spacing after the paragraph to which this style is applied. (Level 7 refers to the level to which this style is automatically applied when using the Word's Outline feature.) An example of how the selected style will format text is also displayed in the Paragraph preview box.

Style Dialog Box

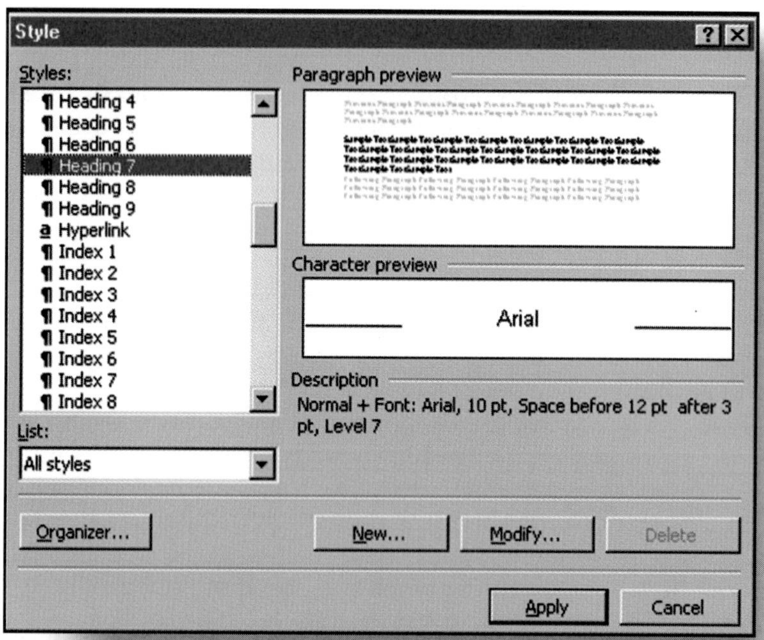

Most of Word's predesigned styles are available in any of its template documents. However, some of Word's template documents also contain additional styles depending on the type of document being created. For example, the memo templates, letter templates, and résumé templates used in previous chapters all contain their own set of specific styles. If you choose a different template document from the New dialog box, click the down arrow to the right of the Style list box on the Formatting toolbar to display the names of styles available for that particular template. If you access the Style dialog box and select *Styles in use* from the List box, you will also see the names of styles available for that particular template.

You may print a list of all the styles contained in a particular template document, including the *Normal.dot* template. The list contains the names of the styles and all the formatting instructions included in each style. To print a list of the available styles in a document, you would complete the following steps:

1. Choose File, then Print.
2. At the Print dialog box, click the down arrow to the right of the Print what list box.
3. Choose Styles from the Print what drop-down list.
4. Click OK or press Enter.

Word contains some styles that are applied automatically to text when you use certain commands. For example, if you use the command to insert page numbers, Word applies a certain style to the page number text. Some other commands for which Word automatically formats text with styles include headers, footers, footnotes, endnotes, indexes, and tables of contents.

Using Word's Brochure Template

The previous version of Word, Word 7, included a brochure template; however, Word 97 does not automatically include this template. If you have upgraded from Office for Windows 95 to Office 97, the documents, templates, and other files from the previous version are preserved in the new version. Click File, New, then click the Office 95 Templates tab to see the templates displayed from the previous version, including the *Brochure.dot* template. If you did not upgrade from Office 95 but installed Office 97 from CD, then you have the ValuPack folder available as mentioned in previous chapters. The ValuPack offers additional templates, including the *Brochure.dot* template. To use this template, copy it from the *ValuPack|Templates|Word* folder on the CD to the *Program Files/Microsoft Office|Templates|Publications* folder on your hard drive.

The brochure template is a letter-fold or three-panel brochure. When the brochure template document is displayed on the screen, it contains instructions and tips on how to create and customize the brochure. Printing these instructions first can be helpful so you can refer to them as you personalize and customize the brochure. After printing the instructional text, you can label the panels and use the printout as your dummy. The instructional text must be deleted when keying the actual brochure content.

The instructional text is formatted as text might appear in a brochure, including columns, headings, subheadings, cover title, and cover graphic image. The formatting instructions for these parts of the brochure are contained in styles that are available to the brochure template document. In exercise 4, you are instructed to create panels 1, 2, and 3 of a brochure using the *Brochure.dot* template as a base. You will insert a file containing the brochure text, you will change the column formatting to three unequal columns, and then you will format specific sections of the text using some of the predefined styles provided in the brochure template.

To apply a style with the Style button on the Formatting toolbar, position the insertion point in the paragraph to which you want the style applied, or select the text, then click the down arrow to the right of the Style button. Click the desired style name in the list to apply the style to the text in the document.

exercise 4

Creating Panels 1, 2, and 3 of a Brochure Using the Brochure Template

1. Create panels 1, 2, and 3 of the brochure shown in figure 6.10 using the *Brochure.dot* template by completing the following steps:
   a. Open the brochure template by completing the following steps:
      (1) Click File, New.
      (2) At the New dialog box, select the Office 95 Templates tab or the Publications tab. (See the previous section for a discussion about the location of this template.)
      (3) Make sure Document is selected in the Create New section.
      (4) Double-click *Brochure.dot* in the Office 95 Templates or Publications list box.
   b. Print a copy of the brochure template instructional text by completing the following steps:
      (1) With the insertion point positioned anywhere on the first page of the brochure, choose File, then Print.
      (2) At the Print dialog box, choose Current Page, then click OK.
      (3) Reinsert the copy of page one into the printer so that the second page of the brochure will print correctly on the back of the first page.
      (4) Position the insertion point anywhere on page 2 and then repeat steps (1) and (2).
   c. Read, fold, and label the brochure panels and use this as your dummy.
   d. Remove all the instructional text by completing the following steps:
      (1) Choose Edit, then Select All or press Ctrl + A.
      (2) Press the Delete key to remove all the instructional text. (This will also eliminate the second page; however, you will recreate the second page when needed.)
   e. Click the Show/Hide ¶ button on the Standard toolbar so that nonprinting characters, such as paragraph symbols and style indicators, display on the screen. (A style indicator is a small black square that usually appears to the left of the text where a style has been applied.)
   f. Adjust the brochure margins by completing the following steps:
      (1) Click File, then Page Setup.
      (2) At the Page Setup dialog box, select the Margins tab.
      (3) Change the left and right margin settings to 0.67 inches. Leave the top and bottom margins as set. (The left and right margin settings were selected because of the unprintable zone that exists on the printer that was used to print the brochure in figures 6.10 and 6.11.)
   g. Turn on automatic kerning for font sizes 14 points and above at the Character Spacing tab of the Font dialog box.
   h. Change the column formatting to three columns of unequal width by completing the following steps:
      (1) With the insertion point positioned at the top of the document, click Format, then Columns.
      (2) At the Columns dialog box, select Three in the Presets section or increase the number to 3 in the Number of columns option.
      (3) Remove the check mark in the Equal column width check box.
      (4) In the Width and spacing section, enter the following amounts in the Width and Spacing text boxes for the columns indicated:

Col #	Width	Spacing
1	2.64	0.7
2	3.00	0.7
3	2.62	

(5) Click OK or press Enter.

i. To insert the file containing the brochure text, complete the following steps:
   (1) With the insertion point located at the beginning of the document, click Insert, then File.
   (2) At the Insert File dialog box, double-click *volunteer text.doc* (located on your student data disk) in the Look in: list box.

j. Apply the predefined styles provided in the *Brochure* template document to specific sections of text in the first panel (or column) of the brochure by completing the following steps:
   (1) With the insertion point at the beginning of the document, choose Edit, then Select All or press Ctrl + A.
   (2) Click the down arrow at the right side of the Style list box located on the Formatting toolbar, then select *Body Text* from the Style drop-down list. Use the vertical scroll bar in this drop-down menu to see all the style names listed. (The *Body Text* style will change the font for all the text in the document to 12-point Garamond. Since the majority of text in this brochure is to be formatted as *Body Text*, applying the style to the whole document will eliminate the need to frequently reapply this style.)
   (3) Click the Zoom button on the Standard toolbar and change the view to 75% or Page Width.
   (4) Format *Giving Is Its Own Reward* by completing the following steps:
      (a) Press Ctrl + Home, then position the insertion point anywhere within the line that reads *Giving Is Its Own Reward.*
      (b) Select *Heading 1* from the Style drop-down list similar to step 1j(2) above.
      (c) Select the title, *Giving Is Its Own Reward . . .*, access the Font dialog box, then change the font size to 27 points, apply a shadow effect, then turn on bold.
      (d) With the title still selected, click once in the style list box on the Formatting toolbar (*Heading 1* should be selected), then press Enter. Make sure *Update the style to reflect recent changes?* is selected, then click OK to redefine the current style for future use.
   (5) Select the line that reads *As a volunteer, you will:*, and select *Emphasis* from the Style drop-down list.
   (6) Select the list of items that begins with *Share your skills and talents* and ends with *Make a difference in other people's lives*, and select *List Bullet* from the Style drop-down list. (If this style does not display in the Style drop-down list, click Format, then Style. At the Style dialog box, click the List: list box, then select All styles.)
   (7) To align the items in the bulleted list that are more than one line of text, complete the following steps:
      (a) If the list of items is not already selected, select the bulleted list.
      (b) Click Format, Paragraph, then select the Indents and Spacing tab.
      (c) Click the Special option list box in the Indentation section, then select *Hanging* from the drop-down list.

(d) Key **0.15** in the By option text box, then click OK or press Enter.

(8) Format *What Do Volunteers Do?* by completing the following steps:

(a) Position the insertion point at the beginning of the line of text that reads *What Do Volunteers Do?* and select *Heading 2* from the Style drop-down list.

(b) Select the same line of text and turn on bold.

(c) Click Format, Paragraph, then select the Indents and Spacing tab.

(d) Change the spacing Before the paragraph to 12 pt and make sure the spacing After is set to 3 pt.

(e) Redefine the *Heading 2* style by following step 1j(4)(d) above.

k. Position the insertion point at the beginning of the line of text that reads *Visitor Services*, then insert a column break to move this text to the top of panel 2.

l. Move the insertion point back to the bottom of panel 1.

m. Insert a text box, then insert and format the decorative symbols at the bottom of panel 1 by completing the following steps:

(1) Click the Text Box button on the Drawing toolbar.

(2) Position the crosshairs at the bottom of panel 1, then click and drag to draw a text box the approximate size and in the approximate location as the symbols shown in panel 1 in figure 6.10.

(3) Click Insert, Symbol, then select the Symbols tab.

(4) Change the Font to Wingdings, then double-click the ☙ symbol located in the fifth row, thirteenth column. Double-click the ❧ symbol immediately to the right (fifth row, fourteenth column), then click Close.

(5) Select the symbols just inserted and apply the following formatting:

(a) Change the font size to 26 points.

(b) Add a shadow effect through the Font dialog box.

(c) Change the paragraph alignment to Center.

(6) Use the sizing handles to adjust the size of the text box so the symbols are completely visible.

n. Format the text box by completing the following steps:

(a) Double-click the text box border to display the Format Text Box dialog box.

(b) Click the Colors and Lines tab, then change the line color to No Line.

(c) Click the Size tab, then change the height to 0.5 inches and the width to 1 inch.

(d) Click the Position tab, then change the horizontal From option to Page and the Horizontal option to 1.4 inches. Change the vertical From option to Page and change the Vertical option to 7.4 inches.

(e) Click OK or press Enter.

o. Apply styles to format the text in panel 2 by completing the following steps:

(1) Position the insertion point anywhere in the line that reads *Visitor Services* and select *Heading 7* from the Style drop-down list.

(2) Position the insertion point anywhere in the line that reads *Patient Services* and select *Heading 7* from the Style drop-down list or press F4 (the repeat key).

(3) To format the block of text at the bottom of panel two, complete the following steps:

(a) Position the insertion point anywhere within the line that reads *"Sharing Responsibility for Your Family's Health"* and select *Block Quotation* from the Style drop-down list.

(b) With the insertion point within the same line of text, change the paragraph alignment to Center.

(c) Select the line of text, change the font size to 16 point, and then apply bold.
(d) Access the Paragraph dialog box, change the line spacing to single and the spacing after the paragraph to 0 pt.
(e) Click Format, Borders and Shading, then click the Shading tab. Change the fill to Gray-25% (second row, third column of the fill color palette). Click OK or press Enter.
(f) Redefine the *Block Quotation* style by following step 1j(4)(d) above.

p. Position the insertion point at the end of the paragraph above the slogan that ends with "*pleasant as possible.*" and press Enter two times.
q. *Staff Services* should be located at the top of the third panel. If not, position the insertion point to the left of *Staff Services* and insert a column break to move the remaining text to the top of panel 3.
r. Apply styles to format the text in panel 3 by completing the following steps:
(1) At the top of panel 3, position the insertion point anywhere within the line that reads *Staff Services* and select *Heading 7* from the Style drop-down list.
(2) Position the insertion point anywhere within the line of text that reads *Who Can Volunteer?* and select *Heading 2* from the Style drop-down list.

s. At the end of the paragraph that starts with *The volunteers at Edward Hospital range . . .*, press Enter.
t. Change the paragraph alignment to Right, change the type size to 11 points, turn on italics, then key **(Continued on back panel)**.
u. Press Enter, then change the paragraph alignment back to left.
v. Position the insertion point at the beginning of the line that reads *About Edward Hospital . . .* and insert a column break.
w. Move the insertion point back to the bottom of panel 3.
x. Copy the text box containing the symbols at the bottom of panel 1 by completing the following steps:
(1) Click the arrow to the right of the Zoom button on the Standard toolbar, then change the viewing mode to Page Width.
(2) Select the text box at the bottom of panel 1.
(3) Position the insertion point on one of the text box borders until it displays as an arrow with a four-headed arrow attached. Hold down the Ctrl key, then click and drag a copy of the text box to the bottom of panel 3, then release the left mouse button.

y. Format the symbol text box at the bottom of panel 3 by completing the following steps:
(1) Double-click the text box border, then click the Position tab.
(2) Change the horizontal From option to Page and the Horizontal option to 8.7 inches. Change the vertical From option to Page and the Vertical option to 7.4 inches.
(3) Click OK or press Enter.

z. Use Print Preview to view your document. Check carefully for the correct placement of text and design elements. Make any adjustments if necessary.

2. Save the brochure and name it c06ex04, panels 1,2,3.
3. You may either print the first page of your brochure now, or wait and print it in exercise 5.
4. Close c06ex04, panels 1,2,3. (When you close the brochure document that is based on the *Brochure.dot* template, you will be prompted with the following message, *Do you want to save the changes you made to Brochure.dot*? Click No so the original brochure template will not change.)

figure 6.10

Giving Is Its Own Reward...

As an Edward Hospital volunteer, you will be involved in new experiences and challenges each day. Volunteering is a job that requires giving of yourself; your pay is in the form of personal reward.

As a volunteer, you will:

- Share your skills and talents
- Develop new interests
- Learn new skills
- Make new friends
- Grow in understanding and self-awareness
- Enjoy the satisfaction that comes from helping others
- Make a difference in other people's lives

What Do Volunteers Do?

Edward Hospital offers volunteer opportunities in three different areas: visitor services, patient services, and staff services.

Visitor Services

At Edward Hospital, we stand by our motto, "Sharing Responsibility for Your Family's Health." We want to show our community that those are not just words, but the way Edward Hospital really operates. Often, a volunteer is the first and last person a hospital visitor encounters. We rely on our volunteers to provide accurate information while, at the same time, acting as goodwill ambassadors for the hospital.

Patient Services

Many volunteer positions involve direct interaction with patients. Many of our volunteers make a difference simply by lending a friendly ear or by performing a small favor when it is most needed and appreciated.

For those volunteers who are uncomfortable dealing directly with patients, there are many ways to help indirectly. Many Edward Hospital volunteers bring a smile to our patients' faces without ever seeing them. For instance, volunteers sew stuffed clowns to give to pediatric patients before surgery. We are always looking to our volunteers for new ideas to help make our patients' hospital stay as pleasant as possible.

"Sharing Responsibility for Your Family's Health."

Staff Services

Many volunteers draw on their past and present work experience to generously assist various hospital departments. Staff service volunteers play an important role in the hospital's team effort to provide cost-efficient, quality healthcare.

Volunteers offer their assistance in the following areas: Business Office, Central Distribution, Fitness Center, Women's Health Center, Employee Health, Human Resources, Laboratory, Edward Institute, Medical Library, Medical Records, Pharmacy, Preadmission Testing, and Surgery.

Who Can Volunteer?

You must be at least 15 years of age to volunteer. We ask our volunteers to commit to a regular weekly schedule. It can be a few hours once a week or several hours each day. Volunteer opportunities are available seven days a week, days and evenings.

The volunteers at Edward Hospital range in age from teenagers to professionals to retirees, bringing a wealth of skill and experience to their volunteer positions.

(Continued on back panel)

In the following exercise, you will create panels 4, 5, and 6 to complete the brochure started in exercise 4. Remember to save periodically as you are creating the panels.

exercise 5

Creating Panels 4, 5, and 6 of a Brochure Using the Brochure Template

1. Open c06ex04, panels 1,2,3.
2. Save the document with Save As and name it c06ex05, volunteer brochure.
3. Create panels 4, 5, and 6 of the brochure shown in figure 6.11 by completing the following steps:
   a. Set the column formatting for the outside panels of the brochure by completing the following steps:
      (1) Position the insertion point at the top of the second page of the brochure to the left of *About Edward Hospital*.
      (2) Click Format, then Columns.
      (3) At the Columns dialog box, make sure the number of columns is set to 3.
      (4) Make sure there is no check mark in the Equal column width check box.
      (5) In the Width and spacing section, enter the following amounts in the Width and Spacing text boxes for the columns indicated (remember: these settings are the opposite of the settings for panels 1, 2, and 3):

Col #	Width	Spacing
1	2.62	0.7
2	3.00	0.7
3	2.64	

      (6) Click the Apply to: list box and select *This point forward*. (This will automatically insert a section break in the document along with the new column formatting.)
      (7) Click OK or press Enter.
   b. Apply styles to format the text in panel 4 by completing the following steps:
      (1) Position the insertion point anywhere within the line of text that reads *About Edward Hospital . . .* and select *Heading 2* from the Style drop-down list.
      (2) With the insertion point in the same line, access the Paragraph dialog box, then change the paragraph spacing before the paragraph to 0 pt for this heading only. Do not redefine the style.
      (3) Position the insertion point anywhere within the line of text that reads *Take The First Step . . .* and select *Heading 2* from the Style drop-down list.
   c. In the paragraph in panel 4 that starts with *For more information*, bold the text that reads *Cindy Bonagura, Volunteer Services Coordinator* and then bold the area code and phone number.
   d. Position the insertion point at the beginning of the line that reads *You can make a difference at Edward Hospital.* and insert a column break at this point.
   e. Apply styles to format the text in panel 5 by completing the following steps: (The decorative symbols will be inserted later.)

(1) Position the insertion point at the top of panel 5 to the left of *You can make a difference . . .*
(2) Press Enter three times.
(3) Format the text in the shaded box by completing the following steps:
(a) Position the insertion point anywhere within the text that reads *You can make a difference at Edward Hospital.* and select *Block Quotation* from the Style drop-down list.
(b) Select the same line of text, then change the type size to 26 points.
(c) Delete the space after *a*, then press Enter.
(d) Delete the space after *at*, then press Enter.
(e) Delete the space after *Edward*, then press Enter.
(4) Position the insertion point below the block quotation at the beginning of the first line of the address that reads *Edward Hospital*, then press Enter seven times.
(5) Select the hospital name and address, choose *Heading 7*, then change the paragraph alignment to Center and the spacing after the paragraph (the selected text) to 0 points.
(6) Select the name of the hospital and change the type size to 14 points. Do not redefine the style.

f. Insert the decorative symbols at the top of panel 5 by completing the following steps:
(1) Click the arrow to the right of the Zoom button on the Standard toolbar, then change the viewing mode to Two Pages.
(2) Select the text box at the bottom of panel 1.
(3) Position the insertion point on one of the text box borders until it displays as an arrow with a four-headed arrow attached. Hold down the Ctrl key, then click and drag a copy of the text box to the top of panel 5, then release the left mouse button.
(4) Double-click the text box border, then click the Position tab. Change the horizontal From option to Page and the Horizontal option to 4.98 inches. Change the vertical From option to Page and the Vertical option to 0.8 inches.
(5) Click OK or press Enter.
(6) Click the arrow to the right of the Zoom button on the Standard toolbar, then change the viewing mode to 75%.

g. At the bottom of panel 5, position the insertion point below the address at the beginning of the line that reads *Edward Hospital* and insert a column break to end panel 5.

h. Insert the title and subtitle into a text box by completing the following steps:
(1) Select both the cover title and subtitle (*Edward Hospital* and *Volunteer Now . . . Giving Is Its Own Reward*).
(2) Click the Text Box button on the Drawing toolbar to insert this text into a text box. The text box and text seem to disappear. Scroll down to the bottom of panel 6, and you will see the text box.

i. Size and format the text box by completing the following steps:
(1) Double-click one of the text box borders to display the Format Text Box dialog box.
(2) Click the Colors and Lines tab, then change the line color to No Line.
(3) Click the Size tab, then change the height of the text box to 1.9 inches and the width to 2.6 inches.
(4) Click the Position tab, then change the horizontal From option to Page and the Horizontal option to 7.82 inches. Change the vertical From option to Page, then change the Vertical option to 0.7 inches.
(5) Click OK or press Enter.

j. Apply styles to the title and the subtitle on the cover (panel 6) by completing the following steps:
   (1) Position the insertion point anywhere within the cover title that reads *Edward Hospital* and select *Title Cover* from the Style drop-down list.
   (2) Select *Edward Hospital*, change the paragraph alignment to Center, change the font size to 18 points, then turn on bold.
   (3) To insert a top border and to adjust the spacing between the borders and the text, complete the following steps:
      (a) Click Format, Borders and Shading, then click the Borders tab.
      (b) In the Preview section, a bottom border should already display. Click the top side of the diagram to insert a top border. Make sure no border displays on the left or right side of the diagram.
      (c) Make sure Paragraph displays in the Apply to list box.
      (d) Click the Options button to display the Borders and Shading Options dialog box.
      (e) In the From text section, change the Top and Bottom options to 8 pt to set the distance from the text to the borders.
      (f) Click OK to close the Borders and Shading Options dialog box, then click OK again to close the Borders and Shading dialog box.
   (4) Click once in the Style list box on the Formatting toolbar, then press Enter.
   (5) Make sure *Update the style to reflect recent changes?* is selected, then click OK to redefine the current style for future use.
   (6) Position the insertion point anywhere within the text that reads *Volunteer Now . . . Giving Is Its Own Reward* and select *Subtitle Cover* from the Style drop-down list.
   (7) Select the subtitle text, then change the paragraph alignment to Center.
   (8) Redefine the *Subtitle Cover* style by repeating steps 3j(4-5).

k. Insert the medical graphic image by completing the following steps:
   (1) Press Ctrl + End to position the insertion point after the subtitle.
   (2) Click Insert, point to Picture, then click From file.
   (3) Change to the folder that contains your student data disk files, then double-click *Medstaff.wmf*. The image will appear at the bottom of panel 6.

l. Size and position the picture by completing the following steps:
   (1) Click once with the left mouse button inside the picture to select it.
   (2) Click Format, then Picture.
   (3) At the Format Picture dialog box, select the Size tab, remove the check mark from the Lock aspect ratio option, then change the height of the image to 4.22 inches and the width to 2.22 inches.
   (4) Click the Position tab, then change the horizontal From option to Page and the Horizontal option to 8.05. Change the vertical From option to Page and the Vertical option to 3.1.
   (5) Choose OK or press Enter to close the dialog box.

m. Use Print Preview to view your brochure. Carefully check your brochure for the correct placement of text and design elements. Make any adjustments if necessary.

4. Save the brochure again with the same name (c06ex05, volunteer brochure).
5. Print both pages of the brochure using both sides of the paper.
6. Close c06ex05, volunteer brochure. Click No in response to the prompt *Do you want to save the changes you made to Brochure.dot?*

figure 6.11

About Edward Hospital . . .

Edward Hospital was established 75 years ago as a respiratory disease sanitorium. Today, Edward Hospital operates as a full-service, not-for-profit hospital with 175 beds. Located on a 60-acre campus, Edward Hospital offers a state-of-the-art, all-private inpatient facility, as well as the Edward Cardiovascular Institute, the Women's Health Center, the Edward Health and Fitness Center, two satellite medical clinics, and Valley View Hospital—a private psychiatric facility. Over 1,500 employees work to make Edward Hospital a success.

Take The First Step . . .

If you are interested in becoming a volunteer at Edward Hospital, you will need to schedule an interview. At the interview, your experience, skills, interests, and availability will be matched to those areas in need of volunteer support. An orientation will be scheduled before you become an active volunteer. Once you start volunteering, you will receive on-the-job training from an experienced hospital employee.

For more information, please call **Cindy Bonagura, Volunteer Services Coordinator,** at: (708) 555-3189.

You can make a difference at Edward Hospital.

Edward Hospital
801 South Washington Street
Naperville, IL 60540-9865

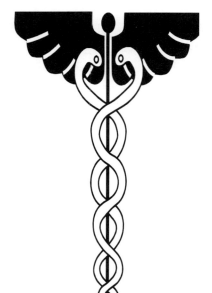

EDWARD HOSPITAL

Volunteer Now . . .
Giving Is Its Own Reward

Character and Paragraph Styles

Two types of styles exist in Word—paragraph styles and character styles. A *paragraph style* applies formatting instructions to an entire paragraph, while a *character style* applies formatting to selected text only. Paragraph styles affect the paragraph that contains the insertion point or selected text. Word considers a paragraph as any text followed by a hard return. This means that even a short line with no punctuation is considered a paragraph. A paragraph style includes formatting instructions such as tabs, indents, borders, paragraph spacing, numbers and bullets, etc. The *Normal* style, as mentioned earlier in this chapter, is the default style and is automatically applied to all paragraphs unless you specify other formatting instructions. Paragraph styles are useful for formatting headings, subheadings, and bulleted lists in a document.

Paragraph Style
A set of formatting instructions that applies to an entire paragraph.

Character Style
A set of formatting instructions that applies to selected text only.

Character styles include options available at the Font dialog box such as font, font size, and font style such as, bold, underlining, and italics. Character styles are useful for formatting single characters, technical words, special names, or phrases.

In the Styles list (accessed through the Style dialog box or the Style button on the Formatting toolbar), paragraph styles are indicated by a ¶ symbol and character styles are preceded by an **a** character. When you used the brochure template document in exercises 4 and 5, the *Heading 1* style was a paragraph style and the *Emphasis* style was a character style. To find out if a particular style has been applied to text, position the insertion point within the line or paragraph, and the style name will display in the Style box on the Formatting toolbar. A character style can even be applied to selected text within a paragraph that has already been formatted with a paragraph style. If this is the case, you need to select the specific text first to see the character style name that has been applied to it.

Creating Styles

A style can be created in two ways. You can create a new style through the Style dialog box or you can create a style from existing text that already contains the formatting you desire. Creating a style from existing text is the easiest method.

When you create your own style, you must give the style a name. When naming a style, try to name it something that gives you an idea what the style will accomplish. Consider the following when naming a style:

- A style name can contain a maximum of 255 characters.
- A style name can contain spaces and commas.
- Do not use a backslash (\), braces ({}), or a semicolon (;) when naming a style.
- A style name is case-sensitive. Uppercase and lowercase letters can be used.
- Avoid using the names already used by Word.

To create a new style from existing text, you would complete the following steps:

1. Key a paragraph of text, such as a heading.
2. Format the text the way you want it to appear, such as changing the font, font size, applying color, paragraph shading, etc.
3. Position the insertion point within the paragraph that contains the desired formatting; or select the text if you are creating a character style.
4. Click the Style box on the Formatting toolbar to select the current style name.
5. Type a new name and then press Enter. The new style name is added to the list of styles available in that document.

The above method of inserting the style name in the Style text box on the Formatting toolbar automatically defines the style as a paragraph style. You must use the Style dialog box to create a character style. You can use the Style dialog box to create both paragraph and character styles from existing text or from scratch. To create a new style using the Style dialog box, you would select text if necessary and then complete the following steps:

1. Choose Format, then Style.
2. At the Style dialog box, choose New.
3. At the New Style dialog box, key a name for the style in the Name text box.
4. Select the Style type option and specify whether you are creating a paragraph or character style.
5. Choose Format, then choose the desired formatting options.
6. When all formatting has been selected, make sure the correct formatting instructions display in the Description section of the New Style dialog box.
7. If you want to assign the style to a keystroke combination, click Shortcut Key to display the Customize Keyboard dialog box. Press the shortcut key combination in the Press new shortcut key text box and then click Assign. Click Close to close the Customize Keyboard dialog box.
8. If you want the style to be available to all new documents based on this template, click the Add to template check box.
9. Choose OK or press Enter.
10. Click Close at the Style dialog box.

When you choose Format at the New Style dialog box, a drop-down list displays with a variety of formatting options. These options, along with the formatting that can be selected with each option, are listed in figure 6.12.

figure 6.12

Style Formatting Options

Choose this:	To select these types of formatting instructions:
Font	Font, style, size, color, effects such as superscript, subscript, outline, shadow, engrave, small caps, etc., and character spacing.
Paragraph	Paragraph alignment, indentations, spacing before and after a paragraph, line spacing, Widow/Orphan control, keep lines together, etc. (Available for paragraph styles only.)
Tabs	Tab stop measurements, alignment, leaders, or clear tabs. (Available for paragraph styles only.)
Border	Border location, color, style, and shading. (Available for paragraph styles only.)
Language	Language that the spell checker, thesaurus, and grammar checker use for the current paragraph. (Available for paragraph styles only.)
Frame	Text wrapping, positioning, and sizing of frames. (Available for paragraph styles only; frames are not used often in this version of Word.)
Numbering	Bulleted, Numbered, and Outlined Numbered paragraphs in various styles. (Available for paragraph styles only.)

Creating a Style Based on an Existing Style

You may also use an existing style as a base for creating a new style. The existing style is then known as the *base style*. The new style inherits all the formatting instructions included in the base style in addition to the formatting currently selected for the new style. If you make a change to the base style, the new style and any other related styles will reflect that change. For example, many of Word's predesigned styles are based on the *Normal* style. If you make a change to the *Normal* style, all styles based on the *Normal* style will be changed also. This may produce some unwanted results in your document if you applied any styles that were based on the *Normal* style. For this reason, **avoid making changes to the Normal style**.

Base Style
A preexisting style that is used as a base for creating a new style.

You can create your own base styles for different elements of your document. For example, suppose you want 14-point Impact headings and 12-point Impact Italic subheadings in your document. You could create a new style that contains an Impact font instruction that will serve as the base style. You could then create two separate styles for the headings and subheadings that include the specific font size and font style choices. Each style would be based on the base style that includes the Impact font selection. If in the future, you decide to change the font to Arial Rounded MT Bold, all you have to do is change the base style and the font will be changed in all the headings and subheadings.

Following One Style with Another

In some situations one set of formatting instructions is immediately followed by another set of formatting instructions. For instance, formatting for a heading is usually followed by formatting for body text. In Word, you can define one style to be immediately followed by another style. Pressing the Enter key after applying the first style will automatically apply the second style to the text that follows. For example, to define a heading style so that it is followed by a body text style, you would complete the following steps:

1. Create the body text style first using either the Style button on the Formatting toolbar or the Style option from the Format menu. (Creating the style that is to follow another style first is the easiest.)
2. Create the heading style using the Style option from the Format menu.
3. At the New Style dialog box, click the down arrow under the Style for following paragraph option, then select the body text style from the drop-down list.
4. Choose OK or press Enter.
5. Choose Close at the Style dialog box.

Applying Styles

A style can be applied before you key text or it can be applied in a document with existing text. Applying styles to existing text is the most convenient method. How you apply a style to existing text depends on the style being used. To apply a character style to existing text, select the text first. If you are formatting text with a paragraph style, position the insertion point anywhere in the paragraph.

The most common methods of applying styles in Word include using the Style button on the Formatting toolbar and the Style command from the Format menu. To apply a style to existing text using the Style button on the Formatting toolbar, you would complete the following steps:

1. Position the insertion point in the paragraph to which you want the style applied, or select the text.
2. Click the down arrow to the right of the Style button on the Formatting toolbar.
3. Click the desired style name in the drop-down list to apply the style to the text in the document.

To apply a style using the Style command from the Format menu, you would complete the following steps:

1. Position the insertion point in the paragraph to which you want the style applied, or select the text.
2. Choose Format, then Style.
3. At the Style dialog box, choose List, then choose *All Styles*.
4. Double-click the desired style name or select the style name and click Apply.
5. If you want to apply the same style to different sections of text in a document, such as applying a heading style to all the headings, apply the style to the first heading. Then, move the insertion point to each of the remaining headings and press F4, Word's Repeat key.

To apply a style before text is keyed, position the insertion point where formatting is to begin and then display the Style dialog box. From the Styles list, select the desired style and then choose Apply. You can also use the Style button on the Formatting toolbar to select a style name. If you apply a style before text is keyed, the style will affect any text you key after the style is applied, even if you begin a new paragraph. You must then apply a different style, such as the *Normal* style, to discontinue the first style.

In addition to applying styles with the Style button on the Formatting toolbar and the Style dialog box, you can use shortcut keys as mentioned above.

Modifying an Existing Style

One of the advantages of using styles within a document is that a style can be modified and all occurrences of that style in the document are automatically updated. Once a style has been created, you can modify the style by changing the formatting instructions that it contains either with the Formatting toolbar or the Style dialog box. When you modify a style by changing the formatting instructions, all text to which that style has been applied is changed accordingly. To modify a style using the Formatting toolbar, you would complete the following steps:

1. Open the document that contains the style you want to modify.
2. Reformat text with the formatting instructions you want changed in the style.
3. Select the reformatted text.
4. Click the down arrow to the right of the Style button on the Formatting toolbar.
5. At the Styles drop-down list, click the style name you want to modify, then press Enter.
6. When Word asks if you want to update the style to reflect recent changes, click OK or press Enter.

You can also modify a style at the Style dialog box. To modify a style at the Style dialog box, you would complete the following steps:

1. Open the document containing the style you want to modify.
2. Choose Format, then Style.
3. At the Style dialog box, select the style name you want to modify in the Styles list box, then choose Modify.
4. At the Modify Style dialog box, add or delete formatting options by choosing Format, and then selecting the appropriate options.
5. When all changes have been made, choose OK or press Enter to close the Modify Style dialog box.
6. Choose Close to close the Style dialog box.

If you would like the modified style to be available in any new document based on the active template (most likely this is the *Normal.dot* template), click Add to template in the Modify Style dialog box to insert a check mark in the check box. For example, if the active template is the Normal template, the modified style is added to that template so that it will be available every time you create a document based on the Normal template.

Additional formatting changes can be made to text even if a style has been previously applied to it. This is useful if you want to make a minor change to specific text without the need to redefine the whole style.

Copying Individual Styles from Other Documents and Templates

When you work on a document, you may want to use a style that already exists in one of Word's templates or in a document you may have created. For example, if you had to create some other promotional material for The Edward Cardiovascular Clinic (see figures 6.17 and 6.18), you could maintain consistency and reinforce the organization's identity by using the same heading and subheading styles that were created for the brochure in exercise 6.

DTP POINTERS
Styles can help to maintain consistency and reinforce an organization's identity.

In Word, the Organizer feature lets you copy individual styles, in addition to macros, toolbars, and AutoText entries, from an existing document or template to another document or template.

For instance, to copy the *teal heading* and the *violet subheading* styles from c06ex06, panels 1,2 to a fictitious document named *fact sheet* using the Organizer dialog box, as shown in figure 6.13, you would complete the following steps:

1. With the insertion point located in *fact sheet*, choose Format, then Style.
2. At the Style dialog box, click Organizer, and then select the Styles tab. By default, the name of the current document, *fact sheet*, displays above a list box on the left side of the Organizer dialog box. The list box shows a list of the styles available in the template attached to that particular document. By default, *Normal* will display as the file name on the right side of the dialog box and the list box below will display the styles available in the Normal template.
3. On the right side of the dialog box, click Close File to change the command button to Open File.
4. Click Open File.
5. Select *c06ex06 panels 1,2*, then click Open or press Enter.

6. In the right list box for *c06ex06, panels 1,2,* select *teal heading,* hold down the Control key, then select *violet subheading.* (Both style names should be selected.)
7. Click Copy. (The *teal heading* and the *violet subheading* styles will now be listed in the *fact sheet* list box on the left side of the dialog box.)
8. Click Close.

Style Organizer Dialog Box

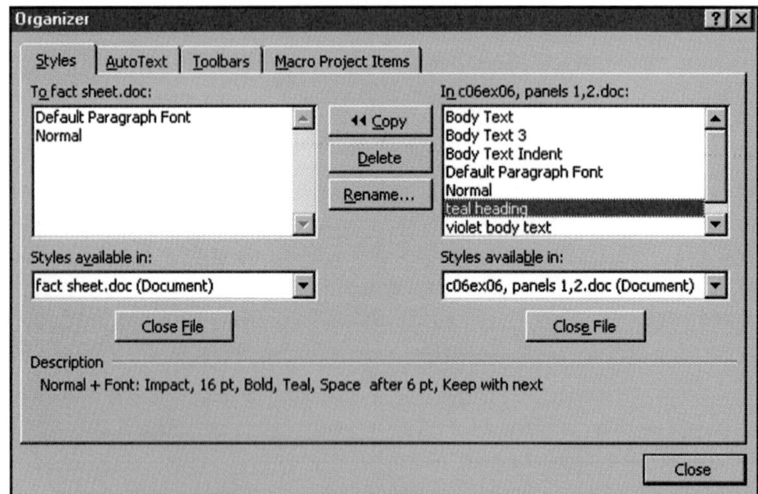

A specific document does not have to be open for you to copy styles from one document or template to another. At the Organizer dialog box, you can select a different document name or template for each list box by clicking the Close File (or Close File) command button below either list box. This changes the command button to an Open File (or Open File) button. Click Open File (or Open File) and select the document or template you want to copy styles to or from.

The styles Organizer dialog box can be confusing because the Copy button displays triangles pointing to the right, making you think that styles must be copied from the left side to the right side. However, styles can be copied from either side. If you select a style in the list box on the right, the triangles on the Copy button change and point to the left, as do the labels above each list box.

Copying All Styles from a Template

Word's Style Gallery feature lets you copy all the styles from a specific template into the current document. To display the Style Gallery dialog box shown in figure 6.14, choose Format, then Style Gallery.

At the Style Gallery dialog box, the template documents are displayed in the Template list box. These are the same template documents that were mentioned in previous chapters, in addition to any you may have created on your own. The document currently open displays in the Preview of box. If you choose a template name from the Template list box, you can see how the formatting from that template would be applied to the current document. If you accessed Style Gallery from a blank screen, the Preview of box will be empty.

At the bottom of the Style Gallery dialog box, the Document option is selected in the Preview section. If you select a template name from the Template list box, and then choose Example from the Preview section, Word will insert a sample of the template document in the Preview of box. As you can see in figure 6.14, *Brochure* is displayed in the Template list box and an example of the brochure template document is displayed in the Preview of box. Choosing Style Samples will cause the styles from the selected template to display in the Preview of box.

To copy all the styles from a specific template into the current document, you would complete the following steps:

1. With the insertion point positioned in the current document, choose Format, then Style Gallery.
2. In the Template list box, select the template name that contains the styles you want to copy.
3. Choose OK or press Enter.

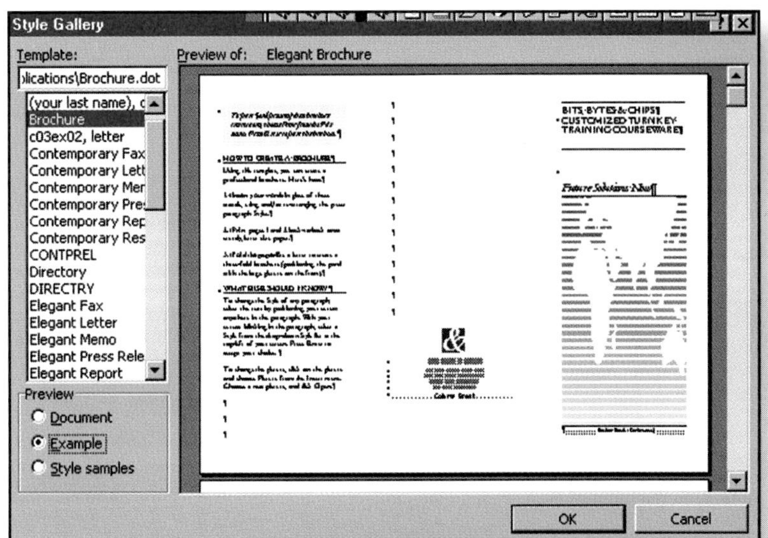

figure 6.14

Style Gallery Dialog Box

Removing a Style from Text

If you wish to remove a style immediately after applying it, click the Undo button on the Standard toolbar. When a style is removed, the style that was previously applied to the text is applied once again (usually this is the *Normal* style). Since only one style can be applied at a time to the same text, you can also remove a style from text by applying a new style. To remove a character style, select the text, then press Ctrl + Spacebar. The text will revert to the *Normal* style.

Using Drop Caps as a Design Element

In publications such as magazines, newsletters, or brochures, a graphics feature called drop cap can be used to enhance the appearance of text. A *drop cap* is the first letter of the first word in a paragraph that is set in a larger font size and set into a paragraph. Drop caps identify the beginning of major sections or parts of a document.

Drop Cap
The first letter of the first word in a paragraph, set in a larger font size and set into the paragraph.

Drop caps look best when set in a paragraph containing text set in a proportional font. The drop cap can be set in the same font as the paragraph text or it can be set in a complementary font. For example, a drop cap can be set in a sans serif font while the paragraph text is set in a serif font. A drop cap can be one character or the entire first word of a paragraph. The examples in figure 6.15 show some of the ways drop caps can be created and formatted.

figure 6.15

Drop Cap Examples

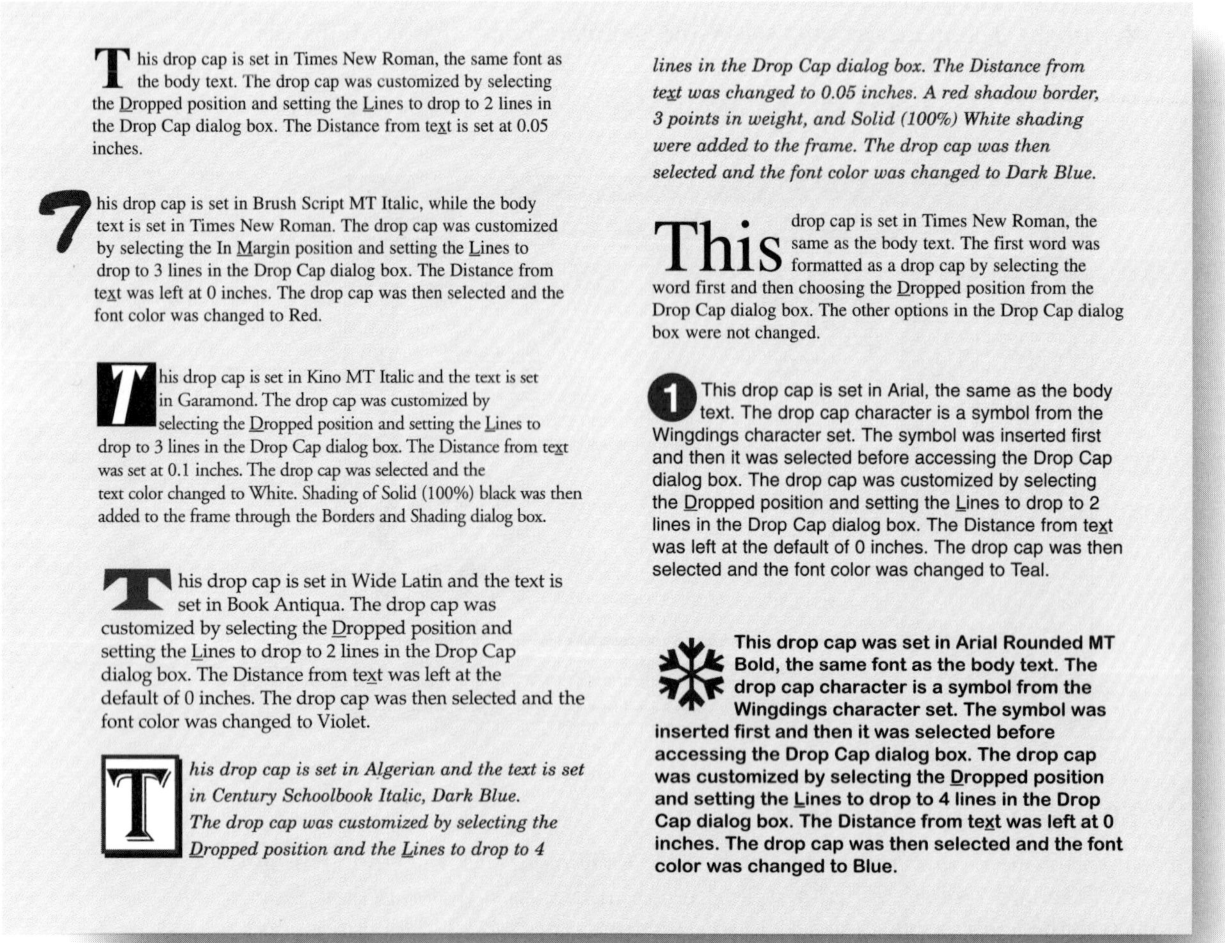

This drop cap is set in Times New Roman, the same font as the body text. The drop cap was customized by selecting the Dropped position and setting the Lines to drop to 2 lines in the Drop Cap dialog box. The Distance from text is set at 0.05 inches.

This drop cap is set in Brush Script MT Italic, while the body text is set in Times New Roman. The drop cap was customized by selecting the In Margin position and setting the Lines to drop to 3 lines in the Drop Cap dialog box. The Distance from text was left at 0 inches. The drop cap was then selected and the font color was changed to Red.

This drop cap is set in Kino MT Italic and the text is set in Garamond. The drop cap was customized by selecting the Dropped position and setting the Lines to drop to 3 lines in the Drop Cap dialog box. The Distance from text was set at 0.1 inches. The drop cap was selected and the text color changed to White. Shading of Solid (100%) black was then added to the frame through the Borders and Shading dialog box.

This drop cap is set in Wide Latin and the text is set in Book Antiqua. The drop cap was customized by selecting the Dropped position and setting the Lines to drop to 2 lines in the Drop Cap dialog box. The Distance from text was left at the default of 0 inches. The drop cap was then selected and the font color was changed to Violet.

This drop cap is set in Algerian and the text is set in Century Schoolbook Italic, Dark Blue. The drop cap was customized by selecting the Dropped position and the Lines to drop to 4 lines in the Drop Cap dialog box. The Distance from text was changed to 0.05 inches. A red shadow border, 3 points in weight, and Solid (100%) White shading were added to the frame. The drop cap was then selected and the font color was changed to Dark Blue.

This drop cap is set in Times New Roman, the same as the body text. The first word was formatted as a drop cap by selecting the word first and then choosing the Dropped position from the Drop Cap dialog box. The other options in the Drop Cap dialog box were not changed.

1 This drop cap is set in Arial, the same as the body text. The drop cap character is a symbol from the Wingdings character set. The symbol was inserted first and then it was selected before accessing the Drop Cap dialog box. The drop cap was customized by selecting the Dropped position and setting the Lines to drop to 2 lines in the Drop Cap dialog box. The Distance from text was left at the default of 0 inches. The drop cap was then selected and the font color was changed to Teal.

❄ **This drop cap was set in Arial Rounded MT Bold, the same font as the body text. The drop cap character is a symbol from the Wingdings character set. The symbol was inserted first and then it was selected before accessing the Drop Cap dialog box. The drop cap was customized by selecting the Dropped position and setting the Lines to drop to 4 lines in the Drop Cap dialog box. The Distance from text was left at 0 inches. The drop cap was then selected and the font color was changed to Blue.**

A drop cap can only be applied to existing text. To create a drop cap, you would complete the following steps:

1. Position the insertion point within the paragraph to be formatted with a drop cap. If a special symbol starts the paragraph, select the symbol first.
2. Choose Format, then Drop Cap.
3. At the Drop Cap dialog box, shown in figure 6.16, select Dropped in the Position section to create a drop cap that is set into the paragraph with the remaining text wrapping around it; or select In Margin to create a drop cap that is positioned in the margin to the left of the paragraph.

4. Choose Font in the Drop Cap dialog box to select the desired font for the drop cap letter only. This does not affect the remaining paragraph text.
5. Choose the Lines to drop option to set the number of lines (from 1–10 lines) that the drop cap will be vertically set into the paragraph. This option affects both the height and width of the drop cap letter.
6. Choose Distance from text to set the amount of distance the drop cap is positioned in relation to the paragraph text.
7. Choose OK or press Enter.
8. The drop cap is placed within a frame in your document. (A frame is similar to a text box except that it is inserted in the text layer rather than the drawing layer. Although text boxes have replaced frames for the most part in Word 97, the drop cap feature still uses a frame to enclose the text.) You can customize the drop cap letter by selecting the letter within the frame and changing the font color and font style. You can also apply other formatting, such as borders and shading, to the frame itself.

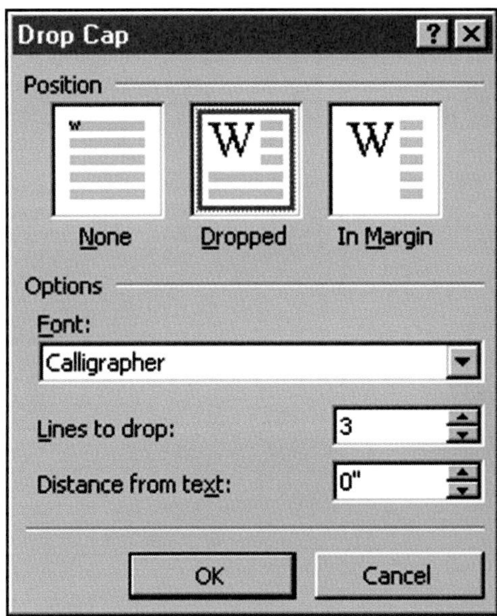

figure 6.16

Drop Cap Dialog Box

Customized drop caps can be an attractive addition to a design, as illustrated in figure 6.15. Practice restraint when using this design element.

In exercise 6, you will create the inside panels of a single-fold brochure using various design and formatting techniques, including a drop cap and styles.

exercise 6

Creating the Inside Panels of a Single-Fold Brochure Using Styles and a Drop Cap

1. Create a dummy for a single-fold brochure using standard size 8½-by-11-inch paper in landscape orientation. Label the panels on one side of the page as Panel 1 (Inside) and Panel 2 (Inside). Label the panels on the other side as Panel 3 (Back) and Panel 4 (Cover).

Refer to the dummy when creating the brochure to ensure that you are keying the appropriate text in the correct location. Remember to save your document periodically as you are working.

2. At a clear document screen, create the inside panels of a single-fold brochure, as shown in figure 6.17, by completing the following steps:
   a. Change the margins and the paper orientation by completing the following steps:
      (1) Choose File, then Page Setup.
      (2) At the Page Setup dialog box, select the Paper Size tab.
      (3) Make sure *Letter* displays in the Paper size list box, then select Landscape in the Orientation section.
      (4) With the Page Setup dialog box still displayed, select the Margins tab. Change the top and bottom margins to 0.5 inches. Change the left and right margins to 0.67 inches. (The left and right margin settings were chosen because of the unprintable zone that exists within the printer that was used to create and print the brochure in figures 6.17 and 6.18. Use these settings for this exercise to work properly with the column widths given.)
      (5) Choose OK or press Enter to close the dialog box.
   b. Turn on automatic kerning for font sizes 14 points and above at the Character Spacing tab of the Font dialog box.
   c. Set up the two-column brochure page layout by completing the following steps:
      (1) Click Format, then Columns.
      (2) At the Columns dialog box, select Two in the Presets section or increase the number to 2 in the Number of columns option.
      (3) Remove the check mark in the Equal column width check box.
      (4) In the Width and spacing section, enter the following amounts in the Width and Spacing text boxes for the columns indicated:

Col #	Width	Spacing
1	4.55	0.7
2	4.41	

      (5) Click OK or press Enter.
   d. Insert the file containing the brochure text by completing the following steps:
      (1) Choose Insert, then File.
      (2) At the Insert File dialog box, double-click *heart text.doc* (located on your student data disk) in the Look in: list box.
   e. Click the Zoom button on the Standard toolbar and change the view to 75% or Page Width.
   f. Format the drop cap paragraph by completing the following steps:
      (1) Click the Show/Hide ¶ button on the Standard toolbar to display nonprinting symbols.
      (2) Select the first paragraph, then change the font to 16-point Arial Italic, Violet.
      (3) With the paragraph still selected, choose Format, Paragraph, then select the Indents and Spacing tab.
      (4) Change the Line Spacing to 1.5 lines, then click OK or press Enter.
      (5) Position the insertion point anywhere within the same paragraph, then choose Format, then Drop Cap.

(6) At the Drop Cap dialog box, choose Dropped in the Position section.
(7) Click the down arrow to the right of the Font list box, then select *Impact* as the font.
(8) Make sure the Lines to drop option displays 3.
(9) Change the Distance from text to 0.1 inches then click OK or press Enter.
(10) Make sure the frame around the drop cap is selected (black sizing handles will display), then display the Font dialog box. At the Font dialog box, change the Font style to Bold and the Color to Teal. Click OK or press Enter to close the dialog box.
(11) Position the insertion point at the end of the same paragraph, then press Enter.

g. Format the first heading, then create a style from the formatted heading by completing the following steps:
   (1) Select *Diabetes: The Latest News* and change the font to 16-point Impact Bold, Teal.
   (2) Choose Format, then Paragraph, and then make the following changes at the Paragraph dialog box:
      (a) Select the Indents and Spacing tab. In the Spacing section, change the spacing After to 6 pt.
      (b) Select the Line and Page Breaks tab. In the Pagination section, click the check box to the left of Keep with next so that the heading will always stay with the paragraph that follows and will not be separated by a column break or a page break.
      (c) Click OK or press Enter.
   (3) Create a style from the formatted heading by completing the following steps:
      (a) Position the insertion point anywhere within the heading just formatted (the heading can still be selected). Click the Style list box on the Formatting toolbar to select the style name that is currently in the box.
      (b) Key **teal heading** and then press Enter. (This heading style will then be added to the list of styles available for this brochure.)

h. Format the first subheading (day, date, name, and title) and then create a style from the formatted subheading by completing the following steps:
   (1) Select *Tuesday, March 9, 1999* and *Katherine Dwyer, M.D.*
   (2) Change the font to 12-point Arial Bold Italic, Violet.
   (3) Choose Format, Paragraph, and then make the following changes at the Paragraph dialog box:
      (a) Select the Indents and Spacing tab. Change the Left Indentation to 0.3 inches.
      (b) Select the Line and Page Breaks tab. In the Pagination section, click the check box to the left of Keep with next.
      (c) Click OK or press Enter to close the dialog box.
   (4) Create a style from the formatted subheading by completing the following steps:
      (a) Position the insertion point anywhere within the subheading just formatted (the subheading can still be selected). Click the Style list box on the Formatting toolbar to select the style name that is currently in the box.
      (b) Key **violet subheading** and then press Enter. (This subheading style will then be added to the list of styles available for this brochure.)

i. Format the body text and then create a style from the formatted body text by completing the following steps:
   (1) Select the paragraph that begins with *One of the best ways . . .* and ends with . . . *new medical recommendations.*

(2) Change the font to 12-point Arial, Violet.

(3) At the Paragraph dialog box, change the Left Indentation to 0.3 inches and change the spacing before the paragraph to 6 pt and the spacing after to 24 pt.

(4) Create a style from the formatted body text by completing the following steps:

(a) Position the insertion point anywhere within the paragraph just formatted (the paragraph can still be selected). Click the Style list box on the Formatting toolbar to select the style name that is currently in the box.

(b) Key **violet body text** and then press Enter. (This body text style will then be added to the list of styles available for this brochure.)

j. Format the second heading by completing the following steps:

(1) Position the insertion point anywhere in the heading that reads *New Advances in Cardiac Surgery*.

(2) Click the down arrow to the right of the Style list box on the Formatting toolbar and select *teal heading* from the Style drop-down list.

k. Format the second subheading by completing the following steps:

(1) Select *Tuesday, March 23, 1999* and *Christine Johnson, M.D.*

(2) Click the down arrow to the right of the Style list box on the Formatting toolbar and select *violet subheading* from the Style drop-down list.

l. Format the second paragraph of body text by completing the following steps:

(1) Position the insertion point within the paragraph that begins with *Advances in minimally* . . . and ends with . . . *leads an informative discussion.*

(2) Click the down arrow to the right of the Style list box on the Formatting toolbar and select *violet body text* from the Style drop-down list.

m. Position the insertion point to the left of *Exercise—Is It the Fountain of Youth?*, and insert a column break.

n. Move the insertion point to the top of panel 2 and apply the *teal heading*, the *violet subheading*, and the *violet body text* styles to the remaining headings, subheads, and body text (up to but not including *All lectures: . . .)* in the brochure as illustrated in figure 6.16. (Hint: You can apply the *teal heading* style to all the headings by applying the first one, then moving the insertion point to each heading and pressing F4. Repeat the process for the subheadings and body text.)

o. Format the lecture information text at the bottom of panel 2 by completing the following steps:

(1) Select from *All lectures:* until the end of the document and change the font to 12-point Arial, Teal.

(2) With the same text still selected, change the left indention to 0.3 inches.

(3) Insert tabs to align the lecture information (time and location) as indicated in figure 6.16.

(4) Position the insertion point after *Naperville, Illinois* and press Enter.

(5) Select the last paragraph, change the font style to italics, and then change the paragraph alignment to Center.

p. Insert the watermark (yellow heart image) by completing the following steps:

(1) Click the Zoom Control button on the Standard toolbar and change the viewing mode to Whole Page.

(2) Click the Text Box button on the Drawing toolbar and draw a text box approximately 3 inches by 3 inches in the center of the page.

(3) Click Insert, point to Picture, then click From File. At the Insert Picture dialog box, double-click the folder containing your student data disk files, then double-click *heart.wmf*.

(4) Change the color of the heart to yellow by completing the following steps:

(a) Double-click inside the heart image to open the image in the Picture editing window.

(b) Click the Zoom button on the Standard toolbar and adjust the view if necessary.

(c) Click the Select Objects button on the Drawing toolbar. Position the mouse pointer outside, above, and to the left of the grid lines surrounding the heart. Click and drag the crosshairs to form an outline around the whole heart, including the grid lines. (The heart should display with selection handles within and on all four sides of the heart.)

(d) Click the Fill Color button on the Drawing toolbar, then select Yellow (fourth row, third column from the left).

(e) Click File, then Close & Return to Document # or name (the document number or name may vary) to return to your document.

(5) Select the picture (black sizing handles should display), click Format, then Object, then customize the picture at the Picture dialog box as follows:

(a) Select the Size tab, then click the Lock aspect ratio check box to remove the check mark. Change the height of the picture to 5 inches and the width to 3.29 inches.

(b) Select the Picture tab, change the Color to Watermark, the Brightness option to 75%, and the Contrast option to 65% in the Image control section.

(c) Click OK or press Enter.

(6) If the picture is cut off, use the text box corner sizing handle to expand the text box until the whole image is visible.

(7) Select the text box (make sure white sizing handles and a dotted border display), double-click one of the text box borders, then make the following changes at the Format Text Box dialog box:

(a) Click the Colors and Lines tab, then change the line color to No Line.

(b) Select the Position tab, then change the horizontal position of the picture to 4 inches from the edge of the page and the vertical position to 1.5 inches from the top of the page. (Remember to change the "From" options first.)

(c) Click OK or press Enter.

(8) Send the picture behind the text by completing the following steps:

(a) Display the Drawing toolbar.

(b) Make sure the text box is still selected, then click the Draw button on the Drawing toolbar.

(c) Click Order, then click Send Behind Text. (The heart should appear as a watermark behind the existing text.)

3. Save panels 1 and 2 of the brochure and name it c06ex06, panels 1,2. (If the document contains a blank second page, delete it so that you are only saving the first page.)
4. Print and then close c06ex06, panels 1,2. (Panels 1 and 2 will also be printed as part of the next exercise.)

figure 6.17

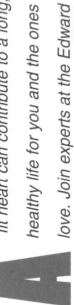

A fit heart can contribute to a long, healthy life for you and the ones you love. Join experts at the Edward Cardiovascular Institute to learn how to keep yours beating strong.

Diabetes: The Latest News

Tuesday, March 9, 1999
Katherine Dwyer, M.D.

One of the best ways to manage any medical condition is to keep abreast of the very latest information. Join endocrinologist Katherine Dwyer, M.D., for an up-to-the-minute discussion of the latest diabetes clinical trials, revised treatment guidelines, and new medical recommendations.

New Advances In Cardiac Surgery

Tuesday, March 23, 1999
Christine Johnson, M.D.

Advances in minimally invasive surgical procedures are helping patients get back to active, healthy lives more quickly—and more safely—than ever. Today, cardiac surgical procedures are marked by shorter hospital stays and recovery times, and lower costs. Learn more about these advances as Christine Johnson, M.D., leads an informative discussion.

Exercise—Is It the Fountain of Youth?

Tuesday, April 6, 1999
Joan Polak, M.D.

Everyone knows that exercise is good for your heart. Now, learn from a cardiologist exactly why it is good for you and what exercises provide the greatest benefits. Learn the specifics behind the "Just Do It" philosophy from Dr. Joan Polak.

Setting Up a Heart-Healthy Kitchen

Tuesday, April 20, 1999
Kaitlin Anzalone, Registered Dietitian

A great start to beginning a heart-healthy diet is doing a heart-check of your kitchen. Join us for practical tips and suggestions for setting up your kitchen.

Diabetes and Cardiovascular Disease

Tuesday, May 4, 1999
Wilma Schaenfeld, M.D.

During this session, we will discuss the clinical features of heart disease in the diabetic, as well as what you can do to reduce the likelihood of future problems.

All lectures: 7:00 to 8:30 p.m.
Edward Cardiovascular Institute
120 Spalding Drive
Naperville, Illinois

The talk is FREE, but because space is limited, please register by calling (708) 555-4941.

In exercise 7, you will create the back and cover (panels 3 and 4) of the heart brochure started in exercise 6. This exercise involves editing the heart image to change the fill color, using text boxes to place text, and using the Text Direction feature to create the rotated return address.

exercise 7

Creating the Back (Panel 3) and Cover (Panel 4) of a Single-Fold Brochure

1. Open c06ex06, panels 1,2.
2. Save the document with Save As and name it c06ex07, heart brochure.
3. Create panels 3 and 4 of the brochure shown in figure 6.18 by completing the following steps:
   a. Press Ctrl + End to move the insertion point to the end of the document, then insert a next page section break.
   b. If center alignment is carried over from the previous page, change to left alignment.
   c. Change the left paragraph indentation to 0 inches at the Paragraph dialog box.
   d. Set the column formatting for the outside panels of the brochure by completing the following steps:
      (1) Click Format, then Columns.
      (2) Make sure the Number of columns option displays 2.
      (3) Make sure there is no check mark in the Equal column width check box.
      (4) In the Width and spacing section, enter the following amounts in the Width and Spacing text boxes for the columns indicated: (Remember: these are the opposite of the settings for panels 1 and 2.)

Col #	Width	Spacing
1	4.41	0.7
2	4.55	

      (5) Click the Apply to: list box and select *This point forward.*
      (6) Click OK or press Enter.
   e. Create the return address on the back (panel 3) of the brochure as illustrated in figure 6.18 by completing the following steps:
      (1) With the insertion point positioned in panel 3, click the Text Box button on the Drawing toolbar.
      (2) Position the crosshairs toward the bottom of panel 3, then click and drag to draw a text box approximately 3½ inches wide and 1½ inches high. (The size and position of the text box will be adjusted later.)
      (3) Key the following information in the format indicated:

EDWARD CARDIOVASCULAR INSTITUTE
One ECI Plaza
120 Spalding Drive, Suite 102
Naperville, IL 60540-9865

(4) Select the text just entered, change the font to 10-point Arial and the color to teal.
(5) Select *Edward Cardiovascular Institute* and apply bold.
(6) Rotate the position of the text by completing the following steps:
  (a) Position the insertion point anywhere within the address.
  (b) Click Format, then Text Direction to display the Text Direction-Text Box dialog box.
  (c) In the Orientation section, click the text direction selection that displays text pointing up and matches the direction of the text in figure 6.18.
  (d) Click OK or press Enter.
(7) With the text box still selected, double-click one of the text box borders, then customize the text box at the Format Text Box dialog box by completing the following steps:
  (a) Click the Colors and Lines tab, change the line color to Violet (third row, seventh column), and then change the line weight to 2.25 pt.
  (b) Click the Size tab, then change the height to 2.9 inches and the width to 0.9 inches.
  (c) Click the Position tab, then change the horizontal distance to 0.4 inches from the edge of the page and the vertical distance to 5.3 inches from the top of the page. (Remember: set the "From" options first.)
  (d) Click OK or press Enter.

f. Click outside the text box to position the insertion point at the top of panel 3, then insert a column break.

g. Create the heart image on the front cover (panel 4) by completing the following steps:
(1) With the insertion point positioned at the top of panel 4, press Enter one time. (This step prevents the picture from jumping to panel 3 after it is inserted.)
(2) Click Insert, point to Picture, then click From File.
(3) In the Insert Picture dialog box, change the folder to the location of your student data disk files, then double-click *heart.wmf* in the Look in: list box.
(4) Change the color of the heart image by completing the following steps:
  (a) Double-click inside the heart image to insert the image into Word's Picture editor.
  (b) Click once in the upper left-hand corner of the heart to select the top half of the heart.
  (c) Click the Fill Color on the Drawing toolbar, then click Teal (second row, fifth column).
  (d) Click once in the bottom pointed area of the heart image to select the bottom half of the heart.
  (e) Click the Fill Color button on the Drawing toolbar, then click Violet (third row, seventh column).
  (f) Click File, then select Close & Return to Document # or name. (The document number or name may vary.)
(5) With the heart selected, click Format, Picture, then make the following changes at the Format Picture dialog box:

(a) Click the Size tab, then click the Lock aspect ratio check box to remove the check mark. Change the height to 6.6 inches and the width to 4.1 inches.

(b) Click the Position tab, then change the horizontal distance to 6.27 inches from the edge of the page and the vertical distance to 1.1 inches from the edge of the page. (Remember to change the "From" options first.)

(c) Click OK or press Enter.

h. Create a text box inside the heart to hold the word *for* by completing the following steps:

(1) Click the Text Box button on the Drawing toolbar.

(2) Position the crosshairs in the upper left portion of the heart. Click and drag to draw a text box that will contain the word *for*. (Do not worry about the exact size or position at this time.)

(3) Change the font to 24-point Impact, yellow.

(4) Key **for**.

(5) Click the Fill Color button, then click No Fill.

(6) Click the Line Color button, then click No Line.

(7) Size the text box with the sizing handles so the text is completely visible, if necessary, then position the text box with the mouse in the approximate position as displayed in figure 6.18.

i. Create a second text box that will contain the word *your* by completing the following steps:

(1) Select the first text box containing *for*.

(2) Position the insertion point on one of the text box borders until it turns into an arrow with a four-headed arrow attached.

(3) Hold down the Ctrl key, then click and drag a copy of the text box to the approximate position of the word *your* in figure 6.18. Release the left mouse button.

(4) Select the word *for*, then key *your*.

(5) Size and position the text box as necessary.

j. Create a third text box that will contain the word *Heart's* by copying the second text box as in steps 3i(1-5), above, except change the font size to 48-point Impact, yellow.

k. Create a fourth text box that will contain the word *sake* by copying the second text box as in steps 3i(1-5).

l. Create a fifth text box to hold the *Presented by:* information by completing the following steps:

(1) Click outside of the heart image to deselect it.

(2) Click the Text Box button on the Drawing toolbar.

(3) Position the crosshairs in the bottom left corner of panel 4. Click and drag to draw a text box that will contain the *Presented by:* information as indicated in figure 6.18. (Do not worry about the exact size or position at this time.)

(4) Key **Presented by:**, then press Enter once.

(5) Select *Presented by:* and change the font to 12-point Impact Italic, Violet.

(6) With the text still selected, display the Paragraph dialog box, then change spacing after the paragraph to 6 pt.

(7) Position the insertion point below *Presented by:*, then key **The Edward Cardiovascular Institute**, ending each line as illustrated in figure 6.18.

(8) Select *The Edward Cardiovascular Institute* and change the font to 16-point Impact Italic, Teal, Small caps.

(9) Size the text box, if necessary, so all the text is visible.

(10) Select *The Edward Cardiovascular Institute*, display the Paragraph dialog box, then change the Line Spacing to Exactly At 14 pt.

(11) Click the Line Color button, then click No Line.

(12) Size and position the text box again with the mouse as needed.

m. Create a sixth text box that will contain the words *Spring 1999* by completing the following steps:

(1) Click the Text Box button on the Drawing toolbar, then draw a text box in the bottom right corner of the brochure cover. (Check the position of this text box in figure 6.18.)

(2) Key **Spring 1999**.

(3) Select *Spring 1999*, then change the font to 22-point Impact, Teal.

(4) Click the Line Color button, then click No Line.

(5) Size and position the text box with the mouse as needed.

4. Save the document again with the same name (c06ex07, heart brochure).
5. Print both pages of the brochure using both sides of the paper. Refer to the directions for printing in exercise 1, if necessary.
6. Close c06ex07, heart brochure.

figure 6.18

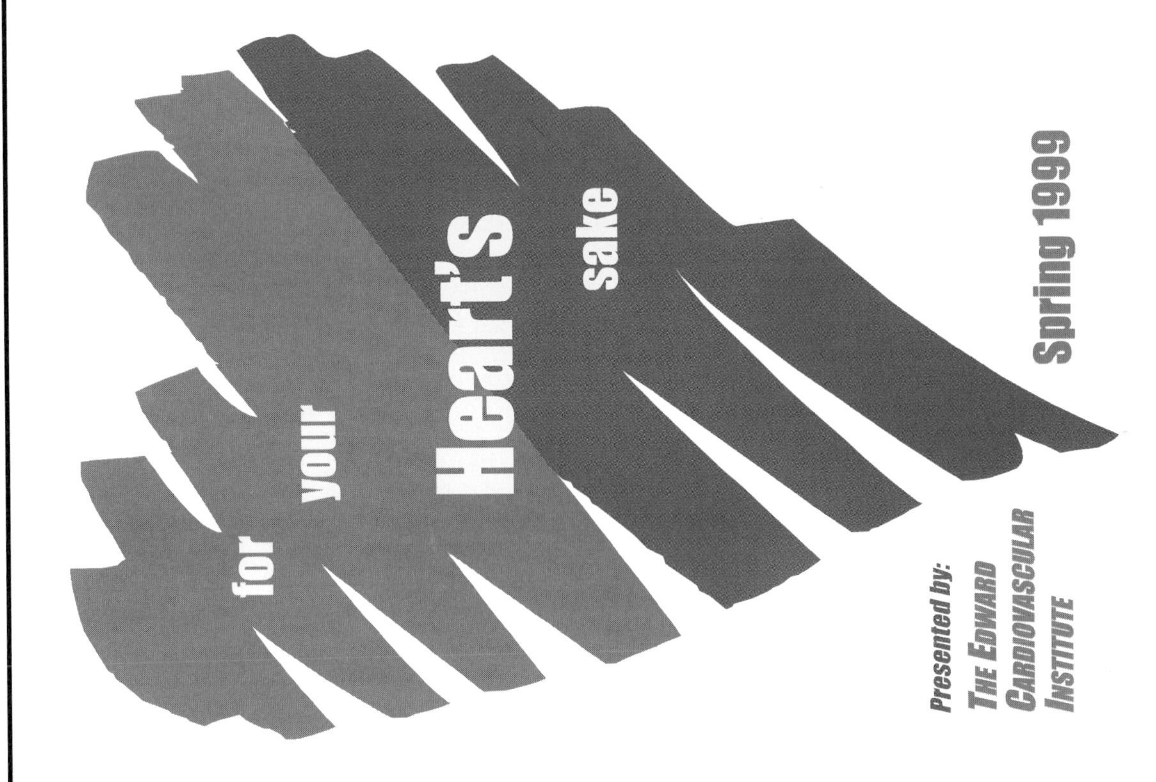
for your
Heart's
sake
Spring 1999
Presented by:
The Edward
Cardiovascular
Institute

EDWARD CARDIOVASCULAR INSTITUTE
One ECI Plaza
120 Spalding Drive, Suite 102
Naperville, IL 60540-9865

chapter summary

- A brochure can be used to inform, educate, promote, or sell. It can also be used to establish an organization's identity and image.
- The manner in which a brochure is folded determines the order in which the panels are set on the page. Folds create distinct sections in which to place blocks of text. The most common brochure fold is called a letter fold.
- A dummy can be created to help determine the location of information on the brochure page layout.
- Consistent elements in a brochure are necessary to maintain continuity in a multipage brochure.
- The easiest method of creating a brochure page layout is to use the Columns feature.
- Column formatting can be varied within the same document by using section breaks to separate the different column formatting sections.
- Reverse text can be created in a document as a design element and usually refers to white text set against a solid black background. Reverse text can also be created with different colors for the text and the background as well as shading.
- The front cover of a brochure sets the mood and tone for the whole brochure. The front cover title must attract attention and let the reader know what the brochure is about.
- Formatting that applies to a variety of documents on a regular basis or that maintains consistency in a single publication can be applied to text using a style.
- A style can be edited and any occurrence of the style in the document is automatically updated to reflect the changes.
- The Normal style from the *Normal* template is automatically applied to any text that is keyed unless you specify other formatting instructions.
- Word provides two types of styles—*character* and *paragraph.* A character style applies formatting to selected text only. A paragraph style affects the paragraph that contains the insertion point or selected text.
- A drop cap is a design element in which the first letter of the first word in a paragraph is set in a larger font size and set into the paragraph.

commands review

	Mouse/Keyboard
Columns dialog box	Format, Columns
Insert a column break	Insert, Break, Column Break; or Ctrl + Shift + Enter
Insert a page break	Insert, Break, Page Break; or Ctrl + Enter
Move insertion point between columns	Position I-beam pointer at desired location, click left button; or Alt + up arrow or Alt + down Arrow (toggles back and forth to top of previous column and to top of next column)

Character Spacing and Kerning	Format, Font, Character Spacing tab
Paragraph Borders and Shading dialog box	Format, Borders and Shading
Display Drawing toolbar	Click Drawing button on Standard toolbar; or right-click Standard toolbar, select Drawing; or View, Toolbars, select Drawing, then press Enter
Draw a Text Box	Click the Text Box button on the Drawing toolbar, click and drag the crosshairs to draw a box
Insert a Text Box	Select text, click the Text Box button on the Formatting toolbar
Size a Text Box	Double-click the text box border, select the Size tab
Position a Text Box	Double-click the text box border, select the Position tab
Format Text Box dialog box	Format, Text Box
Drop Cap dialog box	Format, Drop Cap
Insert Picture dialog box	Insert, Picture
Style dialog box	Format, Style
Style Organizer dialog box	Format, Style, Organizer, Styles tab
Style Gallery dialog box	Format, Style Gallery
Font dialog box	Format, Font; or click the font list box, font size list box, and/or character formatting buttons on the Formatting toolbar
Format Object dialog box	Format, Object

check your understanding

Terms: Match the terms with the correct definitions by writing the letter of the term on the blank line in front of the correct definition.

- A Applying
- B Style
- C Character style
- D Page Layout View
- E Drop cap
- F Dummy
- G Panels
- H Paragraph style
- I Parallel
- J Column Break
- K Columns dialog box
- L Reverse text
- M All Styles
- N Newspaper columns

_____ 1. Folds in a brochure that all run in the same direction.

_____ 2. The sections that divide a brochure page.

_____ 3. A mock-up of a brochure.

_____ 4. In this type of formatting, text flows from top to bottom in the first column, then to the top of the next column, and so on.

_______ 5. Use this dialog box to create columns of unequal width.

_______ 6. This viewing mode allows you to view columns as they will appear when printed.

_______ 7. Insert this (or these) into a document to control where columns end and begin on the page.

_______ 8. A set of formatting instructions saved with a name to be used repeatedly on different sections of text.

_______ 9. Choose this at the Style dialog box to display all the available styles in Word.

_______ 10. The name for the first letter of the first word in a paragraph that is set in a larger font size and set into the paragraph.

_______ 11. The name for white text set against a black background.

Concepts: Write your answers to the following questions in the space provided.

1. What is the purpose of creating a dummy before creating a brochure?

2. What is the biggest advantage of using styles?

3. What is the difference between a paragraph style and a character style?

4. What styles could you create for the text in figure 6.6 to save time and keystrokes in the document creation process?

5. Explain the difference between using the Style Organizer versus the Style Gallery to use styles from other templates or documents.

6. How can drop caps and reverse text serve as design elements in a document?

skill assessments

Assessment 1

1. Create a dummy for a three-panel brochure using standard size 8½-by-11-inch paper in landscape orientation. Label the panels. Refer to the dummy when creating the brochure to ensure that you are keying the appropriate text in the correct location. Remember to save your document periodically as you are working.
2. At a clear document screen, create the brochure panels shown in figure 6.19 by completing the following steps (make any adjustments you feel necessary as you format the text in the brochure):
   a. Change the paper orientation to Landscape.
   b. Change the top and bottom margins to 0.5 and the left and right margins to 0.67 inches.
   c. Format the page for three unequal column widths of 2.64 inches, 3 inches, and 2.62 inches with 0.7 inches spacing between columns.
   d. Turn on kerning for fonts at 14 points and above.
   e. Insert *art text.doc,* located on your student data disk. This file contains the brochure text displayed in figures 6.19 and 6.20.
   f. Click the Zoom button on the Standard toolbar and adjust the view as necessary while working through the remaining steps.
   g. In panel 1, format the first main heading, *SUPPORTING FINE ART*, and create a style from the existing formatting according to the following specifications:
      (1) Change the font to 15-point Garamond, Violet.
      (2) Change the spacing after the paragraph to 42 points.
      (3) Change the alignment to Center.
      (4) Name the style *Violet heading*.
   h. Format the first subheading, *Art League Offerings*, and create a style from the existing formatting according to the following specifications:
      (1) Change the font to 13-point Garamond, Bold Italic.
      (2) Change the spacing after the paragraph to 14 points.
      (3) Change the alignment to Center.
      (4) Name the style *Black subheading*.
   i. Format the first bullet, including the text that follows; create a style from the existing formatting; and apply the style according to the following specifications:
      (1) Select *Studio and Gallery Open to the Public.*
      (2) Display the Bullets and Numbering dialog box, select the Bulleted tab, click the quill pen selection (second row, third column), then choose Customize. (If the quill pen symbol is not displayed as a selection, click any of the other bullet selections, then select Customize.)
      (3) At the Customized Bulleted List dialog box, make the following changes:

(a) Make sure the quill pen symbol is selected as the Bullet character. (If not, click the Bullet button, change the font to Monotype Sorts, then select the quill pen symbol, first row, nineteenth column.)
(b) Change the font size to 12 points.
(c) Change the color to Violet.
(d) In the Text position section, make sure the Indent at text box displays 0.25 inches. Click OK or press Enter.
(e) With the text still selected, use the Font and Font Size button on the Formatting Toolbar to change the font to 12-point Garamond.
(f) Change the spacing after the paragraph to 18 points and select a hanging indent of 0.25 inches.
(g) Name the style *Quill bullet list*.

j. Select the remaining bulleted items in panel 1 and apply the *Quill bullet list* style.
k. Position the insertion point at the beginning of the text to be placed in the next panel and then insert a column break.
l. Insert the paint splat image at the bottom of panel 1 and then edit, size, and position the picture as follows:
(1) Draw a small text box at the bottom of panel 1.
(2) Insert the paint splat image, *splat.wmf*, located on your student data disk.
(3) Double-click the image to access Word Picture editor.
(4) Select the whole paint splat image using the Select Objects button on the Drawing toolbar, then change the fill color to Violet. Close Word Picture.
(5) Remove the text box borders.
(6) Select the picture and use the corner black sizing handles to adjust the size. If necessary, access the Format Object dialog box to change the size more specifically.
(7) Select the text box and use the mouse to position the picture or access the Format Text Box dialog box to position the image more specifically. (Hint: Use the longest line of text, including the bullet, in panel 1 as your guide for centering the image.)

m. Format the text in panel 2 according to the following specifications:
(1) Use the previously created heading style to format the heading.
(2) You may use paragraph borders and shading to create the shaded box or you may use a text box.
(3) Format the first date, *September 13 & 14, 1998,* in the shaded bordered box as a heading and then create a style from the existing formatting according to the following specifications:
(a) Position the insertion point to the left of the first date, then press Enter two times.
(b) Change the font to 12-point Garamond Bold and the alignment to Center.
(c) Change the spacing before the paragraph to 24 pt. (This spacing instruction is included in this style because it is applicable to the majority of date headings in the

shaded box. However, in step 2m(3)(e) below, the spacing instruction will be removed from the first date. Hard returns were used to produce the white space before the first date to accommodate using the Borders and Shading feature to produce the shaded box.)

(d) Name the style *Box heading*.

(e) Access the Paragraph dialog box, then change the spacing before the paragraph to 0 pt. Do not redefine the style.

(4) Format the first event following the date, *Four Corners Art League Art Fair* and *Juried Fine Arts Exhibition and Sale,* and then create a style from the existing formatting according to the following specifications:

(a) Change the font to 12-point Garamond and the alignment to Center.

(b) Name the style *Art body text*.

(5) Use the previously created *Box heading* style to format the remaining date headings.

(6) Use the *Art body text* style to format the remaining events following the dates.

(7) If you are using the Borders and Shading feature to create the shaded box, position the insertion point after the last item in the shaded box and then press Enter to allow for some extra white space. Remember to select the extra paragraph symbols above the first date and below the last item when applying paragraph borders and shading.

(8) Refer to figure 6.19 and format the reaming text in panel 2 using the appropriate styles.

(9) Insert a column break to the left of *CLASSES & WORKSHOPS*, if necessary, to position the text at the top of panel 3.

(10) Copy the paint splat image from the bottom of panel 1 to the bottom of panel 2. Remember to hold down the Ctrl key, then click and drag a copy of the image to the bottom of panel 2. Make any necessary position adjustments.

n. Format the text in panel 3 by completing the following steps:

(1) Use the previously created styles to format headings, subheadings, body text, etc., as you proceed through the panel.

(2) Make any adjustments to paragraph spacing, indentation, or positioning as you deem necessary to create a professional-looking document.

(3) Insert a column break to the left of *JOIN THE ART LEAGUE*, if necessary, to position the text at the top of panel 4.

(4) Copy the paint splat image from the bottom of panel 2 to the bottom of panel 3. Make any necessary position adjustments.

3. Save the inside panels of the art gallery brochure and name it c06sa01, panels 1,2,3.

4. Print and then close c06sa01, panels 1,2,3.

figure 6.19

SUPPORTING FINE ART

Art League Offerings

- Studio and Gallery Open to the Public
- Monthly Lectures and Demonstrations by Professional Artists
- Art Classes, Workshops, & Instruction
- Monthly Exhibits of Juried Fine Art in all Media
- Annual Student Art Show
- Waterfront Art Fair
- Annual Fine Arts Auction
- Annual Christmas Show & Sale
- "Sea and Sand"—Sculpture on the Waterfront by John Dwyer

ANNUAL ART EVENTS

September 13 & 14, 1998
Four Corners Art League Art Fair
Juried Fine Arts Exhibition and Sale

November 28, 1998–January 10, 1999
Christmas Show & Sale
Fine Arts & Crafts
Guest Artists

March 9, 1999
34th Annual Fine Arts Auction

May 11, 1999
Student Art Show
Award Presentation and Open House

Membership

- Participate in all programs
- Exhibit work in the gallery
- Preference for workshops, classes, and demonstrations

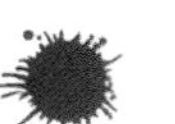

CLASSES & WORKSHOPS

Classes

- Classes for adults and children
- Watercolors
- Pastels
- Oils
- Drawing and composition
- Framing

Class Schedule

Session I
September 25–October 27, 1998
Session II
January 15–February 16, 1999
Session III
March 18–April 19, 1999

Regular Workshops

- Tuesday evening life drawing workshop at the Gallery, 7 p.m.
- Wednesday workshop at the Gallery, 12–4 p.m. All media.

Assessment 2

1. Open c06sa01, panels 1,2,3. Save the document with Save As and name it c06sa02, art brochure.
2. Referring to the dummy created in c06sa01, panels 1,2,3, create panels 4, 5, and 6 shown in figure 6.20 according to the following specifications:
   a. Format the page for three unequal column widths of 2.62 inches, 3 inches, and 2.64 inches with 0.7 inches spacing between columns. Make sure you select *This point forward* from the Apply to: list box at the Columns dialog box.
   b. Format the text in panel 4 as follows:
      (1) Format the heading and subheading with the *Violet heading* and *Black subheading* styles created in Assessment 1.
      (2) Format any body text with *Art body text* style created in Assessment 1. Change the center alignment formatting to left; redefine the style if desired.
      (3) When creating the lines after *Name, Address, Zip,* and *Phone,* set a right tab at the position where the line is to end. When you need to insert a line, turn on underlining, press the Tab key, and then turn underlining off. When creating the Zip and Phone lines, set a left tab where the Zip line is to end. Use underline as stated previously.
      (4) Format the first check box bullet, including the text that follows; create a style from the existing formatting; and apply the style according to the following specifications:
         (a) Select *$5 Junior Membership (Jr./Sr. High).*
         (b) Display the Bullets and Numbering dialog box, then select the Bulleted tab. Create a customized bullet—the check box symbol—from the Wingdings character set (located in the third row, fifth column from the right).
         (c) Change the font size of the bullet to 12 points.
         (d) Make sure the bullet is black and indented 0.25 inches from the text.
         (e) With the text still selected, use the Font and Font Size buttons on the Formatting Toolbar to change the font to 12-point Garamond.
         (f) Change the spacing after the paragraph to 14 points.
         (g) Name the style *Check box bullet list.*
      (5) Select the remaining bulleted membership items in panel 4 and apply the *Check box bullet list* style.
      (6) When creating the two columns following *How would you like to participate in art league activities?* at the bottom of panel 4, insert the text into a two-column table by completing the following steps:
         (a) Select the text that begins with *Gallery volunteer* and ends with *Board Member.*
         (b) Click Table, then Convert Text to Table.
         (c) At the Convert Text to Table dialog box, make sure Paragraphs is selected in the Separate text at section.
         (d) Click OK or press Enter.
         (e) Remove the gridline borders from the table.
      (7) Select the entire table, then apply the *Check box bullet list* style.
      (8) Adjust the spacing between columns if necessary.
      (9) Make any adjustments to spacing or positioning of text as you deem necessary.
   c. Format the remaining text in panel 5 according to the following specifications:

(1) Position the insertion point to the left of *Four Corners Art League*, then insert a column break to position the text at the top of panel 5.
(2) Insert the paint splat image in panel 5 by completing the following steps:
(a) Copy the paint splat image from panel 1, 2, or 3 to the approximate position shown in figure 6.20.
(b) Select the picture (black sizing handles should display), then use one of the corner sizing handles to increase the size of the picture as displayed in figure 6.20.
(c) Select the text box surrounding the picture (white sizing handles should display), then use the mouse to center the image within the panel.
(d) Make sure you change the text wrapping style to none.
(3) Select the text that is to be placed at the bottom of panel 5, then insert a text box.
(4) Format the text within the text box as follows:
(a) Select *Four Corners Art League*, then change the font to 14-point Garamond Bold and the paragraph alignment to Center.
(b) Select the address and phone and fax numbers, then change the font to 12-point Garamond and the paragraph alignment to Center.
(c) Size and position the text box as necessary.

d. Format the text in panel 6 according to the following specifications:
(1) Format the title, *Four Corners Art League*, as follows:
(a) Select *Four Corners Art League*, then insert a text box.
(b) Select the title again, then change the font to 21-point Garamond, Bold Italic, Violet.
(c) Change the paragraph alignment to Center.
(d) Size and position the text box as necessary.
(2) Use the Line button on the Drawing toolbar to draw a line under the title, then change the line style to a 4½ point double line.
(3) Format the subheading, *Studio* and *Gallery* as follows:
(a) Select *Studio* and *Gallery* (including the spaces in between), then insert a text box.
(b) Select the subtitle again, then change the font to 18-point Garamond, Italic.
(c) Size and position the text box as necessary.
(4) Copy one of the paint splat images from the first page and drag it to the cover.
(5) Size and position the picture and text box as necessary.

e. Insert, then size and position the artist image according to the following specifications:
(1) Draw a text box, then insert *artist.wmf*, located on your student data disk.
(2) Size and position the picture and text box as necessary.

3. Save the brochure document again with the same name (c06sa02, art brochure).
4. Print the first page (panels 1, 2, and 3) of the brochure and then print the second page (panels 4, 5, and 6) on the back of the first page. Fold your brochure and check the placement of text and images in relation to the folds. Make any adjustments as necessary to produce a professionally finished product.
5. Close c06sa02, art brochure.

figure 6.20

JOIN THE ART LEAGUE

Membership Application

Name: ______________________________

Address: ____________________________

Zip:__________ Phone: ______________

Dues are payable June 1 for the year ending May 31.

☐ $5 Junior Membership (Jr./Sr. High)

☐ $24 Individual Membership

☐ $30 Family Membership

☐ $50 Contributing Membership

☐ $100 Supporting Membership

How would you like to participate in art league activities?

☐ Gallery volunteer ☐ Committee work

☐ Class instructor ☐ Workshops

☐ Exhibiting ☐ Board Member

Four Corners Art League
240 America's Cup Drive
Newport, RI 02040
(401) 555-2730
Fax: (401) 555-2732

FOUR CORNERS ART LEAGUE

Studio Gallery

Assessment 3

1. You are a member of a fundraising committee for a local charity. Pick a charity, plan an event to raise money, and create a brochure that promotes the charity and advertises the event.
2. Open *document evaluation checklist.doc* located on your student data disk and print one copy.
3. Use the Document Evaluation Checklist to analyze your brochure. Label the exercise as c06sa03.
4. Attach the completed form to the back of your brochure.

creative activity

Visit a place where many brochures are displayed in a rack, such as a college, a chamber of commerce office, a travel agency, a doctor's office, a park district office, a hotel lobby, etc.

- Pick out two brochures that grab your attention. Use the Document Evaluation Checklist (open and print four copies of *document evaluation checklist.doc*) to help you identify the elements that attracted you to pick up the two brochures. Write a short summary for each brochure explaining how these elements are successful.
- Pick out two brochures that failed to grab your attention. Use the Document Evaluation Checklist to help you identify what is wrong with the two brochures. Write a short summary for each brochure that analyzes the design problems and discusses how you would improve them.
- Divide into small groups in class and share your findings with your group.

chapter SEVEN

7 Creating Specialty Promotional Documents

PERFORMANCE OBJECTIVE

Upon successful completion of chapter 7, you will be able to create specialty promotional documents, such as gift certificates, postcards, name tags, business greeting cards, and invitations.

Desktop Publishing Concepts

Templates	Em and en dashes	Balance
Landscape orientation	Layout and design	
Portrait orientation	Color	

Word Features Used

Tables	Mail Merge	Cut and paste
AutoText	Mail Merge Helper	Drag-and-drop
Labels	Data source	Special characters
Pictures	Main document	
Borders	Symbols	

Using Resources for Ideas in Desktop Publishing

By the time you reach this chapter, you will have accumulated a number of different examples of desktop publishing applications. As discussed in chapter 1, studying the work of others is a great way to pick up pointers on interesting uses of fonts, color, text, and graphics. Pick up the newspaper and study the layout of text. Pick up vacation flyers for advertising suggestions. Look at the flyers and the "junk mail" we all regularly receive. Published examples are all around you, and they can help show you how to apply what you have learned to applications in desktop publishing.

Another good source for useful ideas is *The Desktop Publisher's Idea Book* by Chuck Green. In this book, you will find project ideas, tips, and some hard-to-find sources for desktop publishing applications. Also, as mentioned in earlier chapters, paper supply companies offer predesigned papers that make all your communications look more professional.

Using Various Approaches to Creating Documents

You may have already realized that there are many different approaches to creating documents in Word. You must decide which approach is easiest for you to remember and apply. Getting good at a skill takes a lot of practice and experimentation. You may begin thinking of other ways of creating documents that are more efficient or easier to adapt to your setting. Any one of the exercises presented in this chapter can be adapted to just about any business situation. While we typically present one or two different approaches to creating a document, there are usually many other ways to achieve the same result. For instance, consider all the ways you can create a horizontal line in a document:

- Click Format, then Font. At the Font dialog box, click Underline, then select Single, Double, Dotted, Thick, Dash, Dot dash, Dot dot dash, or Wave. Press Tab as many times as necessary to draw a line of a desired length.
- Click the Underline button on the Formatting toolbar, then press Tab.
- Click the down arrow to the right of the Border button on the Formatting toolbar, then select a top, bottom, left, or right border button.
- Click the Line button on the Drawing toolbar and drag to create a line. (Hold down the Shift key if you want to create a straight line.)
- Click the Draw Table button on the Tables and Borders toolbar, then draw a line; or click the arrow on the Borders button on the Tables and Borders toolbar, then select a top, bottom, left, or right border button.
- Press Shift and the hyphen key on the keyboard.

Creating Promotional Documents

Besides flyers and announcements, other promotional documents include gift certificates, postcards, name tags, invitations, and greeting cards. They become promotional documents when a business or organization name is visible or an item is mentioned for sale in a document. Promotional documents are designed to advertise or promote an interest or sale.

Certificates, invitations, and postcards are just a few of the many promotional documents that can be created using tables and text boxes in Word. Figure 7.1 illustrates other promotional documents using the same basic design concepts and Word features used in most of the exercises in this chapter. Whether creating tickets for a charitable event, discount coupons for a house walk, or coasters advertising a local restaurant, Word's desktop publishing features combined with a little imagination can produce endless possibilities.

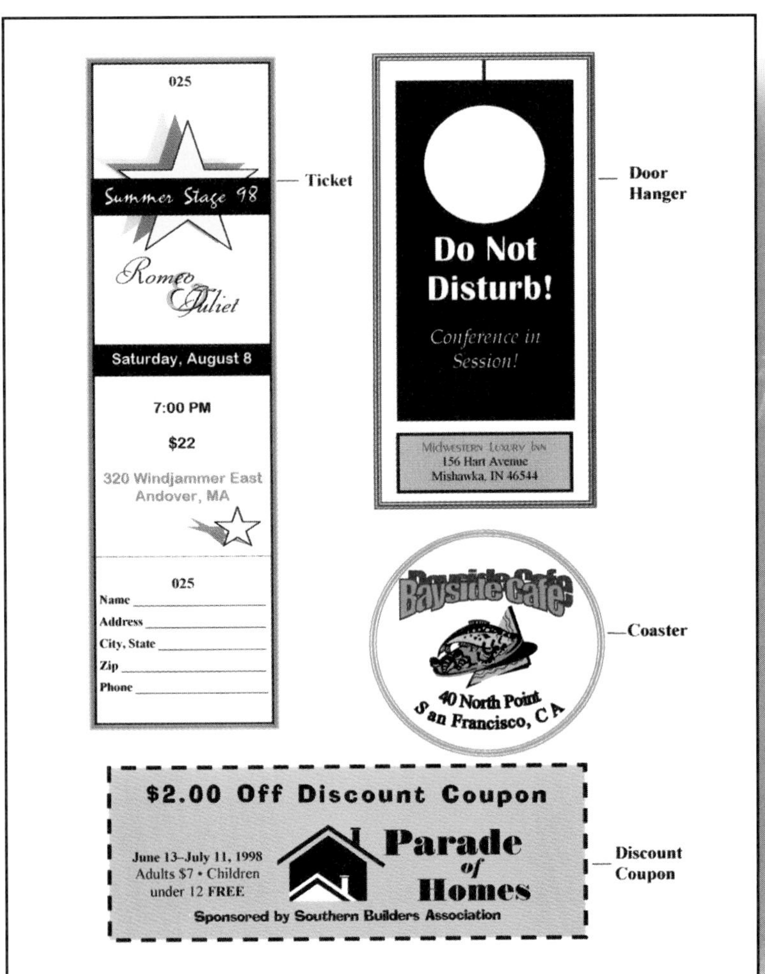

figure 7.1

Using Word to Create Other Promotional Documents

Web pages on the Internet can also be considered promotional in nature. The vast exposure of the World Wide Web provides endless possibilities for advertising products, services, research, data, and more, which may be presented on your company's Web page. In chapter 8, you will learn how to design and lay out a Web page. Many of the same design concepts used for flyers and announcements will be used on Web pages. In addition, animated text and pictures, as well as sound clips and videos can be added to promote interest. More information on Web pages is provided in chapter 8.

Using Tables to Create Promotional Documents

Tables will be used in most of the exercises in this chapter. In Word, name cards and postcards are created using tables in the label feature. Greeting cards are formatted in tables in order to divide the paper into equal sections. A table is effective as a container for information as well as a means for copying the document.

DTP POINTERS
Well-organized and clearly written promotional documents inspire viewer confidence.

Tables can be inserted anywhere in a document. Tables can hold text, numbers, pictures, or formulas in their cells. If you enter text in a cell, the text wraps to the next line based on the width of the cell. If you adjust the width of the cell, the text will adjust to the new cell width.

You can create a table by clicking Table, then Draw a Table; Table, then Insert Table; or you can click the Insert Table button on the Standard toolbar. When you click the Insert Table button, Word automatically sets the width of each column. When you create a table from the Table menu command, you have control over setting the width of each column and the height of each row. Think about how many rows and columns will be needed before you create a table. However, you can insert and delete columns and rows by selecting options from the drop-down list of table commands.

Tables are useful in desktop publishing since they offer options to format several objects consistently and predictably. Tables can give you precise control over layout. If your document needs to be separated by lines or has several areas that share a common border, tables would be the most efficient choice for document layout. Tables require some planning before you can use them in the layout of your document. Tables exist in the text layer and text automatically wraps around them. Like text boxes, tables can hold paragraphs with different indents and alignments and still have the same border around them.

Additionally, cells are easier to copy to other locations, especially if there is a considerable amount of formatting within each cell. To copy a table, select the cell or cells you wish to duplicate by clicking Table, then selecting Row, Column, or Table from the menu list. Click the Copy button on the Standard toolbar, then position the insertion point in the desired location, and click the Paste button on the Standard toolbar or use the Repeat key (F4) to duplicate the last command used. Copying in this manner saves the desktop publisher a considerable amount of time and energy.

Using Text Boxes in Promotional Documents

Additionally, text boxes will be used in many exercises in chapter 7, since they provide an excellent means for positioning elements in a document. However, remember text boxes automatically position elements in the layer above or below the text layer. Occasionally, the cut and paste method of copying and moving can not pick up text boxes along with a considerable amount of formatting and content. Grouping several design elements into a single unit can be helpful in moving and copying.

DTP POINTERS
Use graphics to help emphasize text.

Consider positioning pictures in the text layer by deselecting the *Float over text* option located in the Format Picture dialog box or in the Insert Picture dialog box.

Additionally, consider using the drag-and-drop method of copying and moving elements created in text boxes within tables. Also the AutoText feature may be used to copy elements, such as logos, pictures, and WordArt objects, into labels and other documents formatted in tables and text boxes. This method is discussed later in this chapter.

Creating Gift Certificates to Promote Business

In exercise 1, you will create a gift certificate template that will be used to create certificates in exercise 2 and in various skill and performance assessments later in this chapter. Gift certificates are excellent promotional documents that can be used for promoting further purchases or as rain checks, mini awards, "runner-up" prizes, or warranties. Predesigned and preperforated certificates can be purchased at most paper companies and may be used to accommodate your text. If you are using a predesigned form, you need to make wise decisions about formatting and laying out the text, logo, watermark, or graphics that you have decided to use in your document. You may also consider using light-colored parchment paper or marbleized paper to make the certificate look more official.

A table is being used for this template because of the ease in duplicating the cell to other locations. Using tables is just one approach to creating this type of document—another approach includes using text boxes to build the framework for a gift certificate.

Consult your instructor on whether you should save the exercise as a template or as a document. If you save it to the hard drive as a template, be sure to give the template your name followed by a template name, for instance, *Smith, Gift Certificate*. Another option is to save the form as a document, open the document when needed, and name the newly created document by another name.

DTP POINTERS
Use graphics that are appropriate to the subject of the document and the intended audience.

exercise 1

Creating a Gift Certificate Template

1. At a clear document screen, create a gift certificate template by completing the following steps:
   a. Change all the margins to 0.65 inches.
   b. Click Table, then Insert Table.
   c. At the Insert Table dialog box, change the Number of columns to **2** and the Number of rows to **1**. Click OK or press Enter.
   d. With the insertion point positioned in the first cell, make the following changes:
      (1) Click Table, then Cell Height and Width.
      (2) At the Cell Height and Width dialog box, select the Row tab, then click the down arrow to the right of the Height of row 1 text box and select Exactly. Key **210 pt** in the At text box. (One inch is equal to 72 points. To create a cell approximately 3 inches in height, multiply 72 x 3 = 216 pts. Using 210 points provides additional white space if adjustments need to be made for the unprintable zone.)
      (3) Key **0.2** inches in the Indent from left text box. Make sure Left Alignment is selected. Deselect Allow row to break across pages.
      (4) Select the Column tab. Key **4.75** inches in the Width of column 1 text box. Key **0** inches in the Space between columns text box.
      (5) Click the Next Column button. Key **2.25** inches in the Width of column 2 text box. Make sure **0** displays in the Space between columns text box. Click OK or press Enter.
   e. Click Table, then select Show Gridlines to turn this feature on.
   f. Add a border around the cells by completing the following steps:
      (1) Display the Tables and Borders toolbar.
      (2) Position the insertion point inside the first cell, click the down arrow to the right of the Line Style list box on the Tables and Borders toolbar, then select the seventh line from the top (double line).
      (3) Click the Line Weight list box on the Tables and Borders toolbar and select *¾ pt*.
      (4) Click the selection bar to the left of the table to select both cells.
      (5) Click the down arrow on the Border button on the Tables and Borders toolbar, then click the Outside Border button.
   g. Position the insertion point in the first cell, click Format, then Paragraph.

h. Select the Indents and Spacing tab, then change the Left and Right Indentations to 0.25 inches. Click OK or press Enter.
i. With the insertion point still located in the first cell, press the space bar once, then press Enter. (This is necessary to insert an Enter code inside the first cell.)
j. Position the insertion point in the second cell, then click the Center align button on the Formatting toolbar.

2. Save the certificate form as a template by completing the following steps: (Check with your instructor to see if you should save the certificate as a template to the hard drive or as a document to your student data disk.)
   a. Choose File, then Save As.
   b. At the Save As dialog box, click the down arrow to the right of the Save as type list box, then select *Document Template* from the drop-down list. Make sure *Templates* displays in the Save in: list box.
   c. Double-click *Other Documents* in the folder list box. (Your template should appear in the New dialog box with the Other Documents tab selected.)
   d. Key **(Your Last Name), Certificate** in the File name text box.
   e. Click the Save button.
3. Close (Your Last Name), Certificate.

exercise 2

Creating a Gift Certificate Using the Template Created in Exercise 1

1. Create the gift certificate in figure 7.2 by completing the following steps:
   a. Click File, then New; or if you saved the certificate form created in exercise 1 as a document on your student data disk, open *(Your Last Name), Certificate.doc,* then complete steps 1d and 1e.
   b. At the New dialog box, select the Other Documents tab.
   c. Double-click *(Your Last Name), Certificate.dot.*
   d. Click File, then Save As.
   e. At the Save As dialog box, name your document c07ex02, certificate. Make sure Word Document (*.doc) displays in the Save as type text box, then click Save.
   f. Make sure the default font is 12-point Times New Roman.
   g. Turn on kerning at 14 points.
   h. Create the text and fill-in lines in figure 7.2 by completing the following steps:
      (1) Position the insertion point in the first cell (left side of the certificate), press the down-arrow key once, and then key **Gift Certificate**. Press Enter twice.
      (2) Select *Gift Certificate,* then change the font to 30-point Brush Script MT.
      (3) Press the down-pointing arrow key twice.
      (4) Display the Ruler by choosing View, then Ruler. The Ruler can help you in creating appropriate line lengths.
      (5) Hold down the Ctrl key and press the Tab key four times. Key **Date** and press the space bar once. Create a horizontal line by holding down the Shift key and pressing the hyphen key on the keyboard. The line should be approximately 2.25 inches in length. (This line will copy well in a table.)

(6) Press Enter twice.
(7) Key **This certificate entitles**, press the space bar twice, and then create a line similar to the line in step h5. (The line should end where the previous line ends.) Press Enter twice.
(8) Key **to** and a space, then create another line approximately 2 inches in length as shown in figure 7.2. (If the *t* in *to* automatically capitalizes, click Tools, then AutoCorrect, and then deselect the Capitalize first letter of sentences option.)
(9) Press the space bar once, then key **Dollars** and a space. Key **$** and a space, then create another line. Press Enter twice.
(10) Key **Presented by**, press the space bar twice, and then create a line that ends where the previous lines end. Press Enter twice.
(11) Hold down the Ctrl key and press the Tab key once. Key **Authorized signature** and a space. Create a line that ends where the previous lines end.

i. Create the name and address in figure 7.2 by completing the following steps:
(1) Position the insertion point in the second cell (right side) of the certificate.
(2) Press Enter.
(3) Key the following:

Butterfield Gardens
29 W 036 Butterfield Road
Warrenville, IL 60555
(603) 555-1062
http://www.grower-2-you.com (An automatic link to the Internet may occur when you key this line—the text becomes a Universal Resource Locator which is the code name for a location on the Internet. To remove the hyperlink, press the space bar once after keying *http://www.grower-2-you.com*, then press the backspace key once.)

j. Select *Butterfield Gardens*, then change the font to 20-point Brush Script MT with Shadow.
k. Select the rest of the address and change the font to 10-point Times New Roman. Deselect the text, then press Enter twice.
l. With the insertion point positioned a double space below the address, insert *Buttrfly.wmf* located on your student data disk. (If you need to resize the image, click on any one of the corner sizing handles and drag the sizing handle inward to reduce the size or outward to increase the size proportionately.) Deselect the image.
m. Create two more certificates by completing the following steps:
(1) Position the insertion point anywhere in the certificate, click Table, then Select Row.
(2) Click the Copy button on the Standard toolbar.
(3) Position the insertion point below the first certificate, then press Enter twice.
(4) Click Edit, then Paste Cells.
n. Position the insertion point below the certificate, then press Enter twice.
o. Paste another copy of the certificate.

2. View the document in Print Preview. (Change the top and bottom margins and possibly delete a hard return between the certificates if the certificates do not display on one page.)
3. Save the document again with the same name, c07ex02, certificate.
4. Print and then close c07ex02, certificate.

figure 7.2

Gift Certificate

Date ______________________

This certificate entitles ______________________

to ______________________ Dollars $ ________

Presented by ______________________

Authorized signature ______________________

Butterfield Gardens
29 W 036 Butterfield Road
Warrenville, IL 60555
(603) 555-1062
http://www.grower-2-you.com

Gift Certificate

Date ______________________

This certificate entitles ______________________

to ______________________ Dollars $ ________

Presented by ______________________

Authorized signature ______________________

Butterfield Gardens
29 W 036 Butterfield Road
Warrenville, IL 60555
(603) 555-1062
http://www.grower-2-you.com

Gift Certificate

Date ______________________

This certificate entitles ______________________

to ______________________ Dollars $ ________

Presented by ______________________

Authorized signature ______________________

Butterfield Gardens
29 W 036 Butterfield Road
Warrenville, IL 60555
(603) 555-1062
http://www.grower-2-you.com

Creating Postcards to Promote Business

If you have a brief message to get across to prospective customers, postcards can be an appropriate means of delivering the message. Postcards are inexpensive to create and use. They can be used as appointment reminders, just-moved notes, return/reply cards, display cards, thank you cards, or invitations. Consider purchasing predesigned printed postcards with attractive borders, color combinations, and sizes and weights that meet U.S. Post Office standards. You can purchase blank, prestamped 3½-inch by 5½-inch postcards from the U.S. Post Office at a cost of approximately 20 cents apiece. Or, you can use the Word label feature, which provides a predefined postcard sized at 4 inches by 6 inches. Two postcards will display on a standard-sized sheet of paper when you use Word's postcard label, Avery 5389.

Most postcards are created on 100- to 110-pound uncoated cover stock paper. The paperweight or thickness should be strong enough to hold up in the mail. The front side of the postcard is used for your return address and the recipient's address along with an area reserved for the postage. On the backside, you can create a headline and use a graphic or watermark to emphasize the message. You will need to leave room for your message and optional signature.

Alternatively, use the Table feature in Word to produce four cells that represent four postcard-sized documents. You may want to save the postcards as a template before keying the text content. To create postcards using the Table feature and insert a watermark, as shown in figure 7.3, complete the following steps:

1. Change the Top margin to 0.70 inches and all the remaining margins to 0.5 inches (you may need to adjust your margins based on your nonprintable zone).
2. Change the paper orientation to landscape.
3. Insert a table containing two columns and two rows.
4. Change the height of each row to 248 points and the width of each column to 5 inches. (These measurements will result in four postcards measuring 4 inches by 5 inches—you may need to adjust this measurement based on your nonprintable zone.)
5. Key the text content in the first cell.
6. Insert a picture, but make sure the *Float over text* option at the Insert Picture dialog box has been selected (a checkmark should display inside the checkbox).
7. Select the picture, click the Text Wrapping button on the Picture toolbar, and make sure None is selected.
8. With the picture still selected, click the Image Control button on the Picture toolbar, then select the Watermark option.
9. Click the Draw button on the Drawing toolbar, point to Order, and then click Send Behind Text.
10. Click Table, then Select Row.
11. Click the Copy button on the Standard toolbar.
12. Click Edit, then Paste Cells.
13. Press the F4 (Repeat) key to continue copying the document.

figure 7.3

Creating Postcards Using Word's Table Feature

A. G. Rowe & Sons, Inc. *INVESTMENTS SINCE 1902* Wendy Fausey and Elizabeth Krueper invite you to this FREE workshop *FUNDING YOUR CHILD'S EDUCATION* Wednesday, November 4, 7:00 p.m. or Thursday, November 5, 7:00 p.m. Breckenridge Country Club 3400 Ridgeway Drive Baltimore, MD For reservations, call (410) 555-5132	A. G. Rowe & Sons, Inc. *INVESTMENTS SINCE 1902* Wendy Fausey and Elizabeth Krueper invite you to this FREE workshop *FUNDING YOUR CHILD'S EDUCATION* Wednesday, November 4, 7:00 p.m. or Thursday, November 5, 7:00 p.m. Breckenridge Country Club 3400 Ridgeway Drive Baltimore, MD For reservations, call (410) 555-5132
A. G. Rowe & Sons, Inc. *INVESTMENTS SINCE 1902* Wendy Fausey and Elizabeth Krueper invite you to this FREE workshop *FUNDING YOUR CHILD'S EDUCATION* Wednesday, November 4, 7:00 p.m. or Thursday, November 5, 7:00 p.m. Breckenridge Country Club 3400 Ridgeway Drive Baltimore, MD For reservations, call (410) 555-5132	A. G. Rowe & Sons, Inc. *INVESTMENTS SINCE 1902* Wendy Fausey and Elizabeth Krueper invite you to this FREE workshop *FUNDING YOUR CHILD'S EDUCATION* Wednesday, November 4, 7:00 p.m. or Thursday, November 5, 7:00 p.m. Breckenridge Country Club 3400 Ridgeway Drive Baltimore, MD For reservations, call (410) 555-5132

exercise 3

Creating Postcards Using Word's Label Feature

1. At a clear document screen, create the two postcards in figure 7.4 by completing the following steps:
   a. Turn on kerning at 14 points.
   b. Make sure the default font is 12-point Times New Roman.
   c. Display the Drawing toolbar, the Tables and Borders toolbar, and the Picture toolbar.
   d. Click Tools, then Envelopes and Labels.
   e. At the Envelopes and Labels dialog box, select the Labels tab, then click the Options button.
   f. At the Labels Options dialog box, select *5389 - Post card* in the Product number list box. Click OK or press Enter.
   g. At the Envelopes and Labels dialog box, click the New Document button.
   h. Click Table, then Show Gridlines.
   i. Click the Align Top button on the Tables and Borders toolbar.
   j. With the insertion point located in the first postcard, press the space bar once, then press Enter.
   k. Click the Insert Picture button on the Picture toolbar.
   l. At the Insert Picture dialog box, select the Float over text option (a checkmark should display in the check box). Double-click *Notes.wmf* located on your student data disk.
   m. Select the *Notes* picture, click the Text Wrapping button on the Picture toolbar, and then select None.
   n. With the picture still selected, click the Shadow button on the Drawing toolbar. Select the second shadow in the second row (Shadow Style 6).
   o. Click the Text Box button on the Drawing toolbar. Drag the crosshairs into the label and to the right of the *Notes* picture. Create a text box that measures approximately

0.75 inches in height and 2.70 inches in width. You can verify the box size at the Format Text Box dialog box with the Size tab selected.

p. Select the Colors and Lines tab, select No Lines in the Colors text box in the Line section. Click the down arrow to the right of the Color text box in the Fill section and select *No Fill*, then click OK or press Enter.

q. With the insertion point positioned inside the text box, change the font to 38-point Brush Script MT with Shadow, and then key **Piano Tuning**. (See figure 7.4 for the placement of *Piano Tuning*—drag and position if necessary.)

r. With the insertion point positioned at the top of the label, press the Enter key eight times.

s. Create the postcard text by completing the following steps:
   (1) Click the Center align button on the Formatting toolbar.
   (2) Key **Spring Special**, then press Enter twice.
   (3) Key **$45**, then press Enter twice.
   (4) Key **(Good until May 31, 1999)**, then press Enter twice.
   (5) Select the following text and change the formatting according to the following specifications (do not select the paragraph symbols between the lines of text):

Spring Special	22-point Bookman Old Style
$45	36-point Bookman Old Style in Red with Shadow
(Good until May 31, 1999)	12-point Bookman Old Style Italic

   (6) Press the down arrow key twice to position the insertion point below the last line of text, then click the Align Left button on the Formatting toolbar.
   (7) Click Format, then Paragraph. At the Paragraph dialog box, select the Indent and Spacing tab and change the Left and Right Indentations to **0.25** inches. Click OK or press Enter.
   (8) Change the font to 11-point Bookman Old Style, key **Robert Valecki**, then press Enter.
   (9) Key **Piano Lessons Available**.
   (10) Press Ctrl + Tab five times, then key **(312) 555-8765**.

t. Copy the postcard by completing the following steps:
   (1) Position the insertion point anywhere in the first formatted postcard, click Table, then Select Row.
   (2) Click the Copy button on the Standard toolbar.
   (3) Position the insertion point in the second label (below the first one).
   (4) Click Edit, then Paste Rows. (If an additional cell copies below the second cell, click Table, then Delete Rows.)

u. With the insertion point located in either postcard, create a border by completing the following steps:
   (1) Click Table, then Select Table.
   (2) Click the Line Style list box on the Tables and Borders toolbar, then select the seventh line from the top (double lines).
   (3) Click the Line Weight list box, then select *½ pt* from the drop-down list.
   (4) Click the Border Color button, then select Red in the second row and third column.
   (5) Click the Border button on the Tables and Borders toolbar, then select the All Borders button.

v. View your document at Print Preview. Make sure the elements are located in the postcards as shown in figure 7.4. Make any necessary editing changes. (If the bottom borderline does not display, adjust the top and bottom margins.)

2. Save the document with the name c07ex03, postcard.
3. Print and then close c07ex03, postcard.

Optional: Save the postcard text as an AutoText entry by completing the following steps:

1. Create the postcard text as instructed in exercise 3.
2. When the postcard text is complete, click Table, then Select Row.
3. Click Insert, point to AutoText, then click New.
4. At the Create AutoText dialog box, key **piano** in the AutoText entry text box. Click OK or press Enter.
5. Close the document window without saving.
6. Click Tools, then Envelopes and Labels.
7. At the Envelopes and Labels dialog box, select the Labels tab.
8. Click the Options button and select *5389 - Post card* at the Product number list box. Make sure the option *Full page of the same label* is selected. Click OK or press Enter.
9. Position the insertion point in the Address text box, key **piano**, then press F3.
10. Click the New Document button.
11. The postcard text and picture should copy to both postcards in this label definition. (If a blank postcard displays between the two copies, click Table, then Delete Rows.)

figure 7.4

(Good until May 31, 1999)

Robert Valecki
Piano Lessons Available
(312) 555-8765

Spring Special

$45

(Good until May 31, 1999)

Robert Valecki
Piano Lessons Available
(312) 555-8765

Using Mail Merge in Promotional Documents

Mail Merge is the process of combining variable information with standard text to create personalized documents. Word's Mail Merge feature enables you to create form letters, envelopes, labels, and more. To do so, you merge a *main document*, which contains data such as the text of a form letter or the return address and picture on a postcard, with a *data source*, which contains varying data such as names and addresses. Special codes called *merge fields* in the main document direct Word to collect information from the data source and use it in the main document to create personalized documents. There are three basic processes involved in a mail merge:

1. Create a new main document or edit and designate an existing document as a main document.
2. Create a new data source or choose an existing one.
3. Perform the merge operation.

Main Document
A form that receives the data.

Data Source
Contains variable data such as names and addresses.

Merge Fields
Special codes inserted into the main document instructing Word to collect information from the data source.

Word can create a merge from three different data sources. These sources are: a Word document formatted in a table, tab, or comma-delimited format; an imported application or database such as Microsoft Access, Excel, dBASE, Paradox, etc; and a shared office file such as the Personal Address Book, Outlook, or Microsoft Network lists. You will create a data source formatted in a table.

Using the Mail Merge Helper

Word's Mail Merge Helper includes a series of dialog boxes that guide you through creating or identifying the main document and the data source, then through the merge of the main document and the data source. In exercise 4, you will use Mail Merge Helper to merge addresses onto the reverse side of the two postcards created in exercise 3.

Figure 7.5 illustrates the Mail Merge Helper dialog box, which lays out the three stages in creating a merged document—creating a main document, creating a data source, and completing a merge. Click Tools, then Mail Merge to access this dialog box.

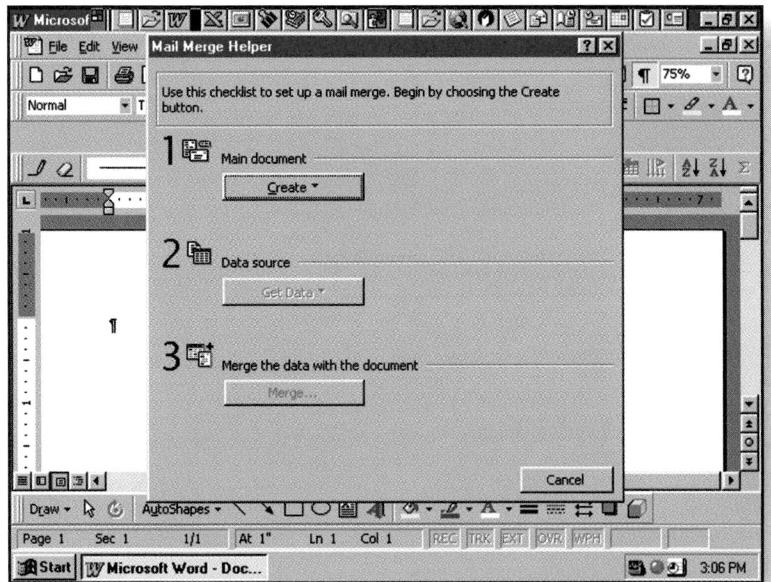

figure 7.5
Mail Merge Helper Dialog Box

Record
Contains all the information for one unit (person, family, or business).

Field
A specific section of variable information, such as title, first name, last name, etc.

Delimiters
Commas, tabs, and cells that separate each field of data.

Creating a Data Source

When creating a data source, consider the present and future uses of this information. The data source contains the variable information about customers, clients, companies, etc. This may include such information as names, addresses, telephone numbers, and products. Information in a data source is usually laid out in a table. Each row of information is known as a *record.* If the data source contains names and addresses of clients, the record contains each individual's name, address, and any other specific information.

Columns of information in a table used as a data source are known as *fields*. Each field, or column, contains one specific type of information about each client. For instance, one field may contain the state and another field may contain the zip code. Word understands commas, tabs, and cells in a table as *delimiters*, which separate each field of data. Variable information in a data source is saved as a record. A record contains all the information in one unit. A series of fields makes one record, and a series of records make a data source.

At the Mail Merge Helper, Word provides predetermined field names that can be used when creating the data source. Field names are used to describe the contents of each field in the data source, as shown in figure 7.6. They are also used to indicate where information goes when it is taken from the data source and placed into a merged document. Field names are limited to 40 characters and they cannot contain spaces. Besides the predetermined field names, you have the option to create your own field names. You can delete any unwanted predetermined fields and insert your own fields at the Field name text box in the Create Data Source dialog box.

When naming the data source file, you may want to add the letters *ds* to the name to identify it as a data source document.

exercise 4

Creating a Data Source

1. At a clear document screen, create the data source shown in figure 7.9 and name it *Post card ds* by completing the following steps:
   a. Click Tools, then Mail Merge.
   b. At the Mail Merge Helper dialog box shown in figure 7.5, click Create. From the drop-down list that displays, click *Mailing Labels*.(You will later select the *5389 - Post card* definition in the Label Options dialog box.)
   c. At the dialog box asking if you want to use the active document or a new document window, select Active Window.
   d. Click Get Data, then, from the drop-down list that displays, click *Create Data Source*.
   e. At the Create Data Source dialog box shown in figure 7.7, the fields provided by Word are shown in the Field names in header row list box. These fields are needed for the data source in this exercise: *Title*, *FirstName*, *LastName*, *Address1*, *City*, *State*, and *PostalCode*.
   f. To remove *JobTitle* or any other unwanted fields, click the down arrow on the vertical scroll bar to the right of the Field names in header row list box until *JobTitle* is visible. Click *JobTitle* in the list box, then click Remove Field Name. When *Job Title* is removed, it will display in the Field name text box. Remove the following unwanted fields from the Field names in header row list box: *Job Title, Company, Address2, Country, HomePhone*, and *WorkPhone*.

g. Click OK or press Enter.
h. At the Save As dialog box, key **Postcard ds** in the File name text box, then click Save.
i. At the dialog box containing the warning that the data source contains no data, click Edit Data Source. This displays the Data Form dialog box shown in figure 7.8.
j. At the Data Form dialog box, key the title **Mrs.** of the first customer shown in figure 7.6, then press the Enter key or the Tab key.
k. Continue keying the information in figure 7.6 for the customer, *Mrs. Peggy McSherry,* in the appropriate fields. Press the Enter key or the Tab key to move to the next field. Press Shift + Tab to move to the preceding field.
l. After entering all the information for *Mrs. Peggy McSherry*, click Add New. This saves the information and displays a blank Data Form dialog box. Continue keying the information for each person in this manner until all records shown in figure 7.6 have been created.
m. After creating the last record for the data source, click View Source and compare your document to figure 7.9.
n. At the data source document, click File, then Save.

2. Close *Postcard ds*.
3. At the clear window, close the document without saving it.

figure 7.6

Data Source Client Information

Title	=	Mrs.
FirstName	=	Peggy
LastName	=	McSherry
Address1	=	3955 Kinzie Court
City	=	St. Louis
State	=	MO
PostalCode	=	50749
Title	=	Mrs.
FirstName	=	Kathleen
LastName	=	Nixon
Address1	=	409 Highland Drive
City	=	St. Louis
State	=	MO
PostalCode	=	50749
Title	=	Mr. and Mrs.
FirstName	=	Eric
LastName	=	Gohlke
Address1	=	3740 North Orchard
City	=	St. Louis
State	=	MO
PostalCode	=	50750
Title	=	Ms.
FirstName	=	Margo
LastName	=	Godfrey
Address1	=	393 River Drive
City	=	St. Louis
State	=	MO
PostalCode	=	50750

figure 7.7

Create Data Source Dialog Box

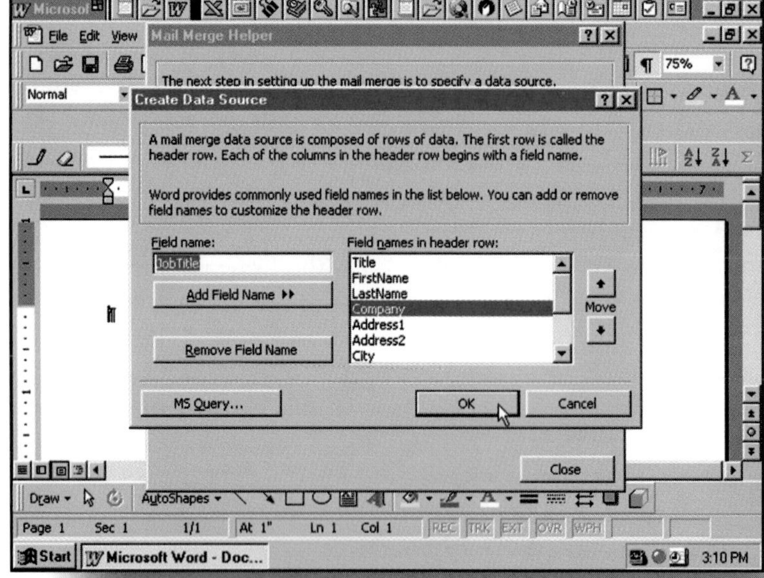

figure 7.8

Data Form Dialog Box

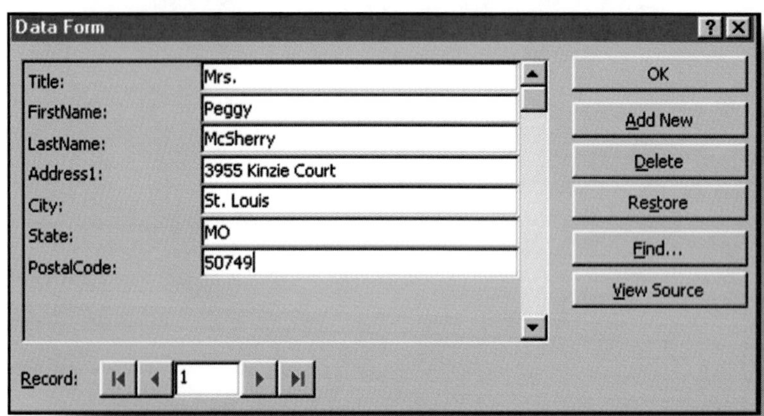

figure 7.9

Postcard ds

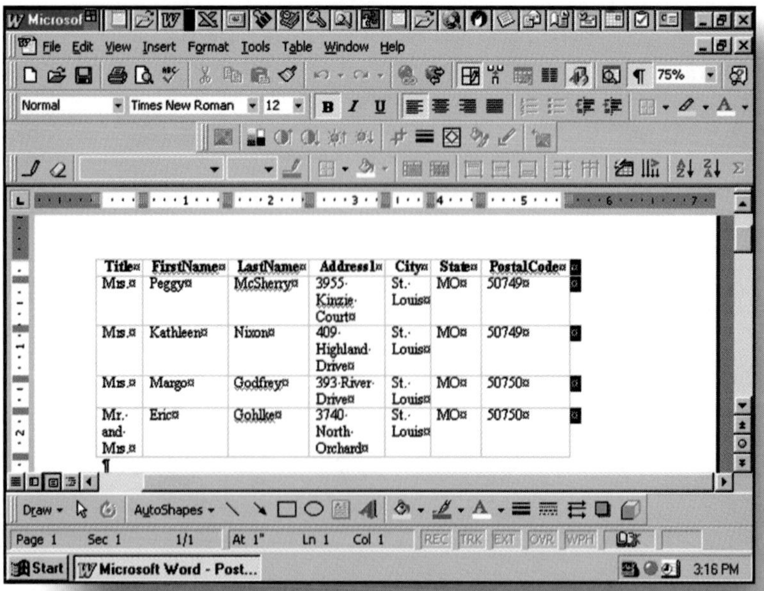

Title	FirstName	LastName	Address1	City	State	PostalCode
Mrs.	Peggy	McSherry	3955 Kinzie Court	St. Louis	MO	50749
Ms.	Kathleen	Nixon	409 Highland Drive	St. Louis	MO	50749
Ms.	Margo	Godfrey	393 River Drive	St. Louis	MO	50750
Mr. and Mrs.	Eric	Gohlke	3740 North Orchard	St. Louis	MO	50750

Creating the Main Document

The main document may be more than just a form letter; it may include a mailing list, catalog, mailing labels, letters, or more. In the next two exercises, you will merge a list of addresses to the backside of the postcard advertising a service for tuning pianos. When the main document is completed and the fields have been keyed into proper locations, your main document will look similar to figure 7.10. To create the main document shown in figure 7.10, complete exercise 5.

When naming a main document, you may want to add the initials *md* to indicate that the file is a main document. Insert spaces between the fields as you would key normal text. For instance, key a comma and space between the <City> field and the <State> field in an address.

exercise 5

Creating a Main Document

1. At a clear document screen, create the main document shown in figure 7.10 by completing the following steps:
   a. Key the following return address in 12-point Times New Roman:

      Mr. Robert Valecki
      32 Lemon Creek Road
      St. Louis, MO 50477

   b. Press Enter twice.
   c. Insert *Flyace.wmf* located on your student data disk.
   d. Resize the picture by completing the following steps:
      (1) Select the picture.
      (2) Click Format, then Picture.
      (3) At the Format Picture dialog box, select the Size tab, then change the Height to 70% and the Width to 70% in the Scale section.
      (4) Select the Position tab, then deselect the Float over text option.
      (5) Click OK or press Enter.
   e. Insert the text inside the banner as shown in figure 7.10 by completing the following steps:
      (1) Double-click the picture to access Microsoft Word Picture. (Click Tools, then Options, and then select the Edit tab and make sure *Microsoft Word* displays in the Picture editor list box. Click OK or press Enter.)
      (2) Click the Text Box button on the Drawing toolbar, then drag and draw a text box that fits inside the *Flyace* picture banner. (Make sure the text box does not interfere with the border of the banner.)
      (3) Remove the border around the text box by choosing *No Line* from the Line button palette on the Drawing toolbar.
      (4) With the insertion point positioned inside the text box, click the Center align button on the Formatting toolbar, change the font to 16-point Times New Roman Bold, then key **Time to Tune!**. (The lines in the banner may not display, so do not be concerned!)

(5) If the text inside the text box is not centered vertically within the banner, position the insertion point before the *T* in *Time to...*, then click Format, Paragraph, select the Indents and Spacing tab, and then key **4 pt** inside the Spacing Before text box. Click OK or press Enter.

(6) Click File, then Close & Return to Document#.

f. Create an AutoText entry by completing the following steps:

(1) Select the return address and the picture (Ctrl + A), then click Insert, point to AutoText, and then click New.

(2) At the Create AutoText dialog box, key **piano** in the AutoText entry Text box.

(3) Click OK or press Enter.

g. Delete the address and picture from the document window.

h. Click Tools, then Mail Merge.

i. At the Mail Merge Helper dialog box, click Create (below Main Document).

j. At the drop-down list that displays, click *Mailing Labels*.

k. At the question asking if you want to use the active document window or a new document, click Active Window.

l. At the Mail Merge Helper dialog box, click Get Data (below Data source).

m. At the drop-down list that displays, click *Open Data Source*.

n. At the Open Data Source dialog box, double-click *Postcard ds* in the list box.

o. At the Microsoft Word dialog box telling you that Word needs to set up your main document, choose Set Up Main Document.

p. At the Label Options dialog box, make sure *5389 - Post card* is selected in the Product number list box, then click OK or press Enter.

q. Position the insertion point in the Sample label text box.

r. Key **piano,** then press F3. (Robert Valecki's return address along with a picture of a banner and an airplane should display.)

s. Press Enter twice.

t. Insert the merge field codes into the Sample Label by completing the following steps:

(1) From the left edge of the Sample Label, press Ctrl + Tab five times.

(2) Click the Insert Merge Field button, click *Title* from the drop-down menu, and then press the space bar once.

(3) Click the Insert Merge Field button, click *FirstName* from the drop-down menu, and then press the space bar once. (The merge fields may wrap to the next line—do not be concerned!)

(4) Click the Insert Merge Field button, click *LastName,* and then press Enter.

(5) Press Ctrl + Tab five times.

(6) Click the Insert Merge Field button, click *Address1*, and then press Enter.

(7) Press Ctrl + Tab five times.

(8) Continue inserting the *City, State*, and *PostalCode* merge fields, including a comma between the city and state and using spaces as you would in regular address text.

(9) Click OK.

(10) Click Close at the Mail Merge Helper.

u. Click Table, then Select Table, then click the Align Top button on the Tables and Borders toolbar.

2. Click File, then Save As.
3. At the Save As dialog box, key **Postcard md** in the File name text box, then click Save or press Enter.
4. Close *Postcard md*.

figure 7.10

Mr. Robert Valecki
32 Lemon Creek Road
St. Louis, MO 50477

Time to Tune!

<<Title>> <<FirstName>> <<LastName>>
<<Address1>>
<<City>>, <<State>> <<Postal Code>>

Mr. Robert Valecki
32 Lemon Creek Road
St. Louis, MO 50477

<<Title>> <<FirstName>> <<LastName>>
<<Address1>>
<<City>>, <<State>> <<Postal Code>>

Merging Information to a Postcard

Once the data source and the main document have been created and saved, they can be merged. Merged documents can be saved in a new document or sent directly to the printer. There are several ways to merge a data source with a main document. A main document and a data source can be merged with buttons on the Mail Merge toolbar or options at the Mail Merge Helper dialog box. To merge a main document with a data source, open the main document, then click the Merge to New Document button (the fifth button from the right on the Mail Merge toolbar—see figure 7.11.)

When the main document is open, you can use buttons on the Mail Merge toolbar to view how the document will look after merging with the first record, the next record, the last record, or a specific record from the data source.

To merge to the printer, open the main document, then click the Merge to Printer button on the Mail Merge toolbar (the fourth button from the right).

Mail Merge Toolbar

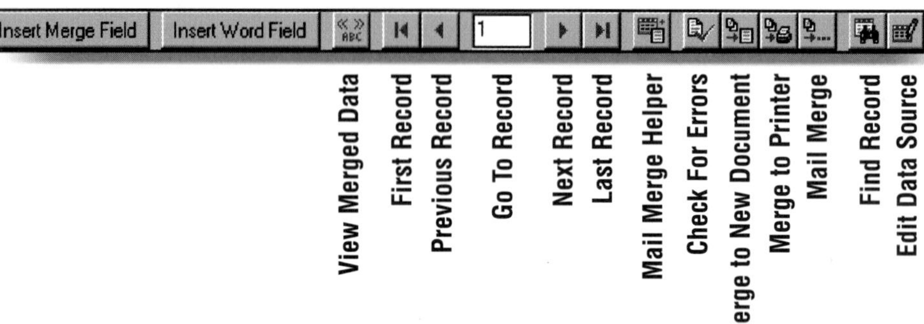

exercise 6

Merging Documents

1. Merge *Postcard md* with *Postcard ds* as shown in figure 7.12 by completing the following steps:
   a. Print two copies of c07ex03, postcard (resulting in four postcards).
   b. Place the printed postcards from step 1a into your printer. (Be careful to position them correctly into the printer so the merge will occur on the backside of each postcard.)
   c. Open *Postcard md*.
   d. Click the Merge to New Document button on the Mail Merge toolbar (fifth button from the right). When the documents are merged, a partial section of a row may display in the document window at the bottom of the first page—do not be alarmed! The postcards should print correctly even though they may not view correctly.
2. When the main document is merged with the data source, save the document and name it c07ex06, merged.
3. View the postcards in Print Preview.
4. Print and then close c07ex06, merged.
5. Close *Postcard md* without saving the changes.

figure 7.12

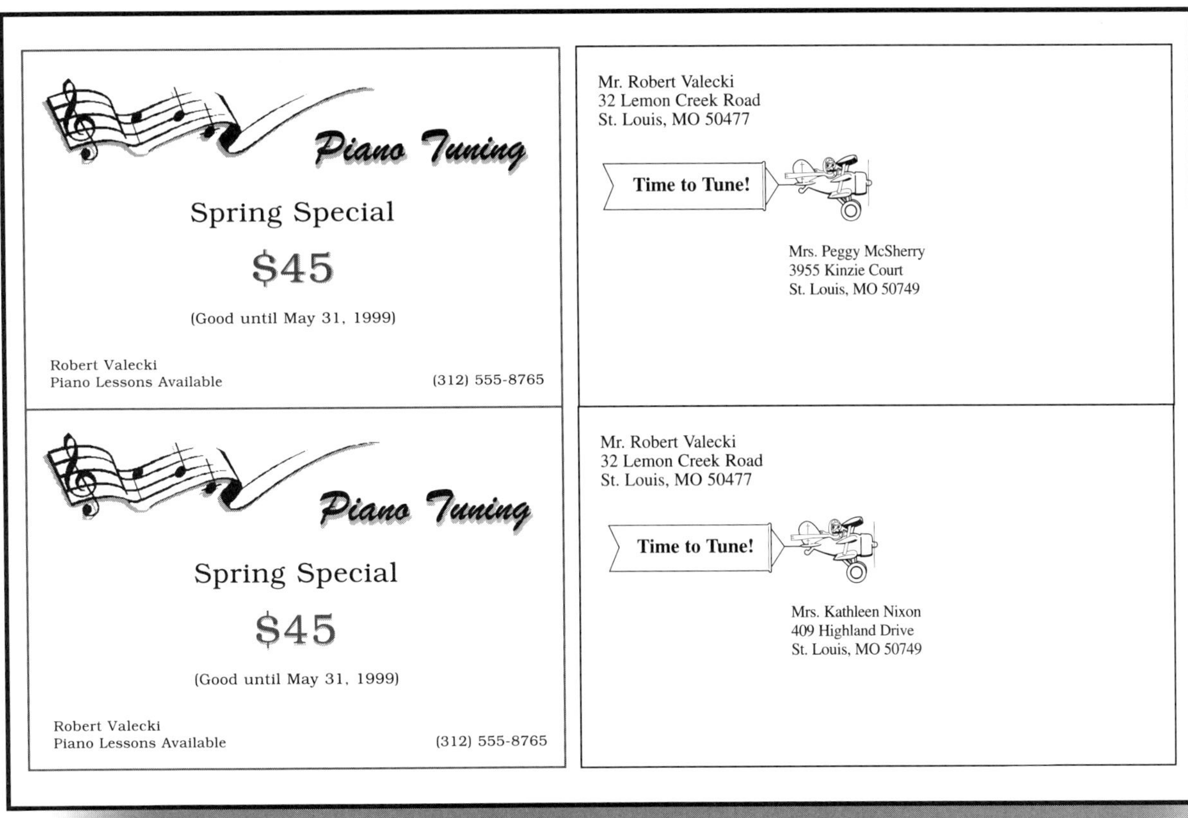

Creating Name Badges

An appropriate name badge (tag) shows your name, your title, and the company or organizations with which you are affiliated. The individual's name should be easy to read and the most dominant element on the name tag. Remembering a person's name is one of the biggest compliments you can pay to that person. However, if you are in a business where you meet a lot of people, remembering names can be difficult. Name badges can definitely reduce the embarrassment of forgetting someone's name.

DTP POINTERS
Use a type size and style that can be read at a glance.

An alternative to choosing labels for name badges is to purchase name tag holders and insert a business card or name badge printed on heavier weight paper inside the holder. The holder is a clear plastic sleeve with a clip or pin on the backside. Holders are usually available through mail order paper companies or office supply companies.

Word includes eight name badge label definitions. The number of labels ranges from six labels to eight labels per sheet. The Avery name badges come in the following sizes: 2.17 inches by 3.5 inches, 2.33 inches by 3.38 inches, and 3 inches by 4 inches.

Typically, more than one name badge is created at a time. If you are creating several badges for many different people, you may want to merge a data source to the label definition (main document) to efficiently produce them. In exercise 7, you will use a data source that has already been prepared for you and saved to your student data disk—*Floral ds*.

Remember to plan your badges with a focal point in mind. The individual's name should be dominant. Choose a font and type size that emphasizes the name. Readability is important, so choose a font that is easy to read at a glance. Since this document is so small, consider using one font for the entire tag. Vary the type style and type size to add interest. Using an appropriate special character or logo with a touch of color will enhance the badge and increase its visual appeal.

exercise 7

Creating Name Badges Using Merge

1. At a clear document screen, create the name badges in figure 7.14 by completing the following steps:
   a. Display the Drawing toolbar and the Tables and Borders toolbar.
   b. Click Tools, then Mail Merge.
   c. At the Mail Merge Helper dialog box, click Create, then select *Mailing Labels* from the drop-down list. At the question asking if you want to use the active document window or a new document, create Active Window.
   d. At the Mail Merge Helper dialog box, click Get Data (below Data Source).
   e. At the drop-down list that displays, click *Open Data Source*.
   f. At the Open Data Source dialog box, double-click *Floral ds.doc* located on your student data disk.
   g. At the Microsoft Word dialog box telling you that Word needs to set up your main document, click the Set Up Main Document button.
   h. At the Label Options dialog box, select *5095 - Name Badge* in the Product number list box, then click OK or press Enter.
   i. At the Create Labels dialog box, click OK. (You will not be keying text in the Sample Label text box.)
   j. At the Mail Merge Helper dialog box, click Edit under the Main document section, then click Mailing Label: Document#.
   k. Format the name badge text and insert merge fields by completing the following steps:
      (1) Make sure table gridlines display.
      (2) Position the insertion point in the first cell, then click the Align Top button on the Tables and Borders toolbar.
      (3) Position the insertion point on the second paragraph symbol that displays. (Turn on Show/Hide ¶.)
      (4) Click the Center align button on the Formatting toolbar, then turn on kerning at 14 points.
      (5) Change the font to 16-point Britannic Bold and turn on Small caps. Click the Insert Merge Field button on the Mail Merge toolbar, then select *Association* from the drop-down list.
      (6) Press Ctrl + Tab, then click Insert, Symbol. Select the Symbols tab, then change the Font to Wingdings. Select the symbol in the fifth row and the tenth column. Click Insert, then Close.

(7) Select the symbol, then change the color to Teal.
(8) Deselect the symbol, then change the font to 11-point Britannic Bold in Black, and then press Enter four times.
(9) Make sure Center alignment is selected, then change the font to 20-point Britannic Bold.
(10) Click the Insert Merge Field button on the Mail Merge toolbar, then select *FirstName* as shown in figure 7.13.
(11) Press the space bar once, click the Insert Merge Field button, and then select *LastName*.
(12) Change the font to 11-point Britannic Bold. Press Enter, then insert the *JobTitle* field.
(13) Press Enter four times, then click the Left Align button on the Formatting toolbar, then insert the *Company* field.
(14) Create a right tab at approximately 3.25 inches on the Ruler.
(15) Press Ctrl + Tab, then insert the *City* and *State* fields separated by a comma and space, as shown in figure 7.13.
(16) Select by dragging from the paragraph symbol above *FirstName*... to the paragraph symbol below *JobTitle*, then click Format, Borders and Shading, and then select the Shading tab. Click the Teal color in the seventh row of the color palette. Make sure *Paragraph* displays in the Apply to text box, then click OK or press Enter.
(17) Select *FirstName LastName* and *JobTitle* and change the font color to White.

l. Save the name badge text as an AutoText entry by completing the following steps:
   (1) Select by dragging through the name badge text beginning with the Enter at the top of the cell and including the last line in the cell.
   (2) With this text selected, click Insert, point to AutoText, and then click New.
   (3) At the Create AutoText dialog box, key **floral** in the Text entry text box. Click OK.
m. Close the document window without saving.
n. At a clear document screen, click Tools, then Mail Merge.
o. At the Mail Merge Helper dialog box, click Create, then select *Mailing Labels*. At the dialog box that displays, click Active Window.
p. Click Get Data, then click *Open Data Source* from the drop-down menu. At the Open dialog box, double-click *Floral ds* located on your student data disk.
q. Click the Set Up Main Document button.
r. Select *5095 - Name Badge* in the Product number section of the Label Options dialog box, then click OK or press Enter.
s. With the insertion point positioned in the Sample label text box, key **floral**, then press F3.
t. Click OK to close the Create Labels dialog box.
u. At the Mail Merge Helper dialog box, click Close.
v. Save the document with Save As and name it *Floral md*.
w. Click the Merge to New Document button on the Mail Merge toolbar (fifth button from the right).

2. Save the name badge document and name it c07ex07, badge.
3. Print and then close c07ex07, badge.
4. Close *Floral md* without saving changes.

figure 7.13

Insert Merge Button and Inserting Merge Codes into a Name Badge

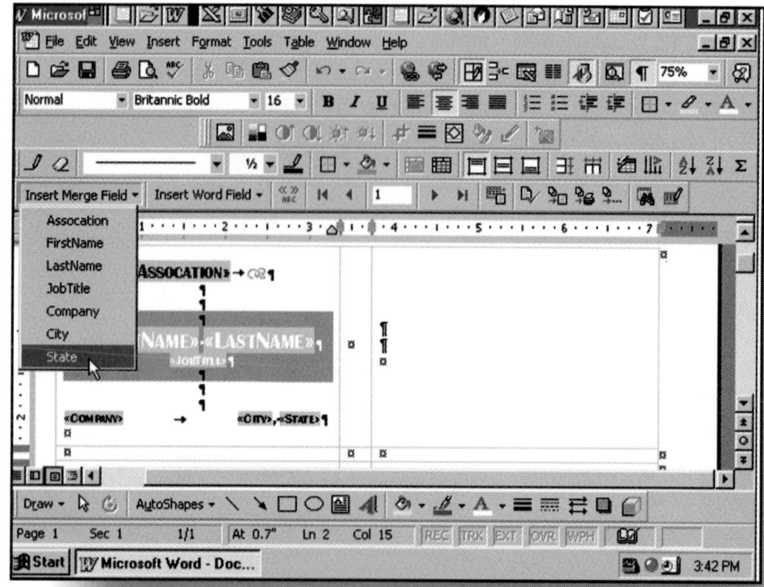

figure 7.14

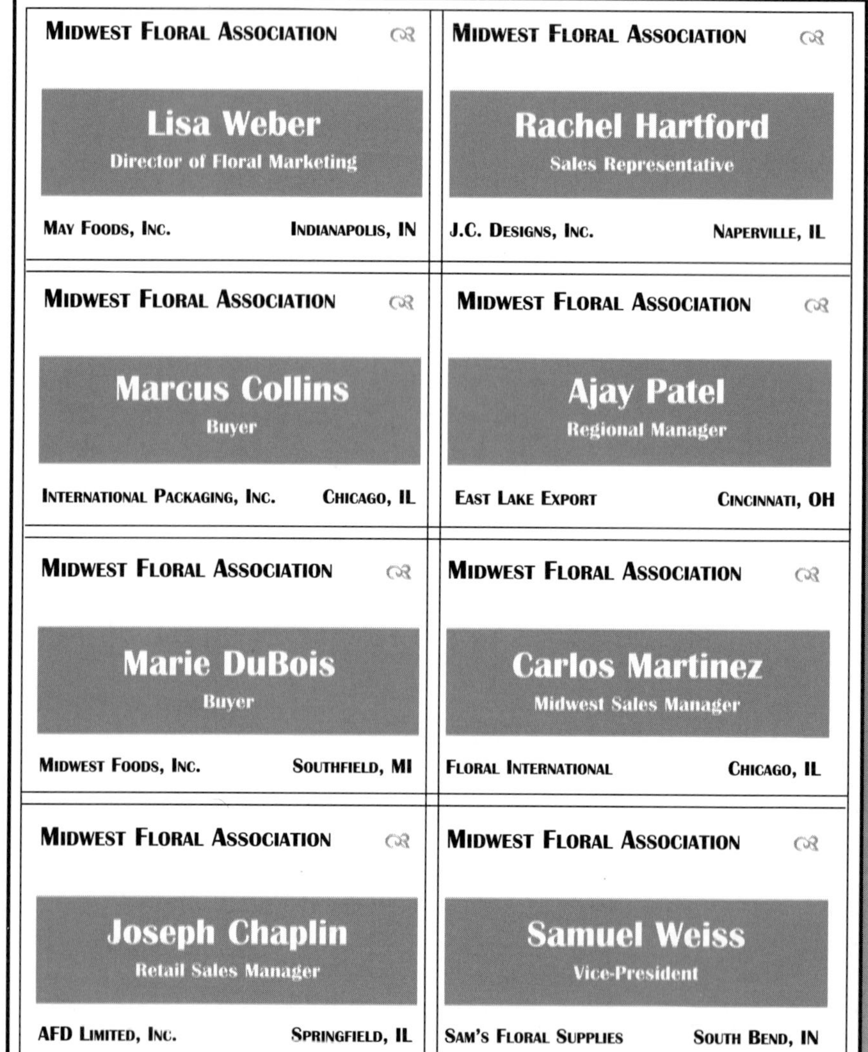

Using Tables to Create Invitations and Greeting Cards

You will be using Word's Table feature to create a table that may be used to format holiday cards, business or personal invitations, seminar or open house announcements, personal notes, or even birth announcements. Figure 7.15 illustrates the result that will be achieved when a standard-sized sheet of paper is divided into four cells using a table, then folded to accommodate text and graphics. Each of the four panels (cells) in figure 7.15 has been identified with a panel number and marked with instructions for rotating text and graphics. In Word, you can rotate text within a text box or table by clicking Text Direction at the Format menu or clicking the Change Text Direction button on the Tables and Borders toolbar. At the Text Direction dialog box, select the option that corresponds with the direction you want your text to display. To rotate a picture or object, select the object then click the Draw button on the Drawing toolbar, point to Rotate or Flip, then select an option to flip the image in a particular direction. Alternatively, click the Free Rotate button on the Drawing toolbar and drag the image by one of the (green) rotating handles. If the Free Rotate tool or the Rotate or Flip option is grayed and inaccessible for a particular clip art image, you may need to ungroup/group the image first.

DTP POINTERS
When sizing a graphic, use the corner sizing handles to keep the image in proportion.

Panel 1 Cover  (Rotate 180 degrees)	Created expressly for you by Rachel Greetings, Ltd. 1998 **Panel 2 Back** (Rotate 180 degrees)
Panel 3 Inside Page (This page is usually blank.)	**Panel 4 Message** (Insert your message here.)

Fold Lines

figure 7.15

Guide for Creating an Invitation, Greeting Card, or Thank You Card on One Sheet of Paper in Portrait Orientation

Alternatively, two invitations or greeting cards can be created on one sheet of paper by changing the paper orientation to landscape, then dividing the paper into four sections using cells in a table. Using this method, you may key, format, and then print the text on one side of a sheet of paper. Then, reinsert the paper into your printer and print text and/or graphics on the reverse side. The last step involves cutting the paper in half, then folding the top to meet the bottom (see figure 7.16).

figure 7.16

Guide for Creating Two Cards on One Sheet of Paper in Landscape Orientation

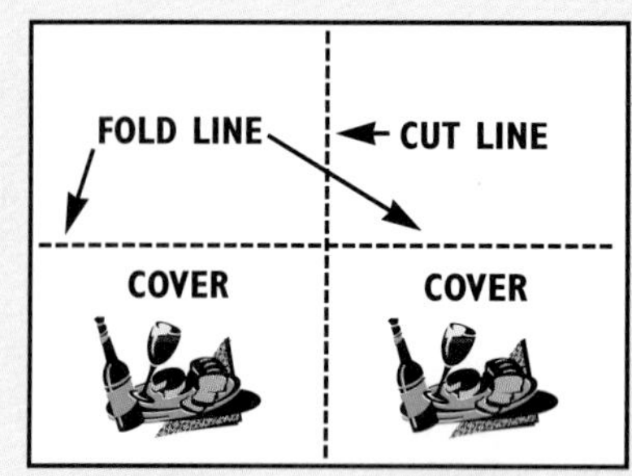

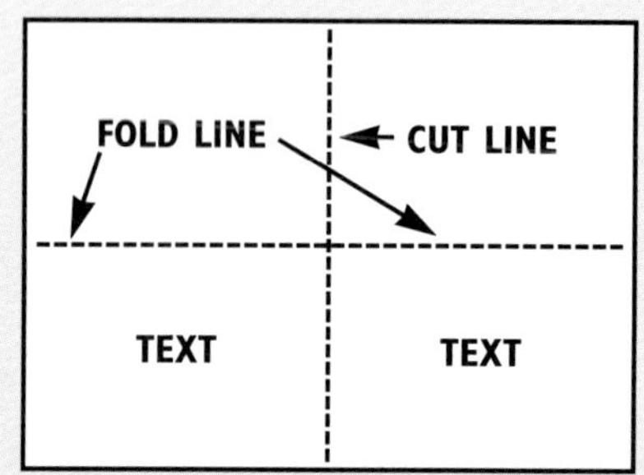

Planning and Designing Cards

In planning and designing your cards, consider focus, balance, proportion, contrast, and directional flow. Since you are working in a small area, remember to allow plenty of white space around design elements. If you are using a graphic image for focus, be sure that the image relates to the subject of the card. Shaded images (watermarks), symbols from the font special character sets, shapes, lines, and freeform designs add interest and individuality to your card design. Promote consistency through the use of color, possibly picking out one or two colors from the graphic image used in your card. If the image appears in black and white, consider adding color to the image at Microsoft Word Picture. Select one or two fonts that match the tone of the document. For a formal invitation, consider using Brush Script MT Italic, Algerian, Colonna MT, or Desdemona. For bold and powerful text, consider Impact, Wide Latin, Braggadocio, or Arial MT Black.

DTP POINTERS
Pick out a color in a graphic to add color to the accompanying text.

DTP POINTERS
Formal invitations often use a symmetrical design.

Your choice of paper is also important—consider using a heavier weight paper, such as 60- or 65-pound uncoated cover stock paper. Another possibility is to use marbleized paper or parchment paper for invitations and other types of cards. Predesigned papers or colored paper can add impact and interest to your document.

If you have a long list of guests, consider creating a master copy and taking it to a commercial printer to have it reproduced and machine folded. For a mass mailing of an invitation or a holiday card, consider creating a data source consisting of names and addresses of your guests, then merge this information onto envelopes or mailing labels.

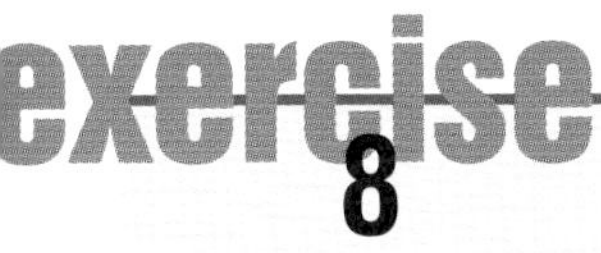

Creating a Greeting Card Using a Table

1. At a clear document screen, create the greeting card shown in figure 7.17 by completing the following steps:
   a. Change all the margins to 0.65 inches.
   b. Turn on kerning at 14 points.
   c. Display the Tables and Borders toolbar, the Drawing toolbar, and the Picture toolbar.
   d. Insert a table and include the following specifications:
      (1) Create a table with two columns and two rows.
      (2) With the insertion point positioned inside the table, click Table, then Cell Height and Width.
      (3) At the Cell Height and Width dialog box, select the Row tab.
      (4) Change the Height of rows 1–2: to *Exactly*, then key **340 pt** in the At text box. Make sure 0" displays in the Indent from left text box and Left is selected in the Alignment section. Deselect the Allow row to break across page option. (You may need to experiment with the point setting to find one that works with your nonprintable zone.)
      (5) Select the Column tab.
      (6) Make sure the Width of column 1 is 3.68 inches and the Space between columns measurement is 0.15 inches.
      (7) Click the Next Column button, then make sure the Width of column 2 is 3.68 inches.
      (8) Click OK to close the dialog box.
   e. Create the cover in the first cell of the first row of the table (Panel 1 as shown in figure 7.15) by completing the following steps:
      (1) With the insertion point positioned in the first cell, insert *bdaycke2.cgm* located on your student data disk. (You must have installed the graphic filter available through a Custom installation to access this picture—your best choice is to Select All in the Custom installation setup. Select a similar picture if this picture is not available.)
      (2) Double-click the picture to access Microsoft Word Picture. (Click Tools, then Options, and then select the Edit tab. Make sure *Microsoft Picture* displays in the Picture editor list box.)
      (3) Change the Zoom to Page width.
      (4) Click the Select Objects button on the Drawing toolbar and drag the crosshairs to create a dashed border around the image beginning in the upper left corner and ending in the bottom right corner (see figure 7.18).
      (5) The picture will display ungrouped; click the Draw button on the Drawing toolbar, then click Group. (If the black area with the colorful streamers does not display ungrouped, you may have to click the Ungroup option so that all the editing points display.)
      (6) With the picture still selected, click the Draw button on the Drawing toolbar, point to Rotate or Flip, then click Flip Vertical as shown in figure 7.19.
      (7) Click File, then Close & Return to Document#.
   f. Select the cake picture, then click Format, then Object.
   g. Select the Position tab, then select the Float over text option to activate this feature. Select the Wrapping tab, and make sure None is selected. Click OK or press Enter. (The picture is now in the layer above the text layer and you can move it anywhere on the page.)

h. Select the cake picture, then drag it to a position similar to figure 7.17.

i. Create the heading on the cover (panel 1) by completing the following steps:
   (1) Click the Insert WordArt button on the Drawing toolbar.
   (2) Select the WordArt style in the second column of the third row, then click OK.
   (3) Key **Happy Birthday!** in 36-point Impact in the Edit WordArt Text box, then click OK.
   (4) Click the WordArt Shape button on the WordArt toolbar, then select the shape in the second column of the fourth row (Deflate).
   (5) Click the Free Rotate button on the WordArt toolbar and rotate the object 180 degrees.
   (6) Drag the cake picture and the WordArt object so they display similar to figure 7.17. *Hint:* Drag the objects off center—you may need to experiment with placement after folding the card.
   (7) Close the WordArt toolbar.
   (8) Select *Happy Birthday*, then click the Draw button on the Drawing toolbar, point to Order, and then select the Send Behind Text option. (This positions the text under the candles on the cake.)

j. Create the text in the second cell in the first row of the table (panel 2—see figure 7.15) by completing the following steps:
   (1) Position the insertion point inside panel 2. Click the Center align button on the Formatting toolbar.
   (2) Click the Insert WordArt button on the Drawing toolbar, select the WordArt style in the third column and first row, and then click OK.
   (3) Change the font to 8 points and key **Created expressly for you**, press Enter, **by Arial Greetings, Ltd.**, press Enter, **1999**. Click OK.
   (4) Click the Free Rotate button on the WordArt toolbar and rotate the object 180 degrees.
   (5) Make sure the None Wrapping style is selected for this WordArt object, then position the text as shown in figure 7.17.

k. The first cell in the second row of the table (panel 3—see figure 7.15) will be blank.

l. Create the text in the second cell in the second row of the table (panel 4—see figure 7.15) by completing the following steps:
   (1) Position the insertion point inside panel 4, then choose Insert, then File.
   (2) Double-click *panel 4, card.doc* located on your student data disk. (The text may display below the table; drag it to a position similar to figure 7.17.)
   (3) Select *Wishing you a* and change the font to 20-point Times New Roman Bold. Select *Bright & Happy Birthday* and change the font to 26-point Times New Roman Bold in Small caps and change the font color as shown in figure 7.17.
   (4) Select *from James Morrison, Agent* and change the font to 14-point Times New Roman Bold.
   (5) Select *Colonial Life Insurance* and change the font to 16-point Times New Roman Bold in Small caps with Shadow.
   (6) Create a text box approximately 1.65 inches in height and 0.65 inches in width. Make sure the Wrapping style is None, then remove the text box border and change the fill to No Fill.
   (7) Position the insertion point inside the text box, then click Insert, then Symbol. Select the Wingdings Font, then click the candle symbol located in the eighth column of the first row. Click Insert, then Close.

(8) Select the candle and change the font size to 100 points. Use the Drag-and-Drop method of copying to duplicate the candle, then add a font color to each of the candles and position them as shown in figure 7.17.

2. View the document in Print Preview. Make sure all the design elements are positioned correctly as shown in figure 7.17.
3. Save the card as c07ex08, card.
4. Print, close, then fold c07ex08, card. (After folding your card, you may need to move some of the design elements.)

Optional: Create the four-paneled card form in portrait orientation and save it as a template. Create a card form in landscape orientation (see figure 7.16) and save it as a template.

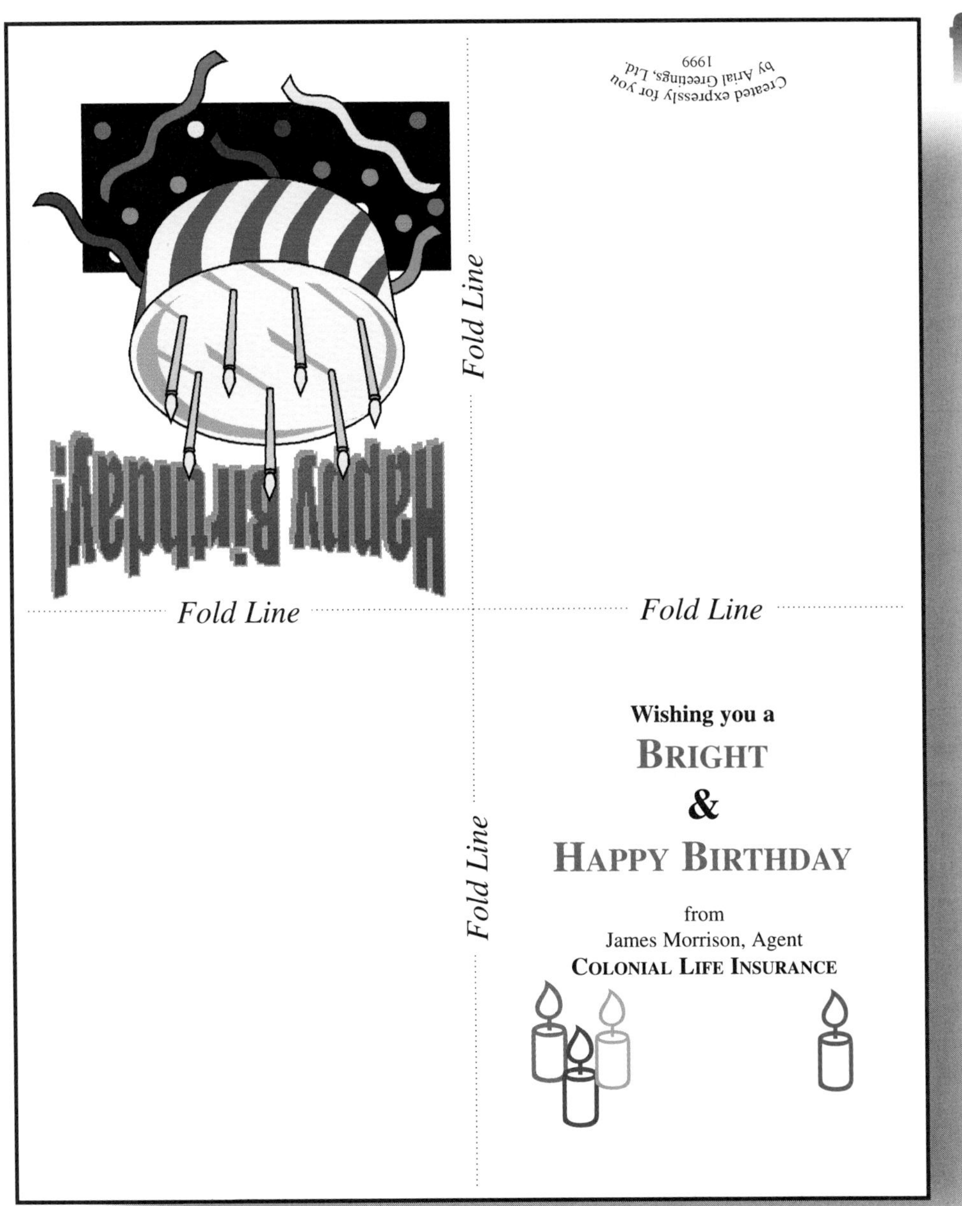

Created expressly for you
by Arial Greetings, Ltd.
1999
Happy Birthday!
Fold Line
Fold Line
Fold Line
Fold Line
Wishing you a
BRIGHT
&
HAPPY BIRTHDAY
from
James Morrison, Agent
COLONIAL LIFE INSURANCE

figure 7.17

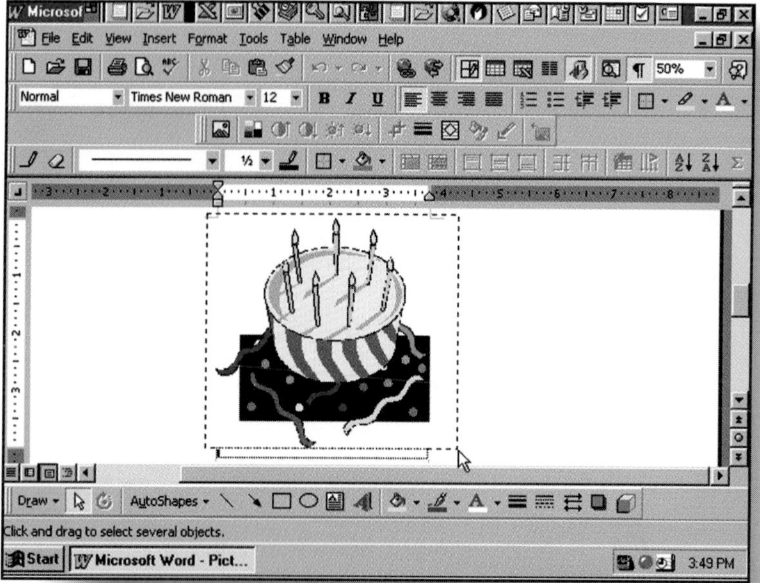

figure 7.18

Using the Select Object Tool in Microsoft Word Picture

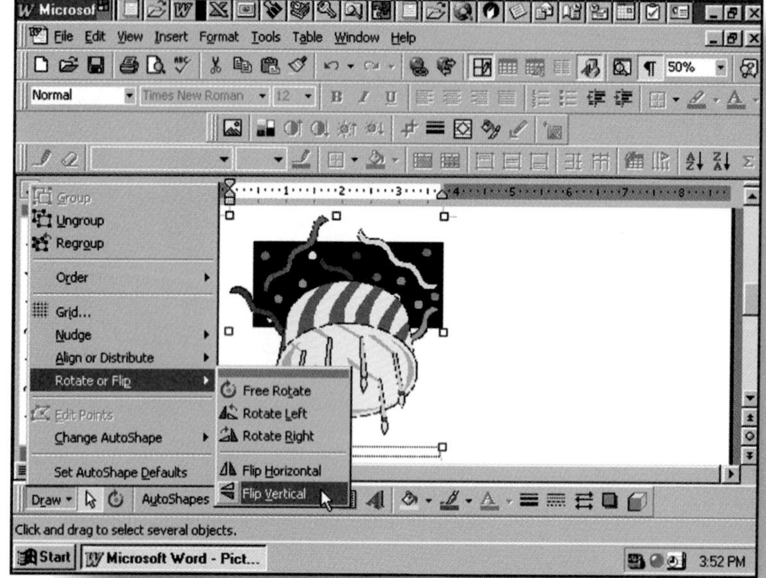

figure 7.19

Flipping an Image in Microsoft Word Picture

chapter summary

- Besides flyers and announcements, other promotional documents include gift certificates, postcards, name badges, and invitations (or greeting cards). They become promotional documents when a business or organization name is visible or an item is mentioned for sale in a document. Promotional documents are designed to advertise or promote an interest or sale.
- The label definition formats your document so that you can print on designated label sheets.
- Use the AutoText feature to assist you in formatting documents created in Word's Label feature.
- Word includes a mail merge feature that you can use to create letters, envelopes, postcards, and much more, all with personalized information.
- A data source document and a main document are needed to perform a merge. A *data source* document contains the variable information. The *main document* contains the standard text along with identifiers showing where variable information is to be inserted. The identifiers are known as *field codes*.
- Any formatting codes you want applied to the merged document should be inserted in the main document.
- Use Word's Mail Merge Helper to assist you in creating the data source and the main document.
- Use the Rotate or Flip option at the Draw menu or use the Free Rotate tool on the Drawing toolbar to rotate pictures or objects.
- Use Microsoft Word Picture (graphic editor) to group an image before flipping it vertically or horizontally.

commands review

	Mouse/Keyboard
Insert Table dialog box	Table, Insert Table
New dialog box	File, New
Envelopes and Labels dialog box	Tools, Envelopes and Labels
AutoText	Insert, AutoText
Mail Merge Helper	Tools, Mail Merge

check your understanding

True/False: Circle the letter T if the statement is true; circle the letter F if the statement is false.

T F 1. A main document is a document that contains variable information about customers, clients, products, etc.

T F 2. Mail Merge is the process of combining information from a database to a data source.

T F 3. FirstName, JobTitle, and Address1 are examples of field names.

T F 4. The data source can be created in a table format or a tab format.

T F 5. The AutoText feature can be used to store text and graphics used to format a label.

T F 6. WordArt text can be sized at the Drawing Object dialog box.

T F 7. You can crop, scale, and size a picture to specific dimensions.

T F 8. Cells in a table can be formatted with options at the Paragraph Borders and Shading dialog box.

T F 9. Tables exist in the text layer and text automatically wraps around them.

T F 10. A watermark can be created inside a cell of a table.

Completion: In the spaces provided, indicate the correct term, command, or number.

1. To position a watermark below the text layer, select this option at the Order menu ____________________.
2. The data source and the main document can be merged to a new document or to the ____________________.
3. A series of ____________________ make a record.
4. FirstName, JobTitle, and Address1 are examples of ____________________.
5. You can merge the source document to the main document by clicking the Merge to New Document button on the ____________________ toolbar.
6. To rotate text inside a table, click this button on the Tables and Borders toolbar ____________________.
7. To rotate a picture 180 degrees, click this option at the Rotate or Flip menu ____________________.
8. The ____________________ document contains variable information about customers, etc.
9. Press ____________________ to insert a tab code within a table.
10. You can group or ungroup a graphic image at Word's graphic editor, which is known as ____________________.

skill assessments

Assessment 1

You are working part time at Hayden's Sporting Center while attending Western Michigan University in Kalamazoo. Your employer has asked you to prepare several $25 gift certificates to be used toward purchases in the store. Please prepare one certificate according to the following specifications. When completed, copy the certificate to fill a page (see figure 7.20).

1. Open the gift certificate template created in exercise 1.
2. Turn on kerning at 14 points.
3. Make sure the default font is 12-point Times New Roman.
4. Display the Drawing toolbar, Picture toolbar, and the Tables and Borders toolbar.
5. Position the insertion point inside the table (certificate form) and merge the two cells by completing the following steps:
   a. Click Table, then Select Row.
   b. Click Table, then Merge Cells.
6. Click Format, then Borders and Shading. Select the Borders tab, then select Box in the Settings section and change the Line Width to 4½ pt.
7. With the insertion point positioned inside the table, change the alignment to Center. Press Enter.
8. Key the text as shown in figure 7.20. Use the Shift and Hyphen keys to create the line (this type of line copies well in a table). Select the text and change the font to Britannic Bold. You determine the appropriate font sizes and add color to the text.
9. Click the Rectangle button on the Drawing toolbar. Drag to create a rectangle that is slightly smaller than the table cell (this box will form the inside border of the certificate).
10. The rectangle shape will display above the certificate—make sure the Wrapping style defaults to None. Change the Line Style to 3 points and add color to the border. If a fill displays inside the box, click the Fill Color button on the Drawing toolbar and select No Fill.
11. Select the rectangle shape, then click the Draw button on the Drawing toolbar, click Order, and then click the Send Behind Text option.
12. Create a text box that is approximately 2.5 inches in height and 2.5 inches in width. (This box will contain the watermark image.) The text box will display above the certificate—make sure the Wrapping style defaults to None. If a fill or border displays, click the Fill Color and Line Color buttons and select No Fill and No Line at each.
13. Insert the picture *Golf.wmf*. Resize the image if necessary to fit inside the certificate. Click the Image Control button on the Picture toolbar and select Watermark.
14. Select the text box containing the watermark, then select the Send Behind Text option at the Order menu (click Draw at the Drawing toolbar, then Order).
15. With the insertion point located in the table, choose Table, then Select Row.
16. Copy and paste the certificate twice.
17. Save the document as c07sa01, sports.
18. Print and then close c07sa01, sports.

figure 7.20

Gift Certificate

Presented to ______________________________

This certificate entitles the bearer to $25 off any purchase at

HAYDEN'S SPORTING CENTER
3290 University Avenue
Kalamazoo, MI 49078

Gift Certificate

Presented to ______________________________

This certificate entitles the bearer to $25 off any purchase at

HAYDEN'S SPORTING CENTER
3290 University Avenue
Kalamazoo, MI 49078

Gift Certificate

Presented to ______________________________

This certificate entitles the bearer to $25 off any purchase at

HAYDEN'S SPORTING CENTER
3290 University Avenue
Kalamazoo, MI 49078

Assessment 2

You are working at Tuscany Realty and have been asked to prepare an announcement of an upcoming open house advertising the sale of a custom-built home on a golf course. The announcement is to be prepared as a postcard and mailed to prospective clients and all homeowners in this neighborhood. This promotional document makes the realtor's name visible to any homeowners in this neighborhood who may be thinking of selling their home or buying a new one. The card will be reproduced at a printing company. Create two postcards similar to the ones shown in figure 7.21. Follow the guidelines given below.

1. Create the formatting and text for the postcard by completing the following steps:
   a. Choose the *Avery 5389 - Post card* definition at the Labels dialog box.
   b. Click the New Document button at the Labels dialog box.
   c. Create the dots in the left top corner and right bottom corner of the postcard by completing the following steps:
      (1) Change the alignment in the cell to Align Top.
      (2) Insert the Wingding symbol found in the third row and the eighth column from the right. The small dots are also in the Wingding character set, located in the fifth row and the sixteenth column from the left.
      (3) Use F4, the repeat key, to save time in duplicating the dots.
   d. The vertical line was drawn into the postcard using the Line button on the Drawing toolbar (be sure to hold down the Shift key as you draw the line).
   e. Create text boxes inside the label (table format) to hold the picture and formatted text.
   f. Access WordArt and key *Tuscany Realty* at the Edit WordArt Text box. Use the Deflate (Bottom) shape in the fourth row and the fourth column of the shape palette. Select the Wide Latin font and change the font color to purple.
   g. Insert the picture *Realest.wmf* located on your student data disk. Size the image as it appears in figure 7.21.
   h. Use Footlight MT Light for the office address and *Open House*. Use Times New Roman for the message text.
   i. Copy the first postcard text to the second postcard.
2. Save the document as c07sa02, house.
3. Print and then close c07sa02, house.

Optional: Create a data source consisting of four of your friends, neighbors, co-workers, or relatives. Create a main document using your return address, the field codes for the data source, and any graphic or symbol that attracts attention and relates to the subject matter in assessment 2. Merge the data source to the main document and print the merged document to the reverse side of the postcards created in assessment 2.

figure 7.21

Tuscany Realty

••••••• Sales Office •••••••

765 Sun Valley Drive
San Diego, CA 73021
(610) 555-9000

You are invited
to an

OPEN HOUSE

Sunday, April 25
from 1–4 p.m.

Come view an exquisite
custom-built home
overlooking
the seventh green at

1702 Granada Drive
Pebblestone Estate
San Diego

Tuscany Realty

••••••• Sales Office •••••••

765 Sun Valley Drive
San Diego, CA 73021
(610) 555-9000

You are invited
to an

OPEN HOUSE

Sunday, April 25
from 1–4 p.m.

Come view an exquisite
custom-built home
overlooking
the seventh green at

1702 Granada Drive
Pebblestone Estate
San Diego

Assessment 3

1. You are working for an accounting firm and have been asked to prepare name badges for your employer and five other employees who will be speaking at a banking conference. Design and create six name badges according to the following specifications (see figure 7.22 for a sample solution):

   - Choose an appropriate badge definition at the Labels dialog box.
   - Seminar name: **Northern Banking Association**
   - Company name: **Rossi, King, & Associates**
   - The office is located in **Portland, ME**
   - Create a company logo—use WordArt, symbols, graphics, or shapes, lines, shadows, 3-D, etc.
   - Speakers' names are as follows:

     Frank Burton
     Rajendram Agtey
     Mary Jane Peterson
     Curtis Brown
     James McSherry
     Susan Howard

2. Save the document and name it c07sa03, badges.
3. Print and then close c07sa03, badges.

figure 7.22

⌘ NORTHERN BANKING ASSOCIATION FRANK BURTON Rossi, King, & Associates *Portland, Maine*	⌘ NORTHERN BANKING ASSOCIATION RAJENDRAM AGTEY Rossi, King, & Associates *Portland, Maine*
⌘ NORTHERN BANKING ASSOCIATION MARY JANE PETERSON Rossi, King, & Associates *Portland, Maine*	⌘ NORTHERN BANKING ASSOCIATION CURTIS BROWN Rossi, King, & Associates *Portland, Maine*
⌘ NORTHERN BANKING ASSOCIATION JAMES MCSHERRY Rossi, King, & Associates *Portland, Maine*	⌘ NORTHERN BANKING ASSOCIATION SUSAN HOWARD Rossi, King, & Associates *Portland, Maine*

Assessment 4

1. You are employed at First Bank and one of your responsibilities is to create an invitation to an *"Evening Out on the Town"* to be sent to several important bank clients. Use Word's table feature and create the invitation in either landscape or portrait orientation. Refer to figures 7.15 and 7.16 in this chapter for two suggested layouts for your invitation. Add graphics, watermarks, lines, borders, symbols, or other enhancements to your document. Use the text and specifications listed below:

   On behalf of First Bank, we would like to cordially invite you to an "Evening Out on the Town" Thursday, May 20, 1998.
   Cocktails - 5:00 p.m.–5:30 p.m.
   Dinner - 5:30 p.m.–7:00 p.m.
   Trattoria 8
   15 North Dearborn Street
   Chicago, Illinois
   Theater - 7:30 p.m.
   Phantom of the Opera
   Chicago Theatre
   175 North State Street
   Chicago, Illinois
   Please RSVP to Victoria Franz, (302) 555-3456 by April 24, 1998

2. Include the following specifications:

   - Consider your audience in creating an appropriate design.
   - Prepare a thumbnail sketch.
   - Use an appropriate font and vary the type size and type style.
   - Change the character spacing in at least one occurrence.
   - Use vertical and horizontal lines, or an appropriate graphic image, graphic border, or symbols to add interest and impact.
   - Use special characters where needed—en or em dashes, bullets, etc.
   - Change the leading if necessary.

3. Save the document and name it c07sa04, bank.
4. Print and then close c07sa04, bank.
5. Evaluate your invitation with the Document Analysis Guide.

creative activity

1. Create a promotional document of your own design or from an example you have saved or found in the mail, at a store, or from any other source. If you are using a sample document, first evaluate the document for good layout and design, a clear and concise message, and proper use of other desktop publishing concepts as outlined in the Document Analysis Guide. Some possible promotional documents include the following examples:

   - Invitation to a new store opening
   - Invitation to a class reunion
   - Bookmark
   - Name badge including a company or organization name or logo
   - Business greeting card
   - Postcard as a follow-up
   - Postcard used to promote a new business (coffee shop, party planner, attorney's office, computer services)
   - Membership card
   - Ticket with a company or organization name or logo
   - Gift certificate
   - Thank you card
   - Employee retirement announcement
   - Company party invitation
   - Postcard advertising a sample sale
   - Raffle ticket for a charity
   - Postcard announcing the opening of a golf course
   - Postcard advertising services at a travel agency

2. Create a copy of the document with any necessary improvements. Try to find unusual, creative documents that were used to promote a business, organization, item, or event.
3. If the sample document was created on odd-sized paper, check to see if your printer can accommodate the paper size. You may need to recreate the document on a standard-sized paper, then trim it to size.
4. Save the completed document and name it c07ca01, promotional.
5. Print and then close c07ca01, promotional—attach the original document if one was used.

8 Creating Web Pages

PERFORMANCE OBJECTIVE

Upon successful completion of chapter 8, you will be able to create a Web home page with hyperlinks using Word 97 and apply basic desktop publishing concepts to the layout and design of the Web page.

Desktop Publishing Concepts

Planning	Balance	Color
Layout and design	Directional flow	Templates
Focus	Consistency	

Word Features Used

Web Page Wizard	Graphics	Sound clips
Blank Web Page template	Web page preview	Online Layout view
Forms	Bullets	Microsoft Word Web site
Hyperlinks	Lines	Tables
Background color	Scrolling text	Alternative text
Web authoring tools	Microsoft Photo Editor	Microsoft Word Picture

In addition to using Word to create promotional documents such as flyers, announcements, brochures, gift certificates, postcards, and more, you can also use Word to create Web pages which may provide promotional information about your company's products, resources, or services. Increasingly, businesses are accessing the Internet to conduct research, publish product or catalog information, communicate, and market products globally. In addition, companies are using Intranets to efficiently share information among employees.

Users access the Internet for several purposes: to communicate using E-mail; to subscribe to news groups; to transfer files; to socialize with other users; and largely to access virtually any kind of information imaginable.

Web Page
A computer file created in HTML and used on the Web.

What is a *Web page*? It is a computer file containing information in the form of text or graphics along with commands in a language called Hypertext Markup Language (HTML). When one of these pages is placed on a "server" computer hooked up to the Internet, it receives a Uniform Resource Locator (URL), which is the address that other users will key in to call up the page.

Understanding Internet and Intranet Terminology

Internet
Worldwide network of computers connected together to share information.

Intranet
An "internal Internet" within an organization that uses Internet technology and tools.

The *Internet* is a worldwide network of commercial, educational, governmental, and personal computers connected together for the purpose of sharing information. An *Intranet* is an "internal Internet" within an organization that uses the same Web technology and tools as the Internet and is also used to share information. Intranets are only accessible to a select audience. An Intranet may provide employees with on-line access to reference material, job postings, phone and address lists, company policies and procedures, enrollment and updates on benefit plans, company newsletters, and other human resource information.

Throughout this chapter, you will simulate creating Web pages for both the Internet and an organization's Intranet. These Web pages will be saved as HTML files to a disk in drive A (or whatever drive you have designated for your student files). You will view each Web page in the Internet Explorer screen.

To use the Internet, you generally need three things—a modem or network connection to an Internet Service Provider (ISP) for access to the Internet, a program to browse the Web (called a Web browser), and a search engine to locate specific data on the Internet.

Modem
Hardware device that allows data to be carried over telephone lines.

A *modem* is a hardware device that allows data to be carried over telephone lines. Modem speed is measured in terms of the number of bits per second data is transferred. A modem or network connection is needed to connect your computer to a receiving computer. An Internet Service Provider (ISP) sells access to the Internet. The ISP is responsible for configuring computers, routers, and software to enable connectivity to every other individual and computer that make up the Internet. A variety of Internet Service Providers are available —local ISPs as well as commercial ISPs, which include *Microsoft Network®, America Online®, AT&T Worldnet Service®*, and *CompuServe®*. To complete exercises in this chapter, you will need access to the Internet through an ISP. Check with your instructor to determine the ISP used by your school to connect to the Internet.

World Wide Web
A set of standards and protocols used to access information on the Internet.

Web Browser
Software program that allows you to move around the Internet.

Once you are connected to the Internet, you can access the *World Wide Web.* The World Wide Web is a set of standards and protocols used to access information available on the Internet. To access the Web and maneuver within the Web, you need a software program called a *Web browser*. Some common Web browsers include *Microsoft Internet Explorer, Netscape Navigator*, and *Mosaic.* A browser allows you to move around the Internet by pointing and clicking with the mouse. The exercises in this chapter are created with the assumption that you will have Microsoft Internet Explorer available. If you use a different Web browser, some of the steps in exercises may vary.

A phenomenal amount of information is available on the Internet. Searching through all the information to find the specific information you need can be an overwhelming task. Software programs, called *search engines*, have been created to help you search more quickly and easily for the desired information. Some common search engines include *NetGuide Live, Infoseek, HotBot, WebCrawler, Lycos, Microsoft, Excite, Yahoo,* and *AltaVista*. The Microsoft Internet Explorer provides simple access to many search engines, as shown in figure 8.1. Search engines are valuable tools to assist a user in locating information on a topic by simply keying a few words or a short phrase. The search engines are particularly helpful when you do not know the specific URL for the information needed.

Search Engine
Software program that helps you quickly access information. Valuable tool when you don't know the specific URL.

As you gain experience searching the Web, you will develop methods to refine your search techniques and tools to limit the time spent browsing. Advanced search features within each search engine can also help you find your needed information.

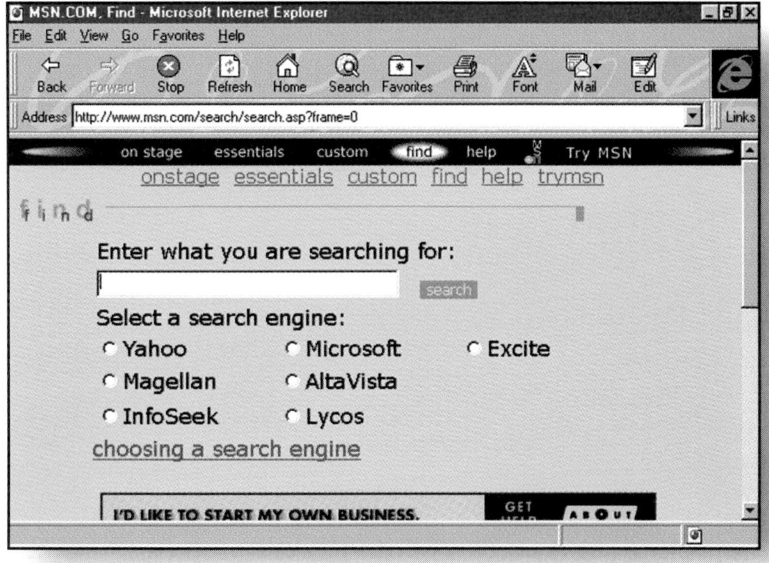

figure 8.1

Different Search Engines

Locating URLs on the Internet

Computer protocols known as TCP/IP (Transmission Control Protocol/Internet Protocol) form the base of the Internet. Protocols are simply agreements on how various hardware and software should communicate with each other. The Internet Service Provider becomes the Domain Name Service (DNS), *the route to the Internet.* The DNS and IP determine how to route your computer to another location/computer on the Internet. Every computer directly linked to the Internet has a unique IP address. Another TCP/IP-related protocol is FTP (File Transfer Protocol). FTP is the means of downloading files to your computer from an FTP server. Typically, an FTP server lists the files in a directory-style listing. The preface for an FTP address would be *ftp://* rather than *http://*.

The Uniform Resource Locators, referred to as URLs, are the method used to identify locations on the Internet. A typical URL is *http://www.microsoft.com*. The first part of the URL, *http://,* identifies the protocol. The letters *http* stand for Hypertext Transfer Protocol, which is the protocol or language used to transfer data within the World Wide Web. The colon and slashes separate the protocol from the server name. The server name is the second component of the

URL. For example, in *http://www.microsoft.com*, the server name is identified as *www.microsoft.* The last part of the URL specifies the domain to which the server belongs—*.com* refers to "commerical," *.edu* refers to "educational," *.gov* stands for "government," and *.mil* refers to "military."

Using the Web Toolbar

If you know the URL for a specific Web site and would like to visit that site, key the URL in the Address section of the Web toolbar. To display the Web toolbar as shown in figure 8.2, click the Web Toolbar button (fourteenth button from the left) on the standard toolbar. Before keying a URL in the Address text box on the Web Toolbar, make sure you are connected to the Internet through your Internet Service Provider. Key the URL exactly as written including any colons (:) or slashes (/).

Home Page
The opening page for a Web site.

Hyperlinks
Colored and underlined text or a graphic that you click to link or connect to another item.

When you are connected to a URL (Web site address), the home page for the specific URL (Web site) displays. The *home page* is the starting point for viewing the Web site. At the home page you can "branch off" to other pages within the Web site or jump to other Web sites. You do this with hyperlinks that are embedded in the home page, as shown in figure 8.3. *Hyperlinks* are colored and underlined text or a graphic that you click to go to a file, a location in a file, an HTML page on the World Wide Web, or an HTML page on an Intranet. Move the mouse pointer on a hyperlink and the mouse pointer becomes a hand. This is one method for determining if something is a hyperlink. Most pages contain a variety of hyperlinks. Using these links, you can zero in on the exact information for which you are searching.

Using the Web toolbar, you can jump forward or backward among the documents you have opened and you can add interesting documents you find on the Web to the Favorites folder to quickly return to them later. Click the Favorites button on the Web toolbar to add the current document or Web page to your Favorites folder. The Refresh button updates any changes you have made to the Web page.

Web Toolbar

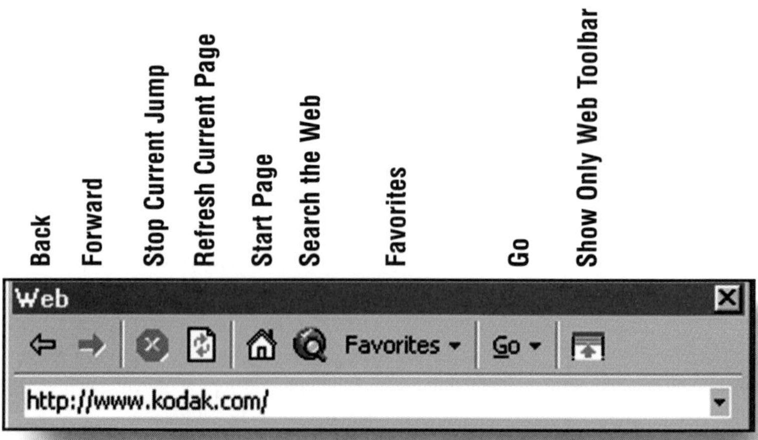

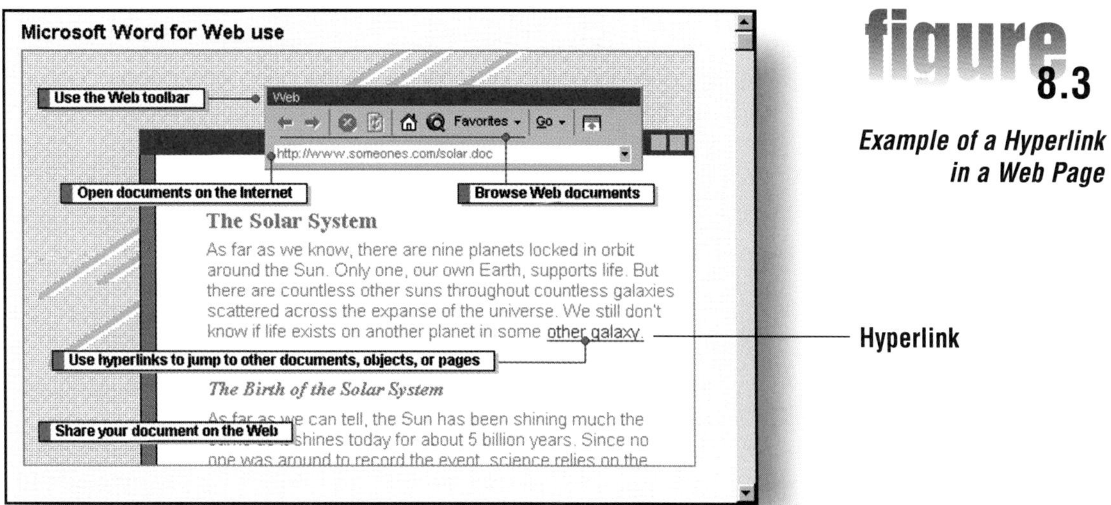

figure 8.3

Example of a Hyperlink in a Web Page

Planning and Designing a Web Page

You can build a Web site yourself, or hire a freelancer or Web access provider. Some advertising consultants develop Web sites for a fee. However, with the help of Word's Web Page Wizard or Word's Blank Web Page template, you can easily create your own Web pages.

Where do you start? Planning is a basic desktop publishing concept that applies to Web pages as well as any other documents created in Word. During the planning stage of your Web page, consider the following items:

- **Clearly identify the purpose of your Web page**. Are you trying to sell? inform? communicate?
- **Assess your target audience**. What will your audience expect from your Web page?
- **Decide what you want your reader to do after reading your Web page**. Do you want some kind of response? Do you want your audience to order something or contact you?
- **Consider your budget**. How much time and money will be available to keep the entries on your Web site current?
- **Review other Web pages**. Decide what designs you like or dislike.
- **Most Web Pages are one page long**. However, you can include much more information by using hyperlinks to other Web pages.
- **Margins, tabs, and columns are not available in HTML.** Use tables to control the layout of a page. Also, use tables to create a multicolumn effect.
- **Fonts are mapped to the closest HTML size.** Use the Increase Font Size and Decrease Font Size buttons on the Formatting toolbar.
- **Organize text on a Web page into chunks or sections using horizontal lines.** Insert graphic horizontal lines to separate as well as decorate.

DTP POINTERS
Look at other Web pages for layout and design ideas.

A starting point for creating a Web site may include viewing existing Web sites for ideas on layout and design of text, banners, logos, graphics, background colors, lines, photos, hyperlinks, etc. Before designing a Web home page consider some of the following questions: Will the home page use a one-column, two-column, or three-column layout? Will the page include an interesting banner with a company logo and name? Will the home page use consistent colors? What will be the focal point on the page? Will the page include a photograph, graphic, or graphic line? Will the information be organized logically and be easy to read? Will the home page be visually appealing? Will the hyperlinks be clearly marked?

Consider using a thumbnail sketch to organize your page layout before actually creating it. Include space for text, photographs, graphics, headlines, divider lines, etc. Instead of including everything on one huge Web front page, consider using hyperlinks to other pages.

DTP POINTERS
Do not overdecorate your Web page.

Remember that the Web site's front door is its home page. This page should contain the elements to achieve the goals the company has set for the Web site. Understand what your goals are before you design the site. Are you creating a Web site on an Intranet to share information among employees or a Web page on the Internet to market a product or service? Know your budget before starting. There are things you can do on any budget, but some things (such as videos and animation) may cost more than you can afford.

DTP POINTERS
Use consistency in design elements on your Web page.

Some Web designers suggest that you create an interesting nameplate or banner to display a logo and company name in an interesting way. Include your company logo to reinforce your company's identity. The site should also include alternative ways to reach the company such as an address, telephone number, E-mail address, and fax number.

DTP POINTERS
Use a company logo to reinforce company recognition.

Graphics are probably the simplest way to make your Web page look better. Be sure to choose a graphic that is appropriate to the subject of the page. Animation, video, scrolling words, and such are eye-catching devices to entice your audience to return to your Web site. But they can take forever to load. You may want to avoid using a graphic that takes longer than 15 to 20 seconds to load. Use small graphics that are less than 30K in size. When in doubt, keep the basic design simple. The main point in designing a Web page is to get the message across! In addition, remember that everything you want to use on your home page must be transferred into computer files. If you want to use a photograph, you may want to scan the photo to convert it to a graphic file. Format main headings with HTML heading styles so a reader can more quickly browse through a document when using the document map in Word's Online Layout view.

DTP POINTERS
Create one dominant focal point.

DTP POINTERS
Too many graphics or large graphics can slow down your Web page.

In exercise 1, you will take a look at a few Web home pages using URLs. As you view each of the Web sites listed in the exercise, pay attention to the layout and design of each home page. For instance, when viewing *http://www.greenpeace*, notice the colorful text, the use of icons for links, the scroll box in the upper right corner, and the graphic border of green trees (the design may change when the page is updated).

exercise 1

Viewing Web Site Home Pages for Design and Layout Ideas

1. Make sure you are connected to the Internet through an Internet Service Provider.
2. Explore several locations on the World Wide Web from within Word by completing the following steps:

a. Display the Web toolbar by clicking the Web Toolbar button (fourteenth button from the left) on the Standard toolbar.
b. Click in the Address text box located on the Web Toolbar. (This will select the current document name in the text box.)
c. Display the home page for the environmental organization, Greenpeace, by keying **http://www.greenpeace.org** and then pressing Enter.
d. In a few moments, the Greenpeace Web site home page will display. The home page will display similar to the one shown in figure 8.4. Home pages are frequently updated, so the Greenpeace home page you are viewing may vary slightly from what you see in figure 8.4. Scroll down the home page studying the layout of the Greenpeace home page.
e. After viewing Greenpeace, view the Web site for Microsoft. To do this, click the current address located in the Address text box, key **http://www.microsoft.com** and then press Enter. Scroll down the home page studying layout and design elements in the Microsoft home page. (The most common component of Web home pages is text—notice the amount of text in this home page.)
f. After viewing the Microsoft page, view the Web site for the White House. Key **http://www.whitehouse.gov**, then press Enter. (Notice the formal layout, elegant script font, photo of the White House, animated flag graphics, varying column layout, icon and text links, graphic line, and the option to choose a graphic or text version of the home page.)
g. After viewing the White House page, view the Web site for the Gap. Key **http://www.gap.com** and then press Enter. (Notice the banner with animated text, two-column layout, photographs, and the interactive link under "gapstyle.")

3. After viewing the information displayed on the Gap home page, return to the Word screen by clicking File, then Close.

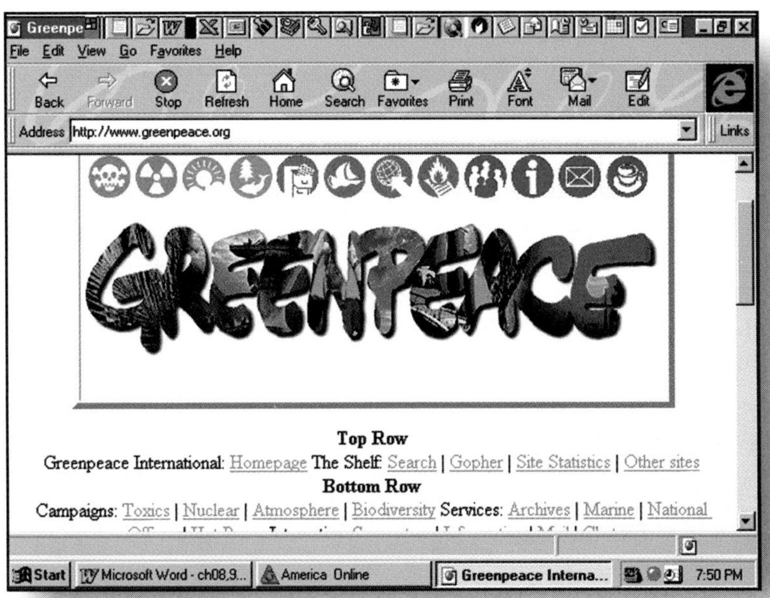

Greenpeace Web Home Page

Using the Internet Explorer Program

In exercise 1, you visited the first Web site by keying the URL in the Address text box in the Web Toolbar. This opened the Internet Explorer program window and also displayed the home page for the Web site. The Internet Explorer program window contains many features similar to the Word window. The Internet Explorer toolbar contains buttons for accessing a variety of commands. The buttons and a description of each button are included in figure 8.5.

Internet Explorer Toolbar Buttons

Button	Description
Back	Displays previous Web page
Forward	Displays next Web page
Stop	Stops loading a page
Refresh	Refreshes (updates contents of current page)
Home	Displays the default Home page
Search	Displays the Search page
Favorites	Displays the Favorites list
Print	Prints the current Web page
Font	Increases or decreases font size of selected text
Mail	Displays Mail and News options
Edit	Lets you make changes to your Web page and then return to Internet Explorer to view the changes

If you create a hyperlink in a document, you can click the Back button on the Internet Explorer Toolbar to display a previous page or location. If you clicked the Back button and then want to go back to the hyperlink, click the Forward button. By clicking the Back button, you can back your way out of any hyperlinks and return to the default Web home page.

As you visit different Web sites, Internet Explorer keeps track of the sites by recording the name and address of the site, the date visited, and when the site was updated. This information is inserted in the history folder. To display this list, click Go on the Internet Explorer Menu bar and then click *Open History Folder* at the drop-down list.

If you find a site that you like to visit on a regular basis, that site can be added to a Favorites list. To do this, display the site, then click the Favorites button on the Internet Explorer toolbar.

Creating a Web Home Page Using the Web Page Wizard

Now that you have spent some time viewing several Web site home pages, you may have a few ideas on how to design an appealing home page. The home pages were designed using a language called Hypertext Markup Language (HTML). This is a language that Web browsers use to read hypertext documents. In the past, a person needed knowledge of HTML to design a home page. Now a home page can be created in Word with the Web Page Wizard or Blank Web Page template, or a Word document can be converted to HTML. To convert an existing Word document to a Web page, click File, then Save as HTML.

Before creating a home page, consider the information you want contained in the home page. Carefully plan the layout of the information and where to position hyperlinks. Good design is a key element to a successful home page. Review the points discussed in the chapter section, *Planning and Designing a Web Page*.

DTP POINTERS
Plan the layout of information on your Web page.

Word provides two methods for creating a home page. You can use a Web page template or the Web Page Wizard. The other method is to create the home page at a Word screen and then convert it to HTML. Several additional Web templates are available for downloading from the Microsoft World Wide Web site. When you download these templates, they are installed in the same folder as the existing Web templates.

Accessing the Web Page Wizard

Word provides a wizard that will help you prepare a Web home page. Using the wizard, you can choose a Web page type and a visual style. From the list of Web types, choose one that best fits the content of the Web page you want to create. You can choose from different layouts and color themes, such as a home page with two columns, a personal home page, a table of contents, a registration form, or a survey form, as shown in figure 8.6. When you use a Web template, you can create and format popular Web page items—such as tables, bulleted or numbered lists, and graphic objects—just as you can with a regular Word document.

DTP POINTERS
Choose a document style that matches the mood of your text.

Access the Web Page Wizard at the New dialog box with the Web Pages tab selected. To use the Web Page Wizard, double-click the Web Page Wizard icon. At the first Web Page Wizard dialog box, choose a Web page type and then click the Next> button. At the second Web Page Wizard dialog box, choose a visual style (as shown in figure 8.7) and then click the Finish button. With the Web site home page displayed, key the desired information.

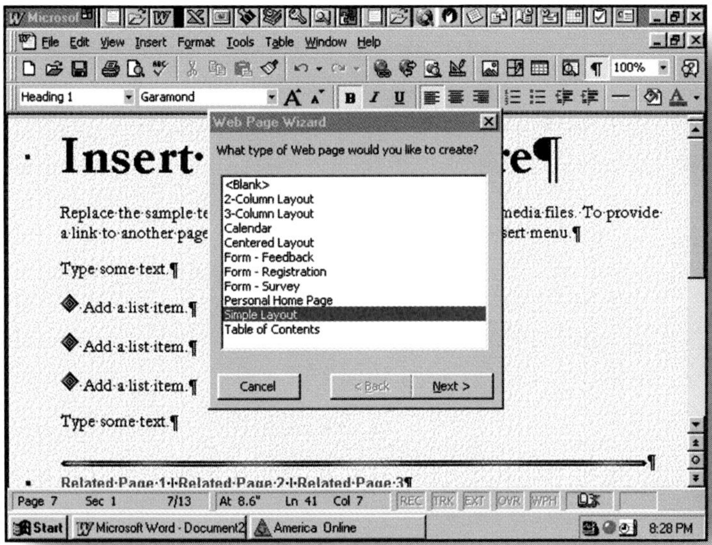

figure 8.6

Types of Web Pages Available in the Web Page Wizard

figure 8.7

Types of Visual Styles in the Web Page Wizard

Using Web Authoring Tools

When you use the Web Page Wizard, you may be prompted to download the latest version of the Web authoring tools. If this prompt should display, click Yes at the dialog box and proceed with the installation. You will need to be connected to the Internet. You can also use the AutoUpdate command on the Tools menu to manually check for the latest version.

Where are the Web authoring tools? These tools are on the Standard and Formatting toolbars (shown in figures 8.12 and 8.13). When the Web authoring features are active, you will notice that the toolbars and menus have been customized for working on Web pages. You must be using a Web page template or wizard, or have converted an existing document to HTML for these tools to be active. You may have to run Setup again and select Web page authoring components if they are not available.

exercise 2

Creating a Web Home Page Using the Web Page Wizard

1. Create a Web home page using the Web Page Wizard by completing the following steps:
   - **a.** At a clear document screen, click File, then New.
   - **b.** At the New dialog box, click the Web Pages tab.
   - **c.** At the New dialog box with the Web Pages tab selected, double-click the Web Page Wizard icon.
   - **d.** If a message displays with the question "*Would you like to access the Internet to check for a new version of Web page authoring tools?*", click the Yes button if you are connected to the Internet; otherwise, click No and update later.

e. At the first Web Page Wizard dialog box, click *Centered Layout* in the list box, then click the Next> button that displays toward the bottom of the dialog box.

f. At the second Web Page Wizard dialog box, click the *Outdoors* visual style in the list box, then click the Finish button that displays toward the bottom of the dialog box.

g. At the Web page document, key the text shown in figure 8.8 by completing the following steps:

(1) Select the text *Insert Heading Here* and key **Butterfield Gardens**.

(2) Select the text *Replace the sample text with your own text, graphics, and multimedia files. To provide a link to another page, select text, and click Hyperlink on the Insert menu.*, then key the text shown in the first paragraph below the heading *Butterfield Gardens* in figure 8.8. (The lines may not end exactly as shown in figure 8.8.)

(3) Select the text *Type some text.* that displays above the first bullet and then key the text shown in the paragraph above the bulleted items.

(4) Select the text *Add a list item.* that displays after the first bullet and then key **Ortho® Online**. (Press Alt + Ctrl + R to create the Registered symbol.)

(5) Select the text *Add a list item.* that displays after the second bullet and then key **New Bio News—Monsanto Company**.

(6) Select the text *Add a list item.* that displays after the third bullet and then key **Bug of the Month Program**.

(7) Select the text *Type some text.* that displays below the last bullet and then key the text shown below the last bullet in figure 8.8.

(8) Select and then delete the text in blue that displays below the *Row of Pebbles.gif (graphic line)* toward the end of the document. This is the text: *Related Page 1* | *Related Page 2* | *Related Page 3*.

2. Save the complete Web home page on your student data disk in the normal manner and name it c08ex02, BG Home Page.html. (This document is saved as an HTML document.)

3. Print and then close c08ex02, BG Home Page.html.

figure 8.8

c08ex02, BGHomePage.html in Online View

Butterfield Gardens

"All the flowers of all the tomorrows are in the seeds of today."

Butterfield Gardens has all the seeds and flowers you may need to make your tomorrows as beautiful as they may be. Butterfield Gardens is a nursery and garden center specializing in annuals, perennials, garden supplies and service, wildflowers, prairie grasses, trees, shrubs, mulch and groundcovers, garden art, gifts, antiques, and birdhouses. We also have an experienced horticulturist on site to help you with your gardening and pest control needs. Ask us about our nonchemical pest control program.

Come visit us and learn more about what is new in gardening:

Ortho® Online

New Bio News—Monsanto Company

 Bug of the Month Program

Stop by and visit us at 29 W 036 Butterfield Road, Warrenville, IL 60555. You can also reach us by telephone at (630) 555-1062, fax at (630) 555-1063, or E-mail at *bgardens@aol.com*. We look forward to serving your gardening needs.

In this chapter, you will be saving your Web home page on your student data disk. For a home page to be available on the Web, you must have access to a Web server. Large businesses usually have their own server and you would have to contact the Information Systems department of the company to arrange for space on the server to store your HTML documents (home pages). The other option is to rent space from an Internet Service Provider (ISP). The ISP you use to access the Web will also arrange to store your Web page. Check out all the fees involved, as there are many different fee structures in existence.

DTP POINTERS
Plan where you want to place a hyperlink to reinforce its effectiveness.

Creating Hyperlinks in a Web Home Page

The business Web sites you visited in exercise 1 included hyperlinks to connect you to other pages or Web sites in different locations. The reader of your document can jump to a location in that document, a different Word document, or a file created in a different program such as an Excel spreadsheet.

The destination document or file can be on your hard drive, on your company's network (Intranet), or on the Internet, such as a page on the World Wide Web. You can create hyperlinks from selected text or graphic objects—such as buttons and pictures. By default, the hyperlink text displays in blue and is underlined. When you return to the document after following a hyperlink, the hyperlink text color changes to purple. You do not have to be on the Internet to use hyperlinks in Word documents.

If an E-mail address is keyed in the Internet format, *yourname@company.com,* at the end of a Web page, Word will automatically create a hyperlink to your default Internet mail program. Additionally, you can create hyperlinks to bookmarks in a document. You can create a bookmark in a document by selecting a word or sentence, then clicking Insert, and then Bookmark. At the Bookmark dialog box, key a short description in the text box, click Add, then click OK. You can then create a hyperlink from another section in the document to the bookmark or from any other document to the bookmark.

Insert Hyperlink

You can create your own hyperlink in your home page. To do this, select the text you want specified as the hyperlink, then click the Insert Hyperlink button (thirteenth button from the left) on the Standard toolbar or click Insert, then Hyperlink. At the Insert Hyperlink dialog box shown in figure 8.9, key the Web site URL or document name in the Link to file or URL text box, then click OK.

Insert Hyperlink Dialog Box

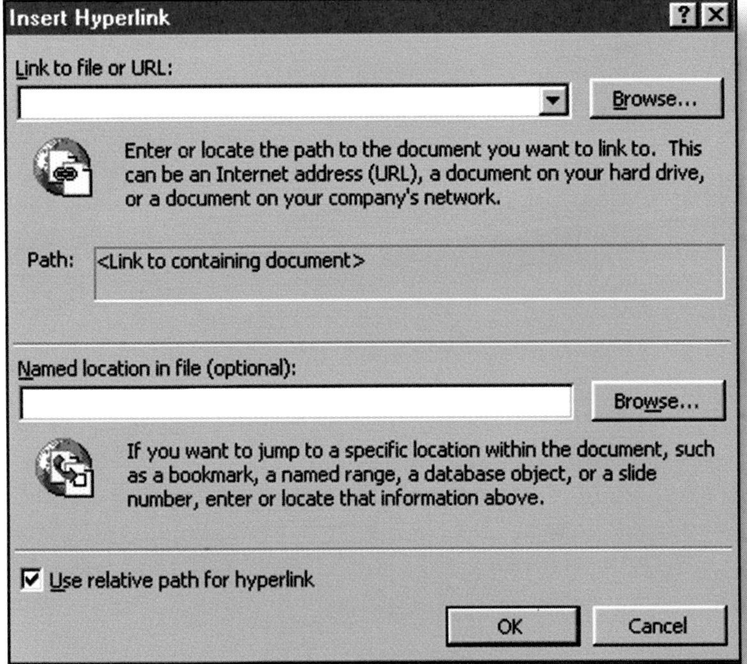

Editing or Deleting a Hyperlink

To edit an existing link, select the hyperlink in Word, then right-click and choose Hyperlink at the shortcut menu. Select the Edit Hyperlink option at the shortcut menu. To delete a hyperlink (but not the document text), click the Remove Link button located in the bottom left corner of the Edit Hyperlink dialog box.

In exercise 3, you will be establishing hyperlinks from the Butterfield Gardens home page to resource sites on the Web as well as to a document saved on your student data disk.

Previewing a Web Page

Web Page Preview

After creating a Web page or converting a Word document to a Web page, you may want to preview the page as it will appear on the Internet Explorer screen. To do this, make sure you have saved the document and then click the Web Page Preview button on the Standard toolbar or click File, then Web Page Preview.

exercise 3

Creating Hyperlinks

1. Open c08ex02, BG Home Page.html.
2. Select the heading, *Butterfield Gardens,* and change the font color to Green as shown in figure 8.10.
3. Select *"All the flowers..."* and change the font to italic and change the font color to Green.
4. Create a hyperlink so that clicking *Ortho® Online* will display the Ortho® Online home page by completing the following steps:
   a. Select the text *Ortho® Online* that displays after the first bullet in the home page document.
   b. Click the Insert Hyperlink button (thirteenth button from the left) on the Standard toolbar.
   c. At the Insert Hyperlink dialog box, key **http://www.ortho.com** in the Link to file or URL text box, then click OK. (This changes *Ortho® Online* text to blue and adds underlining.)
5. Complete steps similar to those in steps 4a to 4c to create a hyperlink from *New Bio News—Monsanto Company* to the URL *http://www.monsanto.com/monpub/index.html.*
6. Create a hyperlink from *Bug of the Month Program* to the Word document saved as *Bug of the Month.html* on your student data disk by completing the following steps:
   a. Select the text *Bug of the Month Program* that displays after the third bullet.
   b. Click the Insert Hyperlink button on the Standard toolbar.
   c. At the Insert Hyperlink dialog box, click the Browse button to the right of the Link to file or URL text box, and locate the file *Bug of the Month.html* located on your student data disk, then click OK. Click OK again.
7. Click File, then Save As and name the document c08ex03, BG Home Page.html.
8. Make sure you are connected to the Internet. (Even if you are not connected to the Internet, you can test your links through your browser—the links will display when you point on them. However, you will not be able to actually link to the other sites and read the home pages without connecting to the Internet.)
9. With your insertion point positioned in the Butterfield Gardens home page within Word 97, click File, then Web Page Preview.
10. Jump to the hyperlink sites by completing the following steps:
    a. Click the hyperlink *Ortho® Online* that displays after the first bullet. (This text displays in blue.)
    b. When the Web site home page displays for *Ortho® Online*, scroll through the home page clicking on any hyperlinks that interest you.
    c. When you have finished viewing the Ortho® Online home page, click the Back button on the Internet Explorer Toolbar until the Butterfield Gardens home page displays.

d. Click each of the other hyperlinks (*New Bio News—Monsanto Company* and *Bug of the Month Program*), and click any hyperlinks that interest you.

11. After viewing the home pages for each hyperlink, close c08ex03, BG Home Page.html and then exit the Internet.

figure 8.10

Web Page in Page Layout View

Butterfield Gardens

"All the flowers of all the tomorrows are in the seeds of today."

Butterfield Gardens has all the seeds and flowers you may need to make your tomorrows as beautiful as they may be. Butterfield Gardens is a nursery and garden center specializing in annuals, perennials, garden supplies and service, wildflowers, prairie grasses, trees, shrubs, mulch and groundcovers, garden art, gifts, antiques, and birdhouses. We also have an experienced horticulturist on site to help you with your gardening and pest control needs. Ask us about our nonchemical pest control program.

Come visit us and learn more about what is new in gardening:

 Ortho® Online

 New Bio News—Monsanto Company

 Bug of the Month Program

Stop by and visit us at 29 W 036 Butterfield Road, Warrenville, IL 60555. You can also reach us by telephone at (630) 555-1062, fax at (630) 555-1063, or E-mail at *bgardens@aol.com.* We look forward to serving your gardening needs.

Applying Formatting to a Web Page

Formatting That HTML Will Support

When creating a Web page in Word, you can use many of the same formatting tools you use for Word documents. For instance, you can apply bold, italic, underline, strikethrough, superscript, and subscript formats to selected text.

DTP POINTERS
Enhance text in a Web page to increase visual appeal.

You can set the colors for text, hyperlinks, and followed hyperlinks for the entire page with the Text Colors dialog box in the Format menu. You can change colors for selected text by clicking the Font Color button on the Formatting toolbar.

You can indent text in 0.25-inch increments by clicking the Increase Indent and Decrease Indent buttons on the Formatting toolbar. In addition, you can change the alignment of text by clicking the Alignment buttons on the Formatting toolbar. A picture can be positioned on a Web page by selecting it first, then clicking an Alignment button. Drawing objects, such as AutoShapes, can be inserted into a Web page by first creating them at the Microsoft Word Picture screen, then saving them to the HTML document.

Formatting That HTML Will Not Support

Formatting that is *not* supported by HTML at this time includes animated text (other than scrolling text), emboss, shadow, engrave, highlighting, line spacing, tabs, font sizes, all caps, small caps, outline effect, character spacing, kerning, text flow settings, and spacing before and after paragraphs. However, paragraphs will automatically contain space before and after them. Additionally, HTML at this time does *not* support margins, newspaper-style columns, paragraph or page borders, page numbering, headers and footers, footnotes and endnotes, master documents, and cross-references.

Periodically, Microsoft will prompt you to download an upgrade to the Web authoring tools. In this case, some of the unsupported formatting effects may then become available.

Using Word's Standard and Formatting Toolbars in HTML

The Standard and Formatting toolbars are available in Word 97 when Word is in HTML editing mode. The features that are available on these toolbars are the Web page authoring tools. If you want to use the Web Page Wizard in the New dialog box and find that the Web Pages tab is not available, you will know that you need to install these tools. To install the Web page authoring features, select the Web Page Authoring (HTML) check box in Setup.

Word is in HTML editing mode when you open an HTML document, save a document with an HTML extension, or choose the Blank Web Page template. When a file is saved in HTML, the basic HTML page structure is in place. You can view this structure, as shown in figure 8.11, by clicking View, then HTML Source. Click Exit HTML Source from the toolbar after viewing the tags.

HTML Tags Behind an HTML Document

```
<HTML>¶
<HEAD>¶
<META·HTTP-EQUIV="Content-Type"·CONTENT="text/html;·charset=windows-1252">¶
<META·NAME="Generator"·CONTENT="Microsoft·Word·97">¶
<TITLE>c08ex02,·BG·Home·Page</TITLE>¶
<META·NAME="Template"·CONTENT="C:\Office·97\Templates\Web·Pages\Web·Page·
Wizard.wiz">¶
</HEAD>¶
<BODY·LINK="#0000ff"·VLINK="#800080"·BACKGROUND="Image3.gif">¶
¶
<B><FONT·SIZE=7><P·ALIGN="CENTER">Butterfield·Gardens</P>¶
</B></FONT><P·ALIGN="CENTER">"All·the·flowers·of·all·the·tomorrows·are·in·the·
seeds·of·today."</P>¶
<P·ALIGN="CENTER">Butterfield·Gardens·has·all·the·seeds·and·flowers·you·may·need·
to·make·your·tomorrows·as·beautiful·as·they·may·be.·Butterfield·Gardens·is·a·
nursery·and·garden·center·specializing·in·annuals,·perennials,·garden·supplies·
and·service,·wildflowers,·prairie·grasses,·trees,·scrubs,·mulch·and·
groundcovers,·garden·art,·gifts,·antiques,·and·bird·houses.·We·also·have·an·
experienced·horticulturist·on·site·to·help·you·with·your·gardening·and·pest·
control·needs.·Ask·us·about·our·non-chemical·pest·control·program.</P>¶
<P·ALIGN="CENTER">Come·visit·us·and·learn·more·about·what·is·new·in·
```

To make formatting changes to an HTML document, click the Format option on the Menu bar, and a drop-down menu displays with options for changing the font, adding bullets or numbering, changing text color case and style, and adding a background. These options are also available on the Word 97 Standard toolbar or the Word 97 Formatting toolbar as shown in figures 8.12 and 8.13. In addition, with some options from the Insert drop-down menu, you can add a horizontal line to a document; add a picture, video, or background sound; and add scrolling text.

> **DTP POINTERS**
> Photos, videos, and background sounds add impact to a Web page, but they create large files and slow down performance.

Word 97 Standard Toolbar With HTML-Related Options

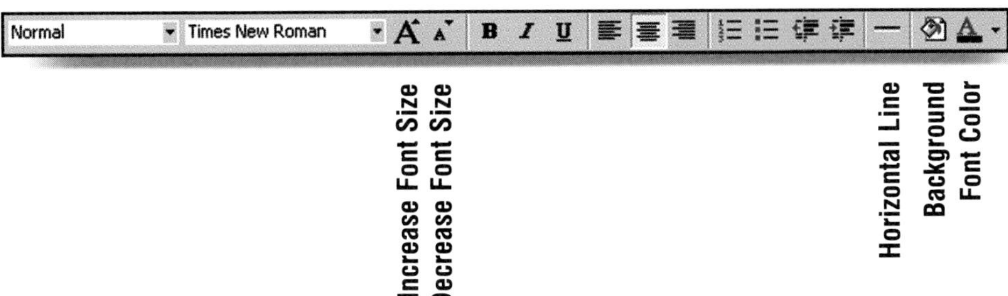

Word 97 Formatting Toolbar With HTML-Related Options

Adding Font Colors and Effects

Font formats are more limited in HTML pages than in Word documents. At the Font dialog box, you can select from six font effects and sixteen colors. However, if you want more colors, format the text in one of the sixteen colors, then modify the color by going into the HTML source code and replace the color code with a color you prefer.

> **DTP POINTERS**
> Use color consistently.

Adding Scrolling Text to a Web Page

You can enhance your Web page with scrolling text, also known as a *marquee*, which travels across a page. At this time, scrolling text is supported in all versions of Microsoft Internet Explorer except version 1.0. Some other Web browsers may not support this feature. At an HTML document screen, add the scrolling text feature by clicking Insert, then Scrolling Text. Type the text that you want to scroll in the *Type the scrolling text here* text box. Select any other options you want—Behavior, Direction, Background Color, Loop, and Speed.

> **Marquee**
> Animated text that displays or travels across a page.

To change font size and color, select the text box containing the scrolling text, then click the Increase Font Size or Decrease Font Size buttons and the Font Color buttons on the Formatting toolbar. To add bold and/or italic, click the corresponding buttons on the Formatting toolbar.

Increase Font Size

Decrease Font Size

If you want to delete the scrolling text from your Web page, complete the following steps:

Font Color

1. At the HTML screen, double-click the text box containing the Scrolling Text.
2. At the Scrolling Text dialog box, select the text in the *Type the Scrolling Text Here* text box.
3. Right-click on the text, then select Delete from the drop-down menu.

Viewing Animated Text

You can create animated text effects—that flash or move—for a document that will be read in Online Layout view only. The animated text will not print and it is not available in HTML documents at this time. This feature is located at the Animation tab of the Font dialog box.

Editing in Online Layout View

Online Layout view enables you to view your document as it might appear online. The Document Map feature is available and it displays to the left of the screen in Online Layout view. Document Map is helpful in jumping between locations in large documents. In order for the Document Map to display the main headings, you must apply HTML heading styles to your heading text.

Adding Bullets and Lines to a Web Page

Bullets can be added to your document lists by clicking the Bullet button on the Formatting toolbar. Additionally, you can change the regular bullets to special graphical bullets for your Web page. Select the bulleted list in your document, then click Bullets and Numbering on the Format menu, select the Bulleted tab, and then select the graphical bullet that you want. Many exciting bullets are available in the Bullets dialog box shown in figure 8.14. Click the More button to view additional bullets. The graphical bullets are saved to your default folder along with your HTML document; however, the bullets are not saved within the HTML file. For example, a graphical bullet may display in the folder as *RedSwirl.gif* or as *Bullet2.gif*.

figure 8.14

Graphical Bullets

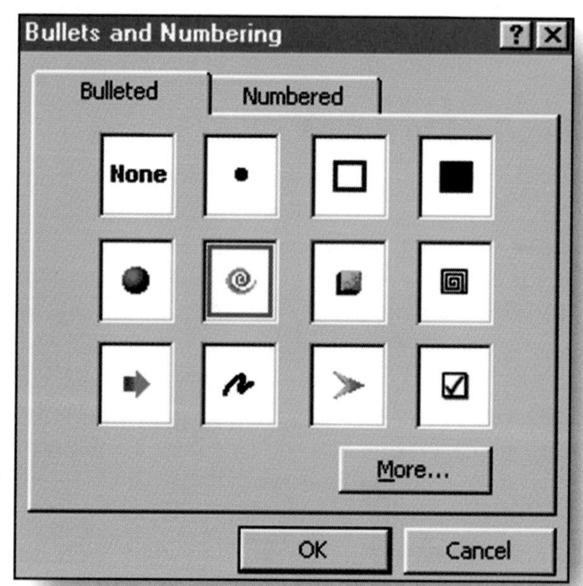

You can also create special horizontal lines for your Web page. To do this, click Horizontal Line on the Insert menu, and then select the line style you want. Figure 8.15 illustrates many of the line styles available to you. Click the More button below the Style list box to view additional graphical lines. An example of a graphical line file is *Neighborhood.gif*.

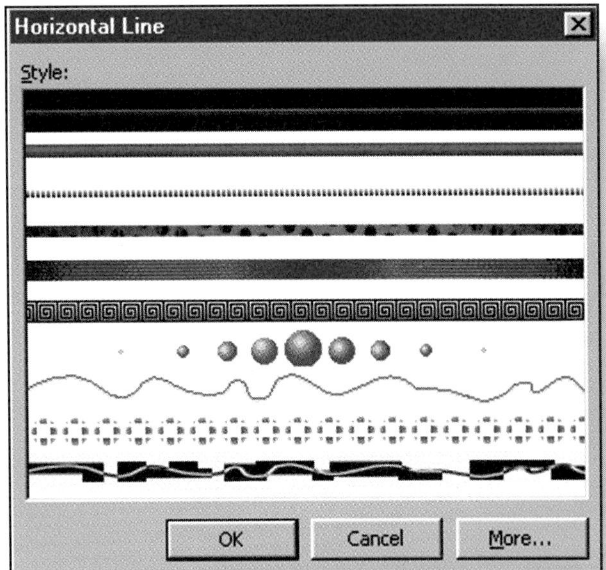

figure 8.15

Graphical Horizontal Lines

Adding Background Color to a Web Page

To make your document more visually appealing to read online, you can add background colors and textures to it. You can see the backgrounds on the screen, but they will not display when the page is printed. To decorate your document with a background, point to Background on the Format menu. Then click the color you want, or click Fill Effects and select a gradient, textured, or patterned background.

DTP POINTERS
Use background color to decorate a Web page.

Inserting Graphics and Objects in a Web Page

HTML currently supports only two graphic file formats: *.gif* and *.jpg* (*jpeg*). However, with Word 97, you can use many other graphic file formats such as .wmf, .tif, .cgm, and .bmp and Word will automatically convert the graphic image to a format suitable for HTML pages when you save the Word document with Save as HTML. Word will save each graphic file as *Image1.gif, Image2.gif,* and so on in the same folder as your Word documents.

Resize your image in Word before saving the document as an HTML file. If you have problems resizing a particular graphic, you may need to load the image into a graphic-editing program such as Microsoft Photo Editor or Microsoft Word Picture. To change to a different graphic editor in Word, click Tools, Options, select the Edit tab, and then select the desired editor in the Picture editor list box. To access the editor, double-click on the image or click Insert, Object, and then select Microsoft Photo Editor 3.0 Photo.

You can change the position of an image on a Web page by selecting the image, then clicking one of the alignment buttons on the Formatting toolbar. Additionally, you can key increments in the Vertical and Horizontal text boxes in the Distance from text section of the Picture dialog box after selecting a Text wrapping option as shown in figure 8.16.

Picture Dialog Box

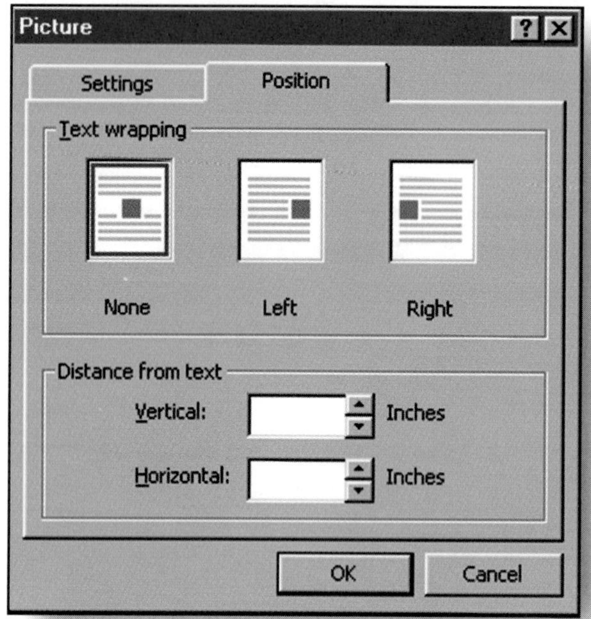

Using Alternative Text in Place of Graphics

You may want to create alternative text that displays when graphics or hyperlinked graphics cannot display. Graphics, photos, and visuals create large files and slow down performance of the Web page. As an alternative, many Web pages will include text in place of the graphic image. To create a text alternative, complete the following steps:

1. Select a nonhyperlinked graphic by clicking on it. Select a hyperlinked graphic by right-clicking on the hyperlinked graphic, then choose Hyperlink, Select Hyperlink.
2. Click Format, then Picture.
3. At the Picture dialog box, select the Settings tab.
4. Type in the Text box the text you want to appear when the graphic does not display.
5. Click OK.

Understanding .GIF and .JPG File Formats and HTML

When a graphical bullet or line, or a clip art image is added to an HTML document, Word automatically saves the bullet, line, or graphic as a *.gif* or *.jpg* file. The file is saved separately from the document HTML file. At this time, HTML does not have the capability to save a graphic file within its format. Therefore, the two file formats that HTML will recognize, *.gif* and *.jpg*, are saved separately from the HTML document, but are saved in the same default folder. Both files must be saved in the same folder if you want the graphics to display in the HTML document when you open it. For instance, if you add the graphical line, *Neighborhood.gif*, to your HTML document, *Neightborhood.gif* will display in the same folder as the document file, but not within the document file. A clip art image will display as *Image1, Image 2, etc.*. Do not delete the *.gif* or *.jpg* files from your folder thinking that they are taking up too much space on your drive or disk. They must remain in the same folder as the HTML document to which they are connected.

Creating Transparent Areas in a Picture

When an image contains a transparent area, the background color or texture of the page shows through the image. If the image is a bitmap file, you can use the Set Transparent Color tool on the Picture toolbar in Word. The following file formats are associated with Microsoft Photo Editor and can be altered in the Photo Editor by either double-clicking on each image or accessing the Photo Editor at the Object dialog box as shown below: gif, .jpg, .pcd, .pcx, .png, .tga, .tif, or .bmp.

DTP POINTERS
Transparency added to a graphic can improve the overall look of the Web page by blending the graphic with the background color.

1. Click Object at the Insert menu, and then select the Create New tab.
2. In the Object type list box, select *Microsoft Photo Editor 3.0 Photo*.
3. Open the graphic or photo to which you want to apply a transparent effect.
4. Click the Set Transparent Color button and position the tool on the desired area and left-click the mouse (see figure 8.17—the area will become clear or transparent).
5. Save the image in the *.gif* format if you want to use it on a Web page.
6. Close the Photo Editor program.
7. Insert the image into your Web page.

Set Transparent Color

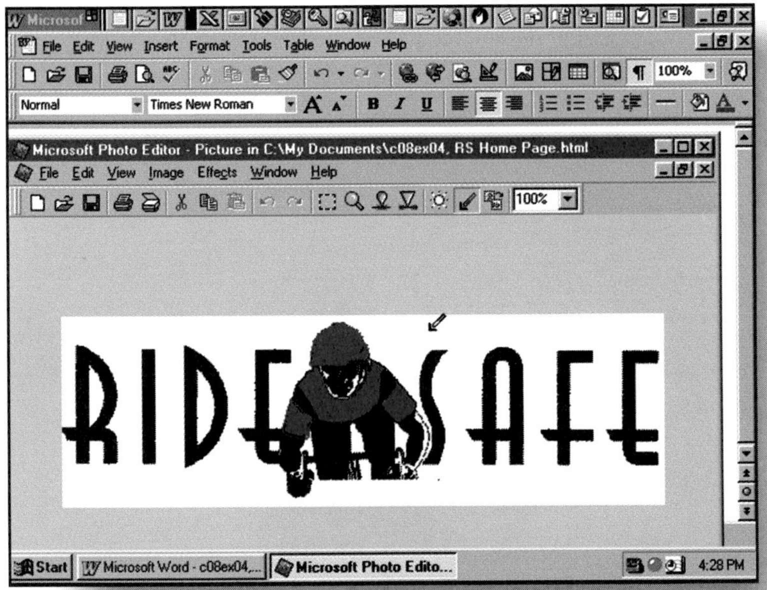

figure 8.17

Using Microsoft Photo Editor to Apply Transparency

Downloading More Graphics and Other Items

Additional images for Web page authoring are available on the World Wide Web. Access the Web, then point to Picture on the Insert menu, and then click Browse Web Art Page. Follow the directions to download the images that you want. One valuable Web URL that contains many images, icons, backgrounds, sounds, fonts, and more is *http://www.microsoft.com/gallery.*

Scanning Pictures for a Web Page

DTP POINTERS
Scanned pictures are generally large files.

If a scanner is attached to your computer, you can use Word and Microsoft Photo Editor to scan your images into Word documents or into documents saved in HTML format. Microsoft Photo Editor is a powerful picture editor that lets you edit scanned (and other) images. When you begin the scan, Photo Editor starts your scanner software, which performs the scan. To scan a picture, complete the following steps:

1. Turn your scanner on, then click Insert, Picture, and then From Scanner. Photo Editor starts, and your scanner software is activated.
2. Follow the instructions for using your scanner and scanner software.
3. The final scanned image will appear in the Photo Editor window. Use Photo Editor to edit the image.
4. At the Photo Editor window, click File, then Save As. Save your image with a *.gif* or *.jpg* format if you are going to use the image on a Web page. (Keep in mind that scanned images may create large files and can slow down your Web page.)

Adding AutoShapes and Other Drawing Objects to a Web Page

Drawing objects, such as AutoShapes, text boxes, and WordArt objects, can be inserted into Web pages. Insert drawing objects into Web pages by first creating a Microsoft Word Picture object and then using the options on the Drawing toolbar, as shown in figure 8.18. To access Microsoft Word Picture, click Insert, Object, and then select Microsoft Word Picture at the Create New tab of the Object dialog box. Click the AutoShapes button on the Drawing toolbar, then point to one of the categories of Autoshapes listed, and then select a particular form. After you draw the form into the Microsoft Word Picture screen, close the Word Picture screen and return to your document window.

WordArt and an AutoShape in a Web Page

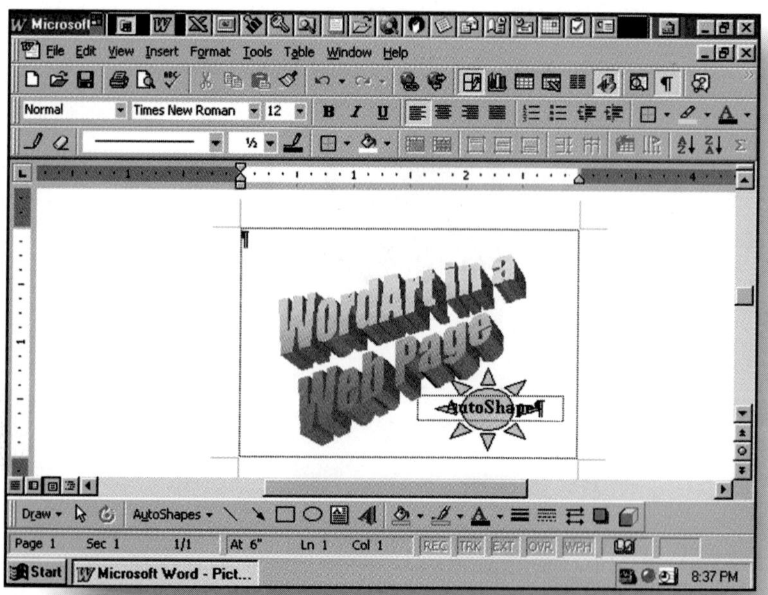

When you save your document with Save as HTML, Word converts the drawing object to a *.gif* image. However, to apply transparency to a drawing object saved as a *.gif* file, you must edit it in the Microsoft Photo Editor program. To verify which editing program is available, click Tools, Options, select the Edit tab, and choose either the Microsoft Photo Editor 3.0 Photo program or the Microsoft Word Picture program at the Picture editor list box.

In exercise 4, you will create an Intranet home page for Ride Safe using a Word document converted to a Web page. When you save the Word document as a Web page, the document closes and then reopens in the HTML format. Formatting not supported by HTML is removed from the document. You will add HTML-related formatting to this document.

exercise 4

Converting a Word Document to HTML and Applying Formatting

1. Open *Ride Safe Home Page.doc.* (This document is located on your student data disk.)
2. Convert the document to a Web page as shown in figure 8.19 by completing the following steps:
   a. Click File, then Save as HTML.
   b. At the Save As HTML dialog box, key **c08ex04, RS Home Page** and then press Enter or click the Save button.
3. When the document displays as an HTML document, format the document by completing the following steps:
   a. Add a textured light blue background to the document by completing the following steps:
      (1) Click Format, then point to Background.
      (2) At the background palette, click Fill Effects.
      (3) At the Texture tab, select the first texture in the third row (Blue tissue paper).
      (4) Click OK.
   b. Make sure you have selected Microsoft Photo Editor as the default Picture editor in Word 97 by completing the following steps:
      (1) Click Tools, then Options.
      (2) Select the Edit tab.
      (3) Select Microsoft Photo Editor 3.0 Photo at the Picture editor list box.
      (4) Click OK.
   c. Insert the Ride Safe logo by completing the following steps:
      (1) Turn on the Show/Hide ¶ button.
      (2) Position the insertion point at the top of the page, then click Insert, point to Picture, then click From File. Select *Ridesf1blue.bmp* located on your student data disk.
      (3) Select the Ride Safe logo, then click the Center align button on the Formatting toolbar.
   d. Save your document with the same name, c08ex04, RS Home Page.html.
   e. Apply transparency to the logo image by completing the following steps:
      (1) Double-click the logo to access Microsoft Photo Editor.
      (2) Click the Set Transparent Color button on the Photo Editor toolbar.
      (3) Drag the Set Transparent Color tool into the white area surrounding the logo, then click the left mouse button.
      (4) At the Change Color to Transparent dialog box, make sure *100%* displays in the Transparency text box, then click OK. (The transparent areas will display checkered on the screen.)

(5) Click File, then Exit and Return to the c08ex04, RS Home Page.html (at the Photo Editor screen).

f. Apply formatting to the title by completing the following steps:
   (1) Select *Welcome to the Ride Safe...*, then click the Increase Font Size button three times.
   (2) Click the Bold button on the Formatting toolbar.
   (3) With the text still selected, click the Font Color button on the Formatting toolbar and select Blue in the second row.

g. Add a horizontal line below the title by completing the following steps:
   (1) Position the insertion point on the paragraph symbol below *Welcome to the Ride Safe Intranet....*
   (2) Click Insert, then Horizontal Line.
   (3) At the Horizontal Line dialog box, click the More button.
   (4) At the Insert Picture list box, double-click *Stained Glass Line.gif.*
   (5) Delete the paragraph symbol above the graphic line.

h. Position the insertion point on the second paragraph symbol below *Welcome to Ride ...*, then create another horizontal line by copying and pasting the line in step 1e.

i. Position the insertion point between the two horizontal lines, then key **Biking and In-Line Skating Safety is Our Goal....**

j. Select *Biking and In-Line...*, click the Italic button and the Center align button on the Formatting toolbar, and then click the Font Color button and select Blue in the second row.

k. Select each of the section headings (*What's New on the Ride Safe Intranet?, etc.*) and apply the *Heading 1* style located in the Style list box on the Formatting toolbar.

l. Select *E-MAIL SUGGESTION BOX* and change the font to Arial Bold and the font color to Blue.

m. Select *Ride Safe, Inc. | Address...* and apply the *Hyperlink* style.

n. Change the bullets as shown in figure 8.19 by completing the following steps:
   (1) Select the two bulleted items below *What's New on the Ride Safe Intranet?.*
   (2) Click Format, then Bullets and Numbering.
   (3) At the Bullets and Numbering dialog box, click the More button.
   (4) Double-click *Stained Glass Ball.gif.*
   (5) With the two bulleted items selected, click the Increase Indent button on the Formatting toolbar.

o. Select the bullets below *Bicycle Helmet Program Guide* and complete steps similar to n(1) to n(5).

p. Select the bullets below *Employee Connections* and complete steps similar to n(1) to n(5).

q. Click File, then Save or click the Save button on the Standard toolbar. (You must save changes to your document before adding hyperlinks.)

r. Create a hyperlink from *Download Forms and Guide to Bicycle Rodeo* to a document located on your student data disk by completing the following steps:
   (1) Select *Download Forms...*, which is located in the *What's New...* section.
   (2) Click the Insert Hyperlink button on the Standard toolbar.
   (3) At the Insert Hyperlink dialog box, click the Browse button to the right of the Link to file or URL text box, and then select *What's New.doc* located on your student data disk.
   (4) Click OK, then click OK again.

s. Create a hyperlink from *What's New.doc* to c08ex04, RS Home Page.html by completing the following steps:

(1) Double click the *Download Forms...* hyperlink you just created in steps r(1) to r(4), then select *Ride Safe Home Page* in the last line at the bottom of the page.
(2) Click the Insert Hyperlink button on the Standard toolbar.
(3) At the Insert Hyperlink dialog box, click the Browse button to the right of the Link to file or URL text box, and then select *c08ex04, RS Home Page.html.*
(4) Click OK, then click OK again.
(5) Close *What's New.doc.* (Save the changes to *What's New.doc.*)

4. Save the formatting to the Web page document by clicking the Save button on the Formatting toolbar.
5. Preview the Web page by clicking the Web Page Preview button on the Standard toolbar, then practice the hyperlinks.
6. Click File, then Close to return to the document in Word.
7. Print and then close c08ex04, RS Home Page.html.

figure 8.19

Welcome to the
Ride Safe Intranet Home Page

Biking and In-Line Skating Safety is Our Goal...

What's New on the Ride Safe Intranet?

- Company Newsletter
- Download Forms and Guide to Bicycle Rodeo

Bicycle Helmet Program Guide:

- How to Run a Successful Program
- Frequently Asked Questions
- Ways to Promote Your Program
- Helpful Resources
- Fees and Product Pricing

Employee Connections:

- Employee Benefits
- Medical
- Vacation Policy

E-MAIL SUGGESTION BOX

If you have any questions or suggestions, please use this e-mail address to send your thoughts to ridesafe@aol.com.

Ride Safe, Inc. | Address | Telephone | Fax |

Creating Forms on a Web Page

You can use forms to collect and present data on your Web page. You can create a form that collects a user's feedback or registration information. You can store this information in a database or in a text file for future use. An easy way to create a form is to select a sample form and modify it to meet your needs by using the Forms toolbar. Sample forms, such as feedback and survey forms, are available from the Web Page Wizard as shown in figure 8.20. If the Wizard does not have a form that will meet your needs, you can create a form by inserting the controls you want from the Control Toolbar.

For our purposes in this chapter, we will not be accessing a database for use with the form controls. If you would like additional information about linking the form controls to a database or query, see your Word 97 or Office 97 reference manuals.

In exercise 5, you will use the Web Page Wizard to create a form requesting information from prospective clients for a free real estate appraisal. You will customize the form to fit your needs. This form will be used for a hyperlink in exercise 6.

exercise 5

Creating a Form Using the Web Page Wizard

1. Create a registration form as shown in figure 8.20 by completing the following steps:
   a. At a clear document screen, click File, then New.
   b. At the New dialog box, click the Web Pages tab, and then double-click the Web Page Wizard icon.
   c. At the first Web Page Wizard dialog box, click *Form - Registration* in the list box, then click the Next> button that displays at the bottom of the dialog box.
   d. At the second Web Page Wizard dialog box, click *Community* in the list box, then click the Finish button that displays toward the bottom of the dialog box.
   e. At the Web page document, key the text shown in figure 8.20.
   f. Select *Forecast Realty,* change the font to Braggadocio, then click the Decrease Font Size button once, and then click the Font Color button on the Formatting toolbar and select Red.
   g. Add text to the list box located below *When are you planning to move?* by completing the following steps:
      (1) Click the Form Design Mode button (eighth button from the right) on the Standard toolbar. The Control Toolbar will display.
      (2) Select the list box below *When are you planning to move?*, then click the Properties button (second button in the first row) on the Control Toolbar.
      (3) At the Properties dialog box, select the Alphabetic tab, then key **6 months; 1 year; not moving** in place of *Option 1, Option 2, Option 3* in the column to the right of the Display Values row and the Values row.
      (4) Close the Properties dialog box by clicking the (X) in the upper right corner.
      (5) Click the Form Design Mode button again to turn this feature off or click the Exit Design Mode button (small dialog box with an X on it).
      (6) Close the Controls dialog box by clicking the (X) in the upper right corner.
2. Save the form with Save As and name it c08ex05, FR Form.html.
3. Click the Web Page Preview button on the Standard toolbar.
4. Click the down arrow to the right of the *When are you planning to move?* list box. The options should display as *6 months; 1 year;* and *not moving.*

5. Make sure *Single, Multi-unit* and *Townhouse/condo* displays as a single line of text. If any one of these items displays on two lines, adjust the cell widths to accommodate the text. (You will need to exit Web Page Preview to make the table adjustments, then view the document again in Web Page Preview to make sure all the options display properly.)
6. In Web Page Preview, select the appropriate checkboxes, then key your name and other personal data in the text boxes on the form.
7. Click File, then Close to close the Web Page Preview screen.
8. Save the form again as c08ex05, FR Form.html.
9. Print and then close c08ex05, FR Form.html.

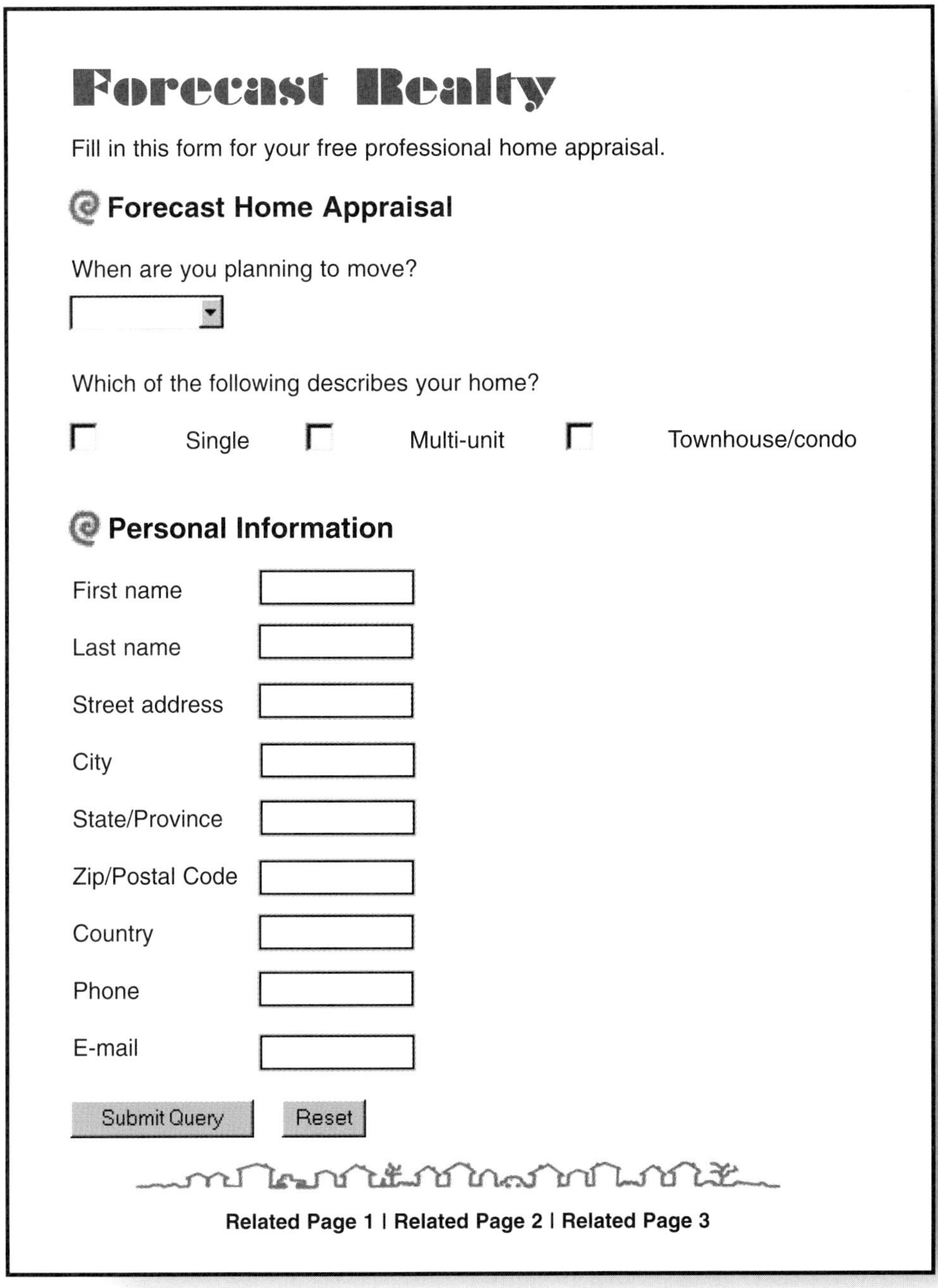

figure 8.20

Forecast Realty

Fill in this form for your free professional home appraisal.

Forecast Home Appraisal

When are you planning to move?

Which of the following describes your home?

Single Multi-unit Townhouse/condo

Personal Information

First name

Last name

Street address

City

State/Province

Zip/Postal Code

Country

Phone

E-mail

Submit Query Reset

Related Page 1 | Related Page 2 | Related Page 3

Designing a Web Page Using a Table

DTP POINTERS
Carefully plan an underlying structure to your document.

Working with tables on Web pages is similar to working with tables in Word documents. You can use Draw Table to create and modify the structure of the table. Tables are often used as a behind-the-scenes layout tool on Web pages—for instance, to arrange text and graphics. You can add borders to tables on Web pages by using the Border command at the Table menu.

You can change the background color or shading in tables by using the Table Properties command at the Table menu. Many other changes can be made to a table by choosing the options listed at the Table menu. As discussed earlier in the chapter, tables can be used to control the layout of a page—margins, tabs, and columns are not available in HTML.

Using Graphics as Hyperlinks

As you browsed the Web sites in exercise 1, did you notice that graphics were sometimes used as hyperlinks to other Web sites or documents? You can hyperlink your graphics just as easily as you created text hyperlinks earlier in this chapter. To hyperlink a graphic to a Web page or document, complete the following steps:

DTP POINTERS
Graphics break up text-intensive areas on a Web page.

1. Insert the graphic.
2. Select the graphic.
3. Click Insert, Hyperlink to display the Insert Hyperlink dialog box, or click the Insert Hypertext button on the Standard toolbar.
4. In the Link to file or URL text box, key the path and file name or URL to the file or Web site to which you want to link. If you do not know the path or URL, click Browse.
5. Click the Use Relative Path for Hyperlink option if you want to be able to move all the linked files to a new location.
6. Click OK.
7. If the graphic is too large and seems to slow down the Web page, create alternative text to substitute for the image. See the section before exercise 4 titled *Inserting Graphics and Objects in a Web Page.*

In exercise 6, you will create a Web home page for a real estate company. The layout of the page will be based on a table structure. You will include graphics related to the subject of the page and use these graphics as hyperlinks to other documents or sites on the Web. You will also create a hyperlink to the form you created in exercise 5.

exercise 6

Creating a Web Page Using a Table

1. Create a Web home page using a table by completing the following steps:
   a. At a clear document screen, click File, then New.
   b. At the New dialog box, click the Web Pages tab.
   c. At the New dialog box with the Web Pages tab selected, double-click the Blank Web Page icon.

d. At the Web document window, create a table layout similar to the one in figure 8.21 by completing the following steps:
   (1) Display the Tables and Borders toolbar.
   (2) Make sure the gridlines display by clicking Table, then Show Gridlines.
   (3) Click the Draw Table button on the Tables and Borders toolbar.
   (4) Draw a table beginning in the upper left corner of the HTML screen and ending in the lower right corner of the screen. (As you enter text into the cells, they will expand to accommodate your text.)
   (5) Draw the cells as shown in figure 8.21.
e. Click Format, point to Background, then click Fill Effects. At the Texture palette, double-click the first texture (Newsprint).
f. Position the insertion point in the top left cell, click the Center Align button on the Formatting toolbar.
g. Save the Web page with Save As and name the document c08ex06, FR Home Page.html.
h. Insert the picture *Realest.wmf* located on your student data disk (size if necessary).
i. Create the text in the cell to the right of the graphic by completing the following steps:
   (1) Position the insertion point in the cell to the right of the graphic, key **Forecast Realty**, and then press Enter.
   (2) Change the Font to Britannic Bold and the Color to Dark Blue by using the appropriate buttons on the Formatting toolbar.
   (3) Key **15 West Ogden Avenue, Naperville, IL 60540**, press Enter, key **http://www.forecastrealty.com**, press Enter, key **Phone: (630) 555-2001**, press the space bar five times, then key **Fax: (630) 555-2004**. (The Internet address will display in blue and underlined—do not delete this formatting.)
   (4) Select *Forecast Realty* and change the font to Braggadocio and change the font color to Red. Click the Increase Font Size button once.
   (5) Select the address, Web address, and phone and fax text, then click the Decrease Font Size button once.
j. Add scrolling text to the Web page by completing the following steps:
   (1) Position the insertion point in the cell below the name and address cell and press Enter.
   (2) Click the Center align button on the Standard toolbar.
   (3) Click Insert, then Scrolling Text.
   (4) At the Scrolling Text dialog box, make the following changes:
      (a) Click the down arrow to the right of the Background Color text box (displays with the word *Auto*), then select *Gray-25%*.
      (b) Select the words *Sample Text* that display in the Type the Scrolling Text Here text box, then key **Forecasting a Smooth Move for You...**, press the space bar ten times, then key **Focus on Naperville!**, press the space bar ten times, then key **Focus on a Family Community!**, press the space bar ten times, then key **Focus on the #1 "Kid-Friendly" City in the U.S.!**
      (c) Click the OK button to close the dialog box.
      (d) Select the scrolling text box, then click the Italic button on the Formatting toolbar.
      (e) With the scrolling text box still selected, click the Font Color button on the Formatting toolbar, then select the Dark Blue color.

(f) If the scrolling text box displays beyond the right border of the table, you may need to click a corner-sizing handle and reduce the horizontal size of the text box.

k. Create the bulleted text in figure 8.22 by completing the following steps: (*Hint*: You can turn off the scrolling text by selecting the text box containing the scrolling text, then right-clicking the mouse, and then clicking Stop from the drop-down menu.)
   (1) Position the insertion point in the cell below the scrolling text, click Insert, then File.
   (2) Insert the document *Naperville.doc* located on your student data disk.
   (3) Select the bulleted text, then click Format, Bullets and Numbering.
   (4) Select the Bullets tab, then click the More button.
   (5) Double-click *Red Swirl.gif* in the list box.
   (6) With the text still selected, click the Increase Indent button on the Formatting toolbar once.

l. Insert graphics and text into the four cells below the bulleted text by completing the following steps:
   (1) Position the insertion point in the first cell, then click Table, then Select Row. Click the Center Align button on the Formatting toolbar.
   (2) With the insertion point located in the first cell, insert the picture *Realtor.wmf* located on your student data disk.
   (3) Resize the image to make it smaller, as shown in figure 8.22.
   (4) Press Enter, then key **Contact Agents**.
   (5) Position the insertion point in the next cell, insert the picture *Schlhse1.wmf* located on your student data disk, press Enter, and then key **Community/Schools**.
   (6) Position the insertion point in the next cell, insert the picture *Lightblb.wmf* located on your student data disk, press Enter, and then key **Tips on Selling Your House**. (You may need to resize the picture.)
   (7) Position the insertion point in the next cell, insert the picture *Moneybag.wmf* located in the Popular Folder (C:\Program Files\Microsoft Office\Clipart\Popular), press Enter, and then key **Free Home Appraisal**. Resize the money bag graphic—it will be huge!
   (8) Position the insertion point anywhere in the row containing the graphics, then click Table, then Select Row.
   (9) With the row selected, change the font to Britannic Bold in Dark Blue and click the Decrease Font Size button once.

m. Create the text at the bottom of the table shown in figure 8.22, by completing the following steps:
   (1) Position the insertion point in the cell below the four cells containing the graphics, then click the Center align button on the Formatting toolbar.
   (2) Click the Decrease Font Size button on the Formatting toolbar and change the font color to Dark Blue, then key **Thank you for visiting us at our new Web site. Come visit us again soon!**.
   (3) Press Enter.
   (4) Click Insert, Horizontal Line, then click the More button.
   (5) Double-click *Neighborhood.gif* in the list box.

n. Save the document with the same name *c08ex06, FR Home Page.html*.

o. Create hyperlinks in the Web page by completing the following steps:
   (1) Select *Naperville* in the second bulleted line.
   (2) Click the Insert Hyperlink button on the Standard toolbar.
   (3) At the Insert Hyperlink dialog box, key **http://chicago.digitalcity.com/naperville** in the Link to file or URL text box, then click OK.
   (4) Complete steps similar to those in o(3) to create a hyperlink from *schools* to the URL *http://chicago.digitalcity.com/naperville.* Click OK.
   (5) Select the picture of the schoolhouse, then create a hyperlink by following steps similar to o(3) and link the picture to the URL *http://chicago.digitalcity.com/naperville.* Click OK.
   (6) Select *Community/Schools* and create a hyperlink to *http://chicago.digitalcity.com/naperville*. Click OK.
   (7) Complete steps similar to those in o(3) to create a hyperlink from *appraisal* in the last bulleted line to *c08ex05, FR Form.html* created in exercise 5 and located on your student data disk (click the Browse button to the right of the Link to file or URL text box to locate your student data disk).
   (8) Complete steps similar to those in o(3) and o(7) to create a hyperlink from *Free Home Appraisal,* located below the moneybag graphic, to the file *c08ex05, FR Form.html.*
   (9) Create a hyperlink from the money bag graphic to *c08ex05, FR Form.html.*

2. Save the Web page again as c08ex06, FR Home Page.html.
3. Make sure you are connected to the Internet.
4. Click the Web Page Preview button on the Standard toolbar.
5. Make any necessary adjustments such as font size, position of elements, etc., then click the hyperlinks.
6. Click File, then Close to close the Web Page Preview screen.
7. You can add table borders to your Web page or leave them off. If you decide to add the borders, click Table, then Borders, and then select Grid in the Presets section. Click OK.
8. Save the Web page again if you made any changes.
9. Print and then close c08ex06, FR Home Page.html.
10. Exit the Internet.

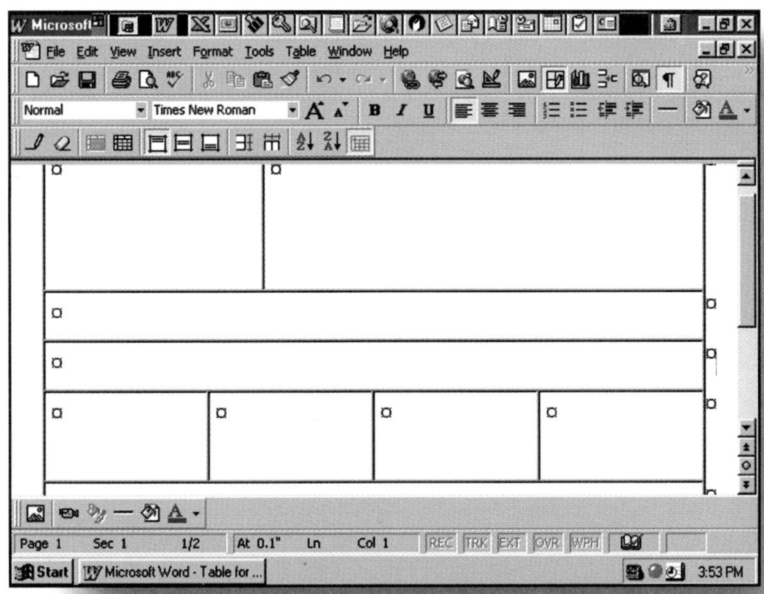

Table Structure for the Forecast Home Page in Exercise 5

8.22

Scrolling Text will Display Here in Online View

Forecast Realty

15 West Ogden Avenue, Naperville, IL 60540

http://www.forecastrealty.com

Phone: (630) 555-2001 Fax (630) 555-2004

- Let us introduce you to one of our helpful, cheerful agents.
- Let us tell you about what's new in Naperville.
- Let us show you the facts about our schools.
- Let us introduce you to a great place to live.
- Let us give you a free, professional appraisal of your home.

Contact Agents

Community/Schools

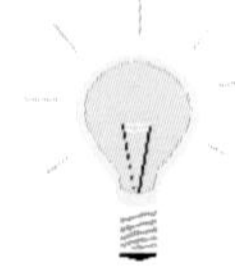

Tips on Selling Your House

Free Home Appraisal

Thank you for visiting us at our new Web site. Come visit us again soon!

chapter summary

- The Internet is a worldwide network of commercial, educational, governmental, and personal computers connected together for the purpose of sharing information.
- An Intranet is an "internal Internet" within an organization that uses the same Web technology and tools as the Internet and is also used for sharing information.
- Word provides the ability to jump to the Internet from the Word document screen.
- The World Wide Web is the most commonly used application on the Internet and is a set of standards and protocols used to access information available on the Internet.
- To locate information on the World Wide Web you need a modem, browser software, and an Internet Service Provider account. An Internet Service Provider sells access to the Internet.
- A modem is a hardware device that carries data over telephone lines.
- A software program used to access the Web is referred to as a Web browser.
- Use a search engine such as Yahoo, InfoSeek, or Excite to locate information on the Internet on a specific topic by keying a few words or a short phrase.
- The Uniform Resource Locators, referred to as URLs, are the method used to identify locations on the Internet.
- Home pages are the starting point for viewing Web sites. Home pages are also documents that describe a company, school, government, or individual and are created using a language called Hypertext Markup Language (HTML).
- A home page can be created in Word and then converted to an HTML document or you can create a Web page using the Web Page Wizard or the Blank Web Page template.
- Plan and design your Web page with a purpose in mind. Review other Web pages on the Internet or an Intranet for design ideas.
- Hyperlinks are colored and underlined text or a graphic that you click to go to a file, a location in a file, an HTML page on the WWW, or an HTML page on an Intranet.
- One method for creating a hyperlink is to select the text and then click the Insert Hyperlink button on the Standard toolbar. At the Insert Hyperlink dialog box, key the URL and then click OK.
- Format a Web page with Menu bar options as well as buttons on the toolbars.
- The Web Page Wizard includes several different types of Web page layouts in addition to many visual styles.
- Word's Web page authoring tools give you all the tools needed to create attractive Web pages.
- Preview a Web page document by clicking the Web Page Preview button on the Standard toolbar.
- HTML does not support all of the Word formatting features.
- HTML does not support all graphic formats. Word automatically converts various graphic files into *.gif* or *.jpg (jpeg)* formats that are suitable for HTML pages.
- When an image contains a transparent area, the background color or texture of the page shows through the image.
- Tables are used to control the layout of a Web page.
- Forms can be used to collect and present data on a Web page.

commands review

	Mouse
Display the Web toolbar	Click Web Toolbar button on Standard Toolbar; or right-click any toolbar, then click *Web*
Display Internet Explorer Search page	Click Search the Web button on the Web toolbar
Save Word document in HTML format	File, Save as HTML
Display the Web Page Wizard	File, New, select the Web Pages tab, then double-click the Web Page Wizard icon
Display a Blank Web Page	File, New, select the Web Pages tab, then double-click the Blank Web Page icon
Insert graphics	Click Insert, point to Picture, then click Clip Art, From File, or Browse Web Art Page
Insert a hyperlink	Click Insert Hyperlink button on the Standard toolbar, or click Insert, then Hyperlink
Preview a Web page	Click Web Page Preview button on Standard toolbar; or click File, then Web Page Preview
Edit a hyperlink	Select the hyperlink, right-click and select Hyperlink, then click Edit Hyperlink
Display Horizontal Line dialog box	With Web page document open, click Insert, Horizontal Line
Display Bullets and Numbering dialog box	With Web page document open, click Format, Bullets and Numbering
Display Scroll Text dialog box	With Web page document open, click Insert, Scrolling Text
Display Background color	Click Format, point to Background, then select a color or fill effect
Tables	Click Table, then Draw a Table or Insert a Table; or click the Draw Table button on the Tables and Borders toolbar; or display Forms toolbar, then click the Draw Table or Insert Table buttons
Forms	Click Insert, point to Forms, then select an option; or display Forms toolbar

check your understanding

Completion: In the space provided at the right, indicate the correct term or command.

1. List three reasons why users access the Internet. ____________

____

____

2. List two of the more popular Web browser software packages. ______________________ ______________________

3. The letters ISP stand for this. ______________________

4. This is a method used to identify locations on the Internet. ______________________

5. This is an "internal Internet" used to share information within an organization. ______________________

6. Click this button on the Standard toolbar to access the Web. ______________________

7. Click this button in the Internet Explorer program window to display the previous page or location. ______________________

8. Click this in a home page to link to another page or location. ______________________

9. List two search engines that can be used to search for specific information on the Internet. ______________________ ______________________

10. A home page on the Web is created using this language. ______________________

11. A home page can be created in Word and then converted to HTML or created with this feature. ______________________

12. Click this button on the Standard toolbar to add a hyperlink to selected text. ______________________

13. Click this button on the Standard toolbar to view the Web page document in the Internet Explorer program window. ______________________

14. Apply background shading to a Web document by clicking Background at this drop-down menu. ______________________

15. This Word feature is used to control the layout of a Web page. ______________________

16. This HTML feature displays text like a marquee of text traveling across the page. ______________________

17. Center a graphic horizontally on a Web page by clicking this button on the Formatting toolbar. ______________________

18. To create a transparent area in a picture, use this Microsoft graphic editor. ______________________

skill assessments

Assessment 1

1. Use the Web Page Wizard to create a Web home page for the Packages Plus Mail Service. Include the following specifications:
   a. At the first Web Page Wizard dialog box, choose *2-Column Layout* in the list box.
   b. At the second Web Page Wizard dialog box, choose *Community* in the list box.
   c. Add the text in figure 8.23.
   d. Select and then delete the text that displays at the bottom of the page.
   e. Save your document with Save As and name it c08sa01, Packages Home Page.html.
   f. Select each of the following carrier companies and create a hyperlink to the Web:

DHL Worldwide Express	*http://www.dhl.com*
Federal Express	*http://www.fedex.com*
United Parcel Service	*http://www.ups.com*
United States Postal Service	*http://www.usps.gov/postofc*

   g. View a home page for one of the carriers, looking for some information that interests you. Print one page of the carrier Web page.
   h. Create a hyperlink for one of the following items: *Search, Download,* or *Feedback*. The hyperlink may consist of a link to an appropriate home page on the Web, a link to a Web page where graphic files may be downloaded, or a link to a simple feedback document you have created. (Or, you may substitute the words, *Search, Download,* and *Feedback*, with clip art images and create graphical hyperlinks.)
2. Save the completed Web home page on your student data disk with the same name, c08sa01, Packages Home Page.html.
3. Print and then attach the page from step 1f.
4. Close c08sa01, Packages Home Page.html, and then exit the Internet.

figure 8.23

Packages Plus Mail Service

Packages Plus Mail Service welcomes you to its Web site home page. We are a mailing center dedicated to helping you with all your mailing needs. We provide a variety of services including one-day and two-day mailing, international services, photocopying (color as well as black and white), sending and receiving fax documents, wrapping fragile packages, and our new desktop publishing service. We also offer mailboxes for our customers who need a mail drop.

We use the following carrier companies for mailing purposes:

DHL Worldwide Express
Federal Express
United Parcel Service
United States Postal Service

Stop by and visit us at 1322 Yuma Street, Phoenix, AZ 85015. You can reach us by telephone at (602) 555-0933 or send us a fax at (602) 555-0941. We look forward to serving your mailing needs.

Assessment 2

1. Assume you are working for a travel vacation company named Paradise Vacations that specializes in selling vacation packages to tropical locations. Your company is setting up a Web page to advertise its travel services. Include the handwritten specifications from figure 8.24 on your Web page. Be sure to create the graphical hyperlinks as shown in figure 8.24. In addition to many graphics and hyperlinks, the background texture and scrolling text may affect the size of this HTML file. If necessary, use alternative text in place of some of the graphics (as discussed in the chapter), eliminate the background texture, or turn off the scrolling text feature to reduce the size of the file before saving the document.
2. Use the *Blank Web Page.dot* template.
3. Create a table as the underlying structure for your Web page. (Figure 8.24 illustrates the Web page with table borders turned on to help you visualize the table structure.)
4. Include the handwritten specifications shown in figure 8.24.
5. Insert the clip art images shown in figure 8.24—located on your student data disk.
6. Save the document as c08sa02, Paradise Home Page.html.
7. View the home page in the Web Page Preview. Click the hyperlinks to the Internet.
8. Print and then close c08sa02, Paradise Home Page.html.

figure 8.24

Tropcsun.wmf — Background - Stationery

BrushScript MT, Blue

Paradise Vacations

Scrolling Text

Fun in the Sun! — Times New Roman

Planes.wmf

[Airplane Schedules](http:www.americanair.com)

key.wmf

[Hotels, Resorts, Condos](http.www.ramada.com/ramada.html)

Ship3.wmf

[Cruises](http:www.1cruise.com)

Fabulous Vacation Destinations! — Times New Roman

BrushScript MT

- ***Caribbean***—Cayman Islands, Virgin Islands
- ***Mexico***—Cancun, Cozumel — Times New Roman
- ***Bahamas*** — Graphic Bullet - Bulleted Tab - third bullet in third row
- ***Florida***—Sanibel Island, Key West
- ***Hawaii***—Maui, Oahu, Kauai

Travel with *Paradise* and Travel with the Best!—Times New Roman

(BrushScript MT, Blue)

- Contact our travel office at: 349 Quincy Drive, Boston, MA 02127 for additional information and travel brochures.
- Call us at: 1-800-555-4671
- E-mail at: http://www.ptravel@aol.com

Assessment 3

1. Create your own personal Web page and include the following specifications: (If you are currently working, assume you are creating your Web page for your company's Intranet.)
   a. Access the Web Page Wizard at the New menu.
   b. At the first Web Page Wizard dialog box, click *Personal Home Page* in the type list box, then click the Next> button.
   c. At the second Web Page Wizard dialog box, choose an appropriate style for your home page, then click Finish.
   d. Key any pertinent data.
   e. Delete any headings or categories that do not pertain to you.
   f. Save your document and name it c08sa03, My Home Page.html.
   g. Create at least two hyperlinks to either another document or to a Web site on the Internet. (The hyperlinks can be graphical or in text.)
   h. If a scanner is available, scan a photo of yourself. If a scanner is not accessible, insert an appropriate clip art image.
   i. Format your text to enhance the Web page—be consistent in the use of fonts and font colors.
   j. Do not overdecorate your Web page!
2. View your Web page at Web Page Preview.
3. Save your document with the same name *c08sa03, My Home Page.html.*
4. Print and then close c08sa03, My Home Page.html.

creative activity

Activity 1

1. Use Word's Office Assistant to learn how to add background sound to a Web page. After reading the information, complete the following steps:
   a. Open c08ex06, FR Home Page.html.
   b. Save the document with Save As and name it c08ca01, FR Home Page.html.
   c. Insert the program CD into your computer CD-ROM drive or consult your instructor as to an alternate location of an audio file.
   d. Access the CD-ROM drive to download an audio file.
   e. Add background sound of your choosing.
   f. Create a hyperlink in your Web page to access the sound file.
2. Save the document again with the same name *c08ca01, FR Home Page.html.*
3. Close c08ca01, FR Home Page.html.

Activity 2

1. Insert a picture (photograph) into a Web page by completing the following steps:
   a. Open c08sa02, Paradise Home Page.html.

b. Save the document with Save As and name it c08ca02, Paradise Home Page.html.
c. Replace *Tropcsun.wmf* with a photograph from Microsoft Clip Gallery (Pictures tab) or from your Word or Office 97 program CD-ROM. Choose an appropriate tropical travel photograph.
2. Save the document again with the same name *c08ca02, Paradise Home Page.html.*
3. Close c08ca02, Paradise Home Page.html.

Activity 3

1. Use Word's Help feature to learn more about Word and the Web by completing the following steps:
   a. Click Help, Contents and Index, and then select the Index tab.
   b. At the Index dialog box, key Getting Results - Word and the Web or Getting Results - Word Web Page.
   c. Select any topics that interest you.
   d. Prepare and give a short presentation to your classmates discussing the information you researched.
   e. If the Getting Results section of the Help feature is not available to you, access the Internet to find out more about the Web by clicking Help, pointing to Microsoft on the Web, then choosing any one of the topics listed. (*Hint:* You may want to spend some time looking at Free Stuff and Best of the Web.)
2. Prepare and give your presentation on the information you learned about in Free Stuff, Best of the Web, etc.

chapter NINE

Creating Presentations Using PowerPoint

PERFORMANCE OBJECTIVE

Upon successful completion of chapter 9, you will be able to create on-screen presentations, overhead transparencies (color or black and white), paper printouts, 35mm slides, notes, handouts, and outlines using PowerPoint's AutoContent Wizard and presentation designs.

Desktop Publishing Concepts

Planning	Balance	White space
Designing	Proportion	Color
Focus	Contrast	Layout and design

Word Features Used

AutoLayout	Notes Page view	Sound
Design Presentations	Slide Show view	Slide master
Slide view	AutoContent Wizard	Animation effects
Outline view	Microsoft Clip Gallery	Build
Slide Sorter view	Slide transitions	

Using PowerPoint to Create a Presentation

If you have access to Microsoft PowerPoint 97, you can continue with chapter 9. Giving a successful presentation, whether using Word or PowerPoint, involves using visual aids to strengthen the impact of the message as well as to organize the presentation. Visual aids can include transparencies, slides, photographs, or an on-screen presentation. Microsoft PowerPoint 97 is a complete presentation graphics program that lets you create on-screen presentations, overhead transparencies (color or black and white), paper printouts, 35mm slides, notes, handouts, and outlines.

The concept of making a presentation and preparing presentation materials has been around for a long time. In the past, presentation materials were designed and created by outside sources, greatly adding to their cost. Today, advances in hardware and software make it possible to create most supporting presentation materials at your desktop, greatly reducing production costs.

In addition to production cost savings, creating your own presentation materials offers other advantages. You maintain total control over designing and producing the materials. Since you can easily make last-minute changes, you can produce a top-quality product right up to the last minute. You have the flexibility of working around your own schedule, not the schedule of others. The only drawback of creating presentation materials on your own, as with other desktop-published documents, is that it takes a great deal of time, practice, effort, and patience.

DTP POINTERS
Creating presentation materials takes time, effort, practice, and patience.

Planning a PowerPoint Presentation

The planning process for a presentation is basically the same as for other documents you have created in this textbook. In the planning stages:

- **Clearly define your purpose**. Do you want to inform? Educate? Sell? Motivate? Persuade? Entertain?
- **Evaluate your audience**. Who will be listening to and watching your presentation? What is the age range? What is their educational level? What knowledge do they have of your topic? What image do you want to project to your audience? And what does your audience expect from your presentation?
- **Decide on content**. Decide on the exact content and organization of your message. Do not try to cover too many topics—this may strain the audience's attention or cause confusion. Identifying the main point of the presentation will help you stay focused and convey a clear message.
- **Determine the medium to be used to convey your message**. Transparencies? Slides/Outlines? Promotional fact sheets? To help decide the type of medium to be used, consider such items as the topic, availability of equipment, the size of the room where the presentation will be made, the number of people who will be attending the presentation, etc.

In this chapter, you will create supporting presentation materials for a company called Ride Safe, Inc. This company promotes and sells a bicycle and in-line skating safety program, along with bicycle helmets and other associated protective outerwear. To view the planning process in a more realistic way, consider the previous items in relation to a Ride Safe presentation.

Purpose: The purpose of a Ride Safe presentation is threefold. The company wants to *educate* audiences on bicycle and in-line skating safety and the importance of wearing protective outerwear to prevent serious injuries. The company wants to *motivate* the audience to take precautionary measures to prevent serious injuries. The company wants to *sell* its program and products.

Audience: Ride Safe presentations are most often made to adult audiences, although the safety program they sell is for children. The audience usually consists of parents, teachers, school administrators, or community program directors. This type of audience is usually well aware that bicycle and in-line skating accidents happen frequently—some serious, some not so serious. The educational levels and backgrounds of the audience members may vary. However, all the parents in the audience are naturally protective of their children and want to feel they are doing their best to protect them from harm.

Content: Content depends greatly on purpose. To achieve their goals, Ride Safe wants to include information about the company history and its goals. Statistics will be included on bicycle-related injuries and deaths. Additional information will be provided on why children have more accidents and why the company's program and protective equipment is the best choice. The company will also include information so individuals can request further information. Samples of the safety curriculum may be included.

Medium: Ride Safe prefers to use overhead transparencies as part of the presentation. Since the company's presentations often take place in schools, an overhead projector is readily available. Also, transparencies work well with their typical audience size of 50 people. Additionally, slides may be produced and then viewed using a slide projector; or an electronic slide presentation may be presented depending on the availability of presentation software, a computer, an overhead projector, and an LCD panel. Handouts, such as an introductory letter, a business card, and a return/reply postcard are also included in the presentation materials.

Selecting a Visual Medium

Selecting a visual medium depends on several factors: the topic, your style, your level of equipment-operating ability, audience size, location of presentation, equipment availability, lighting conditions, etc. Three common visual formats are overhead transparencies, 35mm slides, and electronic slide shows.

DTP POINTERS
Keep the text simple in transparencies and slides.

Transparencies are the most commonly used visual format for both formal and informal presentations. They work well with small- to medium-sized groups. Transparencies are preferred for many reasons. They allow for more interaction between audience and presenter; the lights stay on so the audience is able to take notes; equipment is readily available; overhead projectors are easy to use; additional points can be added or highlighted with a transparency marker; and they are fairly easy and inexpensive to produce. Laser and ink jet printers can print files you create on compatible transparency film. In addition, cardboard frames can be added to transparencies for ease in handling and as visual borders. Another piece of equipment, a transparency maker, can create a transparency from a printed copy of your document.

Thirty-five millimeter (35mm) slides are a popular visual format. Slides maintain high-quality color and can add visual impact to your presentation. Slide presentations work well with medium- to large-sized audiences. In order to produce slides, a special piece of equipment called a film recorder is necessary. This piece of equipment is attached to your computer and films the documents you want converted into slides. The film must then be taken to an outside service to be developed and made into slide images. Slide presentations tend to be more formal. The room needs to be darkened during a slide presentation, making it difficult for the audience to take notes or interact. Making last-minute changes to a slide presentation is difficult—they are more expensive to produce, and the equipment may be more difficult to operate.

Electronic slide shows are gaining popularity due to the array of presentation software on the market. Presentation software features let the user create "slides" for presentations. The slides, containing information and images created by you on the computer, do not have to be developed. The features of the presentation software enable the user to conduct a slide show from the computer screen. The ability to add animation and sound effects to presentations makes electronic slide shows especially attractive and effective. However, to conduct an electronic slide show, you must have a computer available, appropriate presentation software, an overhead projector, and a special computer projecting device called an LCD (liquid crystal display) panel. You also must be comfortable with the operation of the equipment and the software being used.

In addition to careful planning and preparation for your presentation, also consider the actual delivery of the presentation. Are you at ease in front of an audience? Are you fully prepared? Did you practice the presentation? You may want to take time to review a few guidelines for making presentations, as shown in a PowerPoint template named *Presentation Guidelines - Dale Carnegie Training (R).pot.* To access this template, click File, New, then select the Presentation tab. Scroll downward until you see this template icon, then double-click *Presentation Guidelines....* Read the material and apply what you have learned.

Creating Transparencies/Slides

When creating overhead transparencies or slides, consider these guidelines:

Purpose: Ask yourself if the material you want to present clarifies and reinforces the topic being presented.

Typeface: One typeface is fine; use two at the most. Instead of changing typefaces, try varying the type style, such as bold or italics. Legibility is of utmost importance.

Type size: Eighteen points is the minimum. You want everyone in the room to be able to read what you have taken the time to prepare. Choose a thicker font or apply bold to increase the readability of the text.

Headings: Keep titles short if possible; long headings are harder to read. Kern and track if necessary.

Organization: Keep transparencies and slides simple and easy to read. Outline your message to organize ideas and then introduce one main topic or major point per transparency or slide. Each idea or supporting point needs its own line. Limit the number of words per line and the number of lines on a transparency to approximately seven.

DTP POINTERS
Introduce one concept per slide.

Continuity: Be consistent in the design and layout of your transparencies or slides. Repeat specific design elements, such as logo, color, or type of bullets used, in all the transparencies/slides for a particular presentation. Consistent elements help to connect one transparency to the next and contribute to a cohesive presentation.

Color: Use restraint. Color must enhance the message, not detract from it. Color can be used to emphasize important points. Be consistent—if you decide to make a heading black text on a light yellow background, then make all headings black text on a light yellow background. If males are represented by the color green in a chart, then use the same color for males in any other charts. Colors used must look good together. Study pleasing color combinations in brochures, magazines, books, stores, etc.

DTP POINTERS
Be consistent when using color to represent facts in a presentation.

Preparation: Plan and be ready for the unexpected. Will you be providing the audience with handouts? If so, what will they be? How many do you need? What about extras? What would you do if someone forgets the computer, you forget the presentation disk, or the lightbulb goes out in the overhead projector? Be prepared for all logical possibilities.

DTP POINTERS
Audiences appreciate handouts.

Creating a PowerPoint Presentation

PowerPoint provides several methods for creating a presentation. You can use PowerPoint's AutoContent Wizard, which asks you questions and then chooses a presentation layout based on your answers. PowerPoint's presentation designs provide a variety of formatting options for slides. If you want to apply all your own formatting to slides, you can start with a blank presentation screen.

The steps you follow to create a presentation will vary depending on the method you choose. There are, however, basic steps you will complete. These steps are:

1. Load PowerPoint.
2. Create a new presentation using the AutoContent Wizard, Template, or Blank presentation if you want to apply your own formatting. If you were revising a presentation, you would click Open an existing presentation. Click OK.
3. Key the text for each slide, adding additional elements as needed, such as graphic images.
4. Save the presentation.
5. Print the presentation as slides, handouts, notes, or an outline.
6. Run the presentation.
7. Close the presentation.
8. Exit PowerPoint.

Understanding the PowerPoint Window

When PowerPoint has been loaded and you have chosen the specific type of presentation you want to create, you are presented with the PowerPoint window as shown in figure 9.1. What displays in the presentation window will vary depending on what type of presentation you are creating. However, the PowerPoint window contains some consistent elements.

PowerPoint Window

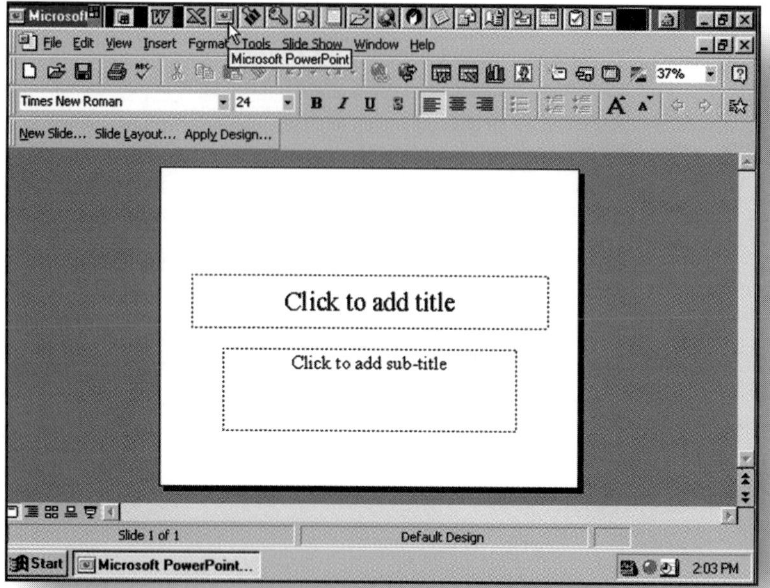

Most of the elements in the PowerPoint window are similar to other Microsoft applications such as Word. The following PowerPoint window elements vary in comparison to the Word window: PowerPoint commands are grouped into options on the Menu bar; the Standard toolbar includes frequently used PowerPoint commands such as inserting a Microsoft Word table, an Excel worksheet, table, or clip art; the vertical scroll box includes a slide indicator that is used to quickly advance through slides; various view buttons display on the horizontal scroll bar; the Drawing toolbar and the Status bar display messages about certain PowerPoint features.

Understanding PowerPoint's Standard and Formatting Toolbars

Many buttons on PowerPoint's Standard toolbar remain consistent with Word and other Microsoft applications, but, as shown in figure 9.2, some buttons differ to represent specific PowerPoint features.

Standard Toolbar

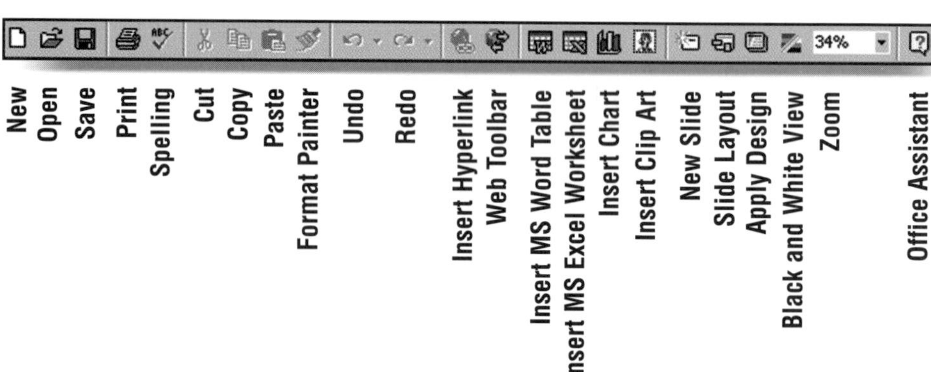

The following buttons on the PowerPoint Standard toolbar differ from other Microsoft applications:

Select this button…	To perform this action:
Insert Hyperlink	Colored and underlined text, that, when clicked, allows you to jump quickly to other documents, objects, or pages on the World Wide Web
Web Toolbar	Allows access to the World Wide Web
Insert Microsoft Word Table	Insert a blank Microsoft Word Table with number of rows and columns you specify
Insert Microsoft Excel Worksheet	Add a blank Microsoft Excel Worksheet to your slide in Slide view
Insert Chart	Embed a chart in a slide using specified data
Insert Clip Art	Insert a clip art image from the Microsoft Clip Gallery
New Slide	Add a new slide to your presentation
Slide Layout	Reapply or change layout of a slide
Apply Design	Apply one of the PowerPoint designs to a presentation
B&W View	Display a presentation in black and white (rather than color)
Zoom	Display the characters on your screen larger or smaller on the screen
Office Assistant	Answers your questions and offers suggestions on more efficient ways to complete a task.

PowerPoint's Formatting toolbar includes a variety of options that are similar to other Microsoft applications, such as changing typeface and size, bold, italics, and underline, as shown in figure 9.3.

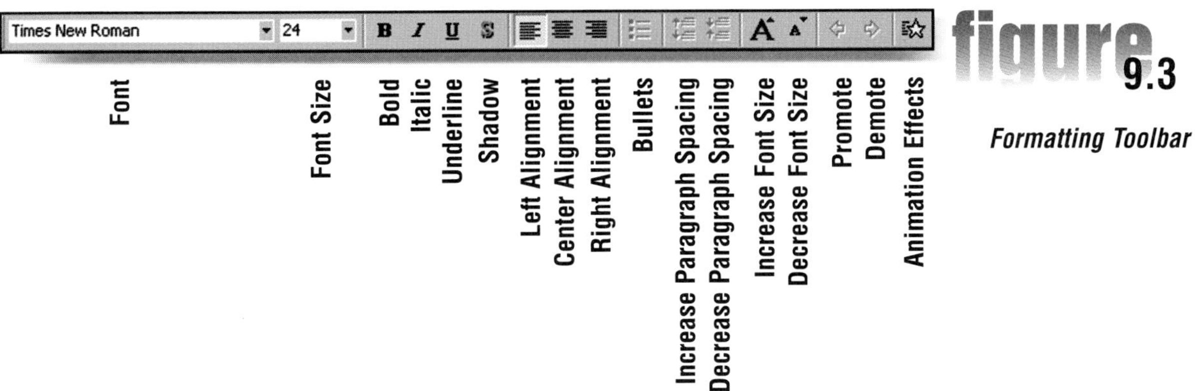

figure 9.3

Formatting Toolbar

The following buttons on the Formatting toolbar activate specific PowerPoint features:

Select this button…	To perform this action:
Text Shadow	Add or remove a shadow to or from selected text
Text Color	Change color of selected text
Increase Paragraph Spacing	Increase spacing between selected paragraphs
Decrease Paragraph Spacing	Decrease spacing between selected paragraphs
Increase Font Size	Increase font size by approximately 4 points

Decrease Font Size	Decrease font size by approximately 4 points
Bullets On/Off	Add or remove bullets to or from selected text
Promote (Indent less)	Move selected text to the previous level (left) in an outline
Demote (Indent more)	Move selected text to the next level (right) in an outline

Viewing a Presentation

PowerPoint provides a variety of viewing options for a presentation. The presentation view can be changed with options from the View drop-down menu or with viewing buttons that display on the View Button Bar located at the left side of the horizontal scroll bar, as shown in figure 9.4.

View Button Bar

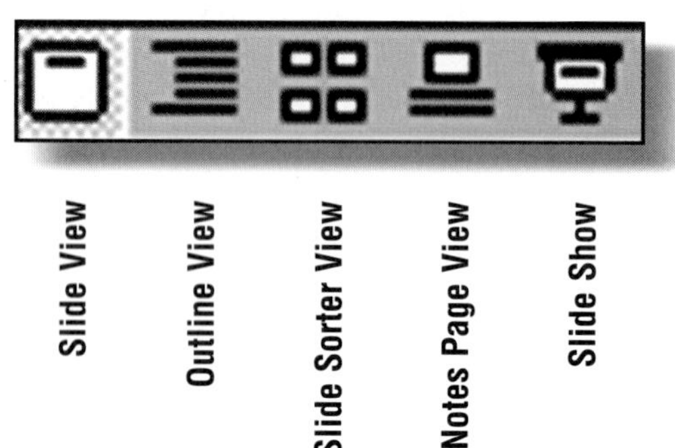

The viewing choices include:

Select this button...	**To perform this action:**
Slide View	Use the Slide view to display individual slides on the screen. This view is useful for determining the effectiveness of individual elements on slides. Editing can also be performed in this view.
Outline View	The Outline view displays the organization of the presentation by headings and subheadings. Editing is probably easiest in Outline view since you simply click in the location you want to edit.
Slide Sorter View	Choosing the Slide Sorter view causes several slides to display on the screen at one time. In this view, you can quickly and easily rearrange the order of slides by moving and dragging slides with the mouse.
Notes Page View	Some presenters provide a hard copy of the information covered in the presentation. With PowerPoint, this can take the form of the slide printed at the top of the page with space available at the bottom of the page for the audience member to write notes. Change to the Notes Page view to see how the slide will display on the page along with the space for taking notes.

Slide Show	Use the Slide Show view to run a presentation. When you choose this view, the slide fills the entire screen.

Previous Slide

Next Slide

In the Slide view and the Notes Page view, change slides by clicking the Previous Slide or Next Slide buttons located at the bottom of the vertical scroll bar. You can also change to a different slide by using the arrow pointer on the scroll box (called the *slide indicator*) on the vertical scroll bar. To do this, position the arrow pointer on the slide indicator, hold down the left mouse button, drag up or down until a box displays with the desired slide number, then release the mouse button.

Slide Indicator
The scroll box in the vertical scroll bar is used to change slides.

The keyboard can also be used to change to a different slide. Press the Page Down key to display the next slide in the presentation or press the Page Up key to display the previous slide in the presentation.

Creating a Presentation Design

When choosing a design for your slides, consider your audience, your topic, and the method of delivery. You wouldn't want to select a design with bright, vibrant colors for an audience of traditionally conservative bankers. Neither would you want to use a design with dark colors or patterns if you plan to photocopy printouts—the colors and patterns may blur.

Understanding the Impact of Color

In addition, studies on the psychology of color suggest that certain colors elicit certain feelings in an audience. For example, red backgrounds in presentations tend to heighten emotions in audiences. The color red evokes feelings of competition, desire, and passion. Red would be an effective color in a sale or marketing presentation. Darker shades of red, such as maroon or burgundy, are better choices for effective business presentations.

Blue backgrounds promote a conservative approach to the information presented and provide a general feeling of calmness. Blue tends to elicit feelings of loyalty and security. Yellow or white text against dark blue or indigo backgrounds are good combinations. Black backgrounds are effective in financial presentations. Black seems to show directness or forcefulness. Green backgrounds project an image of being direct, social, or intelligent. Green acts to stimulate interaction and is a good choice for use in training and educational presentations. Purple or magenta is appropriate in presentations that tend to entertain or represent less conservative or serious topics.

DTP POINTERS
Think about how your audience will respond to the colors in your presentation.

Using a PowerPoint Design Template

To create a presentation using a PowerPoint design, you would complete the following steps:

1. To load PowerPoint, click the Start button on the Windows taskbar, click Programs, then click *Microsoft PowerPoint*.
2. At the PowerPoint dialog box shown in figure 9.5, click Template, then OK.
3. At the New Presentation dialog box shown in figure 9.6, select the Presentation Designs tab.
4. At the New Presentation dialog box with the Presentation Designs tab selected, click the desired design (the design displays in the Preview box

at the right side of the dialog box), then click OK. (The design names include: *Angles, BLUSH, Contemporary, Contemporary Portrait, Dads Tie....)*

5. At the New Slide dialog box shown in figure 9.7, click the desired layout, then click OK. (Click the down-pointing scroll arrow to display twelve additional layouts.)
6. At the slide, key the desired text and/or insert the desired elements.
7. To create another slide, click the New Slide button on the PowerPoint Standard toolbar or click Insert from the Menu bar, then click New Slide. Click the desired AutoLayout, then click OK.
8. When all slides have been completed, save the presentation.

figure 9.5

PowerPoint Dialog Box

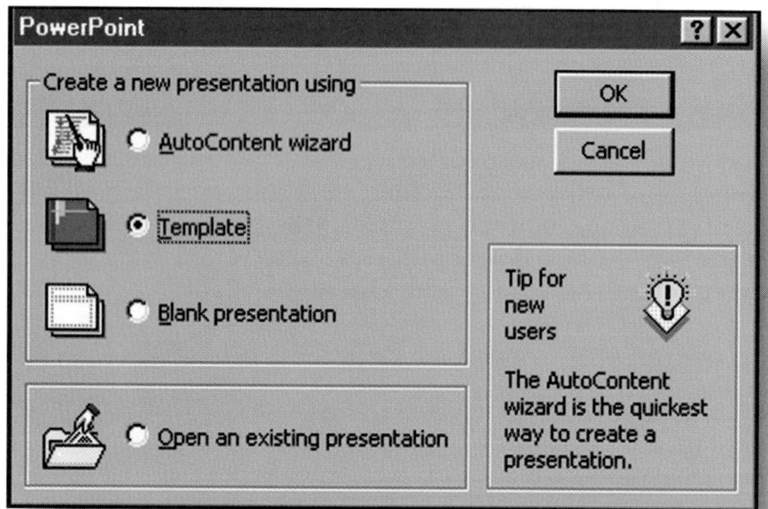

figure 9.6

New Presentation Dialog Box

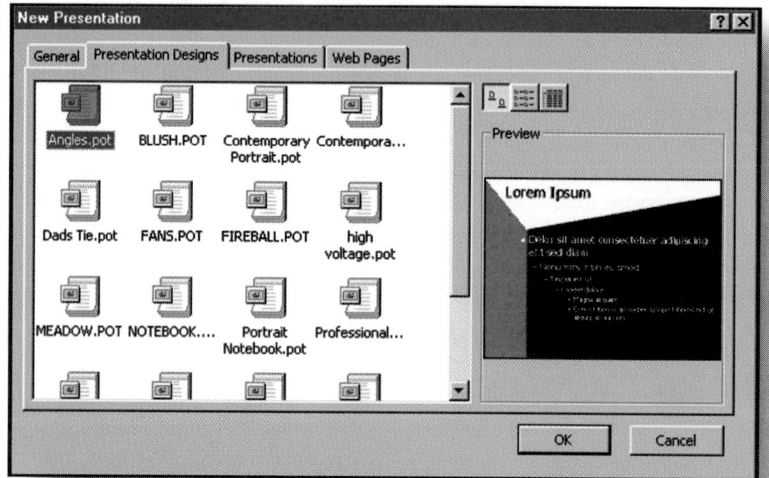

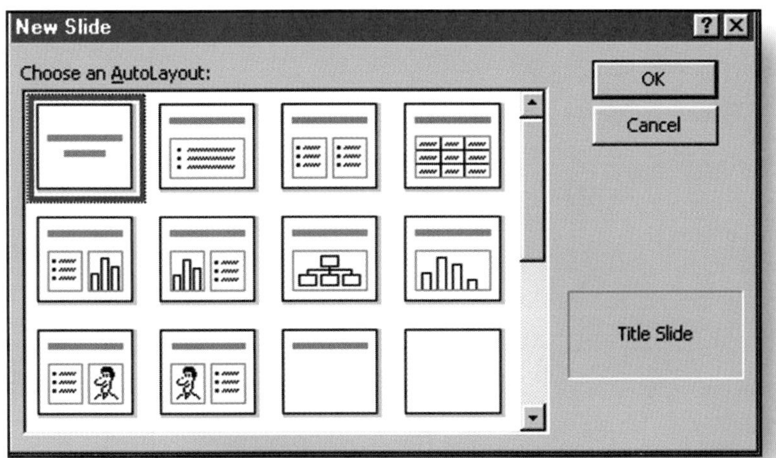

New Slide Dialog Box

Additionally, you can apply a presentation design template from Outline, Slide, or Slide Sorter view by clicking the Apply Design button (fourth button from the right) on the Standard toolbar. You can also access the design templates by clicking Format, clicking Apply Design, clicking the design you want from the Apply Design dialog box, then clicking Apply.

Apply Design

Spell Checking a Presentation

Like Microsoft Word 97, PowerPoint 97 has a feature that will spell check your text automatically as you type. If the word is not in its dictionary, PowerPoint will underscore the word in red. To run the spell checker in PowerPoint, position the insertion point at the beginning of the document, then click the Spelling button (fifth button from the left) on the Standard toolbar; or click Tools, then Spelling from the Menu bar; or press F7.

Spelling

Printing a Presentation

A presentation can be printed in a variety of formats. You can print each slide on a separate piece of paper; print each slide at the top of the page, leaving the bottom of the page for notes; print all or a specific number of slides on a single piece of paper; or print the slide titles and topics in outline form. Use the Print what option at the Print dialog box to specify what you want printed. To display the Print dialog box, shown in figure 9.8, click File, then Print, or press Ctrl + P. At the Print dialog box, click the down arrow at the right side of the Print what text box, then click the desired printing format and click OK.

figure 9.8

Print Dialog Box

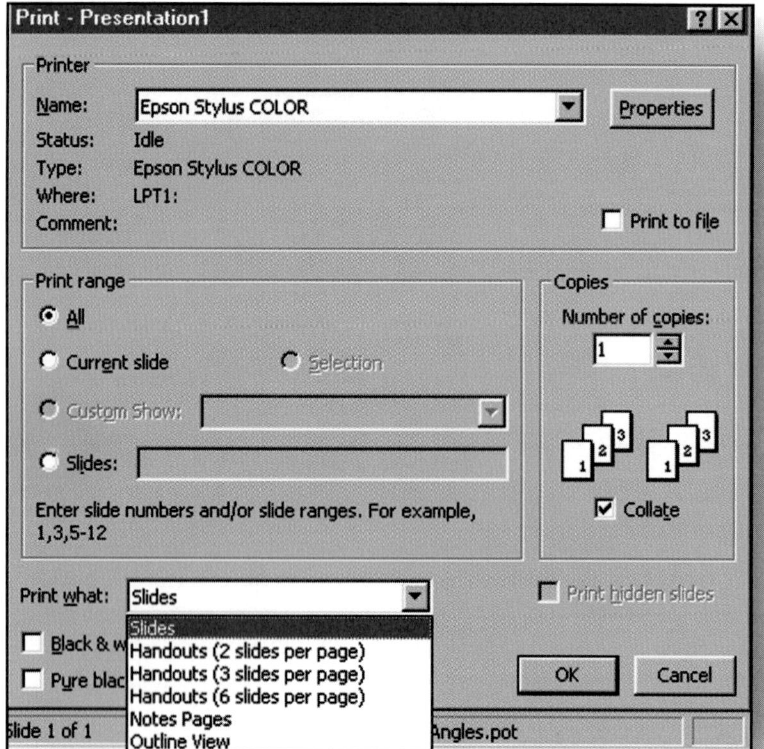

Creating a Presentation Using AutoLayout

When you choose an AutoLayout format, each slide will contain placeholders as shown in the New Slide dialog box in figure 9.7. A placeholder is a location on the slide where information is to be entered. For example, many slides contain a title placeholder. Click in this placeholder and then key the title of the slide. When text is entered into a placeholder, the placeholder turns into a text object.

You can replace an AutoLayout format previously selected for a slide by clicking Format, then Slide Layout. Make a selection from the Slide Layout dialog box, then click the Reapply button.

An AutoLayout format can include some or all of the following placeholders:

- **Title:** Used to hold the title of the slide.
- **Bulleted List:** Used for a bulleted list of related points or topics.
- **2-Column Text**: Bulleted list in two columns.
- **Table:** Used for a table that is inserted from Microsoft Word.
- **Organization Chart:** Used to display an organization chart in a slide.
- **Chart:** Holds a chart, which is a visual representation of data.
- **Clip Art:** Holds a picture in a slide such as a clip art picture.
- **Blank:** Holds an external object such as a picture, text box, movies, and sounds.

exercise 1

Creating and Printing a Presentation

1. Prepare a presentation that promotes membership in the Wheaton Bicycle Club sponsored by Ride Safe, Inc., as shown in figure 9.9, by completing the following steps:
   a. Load PowerPoint by clicking the Start button on the Windows taskbar, pointing to Programs, and then clicking *Microsoft PowerPoint* or click the PowerPoint button on the Microsoft Office Shortcut Bar.
   b. At the PowerPoint dialog box, click Template, then click OK.
   c. At the New Presentation dialog box, select the Presentation Designs tab.
   d. At the New Presentation dialog box with the Presentation Designs tab selected, click the *high voltage.pot* design. Click OK.
   e. At the New Slide dialog box, double-click the first layout in the list box (Title Slide).
   f. At the slide, click the text *Click to add title,* then key **Wheaton Bicycle Club**.
   g. Select *Wheaton Bicycle Club* and then change the font to 60-point (use the Increase Font Size button on the Formatting toolbar).
   h. Click in the text *Click to add sub-title,* then key the following:
      (1) Key **Sponsored by Ride Safe, Inc.**
      (2) Press Enter, then key **Presented by:**.
      (3) Press Enter, then key Your Name.
      (4) Select *Sponsored by Ride Safe, Inc.* and then change the font to 36-point Times New Roman Bold with Text Shadow. (Click the Increase Font Size button and the Bold button on the Formatting toolbar. The Text Shadow option is already active.)
      (5) Select *Presented by:* and then change the font to 28-point Times New Roman with Text Shadow (click the Decrease Font Size button on the Formatting toolbar).
      (6) Select *Your Name* and then change the font to 32-point Times New Roman Bold Italic with Text Shadow.
   i. Create a second slide by completing the following steps:
      (1) Click the New Slide button (sixth button from the right) on the PowerPoint Standard toolbar.
      (2) At the New Slide dialog box, double-click the second layout (Bulleted List) in the list box. (This inserts another slide on the screen.)
      (3) Key the following text inside the placeholders in the second slide:

Title	=	**Our Goal is Healthy Fun!**
Bullets	=	**Good friends**
		Healthy exercise
		Great biking and social events

      (4) Select *Our Goal is Healthy Fun!* and then change the font size to 50-point Impact. Select all the bulleted text, and then change the font to 36-point Times New Roman Bold with Text Shadow.
   j. Create the remaining four slides by completing steps similar to steps i(1) through i(4). Key the text in each slide from the text shown in figure 9.9.
2. Click the Spelling button (fifth button from the left) on the Standard toolbar to spell check your slides.
3. Save the presentation and name it c09ex01, Bicycle Club.ppt.

4. View the presentation at various view screens by completing the following steps:
   a. To move the insertion point to the first slide, press Ctrl + Home, click the Previous Slide button, or click and drag the slide indicator until the first slide displays.
   b. Click View, then Outline or click the Outline View button on the View Button Bar.
   c. Click View, then Slide Sorter or click the Slide Sorter button on the View Button Bar.
   d. Click View, then Zoom. At the Zoom dialog box, change the setting to 100%. Click OK or press Enter.
   e. Click View, then Zoom and change the setting back to 66%. Click OK or press Enter.
   f. Click View, then Notes Page or click the Notes Page View button on the View Button Bar.
   g. Click View, then Slide or click the Slide View button on the View Button Bar.
   h. Click View, then Black and White or click the Black and White View button on the Standard toolbar.
   i. Click the Black and White button to deselect it and return the slides to color.
5. Print all six slides on the same page by completing the following steps:
   a. Click File, then Print.
   b. At the Print dialog box, click the down arrow to the right of the Print what option, then click *Handouts (6 slides per page)* from the drop-down menu.
   c. Click OK.
6. Close c09ex01, Bicycle Club.ppt by clicking File, then Close.

figure 9.9

Wheaton Bicycle Club Presentation

Wheaton Bicycle Club

Sponsored by Ride Safe, Inc.

Presented by:

Your Name

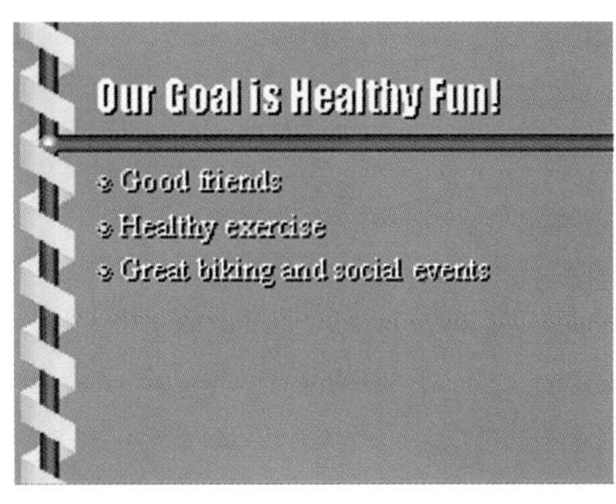

Our Goal is Healthy Fun!
Good friends
Healthy exercise
Great biking and social events

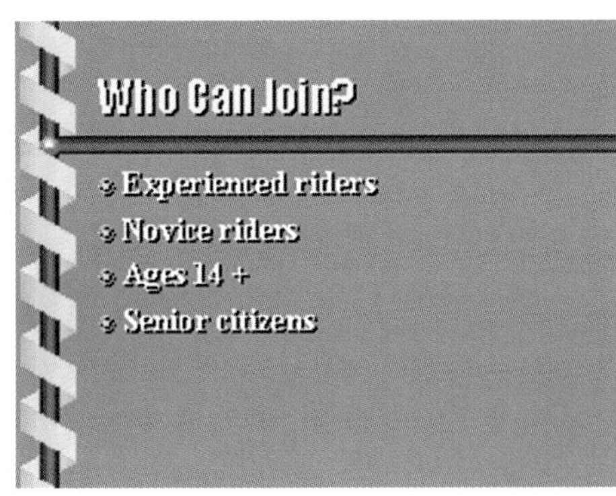

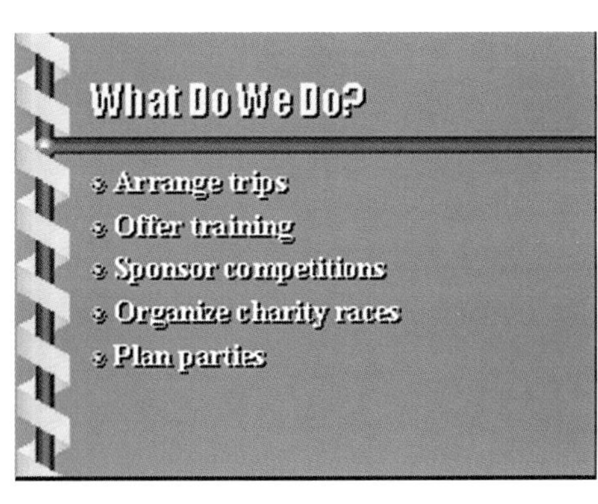

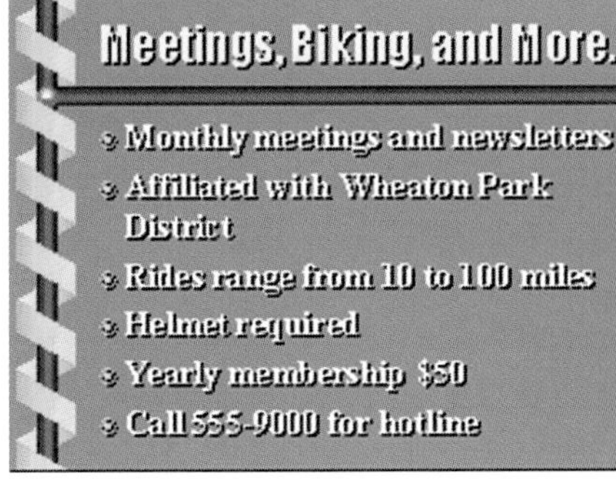

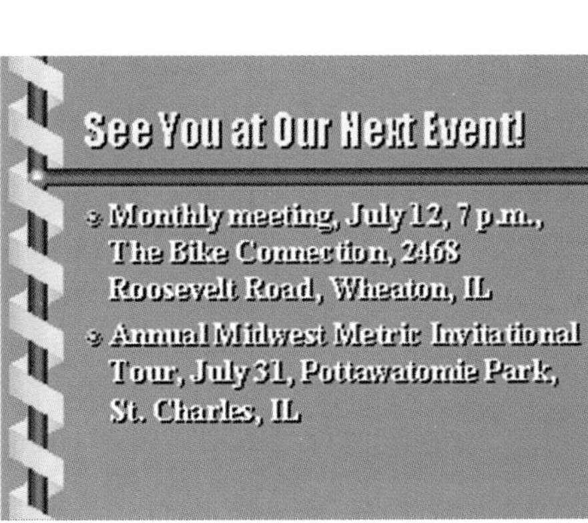

Preparing a Presentation in Outline View

In exercise 1, you created a short slide presentation using a PowerPoint design template in which you inserted a small amount of text on each slide. If you are creating a longer presentation with more slides and text, consider using the Outline view to help organize the topics for the slides without the distractions of colorful designs, clip art, transition effects, or sound.

In the Outline View, the Outlining toolbar displays at the left side of the screen. This toolbar contains the Promote and Demote buttons mentioned in the previous paragraphs along with other buttons, as shown in figure 9.10. A miniature sample of your slide with the design is shown on the right side of the screen.

Outlining Toolbar

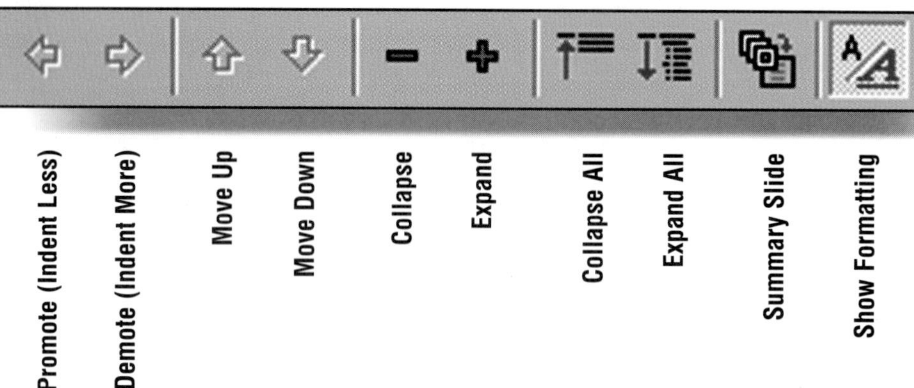

To prepare a presentation in Outline view, you would complete the following steps:

1. Start the PowerPoint program.
2. At the PowerPoint dialog box, click Template.
3. At the New Presentation dialog box, select the Presentation Designs tab, click a specific design, then click OK.
4. At the New Slide dialog box, click an AutoLayout format, then click OK.
5. With the blank slide displayed on the screen, click the Outline View button on the View Button Bar.
6. Key the title of the first slide, then press Enter.
7. Click the Demote (Indent more) button on the Outlining toolbar or press the Tab key to move to the next tab stop, then key the first heading.
8. Continue keying the text for each slide in the presentation. Click the Demote (Indent more) button on the Outlining toolbar or press Tab to move the insertion point to the next tab stop (and automatically change the text formatting), or click the Promote (Indent less) button on the Outlining toolbar or press Shift + Tab to move the insertion point to the previous tab stop. Continue in this manner until all text is entered for the presentation.
9. When the presentation is completed, save it in the normal manner.

Demote

When keying text for a presentation in the Outline View mode, click the Demote (Indent more) button on the Outlining toolbar or press the Tab key to move the insertion point to the next tab stop. This moves the insertion point and also changes the formatting. The formatting will vary depending on the

AutoLayout format you chose at the New Slide dialog box. For many AutoLayout formats, a slide title is set in 44-point Times New Roman Bold. Text keyed at the first tab stop will be set in a smaller point size, such as 32-point Times New Roman.

To move the insertion point to a previous tab stop, click the Promote (Indent less) button on the Outlining toolbar or press Shift + Tab. This moves the insertion point and also changes text formatting. Moving the insertion point back to the left margin will begin another slide. These slides are numbered at the left side of the screen and are preceded by a slide icon.

Promote

Editing Slides

Slides within a PowerPoint presentation can be edited. Text within individual slides can be inserted or deleted, slides can be deleted from the presentation, slides can be inserted into an existing presentation, and slides can be rearranged. Slides can be edited in several views—use the view that makes editing the easiest. For example, rearrange the order of slides in the Slide Sorter view; delete or insert text within slides in the Outline view or the Slide view.

Inserting and Deleting Slides

An entire slide can be deleted from a presentation at the Slide Sorter or Outline views. To delete a slide from a presentation, display the presentation in Slide Sorter view, click the slide you want to delete, then press the Delete key or click Edit, Delete Slide. A slide can also be deleted in Outline view. To do this, change to the Outline view, position the arrow pointer on the slide icon located next to the slide text you want to delete until the arrow pointer turns into a four-headed arrow, then click the left mouse button to select all of the text for the slide. With the text for the slide selected, press the Delete key.

A new slide can be inserted into an existing presentation at the Slide Sorter or Outline view. To add a slide to a presentation in the Slide Sorter view, you would follow these basic steps:

1. Open the presentation to which you want the slide added.
2. Change to the Slide Sorter view.
3. Click to the left of the slide that will immediately precede the new slide. (For example, if you want the new slide to immediately follow slide 3, then click to the left of slide 3.)
4. Click the New Slide button that displays on the Standard toolbar; or click Insert, then New Slide.
5. At the New Slide dialog box, double-click the desired AutoLayout format.
6. At the Slide Sorter view, double-click the new blank slide. (This changes the presentation to the Slide View with only the new slide displayed in the Presentation window.)
7. Add the desired text to the new slide.
8. Save the presentation again.

To insert slides in Outline view, position the insertion point to the left of the text of the slide that will immediately precede the new slide. Click the New Slide button, then double-click an AutoLayout.

Rearranging Slides

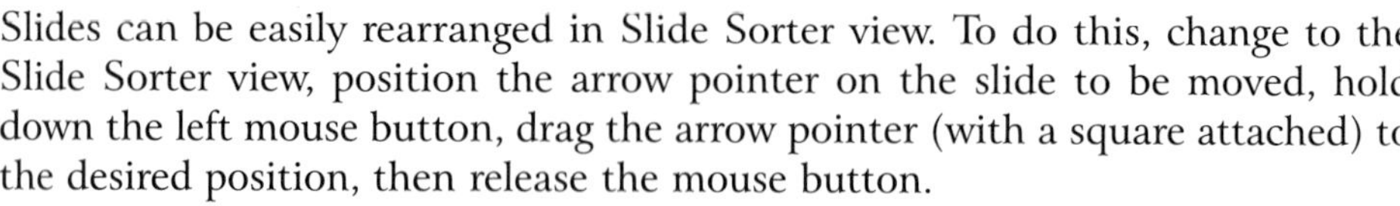

Slides can be easily rearranged in Slide Sorter view. To do this, change to the Slide Sorter view, position the arrow pointer on the slide to be moved, hold down the left mouse button, drag the arrow pointer (with a square attached) to the desired position, then release the mouse button.

Collapse

Expand

Move Down

Move Up

To move a slide created in Outline view, collapse the outline first. To collapse an outline, eliminate or hide all the details or levels of a slide. Click the Collapse button (fifth button from the top) on the Outlining toolbar, and only the title of each slide will display. To expand the outline, click the Expand button (sixth button from the top) on the Outlining toolbar and the titles and all bulleted points of the selected slide will display. A gray line below the text represents the rest of the text. Click anywhere in the title of the slide you want to move. Click the Move Down button to move the slide down or click the Move Up button to move the slide up. Each time you click the Move Up or Move Down button, the selected slide moves up or down one line at a time. Another way to move a slide in Outline view is to collapse the outline, click the icon of the slide you want to move, drag the slide icon to the desired location (note that a black line appears at the slide's new position), and then release the mouse button.

In the following exercise you will create a presentation in outline view, delete slides, insert slides, and rearrange slides.

Preparing a Presentation in Outline View then Rearranging Slides

1. Create a presentation in Outline view by completing the following steps: (If you have already entered PowerPoint, complete the steps listed under step a. If you have not yet entered PowerPoint, follow the steps listed under step b.)
   a. If you are already in PowerPoint, complete the following steps:
      (1) Click File, then New.
      (2) At the New Presentation dialog box, select the Presentations tab.
      (3) Double-click *Company Meeting (Standard).pot* at the list box.
   b. If you have not yet entered PowerPoint, complete the following steps:
      (1) Load PowerPoint.
      (2) At the PowerPoint dialog box, click Template, then click OK.
      (3) At the New Presentation dialog box, select the Presentations tab.
      (4) At the New Presentation dialog box with the Presentations tab selected, double-click *Company Meeting (Standard).pot* at the list box.
   c. With the first slide displayed, click the Outline View button on the View Button Bar.
   d. At the Outline screen, create the outline shown in figure 9.11 by completing the following steps:
      (1) With the "Company Meeting Title" highlighted, key **Changes in the Role of Office Support Personnel** in the first slide title shown in figure 9.11, then double-click the word "Presenter" to highlight it and key Your Name, **Presenter**.
      (2) Double-click the word "Agenda" and key the second slide title shown in figure 9.11, **Office Environment**, then press Enter.

(3) Click the Demote (Indent more) button on the Outlining toolbar or press the Tab key. Key the text after the first bullet in figure 9.11 that begins with **Job Titles/Responsibilities,** then press Enter.

(4) Key **Time, Task and Stress Management,** then press Enter.

(5) Key **Organizational Structure**, then press Enter.

(6) Click the Demote (Indent more) button on the Outlining toolbar or press the Tab key, then key the text after the hyphen bullet (-), **Use PowerPoint 97 to show an Organization**.

e. Delete slides 3 through 13. To do this, click on each slide icon and press the Delete key. (Alternatively, you can select each slide icon while holding down the Shift key, then press Delete to delete all of the slides at once.)

f. Press the Enter key and then click the Promote button on the Outlining toolbar twice or press Shift + Tab twice. This will add a new slide. Key the text for slides 3 and 4 shown in figure 9.11.

g. Rearrange some of the slides in the presentation by completing the following steps:

(1) Change to Slide Sorter view.

(2) Move slide 4 (**Travel Planning**) before slide 3 (**Conference Planning**). To do this, position the arrow pointer on slide 4, hold down the left mouse button, drag the arrow pointer (with a square attached) between slides 2 and 3, then release the mouse button. (A vertical line will display between the two slides.)

(3) Move and copy text within and between slides by completing the following steps:

(a) With the slides still displayed in Slide Sorter view, click slide 4 to select it.

(b) Click the Slide View button on the View Button Bar or double-click slide 4. (This displays only slide 4 in the Presentation window.)

(4) In slide 4, move the first bulleted item **Multinational Meetings** to the end of the list by completing the following steps:

(a) Position the I-beam pointer on any text in the bulleted items, then click the left mouse button. (This selects the object box containing the bulleted text.)

(b) Drag the insertion point through the first item to select the entire line.

(c) Position the insertion point on the selected text. Hold down the left mouse button, drag the arrow pointer (turns into an arrow with a dashed box below it and a thin horizontal line to the right of it) to the end of the last line of text in the list, then release the mouse button.

(d) Deselect the text, then position the insertion point in front of *Multinational*, and then press Enter.

(e) Press Shift + Tab. (Multinational Meetings should display with a small yellow bullet.)

2. Save the presentation with File, Save As and name it c09ex02, Office Support.ppt. (PowerPoint will automatically insert the *.ppt* extension.)

3. Print the outline by displaying the Print dialog box, then changing the Print what option to *Outline View*.

4. Close c09ex02, Office Support.ppt

Changes in the Role of Office Support Personnel before Moving Slides

1 Changes in the Role of Office Support Personnel
Your Name, Presenter

2 Office Environment
- Job Titles/Responsibilities
- Time, Task and Stress Management
- Organizational Structure
  - Use PowerPoint 97 to show an Organization

3 Conference Planning
- Multinational Meetings
- Committee Meetings
  - Use PowerPoint 97 for an Agenda
- Conference or Convention Arrangements
  - Use MS Word 97 for professional-looking documents, MS Excel 97 for tracking participants, MS Access 97 for queries

4 Travel Planning
- Travel Arrangements
  - Air travel, rental car, hotel/motel reservations
  - Possible Internet addresses:
    - http://www. expedia.com/daily/toc/default.htm
    - http://www.thetrip.com/
    - http://www.biztravel.comN4/newhome.cfm
    - http://www.travelocity.com/
- International Travel

Installing Graphic Filters

In the upcoming exercises, you may be instructed to insert graphics located on your student data disk, in Microsoft Clip Gallery, or on the program CD-ROM. These graphics may have file formats other than the Windows Metafile (.wmf) format, which you may be accustomed to using. Some of the graphic files used are saved in the Computer Graphics Metafile (.cgm) format. If you installed Word or Office 97 using a Custom Installation and included the graphic filters, you should be able to insert these files. (The Computer Graphics Metafile [cgm] graphic filter is not available with a Typical Installation.)

To make sure that you installed the necessary graphics filter, click Insert, then point to Picture, and then check the list of filters in the *Files of type* list box. If the filter you need is not listed, run Setup again, and install the filters you need. See the Preface for additional information on graphic filters.

You can substitute any of the (.cgm), (.bmp), or any other graphic files in the chapter exercises with other appropriate graphics. Remember to consider your audience and the subject of your document in choosing appropriate graphics to enhance your documents.

Adding Clip Art to a Slide

To enhance the visual impact of slides in a presentation, consider adding a Microsoft clip art image. Microsoft's clip art images cover a wide range of topics. A clip art image can be inserted into a slide in many different ways. One way is to use a slide layout that contains a clip art placeholder. A clip art placeholder displays in a presentation layout at the New Slide dialog box as a cartoon picture of a man. To insert an image in a clip art placeholder, display the desired layout, then double-click the clip art placeholder. This displays the Microsoft Clip Gallery dialog box as shown in figure 9.12. At this dialog box, click the Clip Art tab, click the desired category, such as Business or People, then double-click a desired image in the list box.

figure 9.12

Microsoft Clip Gallery Dialog Box

A clip art image can also be inserted in a slide that does not contain a clip art placeholder. To do this, select the location in the slide where you want the clip art image inserted, then click the Insert Clip Art button on the Standard toolbar (seventh button from the right). Alternatively, you can click Insert, Picture, then Clip Art. This displays the Microsoft Clip Gallery dialog box where you can choose the desired category and image.

Insert Clip Art

To insert graphic files from your student data disk into your PowerPoint slides, click once in the AutoLayout placeholder containing the clip art icon, then click Insert, Picture, From File from the PowerPoint menu bar. You will need to size the image to fit the placeholder area. Size the image by holding down the Ctrl key as you drag a corner sizing handle inward to reduce the size and outward to increase the size proportionately. A graphic file from your student data disk can also be inserted without selecting a specific AutoLayout with a clip art placeholder. Decide where you want an image to display in your slide, then click Insert, Picture, then From File. Once the image is inserted into your slide, select the graphic image, then size and move it if necessary. It is recommended, however, to add the graphic files from your student data disk to Microsoft Clip Gallery for ease in retrieving and handling these images.

Adding a Graphic Image to the Clip Gallery

If you frequently use a company logo or scanned image in slides, you may want to add these files to the Clip Gallery. To add other images to the Clip Gallery, complete the following steps:

1. Click the Insert Clip Art button (button with the cartoon man on it).
2. At the Microsoft Clip Gallery dialog box, click the Clip Art tab. Click Import Clips....
3. At the Add clip art to Clip Gallery dialog box, change the Look in: to the drive where the file is located. Key the File name: and click Open.
4. Locate the file containing the image you want to add to the Clip Gallery, then click Open.
5. Select a category from the list in the Picture Properties dialog box. Key an optional description. (You can choose one or more categories for a picture, or you can choose to not categorize a picture at all.) Click OK.
6. At the Microsoft Clip Gallery dialog box, click Insert or Close depending on your desired action.

Inserting and Manipulating Graphics in PowerPoint Slides

Cropping an Image

Cropping
The process of trimming vertical and horizontal edges off a picture.

Once an image has been inserted, you can crop, scale, move, copy, or recolor it as you wish. *Cropping* is the process of trimming vertical and/or horizontal edges of a picture. Once an image has been cropped in PowerPoint, it can always be uncropped by using the same command. Photos are often cropped to focus attention on a particular area. To crop an image on a slide, complete the following steps:

1. Make sure the slide is in Slide view.
2. Select the picture you want to crop.
3. Position the arrow pointer on a toolbar and right-click. Left-click on *Picture* to turn on the Picture toolbar shown in figure 9.13.
4. Click Crop on the Picture toolbar.
5. Position the cropping tool over a sizing handle and drag.
6. When you are satisfied with the image, release the mouse button, then press Esc or click outside the selected area to turn off cropping. Close the Picture toolbar.

Picture Toolbar

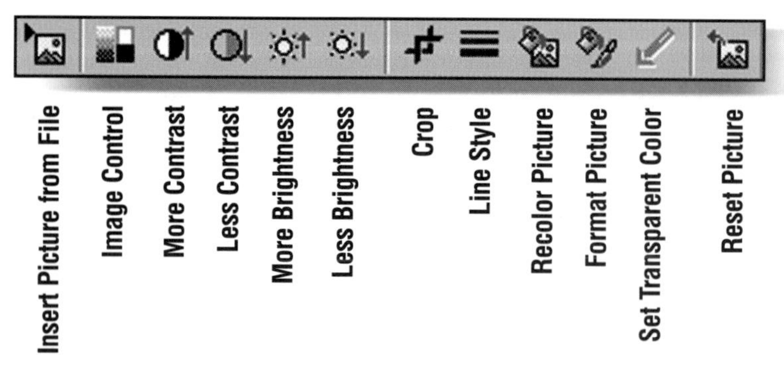

Scaling (Resizing) an Image

To change the size of an image without changing its proportions, hold down the Ctrl key as you drag a corner handle. You can also proportionally scale an image by selecting the image, then clicking Format, Picture, Size tab. Make the desired changes and then click OK.

Moving an Image

To move an image, select it, click anywhere within the image, then drag it to a new location. The image will keep its original dimensions. You can also use the Cut and Paste buttons on the Standard toolbar or click Edit, then Cut, position the insertion point where you want the image to appear, then click Edit, Paste.

In addition, you can move an image in very small increments in Slide or Notes Page view by selecting the image and then pressing an arrow key.

Copying an Image

You can duplicate an image to another slide by completing the following steps:

1. In Slide view, select the image you want to copy.
2. Click Edit, then Copy or click the Copy button on the Standard toolbar.
3. Change to Slide Sorter view, then double-click the slide to which you want to add the image.
4. Click Edit, then Paste or click the Paste button on the Standard toolbar.

Additionally, you can use the Drag-and-Drop option to duplicate an image by completing the following steps:

1. Click Tools, then Options.
2. At the Options dialog box, select the Edit tab, then click the Drag-and-Drop text editing check box to turn this feature on.
3. Select the image, hold down the Ctrl key, and drag the copy to its new location.

Recoloring an Image

To recolor an image, complete the following steps:

1. In Slide view, select the image you want to recolor.
2. Click Format, Picture, Picture tab, then Recolor; or click the right mouse button to access a shortcut menu, click Format Picture, Picture tab, Recolor.
3. At the Recolor Picture dialog box shown in figure 9.14, select the color in the Original column that you would like to change, then click the down arrow in the New column and select a new color.
4. Click Preview to see the color changes.
5. When you are satisfied with the results, click OK.

figure 9.14

Recolor Picture Dialog Box

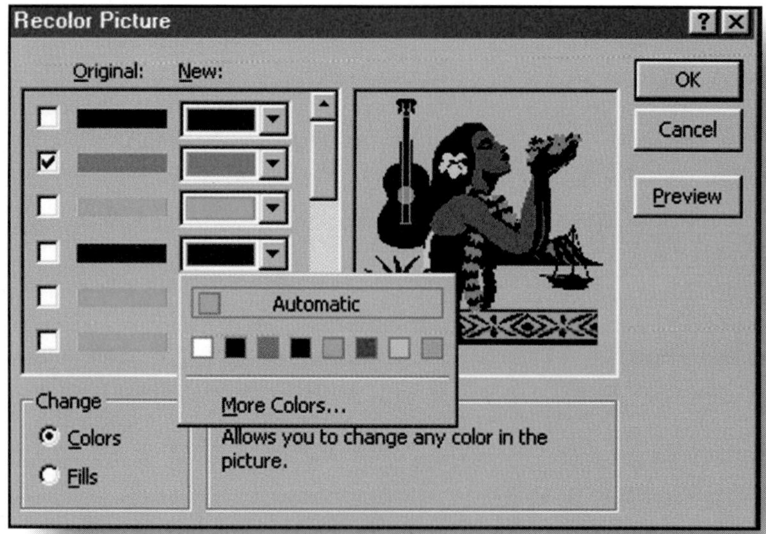

Changing Slide Color Schemes and Backgrounds

The slide color schemes can be changed by completing the following steps:

1. In Slide View, click Format, Slide Color Scheme. There are three choices under the Standard tab. You may also click the Custom tab and make scheme color changes.
2. Click Apply or Apply to All.

To change the backgrounds of the slides, complete the following steps:

1. In Slide View, click Format, Background.
2. In the Background Fill box, click the down arrow, then click Fill Effects....
3. Click the Gradient tab, Two colors radio button.
4. Click the From Title. This makes a nice design.
5. You can also make changes with the Texture and Pattern tabs.

In exercise 3 you will open an existing presentation and add graphic images to enhance the presentation. Although inserting an image in each slide is not necessary, several graphics are added in exercise 3 to demonstrate various techniques in inserting and changing graphics. Too many graphics in a presentation can distract from the message of the presentation.

Steps are given in exercise 3 to insert graphic images from your student data disk. However, you may have added these images to the Microsoft Clip Gallery as discussed earlier. In that case, disregard these steps and insert the images by double-clicking the cartoon man icon in the placeholder to access Microsoft Clip Gallery, then double-clicking the desired image.

exercise 3

Inserting Graphic Images into a Presentation

1. Enhance a presentation with clip art images as shown in figure 9.15 by completing the following steps:
   a. Open *Basic Five Reasons.ppt* from your student data disk by completing the following steps:
      (1) If you are already in PowerPoint, click File, then Open. If you have not yet entered PowerPoint, load PowerPoint, then click Open an Existing Presentation.
      (2) At the Open dialog box, make sure the drive or folder where your student data disk is located displays in the Look in: text box.
      (3) Make sure Presentations and Shows displays in the Files of type: text box.
      (4) Select *Basic Five Reasons* from the File name: list box.
      (5) Click Open.
   b. Save the presentation with File, Save As and name it c09ex03, Five Reasons.ppt. (PowerPoint will automatically insert the *.ppt* extension.)
2. At the first slide, select *Your Name* and key your own name as the presenter. Click the Next Slide button at the bottom of the vertical scroll bar to advance to the second slide.
3. Insert a clip art image into the second slide by completing the following: (Many of the clip art images are found on the program CD-ROM.)
   a. Double-click the cartoon man icon located in the right section of the placeholder.
   b. At the Microsoft Clip Gallery, select *Science and Medicine* from the list displayed in the Clip Art tab of the dialog box. (Click *All Categories* if Science and Medicine is not available.)
   c. Continue clicking the down arrow to the right of the Clip Art list box until a black and white picture of a medical staff displays. Click the Magnify check box and you will see the name of the clip art. Double-click *medstaff.wmf.*
   d. Click outside the image to deselect it.
   e. Click the Next Slide button.
4. Insert a clip art image from your student data disk into the third slide by completing the following steps:
   a. Click once on the cartoon man icon located in the left section of the placeholder in the third slide. Eight sizing handles should display around the placeholder.
   b. Click Insert, point to Picture, then click From File.
   c. Make sure the drive or folder where your student data disk is located displays in the Look in: text box.
   d. From the list box, double-click *certifct.cgm.* (This graphic can also be found on the program CD-ROM as certifct.wmf.)
   e. If the CGM Graphic Import dialog box displays, click OK or press Enter. (The size of the graphic may be too large for the placeholder frame.)
   f. You may need to drag the image into the placeholder frame. Size the image by holding down the Ctrl key and dragging one of the corner handles inward to reduce the image to the approximate size of the placeholder frame. Deselect the image.
   g. Click the Next Slide button.
5. Insert a graphic image into the fourth slide by completing the following steps:
   a. Double-click the cartoon man icon located in the right section of the placeholder.
   b. At the Microsoft Clip Gallery, select *Currency* from the list displayed in the Categories section of the dialog box. (Click *All Categories* if Currency is not available.)

c. At the Clip Art list box, double-click the clip art image of a green bag of money with a dollar symbol in the center of the bag. The description of the graphic is *Reward Accounting*.
d. With the clip art selected, right-click your mouse to access the shortcut menu.
e. Click *Format Picture* from the shortcut menu, select the Picture tab, and then click the Recolor... button.
f. At the Recolor Picture dialog box, click the down arrow to the right of the dark green bar in the New section, then from the drop-down list that displays, select *More Colors*. Click the bright yellow color on the color palette. Click OK. (A check mark will display in the check box to the left of the dark green box in the Original section.)
g. Click the down arrow to the right of the bright green bar and from the color palette that displays, select *More Colors*. Click the purple color.
h. Click OK or press Enter. Click OK at the Format Picture dialog box.
i. Deselect the image.
j. Click the Next Slide button.

6. Add a clip art image to the fifth slide by completing the following steps:
   a. Click once on the cartoon man icon located in the left section of the placeholder in the fifth slide.
   b. Click Insert, point to Picture, then click From File.
   c. Make sure the drive or folder where your student data disk is located displays in the Look in: text box.
   d. Double-click *mntbike2.cgm* in the list box. (The image will take up most of the placeholder area.) If you are unable to insert this image, substitute images can be found in Microsoft Clip Gallery in the Sports and Leisure folder or on the program CD-ROM.)
   e. Drag the image into the placeholder frame. (Resize if necessary by dragging a corner sizing handle.)
   f. Crop the image as shown in figure 9.15 by completing the following steps:
      (1) With the clip art selected, display the Drawing toolbar—right-click your mouse while positioned in a toolbar. Also, display the Picture toolbar.
      (2) Click Crop from the Picture toolbar. (The arrow pointer will display as a cropping tool.)
      (3) Position the cropping tool on the lower-middle sizing handle and drag the tool upward to eliminate the lower half of the image.
      (4) Position the cropping tool on the left-middle sizing handle and drag the tool to the right to eliminate part of the left side of the image.
      (5) Position the cropping tool on the right-middle sizing handle and drag the tool to the left and release the mouse near the cyclist's face.
      (6) Click on the Crop tool to turn it off. Close the Picture toolbar.
   g. Increase the size of the image by dragging one of the corner handles outward to the approximate size of the placeholder frame as shown in figure 9.15. (The placeholder frame may not display at this point.)
   h. Deselect the image.
7. Spell check the presentation.
8. Save the presentation again with the same name, c09ex03, Five Reasons.ppt.
9. Print all six slides on the same page.
10. Close c09ex03, Five Reasons.ppt.

figure 9.15

Five Reasons Presentation

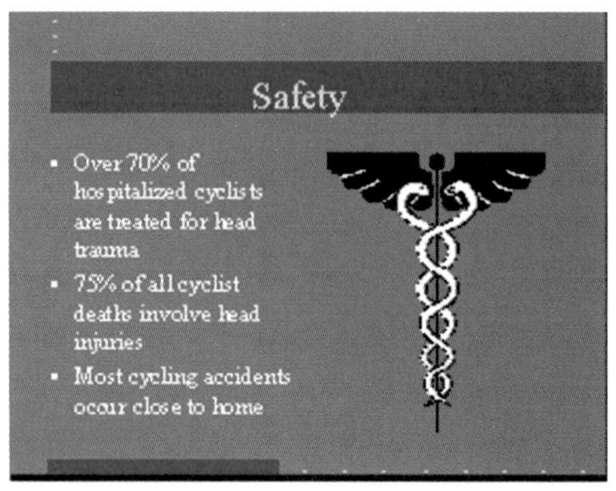

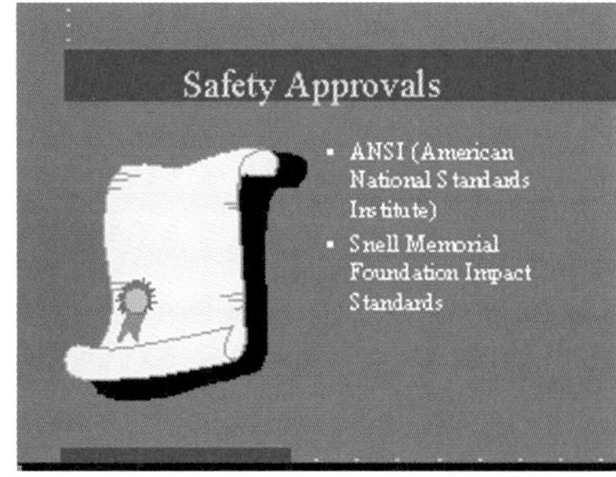

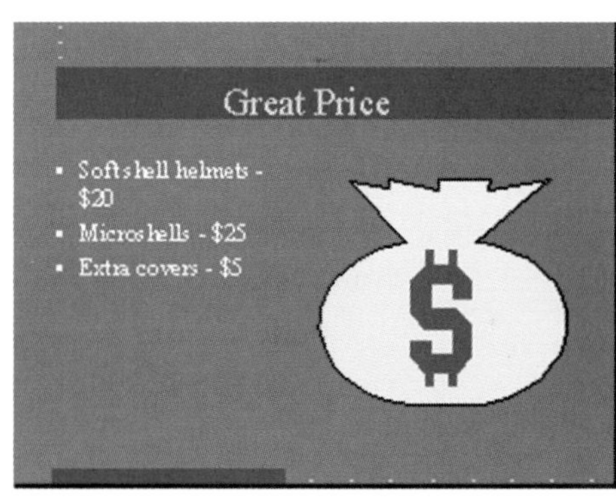

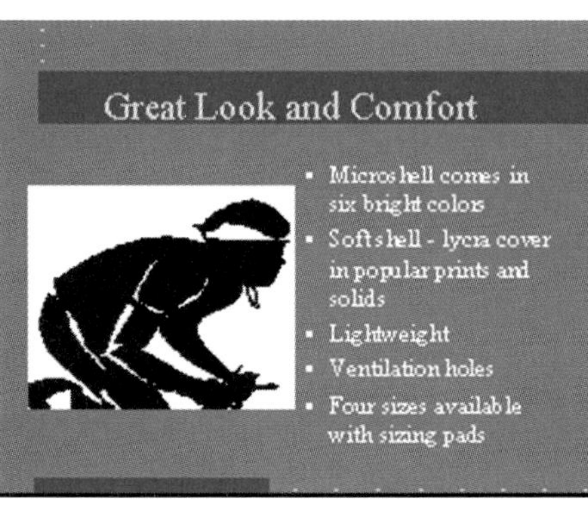

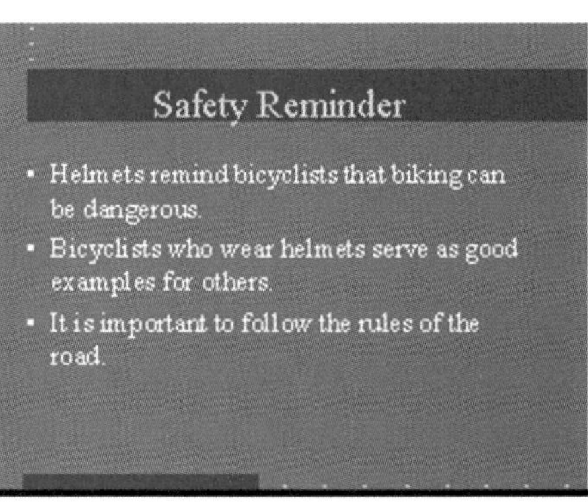

Planning a Presentation with the AutoContent Wizard

DTP POINTERS
Use five to seven words per line on a slide.

DTP POINTERS
Use five to seven lines per slide.

PowerPoint contains an AutoContent Wizard that will help you in the planning and organizing of a presentation. You respond to certain questions from the wizard and, based on your responses you are presented with slides containing information on what to include in your presentation and how to organize it. For example, suppose you are an employee of Ride Safe, Inc., and have been asked to prepare a presentation on selling bicycle and in-line skating helmets; you can use the AutoContent Wizard to help you organize this sales presentation. The wizard also provides additional information on other types of presentations. Consider printing this information for help in creating other presentations.

AutoContent Wizard can be accessed at the PowerPoint dialog box as shown in figure 9.5. Alternatively, you can access AutoContent Wizard by clicking File, then New. Select the Presentations tab at the New Presentation dialog box and double-click the AutoContent Wizard icon.

Running A Slide Show

Several methods can be used to run a slide show. Slides created in PowerPoint can be converted to 35mm slides or transparencies; or the computer screen can display the slides, much like a slide projector. An on-screen presentation saves the expense of producing slides and lets you use the computer's color capability. However, you will need an overhead LCD projector if you are displaying a presentation to more than a few people.

If you are running a slide show in PowerPoint, there are several methods you can choose. You can run the slide show manually (you determine when to advance to the next slide), advance slides automatically, or set up a slide show to run continuously for demonstration purposes.

If you want to run a slide show manually, open the presentation, then click the Slide Show button on the View Button Bar. You can also click View, then Slide Show or click Slide Show at the Menu bar. At the Slide Show dialog box, click Show. To control movement through slides in a slide show, refer to the following table:

To do this...	Perform this action:
Show next slide	Click left mouse button; or press one of the following keys: space bar, N, right arrow, down arrow, or Page Down
Show previous slide	Click right mouse button; or press one of the following keys: backspace, P, left arrow, up arrow, or Page Up
Show specific slide	Key slide number, then press Enter
Toggle mouse on or off	Key A or equal sign (=)
Switch between black screen	Key B or period (.) and current slide
Switch between white screen	Key W or comma (,) and current slide
End slide show and return to PowerPoint	Press one of the following keys: Esc, hyphen (-), or Ctrl + Break

exercise 4

Using AutoContent Wizard for a Sales Presentation

1. Prepare slides to assist in organizing a presentation to sell bicycle and in-line skating helmets, as shown in figure 9.16, by completing the following steps: (If you have not yet loaded PowerPoint, follow the steps listed under step a. If you have already loaded PowerPoint, follow the steps listed under step b.)
   a. Load PowerPoint by click the Start button on the Windows Taskbar, clicking Programs, then *Microsoft PowerPoint.* At the PowerPoint dialog box, click AutoContent wizard, then click OK.
   b. If you have already loaded PowerPoint, complete the following steps:
      (1) Click File, then New.
      (2) At the New Presentation dialog box, select the Presentations tab.
      (3) Double-click the AutoContent Wizard icon.
2. At the first AutoContent Wizard dialog box, read the information presented, then click Next>.
   a. **Presentation type:** At the *Select the type of presentation you're going to give,* make sure the All button is selected, click Recommending a Strategy, then click Next>.
   b. **Output options:** At the *How will this presentation be used?*, make sure the *Presentations, informal meetings, handouts* is selected, then click Next>.
   c. **Presentation Style:** Make sure the *On-screen presentation* is selected and *Yes print handouts* is selected, then click Next>.
   d. **Presentation options:** Key **Ride Safe Helmet Sales** in the *Presentation title* text box. Key your name in the *Your name* text box. Delete the additional information. Click Finish.
3. View the outline provided by Wizard by scrolling the down arrow at the bottom of the vertical scroll bar. Continue reading the information on each slide until all slides have been read.
4. View the slides again by changing to Slide view. Use the slide indicator by completing the following steps:
   a. Position the arrow pointer on the slide indicator (the scroll box) on the vertical scroll bar, hold down the left mouse button, drag the slide indicator on the top of the vertical scroll bar until a white box displays the slide number and the title of the presentation, then release the mouse button. (This displays each slide number in the Presentation window.)
   b. View the slides again using Slide Sorter view by clicking View, then Slide Sorter; or clicking the Slide Sorter View button on the View Button Bar.
5. Run the slide presentation on the screen by completing the following steps:
   a. In Slide Sorter view, click once on Slide 1 or press Ctrl + Home. (This is to ensure that your slide show begins with the first slide.)
   b. Click the Slide Show button on the Menu bar or click the Slide Show button on the View Button Bar. (This should cause Slide 1 to display and fill the entire screen.)
   c. After viewing Slide 1, click the left mouse button. (This causes Slide 2 to display.)
   d. Continue viewing and then clicking the left mouse button until all eight slides have been viewed and the screen returns to the Slide Sorter view.
   e. After viewing the last slide (Slide 8), click the left mouse button again. (This returns the display to Slide Sorter view.)
6. Save the presentation by completing the following steps:
   a. Click the Save button on the Standard toolbar.
   b. At the Save dialog box, key **c09ex04, Helmet Sales.ppt**, then press Enter or click Save.

7. Print the information on the slides provided by the Wizard in Outline view by completing the following steps:
   a. Click File, then Print.
   b. At the Print dialog box, click the down arrow to the right of the Print what option, then click *Outline View* from the drop-down menu.
   c. Click OK.
8. Close c09ex04, Helmet Sales.ppt.

figure 9.16

Helmet Sales Presentation

Your Name

1 Ride Safe Helmet Sales
Your Name

2 Recommending a Strategy
Ideas for Today and Tomorrow

3 Vision Statement
◆ State the vision and long term direction

4 Goal and Objective
◆ State the desired goal
◆ State the desired objective
◆ Use multiple points if necessary

5 Today's Situtation
◆ Summary of the current situation
◆ Use brief bullets, discuss details verbally

6 How Did We Get Here?
◆ Any relevant historical information
◆ Original assumptions that are no longer valid

7 Available Options
◆ State the alternative strategies
◆ List advantages & disadvantages of each
◆ State cost of each option

8 Recommendation
◆ Recommend one or more of the strategies
◆ Summarize the results if things go as proposed
◆ What to do next
◆ Identify Action Items

Running a Slide Show Automatically

Slides in a slide show can be advanced automatically after a specific number of seconds. To do this, specify the seconds at the Slide Transition dialog box shown in figure 9.17. To display this dialog box, open a presentation, change to the Slide Sorter view, select an individual slide or select all slides in the presentation, then click Slide Show, then Slide Transition.

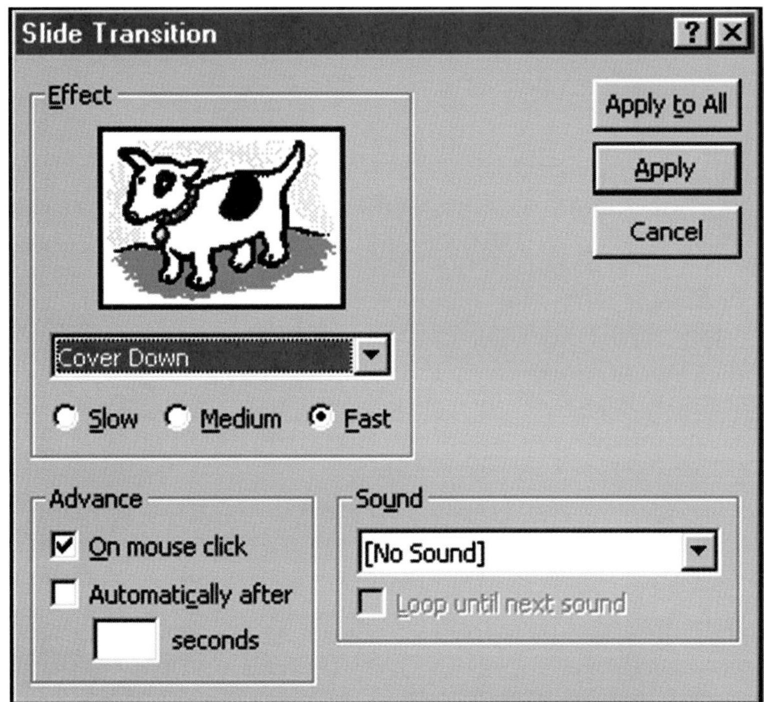

figure 9.17

Slide Transition Dialog Box

If you want to specify a time for an individual slide, select that slide first (by clicking it), then display the Slide Transition dialog box. If you want transition times to affect all slides in the presentation, select all the slides first and then display the Slide Transition dialog box. To select all slides in a presentation, display the slides in Slide Sorter view, hold down the Shift key, then click each slide. You can also select all slides by pressing Ctrl + A, or Edit, Select All. To deselect, hold down the Shift key, then click each slide.

With the desired slides selected, make changes to the Slide Transition dialog box. To automatically advance slides, click Automatically after (in the Advance section), then key the number of seconds. After making changes to the Slide Transition dialog box, click Apply to close the dialog box. You can also click Apply to All to effect all slides.

To automatically run the presentation, be sure Slide 1 is selected. Click the Slide Show button on the View Button Bar. This runs the presentation showing each slide on the screen the specified number of seconds. When a time has been added to a slide (or slides), the time displays at the bottom of the slide (or slides) in Slide Sorter view.

Running a Slide Show in a Continuous Loop

In a continuous-loop slide show, all the slides are viewed over and over again until you stop the show. This feature is especially effective when presenting a new product or service at a trade show or at a new store opening. To run a presentation in PowerPoint in a continuous loop, click Slide Show, then Set Up Show. At the Set Up Show dialog box, click the check box to the left of Loop continuously until 'Esc'. Click OK. When you are ready to run the presentation, click the Slide Show button on the View Button Bar.

When you are ready to end the slide show, press the Esc key on the keyboard. You will then be back to the Slide Sorter view.

Adding Transition and Sound Effects

Transition
How one slide is removed from the screen and the next slide is displayed.

At the Slide Transition dialog box shown in figure 9.17, you can enhance the presentation by adding transition effects and sound. *Transition* refers to what takes place when one slide is removed from the screen during a presentation and the next slide is displayed. Interesting transitions can be added such as blinds, boxes, checkerboards, covers, random bars, strips, and wipes.

To add a transition effect, click the down arrow at the Effect list box in the Slide Transition dialog box, then click the desired transition at the drop-down menu. When you click the desired transition, the transition is displayed at the picture of the dog that changes to a key.

DTP POINTERS
Each slide can have a different transition effect as long as at least one element remains consistent in all the slides.

As a slide is removed from the screen and another slide is displayed, a sound can be added. To add a sound, click the down arrow to the right of the Sound list box, then click the desired sound. You can choose from a list of sounds such as camera, explosion, laser, ricochet, typewriter, and whoosh. When a transition is added, a transition icon displays below the slide (or slides) at the bottom left side.

Setting and Rehearsing Timings for a Presentation

Setting a time at the Slide Transition dialog box sets the time for each selected slide. In some presentations, you may want to specify a different amount of time for each slide and then rehearse the presentation to ensure that the time set is appropriate. This can be accomplished with the Rehearse Timings option at the Slide Show dialog box. To rehearse and set a time for each slide, you would complete these steps:

1. Open the presentation.
2. Change to the Slide Sorter view.
3. Click Slide Show, Rehearse Timings.
4. The first slide in the presentation displays along with a Rehearsal dialog box that displays at the bottom right corner of the screen. The Rehearsal dialog box shows the time for the current slide in the right corner and the entire time for the presentation in the left corner. The timer begins immediately.
5. Click the Next Slide button (displays at the bottom right side of the dialog box with a right-pointing arrow) when the desired time is displayed; click the Pause button (displays with two thick vertical bars) to stop the timer and leave the slide on the screen; or click the Repeat button if you want the time for the current slide to start over.
6. Continue in this manner until the time for all slides in the presentation has been specified.

7. After specifying the time for the last slide, a Microsoft PowerPoint dialog box displays with the total time of the presentation displayed and asks if you want to record the new slide timings. At this dialog box, click Yes to save the new timings. Click Yes or No to review timings in Slide Sorter view.

exercise 5

Running a Presentation Automatically and Establishing Specific Times for Slides

1. Open c09ex01, Bicycle Club.ppt. (This presentation was created in exercise 1.)
2. Save the presentation with File, Save As and name it c09ex05, Rehearsed Bicycle Club.ppt.
3. Add a graphic image to the slides as shown in figure 9.18 by completing the following steps:
   a. At the first slide, select the text box containing the heading *Sponsored by Ride Safe...* and drag it downward approximately one-half inch. (Refer to figure 9.18 for correct placement.)
   b. Select the heading *Wheaton Bicycle Club*, and drag the text box containing the heading downward approximately 1 inch. (The text box should be positioned directly below the horizontal line in the template.)
   c. Click Insert, point to Picture, and then click From File.
   d. At the Insert Picture dialog box, make sure the drive or folder where your student data files are located displays in the Look in: text box.
   e. Double-click *cycling.cgm* at the File name: list box (or use any appropriate substitute image).
   f. If the CGM Graphics Import dialog box displays, click OK or press Enter.
   g. Size the picture by dragging one of the corner sizing handles inward with the double arrow, then drag the picture, with the four-headed arrow, to the top and middle of the horizontal line as shown in figure 9.18. (Holding down the Ctrl key as you drag a sizing handle resizes the image from the center to increase or decrease the size of the image depending on whether you drag inward or outward.)
   h. With the picture still selected, click the Copy button on the Standard toolbar. (This copies the image to the clipboard, so it may be pasted to other slides.)
   i. Click the Next Slide button to display the second slide.
   j. Click the Paste button on the Standard toolbar.
   k. Drag to position the picture as shown in figure 9.18.
   l. Continue copying the picture to the remaining slides by completing steps similar to 3i and 3k. (Resize and position if necessary.)
   m. Press Ctrl + Home to position the insertion point in the first slide.
4. Add transition and sound effects by completing the following steps:
   a. Change to the Slide Sorter view.
   b. Hold down the Shift key, then click each slide; or press Ctrl + A. (This selects all slides in the presentation.)
   c. Click Slide Show, then Slide Transition; or click the Slide Transition button on the Slide Sorter toolbar (first button).
   d. At the Slide Transition dialog box, click Automatically after, then key **5** in the Seconds text box. (Do not close the Slide Transition dialog box.)
   e. Add a transition effect by completing the following steps:
      (1) Click the down arrow to the right of the Effect list box (containing the text *No Transition*).

(2) From the drop-down list that displays, click *Blinds Horizontal*. (Make sure Fast is selected in the Speed section.)

f. Add a sound effect by completing the following steps:

(1) Click the down arrow to the right of the Sound list box (containing the text *[No Sound]*).

(2) From the drop-down list that displays, click *Camera*.

g. Click Apply to All to close the dialog box.

5. Run the presentation automatically by clicking the Slide Show button on the View Button Bar or clicking Slide Show, then View Show. When the presentation is done, the slides display in Slide Sorter view.

6. Set a different specific time for each slide by completing the following steps:

a. Make sure all the slides are selected (press Ctrl + A) and displayed in Slide Sorter view, then click Slide Show, Rehearse Timings; or click the Rehearse Timings button on the Slide Sorter toolbar (a clock displays on the button and it is the third button from the right).

b. With the first slide displayed, wait until the timer at the right side of the Rehearsal dialog box displays 10 seconds, then click the Next Slide button. (The Next Slide button displays at the bottom right side of the dialog box and contains a right-pointing arrow.) If you miss 10 seconds, click the Repeat button at the bottom left side of the dialog box. This restarts the clock for that particular slide. (The middle button at the bottom of the Rehearsal dialog box will pause the timing.)

c. With the second slide displayed, wait until the timer at the right side of the dialog box displays 8 seconds, then click the Next Slide button.

d. Set 8 seconds for the third slide, and 5 seconds for the remaining three slides.

e. After setting the time for the last slide, the Microsoft PowerPoint dialog box displays asking if you want to record the new timings. At this dialog box, click Yes. At the next dialog box asking to review timings, click Yes. (If any of the times are incorrect, you can change them by selecting the slide with the incorrect setting, then clicking Slide Show, then Slide Transition or clicking the Slide Transition button on the Common Tasks toolbar. At the Slide Transition dialog box, click inside the check box to turn on the *Automatically after* option. Key an increment in seconds in the *seconds* text box, then click Apply.)

7. Run the presentation again by completing the following steps:

a. Press Ctrl + Home to display the first slide in the sequence.

b. Click Slide Show, Set Up Show.

c. At the Set Up Show dialog box, click Loop continuously until 'Esc'. Click OK.

d. Click Show on the View Button Bar. (Let the slides change automatically; the first slide will display for 10 seconds, the second and third for 8 seconds, and the remaining three for 5 seconds.) Press the Esc key on the keyboard to end the loop.

8. Save the presentation again with the same name, c09ex05, Rehearsed Bicycle Club.ppt.

9. Click to remove the check mark to the left of Loop continuously until 'Esc' at the Slide Show, Set Up Show dialog box. Click OK.

10. Print the presentation with six slides per page.

11. Close c09ex05, Rehearsed Bicycle Club.ppt.

figure 9.18

Rehearsed Bicycle Club Presentation

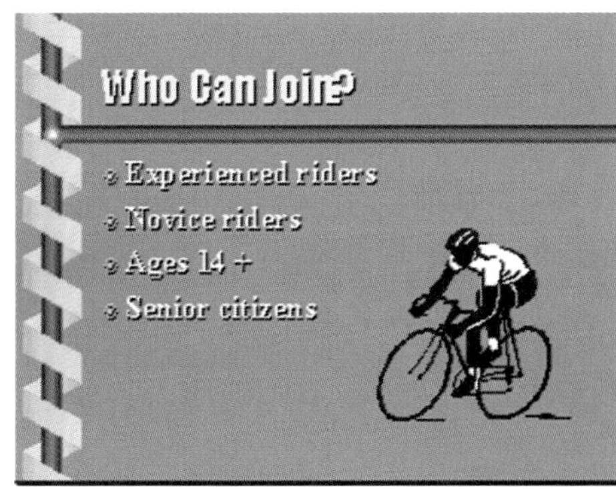

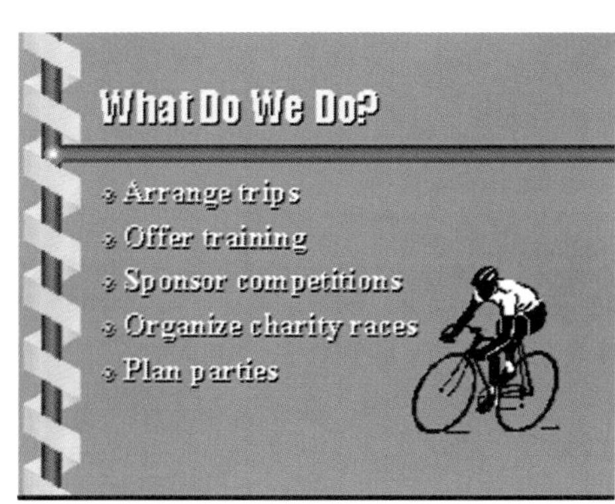

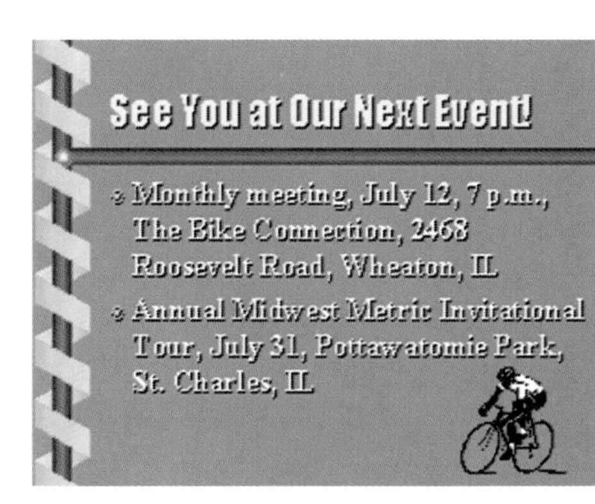

Using a Slide Master

If you use a PowerPoint design, you can choose to use the formatting provided, or you may want to customize the formatting. If you customize formatting in a presentation, PowerPoint's slide master can be very helpful in reducing the steps needed to format all slides in a presentation. For instance, if you want to add a company logo or consistent formatting to all the slides in your presentation, a slide master will save you time and will make it easier to maintain a uniform appearance in your presentation. If you know in advance that you want to change the formatting of slides, display the slide master, make the changes needed, then create the presentation. If the presentation is already created, edit the presentation in a slide master. Any changes made to a slide master will affect all the slides in the presentation. There is also a master for the title slide, handouts, and notes.

DTP POINTERS
Consistency is important in maintaining a uniform appearance.

To display the slide master, change to the Slide view, position the insertion point on the Slide View button on the View Button Bar, hold down the Shift key, then click the left mouse button. This displays a slide master similar to the one shown in figure 9.19. At this slide, make any desired changes, then click the Slide View button (do not hold down the Shift key this time) to exit the slide master. Changes made at a slide master will be reflected in the current slide displayed as well as in the remaining slides in the presentation. Alternatively, the slide master feature can be accessed by clicking View, Master, then Slide Master.

figure 9.19

Slide Master

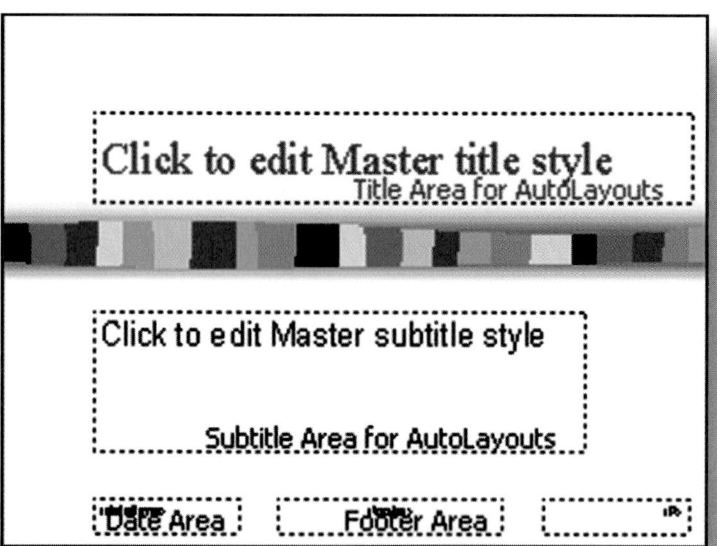

In exercise 6, you will use a slide master to create slides for a presentation.

Formatting Object Boxes

As mentioned earlier, placeholders in PowerPoint design templates consist of object boxes containing specific formatting. Buttons on the Drawing toolbar can be used to customize these object boxes by changing such things as the background color or by adding a border. If you want changes to an object box to affect all slides in a presentation, make the changes at the Slide Master.

Inserting WordArt in PowerPoint

With WordArt, you can apply special effects to text. For instance, WordArt can be used to create interesting logos for a company or product. Like the results of Microsoft Graph and Microsoft Organization Chart, WordArt creations are objects. When a WordArt object is selected, the image is surrounded by handles. (Refer to chapter 4 for a review on WordArt.) You can create WordArt from either Slide view or the Slide Master. The advantage of creating WordArt in a slide master is that it will appear automatically on every slide in the presentation. To create WordArt in PowerPoint complete the following steps:

DTP POINTERS
A logo reinforces a company's identity.

1. Open an existing slide.
2. Right-click on a toolbar to display the list of toolbars. Select the WordArt toolbar. (You can also access WordArt by clicking the WordArt button on the Drawing toolbar or by clicking Insert, pointing to Picture, then clicking WordArt.)
3. Click the Insert WordArt button (first button from the left) on the WordArt toolbar.
4. Select a WordArt style, then click OK.
5. At the Edit WordArt text dialog box, key text in the Enter Your Text Here dialog box. Click OK.
6. Modify your text with various WordArt features.
7. Close WordArt by clicking anywhere on the slide.
8. Close the WordArt toolbar.

exercise 6

Formatting Objects and Creating a Logo in a Slide Master

1. Create the presentation on Ride Safe products shown in figure 9.20 by completing the following steps. (If you have already entered PowerPoint, complete the steps listed under step a. If you have not yet entered PowerPoint, follow the steps listed under step b.):
   a. If you are already in PowerPoint, complete the following steps:
      (1) Click File, then New.
      (2) At the Presentations tab, double-click *Company Meeting (Standard).pot.*
   b. If you have not yet entered PowerPoint, complete the following steps:
      (1) Load PowerPoint.
      (2) At the PowerPoint dialog box, click Template, then click OK.
      (3) At the New Presentation dialog box, select the Presentations tab.
      (4) At the Presentations tab, double-click *Company Meeting (Standard).pot.*
2. Change the Slide Color Scheme by completing the following steps:
   a. Click Format, then Slide Color Scheme.
   b. Select the Standard tab, then click the second Title Bullet in the Color Schemes section.
   c. Select the Custom tab, then complete the following steps:
      (1) Click Text and lines, then click the Change Color... button. Choose the white color in the palette, then click OK.
      (2) Click Accent, then click the Change Color... button. Choose a bright pink color in the palette, then click OK.
      (3) Click Accent and hyperlink, then click the Change Color... button. Choose a bright yellow color in the palette, then click OK.
      (4) Click Accent and followed hyperlink, then click the Change Color... button. Choose a bright blue, then click OK.
      (5) Click Apply to All.

d. Change Background by completing the following steps:
   (1) Click Format, then Background.
   (2) Click the down arrow in the Background fill section. Click the More Colors button, then select the Standard tab. Select the blue color in the top row, second from the right. Click OK. Click Apply to all.

3. Create a slide master for the presentation by completing the following steps:
   a. With the first slide displayed, click View, point to Master, and then click Slide Master. This displays the slide master.
      (1) Turn off bullets by clicking inside *Click to edit Master text styles*. Select all of the levels, then click the Bullets button on the Formatting toolbar. (This action turns off the Bullets feature).
      (2) Click inside the line, *Click to edit Master title style,* then change the font size to 44 points. Click the Center Align button on the Formatting toolbar.
      (3) Select the lines, *Click to edit Master text styles*, *Second Level*, and *Third Level*, then change the font size to 32 points. Turn on bold, then click the Center Align button on the Formatting toolbar.
      (4) Select and then delete the remaining two levels.
   b. Insert a logo for Ride Safe as a WordArt object in the slide master by completing the following steps:
      (1) Display the Drawing toolbar.
      (2) Click the Insert WordArt button on the Drawing toolbar. Select the WordArt style in the fourth row and fourth column. Click OK.
      (3) Key **Ride Safe, Inc.** in the text entry box, then click OK.
      (4) Click the down arrow to the right of the Fill Color button on the Drawing toolbar and click the pink color.
      (5) Move the WordArt object by selecting and dragging it to the bottom of the slide as shown in figure 9.20.
   c. Insert the date and slide number by completing the following steps:
      (1) Click View, then Header and Footer.
      (2) Select the Slide tab, then make sure Date and time is selected. Also, make sure Update automatically is selected.
      (3) Click inside the check box to turn on Slide number, but Footer should not be selected.
      (4) Click Apply to All.
   d. Click the Slide View button on the View Button Bar. (This removes the master slide and displays a slide with the formatted elements.)

4. Key the text in the first slide, as shown in figure 9.20, by completing the following steps:
   a. Click inside *Company Meeting Title.* Highlight this text.
   b. Key **Ride Safe, Inc.**
   c. Click to the left of *Presenter,* then key Your Name.
   d. Change the background of slide 1 by following these steps:
      (1) Click Format, then Background.
      (2) Click the down arrow in the Background fill section, then click Fill Effects.
      (3) Click the Two colors option button.
      (4) Click the From title option button in the Shading styles section.
      (5) Click OK. Click Apply.

5. Delete slides 2-13 since you will not use this information. (Hint: View the slides in Slide Sorter View or Outline View, select each slide while holding down the Shift key, then press Delete.)

6. Click the New Slide button on the Standard toolbar and make sure the first AutoLayout is selected. Click OK at the New Slide dialog box. Key the text in slides 2-6 as shown in figure 9.20.

7. Save the presentation and name it c09ex06, New Products.ppt.
8. Print all six slides on the same page.
9. Close c09ex06, New Products.ppt.

9.20

New Products Presentation

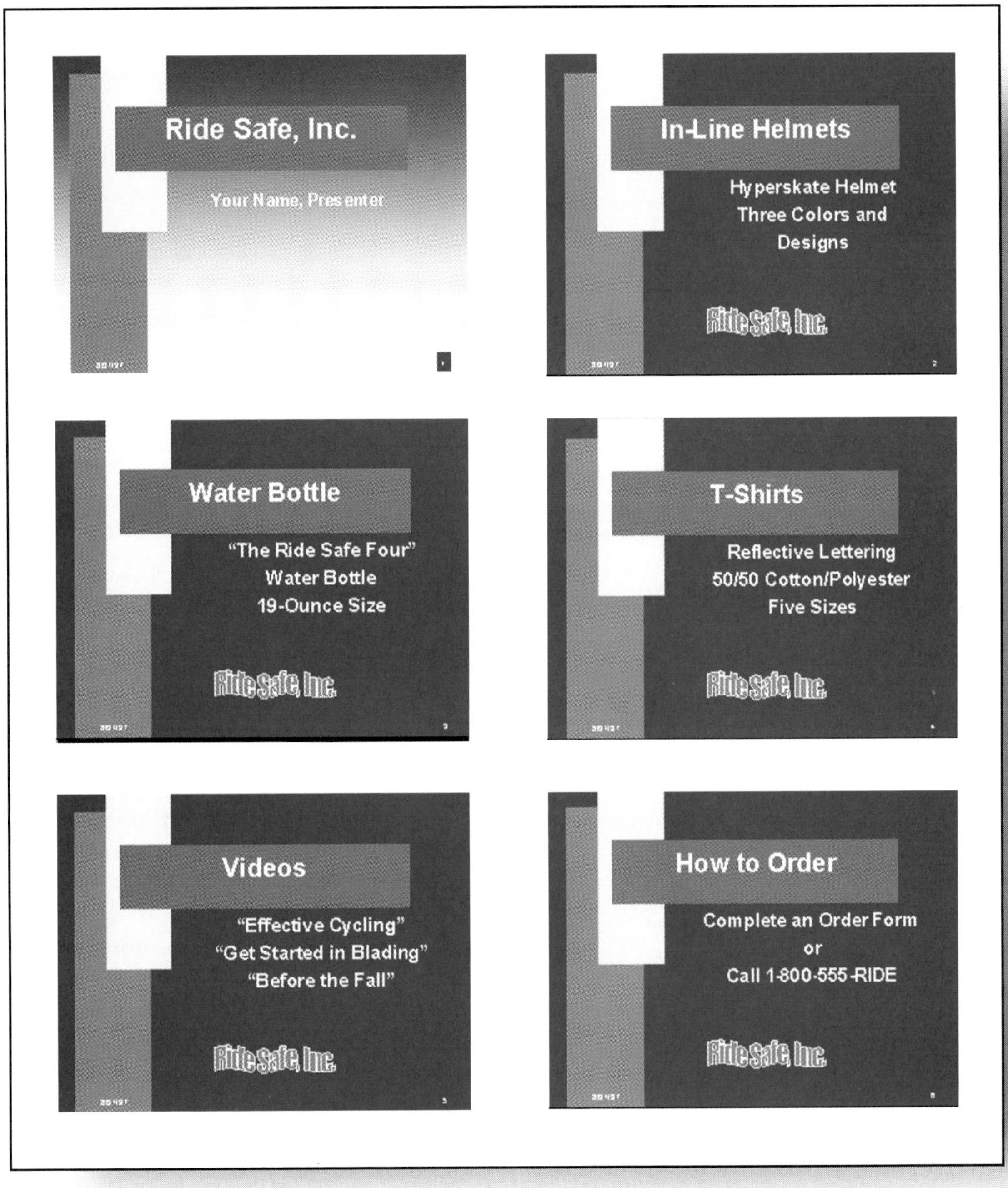

Ride Safe, Inc.
Your Name, Presenter

In-Line Helmets
Hyperskate Helmet
Three Colors and
Designs
Ride Safe, Inc.

Water Bottle
"The Ride Safe Four"
Water Bottle
19-Ounce Size
Ride Safe, Inc.

T-Shirts
Reflective Lettering
50/50 Cotton/Polyester
Five Sizes
Ride Safe, Inc.

Videos
"Effective Cycling"
"Get Started in Blading"
"Before the Fall"
Ride Safe, Inc.

How to Order
Complete an Order Form
or
Call 1-800-555-RIDE
Ride Safe, Inc.

Adding Animation Effects to a Presentation

Animation Effects

With options from the Animation Effects dialog box, you can add animation effects such as having an element fly or drive into a slide, display as a camera effect, or appear one step at a time during a slide show. To display animation choices, open a presentation, select the specific objects within a slide to which you want the animation added, then click the Animation Effects button on the Formatting toolbar. This causes the Animation Effects toolbar to display as shown in figure 9.21.

Animation Effects Toolbar

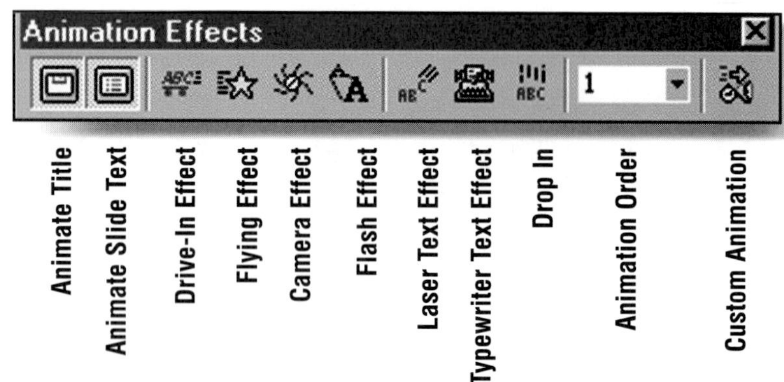

Select this button...	To perform this action:
Animate Title	Drop slide title from top of slide
Animate Slide Text	Have body text appear one step at a time
Drive-In Effect	Make selected text or objects fly in from the right along with the sound of a car
Flying Effect	Have selected text or object fly in from the left with a whoosh sound
Camera Effect	Have selected text or object appear as if a camera shutter was opened
Flash Once	Make selected text or object flash once after last build
Laser Text Effect	Make selected text or object fly in from top right accompanied by the sound of a laser—if text is selected, it appears one letter at a time
Typewriter Text Effect	Make selected text or objects appear one character at a time accompanied by the sound of a typewriter
Drop-In	Make selected text or object drop in from the top of the slide; text appears one word at a time
Animation Order	Select order in which selected text or object appears
Custom Animation	Set options you want to use to build or play an inserted object

Adding a Build to a Slide Presentation

With the buttons on the Animation Effects toolbar, you can display important points on a slide one point at a time, which is known as a build technique. The *build* technique helps the audience stay focused on the point being presented rather than reading ahead. The build technique is very effective in slides containing several points.

Build
A feature that displays information (usually bulleted items) a little at a time.

Options from the Animation Settings dialog box let you customize the build. To display this dialog box, open a presentation, display the desired slide, then click the Custom Animation button on the Formatting toolbar. At the Animation Effects toolbar, click the Custom Animation button.

With the Custom Animation button, you can specify what items display during a build. You can specify that all items display at once or you can specify a level. At the Custom Animation dialog box, you can reverse the order of the build and have another build start when the previous build ends. With options in the Effects section, you can add a build transition effect such as flying, blinds, checkerboard, flash, or stripes; add sound such as a camera, laser, typewriter, or whoosh; or build by paragraph, word, or letter. With other options at the Custom Animation dialog box, you can specify whether the selected text is built first or second and also whether a previous build is dimmed when the next build is displayed.

DTP POINTERS
To add a build effect of both text and graphics on a single slide, hold down the Shift key as you select each object.

You will be using a build technique in exercise 7 in addition to adding animation.

exercise 7

Adding Animation and Build to a Presentation

1. Open *Basic In-Line Presentation.ppt* located on your student data disk.
2. Save the presentation with Save As and name it c09ex07, Animated In-Line.ppt.
3. Add a clip art image to each slide by completing the following steps:
   a. Change to Slide view. (Make sure the first slide is displayed in the Presentation window.)
   b. With the first slide displayed, click Insert, point to Picture, and then click From File.
   c. At the Insert Picture dialog box, make sure the drive or folder where your student data disk is located displays in the Look in: text box.
   d. Double-click *Rollblde.cgm* at the list box (or select an appropriate alternative graphic).
   e. Reduce the size of the image by dragging a corner sizing handle inward. Drag to position the image as shown in figure 9.22.
   f. Add animation effects to the rollerblade image in each slide by completing the following steps:
      (1) With the first slide displayed, click to select the rollerblade image.
      (2) Display the Animation Effects toolbar by clicking the Animation Effects button on the Formatting toolbar (the last button with a star on it).
      (3) Select the rollerblade image, then click the Custom Animation button (last button) on the Animation Effects toolbar.
      (4) At the Custom Animation dialog box, select the Effects tab, click the down arrow to the right of the Entry animation and sound list box and select *Fly From Left*.
      (5) Click the down arrow to the right of the No Sound list box, then select *Screeching Brakes* from the drop-down menu. (If the *Screeching Brakes* sound is not available to you, select the *Whoosh* sound or any other appropriate sound effect.)
      (6) Click OK.

g. With the image selected, click Edit, then Copy. (You are copying the image to the clipboard so that it may be pasted to the other slides in this presentation.)

4. Paste the animated rollerblade image to each slide. (The image has been saved to the clipboard.) Resize the image if necessary and position it by selecting then dragging it to the locations shown in figure 9.22.
5. Add a build effect to each slide by completing the following steps:
   a. With the first slide displayed, select the object box containing the title *International In-Line...Rules of the Road.*
   b. Click the Animate Title button on the Animation Effects toolbar (first button).
   c. Select the object box containing the text *Presented by...*, then click the Laser Text Effect button on the Animation Effects toolbar.
   d. Click the Next Slide button.
   e. With the second slide displayed, select the object box containing the title *Skate Smart*, then click the Animate Title button on the Animation Effects toolbar. Make sure 2 displays in the Animation Order list box.
   f. With the second slide still displayed, add a build technique to the bulleted items on the slide by completing the following steps:
      (1) Click once in the bulleted text.
      (2) Click the Custom Animation button on the Animation Effects toolbar.
      (3) At the Custom Animation dialog box, select the Timing tab.
      (4) Make sure *Text 2* is selected in the Animation order list box, then click the Animate option button in the Start animation section.
      (5) Select the Effects tab, then make sure the Animation order is 1. Picture frame 3, 2. Title 1, 3. Text 2. (Change the order by selecting the line you want to move, then clicking the up or down arrows.)
      (6) Make sure *Text 2* is selected in the Animation order section. Click the down arrow in the first list box in the Effects section, Entry animation and sound, then click *Checkerboard Across* at the drop-down menu.
      (7) Click the down arrow in the next list box in the Effects section (contains the text *[No Sound]*), then select *Chime* from the drop-down list. (If *Chime* is not available, select an appropriate substitute sound.)
      (8) Click the down arrow to the right of the After animation (contains the text *Don't Dim*), then click the light blue color in the first row.
      (9) Click OK to close the Custom Animation dialog box.
   g. Click the Next Slide button.
   h. Format the remaining slides with the same title animation and build technique formatting.
   i. Click the Close button on the Animation Effects toolbar to remove it from the screen.
6. Display the presentation in Slide Sorter view, then click the first slide or press Ctrl + Home.
7. Run the presentation by clicking the Slide Show button on the View Button Bar. Click the left mouse button to advance each slide manually.
8. When the presentation is completed, save the presentation again with the same name, c09ex07, Animated In-Line.ppt.
9. Print the presentation with five slides on one page.
10. Close c09ex07, Animated In-Line.ppt.

Optional: Add different build and transition effects to each slide.

figure 9.22

Animated In-Line Presentation

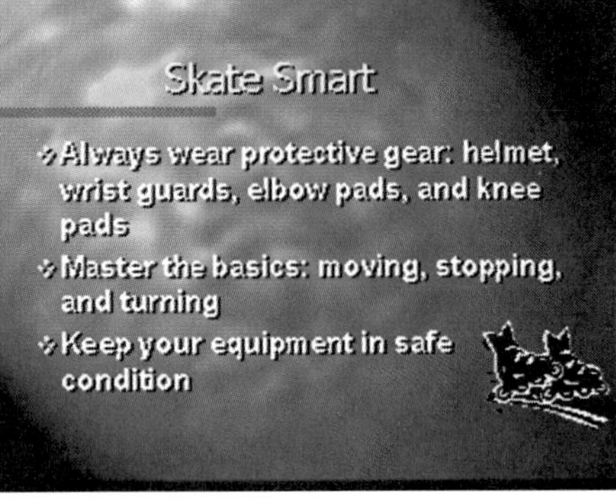

Creating Supporting Handouts for a Presentation

Presentation materials often include handouts for the audience. Handouts might contain an outline of the presentation topics and other supplementary information. Very often supplementary materials include some type of a reply/response card, a fact sheet, a brochure, and a business card. The company or individual making the presentation may even provide a special folder for all of these materials with the organization's name and logo on the front cover. These materials make it easy for individuals to review the materials on their own time and to contact the company or presenter after the presentation is over.

Refrain from handing out copies of materials during your presentation as this can shift the listeners' attention from your presentation to reading ahead. Samples of supporting documents for a Ride Safe presentation can be found in figure 9.23.

figure 9.23

Sample Documents for a Ride Safe Presentation

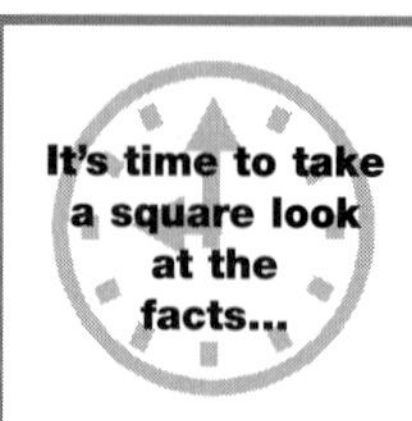

It's time to take a square look at the facts...

The SAFETY ON WHEELS™ PROGRAM from RIDE SAFE® addresses both bicycling and in-line skating—with compelling safety education, as well as quality helmets and protective gear.

It could be the most important safety program you run this year!

- In 1997, an estimated 7,000 people sustained head injuries while in-line skating.
- In-line skating is now the fastest growing recreational sport in America.
- Kids under 15 account for 60% of all in-line skating injuries.
- Each year, over 500,000 people have serious injuries from bicycle crashes.
- Sixty percent of all bicycle/car collisions occur among bicyclists between the ages of 8 and 12.
- Children are more likely to lose their lives as pedestrians and bicyclists than any other way.

FACT SHEET

We are interested in the new Safety on Wheels Program™ from Ride Safe®. Please send us the following information.

- ❑ Safety on Wheels Program™ description and price list
- ❑ Bicycle safety trick shows
- ❑ In-line skating instruction programs
- ❑ Reflective sweatshirts and T-shirts

If you would like a sample helmet and Program Guide, or for *faster responses*, call 800-555-RIDE.

Name ____________________

Address ____________________

City ____________ State ________ ZIP ________

Phone ____________ Fax ____________

Organization Name ____________________

Phone ____________________

RIDE SAFE INC
30 W 2560 BUTTERFIELD ROAD #212
P O BOX 888
WARRENVILLE IL 60555

POSTCARD (FRONT AND BACK)

For Details, Contact:

Dane & Mary Beth Luhrsen
Ride Safe, Inc.
Phone 1-800-555-RIDE (7433)

Ride Safe, Inc.
30 W 2560 Butterfield Road, #212
P.O. Box 888
Warrenville, IL 60555
Phone 1-800-555-RIDE (7433)

Ride Safe News Release

Police Ticketing Program: Local Police to "Ticket" Children Wearing Bicycle Helmets

As part of the Main Street School PTA's Bicycle Safety Program, local police will be stopping and "ticketing" children who are wearing bicycle helmets when they are riding their bicycles.

Your Town, September 24, 1998: Should you keep your children off the streets? NO! These "tickets" are actually coupons that can be redeemed for free ice cream cones at Stewart's Ice Cream Parlor, free movie rentals from Star Video, and free pizza slices from Angelo's Pizzeria.

"The children are extremely excited about this program," said Mary Jones, PTA Health and Safety Coordinator from Main Street School. "We think children will start wearing their bicycle helmets because of the prizes and will continue wearing them because it has become a habit." According to statistics published by the National Safe Kids Coalition, more than 800 people die in bicycle accidents each year. Thousands more receive serious head and brain injuries. A recent study found that wearing a bicycle helmet could reduce the risk of head injuries by 85%.

"We want to do something before our community is faced with a tragic accident," says Ms. Jones. Ms. Jones would like to thank the local police, Stewart's Ice Cream Parlor, Star Video, and Angelo's Pizzeria for their support of the program. Please call Mary Jones at 555-8974 if you have any questions about the program.

For Release 9 a.m. EDT September 24, 1998

PRESS RELEASE

30 W 2560 Butterfield Road, #212
P.O. Box 888
Warrenville, IL 60555

1-800-555-RIDE (7433)

BUSINESS CARD

Ride Safe
Certificate of Achievement

Awarded to

Ride Safe Program Recipient

Congratulations on your outstanding achievement. Please remember the lessons that you have learned, always wear your bicycle or in-line skating helmets whenever you ride your bike or in-line skates.
RIDE SAFE!

Presented by
Ride Safe, Inc.

Thursday, September 24, 1998

PTA President — *School Principal*

Dane & Mary Beth Luhrsen, Ride Safe Owners — *Classroom Teacher*

CERTIFICATE

chapter summary

- A PowerPoint presentation can be created by using the AutoContent Wizard, preformatted presentation design templates, or a blank presentation screen.
- Slides in PowerPoint presentation design templates contain placeholders where specific text or objects are inserted.
- Placeholders can be customized by changing background color or adding a border or shadow.
- If you want changes made to a placeholder to affect all slides in a presentation, make the changes at the slide master.
- PowerPoint provides viewing options for presentations that include: Slide, Outline, Slide Sorter, Notes Page, and Slide Show views.
- When choosing a presentation design for your slides, consider your audience, the topic, and the method of delivery.
- AutoLayout formats can include placeholders that format a title, bulleted list, clip art, chart, organizational chart, table, or object.
- PowerPoint's AutoContent Wizard provides helpful information on planning and organizing a presentation based on the topic and purpose of the presentation.
- Slides in a slide show can be advanced manually or automatically at specific time intervals.
- Transition refers to what action takes place as one slide is removed from the screen during a presentation and the next slide is displayed.
- Preparing a presentation in Outline view helps to organize topics for each slide without the distractions of colorful designs, clip art, transitions, or sound. It is a good view to use when "brainstorming" the creation of a presentation.
- Sound effects and animation create impact in a slide show.
- PowerPoint's build technique displays important points one at a time on a slide.

commands review

Start PowerPoint	Start button on Taskbar, Program, Microsoft PowerPoint
Microsoft Clip Gallery	Insert, Picture, Clip Art; Insert, Object, Microsoft Clip Gallery, OK; click Insert Clip Art button on Standard toolbar; or double-click clip art placeholder in Slide Layout view
Run a slide show	View, Slide Show; Slide Show, View Show; or click Slide Show button
WordArt	Click Insert WordArt button on Drawing toolbar; display WordArt toolbar, click Insert WordArt button; or click Insert, Picture, WordArt
Slide Master	Click Slide View button while holding down Shift key; or View, Master, Slide Master

check your understanding

True/False: Circle the letter T if the statement is true; circle the letter F if the statement is false.

T F 1. PowerPoint templates contain placeholders where specific text or objects are inserted.

T F 2. Slide view displays miniature versions of a presentation.

T F 3. PowerPoint automatically spell checks text as you key the text within a document.

T F 4. If you want changes made to placeholders to affect all slides in a presentation, make the changes at the slide master.

T F 5. At Slide Sorter view, the slide fills the entire screen.

T F 6. An AutoLayout format may contain a Chart placeholder.

T F 7. Scaling an image is the process of trimming vertical and/or horizontal edges of a picture.

T F 8. The AutoContent Wizard provides suggestions on how to plan and organize a presentation based on your responses.

T F 9. To run a presentation, click Format, then Slide Show.

T F 10. You can rearrange slides in Slide Sorter view.

Terms: In the space provided, indicate the correct term(s).

1. Display the ______________________ toolbar to create builds and animate text and objects for a slide show.
2. Click ______________________ view to display several slides on a screen at one time.
3. Click ______________________ view to run a presentation.
4. ______________________ contains formatting that gives each slide in a presentation identical properties.

skill assessments

Assessment 1

As an instructor at the Van Buren Vocational Center, you are in charge of preparing a slide-show presentation promoting the Business Services and Technology Department. Your audience will include students, parents, teachers, school administrators, and school board members. Enhance last year's presentation by adding text color, clip art, transitions, and animation effects. Include the following specifications in designing your presentation. (Figure 9.24 is provided as a sample solution—your presentation should include your choices.)

1. Enhance the Van Buren Vocational Center presentation by completing the following steps: (Refer to figure 9.24 as an example.)
   a. Load PowerPoint.
   b. Open *Vocational Presentation.ppt* located on your student data disk.
   c. Save the presentation and name it c09sa01, Vocational.ppt.

d. Apply an appropriate presentation design.
e. Add appropriate clip art images to each of the slides. The sample solution in figure 9.24 includes the files listed below. You can use any of the listed graphics or select your own—make sure they are appropriate to the subject of the slides and to the intended audience.

	Filename
(1) Slide 1	computer.wmf (located on student data disk)
(2) Slide 2	ceo.wmf (program CD-ROM)
(3) Slide 3	confrnce.wmf (program CD-ROM)
(4) Slide 4	worldair.wmf (program CD-ROM)
(5) Slide 5	cdrom.wmf (program CD-ROM)
(6) Slide 6	grad3.wmf (program CD-ROM)

f. If necessary, size and position the clip art images.
g. Select one of the clip art images, then recolor the image by completing the following steps:
   (1) With the image selected, click the Recolor Picture button on the Picture toolbar.
   (2) At the Recolor Picture dialog box, click the down arrow next to the second box from the top in the New section.
   (3) At the drop-down color palette that displays, select an appropriate color. (A check mark will appear in the check box next to the Original color box.)
   (4) Click OK.
h. Crop one of the images using the Crop button on the Picture toolbar.
i. Change the bullets—you decide on the bullet symbol and add color to the bullets.
j. Use a build for the bulleted items.
k. Apply transition effects to your slides. You decide if you want one type of transition for the whole presentation or if you want a different transition for each slide.
l. Apply a sound to at least 2 slides. (If audio is available to you.)
m. Select Slide 6 and change the slide layout by clicking Format, then Slide Layout.

2. Time the slides. Choose an appropriate layout.
3. Make the slide show a continuous on-screen presentation by completing the following steps:
   a. Click Slide Show, Set Up Show.
   b. At the Set Up Show dialog box, click in the check box to the left of Loop continuously until 'Esc'.
4. Save the presentation again with the same name, c09sa01, Vocational.ppt.
5. Run c09sa01, Vocational.ppt for a fellow student in your class and have the student summarize any good points and bad points about the presentation. Make any necessary changes.
6. Print c09sa01, Vocational.ppt with six slides on one page.
7. Close c09sa01, Vocational.ppt.

figure 9.24

Vocational Presentation Sample Solution

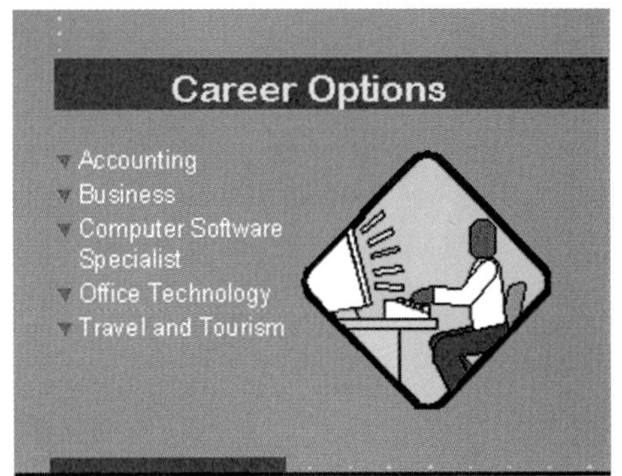

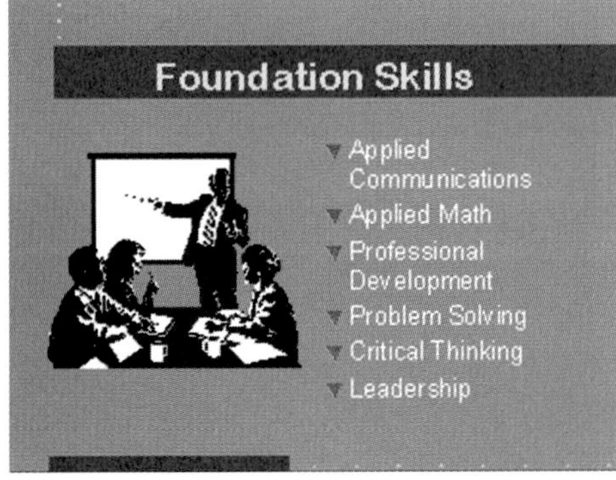

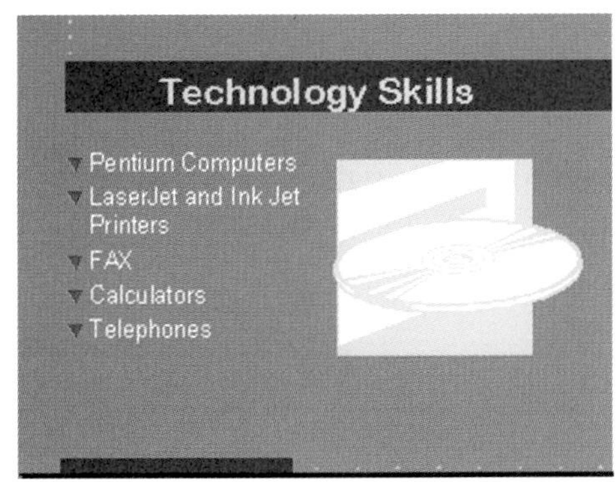

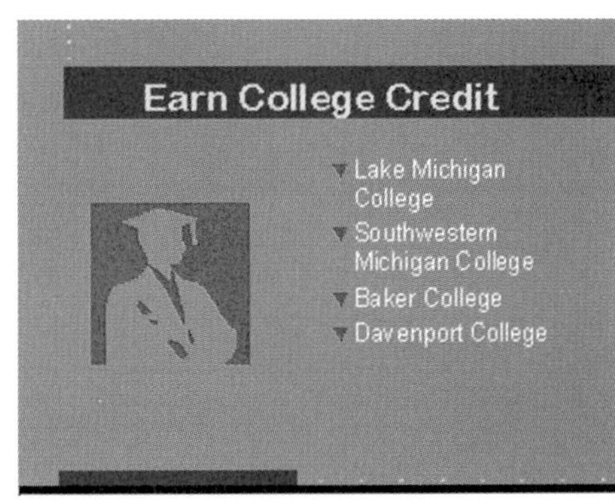

Assessment 2

You work for a travel vacation company named Paradise Vacations that specializes in selling vacation package plans to tropical locations. Your company is setting up a display booth at a well-attended travel trade show. You need to create an electronic slide show to be run continuously in your booth. Your target audience is travel consultants who sell vacation package plans to their clients. Your goal is to inform your audience of the travel plan benefits your company can offer to their travel clients, thereby motivating the travel consultants to promote your vacation packages when selling travel plans to their clients. Using specific text from figure 9.25, create an on-screen presentation in PowerPoint according to the following specifications: (The *Tropical.pot* template from Office 95 is an excellent template for this exercise. If you have the 95 templates available to you, consider using this particular design template.)

1. Use the AutoContent Wizard to help you organize your presentation. Select *Product/Service Overview* as the type of presentation you are going to give. (As you know, the AutoContent Wizard is automatically displayed when PowerPoint is loaded.)
2. When the first slide displays, change to Outline view. Utilizing the information provided in figure 9.25, Paradise Vacations Text, use the ideas supplied in the slide presentation design template to guide you in organizing your presentation. You can also edit the text to fit your needs.
3. After completing your presentation in Outline view, switch to Slide view.
4. Apply an appropriate presentation design.
5. Use a build effect for the bulleted items. You decide on the bullet symbol to be used.
6. Apply transition effects to your slides. You decide if you want one type of transition for the whole presentation or if you want a different transition for each slide.
7. Time the slides to change every 8 seconds.
8. Make the slide show a continuous on-screen presentation by completing the following steps:
   a. Click Slide Show, Set Up Show.
   b. At the Set Up Show dialog box, click in the check box to the left of Loop continuously until 'Esc'.
9. Save the presentation and name it c09sa02, Paradise.ppt.
10. Run the on-screen presentation for a classmate or your instructor.
11. Print and then close c09sa02, Paradise.ppt. (Check with your instructor about printing this presentation. One suggestion is to print six slides per page in Black and White to save on paper and printer ink.)

Optional: Add animation and sound effects to your Paradise Presentation.

figure 9.25

Paradise Vacations Text

Paradise Vacations, specializing in tropical vacations, offers over thirty-five fabulous vacation destinations. You can select from over 225 hotels, resorts, condos, and villas at some of the most popular destinations in the Caribbean, Mexico, the Bahamas, Bermuda, Florida, and Hawaii. Choose from a range of moderate to luxurious accommodations, including several all-inclusive vacation properties.

Departing from over fifty U.S. cities, Paradise Vacations is one of the nation's leading vacation companies. We offer value, quality, variety, reliability, and superior service.

Paradise Vacations include roundtrip airfare, hotel accommodations, roundtrip airport-hotel transfers, hotel taxes, hotel service charges and surcharges, and the services of a Paradise representative at your destination.

Your Paradise Representative is professionally trained, friendly, and reliable. Your representative will direct you to your airport-hotel transfer, acquaint you with your destination, arrange optional excursions, and answer your questions.

Our own Hotel Rating Guide helps you to select the accommodations that best fit your needs. Ratings are based on property location, cleanliness, amenities, service, and room quality.

We offer a free Price Protection Guarantee. Sometimes the price of a vacation package plan changes. We guarantee that once your balance is paid in full, we will not increase the price of your vacation. In addition, we periodically offer special promotion prices on vacation package plans. If we advertise a discounted price on the exact same vacation you have booked, you will automatically receive the savings.

Travel with Paradise and travel with the best! Contact your travel consultant for vacation packages and ask for Paradise Vacations!

Assessment 3

1. Create your own home page using the *Personal Home Page (Standard).pot* template at the New Presentation, Presentations tab dialog box. If you are pursuing a new position in the near future, you may wish to include Education and Experience as Custom Topic A and Custom Topic B.
2. Scan a photo to include on one of the pages.
3. Change the slide Color Scheme, Background, and bullets.
4. Add animation and sound.
5. Save the presentation and name it c09sa03, Home.ppt.
6. Print your home page presentation as slides.
7. Close c09sa03, Home.ppt.

creative activity

Use the Help feature in PowerPoint and the Office Assistant to learn more about PowerPoint and the Web. Create a Web home page on a subject of your choice using PowerPoint. Include the following specifications in your presentation:

1. Click Help, Contents and Index, then select the Index tab.
2. Key **Getting Results - PowerPoint Web Page**, or **Getting Results - Web and PowerPoint**.
3. Print the information from each of these cards.
4. Apply what you have learned about PowerPoint and the Web in creating a Web home page.
5. Include two text hyperlinks in your Web page.
6. Include one graphic hyperlink.
7. Use any graphic bullets and/or graphic horizontal lines that are appropriate to the mood of your Web page.
8. Enhance your presentation with color, fonts, font sizes, etc.
9. Save your Web page as c09ca01, Web Page.html.
10. Print and then close c09ca01, Web Page.html.

Unit two

PERFORMANCE ASSESSMENTS

Assume you are working for a well-known certified public accounting firm, named Winston & McKenzie, CPA. A relatively new department in your firm, Executive Search Services, offers other companies assistance in searching for individuals to fill executive positions. You have been asked to prepare various presentation materials that will be used to inform other partners (owners), staff members, and clients of the scope of this department.

First, you will create a fact sheet highlighting the services of the Executive Search Department and the qualifications of its consultants. Second, you will prepare a self-mailer brochure that lists the services of the Executive Search Department, the benefits to the reader, the way to obtain more information, and a mailing label section. Additionally, you will create a PowerPoint presentation outlining the approach Executive Search Services uses when helping a company conduct an executive search.

Think about the audience of an accounting firm in general, and then think more specifically about the audience that might use Executive Search Services. Before you begin, print *fact sheet text.doc, W&McK text1.doc, W&McK text2.doc*, and *W&McK text3.doc* located on your student data disk. Read the text in these documents to familiarize yourself with the services offered by this company. Include some consistent elements in all your documents. Use a logo, a graphic image, a special character, text boxes, ruled lines, borders, fill, or color to create unity among the documents. Incorporate design concepts of focus, balance, proportion, contrast, directional flow, color, and appropriate use of white space.

Assessment one

Using the text in *fact sheet text.doc*, create a fact sheet highlighting the services offered by Winston & McKenzie's Executive Services according to the following specifications:

1. Create a thumbnail sketch (experiment!) of your proposed page layout and design.
2. Create styles for repetitive formatting, such as for bulleted text or headings.
3. Design a simple logo using the Drawing toolbar, WordArt, or other Word features.
4. Vary the fonts, type sizes, and type styles to emphasize the relative importance of items.

5. Use bullets to list the services offered. You decide on the character to be used as a bullet.
6. You may use any relevant picture, symbols, borders, colors, etc. in your fact sheet. You decide on the position, size, shading, border/fill, spacing, alignment, etc.
7. Save the document and name it u02pa01, fact sheet.
8. Print and then close u02pa01, fact sheet.
9. Print a copy of the Document Evaluation Checklist. Use the checklist to evaluate your fact sheet. Hand in both items.

Assessment two

Using the text in *W&McK text1.doc; W&McK text2.doc;* and *W&McK text3.doc* located on your student data disk, create a three-panel brochure according to the following specifications: (**Note:** Save periodically as you work through this assessment.)

1. Create a dummy of the brochure layout so you know exactly which panel will be used for each section of text. Use *W&McK text1.doc* as the text in panel 1, *W&McK text2.doc* as the text in panel 2, and *W&McK text3.doc* as the text in panel 3. (Panel 3 is actually the information request side of a card the reader can send to the company for more information. The mailing address side, which is panel 4, will be created in step 5.)
2. Prepare a thumbnail sketch of your proposed layout and design.
3. Include the following formatting:
   a. Change the paper size to Letter Landscape.
   b. Change the top, bottom, left, and right margins to 0.5 inches (or as close to this as possible).
   c. Turn on kerning at 14 points.
4. Create the inside panels of the brochure according to the following specifications:
   a. Use the column feature to divide the page into panels using uneven columns.
   b. You decide on appropriate typeface, type size, and type style selections that best reflect the mood or tone of this document and the company or business it represents.
   c. Create a customized drop cap to be used at the beginning of each paragraph in panel 1. You decide on the color, position, the typeface, the number of lines to drop, and the distance from the text.
   d. Create any styles that will save you time and keystrokes, such as styles for headings, body text, and bulleted items.
   e. Itemize any lists with bullets. You decide on the bullet symbol, size, color, spacing, etc.
   f. Use text boxes to specifically position text if necessary or to highlight text in a unique way.
   g. Include ruled lines. You decide on the line style, thickness, placement, color, etc.
5. To make the brochure self-mailable, create the mailing address side of the request for information (created in panel 3) by completing the following steps in panel 4:

a. Include the following text at the top of the panel:

For More Information About Our Executive Search Services: Please call Janet Rankins at (317) 555-6342 or Bill Bush at (317) 555-8989 or complete the attached information request card.

b. Create a dotted line from margin to margin within the panel to represent a cutting line or perforated line. Pay attention to the placement of this dotted line. If the reader were to cut the reply/request card on this line, are the items on the reverse side of the card (panel 3) placed appropriately? If not, make adjustments.

c. Insert the mailing address into a text box, then use Word's Text Direction feature to create the mailing address. You decide on an appropriate font, type size, and color. Key the following address:

Winston & McKenzie, CPA
Executive Search Services
4600 North Meridian Street
Indianapolis, IN 46240

d. Use the mouse to size and position the text box containing the mailing address to an appropriate mailing address position. You can also use the Format Text Box dialog box to position the text box more precisely.

e. Follow steps 5c and 5d to create the return address. Use the same address as in step 5c. Position the return address text box into an appropriate return address position.

6. Create the cover of the brochure by completing the following steps in panel 6:
   a. Key **You Can't Afford to Make the Wrong Hiring Decision!** as the title of the brochure.
   b. Use any appropriate graphic image you have available or create your own logo on the front cover of the brochure. You decide on the position, size, and border/fill, if any. (Some suggestions from Word 97's picture selection include *Agree.wmf, Meeting.wmf,* or *Meeting2.wmf.*)
   c. Decide on an appropriate location and include the company name, address, and the following phone and fax numbers:

Phone:	**(317) 555-8900**
Fax:	**(317) 555-8901**

7. Save the brochure and name it u02pa02, brochure.
8. Print and then close u02pa02, brochure.
9. Print a copy of *document evaluation checklist.doc*. Use the checklist to evaluate your brochure. Make any changes, if necessary. Hand in both items.

Optional: To save on mailing costs, you have to send out postcards to prospective clients. Rewrite and shorten the text in *W&McK text1.doc* so it highlights the pertinent points, but fits onto a 4-by-6-inch postcard. Include the company's name, address, phone, and fax numbers.

Assessment three

In addition to being an employee at Winston & McKenzie, you are also active as a volunteer for the Metropolitan Art League. One of your responsibilities is to create an on-screen presentation highlighting important aspects of the Art League. Create the presentation by completing the following steps: (The *Theater.pot* design template from Office (PowerPoint) 95 is an excellent template for this presentation—if the 95 templates are available to you, consider using this particular template.)

1. Open *Spotlight.ppt* located on your student data disk.
2. Apply an appropriate presentation design.
3. Use a build effect for bulleted items. You decide on the bullet symbol to be used.
4. Apply transition effects to your slides.
5. Make the slide show a continuous on-screen presentation. You decide the time increments for the slides.
6. Enhance the presentation with varying fonts, font sizes, and colors.
7. Use any appropriate clip art images, symbols, pictures, etc. (Hint: *Artist.wmf, Conductr.wmf, Dancers.wmf,* and *Theatre.wmf* located on your student data disk.)
8. Save the presentation and name it u02pa03, spotlight.ppt.
9. Print and then close u02pa03, spotlight.ppt.

Optional: Add an appropriate sound—click Format, point to Movies and Sounds, and insert a sound clip from Microsoft Clip Gallery.

Assessment four

Use the text in the brochure in Assessment 2 (the text is also located on your student data disk as *W&McK text1.doc, W&McK text2.doc, and W&McK text 3.doc*) to create a Web home page for Winston & McKenzie, CPA. The Web page should highlight the services of the Executive Search Department. Include the following specifications:

1. Use the Web Page Wizard, the Blank Web Page template, or create the home page as a Word document and save it in HTML.
2. Create a thumbnail of the Web home page.
3. Use appropriate graphical bullets.
4. Use a graphic horizontal line—choose an appropriate line style.
5. Enhance the text with bold, italic, varying fonts, font sizes, and color.
6. Use a background color or fill effect.
7. Include a graphic or photo.
8. Insert two hyperlinks (graphic links or text links).
9. Include an address, phone number, fax number, and an E-mail address.
10. View the Web page in Web Page Preview.
11. Save the document and name it u02pa04, Web Page.html.
12. Print and then close u02pa04, Web Page.html.

Optional: Include scrolling text or sound.

Unit three

PREPARING PUBLICATIONS

In this unit, you will learn to create newsletters, reports, term papers, and manuals along with a variety of visual enhancements.

s c a n s

The Secretary's Commission on Achieving Necessary Skills

DECISION MAKING

TECHNOLOGY

PROBLEM SOLVING

COMMUNICATIONS

10 Creating Basic Elements of a Newsletter

PERFORMANCE OBJECTIVE

Upon successful completion of chapter 10, you will be able to create newsletters using your own designs based on desktop publishing concepts and Word features such as columns and styles. You will also be able to improve the readability of your newsletters by specifying line spacing, using kerning, adjusting character spacing, and changing alignment.

Desktop Publishing Concepts

Grid
Layout and design
Consistency
Thumbnail sketch
Newsletter elements
Readability
Color
Leading

Word Features Used

Styles
Kerning
Line spacing
Character spacing
Newspaper (snaking) columns
Balanced and unbalanced columns
WordArt
Widow/orphan protection
Paragraph indentation
Em space
Graphics images

The demand for newsletters in the private and business sectors has helped to promote the desktop publishing revolution. Affordable word processing and desktop publishing software, along with laser printers, significantly reduced the cost of producing professional-quality newsletters. Now users with limited budgets can create multipage documents in-house, providing organizations, businesses, or individuals with cost-effective means of communicating.

Newsletters are one of the most common means of communicating information and ideas to other people. Newsletters can be published by individuals, associations, clubs, churches, schools, businesses, consultants, service organizations, political organizations, and other establishments from all over the world.

Designing a newsletter may appear to be a simple task, but newsletters are more complex than they appear. Newsletters can be the ultimate test of your desktop publishing skills. Remember that your goal is to get the message across. Design is important because it increases the overall appeal of your newsletter, but content is still the most important consideration. Whether your purpose for creating a newsletter is to develop better communication within your company or to develop awareness of a product or service, your newsletter must give the appearance of being well planned, orderly, and consistent. In order to establish consistency from one issue of a newsletter to the next, carefully plan your document.

DTP POINTERS
Newsletter design should be consistent from issue to issue.

Defining Basic Newsletter Elements

Successful newsletters contain consistent elements in every issue. Basic newsletter elements divide the newsletter into organized sections to help the reader understand the text, as well as to entice the reader to continue reading. Basic newsletter elements usually include the items described in figure 10.1. Figure 10.2 illustrates the location of these basic elements on a newsletter page. Additional newsletter enhancements and elements are presented in chapter 11.

figure 10.1

Basic Newsletter Elements

- *Nameplate:* The nameplate, or banner, consists of the newsletter's title and is usually located on the front page. Nameplates can include the company logo, a unique typeface, or a graphic image to help create or reinforce a company identity. A *logo* is a distinct graphic symbol representing a company.
- *Subtitle:* A subtitle is a short phrase describing the purpose or audience of the newsletter. A subtitle can also be called a *tagline*. The information in the subtitle is usually located below the nameplate near the folio.
- *Folio:* A folio is the publication information, including the volume number, issue number, and the current date of the newsletter. The folio usually appears near the nameplate, but it can also be displayed at the bottom or side of a page. In desktop publishing, *folio* can also mean page number.
- *Headlines:* Headlines are titles to articles that are frequently created to attract the reader's attention. The headline can be set in 22- to 72-point type or larger and is generally keyed in a sans serif typeface.
- *Subheads (Section Headings):* Subheads are secondary headings that provide the transition from headlines to body copy. Subheads can also be referred to as *Section Headings* since they break up the text into organized sections. Subheads are usually bolded and sometimes keyed in larger type sizes. There may be more space above a subhead than below.
- *Byline:* The byline identifies the author of the article.
- *Body Copy:* The main part of the newsletter is the body copy or text.
- *Graphic Image:* Graphic images are added to newsletters to help stimulate ideas and add interest to the document. They provide visual clues and visual relief from text-intensive copy.

figure 10.2

Basic Elements of a Newsletter

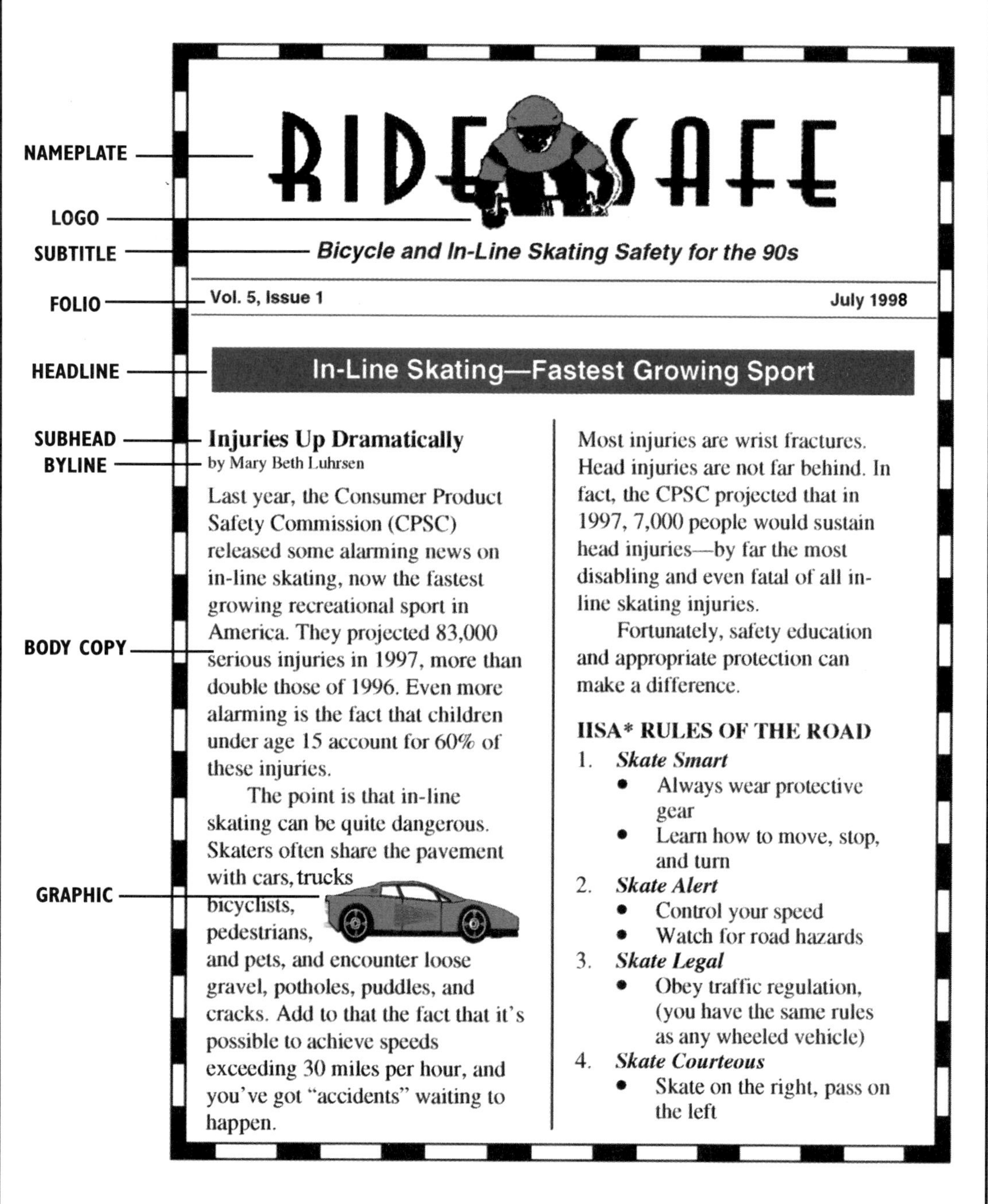

RIDE SAFE

Bicycle and In-Line Skating Safety for the 90s

Vol. 5, Issue 1 July 1998

In-Line Skating—Fastest Growing Sport

Injuries Up Dramatically

by Mary Beth Luhrsen

Last year, the Consumer Product Safety Commission (CPSC) released some alarming news on in-line skating, now the fastest growing recreational sport in America. They projected 83,000 serious injuries in 1997, more than double those of 1996. Even more alarming is the fact that children under age 15 account for 60% of these injuries.

The point is that in-line skating can be quite dangerous. Skaters often share the pavement with cars, trucks bicyclists, pedestrians, and pets, and encounter loose gravel, potholes, puddles, and cracks. Add to that the fact that it's possible to achieve speeds exceeding 30 miles per hour, and you've got "accidents" waiting to happen.

Most injuries are wrist fractures. Head injuries are not far behind. In fact, the CPSC projected that in 1997, 7,000 people would sustain head injuries—by far the most disabling and even fatal of all in-line skating injuries.

Fortunately, safety education and appropriate protection can make a difference.

IISA* RULES OF THE ROAD

1. ***Skate Smart***
   - Always wear protective gear
   - Learn how to move, stop, and turn
2. ***Skate Alert***
   - Control your speed
   - Watch for road hazards
3. ***Skate Legal***
   - Obey traffic regulation, (you have the same rules as any wheeled vehicle)
4. ***Skate Courteous***
   - Skate on the right, pass on the left

Planning a Newsletter

Before creating your newsletter, consider your target audience and your objective for providing the information. Is the goal of your newsletter to sell? inform? explain? or announce? What is the purpose of the newsletter? Companies and organizations often use newsletters to convey a sense of pride and teamwork among employees or members. When planning a company newsletter, consider the following suggestions:

- If a scanner is available, use pictures of different people from your organization in each issue.
- Provide contributor forms requesting information from employees.
- Keep the focus of the newsletter on issues of interest to the majority of employees.
- Make sure you include articles of interest to varying levels of employment.
- Hand out regular surveys to evaluate newsletter relevancy.

If the aim of your newsletter is to promote a product, the focal point may be a graphic image or photograph of the product rather than more general company news. Your aim can also influence the selection of typefaces, type sizes, and visual elements and even the placement of all these elements.

Also consider the following questions when planning your document: What is the image you want to project? How often will the newsletter appear? What is your budget? How much time can you devote to its creation? What items are likely to be repeated from issue to issue? And, will your newsletter accommodate ads, photographs, or clip art in its layout? After answering these questions, you are ready to begin designing your newsletter.

DTP POINTERS
Look at as many publications as you can to get ideas for design.

Designing a Newsletter

Desktop publishing concepts and guidelines discussed in previous chapters will provide you with a good starting point for your newsletter. These guidelines emphasize the use of consistency, balance, proportion, contrast, white space, focus, directional flow, and color. If you are designing a newsletter for a company, make sure the design coordinates with your firm's corporate identity by using the same logo, typefaces, type sizes, column arrangements, and color choices that are used in other corporate correspondence.

Applying Desktop Publishing Guidelines

One of the biggest challenges in creating a newsletter is balancing change with consistency. A newsletter is a document that is typically reproduced on a regular basis, whether monthly, bimonthly, or quarterly. With each issue, new ideas can be presented, new text created, and new graphics or photos used. However, for your newsletter to be effective, each issue must also maintain a consistent appearance. Consistency contributes to your publication's identity and gives your readers a feeling of familiarity.

DTP POINTERS
Many logos are trademarks—before using them, find out whether you need permission.

When designing your newsletter, think about the elements that should remain consistent from issue to issue. Consistent newsletter features and elements may include: size of margins, column layout, nameplate formatting and location, logos, color, ruled lines, formatting of headlines, subheads, and body text. Later in the chapter, you will create styles to automate the process of formatting consistent elements.

Focus and balance can be achieved in a newsletter through the design and size of the nameplate, the arrangement of text on the page, the use of graphic images or scanned photographs, or the careful use of lines, borders, and backgrounds. When using graphic images or photos, use restraint and consider the appropriateness of the image. A single, large illustration is usually preferred over many small images scattered throughout the document. Size graphic images or photos according to their relative importance to the content. Headlines and subheads can serve as secondary focal points as well as provide balance to the total document.

DTP POINTERS
Use graphic accents with discretion.

White space around a headline creates contrast and attracts the reader's eyes to the headline. Surround text with white space if you want the text to stand out. If you want to draw attention to the nameplate or headline of the newsletter, you may want to choose a bold type style and a larger type size. Another option is to use WordArt to emphasize the nameplate title. Use sufficient white space throughout your newsletter to break up gray areas of text and to offer the reader visual relief.

Good directional flow can be achieved by using ruled lines that lead the reader's eyes through the document. Graphic elements, placed strategically throughout a newsletter, can provide a pattern for the reader's eyes to follow.

In figure 10.2, focus, balance, contrast, and directional flow were achieved through the placement of graphic images at the top and bottom of the document, the blue shaded text box with reverse text, and bolded headings.

If you decide to use color in a newsletter, use it sparingly. Establish focus and directional flow by using color to highlight key information or elements in your publication. The use of color as a newsletter enhancement will be discussed in chapter 11.

Creating a Newsletter Page Layout

Typically, page layout begins with size and orientation of the paper and the margins desired for the newsletter. Next, decisions on the number, length, and width of columns become imperative. Typefaces, type sizes, and type styles must also be considered. In addition, graphic images, ruled lines, and shading and coloring decisions must be made.

Choosing Paper Size and Type

One of the first considerations in designing a newsletter page layout is the paper size and type. The number of copies needed and the equipment available for creating, printing, and distributing the newsletter can affect this decision. Most newsletters are created on standard-size 8½-by-11-inch paper, although some are printed on larger sheets such as 8½-by-14 inches. The most economical choice for printing is the standard 8½-by-11-inch paper. Also, consider that 8½-by-11-inch paper is easier to hold and read, cheaper to mail, and fits easily in standard file folders.

Paperweight is determined by the cost, the quality desired, and the graphics or photographs included. The heavier the stock, the more expensive the paper. In addition, pure white paper is more difficult to read because of glare. If possible, investigate other, more subtle colors. Another option is to purchase predesigned newsletter paper from a paper supply company. These papers come in many colors and designs. Several have different blocks of color created on a page to help separate and organize your text.

Creating Margins for Newsletters

DTP POINTERS
Be generous with your margins; do not crowd text.

After considering the paper size and type, determine the margins of your newsletter pages. The margin size is linked to the number of columns needed, the formality desired, the visual elements used, the amount of text available, and the type of binding. Keep your margins consistent throughout your newsletter. Listed here are a few generalizations about margins in newsletters:

- A wide right margin is considered formal. This approach positions the text at the left side of the page—the side where most readers tend to look first. If the justification is set at full, the newsletter will appear even more formal.
- A wide left margin is less formal. A table of contents or marginal subheads can be placed in the left margin giving the newsletter an airy, open appearance.
- Equal margins tend to create an informal look.

DTP POINTERS
Place page numbers on the outside edges when using mirror margins.

If you plan to create a multipage newsletter with facing pages, you may want to use Word's mirror margin feature, which accommodates wider inside or outside margins. Figures 10.3 and 10.4 illustrate mirror margins in a newsletter. Often the inside margin is wider than the outside margin; however, this may be dependent on the amount of space the binding takes up. To create facing pages with mirror margins, click File, then Page Setup. At the Page Setup dialog box, select the Margins tab, then select the Mirror margins option. If you plan to include page numbering, position the numbers on the outside edges of each page.

Gutter
Extra space added to the inside margin to accommodate the binding.

Also consider increasing the *gutter* space to accommodate the binding on a multipage newsletter. To add gutter space on facing pages, add the extra space to the inside edges; on regular pages, add space to the left edges. To add gutters, display the Page Setup dialog box with the Margins tab selected, then select or key a gutter width at the Gutter option. Gutters do not change the margins, but rather add extra space to the margins. However, gutters make the printing area of your page narrower.

figure 10.3

Outside Mirror Margins in Facing Pages of a Newsletter

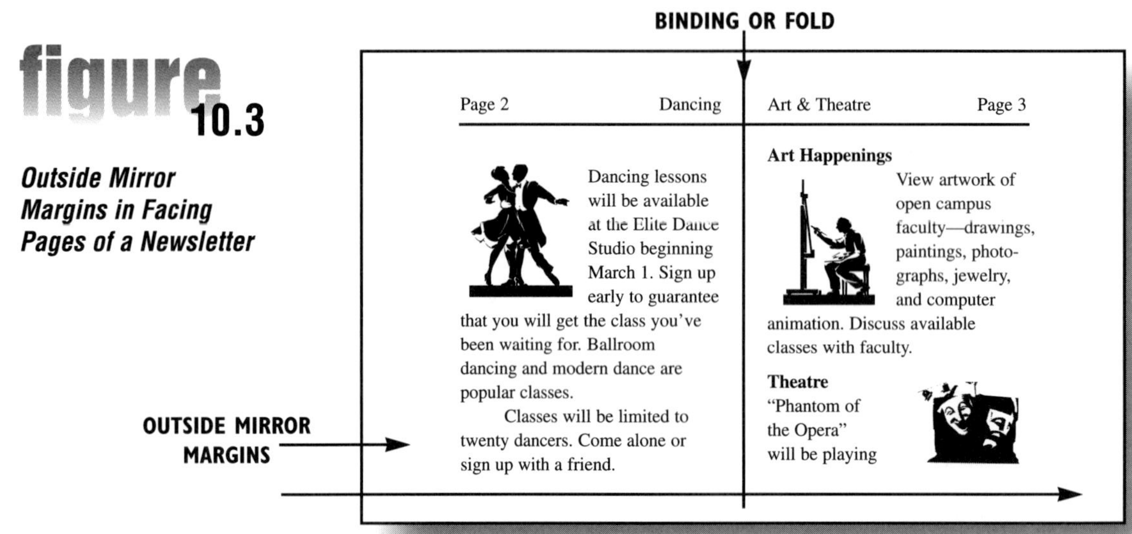

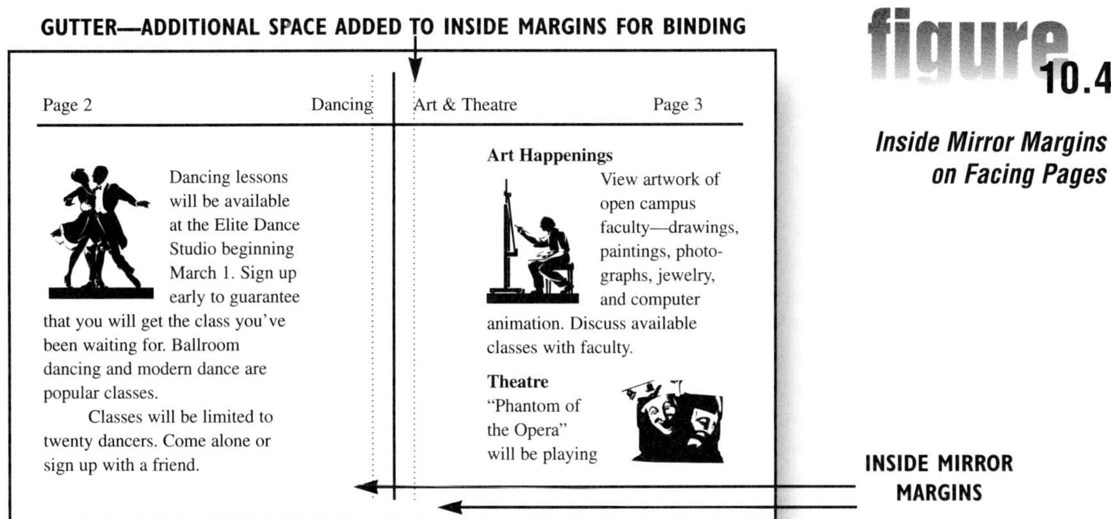

figure 10.4

Inside Mirror Margins on Facing Pages

Objects and text boxes default to the None wrapping style. Pictures default to the Top and Bottom wrapping style. By changing the wrapping style to Square or Tight, or adjusting the Edit Wrap Points to move text closer to an object or box, you are able to position design elements anywhere on a page and have text wrap around them. You can position text, objects, or pictures in the margins of a newsletter or in the middle of two columns to add interest and emphasis. More information will be provided in chapter 11 on creating and positioning design elements such as pull quotes, sidebars, and more.

Creating Newspaper Columns for Newsletters

When preparing newsletters, an important consideration is the readability of the document. *Readability* is the ease with which a person can read and understand groups of words. The line length of text in a document can enhance or detract from the readability of text. To improve readability of newsletters, you may want to set the text in columns.

Readability
The ease with which a person can read and understand a group of words.

Newspaper columns in a newsletter promote the smooth flow of text and guide the reader's eyes. As discussed earlier in chapter 6, Word's newspaper column feature (also called *snaking columns*) allows text to flow up and down columns in the document. In order to work with columns, Word must be set to page layout view. When the first column on the page is filled with text, the insertion point moves to the top of the next column on the same page. When the last column on the page is filled, the insertion point moves to the beginning of the first column on the next page.

Snaking Columns
Another name for newspaper columns where text flows up and down columns.

As you know, newspaper columns can be created using the Columns button on the Standard toolbar or with options from the Columns dialog box. Columns of equal width are created with the Columns button on the Standard toolbar. To create columns of unequal width, use the Columns dialog box shown in figure 10.5. To display this dialog box, click Format, then Columns. Notice the options selected in the Columns dialog box in figure 10.5—three columns of equal width with 0.5-inch Spacing, Line between, and Apply to: This point forward. Generally, keying text first and then formatting it into newspaper columns is considered faster.

Columns Dialog Box

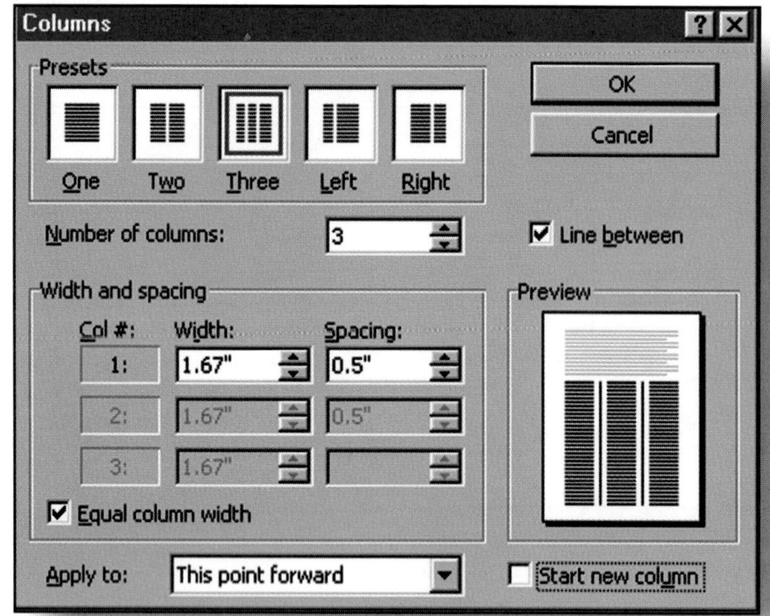

Using Balanced and Unbalanced Columns

Word automatically lines up (balances) the last line of text at the bottom of each column. On the last page of a newsletter, the text is often not balanced between columns. Text in the first column may flow to the bottom of the page, while the text in the second column may end far short of the bottom of the page. Columns can be balanced by inserting a section break at the end of the text by completing the following steps:

1. Position the insertion point at the end of the text in the last column of the section you want to balance.
2. Click Insert, then Break.
3. At the Break dialog box, click Continuous.
4. Click OK or press Enter.

Figure 10.6 shows the last page of a document containing unbalanced columns and a page where the columns have been balanced. If you want to force a new page to start after the balanced columns, click after the continuous break and then insert a manual page break.

Unbalanced and Balanced Columns

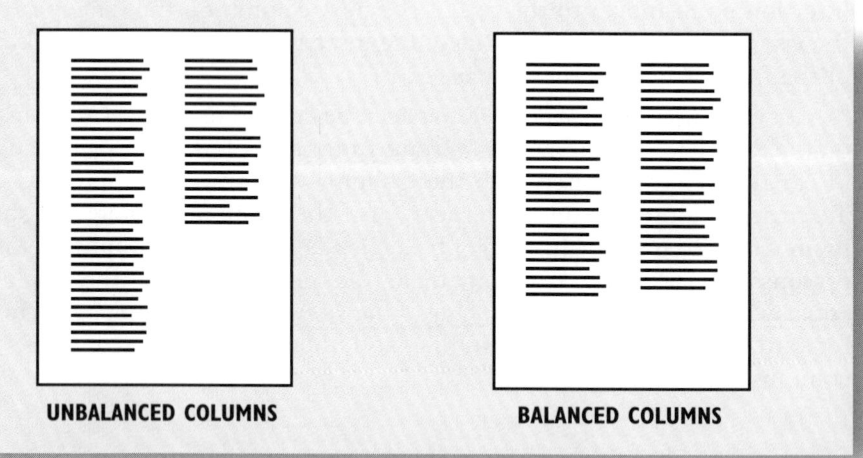

Determining Number of Columns

The number of columns used in newsletters may vary from one column to four or more columns. The size of the paper used, the font and type size selected, the content and amount of text available, and many other design considerations affect this decision.

One-column newsletters are easy to produce since the articles simply follow each other. If you do not have much time to work on your newsletter, this format is the one to use. The one-column format is the simplest to design and work with because it allows you to make changes and additions easily. You will want to use a large type size—usually 12 points—to accommodate the long line length of a one-column design. Be sure to use wide margins with this column layout. Also, keep in mind that an asymmetrically designed page is more interesting to look at than a symmetrical one, as shown in figure 10.7.

Asymmetrical Design

XXXXXXXXXXX
XXXXXX
XXXXXXXXXXX
XXXXXXXXXXX
XXXXXXXXXXX
XXXXXXXXXXX
XXX
XXXXXXXXXXX
XXXXXXXX

XXXXXXXXXXXXXXXXXX
XXXXXXXXXXXXXXXXXX

Symmetrical Design

XXXXXXXXXXXXXXXXXX
XXXXXXXXXXXXXXXXXX
XXXXXXXXXXXXXXXXXX
XXXXXXXXXXXXXXXXXX
XXXXXXXXXXXXXXXXXX

figure 10.7

Asymmetrical and Symmetrical Design in Newsletters

The two-column newspaper format is the most frequently used selection for newsletters. It gives a formal look, especially if used with justified text. Generally use type sizes between 10 and 12 points when using a two-column layout. Be careful to avoid *tombstoning*, which occurs when headings display side by side in adjacent columns. Using an asymmetrical design in which one column is wider than the other and adding graphic enhancements will make this classic two-column format more interesting.

Tombstoning
When headings display side by side in adjacent columns.

A three-column format is successful if you avoid using too much text on the page. This popular format is more flexible for adding interesting design elements. You may use a smaller type size (9 to 11 points) and therefore fit more information on a page. You can also place headings, text, and graphics across one, two, or three columns to create a distinctive flow. Often, one column is reserved for a table of contents, marginal subheads, or a masthead (publication information), thus allowing for more white space in the document and more visual interest.

A four-column design gives you even more flexibility than the three-column layout; however, more time may be spent in putting this newsletter layout together. Leaving one column fairly empty with a great deal of white space to offset more text-intensive columns is a visually appealing solution. This format gives you many opportunities to display headings, graphics, and other design elements across one or more columns. You will need to use a small type size for your text—9 to 10 points.

Using Varying Numbers of Columns in a Newsletter

Section breaks can be used to vary the page layout within a single newsletter. For instance, you can use a section break to separate a one-column nameplate from text that can be created in three-columns as shown in figure 10.8.

There are three ways to insert section breaks into a document. One way is to use the Break dialog box. (To display this dialog box, click Insert, then Break.) Another way to break up your text into sections is to use the Columns dialog box and tell Word to format text into columns from *This point forward* from the location of the insertion point. The third way is to select the text first, then apply column formatting.

10.8

Section Breaks in Newsletters

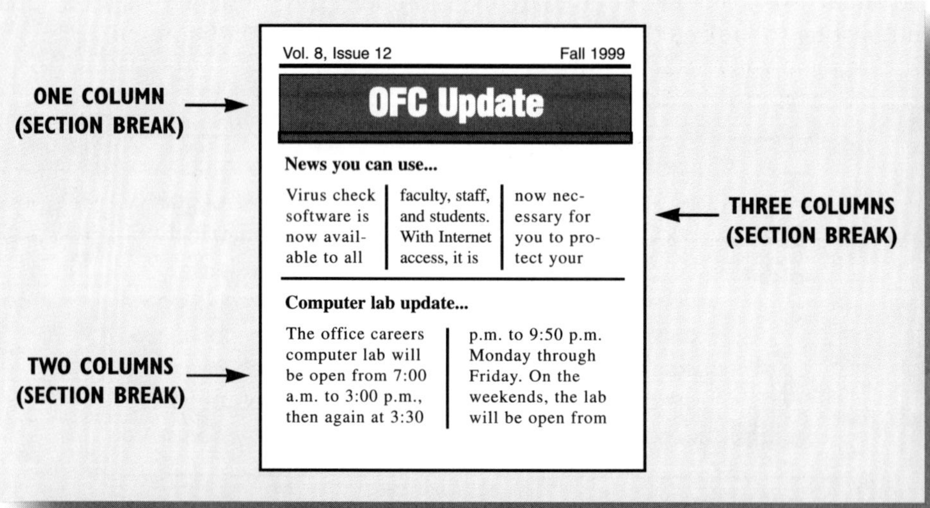

To move the insertion point between columns, use the mouse or press Alt + up arrow to move the insertion point to the top of the previous column, or Alt + down arrow to move the insertion point to the top of the next column.

Additionally, when formatting text into columns, Word automatically breaks the columns to fit the page. If a column break appears in an undesirable location, you can insert a column break into the document to control where the columns end and begin on the page. To insert a column break, position the insertion point where you want the new column to begin, then press Ctrl + Shift + Enter or click Insert, Break, then Column break.

Changing the Number of Columns

To change the number of columns for an entire newsletter, click Edit, then Select All; to change the number of columns for part of a document, select the affected text only; to change the number of columns in several existing sections, click to select the multiple sections. After selecting the areas you want to change, click Format, then Columns, then enter the number of columns desired.

If you want to remove columns in your newsletter, click in the section or select multiple sections you want to change, then click Format, then Columns, and then click One.

Determining Column Width

Column width, type size, and leading are related, in that altering one setting affects the settings of the others. As a general rule, narrow columns are easier to read than wide ones, but the number of words is important. Typically columns contain 5 to 15 words per line. In typesetting, the vertical line spacing, measured from the baseline of one line of text to the baseline of the next line of text, is referred to as *leading*. In general, short lines use minimal leading, whereas long lines require more leading.

Leading
Vertical line spacing measured from the baseline of one line to the baseline of the next line.

One method for determining column width is based on the typeface and point size used. Use a typeface and type size you intend to use in the body text (choose a serif font in a type size between 10 and 12 points). Type a complete lowercase alphabet, print it, measure the length of the alphabet with a ruler, and multiply by 1.5 to determine the column width, as shown in figure 10.9 (Use the desktop ruler attached to the back of this textbook.) Generally, line length should be approximately 1.5 to 2 alphabets or 39 to 52 characters.

Line length in typesetting is usually measured in *picas*. Since 6 picas equals 1 inch, a line length of 5 inches would be measured as 30 picas. A guideline in typesetting is that the line length measured in picas does not exceed twice the point size of the type. For instance, 12-point type looks best in a 20- to 23-pica column.

Picas
Line length in typesetting—6 picas equal 1 inch.

figure 10.9

Determining Column Width

12-point Times New Roman	**12-point Palatia**
abcdefghijklmnopqrstuvwxyz	abcdefghijklmnopqrstuvwxyz
Measures: **2 inches**	Measures: **2.25 inches**
2 x 1.5 = **3 inches**	2.25 x 1.5 = **3.38 inches**
3 inches = 18 picas	**3.38 inches = 22.8 picas**

Changing Column Widths

If your newsletter is divided into sections, click in the section you want to change, then drag the column marker on the horizontal ruler. If an adjacent column is hampering your efforts to change a column width, reduce the width of the adjacent column first. If the column widths are equal, all of the columns will change. If the column widths are unequal, only the column you are adjusting changes. To specify exact measurements for columns widths, use the Columns dialog box.

Adding Vertical Lines Between Columns

Click in the section where you want to add a vertical line, then click Format, Columns. At the Columns dialog box, select the Line between check box and then close the dialog box.

Adding Borders to Newsletter Pages

You can add page borders and text box borders to change the appearance of your newsletters. Borders help separate different articles. To add a page border, click Format, Borders and Shading, select the Page Border tab, and then select a particular line Style, Width, and Color, or select a predesigned Art border.

To change a text box border, select it, double click its edge, select the Colors and Lines tab, and then select various options at the Format Text Box dialog box.

Creating Newsletter Columns with Text Boxes

Newsletters can be formatted with text boxes in place of newspaper (snaking) columns or in conjunction with newspaper columns. Text boxes allow you to start a story on one page and continue it on another, as long as it is in the same document. Suppose you want to begin an article on page 1 of a newsletter and continue it on page 3, you can make this happen by placing the text in text boxes and creating a link between them. The text will flow from one text box to another as you key the text.

Word includes a Newsletter Wizard, which provides many options for the layout of a newsletter. Text boxes are used in the formatting of two of the template styles in the Newsletter Wizard. The third style uses the newspaper column feature in addition to linked text boxes. Since chapter 10 discusses basic newsletter elements, the more advanced features such as the Newsletter Wizard, linked text boxes, table of contents, pull quotes, and more will be introduced in chapter 11.

Preparing a Grid

As mentioned in chapter 1, a grid is a valuable tool for organizing page elements and maintaining consistency in documents. This framework of lines guides the placement of margins, columns, visuals, headlines, subheads, and other elements in a newsletter. Once this layout is determined, it can be reused with slight adjustments. Many desktop publishing programs have on-screen grids to help you visualize layout. However, many word processing programs, such as Word, do not have an on-screen grid feature.

Word does include a drawing grid that helps you align drawing objects, though the gridlines are not visible on the screen. Therefore, you will need to create a rough, penciled-in grid similar to that shown in figure 10.10. Not all columns on a page have to be the same width. For example, you can create a variation of the three-column grid with two uneven columns as shown in figure 10.11. However, this format must remain consistent from page to page as well as from issue to issue.

Typesetters and professional designers measure horizontal space on a page using *picas*. A *pica* is a measurement used for determining line length in desktop publishing; there are 6 picas in a horizontal inch. Pica, inch, and point equivalents are as follows:

1 inch	=	6 picas
1 pica	=	12 points
1 point	=	1/72 inch
12p6	=	12 picas and 6 points or roughly $2^1/_8$ inches

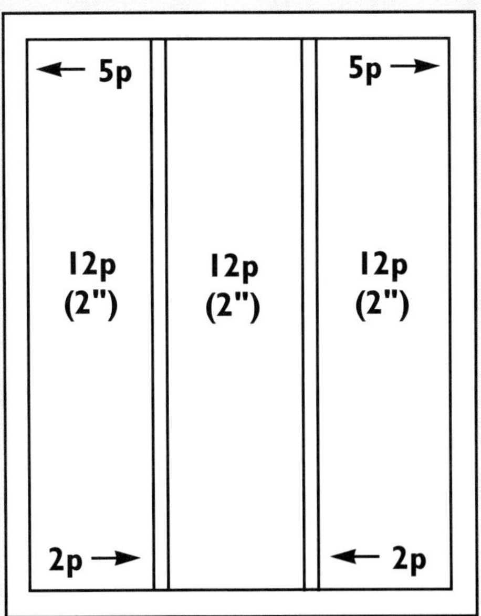

figure 10.10

Sketch of a Column Grid ("p" indicates picas)

Page 2 Underlining Grid | Underlining Grid Page 3

1 2 3 | 1 2 3

figure 10.11

Underlining Three-Column Grid

Creating a Thumbnail Sketch

One of the early steps in designing a newsletter is to plan the overall look of the document. As mentioned in chapter 1, a thumbnail sketch is a very basic, rough sketch used to visualize your design and layout, as shown in figure 10.12. Your sketch need not be anything more than a penciled-in drawing on a sheet of paper. Most designers use wavy lines for headlines, straight lines for text, and large Xs for graphic images or photographs.

A thumbnail sketch is an excellent way to experiment with different layouts and designs. Look at the work of others for hints and suggestions on different layouts. Creating a thumbnail is like "thinking" on paper.

figure 10.12

Thumbnail Sketch

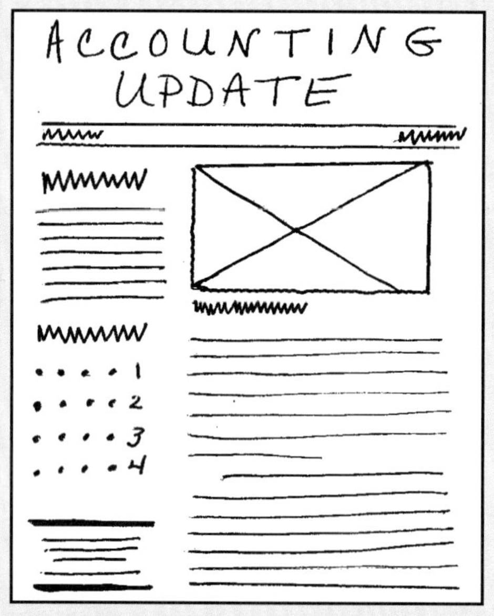

Creating Your Own Newsletter

Using Styles in Newsletters

Styles are especially valuable in saving time, effort, and keystrokes in creating newsletters. Newsletters are typically one of the most frequently created desktop publishing documents. Additionally, certain newsletter elements must remain consistent from page to page as well as from issue to issue. Styles reinforce consistency in documents by saving repetitive formatting instructions with a name so they can be applied over and over. As you will learn in chapter 11, the Newsletter Wizard includes numerous styles.

In addition to predesigned system styles included in many Word template or wizards, you have the option to create your own customized styles either based on system styles or created from scratch as previously discussed in chapter 6. Throughout the creation of the newsletter in figure 10.14, you will use various predesigned system styles and customize them to certain specifications as well as create your own styles based on existing styles. Styles created in one document can be copied to another document by clicking Style on the Format menu and then clicking Organizer.

If you apply a style, then later decide you do not want the style applied to your text, you can modify any part of the style you find undesirable at the Style dialog box, or you can simply apply the Normal style, which will replace the previous style. To apply the Normal style, position your insertion point in the text you want to reformat, click the down arrow to the right of the Style list box on the Formatting toolbar, then select the Normal style from the Style drop-down list. Or, click the Undo button on the Formatting toolbar to undo the insertion of the style.

Word also includes the option to turn on the AutoFormat feature, which automatically applies formatting without your having to select a particular style from a list. AutoFormat analyzes a Word document to identify specific elements, and then formats the text by applying styles from the attached template. AutoFormat As You Type is an option you can turn on that will format headings, numbered and bulleted lists, borders, and numbers. To view the formatting that AutoFormat will automatically apply, click Format, AutoFormat, and then Options.

Adjusting Leading in Newsletters

While creating newsletters, you may find areas where adjustments should be made to increase or decrease white space between lines. This may occur when creating a nameplate, headline, subhead, or body text. Insufficient leading makes the text difficult to read. Extra leading makes a page look less gray; however, too much leading or too little leading can make it difficult to find the beginning of the next line.

DTP POINTERS
When line length increases, line spacing (leading) should also increase.

In Word, you can adjust leading by adjusting the line spacing—single, 1.5 lines, or double—or by specifying an exact amount at the At Least or Exactly settings. Or you can adjust line and paragraph spacing at the Paragraph dialog box. To adjust line and paragraph spacing, click Format, then Paragraph. At the Paragraph dialog box, select the Indents and Spacing tab. Make selections at the Spacing section by selecting or keying a measurement Before or After your line of text.

Normal leading in Word is 120 percent of the type size being used. For example, a 10-point type has 12 points of leading. Large type size has an effect on leading. For instance, if a headline contains two lines both keyed at 30 points, the space between the two lines may be too wide. Reducing the leading will improve the appearance of the heading. Consider the following guidelines when determining leading:

- Large type requires more leading.
- Longer lines need more leading to make them easier to read.
- Sans serif type requires more leading because it does not have serifs that guide the eye along the line.
- Use styles to apply line spacing consistently in newsletters.

Adjusting Character Spacing in Newsletters

Letters in a nameplate can be altered so there is more or less space between the characters by adjusting character spacing at the Font dialog box. Figure 10.13 illustrates a nameplate that shows expanded and condensed character spacing. Kerning is usually applied to headlines and subheads.

Desktop Publishing Expanded 3 points (Matura MT Script Capitals)	Desktop Publishing Condensed 1 point (Book Antiqua)

figure 10.13
Adjusting Character Spacing

Throughout the exercises in this chapter, you will continually build the newsletter shown in figure 10.14. Each exercise involves creating a style for each specific newsletter element. Each exercise builds on the previous one, finally resulting in a completed newsletter with embedded styles and saved as a template to help you create the next issue.

figure 10.14

Ride Safe Newsletter with Elements and Styles Marked

Volume 5, Issue 1 • June 1998 ← *Folio Style*

Subtitle → ***Bicycle and In-Line Skating Safety News for the 90s •***

IN-LINE SKATING—FASTEST GROWING SPORT ← *Headline Style*

Subhead Style

Injuries Up Dramatically

by Mary Beth Luhrsen ← *By line Style*

Last year, the Consumer Product Safety Commission (CPSC) released some alarming news on in-line skating, now the fastest growing recreational sport in America. They projected 83,000 serious injuries in 1997, more than double those of 1996. Even more alarming is the fact that children under age 15 account for 60% of these injuries.

The point is that in-line skating can be quite dangerous. Skaters often share the pavement with cars, trucks, bicyclists,

pedestrians, and pets and encounter loose gravel, potholes, puddles, and cracks. Add to that the fact that it's possible to achieve speeds exceeding 30 miles per hour, and you've got "accidents" waiting to happen.

Most injuries are wrist fractures, followed by elbows or lower arm fractures. Head injuries are not far behind. In fact, the CPSC projected that in 1997, 7,000 people would sustain head injuries—by far the most potentially disabling and even fatal of all in-line skating injuries. ← *RS Body Style*

Fortunately, safety education and appropriate protection can make a difference. The International In-Line Skating Association (IISA) recommends helmets be certified to the ANSI, ASTM, or Snell bicycle helmet safety standards. Remember to think "Safety On Wheels" in 1998.

Subhead Style

A Message to Parents

by Mary Beth and Dane Luhrsen

For the past four years, Ride Safe has been committed to promoting safe bicycling and bicycle helmets. We started with our own four children (ages 2–8), who didn't want to wear helmets because their friends didn't wear them. We thought if we could offer "cool" looking helmets to a group of children, we could diminish this negative peer pressure. Our strategy worked, and the Ride Safe program has already convinced 200,000 people at over 2,000 schools to wear bicycle helmets.

In 1996, we expanded our program to include educational materials and protective gear for another very popular sport—in-line skating. Our new **Safety on Wheels™** program includes safety gear made by Skating—In Line, "the choice of champions."

We hope you will play an active role in your children's "Safety On Wheels" and give serious consideration to purchasing protective equipment for your entire family. If you have any questions about Ride Safe products and services, please call us at 800-555-RIDE.

Subhead Style

Our Ride Safe Guarantee

Ride Safe, Inc., guarantees 100% satisfaction. If anyone becomes dissatisfied with their Ride Safe product at any time, for any reason, it can be returned to Ride Safe for a refund.

Reducing the Size of Your File

The logo used in this newsletter, which is a graphic file located on your student data disk (*Ridesf1blue.bmp*), is a fairly large file. Therefore, you may want to save the document from one exercise to the next under one filename instead of naming each exercise separately and saving each to a disk.

To minimize the size of your document, you can also select the Link to file box at the Insert Picture dialog box. This option links the graphic file to the document rather than embedding it to the document file. Embedding a picture adds significantly to the size of the file. You might want to consider embedding a picture if file size is not an issue and you use a picture in every edition of your newsletter.

Creating a Folio

Creating a folio for your newsletter will be the first step in building the Ride Safe newsletter. The folio will consist of information that will change from issue to issue, such as the volume number, issue number, and date. However, the formatting applied to the folio will remain consistent with each issue. To ensure consistency, prepare a folio style and apply it to the new information keyed into the folio each month. Using this style will reduce time and effort.

Frequently, the folio is preceded or followed by a graphic line that sets the folio information apart from the rest of the nameplate. The folio can appear at the top of the nameplate as in this exercise, although it is more commonly placed below the nameplate. Reverse text can be added for emphasis and interest and text set in italic is often used.

exercise 1

Creating a Folio Style for a Newsletter

1. At a clear document screen, create the folio for the newsletter in figure 10.14 by completing the following steps:
   a. Change all the margins to 0.75 inches.
   b. Change to Page Layout viewing mode, change the Zoom Control to 75%, and click the Show/Hide ¶ button to display nonprinting characters.
   c. With the insertion point located at the beginning of the page, change the font to 13-point Impact and key **Volume 5, Issue 1**, and then press the space bar three times.
   d. Create the bullet symbol (•) as shown on the first line of the newsletter in figure 10.14, by completing the following steps:
      (1) Click Insert, then Symbol.
      (2) At the Symbol dialog box, select the Symbols tab.
      (3) Select the Wingdings font, then select the symbol in the fifth row and the sixteenth column.
      (4) Click Insert, then Close.
   e. Press the space bar three times, then key **June 1998**.
   f. Press Enter.
   g. Select *Volume 5...*, then click Format, then Font.
   h. Select the Character Spacing tab, then change the Spacing to Expanded By: **1 pt**.
   i. Turn on kerning at 13 points, then choose OK or press Enter.

j. With the text still selected, click Format, then Paragraph.
k. At the Paragraph dialog box, select the Indents and Spacing tab.
l. Change the Left Indentation to 0.25 inches, then key **6 pt** in the After text box located in the Spacing section.
m. Click OK or press Enter.
n. Select the symbol between the issue and date, click the Font Color button on the Formatting toolbar, and then select Blue in the second row of the color palette.
o. Create a style from existing text by completing the following steps:
   (1) Position the insertion point anywhere in the folio text.
   (2) Click inside the Style list box on the Formatting toolbar to select the current style name.
   (3) Key **Folio** and press Enter. (The *Folio* style is then added to the list of styles available in this document.)

2. Save the document and name it c10ex01, folio. (You may want to save this exercise and the following Ride Safe newsletter exercises under one filename to reduce disk space.)
3. Close c10ex01, folio. (You will not print until the entire newsletter has been created.)

Creating a Nameplate

A nameplate or banner is the first thing that captures the reader's eyes, and it provides immediate identification of the newsletter. A nameplate is the artwork (graphic, logo, scanned image, cropped image, etc.) or type, including the name of the publication, that is usually placed at the top of the first page of a newsletter. The choice of fonts, type sizes, and the designs of the name are important since they are seen repeatedly by the reader. See figure 10.15 and examine the sample nameplates for varying locations for newsletter elements.

DTP POINTERS
Your nameplate should sell the contents of your newsletter.

The nameplate in exercise 2 consists of the company's name and a logo bordered by two dotted lines created in the same color as the color used in the logo. Ride Safe, Inc., uses two different logo designs in most of their publications. The Ride Safe logos, however, may display in several different colors, such as blue, red, teal, orange, yellow, or purple. Most nameplates remain unchanged from issue to issue; therefore, saving it as a style is not necessary. Moreover, the nameplate should be saved to a newsletter template.

Figure 10.15 illustrates several examples of nameplates. Looking at the work of others can help you develop your own skills in design and layout.

figure 10.15

Sample Nameplates

August 1998

NAPER NEWS

Community Update ❖ Issue 20 Vol. 3

NAMEPLATE USING AN ASYMMETRICAL DESIGN

FOCUS

Desktop Publishing

Volume 2 ◆ Issue 5	News & Notes	March ◆ 1998

NAMEPLATE WITH LAYERED TEXT

Vol. 1, Issue 5 July 1998

News & Views

For Desktop Publishers

Word 97 is a Leader in Word Processing

NAMEPLATE USING WORDART, A FOLIO, A HEADLINE IN REVERSED TEXT, AND A SUBTITLE

Technology Update Volume 2 • Issue 6

August 1998

News

NAMEPLATE USING ROTATED TEXT, A GRAPHIC, AND REVERSED TEXT

figure 10.15 continued

Spring Issue 1998

29 W 036 Butterfield Road
Warrenville, IL 60555
(708) 555-1062
http://www.grower-2-you.com

NAMEPLATE WITH A COMPANY LOGO, REVERSED TEXT, AND CUSTOMIZED LINES

The Law Family Newsletter

1998 A YEAR IN REVIEW

NAMEPLATE WITH ROTATED TEXT IN REVERSE AND WITH A SHADOW

exercise 2

Creating a Nameplate for a Newsletter

1. At a clear document screen, create the nameplate shown in figure 10.14 by completing the following steps:
   a. Open c10ex01, folio.
   b. Save the document with Save As and name it c10ex02, nameplate.
   c. Change to the Page Layout viewing mode, change the Zoom Control to 75%, and click the Show/Hide ¶ button to display nonprinting characters.
   d. Format the nameplate by completing the following steps:
      (1) Position the insertion point on the paragraph symbol below the folio and make sure *Normal* displays in the Style list box on the Formatting toolbar.
      (2) Change the font to 13-point Impact in Blue.
      (3) Click Format, then Paragraph, and then make sure *0 inches* displays in the Left Indentation text box. Click OK or press Enter.
      (4) Click Insert, then Symbol.
      (5) At the Symbol dialog box, select the Symbols tab, then change the font to Wingdings, and select the bullet symbol in the fifth row and the sixteenth column.
      (6) Click the Insert button, then click Close.
      (7) Continue pressing the F4 key until you have created an entire row of blue symbols.
      (8) Press Enter.
   e. Insert the Ride Safe logo by completing the following steps:
      (1) Position the insertion point on the paragraph below the dotted line, click Insert, point to Picture, and then click From File.
      (2) At the Insert Picture dialog box, change the directory in the Look in: box to the location of your student data disk.
      (3) Make sure the Files of type list box displays *All Files* (*.*), and then double-click *Ridesf1blue.bmp.*
      (4) Select the image, then drag it straight and to the center as shown in figure 10.14.
      (5) Deselect the image, position the insertion point on the paragraph symbol after the image, and then press Enter.
   f. Select the blue dotted line (do not select the paragraph symbol at the end of the dotted line).
   g. Click the Copy button on the Formatting toolbar.
   h. Position the insertion point on the first paragraph symbol below the logo, then click the Paste button on the Standard toolbar.
2. Save the document again with the same name, c10ex02, nameplate.
3. Close c10ex02, nameplate. (You may want to wait to print the entire newsletter when it is completed.)

Creating a Subtitle

As the third step in building a newsletter, you will create a subtitle. Since the text in the subtitle will remain consistent from issue to issue, creating a style for the subtitle is not necessary. A subtitle emphasizes the purpose of the newsletter and identifies the intended audience. The subtitle is usually keyed in a sans serif typeface in 14 to 24 points, and kerning should be turned on.

exercise 3

Creating a Subtitle in a Newsletter

1. At a clear document screen, add a subtitle to the newsletter by completing the following steps:
   a. Open c10ex02, nameplate.
   b. Save the document with Save As and name it c10ex03, subtitle.
   c. Change to Page Layout viewing mode, change the Zoom Control to 75%, and click the Show/Hide ¶ button to display nonprinting characters.
   d. Format the subtitle by completing the following steps:
      (1) Position the insertion point on the paragraph symbol below the dotted line, click Format, then Font.
      (2) Change the font to 13-point Impact Italic, and make sure the font color displays in Black.
      (3) Select the Character Spacing tab.
      (4) Change the Spacing to Expanded By: **1 pt**.
      (5) Turn on the kerning at 13 points. Choose OK or press Enter.
      (6) Click Format, then Paragraph.
      (7) At the Paragraph dialog box, select the Indents and Spacing tab.
      (8) Change the Spacing Before to **0 pt**, change the Spacing After to **12 pt**, then click the Tabs button.
      (9) At the Tabs dialog box, key **6.75** inches in the Tab stop position text box, select Right Alignment, click the Set button, and then click OK or press Enter.
      (10) Press Tab.
      (11) Key **Bicycle and In-Line Skating Safety News for the 90s**.
      (12) Press the space bar three times, then click the Italic button on the Formatting toolbar to turn off this feature.
      (13) Click Insert, then Symbol.
      (14) At the Symbol dialog box, select the Symbols tab, change the font to Wingdings, and then select the bullet symbol in the fifth row and the sixteenth column.
      (15) Click the Insert button, then click Close.
      (16) Press Enter.
      (17) Select the symbol and change the font color to Blue.
2. Save the document again with the same name, c10ex03, subtitle.
3. Close c10ex03, subtitle. (You will print when the newsletter is complete.)

Creating a Headline

After completing the folio, nameplate, and subtitle, you will create a headline in exercise 4. Headlines organize text and help readers decide whether they want to read the article. To set the headline apart from the text, use a larger type size, heavier weight, and a different typeface than the body. When determining a type size for a headline, start with 18 points and increase the size until you find an appropriate one. As a general rule, choose a sans serif typeface for a headline. However, this is not a hard-and-fast rule.

DTP POINTERS
Avoid using underlining in a headline or subhead.

Since the headline consists of text that will change with each issue of the newsletter, consider creating a style to format the headline.

Headlines often improve in readability and appearance if leading is reduced. The leading in a headline should be about the size of the type size used to create it. Using all caps (use sparingly) or small caps substantially reduces leading automatically, since capital letters lack descenders.

DTP POINTERS
Avoid all caps; small caps are easier to read.

Headlines and subheads should have more space above than below. This indicates that the heading goes with the text that follows rather than the text that precedes the heading.

exercise 4

Creating a Headline Style for a Newsletter

1. At a clear document screen, create a headline style for the newsletter in figure 10.14 by completing the following steps:
   a. Open c10ex03, subtitle.
   b. Save the document with Save As and name it c10ex04, headline.
   c. Change to Page Layout viewing mode, change the Zoom Control to 75%, and click the Show/Hide ¶ button to display nonprinting characters.
   d. Format the headline by completing the following steps:
      (1) Position the insertion point on the paragraph symbol below the subtitle.
      (2) Change the font to 24-point Britannic Bold. (Make sure italic is turned off.)
      (3) Change the font color to Gray-50%.
      (4) Turn on the Small caps.
      (5) Select the Character Spacing tab, then change Spacing to Expanded By: **1.5 pt**.
      (6) Make sure kerning is turned on at 13 points. Click OK or press Enter.
      (7) Key **In-Line Skating—Fastest Growing Sport**. (Use an em dash.)
      (8) Select *In-Line Skating...*, then click Format, then Paragraph.
      (9) At the Paragraph dialog box, select the Indents and Spacing tab.
      (10) Change the Spacing at the Before text box to **6 pt** and the Spacing After to **18 pt.** Choose OK or press Enter.
      (11) Deselect the text, then press Enter.
   e. Create a style from existing text by completing the following steps:
      (1) Position the insertion point anywhere in the headline text.
      (2) Click inside the Style list box on the Formatting toolbar to select the current style name.
      (3) Key **Headline** and press Enter. (The *Headline* style is then added to the list of styles available in this document.)
2. Save the document again with the same name *c10ex04, headline*.
3. Close c10ex04, headline. (You will print when the newsletter is complete.)

Formatting Body Text in a Newsletter

In exercise 5, you will format the body text for the newsletter you are building in this chapter. You will change the font and type size, create em spaces for paragraph indentations, and turn on the columns feature. Before doing so, take a look at some of the formatting options that apply to body text.

Applying the Widow/Orphan Feature

Widow
A single line of text pushed to the top of the next page.

Orphan
A single line of text appearing by itself at the end of a page.

Word's Widow/Orphan control feature is on by default. This feature prevents the first and last lines of paragraphs from being separated across pages. A *widow* is a single line of a paragraph or heading that is pushed to the top of the next page. A single line of text (whether part of a paragraph or heading) appearing by itself at the end of a page is called an *orphan*. This option is located in the Paragraph dialog box with the Line and Page Breaks tab selected.

Even with this feature on, you should still watch for subheadings that are inappropriately separated from text at the end of a column or page. If a heading displays inappropriately, insert a column break. To insert a column break, position the insertion point where you want a new column to begin, then press Ctrl + Shift + Enter, or click Insert, Break, then Column Break.

Aligning Text in Paragraphs in Newsletters

The type of alignment you choose for a newsletter influences the "color" or tone of your publication. Text within a paragraph can be aligned in a variety of ways. Text can be aligned at both the left and right margins (justified); aligned at the left or right; or centered on a line, causing both the left and right margins to be ragged.

Justified text is common in publications such as textbooks, newspapers, newsletters, and magazines. It is more formal than left-aligned text. For justified text to convey a professional appearance, there must be an appropriate line length. If the line length is too short, the words and/or characters in a paragraph may be widely spaced, causing "rivers" of white space. Remedying this situation requires increasing the line length, changing to a smaller type size, and/or hyphenating long words. Hyphenation will be discussed in greater detail in chapter 11. Text aligned at the left is the easiest to read. This alignment has become popular with designers for publications of all kinds. Center alignment should be used on small amounts of text.

Indenting Paragraphs with Em Spaces

In typesetting, tabs are generally measured by em spaces rather than inch measurements. An em space is a space as wide as the point size of the type. For example, if the type size is 12 points, an em space is 12 points wide. Generally, you will want to indent newsletter text one or two em spaces.

Em space indentations can be created in two ways. One way is to display the Paragraph dialog box with the Indents and Spacing tab selected, then select or key an inch or point increment at the Left or Right Indentation text boxes (be sure to include "pt" when keying a point increment). Or, you can create an em space at the Tabs dialog box. In exercise 5, you will change the default tab setting to 0.25 inches to create an em space indentation for each paragraph preceded with a tab code (0.25 inches is approximately 24 points or 2 em spaces for text keyed in 12-point type size).

Be sure to use em spaces for any paragraph indentations used in newsletters. Also, use em spaces for spacing around bullets and any other indented text in newsletters.

Generally, the first paragraph after a headline or subhead is not indented even though all remaining paragraphs will have an em space paragraph indentation. In figure 10.14, notice the paragraph formatting in the newsletter.

exercise 5

Creating a Body Text Style in a Newsletter

1. At a clear document screen, create a body text style for the newsletter in figure 10.14 by completing the following steps:
   a. Open c10ex04, headline.
   b. Save the document with Save As and name it c10ex05, body.
   c. Change to Page Layout viewing mode, change the Zoom Control to 75%, and click the Show/Hide ¶ button to display nonprinting characters.
   d. Position the insertion point on the paragraph symbol below the headline text. (Make sure the style is *Normal*.)
   e. Insert *ride safe.doc* located on your student data disk, then delete the paragraph symbol at the end of the document.
   f. Create a section break between the headline and the body text by completing the following steps:
      (1) Position the insertion point at the beginning of *Injuries Up Dramatically*.
      (2) Click Insert, then Break.
      (3) At the Break dialog box, choose Continuous in the Section breaks section.
      (4) Click OK or press Enter.
   g. Turn on the columns feature by completing the following steps:
      (1) With the insertion point still positioned at the beginning of *Injuries Up Dramatically*, click Format, then Columns.
      (2) At the Columns dialog box, select Three in the Presets section.
      (3) Click the Line between option (this inserts a line between the columns).
      (4) Make sure the Equal column width option is selected.
      (5) Make sure *This section* displays in the Apply to: list box.
      (6) Click OK or press Enter.
   h. Format the body text by completing the following steps:
      (1) Select all the text in the three columns beginning with *Injuries Up Dramatically* by pressing Ctrl + Shift + End, then change the font to 11-point Garamond.
      (2) With the text still selected, click Format, then Paragraph. At the Paragraph dialog box, select the Indents and Spacing tab. Change Line spacing to At Least, then key **11 pt** in the At: text box.
      (3) Change the Spacing After to **4 pt**.
      (4) To change the paragraph indentions to an em space, click the Tabs button at the Paragraph dialog box.
      (5) At the Tabs dialog box, key **0.25** in the Tab stop position text box, make sure Left is selected in the Alignment section, then click the Set button.
      (6) Click OK or press Enter to close the Tabs dialog box.

i. Create a style to format the body text by completing the following steps:
   (1) Position the insertion point in one of the paragraphs in the body of the newsletter.
   (2) Click the Style box on the Formatting toolbar to select the current name.
   (3) Key **RS Body** and press Enter. (The *RS Body* style is then added to the list of styles available in this document.)

2. Save the document with the same name c10ex05, body.
3. Close c10ex05, body. (You will print when the newsletter is complete.)

Creating Subheads for Newsletters

DTP POINTERS
Do not use narrow typefaces in reverse text. Add bold to increase the thickness.

At times a subhead may appear right after a headline, as is the case with this chapter's newsletter. Refer to figure 10.14 to view the subheads you will create in this exercise. Subheads organize text and expand upon headlines, giving readers more information or clues about the text. In addition, subheads also provide contrast to text-intensive body copy. Marginal subheads are sometimes placed in the left margin or in a narrow column to the left of the body text, providing an airy, open appearance. Subheads can be set in a larger type size, different typeface, or heavier weight than the text. They can be centered, aligned left, or aligned right and formatted in shaded boxes. In exercise 6, you will create a customized style based on an existing style. Figure 10.16 shows a newsletter created with marginal subheads.

figure 10.16

Marginal Subheads

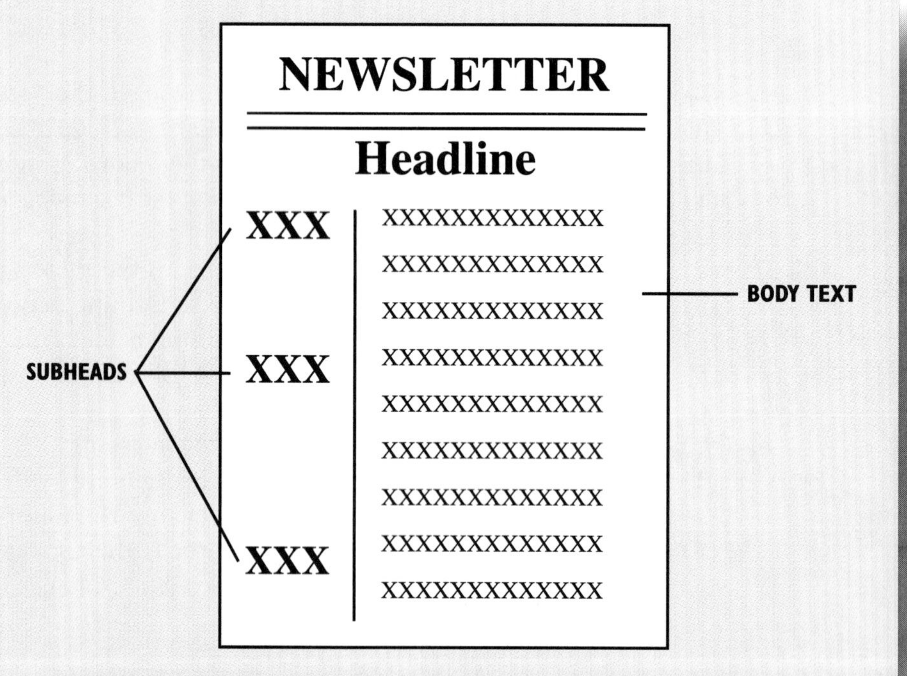

Creating a Subhead Style

1. At a clear document screen, create a subhead style for the newsletter in figure 10.14, by completing the following steps:
   a. Open c10ex05, body.
   b. Save the document with Save As and name it c10ex06, subhead.
   c. Change to Page Layout viewing mode, change the Zoom Control to 75%, and click the Show/Hide ¶ button to display nonprinting characters.
   d. Create a style to format the subhead in the newsletter in figure 10.14 based on an existing style by completing the following steps:
      (1) Select *Injuries Up Dramatically*, then select the *Heading 3* style at the Style list box on the Formatting toolbar. (This will apply the Heading 3 style to the selected text.)
      (2) With *Injuries Up Dramatically* still selected, click Format, then Style.
      (3) At the Style dialog box, make sure Heading 3 is selected in the Styles list box. Make sure Styles in use displays in the List box. Read the description of the style formatting.
      (4) Click the New button at the Style dialog box.
      (5) At the New Style dialog box, key **Subhead** in the Name list box.
      (6) Make sure that *Heading 3* displays in the Based on: list box.
   e. Click the Format button, then select Font at the pop-up list.
   f. At the Font dialog box, change the font to 13-point Britannic Bold.
      (1) Select the Character Spacing tab, then change the Spacing to Expanded By: **0.5 pt**.
      (2) Select *Normal* at the Position list box.
      (3) Turn kerning on at 13 points, then click OK or press Enter.
      (4) Click the Format button, then Paragraph.
      (5) Select the Indents and Spacing tab, make sure that Spacing Before is set at **12 pt** and change the After setting to **6 pt**.
      (6) Change the Alignment to Centered, then click OK or press Enter.
      (7) Click the Format button, click Border, and then select the Shading tab.
      (8) Select the last fill in the first row of the Fill palette (*Gray-12.5%*). Make sure *Paragraph* displays in the Apply to list box. Click OK or press Enter.
      (9) Click OK or press Enter at the New Style dialog box.
      (10) Click Apply at the Style dialog box.
   g. Apply the Subhead style to the other subheadings in the newsletter by completing the following steps:
      (1) Position the insertion point on the heading *A Message to Parents*, located in the second column, then select *Subhead* in the Style list box on the Formatting toolbar. Delete the paragraph symbol before the subheading.
      (2) Apply the Subhead style to the heading *Our Ride Safe Guarantee* in the third column. Delete the paragraph symbol before the subheading.
   h. Position the insertion point in the first subhead *Injuries Up Dramatically*, click Format, then Paragraph. Select the Indents and Spacing tab, then change the Spacing Before to **0 pt**. Click OK or press Enter. (This will eliminate the space before the first subhead at the beginning of the body text. The Subhead style remains unchanged.)
2. Save the document again with the same name, c10ex06, subhead.
3. Close c10ex06, subhead. (You will print when the newsletter is complete.)

Creating a Byline

The next step in the process of building your newsletter is to create the byline. The byline identifies the author of the article. Generally, the byline is set in italic, using the same typeface as the body text. The byline may be the same size as the body typeface, but it may also be set in a type size one or two points smaller.

The byline can be keyed below the headline or subhead depending on which is the title of the article. In addition, the byline can also be keyed as the first line of the body text if it follows a headline or subhead that spans two or more columns. The byline can be keyed at the left margin of a column or it can be keyed flush right in a column.

exercise 7

Creating a Byline Style in a Newsletter

1. At a clear document screen, create a byline style for the newsletter in figure 10.14 by completing the following steps:
   a. Open c10ex06, subhead.
   b. Save the document with Save As and name it c10ex07, byline.
   c. Change to Page Layout viewing mode, change the Zoom Control to 75%, and click the Show/Hide ¶ button to display nonprinting characters.
   d. Create a style to format the byline in the newsletter in figure 10.14 by completing the following steps:
      (1) Select the byline *by Mary Beth Luhrsen* below the first subhead *Injuries Up Dramatically*.
      (2) Change the font to 10-point Garamond Italic.
      (3) At the Paragraph dialog box, change the Spacing Before to **0 pt** and the Spacing After to *6 pt*.
   e. Create a style from existing text by completing the following steps:
      (1) Position the insertion point anywhere in the byline text.
      (2) Click inside the Style list box on the Formatting toolbar to select the current style name.
      (3) Key **Byline** and press Enter. (The *Byline* style is then added to the list of styles available in this document.)
   f. Apply the Byline style to the byline below *A Message to Parents*.
2. Save the document again with the same name, c10ex07, byline.
3. Close c10ex07, byline. (You will print when the newsletter is complete.)

Inserting Graphic Images in Newsletters

DTP POINTERS
Position illustrations close to the text they illustrate.

Clip art added to a newsletter should support or expand points made in the text. Use clip art so that it will give the newsletter the appearance of being well planned, inviting, and consistent. You can modify clip art by using Word's Draw program and Microsoft Word Picture graphic editor. Large and relatively inexpensive selections of clip art can be purchased on CD-ROM. In addition, you may want to scan predesigned company logos (with permission) or photographs that relate to the subject of your newsletter.

The image used in the nameplate in figure 10.14 was scanned professionally and copied to your student data disk in a file format that was compatible with Word 97. Because of the bitmap file format in which it was saved, you cannot alter this image in Microsoft Word Picture. To change the color of the scanned image, you may access Windows Paint or alter a bitmapped image by using the Set Transparent Color option on the Picture toolbar. Complete the following steps to use the Set Transparent Color option:

1. Display the Picture toolbar.
2. Select the bitmapped image.
3. Click the Set Transparent Color button (second from the right) on the Picture toolbar.
4. Drag the transparency tool (mouse pointer) into the area you want to change, then click the left mouse.
5. Click the Fill Color button on the Drawing toolbar and select a color.

Optional steps for using Paint are provided at the end of exercise 8.

exercise 8

Inserting a Graphic Image into a Newsletter

1. At a clear document window, insert a graphic into the newsletter in figure 10.14 by completing the following steps:
   a. Open c10ex07, byline.
   b. Save the document with Save As and name it c10ex08, newsletter.
   c. Change to Page Layout view, change the Zoom Control to 75%, and click the Show/Hide ¶ button to display nonprinting characters.
   d. Display the Picture toolbar.
   e. Position the insertion point near the second sentence in the second paragraph near the text referring to a "car."
   f. Insert *Car.wmf* located in the Popular folder accessed through Insert, Picture, then From File. (The entire path is: C:\Program Files\Microsoft Office\Clipart\Popular\Car.wmf.
   g. Click one of the corner sizing handles and drag it inward to reduce the size similar to figure 10.14.
   h. Select the image, then click the Text Wrapping button on the Picture toolbar, and then select Tight.
   i. If necessary, select then drag the image to the location shown in figure 10.14.
   j. Close the Picture toolbar by clicking the X in the upper right corner of the toolbar.
2. View your newsletter in Print Preview. If the last column is unbalanced with the first and second columns, insert a continuous section break at the end of the last column. (This should result in three balanced columns.)
3. Save the document again with the same name c10ex08, newsletter.
4. Print and then close c10ex08, newsletter.

Optional steps to save the Ride Safe newsletter as a template:

To save time when creating future issues of your newsletter, save your newsletter as a template. To do this, delete all text, pictures, objects, etc., that will not stay the same for future issues. Likewise, leave the nameplate and all text, pictures, symbols, etc., that will remain the same in each issue of your newsletter. For example, to save the Ride Safe newsletter in exercise 8 as a template as shown in figure 10.17, leave the following items and delete the rest:

- Folio (the month and volume/issue numbers will change, but the titles will remain—use the folio text as placeholder text)
- Nameplate
- Subtitle
- Headline (the headline text will change, but the position and formatting will remain—use the headline text as placeholder text)
- Subheads (the subhead text will change, but the formatting will remain—use the subhead text as placeholder text)
- Byline (the byline text will change, but the position and formatting will remain—use the byline text as placeholder text)
- Body Text (the body text will change, but the formatting will remain—leave a paragraph as placeholder text)

Complete the following steps to save c10ex08, newsletter as a template, as shown in figure 10.17:

1. Open c10ex08, newsletter.
2. Delete all text and newsletter elements that will change with each issue (refer to the bulleted items above).
3. Save the newsletter with Save As. At the Save As dialog box, select *Document Template (*.dot)* at the Save as type text box.
4. Double-click the *Publications* folder.
5. Key **Ride Safe Newsletter** in the File name text box.
6. Click Save.
7. Close the document on the screen.
8. To use the template, click File, then New.
9. Select the Publications tab.
10. Double-click *Ride Safe Newsletter.dot.*
11. Select and replace text that needs to be updated. Delete any placeholder text when necessary.

Optional steps to access Windows Paint program to customize a graphic:

1. Click the Start button in the lower left corner.
2. At the Windows menu, select Programs.
3. Select *Accessories* at the Windows pop-up list.
4. Select *Paint*.
5. At the Paint screen, click File, then Open.
6. At the Open dialog box, click the down arrow to the right of the Files of type text box and select All Files.
7. Click the down arrow to the right of the Look in: text box and select the drive where your student data disk is located. Select *Ridesf1blue.bmp*. Click the Open button.
8. At the Paint dialog box, click Image, then Attributes.
9. At the Attributes dialog box, select Colors in the Colors section. Click OK or press Enter. (A color palette should display at the bottom of the screen.)
10. Click the Fill With Color button (jar of paint spilling) on the Paint tool palette. Click any color on the color palette. Position the insertion point inside the helmet area and left click. (The area should display in your chosen color.)
11. Repeat steps 9 and 10 to fill the shirt with the same color.
12. Save the picture with Save As and give the file a name.
13. Click File, then Exit.

10.17

Ride Safe Newsletter Template

Volume 5, Issue 1 • June 1998

Bicycle and In-Line Skating Safety News for the 90s •

In-Line Skating—Fastest Growing Sport

Injuries Up Dramatically

by Mary Beth Luhrsen

Last year, the Consumer Product Safety Commission (CPSC) released some alarming news on in-line skating, now the fastest growing recreational sport in America. They projected 83,000 serious injuries in 1997, more than double those of 1996. Even more alarming is the fact that children under age 15 account for 60% of these injuries.

chapter summary

- Newsletter elements divide the newsletter into organized sections to help the reader understand the text. Basic newsletter elements include nameplate, subtitle, folio, headline, subhead, byline, and body copy.
- Focus and balance can be achieved in a newsletter through the design and size of the nameplate, through the use of graphic images, or through careful use of lines, borders, and backgrounds.
- The margin size for a newsletter is linked to the number of columns needed, the formality desired, the visual elements used, and the amount of text available. Keep margins consistent in a newsletter.
- The line length of text in a newsletter can enhance or detract from the readability of text.
- Section breaks are used to vary the page layout within a single newsletter.
- Typesetters and professional designers measure horizontal space on a page using *picas.* A *pica* is equal to 12 points. One inch is equal to 6 picas.
- The underlying grid of a newsletter must remain consistent from page to page.
- Setting text in columns may improve the readability of newsletters.
- By default, column formatting is applied to the whole document.
- Change to Page Layout viewing mode to view columns as they will appear when printed.
- Word automatically lines up (balances) the last line of text at the bottom of each column. The last page of columns can be balanced by inserting a continuous section break at the end of the text.
- A challenge in creating a newsletter is how to balance change with consistency. Styles assist in maintaining consistency in recurring elements.
- When formatting instructions contained within a style are changed, all the text to which the style has been applied is automatically updated.
- Styles are created for a particular document and are saved with the document.
- A style can be applied using the Style button on the Formatting toolbar or the Style dialog box.
- Word's default leading is equal to approximately 120 percent of the type size used.
- Headlines and subheads should have more leading above than below.
- Set tabs in a typeset document by em spaces rather than inch measurements.
- An em space is a space as wide as the point size of the type.

commands review

	Mouse/Keyboard
Columns dialog box	Format, Columns; or click the Columns button on the Standard toolbar
Character Spacing dialog box	Format, Font, Character Spacing tab
Kerning	Format, Font, Character Spacing tab
Insert a column break	Insert, Break, Column Break; or Ctrl + Shift + Enter
Insert a section break	Insert, Break, Continuous
Insert symbols	Insert, Symbols, Symbols tab
Insert File dialog box	Insert, File
Insert Picture dialog box	Insert, Picture, From File
Leading	Format, Paragraph, Indents and Spacing tab, Spacing—Before and After
Style dialog box	Format, Style
Widow/orphan	Format, Paragraph, Line and Page Breaks
Windows Paint program	Start, Program, Accessories, Paint

check your understanding

True/False: Circle the letter T if the statement is true; circle the letter F if the statement is false.

T F 1. A folio provides information that describes the purpose of the newsletter and/or the intended audience of the newsletter.

T F 2. Column formatting affects the entire document unless your document is divided into sections.

T F 3. Columns are separated by a default setting of 0.25 inches of space.

T F 4. A line length of 4 inches measures 28 picas.

T F 5. A guideline in typesetting is that line length measured in picas does not exceed two times the point size used in the body text of a newsletter.

T F 6. An em space indentation can be created at the Tabs dialog box and keyed in a point or inch increment.

T F 7. Extra leading can make a page look less gray.

T F 8. If a headline contains two lines both keyed in 36 points, the default spacing between the two lines (leading) should be increased to improve readability.

T F 9. One advantage of using styles in formatting a newsletter is that when formatting within a style is changed, the text to which it has been applied changes also.

T F 10. Once a style has been created, the only way to change the style is to rename it and create it again.

Terms: In the space provided, indicate the correct term, command, or number.

1. To create newspaper columns that are approximately equal or balanced, insert a ______________________ at the end of the text.
2. This newsletter element provides immediate identification of the newsletter: ______________________.
3. Insert this (or these) into a document to control where columns end and begin on the page: ______________________.
4. To insert a vertical line between columns, choose this at the Columns dialog box: ______________________.
5. To set a tab at 2 em spaces in a newsletter set in 14-point Times New Roman, key this measurement at the Tabs Set dialog box: ______________________.
6. A set of formatting instructions that are saved with a name and can be used over and over are called a ______________________.
7. If you create a multipage newsletter with facing pages, you may want to use Word's ______________________ margin feature, which accommodates wider inside or outside margins.
8. Avoid ______________________, which occurs when headings display side by side in adjacent columns in a newsletter.
9. Word's ______________________ feature prevents the first and last lines of paragraphs from being separated across pages; this feature is on by fault.
10. The ______________________ identifies the author of an article in a newsletter.

skill assessments

Assessment 1

1. Design and create two nameplates (including subtitle, folio, graphics, etc.) for two newsletters for organizations, schools, or a neighborhood to which you belong (real or fictional). Prepare thumbnail sketches of your designs and attach them to the back of your nameplates. Prepare one nameplate using an asymmetrical design. Also, include a graphic image, scanned image, or special character symbol in at least one of the nameplates.
2. Save the documents and name them c10sa01a, nameplate and c10sa01b, nameplate.
3. Print and then close c10sa01a, nameplate and c10sa01b, nameplate.

Assessment 2

Your neighbor knows you are taking a desktop publishing class, and she would like you to help her create a family newsletter for the holidays. Assume you designed the newsletter shown in figure 10.18, but you forgot to create styles and save it as a template. You know she will ask again next year, so you are going to re-create the newsletter and include styles for all future issues.

1. Include the following specifications in the family newsletter.
   a. Change the top, bottom, left, and right margins to 0.75 inches.
   b. Turn on kerning at 13 points.
   c. Use the graphic, *pointsta.cgm*, located on your student data disk.
   d. Create *1998* in the nameplate in WordArt.
   e. Key **Law Family Newsletter** in 48-point Britannic Bold with the Shadow effect.
   f. Insert a continuous section break.
   g. Create two uneven newspaper columns with a line between the columns.
   h. Insert *family newsletter.doc* located on your student data disk.
   i. Select the body text and change the font to 11-point Times New Roman.
   j. Change the paragraph indentations to an em space.
   k. Change the paragraph spacing to 6 points After (spacing between the paragraphs).
   l. Select *Happy Holidays!* and change the font to 22-point Times New Roman Bold Italic, in Red with shadow, and expanded by 3.5 points.
   m. Select *The Laws* and change the font to 26-point Brush Script MT in Green with shadow.
   n. Select *Mike, Debbie...* and change the font to 20-point Brush Script MT in Black.
2. Save the document and name it c10sa02, family.
3. Print and then close c10sa02, family.
4. Save the newsletter as a template at the publications tab.

Assessment 3

You are working in the office of a computer software company and have been asked to create the company's monthly newsletter. You recently replaced the individual who previously created the newsletters. You found handwritten specifications on a copy, which should help you get started with the task. Complete the following steps:

1. Complete the newsletter shown in figure 10.19 according to the specifications written on the front of the publication. Insert *computer newsletter.doc* from your student data disk.
2. Use your knowledge of leading, character spacing, and type sizes to assist you in making the copy fit on a page.
3. Save the newsletter and name it c10sa03, computer.
4. Print and then close c10sa03, computer.

figure 10.18

Now with the end of 1998 in sight and the holidays just around the corner, we have to wonder where 1998 has gone. Here are a few highlights of our year...

Emily will be 12 in January and now attends Junior High. She is a wonderful young lady and a great source of joy in our lives. We've had so much fun watching her grow from a little girl to a pre-teen—girlfriends coming over (and Mom taking them T.P.ing and participating a little, too), the phone ringing and it always being for her, crushes on a different boy every week—it doesn't seem that long ago that I was doing those things. It sure keeps us going and there never seems to be a dull or quiet moment—and if there is one (on a very rare occasion) you can bet you'll hear Grant yelling, "Mom, where are you?"

Grant is now 7 and he is a character. He is a typical little brother, bugging and teasing Emily and her friends. He really is a lively child and keeps us laughing with his performances.

I don't know who is the bigger kid, Grant or Mike—they are forever pulling jokes on Mom.

We took a much-needed vacation to Disney World and had an absolutely wonderful time. Mike (I think it was the accountant in him) had an agenda for us every day and he took a lot of teasing from us about that—we wanted to buy him a clipboard and whistle!

Mike turned the big "40" this year. We had a great time surprising him with a 40th party celebrated by family and friends. Mike will be with Crowe 16 years this January. He has always enjoyed his work and he works with a great group of people. Mike is also our precinct Committeeman. He worked very hard on the fall campaign. The children were very involved in organizing and passing out literature, watching the debates, and learning about the election process.

Things have changed for Debbie with both the children in school full time. For those of you who knew me at Purdue, you will be surprised (maybe shocked is a better word) that I am taking a real estate class at the local community college—and believe it or not, I am not skipping classes.

Please let us know how you are doing. We think of our family and friends so often—we cherish the times we've shared with you and thank you for the wonderful memories—the best gift one could give another.

Happy Holidays!

The Laws

Mike, Debbie, Emily & Grant

figure 10.19

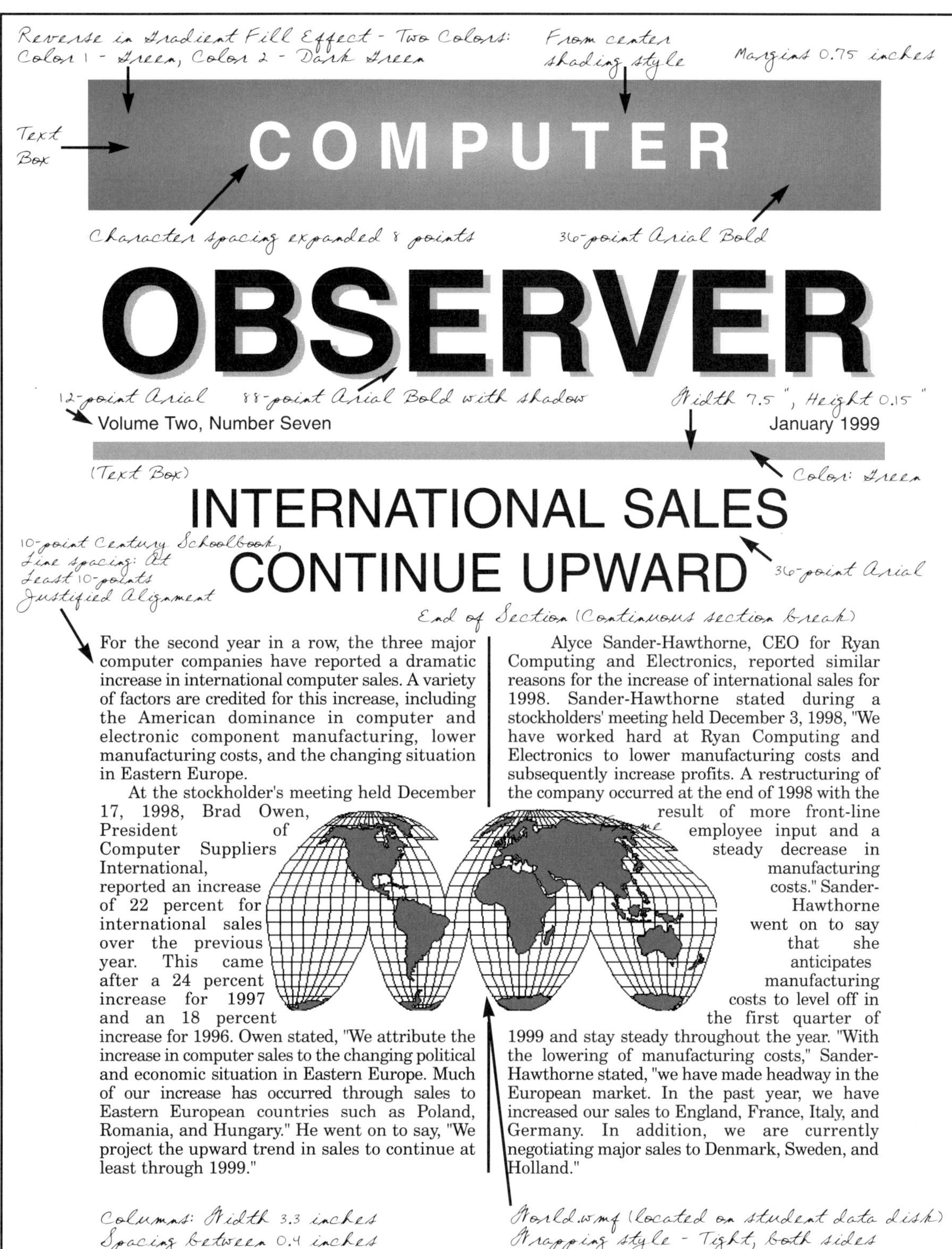

COMPUTER

OBSERVER

Volume Two, Number Seven

January 1999

INTERNATIONAL SALES CONTINUE UPWARD

For the second year in a row, the three major computer companies have reported a dramatic increase in international computer sales. A variety of factors are credited for this increase, including the American dominance in computer and electronic component manufacturing, lower manufacturing costs, and the changing situation in Eastern Europe.

At the stockholder's meeting held December 17, 1998, Brad Owen, President of Computer Suppliers International, reported an increase of 22 percent for international sales over the previous year. This came after a 24 percent increase for 1997 and an 18 percent increase for 1996. Owen stated, "We attribute the increase in computer sales to the changing political and economic situation in Eastern Europe. Much of our increase has occurred through sales to Eastern European countries such as Poland, Romania, and Hungary." He went on to say, "We project the upward trend in sales to continue at least through 1999."

Alyce Sander-Hawthorne, CEO for Ryan Computing and Electronics, reported similar reasons for the increase of international sales for 1998. Sander-Hawthorne stated during a stockholders' meeting held December 3, 1998, "We have worked hard at Ryan Computing and Electronics to lower manufacturing costs and subsequently increase profits. A restructuring of the company occurred at the end of 1998 with the result of more front-line employee input and a steady decrease in manufacturing costs." Sander-Hawthorne went on to say that she anticipates manufacturing costs to level off in the first quarter of 1999 and stay steady throughout the year. "With the lowering of manufacturing costs," Sander-Hawthorne stated, "we have made headway in the European market. In the past year, we have increased our sales to England, France, Italy, and Germany. In addition, we are currently negotiating major sales to Denmark, Sweden, and Holland."

Optional: Use Word's Help feature to learn more about newsletters. Try to find the definition of a *story*. Write the definition on the backside of the computer newsletter. Also, incorporate any changes you may have learned about in the topics you read. The information about linked text boxes will be helpful in the next chapter. To use the Help feature, click Help, and then select Microsoft Word Help. At the prompt *What would you like to do?* key **Newsletters**, then click Search. Make sure you read the following topics:

- Create a newsletter
- Force the start of a new newspaper column
- Create newspaper columns
- Balance column length for newspaper column text
- Delete a linked text box without deleting text

Assessment 4

Open and then print a copy of *Butterfield Gardens.doc* located on your student data disk. Assume you received this newsletter in the mail as a marketing device. The newsletter looks relatively neat and organized, but with closer inspection, you notice there are a few errors in spelling, formatting, and layout and design. Recreate the newsletter according to the following specifications (figure 10.20 is a sample solution—use your own ideas for an interesting newsletter layout and design!):

1. Prepare a thumbnail sketch of your design.
2. Recreate the nameplate or create a nameplate (logo, subtitle, folio) of your own for this company; consider using WordArt in your nameplate design.
3. Create a different layout and design for the newsletter using newspaper columns; use more than one column.
4. Correct all spelling and formatting errors.
5. Use any graphics or scanned images that seem appropriate.
6. Create the recycling icon by inserting the Word picture *Recycle.wmf* located on your student data disk. (A recycle symbol is also available on the program CD-ROM in the Valupack folder and the Font subfolder. The symbol is located in the *Sign MT* font. Print the font preview file located at the top of the list of fonts in the Font subfolder. Some interesting fonts include *Almanac MT, Holiday Mt, Parties MT, Sports Two MT, Sports Three MT, Transport MT,* and *Vacation MT.)*
7. Use any newsletter elements and enhancements that improve the effectiveness and appeal of this newsletter.
8. Save your publication and name it c10sa04, butterfield.
9. Print and then close c10sa04, butterfield. Attach the thumbnail sketch to the back of the newsletter.

The People Who Care

29 W 036 Butterfield Road
Warrenville, IL 60555
(630) 555-1062
http://www.grower-2-you.com

Number 12 *Spring 1999*

"The difficult we do today; the impossible just takes a little longer."

TO MULCH, OR NOT TO MULCH

Mulch can be any number of materials—from straw and leaves to bark, peat moss and plastic film—which can be easily applied to protect the soil surface.

Consider the benefits of mulching. Mulch retains moisture during hot, dry summer months, and repels moisture during periods of heavy rain. Mulching helps control weed growth in the soil between plants, and keeps the soil surface cooler in the summer and warmer in the winter by insulating it from the elements. Good organic mulch, such as cypress, red cedar, cocoa shells, or western bark also looks and smells great.

A three-step process is effective:

- **First, prepare the soil by rotating or spading, then work in a good fertilizer and/or compost such as peat moss or mushroom compost.**
- **Second, clear away leaves, plant debris, and litter from the soil surface. Cultivate and rake smooth.**
- **Third, for effective weed control either use a 4" layer of mulch or a fabric weed barrier covered by 2" of mulch.**

Here are two examples:

1. You want to cover a rectangular area twenty feet by ten feet and control the weeds. This will take 200 square feet of weed barrier and 17 bags (2 cubic feet each) of mulch.

2. The area is circular with a diameter of ten feet. You will need 13 bags of mulch (applied 4" thick).

ON PLANTING YOUR GARDEN

Besides preparing and paying your taxes, what should you be doing to prepare for spring? One thing you can do is plan your garden. To help you, we have booklets covering a wide variety of topics. Some of the booklets include:

Landscape Gardening
Pruning Made Simple
Improving Garden Soils
Beautiful Roses
Beneficial Insects
Growing Perennials

Printed on Recyclable Paper 

creative activity

Activity 1

1. Bring in an example of a newsletter you may have collected, received in the mail, picked up at a local business, or received from an organization of which you are a member. Use the Document Evaluation Checklist (*document evaluation checklist.doc*) to evaluate the newsletter. Revise this newsletter using a completely different layout and design. Incorporate your own ideas and use graphics or scanned images if available. Remember to use consistent elements throughout the document. Create your own styles or use the system styles included in Word to aid in formatting your document. You may want to include this revision in your portfolio along with the original.
2. Save your publication and name it c10ca01, newsletter.
3. Print and then close c10ca01, newsletter. Attach the Document Evaluation Checklist and the original document to the back of your revised version.

Optional: Draw a thumbnail sketch of a different nameplate for this publication. Include the folio and subtitle in the sketch. Add specifications as to which typeface, colors, clip art, etc., should be used in this design.

Activity 2

1. Prepare a one-page newsletter to hand out to your classmates discussing the information you learned about newsletters in the *Getting Results – Newsletters* section of the Help feature. The *Getting Results Book* component may be available on your computer as part of the typical installation of Office 97. However, it may not be available with the typical installation of the standalone Word program. (If you do not have this component available to you, you may want to research creating newsletters on the Internet and develop a newsletter from the information you locate.)
2. To access *Getting Results – Newsletter,* click Help on the menu bar, then click Contents and Index. Select the Index tab, key **Getting Results – Newsletters**, and then click Display.
3. With the topic displayed at your screen, click Options, then Print Topic if you want a hard copy to read.
4. Use a thumbnail sketch and grid to help you layout and design your newsletter.
5. Use WordArt, graphics, and tools on the Drawing toolbar to help you create an interesting design.
6. Create a nameplate with a company name of your choice. For example, *Desktop Designs*, *Newsletter Update*, *Designs for the Desktop, Newsletter 98,* or *DTP Today.*
7. Save your newsletter and name it c10ca02, newsletter.
8. Print a copy for each of your classmates, then close c10ca02, newsletter.

chapter ELEVEN

11 Incorporating Newsletter Design Elements

PERFORMANCE OBJECTIVE

Upon successful completion of chapter 11, you will be able to define, create, and incorporate additional design elements into newsletters, such as headers/footers, tables of contents, mastheads, sidebars, pull quotes, kickers, end signs, jump lines, captions, and color.

Desktop Publishing Concepts

Spot color	Pull quotes	Adding graphics, illustrations, and photos
Headers/footers	Kickers	Mastheads
Sidebars	End signs	Captions
Table of contents	Jump lines	Copy fitting

Word Features Used

Newsletter Wizard	Picture editor	Paragraph spacing
Templates	Color	Line spacing
Newspaper columns	Headers/footers	Character spacing
Text boxes	Symbols	Caption
Linking text boxes	Borders and shading	AutoCaption
Picture	Styles	

Chapter 10 introduced you to the basic elements of a newsletter. Additional elements can be used to enhance the visual impact of a newsletter and to provide the reader with clues to the newsletter content. Newsletter enhancing elements, such as tables of contents, headers/footers, mastheads, pull quotes, kickers, sidebars, captions, ruled lines, jump lines, graphics, illustrations, photos, and end signs are discussed in this chapter.

Adding Visually Enhancing Elements to a Newsletter

The most effective newsletters contain an appealing blend of text and visual elements. As illustrated in figure 11.1, visual elements, such as a table of contents, pull quote, kicker, and sidebar, can be used as focal points to tempt the intended audience into reading more than just the nameplate. Visual elements such as headings, subheadings, tables of contents, headers/ footers, ruled lines, jump lines, and end signs can be used to indicate the directional flow of information in the document. Visual elements such as headings, subheadings, headers/footers, pull quotes, sidebars, and page borders can be used to provide balance, proportion, and contrast in a newsletter. All of these elements, if used in a consistent format and manner, can create unity within a single newsletter and among different issues of a newsletter.

figure 11.1

Visually Enhancing Design Elements

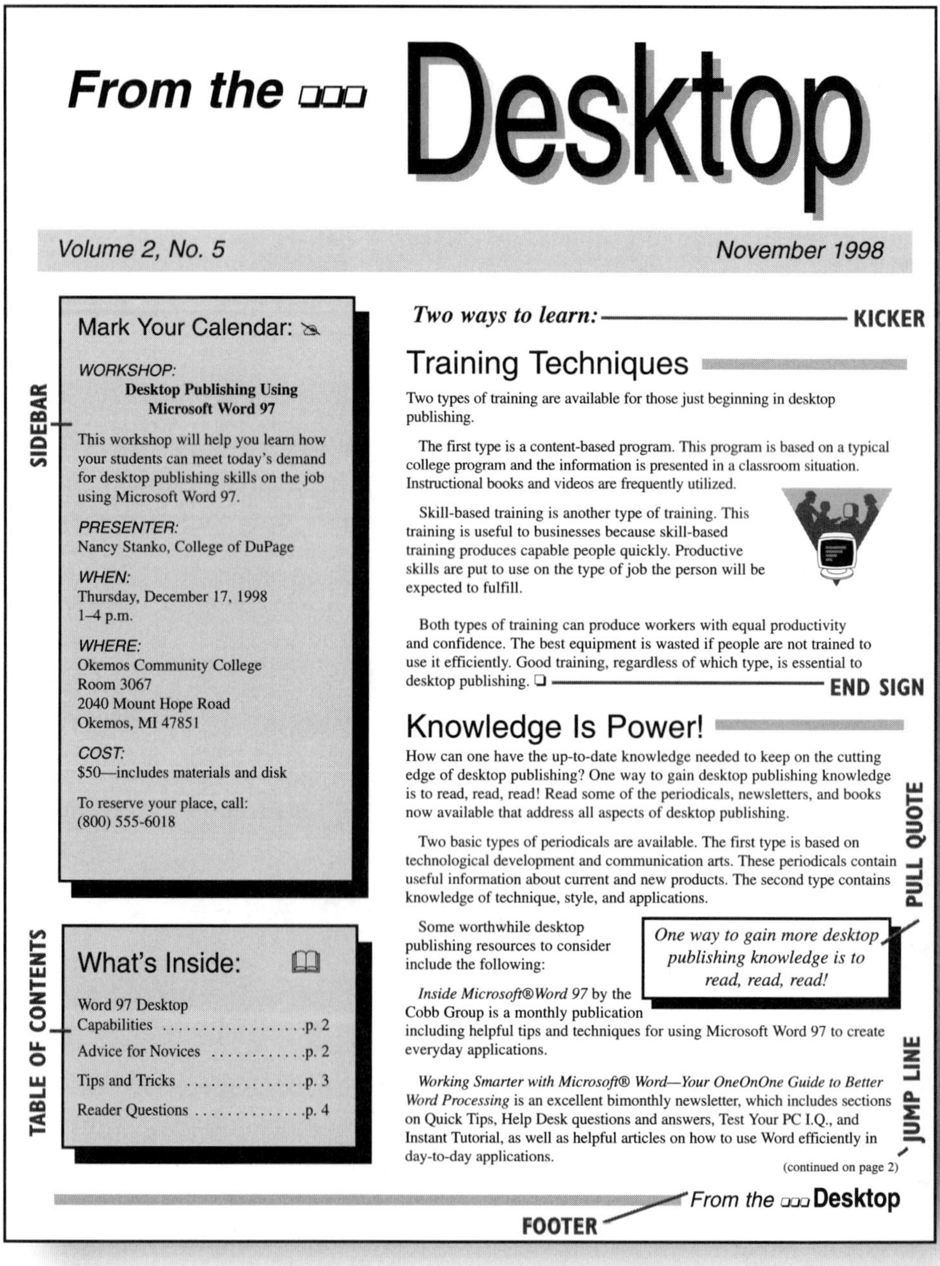

From the Desktop

Volume 2, No. 5 November 1998

SIDEBAR

Mark Your Calendar:

WORKSHOP:
Desktop Publishing Using Microsoft Word 97

This workshop will help you learn how your students can meet today's demand for desktop publishing skills on the job using Microsoft Word 97.

PRESENTER:
Nancy Stanko, College of DuPage

WHEN:
Thursday, December 17, 1998
1–4 p.m.

WHERE:
Okemos Community College
Room 3067
2040 Mount Hope Road
Okemos, MI 47851

COST:
$50—includes materials and disk

To reserve your place, call:
(800) 555-6018

TABLE OF CONTENTS

What's Inside:

Two ways to learn: — KICKER

Training Techniques

Two types of training are available for those just beginning in desktop publishing.

The first type is a content-based program. This program is based on a typical college program and the information is presented in a classroom situation. Instructional books and videos are frequently utilized.

Skill-based training is another type of training. This training is useful to businesses because skill-based training produces capable people quickly. Productive skills are put to use on the type of job the person will be expected to fulfill.

Both types of training can produce workers with equal productivity and confidence. The best equipment is wasted if people are not trained to use it efficiently. Good training, regardless of which type, is essential to desktop publishing. ❑ — END SIGN

Knowledge Is Power!

How can one have the up-to-date knowledge needed to keep on the cutting edge of desktop publishing? One way to gain desktop publishing knowledge is to read, read, read! Read some of the periodicals, newsletters, and books now available that address all aspects of desktop publishing.

Two basic types of periodicals are available. The first type is based on technological development and communication arts. These periodicals contain useful information about current and new products. The second type contains knowledge of technique, style, and applications.

Some worthwhile desktop publishing resources to consider include the following:

One way to gain more desktop publishing knowledge is to read, read, read! — PULL QUOTE

Inside Microsoft® Word 97 by the Cobb Group is a monthly publication including helpful tips and techniques for using Microsoft Word 97 to create everyday applications.

Working Smarter with Microsoft® Word—Your OneOnOne Guide to Better Word Processing is an excellent bimonthly newsletter, which includes sections on Quick Tips, Help Desk questions and answers, Test Your PC I.Q., and Instant Tutorial, as well as helpful articles on how to use Word efficiently in day-to-day applications.

(continued on page 2) — JUMP LINE

From the Desktop — FOOTER

Linking Text Boxes

Newsletters routinely contain articles that start on one page and are continued onto another page. Word 97's text box linking feature makes your job of creating "continued" articles easier. This feature allows text to flow from one text box to another even if the text boxes are not adjacent or on the same page. Any text box can be linked with any other text box. You need at least two text boxes to create a link; however, any number of text boxes can be used to create a chain of linked text boxes. For example, if your article starts on page 1, is continued on page 2, and then finishes on page 4, you can create a chain of three linked text boxes that will contain the article text. When the first text box is filled, the text automatically flows into the second text box, and then into the third text box in the chain. This is especially useful in editing and positioning an article that is continued on another page. If you add or delete text in one of the text boxes, the remaining text in the article in the other text boxes adjusts to the change also. Furthermore, you can establish more than one chain of linked text boxes in a document. For example, you can create a chain of linked text boxes for an article that begins on page 1, and then continues onto pages 3 and 4. In the same newsletter, you can create another chain of linked text boxes for another article that begins on page 2 and then continues on page 4.

Creating the Link

To link text boxes, you must first create two or more text boxes. For example, if you have an article that begins on page 1 and is to be continued on page 2 of a newsletter, create a text box on page 1 and then create another text box on page 2. Size the text boxes to fit appropriately within the allotted column width, then position the text boxes as desired. If necessary, additional size and position adjustments can be made after the text is added to the text boxes. To create a link between the two text boxes, complete these steps:

1. Click the text box that is to be the first text box in the chain of linked text boxes.
2. If the Text Box toolbar does not automatically display, right-click anywhere within the Standard toolbar, then select Text Box or click View, Toolbars, then select Text Box.
3. Click the Create Text Box Link button on the Text Box toolbar as displayed in figure 11.2. The mouse will display as a small upright pitcher.
4. Position the pitcher in the text box to be linked. The pitcher appears tipped with letters spilling out of it when it is over a text box that can receive the link. Click once to complete the link.
5. To create a link from the second text box to a third text box, click the second text box, then repeat steps 3 and 4 above. Repeat these steps to add more links to the chain.

Links can also be established between other shapes, such as circles, banners, and flow charts.

Moving Between Linked Text Boxes

You can use the Next Text Box and the Previous Text Box buttons on the Text Box toolbar to move between linked text boxes. If you select a text box that is at the beginning of a chain of linked text boxes, the Next Text Box button is active and the Previous Text Box button is dimmed. If you select a text box that is at the end of a chain of linked text boxes, only the Previous Text Box button is active. If you select a text box that is in the middle of a chain of linked text boxes, both the Next Text Box and the Previous Text Box buttons will be available. Additionally, if one or both of these buttons are active, you know that the currently selected text box is linked to another text box. If neither of these buttons is active, then the currently selected text box is not linked to any other text box.

figure 11.2

Text Box Toolbar

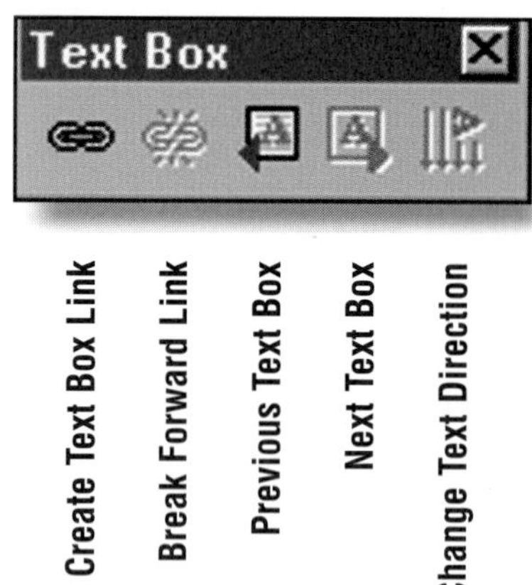

Using the Newsletter Wizard

In Word, you can design your own newsletter from scratch, or you can use Word's Newsletter Wizard to assist you in the setup of a newsletter. This wizard, named *Newsletter Wizard.wiz,* offers three newsletter style templates — *Professional, Contemporary,* and *Elegant*—which you may preview at the Newsletter Wizard dialog box. Other selections offered by the Newsletter Wizard include the title of the newsletter, the date, the volume and issue number, and allowance for mailing label space. Any selections you make can always be edited at a later date. All three of the newsletter templates include styles for headlines, subtitles, section headings, bylines, body text, and more. The *Professional* and *Elegant* newsletter templates use side-by-side text boxes to create a two-column page layout. The *Contemporary* newsletter template uses the columns feature to form the framework of its three-column page layout.

In exercise 1, you will create the first page of a newsletter using the *Newsletter Wizard.wiz* and the *Professional* style template. The title of the newsletter, the date, and the volume and issue number are automatically filled in from information keyed at the Newsletter Wizard dialog box. The two-column format of the resulting newsletter document is achieved through the use of two text boxes positioned side by side in a one-column page layout. The text boxes are used to take advantage of Word's Text Box Linking feature that allows articles to flow continuously across pages.

The newsletter also contains instructional text for using the template. Print a copy of the instructional text before deleting and replacing it with your own newsletter text. In addition, the *Professional* style newsletter template includes a large table of contents (created in a Word table) in the lower left corner of the first page. You will customize the template by inserting article text, applying existing styles, replacing the picture, and changing type size.

Remember, a predefined template is often a perfect starting place for the creation of a document. Once the template framework is displayed on the screen, it becomes a Word document. You can customize it any way you want. You can then save and name it as a regular Word document, or you can save it as a new template document.

exercise 1

Creating a Newsletter Using the Newsletter Wizard

1. At a clear document window, create the first page of a newsletter, as shown in figure 11.3, by completing the following steps:
   a. Use the Newsletter Wizard to help you make the newsletter by completing the following steps:
      (1) Choose File, New, and then select the Publications tab.
      (2) Make sure Document is selected in the Create New section.
      (3) Double-click the Newsletter Wizard.wiz icon.
      (4) At the Newsletter Wizard dialog box that displays, complete the following steps:
         (a) Click Style & Color in the upper left section of the dialog box or click the Next command.
         (b) Select Professional as the newsletter style and make sure Color is selected for your newsletter appearance.
         (c) Click Title Content in the upper left section of the dialog box or click Next.
         (d) Key **From the Desktop** as the title of your newsletter.
         (e) Click the Date check box to insert a checkmark, then key **March 1999** in the corresponding text box.
         (f) Click the Volume and Issue check box to insert a checkmark, then key **Volume 2, Issue 3** in the corresponding text box.
         (g) Click Mailing Label in the upper left section of the dialog box or click Next.
         (h) Click No in response to leaving room for a mailing label.
         (i) Click Finish when done.
         (j) Click OK to the message *The wizard is truncating the title to fit in the page.*
      (5) When the Office Assistant appears asking if you want to do more with the newsletter, click Cancel.
   b. Change the Zoom viewing mode to 75% and then turn on the display of nonprinting characters.
   c. Print one copy of the newsletter and read the instructional text.
   d. To delete the instructional text, complete the following steps: (*Note:* This procedure involves more steps than normal due to the text box format.)
      (1) With the insertion point on the first page of the newsletter, click the Next Page button on the vertical scroll bar to move the insertion point to the top of page 2. (If you choose to scroll to the top of page 2 instead of using the Next Page button, make sure the mouse displays as an I-beam, not a four-headed arrow, before clicking the left mouse button to position the insertion point.)
      (2) Hold the Shift key down, press Ctrl + End to select the remaining text, then press Delete. The insertion point will be positioned at the top of an empty page 2 to the left of a paragraph symbol.
      (3) Press Backspace to delete the blank page 2.
      (4) On page 1, position the insertion point anywhere within the first article in the first column, then click once to select the text box that contains the article. The Text Box toolbar may automatically display. Click and drag it out of the way if necessary.
      (5) Position the insertion point to the left of the heading *Continuing Articles across Pages*. Hold down the Shift key, and press Ctrl + End to select all the text in the text box, then press the Delete key. (Do not worry about the paragraph symbols that are visible in the text box. They are in the text layer below the text box and have no effect on the text box contents.)

(6) Position the insertion point anywhere within the second article in the second column, then click once to select the text box that contains the article.
(7) Position the insertion point to the left of the *Instructions for Using This Template*, hold down the Shift key and press Ctrl End to select all the text in the text box, then the Delete key.
(8) In the table containing the table of contents at the bottom of the first column, select rows 2–4, then press Delete. (Do not delete the first row containing the table of contents heading.)

e. Format the newsletter name, then redefine the applied style by completing the following steps:
(1) Select *From the Desktop*, then change the font size to 40 points.
(2) Click once in the Style list box on the Formatting toolbar to select the *Title-Professional* style name, then press Enter.
(3) Make sure *Update the style to reflect recent changes?* is selected, then click OK.

f. Insert and format the lead-in text (known as a kicker) to the first article by completing the following steps:
(1) Click once inside the first text box in the first column. Click and drag the Text Box toolbar out of the way if necessary.
(2) Key **Desktop Resources . . .**, then press Enter.
(3) Position the insertion point anywhere within *Desktop Resources*, then apply the *Sidebar Head-Professional* style.
(4) Select *Desktop Resources . . .*, then change the font to 10 points.
(5) Click once in the Style list box on the Formatting toolbar to select the *Sidebar Head-Professional* style name, then press Enter. Make sure *Update the style to include recent changes?* is selected, then click OK.

g. Insert and format the article heading by completing the following steps:
(1) Click below the kicker to position the insertion point for the heading.
(2) Key **Knowledge Is Power**, then press Enter.
(3) Position the insertion point anywhere within the article heading, then apply the *Heading 1-Professional* style.
(4) Select Format, then Paragraph and change the spacing after the paragraph to 6 pt.
(5) Click once inside the Style list box on the Formatting toolbar to select the *Heading 1-Professional* style name, then press Enter. Make sure *Update the style to include recent changes?* is selected, then click OK.

h. Insert and format the article text by completing the following steps:
(1) Click once below the article heading to position the insertion point for the article text.
(2) Click Insert, then File. Change to the location of your student data disk files, then double-click *knowledge text.doc*.
(3) Position the insertion point at the beginning of the first paragraph of the article text. Hold down the Shift key, then press Ctrl + End to select all of the article text just inserted. (Selecting the text in this manner includes all of the article text, some of which is hidden because the article text is more than the text box can accommodate. To continue the article, you would draw another text box on the page on which the article is to be continued, then create a link between the two text boxes. The goal of this exercise, however, is to produce the first page only; you will use linked text boxes in a two-page newsletter created later in this chapter.)
(4) Apply the *Body Text-Professional* style to the selected text.

(5) Check the bottom border of the text box. If more text shows (or partially shows) than what is visible in figure 11.3, adjust the height of the text box so that it matches the figure.

i. Insert and format the kicker (lead-in text) to the article in column 2 by completing the following steps:
   (1) Click once inside the text box in the second column. Click and drag the Text Box toolbar out of the way if necessary.
   (2) Press Enter one time.
   (3) Key **Knowledge and Training . . .**, then press Enter.
   (4) Position the insertion point anywhere within *Knowledge and Training*, then apply the *Sidebar Head-Professional* style.

j. Insert and format the article heading by completing the following steps:
   (1) Click below the kicker to position the insertion point for the heading.
   (2) Key **Training Techniques**, then press Enter.
   (3) Position the insertion point anywhere within the article heading, then apply the *Heading 1-Professional* style.

k. Insert and format the article text by completing the following steps:
   (1) Click once below the article heading to position the insertion point for the article text.
   (2) Click Insert, then File. Change to the location of your student data disk files, then double-click *training text.doc*.
   (3) Position the insertion point at the beginning of the first paragraph of the article text, then select the article text just inserted.
   (4) Apply the *Body Text-Professional* style to the selected text.

l. Insert the computer graphic image in the text box in the second column by completing the following steps:
   (1) Position the insertion point in the blank line above *Knowledge and Training ....* (Make sure the Style list box displays *Normal* as the style name.)
   (2) Click Insert, point to Picture, then select From File.
   (3) Change to the location of your student data disk files, then double-click *computer.wmf*.

m. Change the color of the computer screen and add text to the picture by completing the following steps:
   (1) Double-click the computer picture just inserted to switch to Word's Picture editor.
   (2) Click anywhere within the black portion of the computer screen to select this area. (White sizing handles should display around the black part of the screen.)
   (3) Click the Fill Color button on the Drawing toolbar, then change the color to Dark Blue, in the first row, sixth column.
   (4) Select each of the four horizontal gray bars on the computer screen and delete each one.
   (5) Click the Text Box button on the Drawing toolbar, then draw a text box within the boundaries of the computer screen.
   (6) Double-click the text box border and make the following changes at the Format Text Box dialog box:
      (a) Click the Colors and Lines tab, then change the line color to No Line.
      (b) Click the Size tab, then change the height to 0.7 inches and the width to 0.83 inches.
      (c) Click the Position tab, then change the horizontal position to 1.3 inches from the edge of the column and the vertical position to 1.59 inches from the top of the paragraph.

(d) Click the Text Box tab, then change the left and right internal margins to 0.05 inches and the top internal margin to 0.07 inches.
(e) Click OK or press Enter.

(7) Click once inside the text box to position the insertion point.
(8) Key **Good training is essential!**
(9) Select the text just entered, change the alignment to center, then change the font to 10-point Arial Bold and the color to White.
(10) With the text box selected, click the Fill Color button on the Drawing toolbar to change the fill color to Dark Blue.
(11) Click File, then Close & Return to Document # or Name (document number or name may vary).

n. If the text *continued on page 3* appears at the bottom of the text box in the second column, select the text and then delete it.

o. Insert the table of contents in the table reserved for this purpose by completing the following steps:

(1) Position the insertion point below the table of contents heading, *Inside This Issue,* in the second row, first column of the table, then key **1**.
(2) Press the tab key to move to the second column, then key **Knowledge Is Power**.
(3) Key the remaining page numbers and article names in the table as follows:

1	**Training Techniques**
2	**Tips and Tricks**
2	**How to Save Time and Keystrokes**
2	**Upcoming Events**

p. Insert the promotional text below the table of contents by completing the following steps:

(1) Click the Text Box button on the Drawing toolbar and draw a text box below the table of contents.
(2) Double-click the text border and make the following changes at the Format Text Box dialog box:
(a) Click the Colors and Lines tab, then change the line color to No Line.
(b) Click the Size tab, then change the height to 0.6 inches and the width to 3.5 inches.
(c) Click the Position tab, then change the horizontal position to 0 inches from the edge of the column and the vertical position to 9.4 inches from the top of the page. (Remember to change the "From" options first.)
(d) Click OK or press Enter.

(3) Click inside the text box to position the insertion point, then key the following text pressing Enter after the first two lines:

Desktop Publishing Using Microsoft Word 97
May 18, 1999
(See p. 2)

(4) Select the first two lines of the text just entered, then change the font to 11-point Arial Bold Italic, the color to Dark Blue, and the alignment to Center.
(5) Select the last line of text, then change the font to 10-point Arial Bold, the color to Dark Blue, and the alignment to Center..

2. Save and name the newsletter c11ex01, desktop nwsltr.
3. Print and then close c11ex01, desktop nwsltr.

figure 11.3

From the Desktop

Volume 2, Issue 3 March 1999

DESKTOP RESOURCES . . .

Knowledge Is Power

How can one have the up-to-date knowledge needed to keep on the cutting edge of desktop publishing? One way to gain desktop publishing knowledge is to read, read, read! Read some of the periodicals, newsletters, and books now available that address all aspects of desktop publishing.

Two basic types of periodicals are available. The first type is based on technological development and communication arts. These periodicals contain useful information about current and new products. The second type contains knowledge of technique, style, and applications.

Many newsletters and books are available. Your local library and bookstores can be good sources for resource material. Listed below are some newsletters and books that can help you as a desktop publisher.

Inside Microsoft®Word 97 by the Cobb Group is a monthly publication including helpful tips and techniques for using Microsoft Word 97 to create everyday applications.

continued on page 2

INSIDE THIS ISSUE

Desktop Publishing Using Microsoft Word 97
May 18, 1999
(see p. 2)

Good training is essential!

KNOWLEDGE AND TRAINING . . .

Training Techniques

Two types of training are available for those just beginning in desktop publishing.

The first type is a content-based program. This program is based on a typical college program and the information is presented in a classroom situation. Classroom time is usually divided between the presentation of concepts or theory and directed hands-on training. Instructional books and videos are frequently utilized.

Skill-based training is another type of training. This training is useful to businesses because skill-based training produces capable people quickly. Productive skills are put to use on the type of job the person will be expected to fulfill.

Both types of training can produce workers with equal productivity and confidence. The best equipment is wasted if people are not trained to use it efficiently. Good training, regardless of which type, is essential to desktop publishing.

From the Desktop 1

The newsletter created in exercise 1 uses a symmetrical nameplate and page layout. The table of contents is located in the bottom left corner of the page and is easily identified as a separate section since it is separated from the article text by a heavier dark blue top border. The table of contents heading, set in small caps and in a larger and bolder font than the body text, adds more emphasis to this area. The promotional text below the table of contents was added to take up some excessive white space in this location. Remember, if a part of a template does not meet your needs, you can always customize it to your liking.

Using Spot Color

Spot Color
Using another color, in addition to black, as an accent color in a publication.

Spot color refers to using one other color, in addition to black, as an accent color in a publication. The more colors used in a publication, the more expensive it is to produce. Using spot color can be an inexpensive way to make a black-and-white publication more appealing. If you have a color printer, you can see the results of using a second color immediately. You can then take the newsletter to be professionally printed on high-quality paper.

Spot color can be applied to such elements as graphic lines, graphic images, borders, background fill, headings, special characters, and end signs. If your logo or organizational seal contains a particular color, use that color as a unifying element throughout your publication. Just as an all black-and-white page may have a gray look to it, using too much spot color can give the appearance of all one color, which defeats the purpose of using spot color for emphasis, contrast, and/or directional flow. Variations of the spot color used can be obtained by *screening*, or producing a lighter shade of the same color. You can also apply spot color to the background in a reverse text box or to a drop cap. Refer to the two newsletter samples in figure 11.4 to see how spot color can really add to the visual appeal of a publication.

Screening
Decreasing the intensity of a color to produce a lighter shade.

In exercises 2 through 10, you will build a two-page newsletter, as shown in figure 11.18, adding visual enhancements as you proceed. In addition, you will use copy-fitting techniques and add spot color to the newsletter throughout the range of exercises.

figure 11.4

Newsletter with and without Spot Color

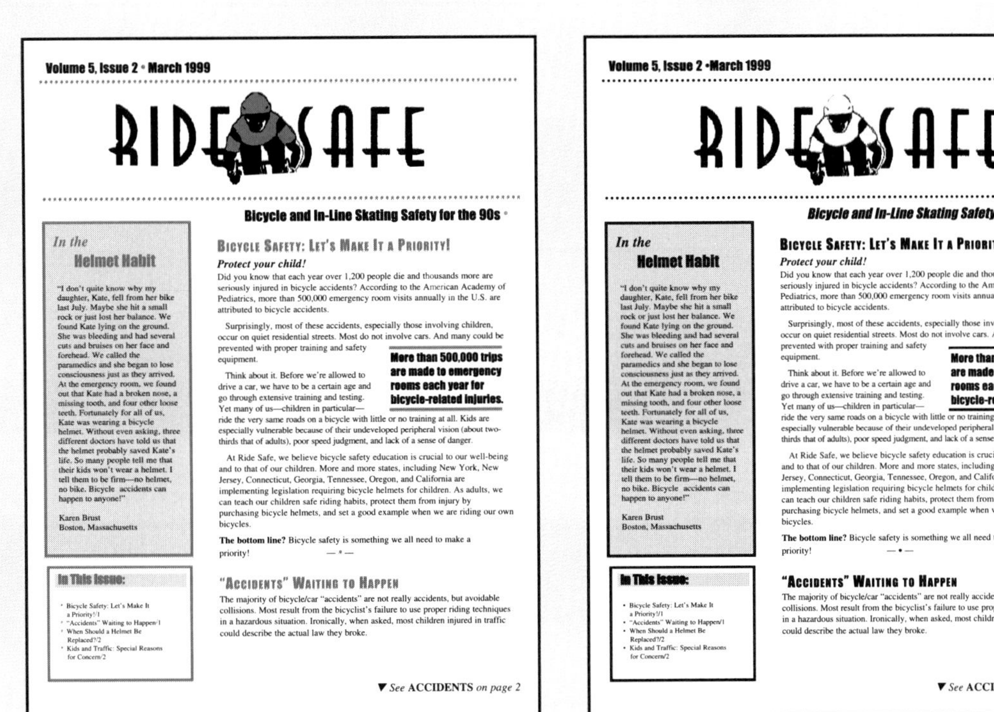

Volume 5, Issue 2 • March 1999

RIDE SAFE

Bicycle and In-Line Skating Safety for the 90s •

In the

Helmet Habit

"I don't quite know why my daughter, Kate, fell from her bike last July. Maybe she hit a small rock or just lost her balance. We found Kate lying on the ground. She was bleeding and had several cuts and bruises on her face and forehead. We called the paramedics and she began to lose consciousness just as they arrived. At the emergency room, we found out that Kate had a broken nose, a missing tooth, and four other loose teeth. Fortunately for all of us, Kate was wearing a bicycle helmet. Without even asking, three different doctors have told us that the helmet probably saved Kate's life. So many people tell me that their kids won't wear a helmet. I tell them to be firm—no helmet, no bike. Bicycle accidents can happen to anyone!"

Karen Brust
Boston, Massachusetts

In This Issue:

- Bicycle Safety: Let's Make It a Priority!/1
- "Accidents" Waiting to Happen/1
- When Should a Helmet Be Replaced?/2
- Kids and Traffic: Special Reasons for Concern/2

BICYCLE SAFETY: LET'S MAKE IT A PRIORITY!

Protect your child!

Did you know that each year over 1,200 people die and thousands more are seriously injured in bicycle accidents? According to the American Academy of Pediatrics, more than 500,000 emergency room visits annually in the U.S. are attributed to bicycle accidents.

Surprisingly, most of these accidents, especially those involving children, occur on quiet residential streets. Most do not involve cars. And many could be prevented with proper training and safety equipment.

More than 500,000 trips are made to emergency rooms each year for bicycle-related injuries.

Think about it. Before we're allowed to drive a car, we have to be a certain age and go through extensive training and testing. Yet many of us—children in particular—ride the very same roads on a bicycle with little or no training at all. Kids are especially vulnerable because of their undeveloped peripheral vision (about two-thirds that of adults), poor speed judgment, and lack of a sense of danger.

At Ride Safe, we believe bicycle safety education is crucial to our well-being and to that of our children. More and more states, including New York, New Jersey, Connecticut, Georgia, Tennessee, Oregon, and California are implementing legislation requiring bicycle helmets for children. As adults, we can teach our children safe riding habits, protect them from injury by purchasing bicycle helmets, and set a good example when we are riding our own bicycles.

The bottom line? Bicycle safety is something we all need to make a priority! — • —

"ACCIDENTS" WAITING TO HAPPEN

The majority of bicycle/car "accidents" are not really accidents, but avoidable collisions. Most result from the bicyclist's failure to use proper riding techniques in a hazardous situation. Ironically, when asked, most children injured in traffic could describe the actual law they broke.

▼ *See* ACCIDENTS *on page 2*

Volume 5, Issue 2 • March 1999

RIDE SAFE

Bicycle and In-Line Skating Safety for the 90s •

In the

Helmet Habit

"I don't quite know why my daughter, Kate, fell from her bike last July. Maybe she hit a small rock or just lost her balance. We found Kate lying on the ground. She was bleeding and had several cuts and bruises on her face and forehead. We called the paramedics and she began to lose consciousness just as they arrived. At the emergency room, we found out that Kate had a broken nose, a missing tooth, and four other loose teeth. Fortunately for all of us, Kate was wearing a bicycle helmet. Without even asking, three different doctors have told us that the helmet probably saved Kate's life. So many people tell me that their kids won't wear a helmet. I tell them to be firm—no helmet, no bike. Bicycle accidents can happen to anyone!"

Karen Brust
Boston, Massachusetts

In This Issue:

- Bicycle Safety: Let's Make It a Priority!/1
- "Accidents" Waiting to Happen/1
- When Should a Helmet Be Replaced?/2
- Kids and Traffic: Special Reasons for Concern/2

BICYCLE SAFETY: LET'S MAKE IT A PRIORITY!

Protect your child!

Did you know that each year over 1,200 people die and thousands more are seriously injured in bicycle accidents? According to the American Academy of Pediatrics, more than 500,000 emergency room visits annually in the U.S. are attributed to bicycle accidents.

Surprisingly, most of these accidents, especially those involving children, occur on quiet residential streets. Most do not involve cars. And many could be prevented with proper training and safety equipment.

More than 500,000 trips are made to emergency rooms each year for bicycle-related injuries.

Think about it. Before we're allowed to drive a car, we have to be a certain age and go through extensive training and testing. Yet many of us—children in particular—ride the very same roads on a bicycle with little or no training at all. Kids are especially vulnerable because of their undeveloped peripheral vision (about two-thirds that of adults), poor speed judgment, and lack of a sense of danger.

At Ride Safe, we believe bicycle safety education is crucial to our well-being and to that of our children. More and more states, including New York, New Jersey, Connecticut, Georgia, Tennessee, Oregon, and California are implementing legislation requiring bicycle helmets for children. As adults, we can teach our children safe riding habits, protect them from injury by purchasing bicycle helmets, and set a good example when we are riding our own bicycles.

The bottom line? Bicycle safety is something we all need to make a priority! — • —

"ACCIDENTS" WAITING TO HAPPEN

The majority of bicycle/car "accidents" are not really accidents, but avoidable collisions. Most result from the bicyclist's failure to use proper riding techniques in a hazardous situation. Ironically, when asked, most children injured in traffic could describe the actual law they broke.

▼ *See* ACCIDENTS *on page 2*

Creating Headers and Footers for a Newsletter

Headers and/or footers are commonly used in newsletters, manuscripts, textbooks, reports, and other publications. The term *header* refers to text that is repeated at the top of every page. Alternately, the term *footer* refers to text that appears at the bottom of every page. In figure 11.1, a horizontal, gray-shaded ruled line and a small version of the nameplate text are included in a footer at the bottom of the page. In a newsletter, information such as page number, the name of the newsletter, the issue or date of the newsletter, and the name of the organization producing the newsletter are often included in a header or footer as illustrated in the header and footer examples in figure 11.5.

Header
Text repeated at the top of every page.

Footer
Text repeated at the bottom of every page.

figure 11.5

Examples of Headers and Footers

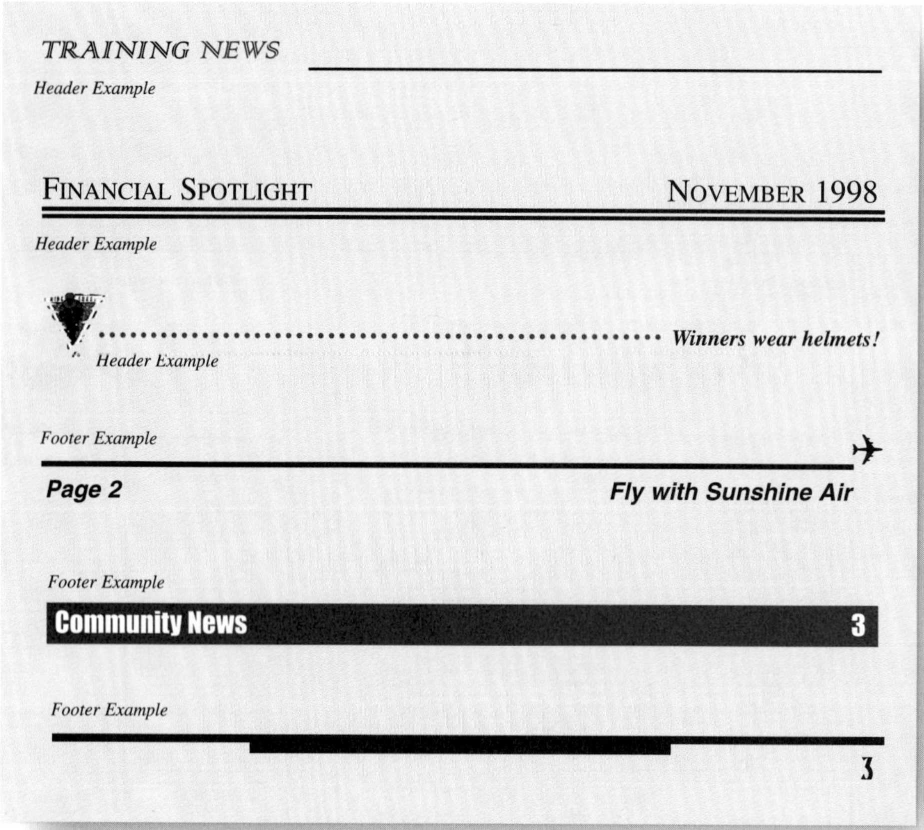

TRAINING NEWS

Header Example

FINANCIAL SPOTLIGHT NOVEMBER 1998

Header Example

Winners wear helmets!

Header Example

Footer Example

Page 2 **Fly with Sunshine Air**

Footer Example

Community News 3

Footer Example

3

DTP POINTERS
Use a header or footer to reinforce company identity. Consistent formatting of a header/footer helps to establish unity in a publication.

Since a header or footer is commonly repeated on every page starting with the second page, it provides the perfect place to reinforce the identity of a company or organization. For example, including the company or organization name, a very small version of the nameplate, or a logo in a header or footer can increase a reader's awareness of your identity. In figure 11.5, the Ride Safe header includes both the company logo and their slogan, while the Community News footer includes the newsletter name and the page number.

Headers or footers, consistently formatted, help to establish unity among the pages of a newsletter, as well as among different issues of a newsletter. In addition, they serve as landmarks for the reader, adding to the directional flow of the document.

Horizontal ruled lines are frequently placed in headers or footers. These serve as a visually contrasting element that clearly identifies the top or bottom of each page. Different effects can be achieved by varying the weight (thickness) of the line, the number of lines, and the arrangement of the lines.

To create a header or footer, you would complete the following steps:

1. Choose View, then Header and Footer.
2. Key the desired header text in the header pane. If you are creating a footer, click the Switch Between Header and Footer button on the Header and Footer toolbar, then key the desired footer text in the footer pane.
3. Click Close on the Header and Footer toolbar.

When you access the header and footer feature, Word automatically changes the viewing mode to Page Layout, and your document text is dimmed in the background. After you insert text in the header and/or footer pane and then click Close on the Header and Footer toolbar, the document text is displayed in black and the header and/or footer is dimmed. If the Normal viewing mode was selected before the header and/or footer was created, you are returned to the Normal viewing mode. In the Normal viewing mode, a header or footer does not display on the screen. Change to Page Layout viewing mode to view the header or footer text dimmed, or use Print Preview to view how a header and/or footer will print.

Placing Headers/Footers on Different Pages

By default, Word will insert a header or footer on every page in the document. You can create different headers and footers in a document. For example, you can do the following:

- create a unique header or footer on the first page;
- omit a header or footer on the first page;
- create different headers or footers for odd and even pages; or
- create different headers or footers for sections in a document.

A different header or footer can be created on the first page of a document. To do this, position the insertion point anywhere in the first page, choose View, then Header and Footer. (If you are creating a footer, click the Switch Between Header and Footer button.) Click the Page Setup button on the Header and Footer toolbar. Make sure the Layout tab is selected, choose Different first page, then choose OK or press Enter. Key the desired text for the first page header or footer. Click the Show Next button on the Header and Footer toolbar to open another header or footer pane. Key the text for the other header or footer that will print on all but the first page, then choose Close at the Header and Footer toolbar. You can follow similar steps to omit a header or footer on the first page. Simply do not key any text when the first header or footer pane is opened.

The ability to place different headers and footers on odd and even pages is useful when numbering pages in a multipage newsletter. Odd page numbers can be placed on the right side of the page and even page numbers can be placed on the left side of the page. For example, in a four-page newsletter, a footer can be created that includes right-aligned page numbering that will appear on the odd pages only. Alternately, another footer can be created that contains left-aligned page numbering that will appear on even pages only.

To create a different header and/or footer on odd and even pages, choose View, then Header and Footer. (If you are creating a footer, click the Switch Between Header and Footer button.) Click the Page Setup button on the Header and Footer toolbar, and then select the Layout tab. Make sure there is no check mark in the Different first page option. Choose Different odd and even, then choose OK or press Enter. Key the desired text at the header or footer pane. Click the Show Next button on the Header and Footer toolbar. At the even header or footer pane, key the desired text, then click the Close button on the Header and Footer toolbar.

exercise 2

Creating a Header and Footer in a Newsletter

1. At a clear document window, add a header and footer to the beginning stages of a newsletter, as shown in figure 11.6, by completing the following steps:
   a. Open *newsletter banner.doc* located on your student data disk.
   b. Save the document with Save As and name it c11ex02, header&footer.
   c. Change the Zoom viewing mode to 75%, and then turn on the display of nonprinting characters.
   d. Select the month and year in the folio and key the current month and year.
   e. Select one of the dotted lines in the banner and click the Copy button on the Standard toolbar. (This line will be pasted in the header later.)
   f. With the insertion point located at the beginning of the document, create a header that will start on the second page of the newsletter by completing the following steps:
      (1) Choose View, then Header and Footer.
      (2) With the insertion point in the Header pane, choose Insert, point to Picture, then select From File.
      (3) At the Insert Picture dialog box, change to the location of your student data disk files in the Look in: list box, then double-click *Ridesf2teal.bmp*.
      (4) Format the picture by completing the following steps:
         (a) Select the image and choose Format, then Picture.
         (b) At the Format Picture dialog box, select the Size tab, then change the Height and Width in the Scale section to 35%.
         (c) Click OK or press Enter.
         (d) Click once to the right of the image to deselect it.
      (5) Click the Text Box button on the Drawing toolbar, then draw a text box that will accommodate the dotted line and slogan to the right of the Ride Safe logo just inserted.
      (6) Double-click the text box border to display the Format Text Box dialog box, then make the following changes:
         (a) Click the Colors and Lines tab, then change the line color to No Line.
         (b) Click the Size tab, then change the height to 0.3 inches and the width to 7.1 inches.
         (c) Click the Position tab, then change the horizontal position to 0.9 inches from the left edge of the page and the vertical position to 0.7 inches from the top of the page. (Remember to set the "From" options first.)
         (d) Click the Text Box tab, then change the left and right internal margins to 0 inches.
         (e) Click OK or press Enter.
      (7) Insert the dotted line and slogan by completing the following steps:
         (a) Click once inside the text box to position the insertion point.
         (b) Click the Paste button on the Standard toolbar to insert the dotted line copied from the nameplate in step 1e. (The line length will be adjusted in the following steps.)
         (c) Position the insertion point in the middle of the dotted line, then press the Delete key until the paragraph symbol displays at the end of the dotted line

within the text box. Continue pressing the Delete key until there is approximately enough space at the end of the line to key the slogan within the text box.

(d) Position the insertion point at the end of the dotted line, then key **Winners wear helmets!**. (If some of the text disappears, delete more of the dotted line until the entire slogan is visible.)

(8) Select the slogan, access the Font dialog box, then make the following changes:

(a) Click the Font tab, then change the font to 12-point Times New Roman Bold Italic and the color to Black.

(b) Click the Character Spacing tab, then click the down arrow in the Position list box and select Raised. Make sure 3 pt displays in the By box. (This raises the slogan to be in alignment with the dotted line.)

(c) Click OK or press Enter.

(9) If the slogan wraps to the next line, delete more of the dotted line until the slogan fits in the text box. If you delete more than necessary, click the Undo button on the Standard toolbar. If the slogan does not extend to the right margin, select a section of the line, and copy and paste it to the existing line.

g. Create the footer that will begin on the second page by completing the following steps:

(1) Click the Switch Between Header and Footer button on the Header and Footer toolbar to switch to the footer pane.

(2) Insert the round bullets by completing the following steps:

(a) Change the justification to center.

(b) Click Insert, Symbol, then select the Symbols tab.

(c) Change the Font to Wingdings and select the round bullet in the third row, twenty-first column.

(d) Click Insert two times to insert two bullets, and then click Close.

(e) Select the two bullets and change the font to 14-point Impact and the Color to Teal.

(3) Insert and format automatic page numbering by completing the following steps:

(a) Position the insertion point in between the two bullets.

(b) Click the Insert Page Number button on the Header and Footer toolbar to automatically insert a page number. (At this point, do not be concerned if the number 1 displays even though the footer is to begin on page 2. This adjustment will made in future steps.)

(c) Select the page number and change the font size to 16-point Impact and change the Color to Black.

(d) Insert a space before and after the page number.

(4) Click the Page Setup button on the Header and Footer toolbar, then select the Margins tab. In the From Edge section, change the distance from the bottom edge of the page to the Footer to 0.7". (Within the existing bottom margin setting, the footer would be partially cut off when printed, making this adjustment necessary.) Choose OK or press Enter.

(5) To insert the horizontal lines on each side of the bullets and page number, complete the following steps:

(a) Display the Drawing toolbar, and then click the Line button on the Drawing toolbar.

(b) Position the crosshairs to the left of the bullets and page number, hold the Shift key down, and draw a line the approximate length and in the approximate location indicated in figure 11.6.

(c) Repeat these same steps to draw the horizontal line on the right side of the bullets and page number.

(6) Double-click the horizontal line on the left and make the following changes at the Format AutoShape dialog box:

(a) Click the Colors and Lines tab, then change the line Weight to 2 points.

(b) Click the Size tab, then change the Width of the line to 3.4 inches.

(c) Click the Position tab, then change the horizontal position to 0.5 inches from the left edge of the page and the vertical position to 10.2 inches from the top edge of the page. (Remember to change the "From" options first.)

(d) Click OK or press Enter.

(7) Double-click the horizontal line on the right, then repeat steps 6(a) through 6(d) above, except change the horizontal position of the line to 4.6 inches from the left edge of the page.

(8) To instruct Word to start the header and footer on page 2, complete the following steps:

(a) Deselect the horizontal line, click the Page Setup button on the Header and Footer toolbar, and then select the Layout tab.

(b) In the Headers and Footers section, click in the check box to the left of Different first page to activate this option.

(c) Click OK or press Enter. The footer text will disappear from the first page and a First Page Footer pane will display. This will remain empty so that no footer text will appear on the first page. If you click the Switch Between Header and Footer button on the Header and Footer toolbar, an empty First Page Header pane will display also.

(d) Click Close on the Header and Footer toolbar.

(9) Press Ctrl + End to position the insertion point at the end of the document and then press Ctrl + Enter to create a second page displaying the header and footer.

2. Save c11ex02, header&footer.
3. Position the insertion point on page 2 to print the page displaying the header and footer. Click File, Print, and then select Current page in the Page range section of the Print dialog box. Click OK or press Enter.
4. Close c11ex02, header&footer.

figure 11.6

Volume 5, Issue 2 • March 1999
RIDE SAFE
Bicycle and In-Line Skating Safety for the 90s •

Look at a hard copy of c11ex02, header&footer, and notice how the triangular logo in the header repeats the image of the bicyclist in the nameplate. In addition, the dotted line in the header on page 2 is consistent in style and color with the dotted lines located within the nameplate on page 1 and the typeface used for the slogan is the same that will be used for the body text. The footer repeats the round bullet symbols found in the nameplate, the header, and the end sign which will later be used within the body copy to indicate the end of an article. As you can see, headers and footers can help to make separate pages a part of a whole unit.

Creating Sidebars in a Newsletter

A *sidebar* is a block of information or a related story that is set off from the body text in some type of a graphics box. In figure 11.1, a sidebar is included in the first column. A sidebar can also include a photograph or a graphic image along with the text. Frequently, the sidebar contains a shaded or *screened* background. A screened (lighter) version of the main color used in a newsletter can serve as the background screen. The sidebar can be set in any position relative to the body text. In Word, sidebars can easily be created by creating a text box and inserting text.

Sidebar
Information or a related story set off from the body text.

In exercise 3, you will set up the column format for the newsletter begun in exercise 2 and create a sidebar. The newsletter page layout will include two columns based on an underlying three-column grid. In later exercises, you will add more visually enhancing elements to the same newsletter.

exercise 3

Inserting a Sidebar in a Newsletter

1. At a clear document window, create column formatting and insert a sidebar in the newsletter from exercise 2, as shown in figure 11.7, by completing the following steps:
   a. Open c11ex02, header&footer.
   b. Save the document with Save As and name it c11ex03, sidebar.
   c. Change the Zoom viewing mode to 75%, then turn on the display of nonprinting characters.
   d. Position the insertion point to the left of the Page Break on page 1 and press Delete to delete the empty page 2. (Working with one page is easier at this point.)
   e. Access the Paragraph dialog box, then change the spacing after the paragraph to 0 points. (The spacing instruction was associated with the folio but is no longer needed.)
   f. Turn on Kerning for fonts 14 Points and above.
   g. Change the column format to two columns by completing the following steps:
      (1) Press Ctrl + End to position the insertion point.
      (2) Click Format, then Columns.
      (3) Change the Number of columns to 2.
      (4) Make sure there is no check mark in the Equal column width check box.
      (5) In the Width and Spacing section, change the Width of column 1 to 2.4 inches.
      (6) Change the Spacing in between columns to 0.25 inches.
      (7) Click in the Width text box for column 2 and make sure it displays 4.85 inches.
      (8) Click Apply to, then select *This point forward*.
      (9) Choose OK or press Enter.
   h. Create the sidebar text box in the first column by completing the following steps:
      (1) Choose Insert, then File. Change to the location of your student data disk files, then double-click *helmet habit text.doc*.
      (2) Make sure the text just inserted is set in 10-point Times New Roman.
      (3) Select the text just inserted (do not include the paragraph symbol below the last paragraph), then click the Text Box button on the Drawing toolbar to insert the text in a text box.
      (4) Using the center sizing handle on the bottom border of the text box, stretch the size of the text box vertically until all the text is visible.
      (5) Double-click the text box border and make the following changes at the Format Text Box dialog box:
         (a) Click the Colors and Lines tab, then change the line color to Teal and the line style to 1½ pt.
         (b) Click the Size tab, then change the height to 5.31 inches and the width to 2.2 inches.
         (c) Click the Position tab and change the horizontal position to 0.5 inches from the edge of the page and the vertical position to 3.17 inches from the top of the page. (Remember to change the "From" options first.)
         (d) Click OK or press Enter.
   i. Format the title of the sidebar text by completing the following steps:
      (1) Change the Zoom viewing mode to 100%.

(2) Position the insertion point at the beginning of the title, *In the Helmet Habit*, and press Enter.
(3) Select *In the*, then change the font to 12-point Times New Roman Bold Italic and the color to Teal.
(4) Position the insertion point after *In the*, delete the space, and then press Enter.
(5) Select *Helmet Habit* and make the following changes:
(a) Change the alignment to center.
(b) Change the font to 14-point Impact, the color to Teal, and expand the character spacing to 1.2 pt.
(6) Position the insertion point after *In the*, access the Paragraph dialog box, then change the Line spacing to Exactly At 10 points.
(7) Position the insertion point after the word *Habit* and change the spacing after the paragraph to 6 points.

j. For use in future issues, create styles for the sidebar heading by completing the following steps:
(1) Position the insertion point anywhere within *In the*, then click the Style list box on the Formatting toolbar.
(2) Key **Sidebar Heading-1**, then press Enter.
(3) Position the insertion point anywhere within *Helmet Habit*, then follow similar steps to j(1-2) and name this style **Sidebar Heading-2**.

k. Position the insertion point after *...anyone!"* in the last line of the article text, press Delete to eliminate an extra hard return, and change the spacing after the paragraph to 6 points.

l. Create a screened background in the text box by completing the following steps: (Since the screened background makes the text harder to read on the screen, this step is placed at this point in the exercise rather than in step 1h(5) above.)
(1) With the text box still selected, click the down arrow to the right of the Fill button on the Drawing toolbar.
(2) Click Fill Effects, then select the Pattern Tab.
(3) In the Pattern section, select the 25% shading selection in the fourth row, first column.
(4) Click the Foreground list box, then select Gray-40% in the third row, last column.
(5) Click the Background list box, then select White in the last row, last column.
(6) Click OK or press Enter.

2. Save c11ex03, sidebar.
3. Print and then close c11ex03, sidebar. (This newsletter continues to build throughout the remaining chapter exercises. Saving each exercise as a separate document takes up a tremendous amount of disk space. As an alternative, open c11ex03, sidebar and save the document with Save As and name the document c11newsletter. Continue completing the remaining exercises and save each exercise with the same name [c11newsletter] as you progress through the exercises. Consult with your instructor about this recommendation.)

figure 11.7

Volume 5, Issue 2 • March 1999

Bicycle and In-Line Skating Safety for the 90s •

In the

Helmet Habit

"I don't quite know why my daughter, Kate, fell from her bike last July. Maybe she hit a small rock or just lost her balance. We found Kate lying on the ground. She was bleeding and had several cuts and bruises on her face and forehead. We called the paramedics and she began to lose consciousness just as they arrived. At the emergency room, we found out that Kate had a broken nose, a missing tooth, and four other loose teeth. Fortunately for all of us, Kate was wearing a bicycle helmet. Without even asking, three different doctors have told us that the helmet probably saved Kate's life. So many people tell me that their kids won't wear a helmet. I tell them to be firm—no helmet, no bike. Bicycle accidents can happen to anyone!"

Karen Brust
Boston, Massachusetts

Creating a Newsletter Table of Contents

A *table of contents* is optional in a one- or two-page newsletter. However, in multipage newsletters, a table of contents is an important and necessary element. A table of contents lists the names of articles and features in the newsletter, along with their page numbers. The information in the table of contents greatly influences whether the reader moves beyond the front page of the newsletter, so the table of contents needs to stand out from the surrounding information. It must also be legible and easy to follow.

Table of Contents
A list of articles and features and their page numbers.

A table of contents is usually located on the front page of a newsletter. It is often placed in the lower left or right corner of the page. It can, however, be placed closer to the top of the page on either side or even within an asymmetrically designed nameplate. If a newsletter is designed to be a self-mailer, the table of contents can be placed in the mailing section so the reader is invited into the newsletter before it is even opened.

DTP POINTERS
The table of contents must:
- stand out from the surrounding text;
- be legible;
- be easy to follow;
- be consistent from issue to issue.

The table of contents in figure 11.1 is located in the lower left corner. The shadow box format and the background fill, or screen, make the table of contents easily identifiable while adding visual interest to the page. The table of contents, along with the shadow box above it, also adds weight to the left side of the page. This added weight balances the heavier right side of the nameplate and the body copy below.

There are many ways to format a table of contents to make it easy to find and visually interesting. As illustrated in figure 11.8, a table of contents can easily be made by inserting text in a text box and then adding various borders, screened backgrounds, fonts, graphics lines, reverse text, and special characters. You can also use paragraph borders and shading to highlight text in a table of contents.

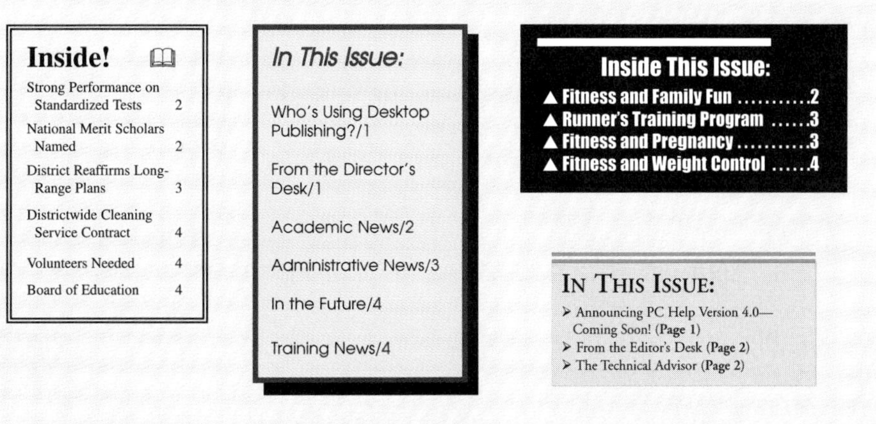

Inside!
Strong Performance on Standardized Tests 2
National Merit Scholars Named 2
District Reaffirms Long-Range Plans 3
Districtwide Cleaning Service Contract 4
Volunteers Needed 4
Board of Education 4
In This Issue:
Who's Using Desktop Publishing?/1
From the Director's Desk/1
Academic News/2
Administrative News/3
In the Future/4
Training News/4
Inside This Issue:
▲ Fitness and Family Fun 2
▲ Runner's Training Program 3
▲ Fitness and Pregnancy 3
▲ Fitness and Weight Control 4
IN THIS ISSUE:
➤ Announcing PC Help Version 4.0—Coming Soon! (Page 1)
➤ From the Editor's Desk (Page 2)
➤ The Technical Advisor (Page 2)

figure 11.8
Examples of Tables of Contents

exercise 4

Inserting a Table of Contents in a Newsletter

1. At a clear document window, add a table of contents to the newsletter from exercise 3, as shown in figure 11.9, by completing the following steps:
   a. Open c11ex03, sidebar.doc.
   b. Save the document with Save As and name it c11ex04, table of contents.
   c. Change the Zoom viewing mode to 75%, then turn on the display of nonprinting characters.
   d. Press Ctrl + End to position the insertion point at the end of the document (below the sidebar), then press Enter.
   e. Insert the table of contents text in a text box by completing the following steps:
      (1) Insert the file *table of contents text.doc* located on your student data disk.
      (2) Select the table of contents text (do not include the paragraph symbol below the last line of text), then click the Text Box button on the Drawing toolbar.
   f. Double-click the text box border and make the following changes at the Format Text Box dialog box:
      (1) Click the Colors and Lines tab, then change the line color to Teal and the line style to 1½ pt.
      (2) Click the Size tab, then change the height to 1.65 inches and the width to 2.2 inches.
      (3) Click the Position tab, then change the horizontal position to 0.5 inches from the edge of the page and the vertical position to 8.65 inches from the top edge of the page. (Remember to set the "From" options first.)
      (4) Click the Wrapping tab, then select Top & Bottom in the Wrapping style section.
      (5) Click OK or press Enter.
   g. Format the table of contents title by completing the following steps:
      (1) Change the Zoom viewing mode to 100%.
      (2) Position the insertion point to the left of *In This Issue:*, then press the space bar once.
      (3) Select *In This Issue:* and make the following changes at the Font dialog box:
         (a) Click the Font tab, then change the font to 12-point Impact and the color to Teal.
         (b) Click the Character Spacing tab, then change the Spacing to Expanded By 1.2 pt.
         (c) Click OK or press Enter.
      (4) Position the insertion point after the colon in *In This Issue:*, access the Paragraph dialog box, then change the spacing after the paragraph to 8 points. Click OK or press Enter.
      (5) Position the insertion point anywhere within the title, then create the shaded background by completing the following steps:
         (a) Click Format, then Borders and Shading
         (b) Click the Shading tab, then select Gray -25% in the second row, third column of the Fill section.
         (c) Click OK or press Enter.

h. For use in future issues, create a style from the formatted title by completing the following steps:
   (1) Position the insertion point within *In This Issue:*, then click the Style list box on the Formatting toolbar.
   (2) Key **ToC Heading**, then press Enter.

i. Format the bulleted text in the table of contents by completing the following steps:
   (1) Select the remaining text below the title and change the font to 11-point Times New Roman. (Do not be concerned if some of the text is not visible at this point.)
   (2) With the text still selected, access the Paragraph dialog box, then make the following changes:
      (a) Change the spacing after the paragraph to 2 points.
      (b) Change the Line Spacing to Exactly 10 points.
   (3) With the text still selected, add bullets to each article name by completing the following steps:
      (a) Choose Format, Bullets and Numbering, and then select the Bulleted tab.
      (b) Click the first bulleted selection and then click Customize.
      (c) At the Customize Bulleted List dialog box, click Font, then change the font size to 14 points and the color to Teal.
      (d) Click OK or press Enter.
      (e) Click Bullet, then change the Font to Wingdings. Select the round bullet in the fifth row, sixteenth column.
      (f) Click OK or press Enter to close the Symbol dialog box and then click OK again to close the Customize Bulleted List dialog box.
   (4) Select the slash mark in each table of contents item, change the color to Teal, and apply bold. (*Hint:* Use Format Painter to repeat the formatting.)
   (5) Bold the page number in each table of contents item.

j. For use in future issues, create a style for the bulleted items in the table of contents by completing the following steps:
   (1) Position the insertion point anywhere within the first bulleted item.
   (2) Click once in the Style list box on the Formatting toolbar to select the current style name.
   (3) Key **ToC bullets** as the new style name, then press Enter.

2. Save c11ex04, table of contents.
3. Print and then close c11ex04, table of contents. (You may want to wait and print the whole newsletter when it is completed in exercise 10.)

figure 11.9

Volume 5, Issue 2 • March 1999

Bicycle and In-Line Skating Safety for the 90s •

In the

Helmet Habit

"I don't quite know why my daughter, Kate, fell from her bike last July. Maybe she hit a small rock or just lost her balance. We found Kate lying on the ground. She was bleeding and had several cuts and bruises on her face and forehead. We called the paramedics and she began to lose consciousness just as they arrived. At the emergency room, we found out that Kate had a broken nose, a missing tooth, and four other loose teeth. Fortunately for all of us, Kate was wearing a bicycle helmet. Without even asking, three different doctors have told us that the helmet probably saved Kate's life. So many people tell me that their kids won't wear a helmet. I tell them to be firm—no helmet, no bike. Bicycle accidents can happen to anyone!"

Karen Brust
Boston, Massachusetts

In This Issue:

Creating Pull Quotes in a Newsletter

A *pull quote,* as illustrated in figure 11.1, acts as a focal point, helps to break up lengthy blocks of text, and provides visual contrast. A pull quote (also called a *pull out* or *call out*) is a direct phrase, summarizing statement, or important point associated with the body copy of a newsletter. Using pull quotes is an excellent way to draw readers into an article.

Pull Quote
A short, direct phrase, statement, or important point formatted to stand out from the rest of the body copy.

Effective pull quotes are interesting, brief, and formatted to stand out from the rest of the body copy. Keep in mind the following tips when creating pull quotes for a newsletter:

- Include relevant and interesting text in a pull quote. Edit any direct quotes so they will not be taken out of context when read individually as a pull quote.
- Pull quotes should be brief—approximately 10 to 15 words and never longer than a few lines.
- Choose a font that contrasts with the font used for the article text.
- Increase the type size.
- Vary the type style by bolding and/or italicizing the pull quote text.
- Set the pull quote off from the rest of the body text with ruled lines or a graphics box.
- Be consistent. Use the same format for other pull quotes throughout the newsletter and throughout future issues of the same newsletter.

DTP POINTERS
Pull quotes should be brief, be interesting, and stand out from the rest of the text.

The text boxes displayed in figure 11.10 show some different ways that pull quotes can be customized to attract the reader's attention. This list of boxes is only a small representation of the methods for customizing pull quotes.

figure 11.10

Pull Quote Examples

In design, function dictates form ...

Pull Quote 1: Created in a text box, no border. Text set in 14-point Arial Black and center-aligned. Paragraph borders selected from the borders styles; border width set at 3 pt; paragraph shading set at Gray-30%; distance from text to top border set at 2 pt.

In design, function dictates form ...

Pull Quote 2: Created in a text box, no border. Text set in 16-point Kino MT and center-aligned. Paragraph borders selected from the borders styles; border width set at 3 pt; color Dark Red; distance from text to top and bottom borders set at 4 pt.

In design, function dictates form ...

Pull Quote 3: Created in a text box with a Black shadow effect, Plum fill, and an internal top margin set at 0.1 inches. Text set in 20-point Book Antiqua Italic White and center-aligned.

IN DESIGN, FUNCTION DICTATES FORM ...

Pull Quote 4: Created in an AutoShape from the Basic Shapes selection, with Teal line color, White fill, and an internal top margin set at 0.1 inches. Text set in 18-point Britannic Bold Italic Teal, Small Caps, and center-aligned.

Creating Shortcuts to Formatting in a Newsletter

As mentioned several times previously, styles and templates can save you time and keystrokes. Knowing when to create a style or to save a document as a template is just as important as knowing how to create and use styles and templates.

Understanding style formatting limitations can help you determine when to make a style. Formatting selections from the following dialog boxes can be included in a style: Font, Paragraph, Tabs, Paragraph Borders and Shading, Language, Frame, and Bullets and Numbering. For example, you can include formatting for text that is to be inserted in a text box, but you cannot include the text box itself in the style. In addition, you cannot save any text or pictures within a style. On the other hand, you can save text boxes, pictures, and/or text as part of a template document.

DTP POINTERS
Create styles for repetitive formatting.

In general, create styles for any repetitive formatting within a document or that will be consistently repeated in future documents. For example, a style can easily be created for article headings within a newsletter. Creating and applying an article heading style will assure you that all your headings will be consistently formatted in the same manner, even in future issues of your newsletter. When creating a style for headings, include font selection, font size and style, font color, and any associated spacing before or after the paragraph symbol.

Other styles can be created for a newsletter banner, subtitle, folio, body copy, sidebar, table of contents, pull quote, bulleted list, etc. For example, styles were created for the sidebar headings in exercise 3 and the table of contents title in exercise 4 so that these styles can be used in future issues of the newsletter. However, many times it may be more efficient to create certain styles and then to save the document as a template. Saving a newsletter as a template lets you save any formatting and/or text that does not change from issue to issue. For instance, a newsletter published on a regular basis includes some elements that remain the same from issue to issue, such as the newsletter banner and headers and footers. When saving a document as a template, omit any text or graphics that will change from issue to issue and leave all text, graphics, and formatting that will remain the same. For instance, if the table of contents text box, position, and title will stay the same from issue to issue, delete the page numbers and the corresponding article names only. Leave the title and text box so that it may be saved as part of the template. Any styles created for any formatting in the newsletter will be saved along with the template.

In exercise 5, you will insert the first newsletter article, format the article heading and article text, and create a pull quote. Since these particular elements may be repeated throughout the newsletter, you will then create styles for these elements.

exercise 5

Creating Styles and a Pull Quote in a Newsletter

1. At a clear document window and using the newsletter from exercise 4, insert text and a pull quote and create styles, as shown in figure 11.11, by completing the following steps:
   a. Open c11ex04, table of contents.doc.
   b. Save the document with Save As and name it c11ex05, pull quote.

c. Change the Zoom viewing mode to 75%, then turn on the display of nonprinting characters.
d. Position the insertion point to the left of the paragraph symbol at the top of the second column, then insert the file *bicycle safety text.doc* located on your student data disk.
e. Format the first article heading by completing the following steps:
   (1) Select *Bicycle Safety: Let's Make It a Priority!* and make the following changes at the Font dialog box:
      (a) Click the Font tab, then change the font to 18-point Impact, change the color to Teal, and select Small caps in the Effects section.
      (b) Click the Character Spacing tab, then change the Spacing to Expanded By 1.2 pt.
      (c) Click OK or Press Enter.
   (2) Choose Format, Paragraph, and then select the Indents and Spacing tab. Change the spacing before the paragraph to 8 points and the spacing after the paragraph to 6 points. Choose OK or press Enter.
f. Create a style for future article headings by completing the following steps:
   (1) Make sure the insertion point is positioned within the article heading.
   (2) Click once in the Style list box located on the Formatting toolbar to select the current style name.
   (3) Key **Article Head** as the new style name and then press Enter.
g. Format the article text for the first article by completing the following steps:
   (1) Position the insertion point at the beginning of the line *Did you know . . .* and select all of the article text.
   (2) Change the font to 11-point Times New Roman.
   (3) Click Format, Paragraph, and then make the following changes at the Paragraph dialog box:
      (a) Click the Indents and Spacing tab, then change the spacing after the paragraph to 3 points in the Spacing section.
      (b) In the Indentation section, change the Special option to First Line By 0.2 inches to indent the first line of each paragraph.
      (c) Click OK or press Enter.
h. Create a style for the article text by completing the following steps:
   (1) With the article text still selected, click once in the Style list box located on the Formatting toolbar to select the current style name.
   (2) Key **Article Text** as the style name and then press Enter.
i. Create a style for the first paragraph of the article that eliminates the first line indentation by completing the following steps:
   (1) Position the insertion point within the first paragraph of article text.
   (2) Click Format, Paragraph, then select the Indents and Spacing tab. In the Indentation section, change the Special option to (none). Click OK or press Enter.
   (3) Click once in the Style list box on the Formatting toolbar to select the current style name.
   (4) Key **1st Paragraph** as the style name and then press Enter.
j. Insert a pull quote by completing the following steps:
   (1) Click the Text Box button on the Drawing toolbar, position the crosshairs on the right side of the third paragraph and draw a text box the approximate size and position of the pull quote in figure 11.11.
   (2) Double-click the text border and make the following changes at the Format Text Box dialog box:

(a) Click the Colors and Lines tab, then change the line color to No Line.
(b) Click the Size tab, then change the height to 1 inch and the width to 2 inches.
(c) Click the Position tab, then change the horizontal position to 6 inches from the edge of the page and the vertical position to 5.2 inches from the top of the page. (Remember to change the "From" options first.)
(d) Click the Wrapping tab, then change the wrapping style to Tight.
(e) Click the Text box tab, then change the top and bottom internal margins to 0 inches.

(3) Insert and format the pull quote text by completing the following steps:
(a) Click once in the text box to position the insertion point.
(b) Key **More than 500,000 trips are made to emergency rooms each year for bicycle-related injuries.**
(c) Select the text just entered and change the font to 13-point Impact.

(4) Add the top and bottom borders by completing the following steps:
(a) Click Format, Borders and Shading, then select the Borders tab.
(b) Click Color, then select Teal as the border color.
(c) Click Width, then select 2¼ pt as the line width.
(d) In the Preview section, click the top and bottom of the diagram to insert borders in these areas; the left and right sides of the diagram should be borderless.
(e) Click OK or press Enter. (Increase the height of the text box if the bottom border is not entirely visible.)

k. Create a style for the pull quote by completing the following steps:
(1) With the insertion point located within the pull quote text, click once in the Style list box on the Formatting toolbar to select the current style name.
(2) Key **Pull Quote** as the new style name and press Enter.

l. In the last paragraph, select and bold *The bottom line?*. Then select and italicize the last sentence, *Bicycle safety is something we all need to make a priority.*

2. Save c11ex05, pull quote.
3. Print and then close c11ex05, pull quote. (You may want to wait and print the whole newsletter when it is completed in exercise 10.)

figure 11.11

Volume 5, Issue 2 • March 1999

Bicycle and In-Line Skating Safety for the 90s •

In the

Helmet Habit

"I don't quite know why my daughter, Kate, fell from her bike last July. Maybe she hit a small rock or just lost her balance. We found Kate lying on the ground. She was bleeding and had several cuts and bruises on her face and forehead. We called the paramedics and she began to lose consciousness just as they arrived. At the emergency room, we found out that Kate had a broken nose, a missing tooth, and four other loose teeth. Fortunately for all of us, Kate was wearing a bicycle helmet. Without even asking, three different doctors have told us that the helmet probably saved Kate's life. So many people tell me that their kids won't wear a helmet. I tell them to be firm—no helmet, no bike. Bicycle accidents can happen to anyone!"

Karen Brust
Boston, Massachusetts

In This Issue:

BICYCLE SAFETY: LET'S MAKE IT A PRIORITY!

Did you know that each year over 1,200 people die and thousands more are seriously injured in bicycle accidents? According to the American Academy of Pediatrics, more than 500,000 emergency room visits annually in the U.S. are attributed to bicycle accidents.

Surprisingly, most of these accidents, especially those involving children, occur on quiet residential streets. Most do not involve cars. And many could be prevented with proper training and safety equipment.

Think about it. Before we're allowed to drive a car, we have to be a certain age and go through extensive training and testing. Yet many of us—children in particular—ride the very same roads on a bicycle with little or no training at all. Kids are especially vulnerable because of their undeveloped peripheral vision (about two-thirds that of adults), poor speed judgment, and lack of a sense of danger.

More than 500,000 trips are made to emergency rooms each year for bicycle-related injuries.

At Ride Safe, we believe bicycle safety education is crucial to our well-being and to that of our children. More and more states, including New York, New Jersey, Connecticut, Georgia, Tennessee, Oregon, and California are implementing legislation requiring bicycle helmets for children. As adults, we can teach our children safe riding habits, protect them from injury by purchasing bicycle helmets, and set a good example when we are riding our own bicycles.

The bottom line? *Bicycle safety is something we all need to make a priority!*

Creating Kickers and End Signs in a Newsletter

Kicker
A lead-in phrase or sentence that precedes the beginning of an article.

End Sign
A symbol or special character indicating the end of an article.

Additional elements, such as kickers and end signs, can also be used in a newsletter. A *kicker* is a brief sentence or phrase that is a lead-in to an article. Generally, it is set in a size smaller than the headline but larger than the body text. It is often stylistically distinct from both the headline and the body text. Kickers can be placed above or below the headline or article heading. In figure 11.1, a kicker is placed above the first article heading and serves as a lead-in to the first article.

Symbols or special characters used to indicate the end of a section of text are known as *end signs*. In figure 11.1, an end sign follows the last paragraph in the first article. It mimics the shadow boxes used for the sidebar, the table of contents, and the pull quote within the newsletter. Appropriate special characters or combinations of these characters, such as •, ■, ❑, ▼, ❖, ◆, ➢, and ✓ from the Monotype Sorts or Wingdings font selection, may be used as end signs.

In exercise 6, you will add a kicker and an end sign to the Ride Safe newsletter from exercise 5.

exercise 6

Creating a Kicker and an End Sign in a Newsletter

1. At a clear document window, insert the kicker and end sign shown in figure 11.12 to the newsletter from exercise 5 by completing the following steps:
   a. Open c11ex05, pull quote.doc.
   b. Save the document with Save As and name it c11ex06, end sign.
   c. Change the Zoom viewing mode to 75%, and then turn on the display of nonprinting characters.
   d. Create the kicker by completing the following steps:
      (1) Position the insertion point at the beginning of the first paragraph below the article heading.
      (2) Key **Protect your child!** and then press Enter.
      (3) Select *Protect your child!* and change the font to 14-point Times New Roman Bold Italic.
   e. Create a style for the kicker formatting by completing the following steps:
      (1) Position the insertion point anywhere within the kicker.
      (2) Click once in the Style list box on the Formatting toolbar to select the current Style name.
      (3) Key **Kicker** and press Enter.
   f. Create the end sign by completing the following steps:
      (1) Position the insertion point at the end of the first article, then press the Tab key three times. (Make sure Italic formatting is turned off.)
      (2) Click Insert, Symbol, then select the Special Characters tab.
      (3) Double-click the Em Dash selection, and then select the Symbols tab.
      (4) Change the Font selection to Wingdings, then double-click the round bullet in the third row, twenty-first column.
      (5) Click the Special Characters tab again, then double-click the Em Dash selection and click Close.
      (6) Insert one space on each side of the bullet.
      (7) Select the end sign and change the font to 11-point Impact. (Remove Italic formatting, if any.)
      (8) Select the round bullet and change the color to Teal.
2. Save c11ex06, end sign (or save as c11newsletter as suggested in exercise 3, step 3).
3. Print and then close c11ex06, end sign. (You may want to wait and print the whole newsletter when it is completed in exercise 10.)

figure 11.12

Volume 5, Issue 2 • March 1999

Bicycle and In-Line Skating Safety for the 90s •

Bicycle Safety: Let's Make It a Priority!

Protect your child!

Did you know that each year over 1,200 people die and thousands more are seriously injured in bicycle accidents? According to the American Academy of Pediatrics, more than 500,000 emergency room visits annually in the U.S. are attributed to bicycle accidents.

Surprisingly, most of these accidents, especially those involving children, occur on quiet residential streets. Most do not involve cars. And many could be prevented with proper training and safety equipment.

Think about it. Before we're allowed to drive a car, we have to be a certain age and go through extensive training and testing. Yet many of us—children in particular—ride the very same roads on a bicycle with little or no training at all. Kids are especially vulnerable because of their undeveloped peripheral vision (about two-thirds that of adults), poor speed judgment, and lack of a sense of danger.

More than 500,000 trips are made to emergency rooms each year for bicycle-related injuries.

At Ride Safe, we believe bicycle safety education is crucial to our well-being and to that of our children. More and more states, including New York, New Jersey, Connecticut, Georgia, Tennessee, Oregon, and California are implementing legislation requiring bicycle helmets for children. As adults, we can teach our children safe riding habits, protect them from injury by purchasing bicycle helmets, and set a good example when we are riding our own bicycles.

The bottom line? *Bicycle safety is something we all need to make a priority!*

— • —

In the

Helmet Habit

"I don't quite know why my daughter, Kate, fell from her bike last July. Maybe she hit a small rock or just lost her balance. We found Kate lying on the ground. She was bleeding and had several cuts and bruises on her face and forehead. We called the paramedics and she began to lose consciousness just as they arrived. At the emergency room, we found out that Kate had a broken nose, a missing tooth, and four other loose teeth. Fortunately for all of us, Kate was wearing a bicycle helmet. Without even asking, three different doctors have told us that the helmet probably saved Kate's life. So many people tell me that their kids won't wear a helmet. I tell them to be firm—no helmet, no bike. Bicycle accidents can happen to anyone!"

Karen Brust
Boston, Massachusetts

In This Issue:

Creating Jump Lines in a Newsletter

Jump Line
Text telling the reader that an article continues on another page.

A *jump line* in a newsletter indicates that an article or feature continues on another page. Jump lines enable the creator of a newsletter to feature the beginning of several articles on the front page, increasing the chances of attracting readers. A jump line also solves the problem of what to do with lengthy articles that might not fit on one page.

As an aid in the directional flow of information in a document, a jump line must be distinguishable from surrounding text so the reader can easily find it. A jump line is commonly set in small italic type, approximately two points smaller than the body copy type. As an option, jump lines can also be enclosed in parentheses.

As mentioned earlier in this chapter, using linked text boxes for articles that are to be continued on another page makes editing and the positioning of continued articles easier. This feature allows text to flow from one text box to another even if the text boxes are not adjacent or on the same page.

exercise 7

Creating a Jump Line in a Newsletter

1. At a clear editing window, add an article and a jump line to the newsletter from exercise 6, as shown in figure 11.13, by completing the following steps:
   a. Open c11ex06, end sign. Save the document with Save As and name it c11ex07, jump line.
   b. Change the Zoom viewing mode to 75% and turn on the display of nonprinting characters.
   c. Press Ctrl + End to position the insertion point below the line containing the end sign.
   d. Click Insert, then Break. Select Column break, then click OK. A second page will be generated and the insertion point will move to the top of page 2.
   e. Insert text boxes to contain the second article on page 1 and to be continued on page 2 by completing the following steps:
      (1) Scroll to the bottom of page 1.
      (2) Click the Text Box button on the Drawing toolbar, then draw a text box below the column break to hold the beginning of the second article. Adjustments will be made to the size and position of the text box in exercise 10.
      (3) Position the insertion point at the top of the first column on page 2, then click the Text Box button again and draw a second text box to hold the remaining article text. Adjustments will be made to the size and position of the text box in future steps.
   f. Create a link between the two text boxes by completing the following steps:
      (1) Select the first text box, then click the Create Text Box Link button on the Text Box toolbar. If the toolbar is not displayed, right-click anywhere within the Standard toolbar, then select Text Box from the list of toolbars.
      (2) Position the mouse, which displays as an upright pitcher, in the second text box until it displays as a pouring pitcher, then click once to complete the link.
   g. Double-click the border of the first text box in the link (at the bottom of page 1, second column) and make the following changes at the Format Text Box dialog box:

(1) Click the Colors and Lines tab, then change the line color to No Line.
(2) Click the Size tab, then change the height of the text box to 1.6 inches and the width to 5 inches.
(3) Click the Position tab, then change the horizontal position to 3.1 inches from the left edge of the page and the vertical position to 8.7 inches from the top edge of the page. (Remember to change the "From" options first.)
(4) Click the Text Box tab, then change the left, right, top, and bottom internal margins to 0 inches.
(5) Click OK or press Enter when done.
(6) Click once inside the first text box to position the insertion point, then insert the file *accident text.doc* located on your student data disk.
(7) Check the text box on page 2 and make sure the remaining article text is visible. If not, use the sizing handles to enlarge the box.

h. Format the title of the second article by completing the following steps:
(1) Position the insertion point anywhere within the title *"Accidents" Waiting to Happen*.
(2) Click the down arrow to the right of the Style list box located on the Formatting toolbar and select *Article Head* from the Style drop-down list.

i. Format the article text by completing the following steps:
(1) Position the insertion point at the beginning of the line *The majority of bicycle/car "accidents"...*, hold the Shift key down, and press Ctrl + End to select all of the article text in both text boxes.
(2) Click the down arrow to the right of the Style list box located on the Formatting toolbar and select *Article Text* from the Style drop-down list.
(3) Position the insertion point anywhere within the first paragraph and apply the *1st Paragraph* style from the Style list box on the Formatting toolbar.

j. Insert and format the jump line by completing the following steps:
(1) Position the insertion point at the end of the first paragraph and press Enter one time.
(2) Change the paragraph alignment to right.
(3) Access the Symbol dialog box, change the font to Monotype Sorts, then insert the triangle symbol in the fourth row, first column.
(4) Press the space bar once, then key **See ACCIDENTS on page 2.**
(5) Select *See* then apply italics.
(6) Select *ACCIDENTS*, then apply bold.
(7) Select *on page 2*, then apply italics.
(8) Select the entire jump line and change the font to 10-point Times New Roman.

k. Create an AutoText entry out of the formatted jump line by completing the following steps: (An AutoText entry is created here instead of a style because the jump line contains mixed formatting and text that can be used in other jump lines.)
(1) Select the entire jump line, including the triangle symbol.
(2) Click Insert, point to AutoText, then click New.
(3) At the Create AutoText dialog box, key **jump line**.
(4) Click OK or press Enter.

2. Save c11ex07, jump line.
3. Print the first page of the newsletter and then close c11ex07, jump line. (You may want to wait and print the whole newsletter when it is completed in exercise 10.)

figure 11.13

Volume 5, Issue 2 • March 1999

Bicycle and In-Line Skating Safety for the 90s •

In the

Helmet Habit

"I don't quite know why my daughter, Kate, fell from her bike last July. Maybe she hit a small rock or just lost her balance. We found Kate lying on the ground. She was bleeding and had several cuts and bruises on her face and forehead. We called the paramedics and she began to lose consciousness just as they arrived. At the emergency room, we found out that Kate had a broken nose, a missing tooth, and four other loose teeth. Fortunately for all of us, Kate was wearing a bicycle helmet. Without even asking, three different doctors have told us that the helmet probably saved Kate's life. So many people tell me that their kids won't wear a helmet. I tell them to be firm—no helmet, no bike. Bicycle accidents can happen to anyone!"

Karen Brust
Boston, Massachusetts

In This Issue:

Bicycle Safety: Let's Make It a Priority!

Protect your child!

Did you know that each year over 1,200 people die and thousands more are seriously injured in bicycle accidents? According to the American Academy of Pediatrics, more than 500,000 emergency room visits annually in the U.S. are attributed to bicycle accidents.

Surprisingly, most of these accidents, especially those involving children, occur on quiet residential streets. Most do not involve cars. And many could be prevented with proper training and safety equipment.

Think about it. Before we're allowed to drive a car, we have to be a certain age and go through extensive training and testing. Yet many of us—children in particular—ride the very same roads on a bicycle with little or no training at all. Kids are especially vulnerable because of their undeveloped peripheral vision (about two-thirds that of adults), poor speed judgment, and lack of a sense of danger.

More than 500,000 trips are made to emergency rooms each year for bicycle-related injuries.

At Ride Safe, we believe bicycle safety education is crucial to our well-being and to that of our children. More and more states, including New York, New Jersey, Connecticut, Georgia, Tennessee, Oregon, and California are implementing legislation requiring bicycle helmets for children. As adults, we can teach our children safe riding habits, protect them from injury by purchasing bicycle helmets, and set a good example when we are riding our own bicycles.

The bottom line? *Bicycle safety is something we all need to make a priority!*

— • —

"Accidents" Waiting to Happen

The majority of bicycle/car "accidents" are not really accidents, but avoidable collisions. Most result from the bicyclist's failure to use proper riding techniques in a hazardous situation. Ironically, when asked, most children injured in traffic could describe the actual law they broke.

▼ *See* **ACCIDENTS** *on page 2*

Inserting Graphics, Illustrations, and Photographs in a Newsletter

If used appropriately, headers, footers, sidebars, tables of contents, pull quotes, kickers, end signs, and jump lines can help to achieve focus, balance, proportion, contrast, directional flow, and consistency within a newsletter. Graphic images, illustrations, charts, diagrams, and photographs can help to achieve these same goals.

Word includes close to 100 predesigned graphic images in its program that you can insert into any document. If you installed Word as part of Microsoft Office from a CD, additional graphic files are available on the CD which you can access through the Insert Picture dialog box. In addition, a variety of clip art is available on the market that includes thousands of ready-made illustrations, in both color and black and white, for almost any subject area. For example, you can purchase clip art for holidays, special events, occupations, sports, geography, entertainment, etc. You can also insert graphic images created in draw programs, such as Corel Draw or Windows Paintbrush.

Word graphics files are identified by a *.wmf* file extension. However, Word is compatible with many other popular graphics file formats. Word can insert some graphics file formats directly whereas other graphics file formats require a specific graphics filter to be installed. The following graphics file formats do not require a separate graphics filter to be installed:

Enhanced Metafile (.emf)
Joint Photographic Experts Group (.jpg)
Portable Network Graphics (.png)
Windows Bitmap (.bmp, .rle, .dib)
Windows Metafile (.wmf)

A separate graphics filter is necessary to install the following graphics file formats:

AutoCAD format 2-D (.dxf)
Computer Graphics Metafile (.cgm)
CorelDraw (.cdr)
Encapsulated PostScript (.eps)
Graphics Interchange Format (.gif)
HP Graphics Language (.hgl, .plt)
Kodak Photo CD (.pcd)
Macintosh PICT (.pct)
Micrografx Designer/Draw (.drw)
PC Paintbrush (.pcx)
Tagged Image File Format (.tif)
Targa (.tga)
WordPerfect Graphics (.wpg)

If the required graphics filter is installed, you can insert any of the previously listed graphic file formats by choosing Insert, pointing to Picture, then selecting From File. Change to the directory location of the desired graphic files and then select the desired filename.

If you cannot import a graphic file with any of the above extensions, your system may be missing some graphic file filters. To determine which filters have been installed, click Insert, point to Picture, then select From File. In the Insert Picture dialog box, click the Files of type list box. If all the file extensions listed above are not listed, you need to install a separate graphics filter. Refer to the Preface to add individual components to Word 97 or refer to the Word 97 reference manual to add filters.

However, you may want to import a graphic that is not supported by any of the graphics filters provided with Word. In order to import an unsupported graphic file format, open the graphic file in the program from which the graphic file originated or a drawing program such as Windows Paint, then save the graphic in an acceptable Word graphic file format. Or you can select the graphic, copy it, and paste it into your document. The graphic then becomes a Windows metafile (*.wmf*).

Photographs can also be added to a newsletter. As the old saying goes, a picture is worth a thousand words, and sometimes just saying the words is not enough. Readers relate to the "realness" of photographs as opposed to clip art or computer-generated images. Photos best describe events or people because they can accurately depict a scene or an expressed emotion. Black-and-white photographs scan better than color photographs. Select only those photos that are clearly defined, in focus, and correctly exposed.

Some information is better understood in a visual format. Whenever possible, include illustrations, charts, tables, and diagrams when presenting technical, numerical, and detailed information.

Using Scanned Images in a Newsletter

Scanner
Converts a photograph, drawing, or text into a compatible digital file format that can be retrieved into specific programs.

Noncomputer-generated images, such as photographs, illustrations, and diagrams, can be included in a newsletter through the use of a scanner. A *scanner* converts a photograph, drawing, or text into a compatible digital file format that can be retrieved into a program such as Word.

In order to use a scanner, you must have an accompanying software program loaded into your computer to scan the image or text and to convert it into a compatible file format. Most scanners work in this manner:

1. Place the photograph or illustration face down on the image scanner.
2. Open the scanning software program.
3. Retrieve the image.
4. Prescan the image.
5. Set the desired scanned image size.
6. Select the desired scan mode.
7. Select the desired resolution.
8. Execute the scan.
9. Save and name the file giving it a compatible file format extension, such as .bmp, .tif, or .wmf.
10. Exit the scanning software program.
11. Open Word.

12. Insert the scanned image into a Word document by choosing Insert, pointing to Picture, then selecting From File. Change to the directory location of the scanned image and select the desired file name.

One very important factor to keep in mind is that you must get permission to use artwork, photos, or illustrations before you can legally scan them into a document. When you purchase clip art and stock photography, you generally buy the right to use it and even modify it, but you may not resell the images themselves as hard copy or computer images. When purchasing these items, read the copyright information provided in the front of the accompanying documentation.

DTP POINTERS
Find out about copyright restrictions on any images to be scanned and request permission, if necessary.

When using photographs in a newsletter, you can scan the photographs, save them in a compatible graphic file format, and then insert them into your newsletter. Or you can insert a placeholder, such as a text box, in your newsletter. You can then print your newsletter, paste a photograph into the area reserved by the text box, and have a commercial printer duplicate your newsletter.

When trying to determine if your photographs should be professionally scanned, keep the following two points in mind:

- If you do not need high-quality output, using images scanned from a desk model scanner is acceptable.
- If you need high-quality output, use a service bureau to have your photos professionally scanned into your newsletter.

exercise 8

Inserting a Picture Placeholder in a Newsletter

1. At a clear document window, add a placeholder for a photograph and caption text to the second page of the newsletter from exercise 7, as shown in figure 11.14, by completing the following steps:
   a. Open c11ex07, jump line.
   b. Save the document with Save As and name it c11ex08, picture.
   c. Change the Zoom viewing mode to 75% and then turn on the display of nonprinting characters.
   d. Insert a text box that will contain the title, the picture placeholder box, and the caption (this page is easier to create using text boxes) by completing the following steps:
      (1) Position the insertion point at the top of page 2.
      (2) Click the Text Box button on the Drawing toolbar, then position the crosshairs at the approximate location of the top of the second column (use the horizontal ruler as a guide).
      (3) Draw a text box the approximate size and in the approximate location as the title and the placeholder box shown in figure 11.14.
   e. Double-click the text box just inserted and make the following changes at the Format Text Box dialog box:
      (1) Click the Colors and Lines tab, then change the line color to No Line.
      (2) Click the Size tab, then change the height of the text box to 4.1 inches and the width to 4.85 inches.

(3) Click the Position tab, then change the horizontal position to 3.1 inches from the left edge of the page and the vertical position to 1.1 inches from the top of the page.
(4) Click the Text Box tab, then change the left and right internal margins to 0 inches, the top internal margin to 0.3 inches, and the bottom internal margin to 0 inches.
(5) Click OK or Press Enter.

f. Insert and format the title by completing the following steps:
(1) Click once in the text box to position the insertion point.
(2) Key ☞**Who Says Helmets Aren't Cool?**➩ (use the arrow symbols from the Wingdings font, seventh row, second and third columns), then press Enter.
(3) Position the insertion point within the title just keyed, then apply the *Article Head* style.
(4) Select each of the arrow symbols and change the color to black.
(5) With the insertion point still within the title, access the Paragraph dialog box, then change the spacing before the paragraph to 0 inches.

g. Insert the placeholder text by completing the following steps:
(1) Click once below the title to position the insertion point.
(2) Press Enter eight times, then change the alignment to center.
(3) Key **Insert picture of children from Silverton, Oregon here.**, then press Enter.
(4) Change the paragraph alignment to left, then press Enter six times.

h. Create the border that defines the photograph placeholder by completing the following steps:
(1) Position the insertion point to the left of the first paragraph symbol below the title.
(2) Select all the paragraph symbols, except for the last paragraph symbol, from this point to the end of the text box.
(3) Click Format, Borders and Shading, then select the Borders tab.
(4) In the Setting section, click Box, then change the border Color to Teal and the Width to 1½ pt.
(5) Click OK or press Enter.

i. Insert and format the caption under the placeholder box by completing the following steps:
(1) Position the insertion point to the left of the last paragraph symbol.
(2) Insert the file *picture text.doc* located on your student data disk.
(3) Select the text just inserted and change the font to 10.5-point Times New Roman Bold Italic.
(4) With the insertion point within the caption text, access the Paragraph dialog box and change the spacing before the paragraph to 4 pt.

2. Save c11ex08, picture.
3. Position the insertion point on page 2. Print page 2 only and then close c11ex08, picture. (You may want to wait and print the whole newsletter when it is completed in exercise 10.)

Winners wear helmets!

Research indicates that 60% of all U.S. bicycle-car collisions occur among bicyclists between the ages of 8 and 12. Still, an average of only $1 is spent per child between birth and age 15 teaching traffic education. Children are permitted to travel with only a *"look both ways before you cross the street"* and *"make sure you stop at all stop signs"* warning. Obviously these "warnings" are not enough.

Who Says Helmets Aren't Cool?

Insert picture of children from Silverton, Oregon here.

Certainly not the children of Silverton, Oregon! One of the biggest reasons children don't wear bicycle helmets is because their friends don't wear them. By getting all the children in your school or neighborhood to order bicycle helmets at the same time, you can help turn this peer pressure from negative to positive. Suddenly wearing a bicycle helmet becomes the "cool" thing to do.

2

Creating a Newsletter Masthead

Masthead
A list of all those contributing to the production of a newsletter and other general information.

The *masthead* is a repeating element that adds consistency among newsletter issues. A masthead (see figure 11.15) usually contains the following information:

- the company or organization (and address) producing the newsletter
- the newsletter's publication schedule, such as weekly, monthly, biannually, etc.
- the names of those contributing to the production of the newsletter, such as editor, authors, and graphic designers
- copyright information

DTP POINTERS
Be consistent in the design and layout of the masthead from issue to issue.

The masthead can also contain a small logo, seal, or other graphic identifier. A masthead is commonly located on the back page of a newsletter, although you will sometimes find it on the first page. Wherever you decide to place the masthead, be consistent from issue to issue in the masthead's design, layout, and location.

figure 11.15

Examples of Mastheads

From the ▫▫▫ Desktop

Editor: **Martha Ridoux**
Design and Layout:
Grace Shevick
Contributing Authors:
Jonathan Dwyer
Nancy Shipley
Christine Johnson
Published Monthly by:
DTP Training, Inc.
4550 North Wabash St.
Chicago, IL 60155
312 555-6840
Fax: 312 555-9366
http://www.dtp.com
©Copyright 1998 by:
DTP Training, Inc.
All rights reserved.

From the ▫▫▫ Desktop

Editor:
Martha Ridoux
Design and Layout:
Grace Shevick
Authors:
Jonathan Dwyer
Nancy Shipley
Christine Johnson
Published Monthly by:
DTP Training, Inc.
4550 North Wabash St.
Chicago, IL 60155
312 555-6840
Fax: 312 555-9366
http://www.dtp.com
©Copyright 1998 by:
DTP Training, Inc.
All rights reserved.

exercise 9

Creating a Newsletter Masthead

1. At a clear document window, add a masthead to the second page of the newsletter from exercise 8, as shown in figure 11.16, by completing the following steps:
   a. Open c11ex08, picture.
   b. Save the document with Save As and name it c11ex09, masthead.
   c. Insert a text box to hold the masthead text by completing the following steps:
      (1) Change the Zoom viewing mode to Whole Page, and then turn on the display of nonprinting characters.

(2) Click the Text Box button on the Drawing toolbar.
(3) Position the cross hairs toward the bottom half of the first column on page 2, then draw a text box the approximate size and in the approximate location as illustrated in figure 11.16.

d. Double-click the text box border and make the following changes at the Format Text Box dialog box:
(1) Click the Colors and Lines tab, then change the line color to Teal and the line style to 1½ pt.
(2) Click the Size tab, then change the height of the text box to 2.85 and the width to 2.2 inches.
(3) Click the Position tab, then change the horizontal position to 0.5 inches from the left edge of the page and the vertical position to 7.2 inches from the top edge of the page. (Remember to change the "From" options first.)
(4) Click OK or press Enter.
(5) Change the Zoom viewing mode to 100%.
(6) Click once inside the text box to position the insertion point, then insert the file *masthead text.doc* located on your student data disk. (All the text will be visible after formatting is completed in the following steps.)

e. Format the masthead title by completing the following steps:
(1) Select *Ride Safe* and make the following changes at the Font dialog box:
(a) Click the Font tab, then change the font to 11-point Impact and the color to Teal.
(b) Click the Character Spacing tab, then expand the character spacing to 1.2 points.
(c) Click OK or press Enter.
(2) Change the paragraph alignment to center.
(3) At the Paragraph dialog box, change the spacing after the paragraph to 6 points.
(4) Add a shaded background to the title by completing the following steps:
(a) With the insertion point within the title, click Format, then Borders and Shading.
(b) Click the Shading tab, then select Gray 25% in the second row, third column of the Fill Section.
(c) Click OK or press Enter.

f. Format the remaining masthead text by completing the following steps:
(1) Select the remaining masthead text and change the alignment to center. (*Hint:* Hold down the Shift key, then press Ctrl + End to select the remaining text in the text box, even if some of the text is not completely visible.)
(2) With the text still selected, change the font to 9-point Times New Roman.
(3) Bold the following: *Editor:*, *Design and Layout:*, *Authors:*, *Published quarterly by:*, and *©Copyright 1999 by:*.
(4) Apply italics to the remaining text.
(5) Adjust the paragraph spacing and line spacing (leading) by completing the following steps:
(a) Position the insertion point after the following items and change the spacing after the paragraph to 1 point at the Paragraph dialog box: *Chris Urban*, *Cassie Lizbeth*, *Amanda Knicker*, and *Fax: ....* (*Hint:* Use F4 after you have formatted the first item to quickly repeat the formatting.)
(b) Select all of the masthead text, except for the heading, and change the Line Spacing to Exactly At 10 points at the Paragraph dialog box.

2. Save c11ex09, masthead.
3. Print page 2 only and then close c11ex09, masthead. (You may want to wait and print the whole newsletter when it is completed in exercise 10.)

figure 11.16

Winners wear helmets!

Research indicates that 60% of all U.S. bicycle-car collisions occur among bicyclists between the ages of 8 and 12. Still, an average of only $1 is spent per child between birth and age 15 teaching traffic education. Children are permitted to travel with only a *"look both ways before you cross the street"* and *"make sure you stop at all stop signs"* warning. Obviously these "warnings" are not enough.

Who Says Helmets Aren't Cool?

Insert picture of children from Silverton, Oregon here.

Certainly not the children of Silverton, Oregon! One of the biggest reasons children don't wear bicycle helmets is because their friends don't wear them. By getting all the children in your school or neighborhood to order bicycle helmets at the same time, you can help turn this peer pressure from negative to positive. Suddenly wearing a bicycle helmet becomes the "cool" thing to do.

Ride Safe

Editor:
Chris Urban
Design and Layout:
Cassie Lizbeth
Authors:
Brandon Keith
Brian Stetler
Amanda Knicker
Published quarterly by:
Ride Safe, Inc.
P.O. Box 888
Warrenville, IL 60555
800-555-RIDE
Fax: 630-555-9068

2

Using Captions

Think of all the times you pick up a newspaper, newsletter, or magazine. How many times do you look at a photograph and immediately read the accompanying explanation? Many graphics images can stand on their own; however, most photographs, illustrations, and charts need to be explained to the reader. Remember that your reader's eyes are automatically drawn to images or elements that stand out on the page. Adding an explanation to your image or photo quickly gives your reader an idea of what is going on. It may even entice your reader to read an accompanying article. Descriptions or explanations of graphics images, illustrations, or photographs are referred to as *captions*.

Caption
A description or explanation of a graphic image, illustration, or photograph.

Captions should explain their associated images while at the same time establish a connection to the body copy. Make the caption text different from the body text by bolding and decreasing the type size slightly. Legibility is still the key. Keep captions as short as possible and consistent throughout your document.

Elements, such as a Word Picture, a Word Table, an Excel Worksheet, a PowerPoint Presentation, a PowerPoint slide, a graph, etc., can be labeled and numbered using Word's Caption feature. To use this feature, click Insert, then Caption. At the Caption dialog box, choose from Word's default labels (Figure, Table, and Equation) or create your own labels. In addition to the label, identifying text can be added to the label. You can also choose the numbering method (Arabic numbers, letters, or Roman numerals) and the position of the caption (below or above).

While the above method labels and numbers certain elements individually, Word's AutoCaption feature automatically adds captions when specific elements are inserted into a document. To use the AutoCaption feature, choose Insert, Caption, and then click AutoCaption at the Caption dialog box. At the AutoCaption dialog box, select the desired elements (such as a Word table or picture) in the Add caption when inserting list box. For example, if Microsoft Word Picture is selected in the AutoCaption dialog box, a numbered and labeled caption, such as *Figure 1*, will automatically be added every time you insert a Microsoft Picture. (See figure 11.17.) The caption numbers will increase automatically as additional Microsoft Pictures are added to a document.

Word's Caption feature is useful because you can individually or automatically number specific elements in sequence. In addition, if one element is deleted or moved, the numbering method of the remaining elements is automatically updated. If you want to add captions to all items of a specific type, such as all tables or all figures in a document, the AutoCaption feature can save you a lot of time.

One drawback to the Caption feature is that you cannot label items without a number being assigned to the label. If elements do not have to be numbered, such as photographs in a newsletter, the easiest way to create a caption is to position the insertion point below the element and key and format the desired caption as you did in exercise 8.

Caption Examples

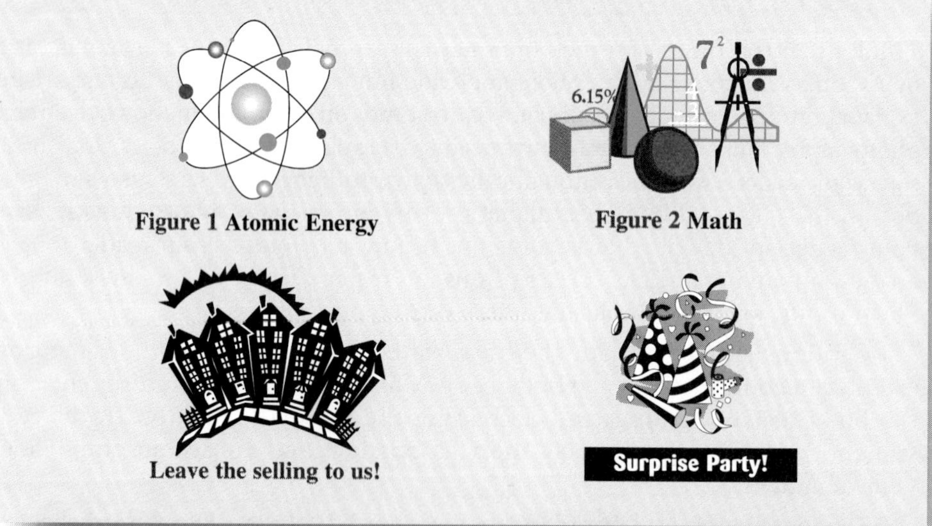

Figure 1 Atomic Energy
Figure 2 Math
Leave the selling to us!
Surprise Party!

Using Additional Enhancements for Starting Paragraphs

In a previous chapter, you learned about the Drop Cap feature. This design element can be used to indicate the beginning paragraph of a new article. Other types of paragraph enhancements can also be included in a newsletter. The following is a short list of paragraph enhancements—you may think of many more:

- Set the first few words of the beginning paragraph in all caps.
- Set the first line of the beginning paragraph in all caps.
- Set the first word of the beginning paragraph in small caps.
- Set the first line of the beginning paragraph in color.
- Use a larger type size with more leading in the first line of the beginning paragraph.

Understanding Copy Fitting

Publications such as magazines and newsletters contain information that varies from issue to issue. Though there is structure in how the articles or stories are laid out on the page (such as the unequal two-column format in the Ride Safe newsletter), there may be times when more or less text is needed to fill the page. Making varying amounts of text or typographical enhancements fit in a fixed amount of space is referred to as *copy fitting*. Many copy fitting techniques have been used in the exercises throughout this textbook. Some copy-fitting suggestions include the following:

Copy Fitting
Fitting varying amounts of text or typographical enhancements into a fixed amount of space.

To create more space:

- Change the margins.
- Change the justification.
- Use hyphenation.
- Change the typeface, type size, or style. Limit body type size to a minimum of 9 points.

- Reduce the spacing between paragraphs.
- Condense the spacing between characters.
- Reduce the leading (line spacing) in the body copy.
- Reduce the spacing before and after paragraphs (or hard returns) to reduce the spacing around the nameplate, headlines, subheads, frames, or text boxes.
- Remove a sidebar, pull quote, kicker, or end sign.
- Edit the text, including rewriting and eliminating sections.

To fill extra space:

- Adjust margins.
- Change justification.
- Change font size. Limit body type size to a maximum of 12 points.
- Increase the spacing between paragraphs.
- Adjust the character spacing.
- Increase the leading (line spacing) in the body copy.
- Increase the spacing around the nameplate, headlines, subheads, text boxes or graphic images.
- Add a sidebar, pull quote, kicker, end sign, graphic lines, clip art, photo, etc.
- Add text.

Be consistent when making any copy-fitting adjustments. For example, if you increase the white space after a headline, increase white space after all headlines. Or, if you decrease the type size of the body copy in an article, decrease the point size of all body copy in all articles. Adjustments are less noticeable when done uniformly. Also, adjustments often can be very small. For instance, rather than reducing type size by a whole point, try reducing it a half or quarter point. In addition, Word includes a Shrink to Fit feature that automatically "shrinks" the contents of the last page in a document onto the previous page if there is only a small amount of text on the last page. To access this copy-fitting feature, click the Print Preview button on the Standard toolbar (or click File, then Print Preview), then click the Shrink to Fit button (seventh button from the left) on the Print Preview toolbar. Word will automatically reduce the point size in order to fit the text on the previous page. Carefully check your document after using the Shrink to Fit feature, as the results are not always desirable.

DTP POINTERS
Copy fitting adjustments are less noticeable when done uniformly throughout the whole document.

In the Ride Safe newsletter created in the previous exercises, adjustments were made to the typeface, type size, type style, spacing above and below the article headings, spacing between paragraphs, spacing within the paragraphs (leading), and size and position of text boxes.

In the next exercise, you will position the linked text box and add two more articles to the second page of the Ride Safe newsletter. You will also apply styles and insert a clip art image. These articles are selected and adjusted to "fit" into the remaining space.

exercise 10

Employing Copy-Fitting Techniques

1. At a clear document window, add two articles and complete the "continued" article on the second page of the newsletter from exercise 9, as shown in figure 11.18, by completing the following steps: (Make your own minor adjustments if necessary to fit the articles in their respective locations.)
   a. Open c11ex09, masthead.
   b. Save the document with Save As and name it c11ex10, newsletter.
   c. Change the Zoom viewing mode to Whole Page, and then turn on the display of nonprinting characters.
   d. To make room for *The Light Bulb Test* article at the beginning of page 2, click and drag the linked text box located on page 2 that contains the remaining text from the "Accidents" article to the open space in the second column. This text box will be formatted in future steps.
   e. Position the insertion point at the top of page 2, then click the Text Box button on the Drawing toolbar. Draw a text box to hold *The Light Bulb Test* article in the approximate size and in the approximate location as shown in figure 11.18.
   f. Double-click the text box border and make the following changes at the Format Text Box dialog box:
      (1) Click the Colors and Lines tab, then change the line color to No Line.
      (2) Click the Size tab, then change the height to 3.5 inches and the width to 2.4 inches.
      (3) Click the Position tab, then change the horizontal position to 0.5 inches from the left edge of the page and the vertical position to 1.1 inches from the top of the page. (Remember to set the "From" options first.)
      (4) Click the Text Box tab, then change the left, right, top, and bottom internal margins to 0 inches.
      (5) Click OK or press Enter.
   g. Change the Zoom viewing mode to 75%.
   h. Click once inside the text box to position the insertion point, then insert the file *light bulb test.doc* located on your student data disk.
   i. Format the article heading by completing the following steps:
      (1) Position the insertion point within the heading *The Light Bulb Test*, then apply the *Article Head* style.
      (2) With the insertion point still within the heading, access the Paragraph dialog box, then change the spacing before the heading to 0 points.
   j. Insert the light bulb image by completing the following steps:
      (1) Position the insertion point between *Light* and *Bulb* in the heading, then press the space bar one time.
      (2) Make sure the insertion point is positioned between the two spaces, then click Insert, point to Picture, then select From File.
      (3) At the Insert Picture dialog box, change to the folder containing your student data disk files, then double-click *Lightblb.wmf*.
      (4) Format the light bulb image by completing the following steps:

(a) Select the light bulb picture, then click Format and then Picture.
(b) Click the Size tab, then change the height of the picture to 0.3 inches and the width to 0.27 inches.
(c) Click OK or press Enter.

k. Position the insertion point within the first paragraph, and apply the *1st Paragraph* style.
l. Position the insertion point within the second paragraph, then apply the *Article Text* style.
m. Create the end sign at the end of the article by completing the following steps:
   (1) On page 1, select the end sign at the end of the first article.
   (2) Click the Copy button on the Standard toolbar.
   (3) Position the insertion point at the end of *The Light Bulb Test* article, press the space bar three times, then click the Paste button on the Standard Toolbar.
n. Format the linked text box containing the rest of the *Accident* article from page 1 by completing the following steps:
   (1) Double-click the border of the linked text box and make the following changes at the Format Text Box dialog box:
      (a) Click the Colors and Lines tab, then change the line color to No Line.
      (b) Click the Size tab, then change the height of the text box to 2.3 inches and the width to 2.4 inches.
      (c) Click the Position tab, then change the horizontal position of the text box to 0.5 inches from the left edge of the page and the vertical position to 4.75 inches from the top of the page. (Remember to set the "From" options first.)
      (d) Click the Text Box tab, then change the left, right, top, and bottom internal margins to 0 inches.
      (e) Click OK or press Enter.
o. Insert and format the jump line at the top of the article by completing the following steps:
   (1) Position the insertion point at the beginning of the article.
   (2) Click Insert, point to AutoText, point to Normal, then click *jump line*. (If *jump line* is not listed, select AutoText instead of pointing to Normal, then select *jump line* from the AutoText entry list box at the AutoText tab located in the AutoCorrect dialog box.)
   (3) Change the alignment to left.
   (4) Delete the word *See*.
   (5) Select the word *on* and key **from**.
   (6) Select the number *2*, then key **1**.
   (7) With the insertion point still positioned within the jump line, access the Paragraph dialog box, then change the spacing after the paragraph to 3 pt.
   (8) Access the Borders and Shading dialog box. Change the Color to Teal, change the Width to 1 pt, then click the top of the diagram in the Preview section to insert a top border. Make sure no borders display on the remaining sides of the diagram.
p. Copy and paste the end sign from the *Light Bulb Test* article to the end of this article by following steps similar to m(1)-(3) above.
q. Save c11ex10, newsletter.
r. Insert an article in the remaining space in the second column, as shown in figure 11.18, by completing the following steps:
   (1) Click the Text Box button on the Drawing toolbar, then draw a text box to hold the *When Should a Helmet Be Replaced?* article in the approximate size and location as shown in figure 11.18.

(2) Double-click the border of the text box and make the following changes at the Format Text Box dialog box:
  (a) Click the Colors and Lines tab, then change line color to No Line.
  (b) Click the Size tab, then change the height of the text box to 4.7 inches and the width to 5 inches.
  (c) Click the Position tab, then change the horizontal position to 3.1 inches from the left edge of the page and the vertical position to 5.3 inches from the top edge of the page. (Remember to set the "From" options first.)
  (d) Click the Text Box tab, then change the left, right, top, and bottom internal margins to 0 inches.
(3) Click once inside the text box to position the insertion point, then insert the file *replace helmet text.doc* from your student data disk.
(4) Apply styles to the article text just inserted by completing the following steps:
  (a) Position the insertion point within the title *When Should A Helmet Be Replaced?*, then apply the *Article Head* style.
  (b) Select all the paragraph text, then apply the *1st Paragraph* style.
(5) Position the insertion point within the article heading, access the Paragraph dialog box, then change the spacing before the paragraph to 0 points.
(6) Insert the bullet and bold the text at the beginning of each paragraph by completing the following steps:
  (a) With the insertion point positioned at the beginning of the first paragraph, select all of the article text.
  (b) Click Format, Bullets and Numbering, and then select the Bulleted tab.
  (c) Select the first bulleted example and then click Customize.
  (d) In the Bullet character section, click Font, then change the font size to 11 points and the color to Teal. Click OK.
  (e) Click Bullet, change the Font to Wingdings, and then select the round bullet in the third row, twenty-first column. Click OK.
  (f) Click OK again to close the Customize Bulleted List dialog box.
  (g) Select the phrase *After a crash.* and change the font to 11-point Impact.
  (h) Repeat the previous step to format the three remaining phrases at the beginning of each bulleted item. (A style could be created for this formatting, if desired; otherwise, press F4 to repeat the formatting.)
(7) Scroll through the newsletter and make any copy-fitting adjustments as necessary.

2. Save c11ex10, newsletter.
3. Print both pages of the Ride Safe newsletter and then close c11ex10, newsletter.

figure 11.18

Volume 5, Issue 2 • March 1999

Bicycle and In-Line Skating Safety for the 90s •

In the

Helmet Habit

"I don't quite know why my daughter, Kate, fell from her bike last July. Maybe she hit a small rock or just lost her balance. We found Kate lying on the ground. She was bleeding and had several cuts and bruises on her face and forehead. We called the paramedics and she began to lose consciousness just as they arrived. At the emergency room, we found out that Kate had a broken nose, a missing tooth, and four other loose teeth. Fortunately for all of us, Kate was wearing a bicycle helmet. Without even asking, three different doctors have told us that the helmet probably saved Kate's life. So many people tell me that their kids won't wear a helmet. I tell them to be firm—no helmet, no bike. Bicycle accidents can happen to anyone!"

Karen Brust
Boston, Massachusetts

In This Issue:

Bicycle Safety: Let's Make It a Priority!

Protect your child!

Did you know that each year over 1,200 people die and thousands more are seriously injured in bicycle accidents? According to the American Academy of Pediatrics, more than 500,000 emergency room visits annually in the U.S. are attributed to bicycle accidents.

Surprisingly, most of these accidents, especially those involving children, occur on quiet residential streets. Most do not involve cars. And many could be prevented with proper training and safety equipment.

Think about it. Before we're allowed to drive a car, we have to be a certain age and go through extensive training and testing. Yet many of us—children in particular—ride the very same roads on a bicycle with little or no training at all. Kids are especially vulnerable because of their undeveloped peripheral vision (about two-thirds that of adults), poor speed judgment, and lack of a sense of danger.

More than 500,000 trips are made to emergency rooms each year for bicycle-related injuries.

At Ride Safe, we believe bicycle safety education is crucial to our well-being and to that of our children. More and more states, including New York, New Jersey, Connecticut, Georgia, Tennessee, Oregon, and California are implementing legislation requiring bicycle helmets for children. As adults, we can teach our children safe riding habits, protect them from injury by purchasing bicycle helmets, and set a good example when we are riding our own bicycles.

The bottom line? *Bicycle safety is something we all need to make a priority!* — • —

"Accidents" Waiting to Happen

The majority of bicycle/car "accidents" are not really accidents, but avoidable collisions. Most result from the bicyclist's failure to use proper riding techniques in a hazardous situation. Ironically, when asked, most children injured in traffic could describe the actual law they broke.

▼ *See* **ACCIDENTS** *on page 2*

figure 11.18 continued

The Light Bulb Test

To illustrate the effectiveness of a bicycle helmet, try the following. Wrap a light bulb in plastic wrap, seal the bottom with a rubber band and place it in a bicycle helmet. Secure the light bulb with tape and drop the helmet onto a flat, hard surface from above your head. The light bulb will not break. In most cases, it will even still light. Now, drop the light bulb without the protection of the helmet. The light bulb will produce a sick thud as it breaks. Helmets *can* make a difference.

Caution: Parents, this experiment is meant to be done by you or under your close supervision. — ● —

▼ ACCIDENTS *from page 1*

Research indicates that 60% of all U.S. bicycle-car collisions occur among bicyclists between the ages of 8 and 12. Still, an average of only $1 is spent per child between birth and age 15 teaching traffic education. Children are permitted to travel with only a *"look both ways before you cross the street"* and *"make sure you stop at all stop signs"* warning. Obviously these "warnings" are not enough. — ● —

Ride Safe

Editor:
Chris Urban
Design and Layout:
Cassie Lizbeth
Authors:
Brandon Keith
Brian Stetler
Amanda Knicker
Published quarterly by:
Ride Safe, Inc.
P.O. Box 888
Warrenville, IL 60555
800-555-RIDE
Fax: 630-555-9068

Who Says Helmets Aren't Cool?

Insert picture of children from Silverton, Oregon here.

Certainly not the children of Silverton, Oregon! One of the biggest reasons children don't wear bicycle helmets is because their friends don't wear them. By getting all the children in your school or neighborhood to order bicycle helmets at the same time, you can help turn this peer pressure from negative to positive. Suddenly wearing a bicycle helmet becomes the "cool" thing to do.

When Should a Helmet Be Replaced?

- **After a crash.** Almost all bicycle helmets are designed to absorb the impact of a crash so that your head is protected. This damages the foam liner and reduces its ability to protect in the future. If you are involved in a crash and your helmet hits the pavement, it should be carefully inspected and/or replaced. Most manufacturers offer free inspection services and sometimes even free crash replacement policies.
- **When it doesn't fit.** Bicycle helmets must fit correctly to offer the intended protection. See your owner's manual for information on how to achieve a correct fit.
- **After three to five years.** The Snell Memorial Foundation recommends that you replace your helmet after five years. Due to advances in technology and performance, we suggest your helmet be evaluated after three years. Normal wear and tear due to drops and exposure gradually reduces a helmet's strength and protection capabilities. Helmets that receive extremely rough treatment should be considered for replacement even earlier. Does your child carefully hang up his/her helmet or is it tossed in the corner?
- **When it isn't being worn.** For whatever reason (not comfortable, too hot, too heavy, too old, doesn't match the new hat or coat, etc.), it may be time for a new helmet. Manufacturers have made dramatic improvements in style, weight, ventilation and cost over the last few years. If you and your children are not wearing helmets, there is nothing like a brand-new one to renew your interest and commitment.

Saving Your Newsletter as a Template

To save time when creating future issues of your newsletter, save your newsletter as a template document. To do this, delete all text, text boxes, pictures, objects, etc. that will not stay the same for future issues. Likewise, leave all text, pictures, symbols, text boxes, headers and footers, etc. that will remain the same in each issue of your newsletter. For example, to save the Ride Safe newsletter as a template, leave the following items and delete the rest:

- Folio
- Nameplate
- Headers and footers
- Sidebar with the title since this will be a feature article every month; delete the sidebar article text only
- Table of contents and heading; delete the table of contents text only
- Masthead
- Remaining text boxes; delete the articles in each text box, but leave the text boxes. The text boxes will most likely need to be reformatted each time you create a new issue of your newsletter; however, they serve as a basic framework for future issues.

Once you have deleted the text and elements that will change every month, save the newsletter with Save As. At the Save As dialog box, click the down arrow to the right of the Save as type: list box and select *Document Template (*.dot)* as the file type. Double-click the Publications folder, key a name for your newsletter template, and then click OK. To use the newsletter template, choose File, New, then select the Publications tab. Double-click the name of your newsletter template. The stripped-down version of your newsletter will display on the screen. Select and replace the month, date, and volume number in the folio. Key article headings and text to complete your newsletter. Delete any placeholder hard returns when necessary. Remember to update the authors' names in the masthead. Save your completed newsletter with a new name, such as RideSafe Oct newsletter. See figure 11.19 for an example of how the Ride Safe newsletter might look if saved as a template.

figure 11.19

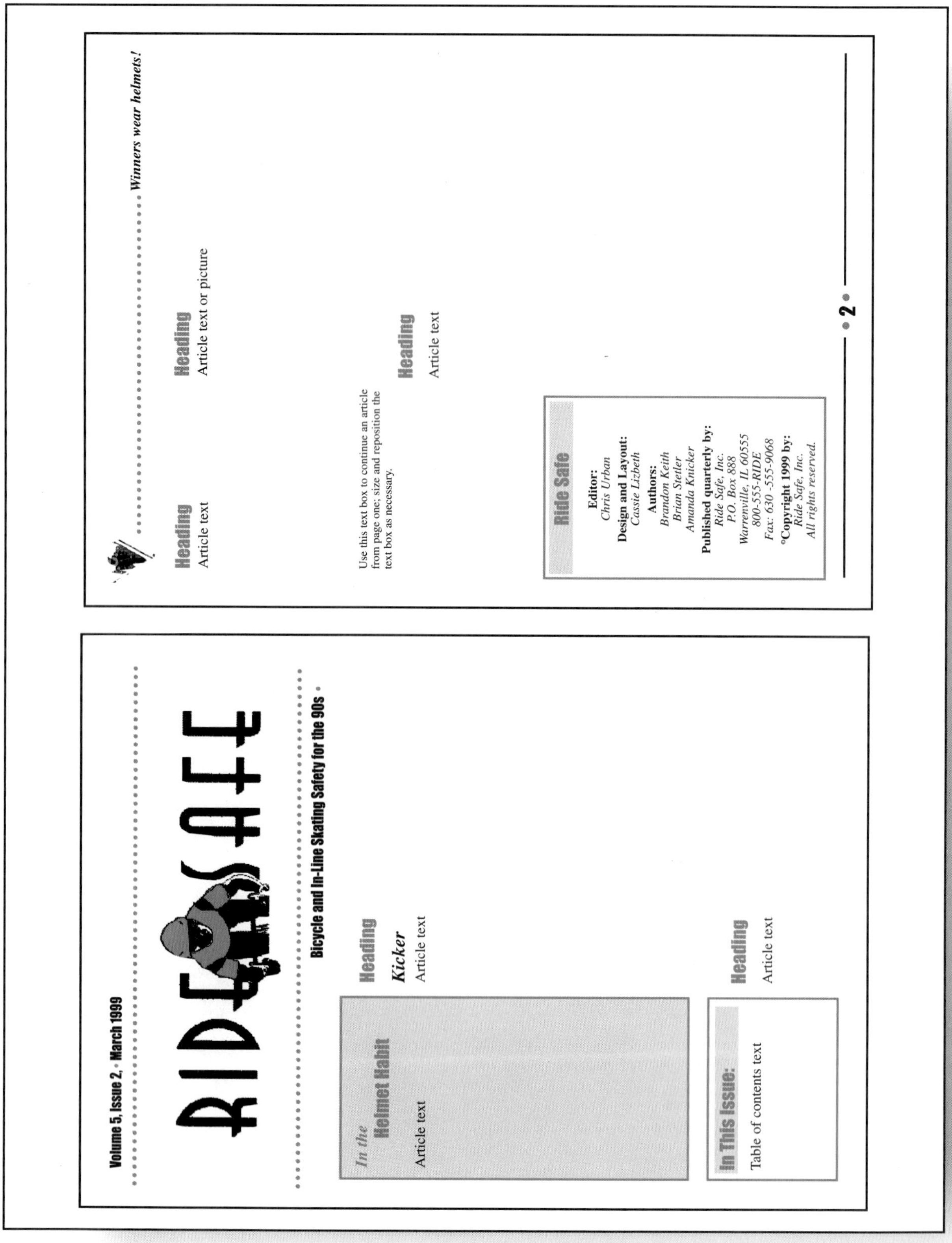

Volume 5, Issue 2, • March 1999

RIDE SAFE

Bicycle and In-Line Skating Safety for the 90s •

In the
Helmet Habit

Article text

Heading

Kicker

Article text

In This Issue:

Table of contents text

Heading

Article text

Winners wear helmets!

Heading

Article text

Heading

Article text or picture

Use this text box to continue an article from page one; size and reposition the text box as necessary.

Heading

Article text

Ride Safe

Editor:
Chris Urban
Design and Layout:
Cassie Lizbeth
Authors:
Brandon Keith
Brian Stetler
Amanda Knicker
Published quarterly by:
Ride Safe, Inc.
P.O. Box 888
Warrenville, IL 60555
800-555-RIDE
Fax: 630 -555-9068
©Copyright 1999 by:
Ride Safe, Inc.
All rights reserved.

• 2 •

chapter summary

- Elements can be added to a newsletter to enhance the visual impact, including tables of contents, headers and/or footers, mastheads, pull quotes, kickers, sidebars, captions, ruled lines, jump lines, page borders, and end signs.
- Use spot color—a color in addition to black—in a newsletter as an accent to such features as graphics lines, graphics images, borders, backgrounds, headings, and end signs.
- Headers and footers are commonly used in newsletters. Headers/footers can be placed on specific pages, only odd pages, or only even pages and can include page numbering, a slogan, a logo, or a horizontal ruled line.
- A sidebar is set off from the body text in a text box and can include a photograph or graphics image along with text.
- In multipage newsletters, a table of contents is an important element and is generally located on the front page in the lower left or right corner.
- A pull quote acts as a focal point, helps to break up lengthy blocks of text, and provides visual contrast.
- A masthead is a repeating element that usually contains the company address, newsletter publication schedule, names of those contributing to the production, and copyright information. It is generally located on the back page of a newsletter.
- A kicker is generally set in a smaller type size than the headline but larger than the body text and is placed above or below the headline or article heading.
- Symbols or special characters used to indicate the end of a section of text are called end signs.
- In a newsletter, a jump line indicates a continuation of an article or feature to another page and enables the creator of the newsletter to feature the beginning of several articles on the front page.
- Graphics images, illustrations, charts, diagrams, and photographs can add focus, balance, proportion, contrast, directional flow, and consistency to a newsletter. Graphics images include line art and continuous-tone art.
- Noncomputer-generated images such as photographs and illustrations can be scanned and then inserted in a newsletter.
- Captions can be added to images to establish a connection to the body copy. Bold caption text and set it in a smaller point size to make it different from the body text.
- Copy fitting refers to making varying amounts of text or typographical enhancements fit in a fixed amount of space.

commands review

	Mouse/Keyboard
New dialog box to access a template	File, New, select desired tab
Newsletter Wizard	File, New, Publications tab
Insert File dialog box	Insert, File
Insert Picture dialog box	Insert, point to Picture, then click From File or Clipart
Format Picture dialog box	Select picture, click Format, then Picture
Headers and footers	View, Header and Footer; click Switch Between Header and Footer to display Header or Footer pane
Display Drawing toolbar	Click Drawing button on Standard toolbar or right-click in the Standard toolbar, select Drawing
Draw a text box	Click the Text Box button on the Drawing toolbar or click Insert, then Text Box
Insert a text box around selected text	Select text, click Text Box button on Drawing toolbar
Format Text Box dialog box	Select text box, Format, Text Box
Format Object dialog box	Select object, Format, Object
Paragraph Borders and Shading dialog box	Format, Borders and Shading dialog box
Kerning (character spacing of specific pairs of characters)	Format, Font, Character Spacing tab, Kerning for fonts, enter specific amount of Points and above to be kerned
Tracking (character spacing)	Format, Font, Character Spacing tab, Spacing, Expand or Condense or Normal, enter point By: amount in point increments
Paragraph spacing	Format, Paragraph
Insert special characters	Insert, Symbol
Style dialog box	Format, Style
Insert a column break	Insert, Break, Column Break
Bullets and Numbering dialog box	Format, Bullets and Numbering

check your understanding

Terms: Match the terms with the correct definitions by writing the letter of the term on the blank line in front of the correct definition.

A	Caption	E	Header	I	Pull quote
B	Copy fitting	F	Jump line	J	Scanner
C	End sign	G	Kicker	K	Sidebar
D	Footer	H	Masthead	L	Spot color

_______ 1. A repeating element that can add consistency among newsletter issues and that contains the company address, newsletter publication schedule, names of those contributing to the production of the newsletter, and copyright information.

_______ 2. Description or explanation of a graphics image, illustration, or photograph.

_______ 3. Text that is repeated at the top of every page.

_______ 4. A block of information or a related story that is set off from the body text in a graphics box.

_______ 5. A color in a newsletter, other than black, used as an accent.

_______ 6. A brief direct phrase, summarizing statement, or important point associated with the body copy of a newsletter.

_______ 7. A symbol or special character used to indicate the end of a section of text.

_______ 8. Indicates a continuation of an article or feature to another page.

_______ 9. A brief sentence or phrase that is a lead-in to an article.

_______ 10. A piece of equipment that converts a photograph, drawing, or text into a compatible digital file format.

Concepts: Write your answers to the following questions in the space provided.

1. List at least five tips to consider when creating a pull quote.

2. What graphics file extensions are compatible with Word? (List at least ten.)

3. List at least six copy-fitting ideas to create more space in a document.

4. List at least six copy-fitting ideas to fill extra space in a document.

5. List at least four paragraph enhancements that can be included in a newsletter.

skill assessments

Assessment 1

1. Find two newsletters from two different sources. Review the newsletters for the items listed below. Label those items that you find in each newsletter.

   Nameplate
   Subtitle
   Folio
   Headlines
   Subheads
   Table of contents
   Masthead
   Header
   Footer
   Sidebar
   Pull quote
   Kicker
   End sign
   Jump line
   Caption
   Spot color

Optional: Write a summary explaining which of the two newsletters is the most appealing and why.

Assessment 2

In this assessment, you are to redesign the first page of a newsletter located on your student data disk. Two pages of text are provided. You only need to redesign the first page, but you may use any of the text on the second page for copy-fitting purposes.

1. Redesign a basic newsletter named *redesign text.doc* located on your student data disk according to the following specifications:
   a. Create a new nameplate, subtitle, and folio. Experiment with thumbnail sketches.
   b. Create the body of the newsletter using an asymmetrical column layout.
   c. Include the following:
      Header and footer
      Table of contents
      Sidebar
      Pull quote
      Graphic with caption
      Spot color (or varying shades of gray)

d. Use a kicker, end signs, jump line, clip art, text box placeholder for a photo, etc., if desired or needed for copy fitting.
e. Use tracking (character spacing), leading (line spacing), paragraph spacing before and after, text boxes, etc., to set the body copy attractively on the page.

2. Save and name the new newsletter c11sa02, redesign nwsltr.
3. Print and then close c11sa02, redesign nwsltr.
4. In class, edit each other's newsletters by completing the following steps:
   a. Independently choose an editor's name for yourself and do not share it with the rest of the class. (This is your chance to be really famous!)
   b. Your instructor will collect all the newsletters and randomly distribute a newsletter to each class participant.
   c. Sign your individual editor's "name" on the back of the newsletter and make editorial comments addressing such items as: target audience, visual appeal, overall layout and design, font selection, graphics image selection, focus, balance, proportion, contrast, directional flow, consistency, and use of color.
   d. Rotate the newsletters so that you have an opportunity to write editor's comments on the back of each newsletter, identified by your individual editor's name only.
   e. Review the editor's comments on the back of your own newsletter and redo your newsletter.
5. Save and name the revised version of your newsletter c11sa02, revised.
6. Print c11sa02, revised.
7. Evaluate your redesigned newsletter with the *Document Evaluation Checklist (document evaluation checklist.doc)*.

Assessment 3

Assume that you are an employee of Ride Safe, Inc., and are responsible for creating their newsletter. You have already completed an issue of this newsletter in c11ex10, and now you have to create the next issue. Using articles from your student data disk and the Ride Safe newsletter already created, create the next issue of the RideSafe newsletter according to the following specifications:

1. Print *RideSafe issue2 text.doc* located on your student data disk.
2. Review the printout of possible articles to be used for the second issue of your newsletter. Decide what articles you would like to include. Save the rest for possible fillers.
3. Make a thumbnail sketch of a possible layout and design. You can open *c11ex10, newsletter.doc* and use the framework of that newsletter to create this second issue. Be consistent in column layout and design elements used. Include the following items:

   Masthead
   Sidebar
   Pull quote
   End sign
   Caption
   Picture
   Spot color

4. For the masthead, use your instructor's name as the editor and your name for the design and layout.
5. Create a style for the article headings.
6. You decide on the order and placement of articles. Use bullets, bold, italics, reverse text, etc., if appropriate to the design and layout of the next issue of your newsletter.
7. Make any copy-fitting adjustments as necessary.
8. Save and name the document c11sa03, ride safe issue2.
9. Print and then close c11sa03, ride safe issue2.
10. Evaluate your newsletter with the Document Evaluation Checklist (*document evaluation checklist.doc*).

Optional: Rewrite and redesign all the article heads to be more clever, interesting, and eye-catching.

creative activity

With a partner, find a poor example of a newsletter and redesign the first page, including the nameplate. Use a different column layout and copy-fitting techniques to produce a newsletter that entices people to actually read your publication. Rewrite the text copy to make it more interesting. Recreate, save, and print c11ca01, then close it. In class, break up into small groups of four to six students and present the before and after versions of your newsletter. Give a brief explanation of the changes made, problems encountered, and solutions found. Vote on the most creative copy and the most creative design.

chapter TWELVE

12 Preparing Reports and Manuals

PERFORMANCE OBJECTIVE

Upon successful completion of chapter 12, you will be able to prepare reports, term papers, manuals, and forms containing elements such as a cover page, table of contents, title page, and index.

Desktop Publishing Concepts

Cover	Back matter	Directional flow
Front matter	Back cover	Balance
Body text	Consistency	

Word Features Used

Templates	Word Picture Editor	Page numbering
Styles	AutoShapes	Headers and footers
Insert file	Borders and shading	Index and tables
Insert picture	Gradient	Document map
Format picture	Drop caps	Tables

Structured publications such as reports, manuals, and directories are text-intensive, multipage documents containing repeating elements, such as headers or footers, and consistently styled title and text pages. Structured publications may contain all or some of the following elements in the order shown:

Cover
Front matter
Title page
Copyright page
Preface

Table of contents
Body text
Sections/chapters
Back matter
Appendix
Bibliography
Glossary
Index
Back cover

Not all structured publications contain each element. The elements are determined by the contents, length, and type of document. For example, a company manual may contain a title page, table of contents, index, and appendix, while a company catalog may contain all elements. Each element is described as follows:

Cover: The cover of a report, manual, or booklet is generally the first thing a reader notices. It should be attractively designed and draw a person's interest and attention. A cover may be multicolored while the inside text is printed in one color. It may be designed and produced by the desktop publisher or sent to a graphic designer for production. For some projects a cover is printed on the same stock as the other pages, while for others a heavier stock is used.

Title Page: The title page of a structured publication generally contains the full title of the publication (including any subtitles), the full name of the author, editor, and publisher, and possibly the publisher's address. If the structured publication is bound, the title page is printed on a right-hand page.

Copyright Page: A copyright page generally includes elements such as copyright dates, copyright permissions, name of the country where the structured publication is published, Library of Congress Cataloging-in-Publication (CIP) data, and the International Standard Book Number (ISBN). A copyright page is generally printed on the reverse side of the title page.

Preface: A preface is a statement by the author about the publication and may include acknowledgments. A preface usually begins on an odd-numbered page. A preface is sometimes referred to as the *foreword* and may be eliminated in technical or short publications.

Table of Contents: The table of contents for a report, manual, or booklet contains the name of each chapter or section and the page number on which each begins. The first page of a table of contents is generally designed like the first page of a chapter or section and begins on an odd-numbered page. Page numbers in a table of contents can be placed immediately after an item, separated by a comma, or separated from an item by leaders. Leaders are characters (generally periods) that print from the item to the page number, which is aligned at the right side of the page. The leaders help guide the reader's eyes across the page to the proper page number.

Body Text: When creating body text for a structured publication, consider such elements as the font, margin widths, running headers/footers, and page numbering. Set body text in approximately 11- or 12-point size and use a serif typeface for easy readability. Set headings and subheadings in a larger point size and consider using a typeface that complements the typeface used for the body text. Add a type style such as bold and/or italics to enhance headings and/or subheadings.

Appendix: Appendices include information that is not essential to the text but may help clarify the information presented. Appendices appear after the body text and usually begin on an odd-numbered page. The beginning page of an appendix is designed in the same manner as the first page of chapters or sections.

Preparing a Report

A report is a structured publication containing consistently styled title and text pages. Word provides three report templates to help you create a formatted report. The three report templates are labeled Contemporary Report, Elegant Report, and Professional Report. Word formats the pages of each of these reports using fonts and design enhancements similar to those in the memo, letter, and newsletter templates carrying the same descriptive names.

DTP POINTERS
Plan and organize the content of a report ahead of time.

In exercise 1, you will prepare a report using the *Contemporary Report* template. This template contains the formatting for a cover page, a chapter or section title page, headings, body text, and more. Instructions on how to use and customize the report template are included in the template. The instructional text is formatted using many of the styles saved with this template, enabling you to visualize the formatting options available in this template. One suggestion when using any of the report templates is to print a hard copy of the template and read the instructional text before creating your own document from the template. Another suggestion is to display all the style names next to the appropriate paragraphs and then write the style names next to the corresponding text on the hard copy of the template document. This way, when you delete the instructional text, you will know what styles were applied to specific sections of text. To display a list of all the style names, click the Normal View button on the horizontal scroll bar. Click Tools, Options, and then click the View tab. In the Window section, insert the desired width of the style name display in the Style area width box, then click OK. The style names will appear on the left side of the screen next to the corresponding paragraphs.

Browsing in Multipage Documents

You may be familiar with several methods of scrolling, browsing, or moving from one location to another in a document. However, there are some methods that are especially useful when creating or editing lengthy reports or manuals.

Using the Select Browse Object Button

Click the Select Browse Object button located at the bottom of the vertical scroll bar between the Previous Page and the Next Page buttons to display a palette of browsing methods as shown in figure 12.1. Point to any browsing option in the palette, and the option name will display below the option. As illustrated in figure 12.1, you can browse by fields, endnotes, footnotes, comments, sections, pages, edits, headings, graphics, and tables, and also by the Go To and Find features. For example, if you select the Browse by Heading option, the insertion point moves to the next heading in the document that is formatted with any of the built-in heading styles *(Heading 1* through *Heading 9)* provided by Word. In addition, the Previous Page and Next Page buttons on the vertical scroll bar change to Previous Heading and Next Heading and the color of the double arrows changes to blue. Click the Previous Heading or Next Heading button to move to the previous or next heading formatted with one of the heading styles. Figure 12.2 lists the results of using the browse options located in the Select Browse Object palette.

Select Browse Object

figure 12.1

Select Browse Object Palette

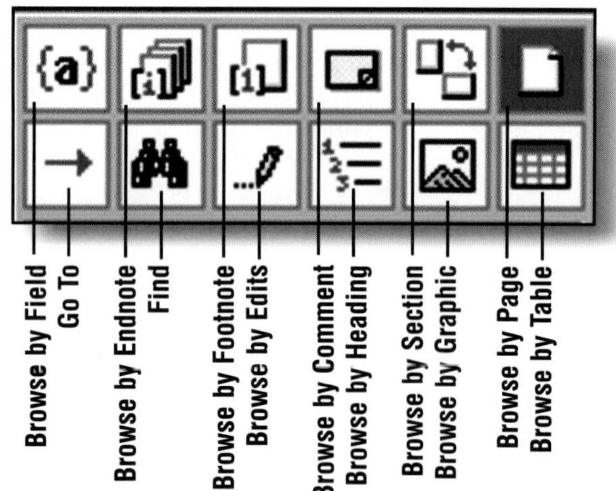

figure 12.2

Select Browse Object Options

Click this browsing option:	To:
Browse by Field	Move the insertion point to the next field in the document; previous and next buttons change to Previous Field and Next Field.
Browse by Endnote	Move the insertion point to the next endnote in the document; previous and next buttons change to Previous Endnote and Next Endnote.
Browse by Footnote	Move the insertion point to the next footnote in the document; previous and next buttons change to Previous Footnote and Next Footnote.
Browse by Comment	Move the insertion point to the next comment in the document; previous and next buttons change to Previous Comment and Next Comment.
Browse by Section	Move the insertion point to the next section in the document; previous and next buttons change to Previous Section and Next Section.
Browse by Page	Move the insertion point to the next page in the document; previous and next buttons change to Previous Page and Next Page.
Go To	Open the Find and Replace dialog box with the Go To tab displayed.
Find	Open the Find and Replace dialog box with the Find tab displayed.

Browse by Edits	Move the insertion point to the next place in the document where text was edited; previous and next buttons change to Previous Edit and Next Edit.
Browse by Heading	Move the insertion point to the next heading in the document that is formatted with a heading style; previous and next buttons change to Previous Heading and Next Heading.
Browse by Graphic	Move the insertion point to the next graphic in the document; previous and next buttons change to Previous Graphic and Next Graphic.
Browse by Table	Move the insertion point to the next table in the document; previous and next buttons change to Previous Table and Next Table.

Using the Document Map Feature

The Document Map is an outline of a document's headings. As mentioned in chapter 8, the Document Map in a Web document displays an outline of any headings formatted with HTML styles. In a regular Word document, the Document Map displays an outline of any headings formatted with Word's built-in heading styles *(Heading 1* through *Heading 9)* or outline-level paragraph formats *(Level 1* through *Level 9)*. You can use the Document Map feature to quickly move to the location of any these headings in your document.

Word automatically displays the Document Map when you switch to Online Layout view; however, you can display it in any view. To use the Document Map feature, click the Document Map button on the Standard toolbar (or click View, then Document Map). An outline of the document's headings are displayed in a separate pane on the left side of the screen, as shown in figure 12.3. Click any heading in the Document Map and the heading will display at the top of the screen. For example, in figure 12.3 *Multimedia PC* is selected in the Document Map and the heading *Multimedia PC* is displayed at the top of the screen.

Document Map

Notice in figure 12.3 that the Document Map pane is not wide enough to fully display some of the headings. To view any heading that is not displayed in full, position the arrow pointer on the heading to view the entire heading. As an alternative, you can adjust the size of the Document Map. To do this, position the arrow pointer on the right edge of the pane until it displays as left- and right-pointing arrows (labeled resize), then click and drag to the left or right.

By default, all levels of headings formatted with Word's built-in heading styles display in the Document Map. However, you can choose the levels of headings to be displayed. For example, you can "collapse" or hide subordinate headings and only display headings formatted with the *Heading 1* style to see a general overview of your document's structure. To collapse the subordinate headings under a heading, click the minus sign (-) next to the heading in the Document Map. To display the subordinate headings under a heading (one level at a time), click the plus sign (+) next to the heading. You can also right-click a heading in the Document Map and then select the number of the levels you wish to display in the Document Map. For instance, click *Show Heading 3* to display heading levels 1 through 3.

To close the Document Map, click the Document Map button on the Standard toolbar or click View, then Document Map.

figure 12.3

Document Map Displayed in Page Layout View

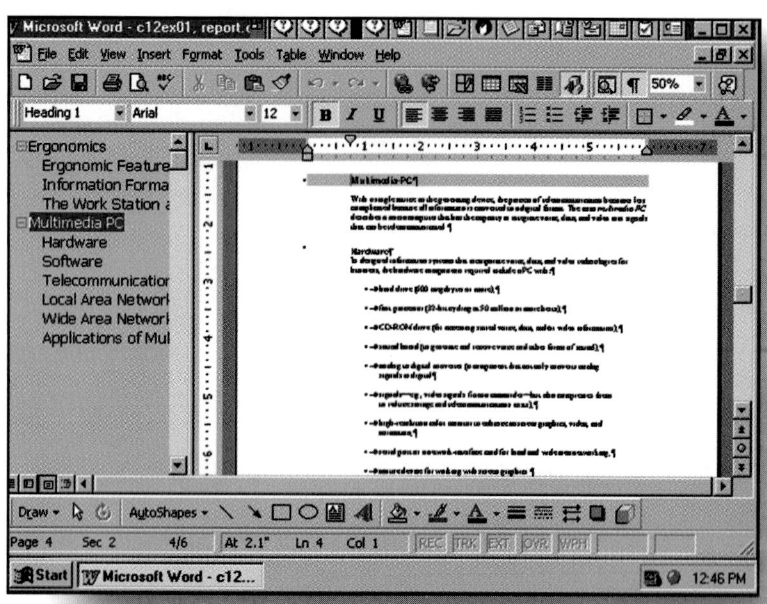

In exercise 1, you will insert text and use the *Contemporary Report* template's styles to format the text into a report layout.

exercise 1

Creating a Report Using the Contemporary Report Template

1. Prepare a report using the *Contemporary Report* template, as shown in figure 12.4, by completing the following steps:
   a. Click File, then New.
   b. At the New dialog box, select the Reports tab and then double-click the Contemporary Report icon. (If this report template is unavailable and you installed Word from a CD, you can copy the report template from the CD [D:\Template\Reports] into Word's Template/Reports folder [C:\Program Files\Microsoft Office\Templates\Reports]. If you updated from Office 95 to Office 97, click the Office 95 Templates tab to find the report templates.)
   c. Print a copy of the report template document and read the instructional text.
   d. Display the style names next to each paragraph by completing the following steps:
      (1) Click the Normal View button on the horizontal scroll bar.

(2) Click Tools, Option, then click the View tab.
(3) In the Window section, change the Style area width to 1 inch. (This amount can vary depending on the length of the style names to be viewed.)
(4) Click OK or press Enter.
(5) Scroll through the document and write the style names next to the paragraphs on the printed copy.
(6) Click Tools, Option, then click the View tab. In the Window section, change the Style area width to 0 inches. (Or you can skip this step and directly change to Page Layout View.)
(7) Click the Page Layout View button on the horizontal toolbar to continue working in the document.

e. Insert the company name and address by completing the following steps:
(1) Move the insertion point to the upper right corner of the first page and click once in the shaded area containing the words *Type Address Here*. A frame will display. (The creator of the template used a frame instead of a text box here. A frame is similar to a text box except that it exists in the text layer.)
(2) Click the border of the frame to display black sizing handles, then key the following (selecting the existing text is not necessary):

Global Communications, Inc.
73 West 22nd Street *(the nd will automatically superscript)*
Oak Brook, IL 60555
Phone: (630) 555-5647
Fax: (630) 555-6521

f. Insert the company name, cover title, and subtitle by completing the following steps:
(1) Select *blue sky associates* (*Company Name* should display in the Style list box on the Formatting toolbar), then key **global communications, inc.**
(2) Scroll down and select the cover title, *Film Watch Division Marketing Plan* (*Title Cover* should display in the Style list box on the Formatting toolbar), then key **Communications Systems**.
(3) Scroll down and select the cover subtitle, *Trey's Best Opportunity to Dominate Market Research for the Film Industry*, excluding the End of Section and Page Break identifiers (*Subtitle Cover* should display in the Style list box on the Formatting toolbar).
(4) Key the following, pressing Shift + Enter as indicated:

Prepared by: (Shift + Enter)
Your name (Shift + Enter)
Current date

g. On page two, insert the title, subtitle, and the first heading by completing the following steps:
(1) Select the title, *FilmWatch Division Marketing Plan* (*Title* should display in the Style list box on the Formatting toolbar), then key **Communications Systems**.
(2) Select the subtitle, *Trey's Best Opportunity to Dominate Market Research for the Film Industry*, (*Subtitle* should display in the Style list box on the Formatting toolbar), then key **Telecommunications at Work**.
(3) Select the first heading, *How To Use This Report Template*, (*Heading 1* should display in the Style list box on the Formatting toolbar), then key **Ergonomics**.

h. Insert the first section of report text by completing the following steps:
(1) Position the insertion point at the beginning of the first paragraph of instructional text located below the heading *Ergonomics*.

(2) Select the remaining text and press the Delete key. (*Hint:* Hold down the Shift key, then press Ctrl + End to select the remaining text.)
(3) Press Enter.
(4) Insert the file *report text1.doc* located on your student data disk.

i. Format the report text and headings by completing the following steps:
(1) Select all of the report text just inserted and apply the *Body Text* style from the Style list box located on the Formatting toolbar.
(2) Position the insertion point anywhere within the following headings and apply the *Heading 2* style from the Style list box located on the Formatting toolbar:

Ergonomic Features
Information Formats
The Work Station as a Focal Point

j. Emphasize specific items in the report text with bullets by completing the following steps:
(1) In the section titled *The Work Station as a Focal Point*, select the two lines that read *the realization that the microcomputer can be used for multiple business purposes;* and *the anticipation of a one-to-one ratio of workers to PCs*.
(2) Apply the *List Bullet* style from the Style list box located on the Formatting toolbar.
(3) In the same section, select *how the information is created;* and *how the information is delivered.*
(4) Repeat step (2) or press F4.

k. Press Ctrl + End to position the insertion point at the end of the document.

l. Press Ctrl + Enter to insert a hard page break.

m. To maintain consistency from the first section title page to the second title page, copy the vertical dotted line by completing the following steps:
(1) At the top of page 2, position the insertion point in the vertical dotted line above the heading, then click once to select the AutoShape containing the dotted line.
(2) Position the insertion point on the AutoShape border until it displays as an arrow with a four-headed arrow attached, then click once. The border should display as a series of small dots.
(3) Click the Copy button on the Standard toolbar.
(4) Position the insertion point at the top of page 4, then click the Paste button on the Standard toolbar.
(5) Click to the left of the AutoShape to deselect it.
(6) Press the Enter key until the Status bar displays 1.6 inches (or as close to this as possible).

n. Insert and format the section subtitle by completing the following steps:
(1) Key **Communications Equipment**, then press Enter.
(2) Position the insertion point on any character within the subtitle, *Communications Equipment*, then apply the *Subtitle* style from the Style list box located on the Formatting toolbar.

o. Insert and format the first heading by completing the following steps:
(1) Position the insertion point a line below the subtitle, key **Multimedia PC**, and then press Enter.
(2) Position the insertion point on any character within the heading, *Multimedia PC*, then apply the *Heading 1* style from the Style list box located on the Formatting toolbar.

p. Position the insertion point a line below the heading, insert the file *report text2.doc* located on your student data disk.

q. Format the report text and headings by completing the following steps:
(1) Select all of the report text just inserted and apply the *Body Text* style from the Style list box located on the Formatting toolbar.

(2) Position the insertion point anywhere within the following headings and apply the *Heading 2* style from the Style list box located on the Formatting toolbar: (After the first style has been applied, you can easily repeat the style by pressing F4 at each heading location.)

Hardware
Software
Telecommunications Links
Local Area Networks
Wide Area Networks
Applications of Multimedia PC

r. Select and apply the *List Bullet* style from the Style list box located on the Formatting toolbar to the following items:
(1) In the section titled *Hardware* on page 4, all the items following *In designed information... include a PC with:*.
(2) In the section title *Software* on pages 4 and 5, all the items following *The software... environment includes:*.
(3) In the section titled *Telecommunications Links* on page 5, all the items following *The following questions... basic options:*.
(4) In the section titled *Local Area Networks* on page 5, all the items following *Consider the following... area networking:*.

s. In the section titled *Wide Area Networks* on page 5, select and apply the *List Number* style from the Style list box located on the Formatting toolbar to the two paragraphs following *The alternatives... service providers:*.

t. In the same section, emphasize the two categories identified by the numbers by completing the following steps:
(1) Select *Media*, the first word after the number 1.
(2) Apply the *Emphasis* style from the Style list box located on the formatting toolbar.
(3) Select *Service providers*, the first two words after the number 2, then repeat step (2).

u. To accommodate correct page numbering, make the following changes:
(1) Replace the continuous section break and page break on the first page with a next page section break by completing the following steps:
(a) On the first page, position the insertion point at the beginning of the Section Break to the right of the paragraph symbol. (Turn on the display of nonprinting characters if it is not already on.)
(b) Press Delete two times to delete the Section Break and the Page Break. (After pressing the Delete key one time, it seems as though both breaks have been deleted; however, the page break is hidden making it necessary to press Delete again.)
(c) With the insertion point positioned one line below the date, click Insert, then Break. In the Section breaks section, click Next page.
(d) Click OK or press Enter.
(2) Turn off different odd/even headers and footers by completing the following steps:
(a) Click File, Page Setup, then select the Layout tab.
(b) Remove the check mark from the Different odd even option in the Headers and Footers section.
(c) Click OK or press Enter.

v. Adjust the page numbering so that the first page of the report does not display a page number but is counted as page 1 and the remaining pages are numbered accordingly by completing the following steps:

(1) With the insertion point positioned on page 2 (Status bar reads *Page 1 Sec 2 2/6*), click Insert, then Page Numbers.
(2) Make sure the Position list box displays *Bottom of page (Footer)*.
(3) Click the Alignment list box, then select *Center*.
(4) Make sure the Show number on first page check box is empty.
(5) Click Format, then make sure the Start at list box displays as number 1.
(6) Click OK to close the Page Numbers Format dialog box, then click OK again to close the Page Numbers dialog box.
(7) Using Print Preview, view the bottom of the second page; no page number should display. View the bottom of the third page; a number 2 should display. View the remaining pages; the numbers should follow in sequence. If the page numbers are only partially visible or not visible at all, try adjusting the distance from the footer to the edge of the page (File, Page Setup, Margins tab, From edge section).

2. Save the report and name it c12ex01, report.
3. Practice using the Select Browse Object options and the Document Map to move to specific locations in the report by completing the following steps:
   a. With the insertion point located at the beginning of the document, click the Select Browse Object button on the vertical scroll bar to display the browsing options.
   b. Browse the report by headings by completing the following steps:
      (1) Click the Browse by Heading option located in the second row, fourth column (see figure 12.1). (The options in your Select Browse Object palette may be displayed in a different order.) The insertion point will jump to the first heading, *Ergonomics*.
      (2) Click the Next Heading button on the vertical scroll bar to move the insertion point to the next heading, *Ergonomic Features*.
      (3) Continue clicking the Next Heading button to move the insertion point to every heading in the report that is formatted with a built-in heading style *(Heading 1* through *Heading 9)*.
      (4) Practice using the Previous Heading button to move the insertion point to previous headings in the report.
   c. Use the Document Map feature to move to specific locations in the report by completing the following steps:
      (1) With the insertion point located on any page in the report, click the Document Map button on the Standard toolbar or click View, then Document Map.
      (2) In the Document Map displayed at the left side of the screen, point to *The Work Station ....* Notice how the heading displays in its entirety.
      (3) Click *The Work Station as a Focal Point* to move the insertion point to this heading in the report. The heading will be displayed at the top of the screen.
      (4) Practice moving the insertion point to other locations by clicking any heading in the Document Map.
   d. Collapse and then expand the Document Map outline by completing the following steps:
      (1) Click the minus (-) sign to the left of *Ergonomics* and then click the minus sign to the left of *Multimedia PC*. Only level 1 headings will display in the Document Map.
      (2) Click the plus (+) sign to the left of *Ergonomics* to display the subordinate headings.
      (3) As an alternate method for displaying levels of headings, right-click *Multimedia PC*, then click *Show Heading 2* to display heading levels 1 and 2.
4. Print and then close c12ex01, report. Depending on the print quality of your printer, the globe on the first page may not be visible and any shading may be very light. To change the intensity or color of the globe or shading, refer to exercise 2. In addition, if the page numbers are not printing, try adjusting the distance from the footer to the edge of the page (File, Page Setup, Margins tab, From edge section).

Global Communications, Inc.
73 West 22nd Street
Oak Brook, IL 60555
Phone: (630) 555-5647
Fax: (63) 555-6521

global communications, inc.

Communications Systems

Prepared by:
Your name
September 21, 1998

Communications Systems

Telecommunications at Work

Ergonomics

Upon your arrival at work today, you seat yourself at the ergonomically designed work station where most of your activities are conducted. *Ergonomics* is the science of helping individuals interface with their immediate office environment so they can function at their highest levels.

Ergonomic Features

Features that contribute to productivity are chairs that are comfortable and that offer good back support, sufficient lighting to minimize eye strain, panels that provide visual privacy, and sufficient space to do the jobs required. Another component of your work station is a multifunction display terminal that can generate, store, transmit, and receive voice, data, word, image, and video information. A terminal should have a filter to eliminate glare from windows or lighting systems, and the top of the screen should be at eye level.

Information Formats

Not all the information you receive at work arrives in an electronic format. You use a laser scanner—another component of your work station—to convert information into an electronic format so it can be acted upon, distributed to others, or stored for future reference.

Documents and information that you create are dictated to your voice-actuated display terminal. Words appear on your terminal display for editing and revision. This activity can be done on your keyboard or with an electronic pointer device that allows you to make changes orally. Once the document is completed, you direct the system to check for spelling, grammar, and syntax errors. For example, if you had dictated a sentence starting with "You is," which is grammatically incorrect, the system would change it to "You are." And when you dictated that "too few people were involved in the activity," the system would use the correct "too," and not "to" or "two."

The completed document or information can now be distributed via electronic mail to one or more individuals anywhere in the world. An electronic copy of what you created is automatically stored in the optical digital disk storage system. If the document or information has legal value, you store it using Wrote Once Read Many (WORM) optical disk technology. Otherwise, the information is stored on the erasable optical disk system so it can be purged when no longer of value.

The Work Station as a Focal Point

The microcomputer has entered its second decade. The dynamic changes that took place in microcomputers in the first decade were astonishing. The power, speed, capacity, and applications of these systems increased tenfold. By all indications, the PC's second decade will be even more dramatic than the first. Here are two reasons:

- the realization that the microcomputer can be used for multiple business purposes;
- the anticipation of a one-to-one ratio of workers to PCs.

Two basic factors that determine the effectiveness of business information systems are

- how the information is created;
- how the information is delivered.

Historically, voice, data, and video applications have been generated by separate devices and, when appropriate, brought together to be telecommunicated. While the integration of voice, data, and video telecommunications will continue to function in this fashion, another alternative has emerged: integration of these technologies using the microcomputer. The microcomputer equipped with the appropriate hardware and software components can be used to create voice, data, and video information.

2

Communications Equipment

Multimedia PC

With a single source as the generating device, the process of telecommunication becomes less complicated because all information is converted to a digital format. The term *multimedia PC* describes a microcomputer that has the capacity to integrate voice, data, and video into signals that can be telecommunicated.

Hardware

In designed information systems that incorporate voice, data, and video technologies for business, the hardware components required include a PC with:

- hard drive (600 megabytes or more);
- fast processor (32-bit cycling at 50 million or more hertz);
- CD-ROM drive (for accessing stored voice, data, and/or video information);
- sound board (to generate and receive voice and other forms of sound);
- analog to digital converter (a component that not only converts analog signals to digital signals—e.g., video signals from a camcorder—but also compresses them to reduce storage and telecommunications costs);
- high-resolution color monitor to enhance onscreen graphics, video, and animation;
- serial port or a network-interface card for local and wide area networking;
- mouse device for working with screen graphics.

Software

The software required to function in a multimedia environment includes:

- a work station operating system (examples include DOS, OS/2, and UNIX);
- communications software (for local area networking or wide area networking);
- device driver software (e.g., disk drivers, mouse drivers, etc.);
- graphical user interface software (e.g., Windows);
- applications software packages (must be suited for the environment, e.g., packages designed for particular operating systems, graphical user interfaces, networking).

3

Telecommunications Links

Once the information to be communicated is digitized and compressed, where appropriate, the next step is telecommunications. The deciding factor is distance. The following questions will help you choose among basic options:

- Will the telecommunications be internal so that a local area network is the only consideration?
- Will the telecommunications be external, requiring the services of a wide area network?
- Will the telecommunications be a combination of the two?

Local Area Networks

Consider the following alternatives for local area networking:

- cable-based or wireless transmission (wireless transmission featuring radio-wave communications may be appropriate, but the number of work stations required and obstacles associated with building construction and location could be obstacles);
- network media (while twisted pair wire and coaxial cable may be sufficient, in cable-based systems, fiber optics offers the highest speed and bandwidth capacities);
- baseband/broadband (baseband can be used effectively for transmitting the integrated information; while broadband provides multiple channels for communications, it requires more hardware and is a more complex operation involving frequency division multiplexing).

Wide Area Networks

The alternatives for wide area networking can be divided into two categories, media and service providers:

1. **Media** (since the information to be transmitted is in a digital format and, where appropriate, compressed, the available media includes twisted pair wire, coaxial cable, optical fiber, microwave, satellite, and laser). Consider cost, ease of use, distance, distribution, security required, and availability in making a media choice.
2. **Service providers** (*common carriers*—telephone companies; *value added carriers*—companies that provide special features; *bypass*—company sets up its own communication links to avoid the continuing costs of local and long distance services).

Applications of Multimedia PC

There are numerous applications for the multimedia PC. Think for a moment of a computer manufacturer that has multiple U.S. locations. Assume that this organization's research and development division produces new components for use in their computers and corrects problems encountered in the manufacturing process.

Through the use of multimedia PC, an e-mail message that incorporates data, video, and voice could be sent to all plant locations. The data would be the text stating a computer component

4

change. The video would be a picture of the current component that has been recorded on CD-ROM disk. A copy of the picture can be extracted from the CD-ROM disk and added to the memo. The voice could be a voice message explaining what has been changed.

A video camera can be used to show the new component, and the installation process can be videotaped. The video signals can be compressed using the analog-to-digital conversion/ compression card in the multimedia PC. This information is also added to the e-mail message. Through an uplink satellite dish, the e-mail message containing voice, data, and video information is transmitted to a satellite transponder, then downlinked to satellite dishes at each plant location.

Projected uses of multimedia PC are limited only by imagination. Currently, multimedia PCs are popularly used to develop and telecommunicate training materials to local or distant sites. Whether the information to be telecommunicated comes from a single source, such as a multimedia PC, or from a variety of devices, knowing the alternatives available and the features and benefits of each will help you make the right choice.

5

DTP POINTERS
Use serif typefaces for text-intensive documents.

The *Contemporary Report* template uses several consistent elements to contribute to a unified appearance. The cover title and the report headings are set in Arial, while the subtitles are set in Times New Roman. The body text of the report is set in 10-point Times New Roman, which is a serif typeface—an appropriate choice for such a text-intensive document. The vertical dotted line at the top of the cover page is repeated at the top of the first section title page (page 2) and then again at the top of the second section title page (page 4). A horizontal variation of the dotted line is also included in the middle of the cover page. The shaded boxes located at the top and bottom of the cover page are repeated in the form of paragraph shading in the *Heading 1* style. A miniature version of the shaded text box is also included at the top of the section title page.

Customizing a Report

DTP POINTERS
Use a template as a base and modify it to fit your needs.

The report templates let you easily and quickly create a very professional-looking report. However, if you do not like all the formatting choices included in a specific template, or if you want a more customized report, you can use a report template as a base and then modify it to fit your needs or liking. For example, if you created the report in exercise 1, you might like to replace the globe with a different image or exclude the image completely. Or maybe you would like to use a different typeface for the report headings, add color to the shaded boxes, or move the horizontal dotted line on the front cover. All of these revisions can be made easily, including modifying styles, while still maintaining the initial framework of the report template. In addition, you can include other report elements such as a preface, table of contents, or index.

exercise 2

Customizing a Report Created with a Report Template

1. Customize the cover and section title pages of the report created in exercise 1, as shown in figure 12.5, by completing the following steps:
   a. Open c12ex01, report.
   b. Use Save As and name the report c12ex02, custom report.
   c. Add color to the AutoShape (shaded rectangle) located behind the company name by completing the following steps:
      (1) On the cover page (page 1), position the insertion point in the shaded AutoShape on either side of *global communications, inc.* until it displays as an arrow pointer with a four-headed arrow attached, then click once to select the shape.
      (2) Click the arrow to the right of the Fill button on the Drawing toolbar, click Fill Effects, and then click the Gradient tab.
      (3) In the Colors section, select One color, then click the Color 1 list box and select Dark Blue in the first row, sixth column.
      (4) Click and drag the Dark/Light slider button all the way to the right toward Light.
      (5) In the Shading styles section, click Horizontal.
      (6) In the Variants section, make sure the first variation in the first row is selected.
      (7) Click OK or press Enter.
   d. Scroll down and select *Prepared by:*, then change the type size to 16 points.
   e. Add color to the globe by completing the following steps:
      (1) Position the insertion point inside the globe image until it displays as an arrow pointer with a four-headed arrow attached, then double-click to display the image in Word's Picture editor.
      (2) Group the globe image by completing the following steps:
         (a) In Microsoft Word Picture, click the left side of the globe, hold down the Shift key, and then click the right side of the globe.
         (b) Click Draw, then click Group to make the image one unit.
      (3) Add fill color to the globe by completing the following steps:
         (a) Click the down arrow to the right of the Fill button on the Drawing toolbar, then click Fill Effects.
         (b) At the Fill Effects dialog box, select the Pattern tab.
         (c) Click the Foreground list box, then select Dark Blue in the first row, sixth column.
         (d) Click the Background list box, then select White in the fifth row, eighth column.
      (4) In the Pattern list box, select 25% in the fourth row, first column.
      (5) Choose OK to close the dialog box.
      (6) Click File, then Close & Return to c12ex02, custom report.doc.
   f. Select the shaded AutoShape located at the bottom of the title page and follow steps c(2) through c(7) above to add gradient shading to this shape.
   g. Move the AutoShape containing the horizontal dotted line, located between the cover title and cover subtitle, by completing the following steps:
      (1) Position the arrow pointer anywhere within the dotted line, then click once to select the AutoShape containing the dotted line. (The AutoShape is invisible until it is selected because it has no fill and no borders.)

(2) Position the pointer arrow on the AutoShape border, then double-click to access the Format AutoShape dialog box.
(3) At the Format AutoShape dialog box, select the Position tab.
(4) Change the Horizontal position to 0.5 inches from the edge of the page, then change the Vertical position to 9 inches from the top of the page. (Remember to change the "From" options first.)
(5) Choose OK to close the dialog box.
(6) Use the Print Preview button to see the new location of the line.

h. Move the insertion point to page 2, select the shaded AutoShape (narrow rectangle) located in the top right corner of the page, then press Delete. (This element seems out of place.)
i. On the same page, select the heading *Ergonomics*, and then change the font size to 14 points.
j. Add color to the paragraph shading surrounding the heading *Ergonomics* by completing the following steps:
(1) Position the insertion point anywhere within the heading *Ergonomics*.
(2) Display the Borders and Shading dialog box, then select the Shading tab.
(3) In the Fill section, select Dark Blue in the seventh row, first column.
(4) In the Patterns section, click the Style list box, then select 37.5%.
(5) Click the Color list box, then select White.
(6) Choose OK to close the dialog box.

k. Click the Document Map button on the Standard toolbar, then click *Multimedia PC* in the Document Map to move the insertion point to this heading.
l. With the insertion point at the beginning of *Multimedia PC*, press F4 to repeat the shading formatting.
m. Select *Multimedia PC*, then change the font size to 14 points. (The style could also be redefined, if desired.)
n. Click the Document Map button to close this feature.

2. Save the customized report with the same name, c12ex02, custom report.
3. Print and then close c12ex02, custom report.

figure 12.5

Cover Page and Pages 1 and 3

Global Communications, Inc.
73 West 22nd Street
Oak Brook, IL 60555
Phone: (630) 555-5647
Fax: (630) 555-6521

global communications, inc.

Communications Systems

Prepared by:
Your name
September 21, 1998

Communications Systems

Telecommunications at Work

Ergonomics

Upon your arrival at work today, you seat yourself at the ergonomically designed work station where most of your activities are conducted. *Ergonomics* is the science of helping individuals interface with their immediate office environment so they can function at their highest levels.

Ergonomic Features

Features that contribute to productivity are chairs that are comfortable and that offer good back support, sufficient lighting to minimize eye strain, panels that provide visual privacy, and sufficient space to do the jobs required. Another component of your work station is a multifunction display terminal that can generate, store, transmit, and receive voice, data, word, image, and video information. A terminal should have a filter to eliminate glare from windows or lighting systems, and the top of the screen should be at eye level.

Information Formats

Not all the information you receive at work arrives in an electronic format. You use a laser scanner—another component of your work station—to convert information into an electronic format so it can be acted upon, distributed to others, or stored for future reference.

Documents and information that you create are dictated to your voice-actuated display terminal. Words appear on your terminal display for editing and revision. This activity can be done on your keyboard or with an electronic pointer device that allows you to make changes orally. Once the document is completed, you direct the system to check for spelling, grammar, and syntax errors. For example, if you had dictated a sentence starting with "You is," which is grammatically incorrect, the system would change it to "You are." And when you dictated that "too few people were involved in the activity," the system would use the correct "too," and not "to" or "two."

The completed document or information can now be distributed via electronic mail to one or more individuals anywhere in the world. An electronic copy of what you created is automatically stored in the optical digital disk storage system. If the document or information has legal value, you store it using Wrote Once Read Many (WORM) optical disk technology. Otherwise, the information is stored on the erasable optical disk system so it can be purged when no longer of value.

The Work Station as a Focal Point

The microcomputer has entered its second decade. The dynamic changes that took place in microcomputers in the first decade were astonishing. The power, speed, capacity, and applications of these systems increased tenfold. By all indications, the PC's second decade will be even more dramatic than the first. Here are two reasons:

Communications Equipment

Multimedia PC

With a single source as the generating device, the process of telecommunication becomes less complicated because all information is converted to a digital format. The term *multimedia PC* describes a microcomputer that has the capacity to integrate voice, data, and video into signals that can be telecommunicated.

Hardware

In designed information systems that incorporate voice, data, and video technologies for business, the hardware components required include a PC with:

- hard drive (600 megabytes or more);
- fast processor (32-bit cycling at 50 million or more hertz);
- CD-ROM drive (for accessing stored voice, data, and/or video information);
- sound board (to generate and receive voice and other forms of sound);
- analog to digital converter (a component that not only converts analog signals to digital signals—e.g., video signals from a camcorder—but also compresses them to reduce storage and telecommunications costs);
- high-resolution color monitor to enhance onscreen graphics, video, and animation;
- serial port or a network-interface card for local and wide area networking;
- mouse device for working with screen graphics.

Software

The software required to function in a multimedia environment includes:

- a work station operating system (examples include DOS, OS/2, and UNIX);
- communications software (for local area networking or wide area networking);
- device driver software (e.g., disk drivers, mouse drivers, etc.);
- graphical user interface software (e.g., Windows)
- applications software packages (must be suited for the environment, e.g., packages designed for particular operating systems, graphical user interfaces, networking).

3

Preparing a Table of Contents

A report, manuscript, book, or textbook often includes sections such as a table of contents, index, and table of figures. Creating these sections in a document can be accomplished quickly and easily with Word's automated features. As mentioned earlier, a table of contents appears at the beginning of a report, manuscript, or book and contains headings and subheadings with corresponding page number locations.

To create a table of contents in Word, you must first mark or identify all the items in your document that you want to include in your table of contents. Then Word must be instructed to build the table of contents from the marked text. You can build a table of contents from headings formatted with Word's built-in heading styles *(Heading 1* through *Heading 9),* from headings formatted with Word's outline-level styles, from headings formatted with custom styles, and from fields. Building a table of contents from Word's built-in heading styles, from custom styles, and from fields will be discussed in this chapter. See Word's reference manual to build a table of contents from Word's outline-level styles.

Using Styles to Mark Table of Contents Entries

When instructed to build a table of contents, Word automatically includes any items formatted by its built-in heading styles (labeled *Heading 1* through *Heading 9*). Word uses the heading style numbers to determine what level the item will occupy in the table of contents. For example, an item formatted with a *Heading 1* style will be formatted as a level one heading in the table of contents. An item formatted with a *Heading 2* style will be formatted as a level two heading in the table of contents, and so on, as illustrated in figure 12.6. The advantage of using styles to mark text for a table of contents is that it is quick and easy. The disadvantage is that the appropriate heading styles must be applied to the desired items in your document for this feature to work. In addition, you are limited to the formatting included in the heading styles unless you want to modify and redefine some of these styles.

Sample Table of Contents

TABLE OF CONTENTS

LEVEL ONE HEADING 1
LEVEL TWO HEADING 1
Level Three Heading 1
Level Three Heading 2
Level Three Heading 2

To apply styles for a table of contents you would complete these steps:

1. Position the insertion point on any character in the text you want included in the table of contents.
2. Click the down arrow to the right of the Style button on the Formatting toolbar, then click the desired style name, such as *Heading 1*.
3. Continue applying the appropriate numbered heading styles to the remaining items to be included in your table of contents.

To compile a table of contents from Word's built-in heading styles you would complete these steps:

1. After the necessary heading styles have been applied, position the insertion point where you want the table of contents to appear.
2. Choose Insert, Index and Tables, and then select the Table of Contents tab.
3. In the Formats list box, select one of the table of contents formats.
4. Choose OK to close the dialog box.
5. Word compiles the table of contents and then inserts it at the location of the insertion point with the formatting selected at the Index and Tables dialog box.

When you select a format, you can view how your table of contents will be formatted in the Preview box. You can also vary the selected table of contents format by changing the options located at the bottom of the dialog box. These options include showing page numbers, right aligning page numbers, showing a specific number of levels, and using dot leaders. The settings for these options may vary, depending on which format you have selected for your table of contents.

If you want the table of contents to print on a page separate from the document text, position the insertion point in the desired location (commonly the bottom of the cover page), choose Insert, then Break. Select Next Page to insert a section break that begins a new page between the cover or title page and the body of the document. Use section breaks instead of regular page breaks between different sections of your document such as the cover, table of contents, chapters, etc., to accommodate the different page numbering formats that may be necessary in your document. Since a table of contents is generally numbered with lowercase Roman numerals, the page numbering method must be changed for that specific page. In addition, the starting page number for the body of the report should be set as page 1 even though the number is usually not printed on the first page of a publication.

DTP POINTERS
A table of contents is usually numbered with Roman numerals.

The items in the table of contents display with a gray background. When Word compiles a table of contents, the whole table is actually a field; hence, the gray background. The gray background does not mean the table of contents is selected. You can select, insert, delete, and format any of the text as normal.

Creating a Customized Style List to Mark Table of Contents Entries

By default, Word uses the built-in heading styles *(Heading 1* through *Heading 9)* to compile a table of contents automatically. In many instances, however, styles with different names other than *Heading 1*, *Heading 2*, etc., can be applied to text in a document that you want to include in a table of contents. You can customize the list of styles Word uses to build a table of contents in a document. For instance, if a style named *Subtitle* is applied to text that you would like to be included in a table of contents as a level one heading, you can instruct Word to recognize the *Subtitle* style as a level one heading.

To customize the list of styles Word uses to build a table of contents you would complete these steps:

1. Position the insertion point where you want the table of contents to appear.
2. Choose Insert, then Index and Tables, then select the Table of Contents tab.
3. Select the desired table of contents format from the Formats list box.
4. Make any desired changes to the available formatting options, such as Show page numbers, Right align page numbers, Show levels, and Tab leader.
5. Choose Options. The Table of Contents Options dialog box lists all the styles available in your document, as shown in figure 12.7. The list of styles will vary depending on what document is displayed on the screen.
6. Find the style name that you want to be included as a level one heading in your table of contents and key 1 in the corresponding TOC level text box.
7. Find the style name that you want to be included as a level two heading in your table of contents and key 2 in the corresponding TOC level text box.
8. Repeat this process for each style you want Word to use when it builds your table of contents. (Make sure the TOC level text box is empty for any style you do not want to be included.)
9. If your table of contents is to be compiled completely from styles, make sure the Styles check box displays with a check mark and the Table entry fields check box is empty. If your table of contents is to be compiled from a combination of styles and field entries, select the Table entry fields check box to insert a check mark.

Table of Contents Options Dialog Box

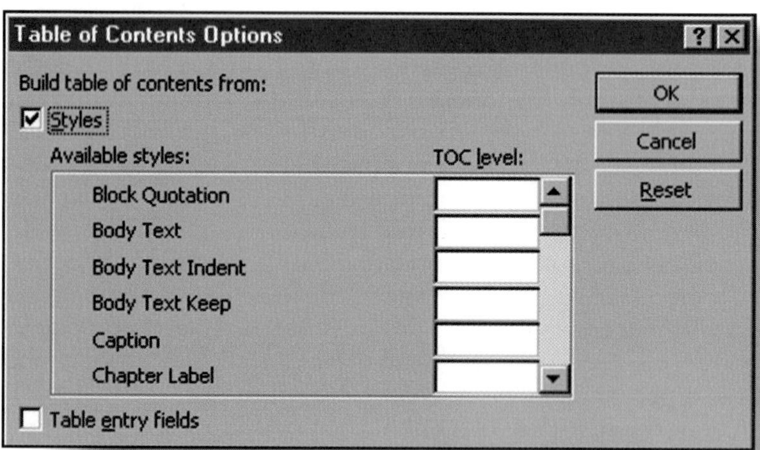

Using Fields to Mark Table of Contents Entries

If you do not want style formatting to be applied to the title, headings, or subheadings in a document, but you do want to include a table of contents, manually mark text for the table as fields. When text is marked for a table of contents as a field, a field code is inserted in the document. For example, a field code entry for a heading such as *Telecommunications at Work* would look like { *TC "Telecommunications at Work" \f C \l "1"* } in your document. (If this code is not visible, click the Show/Hide ¶ button on the Standard toolbar.) The *TC* in the code identifies the text that follows as a table of contents entry. The text in quotation marks is the text that is to appear in the table of contents. The backslash followed by a lowercase letter is referred to as a *switch*. In this case, the *\f* switch tells Word that the character after the switch (in this case, *C*) is the specific type of table in which the entry is to be placed. The letter *C* identifies the specific type of table as a table of contents. This switch, *\f*, and the table identifier, *C*, is only necessary in documents with multiple tables and is inserted as a default when marking entries through the Mark Table of Contents Entry dialog box. The *\l* switch tells Word that the character after the switch is the heading level that will be assigned to this entry in the table of contents, in this case, a level one. Word can then be instructed to compile a table of contents from text entry fields rather than from styles. This method takes more time than the style method but can be useful when you want to create a table of contents from text that has not been formatted with styles.

To mark text as a field in a table of contents you would complete these steps:

1. Select the text you want included in the table of contents, or position the insertion point at the beginning of the text to be included.
2. Press Alt + Shift + O to access the Mark Table of Contents Entry dialog box, shown in figure 12.8.
3. If the text was selected first, it will appear in the Entry text box, along with any character formatting. If the text was not selected first, key the text to be included in the table of contents in the Entry text box.
4. Make sure the Table identifier displays *C*. (This tells Word the marked entry belongs in a table of contents, versus a table of figures or a table of authorities.)
5. Key or select a table of contents heading Level.
6. Choose Mark to close the dialog box.

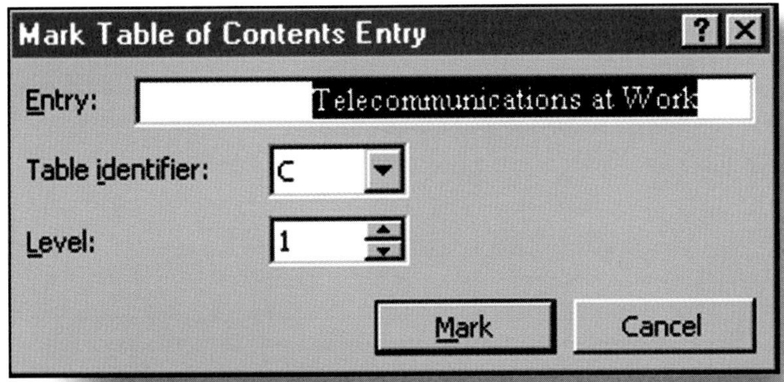

figure 12.8

Mark Table of Contents Entry Dialog Box

To compile a table of contents from entries marked as fields you would complete these steps:

1. Follow the same steps you would take to compile a table of contents from heading styles.
2. Before closing the dialog box, select Options at the Index and Tables dialog box.
3. In the Table of Contents Options dialog box, select the Table entry fields check box to insert a check mark.
4. Remove the check mark from the Styles check box.
5. Choose OK to close the dialog box, then choose OK again to close the Index and Tables dialog box.

Using a Table of Contents to Access Parts of a Document

When you use Word to automatically compile a table of contents in a document, you can quickly access parts of your document through the table of contents. To do this, open the file containing your document that includes a table of contents. Position the insertion point on the table of contents page and click any page number in the table of contents to move the insertion point to the corresponding heading in the document. This feature is especially useful when trying to access sections of a lengthy document to make revisions.

Updating a Table of Contents

DTP POINTERS
Update the table of contents after making final revisions to your document.

Creating the table of contents should be the last step in creating any publication. Try to make all changes that affect pagination before you compile the table of contents. However, if you make changes to a document after compiling a table of contents, you can either update the existing table of contents or replace the entire table of contents with a new one.

Since the table of contents is actually a field, you can update the table of contents by updating the field. To do this, position the insertion point anywhere within the current table of contents (this causes the table of contents to display with a gray background), then press F9, the Update Field key. At the Update Table of Contents dialog box shown in figure 12.9, click Update page numbers only if the changes occur only to the page numbers, or choose Update entire table if changes were made to headings or subheadings within the table. Choose OK or press Enter to close the Update Table of Contents dialog box.

figure 12.9

Update Table of Contents Dialog Box

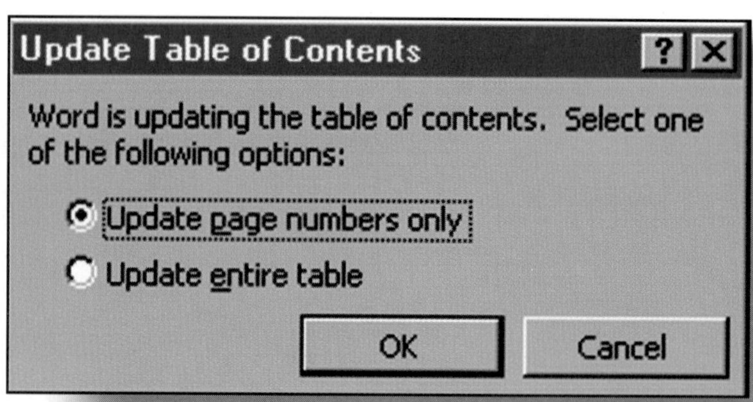

If you make extensive changes to the document, you may want to replace the entire table of contents. To do this, position the insertion point anywhere within the current table of contents (this causes the table of contents to display with a gray background), and then click Insert, then Index and Tables. At the Index and Tables dialog box, make sure the Table of Contents tab is selected, then choose OK or press Enter. At the prompt asking if you want to replace the existing table of contents, click Yes. Any special formatting applied to the table of contents after it was compiled will be lost in the replacement process.

Deleting a Table of Contents

A table of contents that has been compiled in a document can be deleted. To do this, select the entire table of contents using the mouse or keyboard, and then press the Delete key. Even though the table of contents displays with a gray background when the insertion point is positioned on any character in the table, the contents still need to be selected in the normal manner.

exercise 3

Creating a Table of Contents Using Styles to Mark Entries

1. Open c12ex02, custom report.
2. Save the document with Save As and name it c12ex03, table of contents.
3. Create the table of contents shown in figure 12.10 by completing the following steps:
   a. Insert and format a blank page for the table of contents by completing the following steps:
      (1) Position the insertion point at the beginning of page 2 (Status bar reads *Page 1 Sec 2 2/6*) to the left of the first paragraph symbol.
      (2) Click Insert, Break, and then Next page to insert a section break.
      (3) Click OK or press Enter.
   b. Position the insertion point at the top of the blank page to the left of the section break (Status bar reads *Page 1 Sec 2 2/7*), then key **TABLE OF CONTENTS** and press Enter two times.
   c. Compile and insert a table of contents from a custom list of styles by completing the following steps:
      (1) Click Insert, then Index and Tables.
      (2) At the Index and Tables dialog box, choose the Table of Contents tab.
      (3) Select *Formal* in the Formats list box.
      (4) Click Options.
      (5) At the Table of Contents Options dialog box, make sure there is a check mark in the Styles check box.
      (6) Make sure there is no check mark in the Table entry fields check box.
      (7) In the Available styles list box, use the vertical scroll bar to display the *Title* style name.
      (8) Key **1** as the level in the *Title* style's corresponding TOC level text box.
      (9) Use the vertical scroll bar to display the *Subtitle* style name.
      (10) Key **2** as the level in the *Subtitle* style's corresponding TOC level text box.
      (11) Display the *Section Heading* style name.
      (12) Delete the number in *Section Heading* style's corresponding TOC level text box.
      (13) Use the vertical scroll bar to display the *Heading 1* style name.
      (14) Select any existing number in the *Heading 1* style's corresponding TOC level text box, then key **3**.
      (15) Display the *Heading 2* style name.
      (16) Select any existing number in the *Heading 2* style's corresponding TOC level text box, then key **4**.
      (17) Display the *Heading 3* style name.
      (18) Delete the number in *Heading 3* style's corresponding TOC level text box.
      (19) Scroll through the list of available styles and make sure the TOC level text boxes are empty for all styles you do not want to be included.

(20) Click OK to close the Table of Contents Options dialog box, then click OK again to close the Index and Tables dialog box.

d. Adjust the page numbering in the report to accommodate the table of contents by completing the following steps:
   (1) With the insertion point positioned anywhere in the Table of Contents page, click Insert, then Page Numbers.
   (2) Make sure the Position list box displays *Bottom of page (Footer)*.
   (3) Click the Alignment list box, then select *Center*.
   (4) Click in the Show number on first page check box to insert a check mark.
   (5) Click Format, then click the Number format list box and choose *i, ii, iii, ...* from the drop-down list.
   (6) Click Start at and then change the starting number to *ii*.
   (7) Click OK to close the Page Numbers Format dialog box, then click OK again to close the Page Numbers dialog box.
   (8) Using Print Preview, view the bottom of the table of contents page; a lowercase Roman numeral *ii* should display.
   (9) Scroll through the rest of your document to check the page numbering. The first page of the report text will be counted as page number 1 but will not display a page number. The second page of the report text should display with a number 2 and so on.)
   (10) Check the table of contents items and make sure the correct page numbers are being displayed.

e. Format the table of contents heading by completing the following steps:
   (1) Position the insertion point anywhere within the title *TABLE OF CONTENTS*.
   (2) Apply the *Heading 1* style from the Style list box located on the Formatting toolbar.
   (3) Display the Paragraph dialog box, then select the Indents and Spacing tab.
   (4) In the Indentation section, change the Special option to (none).
   (5) Choose OK to close the dialog box.
   (6) Display the Borders and Shading dialog box, then select the Shading tab.
   (7) In the Fill section, select Dark Blue in the seventh row, first column.
   (8) In the Patterns section, click the Style list box, then select 37.5%.
   (9) Click the Color list box, then select White.
   (10) Choose OK to close the dialog box.

f. Select the page number corresponding to the *Ergonomics* entry and remove italic formatting. Repeat the process for the page number corresponding to the *Multimedia PC* entry. (If a hand symbol displays as you attempt to select the page numbers and you click the left mouse button, the insertion point will move to the page number and entry that is being referenced. To avoid moving to another location in your document while trying to select the page numbers, click anywhere in the dotted line to the left of the page number and to the right of the tab symbols to position the insertion point for selecting.)

g. If the page numbers in the table of contents change to all zeroes, press F9 to update the table of contents field.

4. Save the report again with the same name, c12ex03, table of contents.
5. Print the table of contents page. (Check with your instructor to see if you should print the other pages of the document for your portfolio.)

figure 12.10

TABLE OF CONTENTS

COMMUNICATIONS SYSTEMS **1**
TELECOMMUNICATIONS AT WORK 1
Ergonomics 1
Ergonomic Features 1
Information Formats 1
The Work Station as a Focal Point 1
COMMUNICATIONS EQUIPMENT 3
Multimedia PC 3
Hardware 3
Software 3
Telecommunications Links 4
Local Area Networks 4
Wide Area Networks 4
Applications of Multimedia PC 4

Preparing a Manual

Many companies prepare publications for employees and/or customers. These publications may include policies and procedures manuals, benefits manuals, training manuals, and product and client information. A manual is a structured publication that may include some or all of the elements described earlier such as a cover, title page, table of contents, headers/footers, page numbering, glossary, and index.

Preparing a Manual Cover

When planning a cover, consider the contents of the manual. Choose a layout that is appealing and attractive. Choose a font that complements or harmonizes with the contents of the manual. Consider using a picture or graphic image on the cover. Remember all graphic images or clip art need to be relevant to the subject matter. Use large type with one or two words. Text lines set at a 90-degree angle can add visual appeal to a cover. Consider the desktop publishing concepts presented in chapter 1 when designing a cover. Determine the focus (such as a photograph, graphic image, or large display type); create a logical directional flow; maintain consistency with inside elements; and provide contrasting elements. Figure 12.11 illustrates some sample cover designs.

DTP POINTERS
When planning a cover, consider the contents of the manual.

In exercise 4, you will create a manual cover page and title page for a Word 97 training manual using a template called *Manual.dot*. This manual template is not included in Word 97's default template folder. However, you may find the manual template in one of two locations. If you updated to Office 97 from Office 95, the manual template is available by clicking File, New, and then clicking the Office 95 Templates tab. If you installed the CD-ROM version of Word 97 or Office 97, the manual template file is located in the ValuPack\Template\Word folder located on the CD. To use the manual template from the CD, copy the *manual.dot* file to the default Templates folder (or an appropriate subfolder) located on your hard drive. Refer to the section *Read This Before You Begin* located in the front of this textbook for details on how to copy the ValuPack template files into Word's Templates folder.

There are some minor differences between the CD version of the manual template and the Office 95 Templates version. For instance, the *List Bullet* style inserts round bullets in the Office 95 version and square bullets in the CD version. The manual template file located in the ValuPack\Template\Word folder on the CD will be used for this exercise and any associated figures.

In exercise 5, you will prepare the body text for the manual; in exercise 6, you will create a concordance file for an index; in exercise 7, you will create an index for the manual; and, in exercise 8, you will compile a table of contents for the manual.

figure 12.11

Cover Designs

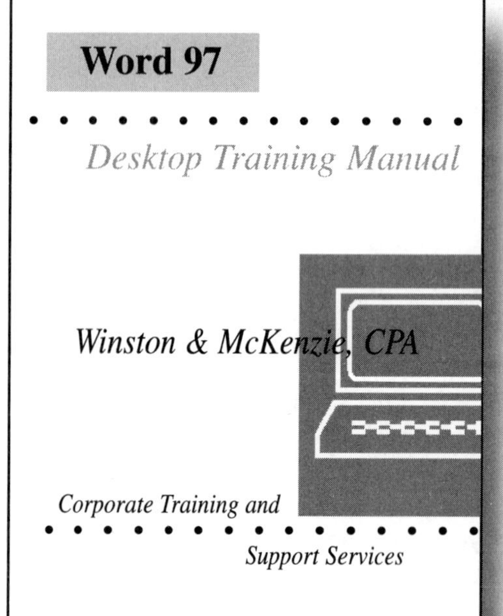

exercise 4

Creating a Manual Cover Page and Title Page

1. Create a manual cover page and title page using the *Manual* template, as shown in figure 12.12, by completing the following steps:
   a. Click File, then New. Select the tab (such as Other Documents or Office 95 Templates) containing the manual.dot template, then double-click the Manual.dot icon. (See the text immediately preceding this exercise for a discussion of the location of the *Manual.dot* template.)
   b. Print and read a copy of the manual template document.
   c. Display the style names next to each paragraph by completing the following steps:
      (1) Click the Normal View button on the horizontal scroll bar.
      (2) Click Tools, Option, then click the View tab.
      (3) In the Window section, change the Style area width to 1 inch. (This amount can vary depending on the length of the style names to be viewed.)
      (4) Click OK or press Enter.
      (5) Scroll through the document and write the style names next to the paragraphs on the printed copy.
      (6) Click Tools, Option, then click the View tab. In the Window section, change the Style area width to 0 inches. (Or, you can skip this step and directly change to Page Layout View.)
      (7) Click the Page Layout View button on the horizontal toolbar to continue working in the document.
   d. Change the Zoom Control to Page Width. Continue to adjust the viewing mode as needed as you progress through this exercise.
   e. Replace the framed text on the cover page with a picture by completing the following steps:
      (1) With the insertion point positioned within the framed text *(Volume 3)* in the upper right corner of the cover page (use the horizontal scroll bar to display this portion of the screen), select the frame border, then press Delete.
      (2) Click Insert, point to Picture, then select From File.
      (3) At the Insert Picture dialog box, change the folder in the Look in: list box to the location of your student data disk files, then double-click *Computer.wmf* in the Name list box.
      (4) Size and position the picture by completing the following steps:
         (a) Click once in the picture to select it.
         (b) Click Format, then Picture.
         (c) At the Format Picture dialog box, click the Size tab and change the Scaling Height and Width to 115%.
         (d) Click the Position tab, then change the horizontal position of the picture to 6.5 inches from the left edge of the page and the vertical position to 0.8 inches from the top of the page. (Remember to change the "From" options first.)
         (e) Choose OK to close the dialog box.
   f. Insert the company name, the cover subtitle, and the cover title by completing the following steps:
      (1) Scroll down and select *INSPIRED TECHNOLOGIES* and then key **WINSTON & MCKENZIE, CPA** as the company name. (The style includes All Caps as a formatting instruction, so the text may be keyed in lower case, if desired.)
      (2) Select *Corporate Graphics and Communications* and then key **Corporate Training and Support Services** as the cover subtitle.

(3) Scroll toward the bottom of the cover page, select *Administrative Stylesheet Guide*, and then key **Word 97 Desktop Training Manual** as the cover title.

g. With the insertion point positioned within *Word 97 Desktop Training Manual*, adjust the character spacing of the cover title (the *Title Cover* style includes a formatting instruction to condense the text by 9 points) by completing the following steps:

(1) Select the cover title, then choose Format, then Font.

(2) At the Font dialog box, select the Character Spacing tab.

(3) Change the Spacing to Condensed By 4.2 points, then click OK or press Enter.

h. Display the Paragraph Borders and Shading dialog box, then change the Shading Pattern Style to 20%.

i. Customize the title page (Status bar reads *Page i Sec 2 2/9*) by completing the following steps:

(1) Position the insertion point on page 2.

(2) Select *CORPORATE GRAPHICS AND COMMUNICATIONS*, then key **CORPORATE TRAINING AND SUPPORT SERVICES** as the title page subtitle.

(3) Select *Administrative Stylesheet Guide*, then key **Word 97 Desktop Training Manual** as the title for the title page.

(4) Scroll down and select the company name and address, then key:

Winston & McKenzie, CPA
4600 North Meridian Street
Indianapolis, IN 46240

2. Save the document and name it c12ex04, manual cover.
3. Print the cover page and the title page only, and then close c12ex04, manual cover.

figure 12.12

WINSTON & MCKENZIE, CPA
Corporate Training and Support Services

Word 97 Desktop Training Manual

CORPORATE TRAINING AND SUPPORT SERVICES
Word 97 Desktop Training Manual

Winston & McKenzie, CPA
4600 North Meridian Street
Indianapolis, IN 46240

In exercise 5, you will insert the body text for the manual started in exercise 4. You will apply styles included in the manual template to various sections of the inserted text.

exercise 5

Inserting and Formatting the Body Text for a Manual

1. Open c12ex04, manual cover.
2. Save the document with Save As and name it c12ex05, manual.
3. Insert and format the body text for the manual started in exercise 4 by completing the following steps:
   a. Customize the framed chapter label on the first page of the body of the manual, as shown in figure 12.13, by completing the following steps:
      (1) On the fourth physical page (status bar will read *Page 1 Sec 5 4/9*), position the insertion point in the frame that contains *Chapter 1* in the upper right corner of the page. (Depending on the location of the insertion point on this page, the status bar may display *Sec 5* or *Sec 6*.)
      (2) Select *Chapter*, then key **Section**.
   b. Edit the header text by completing the following steps:
      (1) Click View, then Header and Footer.
      (2) At the Header-Section 5 pane, select *DESIGN CUSTOMIZATION*, then key **WORD 97**.
      (3) Click the Page Setup button on the Header and Footer toolbar and change the left margin setting to 2.33 inches.
      (4) Click Close on the Header and Footer toolbar.
   c. On the same page, position the insertion point to the left of *Seven Keys to Creating*, select all the instructional text, including the index, and then press Delete. (*Hint:* Hold down the Shift key, then press Ctrl + End to quickly select all of the remaining text.)
   d. Insert the manual text for Section 1 by completing the following steps:
      (1) With the insertion point located at the left margin below the framed *Section 1* title, select *Normal* from the Style list box on the Formatting toolbar.
      (2) Insert the file named *manual text1.doc* located on your student data disk.
      (3) Select the text just inserted and apply the *Body Text* style.
   e. Format the section title and subtitle by completing the following steps:
      (1) Position the insertion point on any character within the title *Using Word's Letterhead Templates*, then apply the *Chapter Title* style from the Style list box on the Formatting toolbar.
      (2) Position the insertion point on any character within the subtitle, *Using Word's letterhead templates is an easy way for you to establish identity and consistency among both your internal and external business documents.*, then apply the *Chapter Subtitle* style from the Style list box.
   f. Change the first letter of the first paragraph into a drop cap by completing the following steps:
      (1) Position the insertion point to the left of *Word* in the first paragraph.
      (2) Choose Format, then Drop Cap.
      (3) At the Drop Cap dialog box, choose Dropped in the Position section.
      (4) Choose OK to close the dialog box.
   g. Below the first paragraph, select the text *Letter Wizard...* through *Professional Letter*, then apply the *List Bullet 3* style. (Depending on the source of your manual template, the *List Bullet 3* style may include round bullets or square bullets.)

h. Position the insertion point on any character within the following headings, then apply the *Heading 1* style to each heading:

Understanding Template Styles
Using the Letter Wizard
Using the User Information Feature

i. Press Ctrl + End to position the insertion point at the end of the document. The insertion point should be located below the last line of text; if not, press Enter to position the insertion point correctly.

j. Choose Insert, then Break. At the Break dialog box select Next page in the Section Breaks section, then click OK or press Enter.

k. With the insertion point positioned on the first page of Section 2 (displays as *Page 1 Sec 7 7/7* in the Status bar), adjust the header text for this section of the manual by completing the following steps:
   (1) Click View, then Header and Footer.
   (2) With the insertion point positioned within the First Page Header for Section 7, click the Page Setup button on the Header and Footer toolbar.
   (3) Click the Layout tab, then remove the check mark in the Different first page check box in the Headers and Footers section.
   (4) Click OK or press Enter. *Word 97* should now appear as the header text.
   (5) Click Close on the Header and Footer toolbar.

l. With the insertion point positioned on the same page, insert the file *manual text2.doc* located on your student data disk.

m. Select the text just inserted and apply the *Body Text* style.

n. Position the insertion point to the left of the first heading *(Styles)* and create the framed section number by completing the following steps:
   (1) Key **Section** and then press Enter.
   (2) With the insertion point positioned within *Section*, apply the *Part Title* style. (*Section* will then be displayed in a frame in the upper right corner of the page.)
   (3) Position the insertion point at the end of the word *Section*, then press Enter.
   (4) Key **2**. (The *Part Title* style contains an instruction that it should automatically be followed by the *Part Label* style; hence, you do not have to manually apply a style to the section number.)

o. Position the insertion point on any character within the section title, *Styles*, then apply the *Chapter Title* style.

p. Position the insertion point on any character within the subtitle *You can save time... repetitive formatting.*, then apply the *Chapter Subtitle* style.

q. Position the insertion point on any character within the following headings, then apply the *Heading 1* style to each heading. (Note: after applying the style to the first heading, you can press F4 at each heading location to repeat the style.)

Understanding the Relationship Between Styles and Templates
Character and Paragraph Styles
Creating Styles
Applying Styles
Modifying an Existing Style
Removing a Style from Text

r. Position the insertion point to the left of *Documents*, the first word in the first paragraph of Section 2, then repeat steps 3 f(2) through (4) to create a drop cap.

s. Apply bullets to a list of items by completing the following steps:

(1) Find the heading *Creating Styles*. (*Hint:* Use the Document Map feature to move the insertion point to different parts of your document.)
(2) In the text that follows this heading, select the five items that follow *Consider the following when naming a style:*.
(3) Apply the *List Bullet* style. (Depending on the source of your manual template, the *List Bullet* style may include round or square bullets.)

t. Select the following items and apply the *List Number* style (Depending on the source of your manual template, the *List Number* style may either include bolded or unbolded numbers.):
(1) In the *Creating Styles* section, the five steps following *To create a new style from existing text, you would complete the following steps:*.
(2) In the *Creating Styles* section, the ten steps following *To create a new style using the Style dialog box, you would select text if necessary and then complete the following steps:*.
(3) In the *Applying Styles* section, the three steps following *To apply a style to existing text using the Style button on the Formatting toolbar, you would complete the following steps:*.
(4) In the *Applying Styles* section, the four steps following *To apply a style using the Style command from the Format menu, you would complete the following steps:*.
(5) In the *Modifying an Existing Style* section, the six steps following *To modify a style using the Formatting toolbar, you would complete the following steps:*.
(6) In the *Modifying an Existing Style* section, the seven steps following *To modify a style at the Style dialog box, you would complete the following steps:*.

u. In the last sentence of the last paragraph of the *Creating Styles* section, select *avoid making changes to the Normal template*, then apply the *Emphasis* style.

v. Adjust the page numbering so that the first page of the report does not display a page number but is counted as page 1 and the remaining pages are numbered accordingly by completing the following steps:
(1) Position the insertion point on the first page of Section 1 (displays as *Page 1 Sec 6 4/13* in the Status bar. Depending on the location of the insertion point on this page, the Status bar may display *Sec 5* or *Sec 6*.)
(2) Click Insert, then Page Numbers.
(3) Make sure the Position list box displays *Bottom of page (Footer)*.
(4) Click the Alignment list box, then select *Center*.
(5) Make sure the Show number on first page check box is empty.
(6) Click Format, then make sure the Start at list box displays as number 1.
(7) Click OK to close the Page Numbers Format dialog box, then click OK again to close the Page Numbers dialog box.

w. Make the page numbering continuous from Section 1 to Section 2 of the manual by completing the following steps:
(1) Position the insertion point on the first page of Section 2 (*Page 1 Sec 7 7/13* will display in the Status bar).
(2) Click Insert, then Page Numbers.
(3) At the Page Numbers dialog box, click Format, and then select Continue from previous section in the Page numbering section.
(4) Click OK or press Enter.

x. Use Print Preview to check the page numbering in both sections of the report. A page number should not display on the first page of Section 1. Sections 1 and 2 should be numbered consecutively from 1 through 10.

4. Save the manual with the same name, c12ex05, manual.
5. Print and then close c12ex05, manual. (Check with your instructor before printing this document. You may want to postpone printing until the table of contents and index have been created in the next two exercises.)

figure 12.13

Exercise 5 Sample Pages

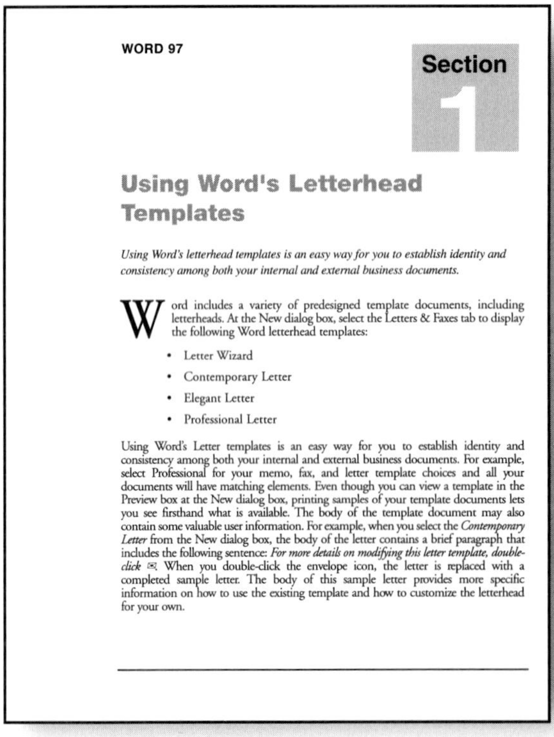

WORD 97

Section 1

Using Word's Letterhead Templates

Using Word's letterhead templates is an easy way for you to establish identity and consistency among both your internal and external business documents.

Word includes a variety of predesigned template documents, including letterheads. At the New dialog box, select the Letters & Faxes tab to display the following Word letterhead templates:

- Letter Wizard
- Contemporary Letter
- Elegant Letter
- Professional Letter

Using Word's Letter templates is an easy way for you to establish identity and consistency among both your internal and external business documents. For example, select Professional for your memo, fax, and letter template choices and all your documents will have matching elements. Even though you can view a template in the Preview box at the New dialog box, printing samples of your template documents lets you see firsthand what is available. The body of the template document may also contain some valuable user information. For example, when you select the *Contemporary Letter* from the New dialog box, the body of the letter contains a brief paragraph that includes the following sentence: *For more details on modifying this letter template, double-click* ✉. When you double-click the envelope icon, the letter is replaced with a completed sample letter. The body of this sample letter provides more specific information on how to use the existing template and how to customize the letterhead for your own.

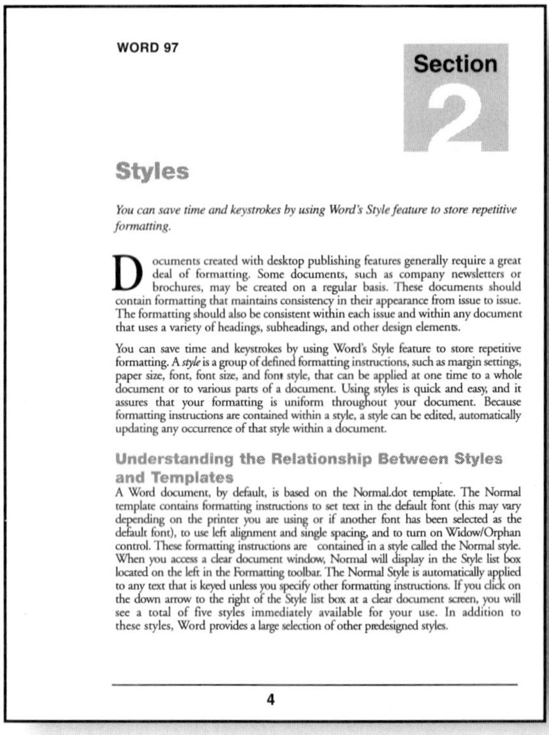

WORD 97

Section 2

Styles

You can save time and keystrokes by using Word's Style feature to store repetitive formatting.

Documents created with desktop publishing features generally require a great deal of formatting. Some documents, such as company newsletters or brochures, may be created on a regular basis. These documents should contain formatting that maintains consistency in their appearance from issue to issue. The formatting should also be consistent within each issue and within any document that uses a variety of headings, subheadings, and other design elements.

You can save time and keystrokes by using Word's Style feature to store repetitive formatting. A *style* is a group of defined formatting instructions, such as margin settings, paper size, font, font size, and font style, that can be applied at one time to a whole document or to various parts of a document. Using styles is quick and easy, and it assures that your formatting is uniform throughout your document. Because formatting instructions are contained within a style, a style can be edited, automatically updating any occurrence of that style within a document.

Understanding the Relationship Between Styles and Templates

A Word document, by default, is based on the Normal.dot template. The Normal template contains formatting instructions to set text in the default font (this may vary depending on the printer you are using or if another font has been selected as the default font), to use left alignment and single spacing, and to turn on Widow/Orphan control. These formatting instructions are contained in a style called the Normal style. When you access a clear document window, Normal will display in the Style list box located on the left in the Formatting toolbar. The Normal Style is automatically applied to any text that is keyed unless you specify other formatting instructions. If you click on the down arrow to the right of the Style list box at a clear document screen, you will see a total of five styles immediately available for your use. In addition to these styles, Word provides a large selection of other predesigned styles.

4

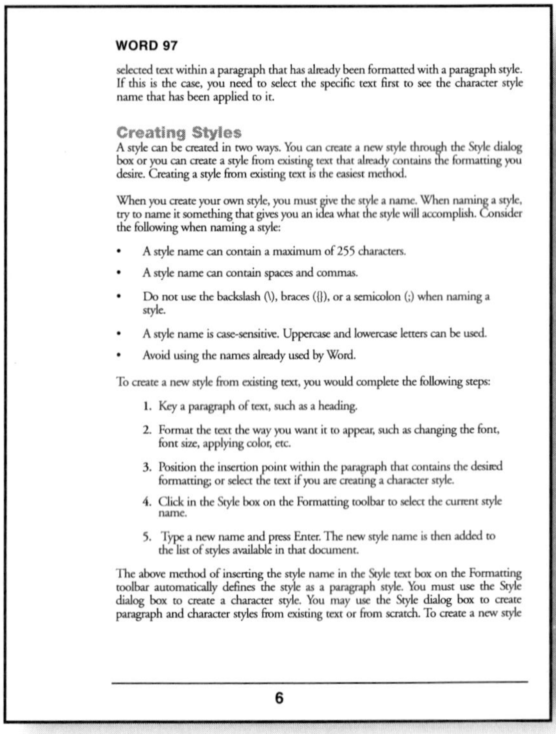

WORD 97

selected text within a paragraph that has already been formatted with a paragraph style. If this is the case, you need to select the specific text first to see the character style name that has been applied to it.

Creating Styles

A style can be created in two ways. You can create a new style through the Style dialog box or you can create a style from existing text that already contains the formatting you desire. Creating a style from existing text is the easiest method.

When you create your own style, you must give the style a name. When naming a style, try to name it something that gives you an idea what the style will accomplish. Consider the following when naming a style:

- A style name can contain a maximum of 255 characters.
- A style name can contain spaces and commas.
- Do not use the backslash (\), braces ({}), or a semicolon (;) when naming a style.
- A style name is case-sensitive. Uppercase and lowercase letters can be used.
- Avoid using the names already used by Word.

To create a new style from existing text, you would complete the following steps:

1. Key a paragraph of text, such as a heading.
2. Format the text the way you want it to appear, such as changing the font, font size, applying color, etc.
3. Position the insertion point within the paragraph that contains the desired formatting; or select the text if you are creating a character style.
4. Click in the Style box on the Formatting toolbar to select the current style name.
5. Type a new name and press Enter. The new style name is then added to the list of styles available in that document.

The above method of inserting the style name in the Style text box on the Formatting toolbar automatically defines the style as a paragraph style. You must use the Style dialog box to create a character style. You may use the Style dialog box to create paragraph and character styles from existing text or from scratch. To create a new style

6

Preparing an Index Using Word

As mentioned earlier, an index lists the topics covered in a publication and the pages where those topics are discussed. Word lets you automate the process of creating an index in a manner similar to that used for creating a table of contents. When creating an index, you mark a word or words that you want included in the index. Creating an index takes some thought and careful planning. You must determine what text will be used as main entries and what text will be used as subentries listed under main entries. In doing this, plan your index around the needs of your readers. Does the index need to be extremely detailed? Do you want to cross-reference index items for your readers? How many levels (nine maximum) do you want to include in the index? An index can include such items as the main idea of a document, the main subject of a chapter or section, variations of a heading or subheading, and abbreviations. Figure 12.14 shows an example of an index. In Word, the items located at the left margin in figure 12.14 are known as main entries. The items indented from the left margin under specific main entries are known as subentries.

DTP POINTERS
An index requires thought and careful planning.

There are two ways to mark text for inclusion in an index. Text can be marked automatically using a concordance file or text can be marked manually. The most efficient way to create an index would be to first create a concordance file to mark text for an index and then manually mark any remaining items that you may have missed.

figure 12.14

Sample Index

INDEX

A
Alignment, 12, 16
ASCII, 22, 24, 35
    word processing, 39
    data processing, 41

B
Backmatter, 120
    page numbering, 123
Balance, 67-69
Banners, 145

C
Callouts, 78
Captions, 156
Color, 192-195
    ink for offset printing, 193
    process color, 195

D
Databases, 124-128
    fields, 124
    records, 124
Directional flow, 70-71

Marking Text Using a Concordance File

The quickest and easiest way to mark text as index entries is to create a *concordance file*. A concordance file is a regular Word document containing a single, two-column table with no text outside the table, as shown in figure 12.15. In the first column of the table, you enter the word(s) you want Word to search for and mark as an index entry. The words listed in this column must be entered exactly as they appear in your document, including capitalization and punctuation. For example, if you want to index the word *software* on one

Concordance File
A file containing words and/or phrases used in marking text for an index.

page and *Software* on another page, you must include them as two separate entries in your concordance file because of the difference in capitalization. In addition, you must list all forms of the text you want Word to search for, such as *copy* and *copying*. In the second column, key the index entry for the text in the first column. If you want the item in the first column to be a main entry in your index, key the item in the second column exactly the way you want it to appear in the index. For example, in figure 12.15, *software* in the first column is to be listed as a main entry in the index as *Software*. If you want the item in the first column to be a subentry of a main entry, key the main entry item in the second column followed by a colon. Then key the subentry item exactly as you want it to appear in your index. For instance, in figure 12.15 CD-ROM is to appear in the index as a subentry of the main entry *Hardware*.

Remember to spellcheck and proofread the concordance file before using it to mark your document.

To mark text for an index using a concordance file you would complete these steps:

1. Open the document containing text you want marked for the index.
2. Click Insert, then Index and Tables, and then select the Index tab.
3. At the Index and Tables dialog box, choose AutoMark.
4. At the Open Index AutoMark File dialog box, select the concordance file name in the Look in: list box.
5. Click Open or press Enter.

Creating a concordance file can be a very tedious process. One suggestion is to open the concordance file and the document to be indexed and then display both documents on the screen at the same time. To see both documents at the same time, click Window, then Arrange All. You can then copy text you want to index into the first column of the concordance file.

Sample Concordance File

Multifunction display	Terminal: multifunction display
voice-activated	Terminal: voice-activated
pointer	Electronic: pointer
copy	Electronic: copy
digital	Optical Disk: digital
erasable	Optical Disk: erasable
voice	Applications: voice
Hardware	Hardware
hard drive	Hardware: hard drive
processor	Hardware: processor
sound board	Hardware: sound board
CD-ROM	Hardware: CD-ROM
software	Software
Software	Software

Marking Text Manually

Even though using a concordance file is a quick and efficient method of creating an index, there may be times when text needs to be marked manually. For instance, a concordance file marks every occurrence of an item listed in the first column, even though you may not want every occurrence marked. To avoid this, the text to be included in the index may need to be marked manually. In addition, manually marking text allows you to add some remaining items to the index that may have been missed in the concordance file.

A selected word or words can be marked for inclusion in an index. To manually mark text for an index, you would complete the following steps:

1. Select the word or words you want included in the index.
2. Click Insert, then Index and Tables, and then select the Index tab.
3. At the Index and Tables dialog box, click Mark Entry.
4. At the Mark Index Entry dialog box, the selected word(s) display in the Main entry text box. If the text is a main entry, leave it as displayed. If the text is a subentry, key the text in the Subentry text box, then key the appropriate main entry in the Main entry text box.
5. Click Mark.
6. Click Close to close the Mark Index Entry dialog box.

When you choose Mark at the Mark Index Entry dialog box, Word automatically turns on the display of nonprinting characters and displays the corresponding index field code to the right of the selected text, as shown in the example in figure 12.16.

The main entry and subentry do not have to be the same as the selected text. You can select text for an index, type the text the way you want it to display in the Main entry or Subentry text box, then choose Mark.

At the Mark Index Entry dialog box, you can apply bold and/or italic formatting to the page numbers that will appear in the index.

The Options section of the Mark Index Entry dialog box contains several options, with Current page as the default. At this setting, the current page number will be listed in the index for the main and/or subentry. If you choose Cross-reference, you would key the text you want to use as a cross-reference for the index entry in the Cross-reference text box. Choose the Mark All button at the Mark Index Entry dialog box to mark the first occurrence of the selected text in each paragraph whose uppercase and lowercase letters exactly match the index entry.

A·template·may·include·several·components,·such·as·styles·{·XE·"Templates:·styles"·},·text,·graphics,·AutoText·entries,·and·macros.·Word·automatically·bases·a·new·document·created·at·a·blank·screen·on·the·*Normal.dot*·template{·XE·"Templates:·normal.dot·template"·}.·This·template·initially·contains·five·styles,·including·one·called·the·*Normal*·style{·XE·"Styles:·normal·style"·}.·The·Normal·style·contains·formatting·instructions·to·

figure 12.16

Sample of Index Entry Field Codes

Compiling an Index

After all entries have been marked for the index, establish the location of the index in the document. An index should appear at the end of a document, generally on a page by itself. To establish the index location, position the insertion point at the end of the document, then insert a page break. With the insertion point positioned below the page break, key **Index** centered and bolded, then press the Enter key. With the insertion point positioned at the left margin, you are now ready to compile the index.

To compile an index you would complete the following steps:

1. Click the Show/Hide ¶ button on the Standard toolbar to turn off the display of nonprinting characters. (If index entry field codes are displayed, page numbering in the index may be incorrect.)
2. Click Insert, then Index and Tables, and then select the Index tab.
3. Select the desired index formatting, such as indented subentries, predesigned index formats, page number alignment, number of columns, and tab leaders.
4. Click OK or press Enter.

Word collects the marked index entries, sorts them alphabetically, references their page numbers, finds and removes duplicate entries from the same page, and then displays the index in the document at the location of the insertion point with the formatting selected at the Index and Tables dialog box.

Changing and Deleting Index Entries

Word displays index entries as *XE* field codes, as illustrated in figure 12.16. To change or delete an index entry field, the display of nonprinting characters must be turned on (click the Show/Hide ¶ button on the Standard toolbar) to make the fields visible. To change an index entry, simply edit or format the text within the quotation marks. To delete an index entry field, select the entire index entry field, including the brackets {}, and then press the Delete key.

Updating or Replacing an Index

If you make changes to a document after inserting an index, insert or delete the desired entries in the concordance file and then save the concordance file with the changes. Repeat the original steps to mark the text for an index using a concordance file. As an alternative, you can manually mark or remark any new or revised entries in your document. You can then either update the existing index or replace the index with a new one. To update an index, position the insertion point anywhere within the index (displays with a gray background), then press F9. Any text or formatting you added to the finished index is lost.

Replace an index in the same manner as you would replace a table of contents. To do this, position the insertion point anywhere within the current index (index displays with a gray background), then choose Insert, then Index and Tables. At the Index and Tables dialog box, make sure the Index tab is selected, then choose OK or press Enter. At the prompt asking if you want to replace the existing index, choose Yes.

Deleting an Index

An index that has been compiled in a document can be deleted. To delete an index, select the entire index using either the mouse or the keyboard, then press the Delete key.

Creating a Concordance File

1. At a clear document screen, create a concordance file with the text shown in figure 12.17, for the manual created in exercise 5, by completing the following steps:
   a. Create a two-column table by completing the following steps:
      (1) Click Table, then Insert Table.
      (2) At the Insert Table dialog box, choose OK to accept the default of two columns and two rows.
   b. Key the text in each cell as shown in figure 12.17. Press the Tab key in the last cell of the table to create new rows as you need them. Pay careful attention to capitalization and punctuation.
2. Save the concordance file and name it c12ex06, concordance.
3. Close c12ex06, concordance.

Templates	Templates
letterhead	Templates: letterhead
Styles	Styles
styles	Templates: styles
Normal template	Templates: normal.dot template
Normal style	Styles: normal style
Letter Wizard	Letter Wizard
Letter Wizard	Templates: letter wizard
User Information	User Information
User Information	Letter Wizard: user information
paragraph style	Paragraph Style
paragraph style	Styles: paragraph style
character style	Character Style
character style	Styles: character style
Creating a style	Styles: creating styles
Style dialog box	Styles: style dialog box
naming a style	Styles: naming styles
base style	Styles: base style
Applying Styles	Styles: applying styles
Style command	Styles: style command
Modifying an Existing Style	Styles: modifying styles
Removing a Style from Text	Styles: removing styles

In exercise 7, you will use the concordance file created in exercise 6 to compile an index for the *Word 97 Desktop Training Manual* created in previous exercises.

exercise 7

Creating an Index Using a Concordance File

1. Open c12ex05, manual.
2. Use Save As and name the document c12ex07, index.
3. Create an index for the *Word 97 Desktop Training Manual* using a concordance file, as shown in figure 12.18, by completing the following steps:
   a. Mark text as index entries by completing the following steps:
      (1) Position the insertion point anywhere within the document
      (2) Click Insert, then Index and Tables, and then click the Index tab.
      (3) Click AutoMark.
      (4) At the Open Index AutoMark File dialog box, display the folder containing *c12ex06, concordance* in the Look in: list box.
      (5) Select *c12ex06, concordance*, then choose Open. (If you scroll through your document, you will see that Word has automatically inserted XE index entry field codes in your document that correspond to the entries in the concordance file. These codes will not print.)
   b. Prepare a separate page for the index by completing the following steps:
      (1) Press Ctrl + End to position the insertion point at the end of the document.
      (2) Press Ctrl + Enter to insert a page break.
      (3) Key **Index**, then press Enter.
      (4) Position the insertion point anywhere within the *Index* heading, then apply the *Section Label* heading.
   c. Compile the index by completing the following steps:
      (1) Click the Show/Hide ¶ button on the Standard toolbar to turn off the display of nonprinting characters. (This will hide the index entry field codes. This step is necessary because the index entry fields take up space in the document, having an effect on page breaks and the location of specific text. As a result, when you instruct Word to build an index, some incorrect page numbers may be listed in the index.)
      (2) Position the insertion point at the left margin below the *Index* heading, click Insert, then Index and Tables, and then select the Index tab.
      (3) In the Formats section, make sure *From Template* is selected.
      (4) Click OK to compile the index. (The index will display in a two-column format with a gray background.)
   d. Position the insertion point to the left of the first indexed item, *Character Style*, then change the column format to one column by clicking Format, then Columns, and then change the number of columns to one. (The two column formatting is a result of a column formatting instruction in the original template.)
   e. Check the index displayed on the screen (or print a hard copy of the index page) for all entries listed in figure 12.17. If any entries are missing, complete the following steps:
      (1) Open *c12ex06, concordance* and make any necessary revisions.
      (2) Save and then close c12ex06, concordance.
      (3) With the compiled index displayed on the screen, repeat steps 3 a(1) through (5) to re-mark the text for index entries.

(4) Position the insertion point anywhere within the index (displays with a gray background), then press F9 to update the index.

4. Save the document with the same name, c12ex07, index.
5. With the insertion point positioned on the Index page, display the Print dialog box, then select Current Page to print the Index page.
6. Close c12ex07, index.

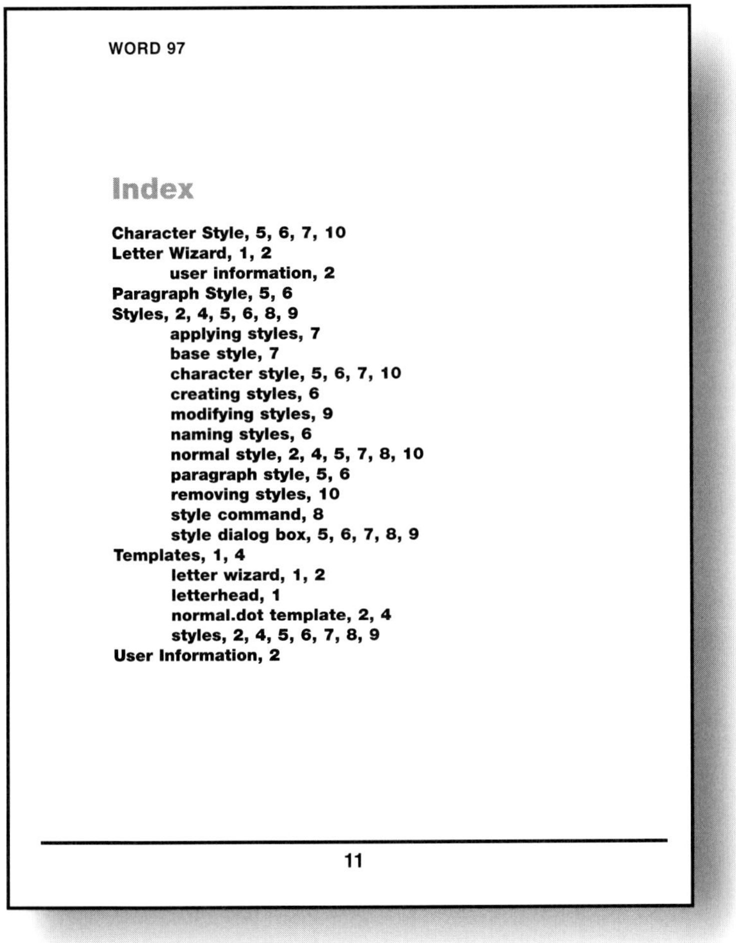

WORD 97

Index

Character Style, 5, 6, 7, 10
Letter Wizard, 1, 2
    user information, 2
Paragraph Style, 5, 6
Styles, 2, 4, 5, 6, 8, 9
    applying styles, 7
    base style, 7
    character style, 5, 6, 7, 10
    creating styles, 6
    modifying styles, 9
    naming styles, 6
    normal style, 2, 4, 5, 7, 8, 10
    paragraph style, 5, 6
    removing styles, 10
    style command, 8
    style dialog box, 5, 6, 7, 8, 9
Templates, 1, 4
    letter wizard, 1, 2
    letterhead, 1
    normal.dot template, 2, 4
    styles, 2, 4, 5, 6, 7, 8, 9
User Information, 2

11

figure 12.18

In exercise 8, you will create a table of contents for the *Word 97 Desktop Training Manual*. As part of the original Manual template, a table of contents already occupies the third physical page of the manual created in exercises 4 through 7. The original table of contents needs to be deleted before a new table of contents can be compiled. The table of contents will be built from a customized style list that designates the *Chapter Title* style as a level one table of contents heading, the *Heading 1* style as a level two heading, and the *Heading 2* style as a level three heading. After the table of contents is compiled, you will manually insert section headings, and you will modify the *Heading 2* style to include a left indent formatting instruction. Since a table of contents page is usually numbered using lowercase Roman numerals, you will adjust the page numbering to display and print a Roman numeral *i* at the bottom of the table of contents page.

exercise 8

Compiling a Table of Contents for a Manual

1. Open c12ex07, index.
2. Use Save As and name the document c12ex08, table of contents.
3. Create a table of contents for the *Word 97 Desktop Training Guide* as displayed in figure 12.19 by completing the following steps:
   a. Prepare the table of contents page as follows:
      (1) Click the Show/Hide ¶ button on the Standard toolbar to turn on the display of nonprinting characters.
      (2) Display the page titled *Table of Contents* (displays as *Page i Sec 3 3/14* in the Status bar). Under the *Table of Contents* title, position the insertion point to the left of *Introduction*.
      (3) From this point forward, select all the text on this table of contents page. Do not include the Section Break (Next Page) in the selection.
      (4) Press the Delete key.
   b. With the insertion point positioned below the heading at the left margin to the left of the Section Break, compile the table of contents by completing the following steps:
      (1) Turn off the display of nonprinting characters by clicking the Show/Hide ¶ button on the Standard toolbar.
      (2) Click Insert, then Index and Tables, and then select the Table of Contents tab.
      (3) Make sure *From Template* is selected in the Formats list box.
      (4) Click Options.
      (5) At the Table of Contents Options dialog box, make sure there is a check mark in the Styles check box in the Build table of contents from styles section.
      (6) Make sure there is no check mark in the Table entry fields check box.
      (7) In the Available Styles list box, use the vertical scroll bar to display the *Chapter Title* style name.
      (8) Key **1** as the level in the *Chapter Title* style's corresponding TOC level text box.
      (9) Use the vertical scroll bar to display the *Heading 1* style name.
      (10) Select any existing number in the *Heading 1* style's corresponding TOC level text box, then key **2**.
      (11) Display the *Heading 2* style name.
      (12) Select any existing number in the *Heading 2* style's corresponding TOC level text box, then key **3**.
      (13) Display the *Heading 3* style name.
      (14) Delete the number in *Heading 3* style's corresponding TOC level text box.
      (15) Scroll through the remaining available styles and make sure the TOC level text boxes are empty for all styles you do not want to be included.
      (16) Click OK to close the Table of Contents Options dialog box, then click OK again to close the Index and Tables dialog box. The table of contents will display with a gray background.
   c. Adjust the page numbering in the manual to accommodate the table of contents by completing the following steps:

(1) With the insertion point positioned anywhere in the Table of Contents page, click Insert, then Page Numbers.
(2) At the Page Numbers dialog box, make sure *Bottom of page (Footer)* displays in the Position list box and *Center* displays in the Alignment list box.
(3) Click Format, then make sure *i, ii, iii . . .* displays in the Number format list box.
(4) Change the Start at option to *iii*.
(5) Click OK to close the Page Number Format dialog box and click OK again to close the Page Numbers dialog box.

d. Scroll to the bottom of the table of contents page. The page number should display as *iii*.
e. Scroll through the rest of your document to check the page numbering. The first page of the report should be counted as number *1*, but a number will not display. The second page of the report should display with a number *2* and so on.
f. Check the table of contents items and make sure the correct items and corresponding page numbers are being displayed. If any of the page numbers referenced are incorrect, turn off the display of nonprinting characters, then update the page numbers by pressing F9.
g. Modify the *TOC 2* style so that all items at this level are indented by completing the following steps:
(1) Click Format, then Style.
(2) At the Styles dialog box, select *TOC 2* from the Styles list box.
(3) Click Modify.
(4) At the Modify Style dialog box, choose Format.
(5) From the Format drop-down list, choose Paragraph, and then select the Indents and Spacing tab.
(6) In the Indentation section, display or key **0.1** in the Left text box.
(7) Click OK to close the Paragraph dialog box.
(8) Click OK to close the Modify Style dialog box.
(9) Click Close to close the Style dialog box. (Any table of contents item formatted by the *TOC 2* style should now be indented.)

h. Include section titles in the table of contents by completing the following steps:
(1) Position the insertion point to the left of the first table of contents entry, *Using Word's Letterhead Templates*.
(2) Key **section 1**, then press Enter.
(3) Position the insertion point anywhere within *section 1*, then apply the *Section Heading* style.
(4) Position the insertion point to the left of the word *Styles*.
(5) Key **section 2**, then press Enter.
(6) Position the insertion point anywhere within *section 2*, then apply the *Section Heading* style.

4. Save the document with the same name, c12ex08, table of contents.
5. Print c12ex08, table of contents. (Check with your instructor about printng the whole manual or just printing the table of contents page. If you try to print the table of contents page and the page numbers change to zero on the screen, position the insertion point within the table and press F9 to update the page numbers.)
6. Close c12ex08, table of contents.

Table of Contents

iii

Binding Publications

The final finishing process for a publication is binding. A wide variety of bindings can be used. Some can be finished in the office and others can be finished with more sophisticated options at commercial binders. In the office, binding can include stapling the publication or three-hole punching the paper for use in a ring notebook or report cover. In addition, some offices may have equipment that can bind pages with a plastic spiral binding.

chapter summary

- Structured publications such as reports, manuals, and booklets are text-intensive, multipage documents containing repeating elements, such as headers or footers, and consistently styled title and text pages.
- Structured publications can contain all or some of the following elements: a front cover; front matter such as a title page, copyright page, preface, and table of contents; body text; back matter such as an appendix, bibliography, glossary, and index; and a back cover.
- Word provides three report templates—Contemporary, Elegant, and Professional.
- When creating a table of contents in Word, two basic steps are completed: the title, headings, and subheadings are marked automatically or manually in the document then the table of contents is compiled.
- When creating an index in Word, two basic steps are completed: the words or phrases are marked automatically or manually as main entries or subentries, then the index is compiled.
- Words or phrases that appear frequently in a document can be entered into a Word table and saved as a concordance file. This file is then used when creating the index.
- When including a table of contents or index, adjust page numbering in your document to accommodate these items.
- A table of contents and an index compiled by Word are considered fields and can be updated.

commands review

	Mouse/Keyboard
New dialog box to access a template	File, New, select desired tab
Insert File dialog box	Insert, File
Format an AutoShape	Format, AutoShape
Word Picture	Double-click the picture
Borders and Shading dialog box	Format, Borders and Shading
Index and Tables dialog box	Insert, Index and Tables
Table of Contents Options dialog box	Insert, Index and Tables, Table of Contents tab, Options
Mark Table of Contents dialog box	Alt + Shift + O
Update Table of Contents dialog box	Position insertion point within table, press F9
Page Numbers dialog box	Insert, Page Numbers
Insert Picture dialog box	Insert, Picture, From File or Clip Art
Headers and Footers dialog box	View, Header and Footer
Drop Cap dialog box	Format, Drop Cap
Mark Index dialog box	Insert, Index and Tables, Index tab, Mark Entry
Insert a table	Table, Insert Table

check your understanding

Terms: Match the terms with the correct definitions by writing the letter of the term on the blank line in front of the correct definition.

- **A** Appendix
- **B** Bibliography
- **C** Select Browse Object
- **D** Glossary
- **E** Copyright page
- **F** Document Map
- **G** Preface
- **H** Table of Contents
- **I** Title page
- **J** Index

_____ 1. A statement by the author about the publication that may include acknowledgments.

_____ 2. Information that is not essential to the text but may help clarify the information presented.

_____ 3. The full title of the publication (including any subtitles) and the full name of the author, editor, and publisher.

_____ 4. A set of definitions for specialized terms used in the publication.

_____ 5. A list of topics contained in the publication with the pages on which those topics are discussed.

_____ 6. A list of sources or suggestions for further reading.

_____ 7. A list of the names of each chapter or section and the page number on which each begins.

_____ 8. This page generally includes where the publication is published, Library of Congress Cataloging-in-Publication (CIP) data, ISBN number, copyright dates, and copyright permissions.

_____ 9. Use this feature to display an outline of any document headings formatted with Word's built-in heading styles, *Heading 1* through *Heading 9*.

_____ 10. To move to different parts of your document, such as pages, headings, footnotes, graphics, or tables, click this button on the vertical scroll bar.

Concepts: Write your answers to the following questions in the space provided.

1. Name the three report templates provided by Word.

2. By default, what styles does Word use to automatically compile a table of contents?

3. Name the file that can be created that contains words or phrases in a Word table to be included in an index.

4. Explain the steps necessary to update or replace a table of contents or an index.

5. An index appears at this location in a publication.

6. Name the two basic steps to follow when creating a table of contents or an index for a document using Word.

skill assessments

Assessment 1

1. At a clear editing window, prepare a report using the *Elegant Report* template. You may want to print and read the report instructional text first. You may also want to note on the hard copy the style names used.
2. Format the cover page according to the following specifications:
   a. Click in the prompt CLICK **HERE** AND TYPE COMPANY NAME and key **Communications Solutions, Inc.** (An All Caps formatting instruction is included in the style.)
   b. Individually select the title and subtitle, and then replace with the following:

      Title: Alternative Services
      Subtitle: Prepared by: (Your name here) (press Shift + Enter)
      Current date

   c. Click File, Page Setup, then select the Layout tab. Click the Different odd and even check box in the Headers and Footers section to remove the check mark.
   d. Position the insertion point to the left of the continuous section break and to the right of the paragraph mark, then press delete two times. (This will delete both the section break and the page break.)
   e. Access the Break dialog box, then insert a Next Page section break. (This step is necessary to accommodate the necessary page numbering formatting in this report.)

3. Insert and customize a graphic image on the cover page by completing the following steps:
   a. On the cover page, position the insertion point to the left of the Next Page section break.
   b. Access the Insert Picture dialog box and insert the *Arrows 7.wmf* picture located in the *Clipart|Popular* folder.
   c. Size and position the arrow image according to the following specifications:
      (1) Change the height of the picture to 3.17 inches and the width to 4.25 inches.
      (2) Change the position of the picture to 2.2 inches from the left edge of the page and the vertical position to 5.7 inches from the top edge of the page. (Remember to change the "From" options first.)
   d. Change the color of the arrow image by completing the following steps:
      (1) Double-click the image to access Word Picture.
      (2) Change the Zoom viewing mode to 50%.
      (3) Click the shadow section (displays as a dark green) of the arrow image. Sizing handles should display on the dotted border surrounding the picture.
      (4) Click the down arrow to the right of the Fill button on the Drawing toolbar, then change the color to Gray-25% in the fourth row, eighth column.
      (5) Click the main section (displays as a bright green) of the arrow image. Sizing handles should display inside the dotted border surrounding the picture.
      (6) Click the down arrow to the right of the Fill button on the Drawing toolbar, then change the color to Gray-40% in the third row, eighth column.
      (7) Click File, then Close & Return to Document #. (The number may vary.)
   e. Scroll to the bottom of the cover page, then click the number 1 that is displayed at the bottom of the page. Click the frame border to select it, then press Delete.
4. Create the body of the report according to the following specifications:
   a. On the first page of the report (Status bar will display *Page 1 Sec 2 2/3*), select the title *PROPOSAL AND MARKETING PLAN,* then key **Teleports**.
   b. Delete *Blue Sky's Best Opportunity For East Region Expansion*.
   c. Select *How To Use This Report Template* and key **A "One-Stop Shopping" Telecommunications Solution**.
   d. Delete the text in the report from the paragraph that begins *Change the information...* to the end of the document.
   e. Press Enter to place the insertion point below the heading.
   f. Insert the file named *chapter1 text.doc* located on your student data disk into the report.
   g. Select the text just inserted and apply the *Body Text* style.

h. Apply the *Heading 2* style to the following headings:

Evolution of Teleports
Types of Teleports
Teleport Services

i. Apply the *List Bullet* style to the following items:
   (1) At the end of the first paragraph, the five items following *There are a number of reasons for unacceptable service:.*
   (2) In the *Types of Teleports* section, the two items following *There are two types of teleports:.*
   (3) In the *Teleport Services* section, the six items following *Here are some examples of the services provided by teleports:.*

j. Move the insertion point to the end of the document, then press Enter.

k. Click Insert, then Break. Choose Next page in the Section breaks section.

l. With the insertion point positioned at the top of page 4 (Status bar displays *Page 1 Sec 3 4/4*), key **Integrated Services Digital Network** as the title, then press Enter.

m. Apply the *Title* style to *Integrated Services Digital Network*.

n. Position the insertion point at the left margin below the title, key **An Alternative Source for Transmitting Communications**, then press Enter.

o. Apply the *Heading 1* style to the heading keyed in step 4n.

p. Position the insertion point below the heading, then insert the file named *chapter2 text.doc* located on your student data disk into the report.

q. Select the text just inserted and apply the *Body Text* style.

r. Apply the *Heading 2* style to the following headings:

ISDN Services
ISDN Operations
ISDN Benefits

s. In the *ISDN Benefits* section, apply the *List Bullet* style to the seven items following *ISDN implementation has many potential benefits:.*

5. Adjust the page numbering so that the first page of the report text does not display a page number but is counted as page 1 (rather than page 2, as it is now) by completing the following steps:
   a. Position the insertion point on the first page of the report text (titled *TELEPORTS*; Status bar will display *Page 1 Sec 2 2/5*), then click Insert, then Page Numbers.
   b. Make sure the Position list box displays *Bottom of page (Footer)*.
   c. Click the Alignment list box, then select *Center*.
   d. Make sure the Show number on first page check box is empty.
   e. Click Format, then make sure the Start at list box displays as number one.
   f. Click OK to close the Page Number Format dialog box, then click OK again to close the Page Numbers dialog box.

6. Make the page numbering continuous from the first section (*TELEPORTS*) of the report to the second section (*INTEGRATED SERVICES DIGITAL NETWORK*) by completing the following steps:

a. Position the insertion point on the fourth page (Status bar displays as *Page 1 Sec 3 4/5*) of the report.
b. Click Insert, then Page Numbers.
c. Click in the Show number on first page check box to insert a checkmark.
d. Click Format and then click Continue from previous section in the Page numbering section of the Page Number Format dialog box.
e. Click OK to close the Page Number Format dialog box and then click OK again to close the Page Numbers dialog box.

7. Create a table of contents according to the following specifications:
   a. Position the insertion point at the top of the second page to the left of the title *TELEPORTS*, then insert a Next Page section break to create a separate page for the table of contents between the cover page and the first page of the report.
   b. With the insertion point located at the beginning of the blank page (Status bar displays *Page 1 Sec 2 2/6*), change the style to Normal.
   c. Title the page *Table of Contents*, then press Enter two times. (The *Title* style will be applied to this heading *after* the table of contents is compiled to eliminate it from being included as an entry in the table of contents.)
   d. Mark the text for a table of contents using a customized style list as follows:
      (1) Use the *Title* style as a first-level table of contents heading.
      (2) Use the *Heading 1* style as a second-level table of contents heading.
      (3) Use the *Heading 2* style as a third level table of contents heading.
      (4) Remove *Heading 3* from the table of contents level listing.
      (5) At the Table of Contents Options dialog box, remember to delete any style names from the list of available styles that are not to be used as table of contents entries.
   e. Compile the table of contents using *Formal* as the table of contents format.
   f. Select the page numbers in each item formatted by the *TOC 3* style, then remove the italics. (*Hint:* Click to the left of each number to position the insertion point, then select the number. If a hand symbol displays as you attempt to select each of these numbers and you click the left mouse button, the insertion point will move to the referenced location.)
   g. Select the table of contents, then change the font to 11-point Garamond.
   h. Check the page numbers listed in the table of contents for accuracy; update the table of contents if necessary.
8. On the table of contents page, change the page numbering format to Roman numerals and the starting number to *ii* by completing the following steps:
   a. With the insertion point positioned on the table of contents page, click Insert, then Page Numbers.
   b. In the Page Numbers dialog box, click in the Show number on first page check box to insert a checkmark.

c. Click Format, then change the Number format to Roman numerals (*i, ii, iii, …*).
d. Click Continue from previous section in the Page numbering section.
e. Click OK to close the Page Number Format dialog box and then click OK again to close the Page Numbers dialog box. (The Roman numeral will display in small caps (*II*) since the footer style includes a small caps formatting instruction.)

9. Apply the *Title* style to the table of contents heading.
10. Check all page numbering in the document; make adjustments if necessary.
11. Save the report and name it c12sa01, communications report.
12. Print and then close c12sa01, communications report.

Optional: Write a one-paragraph summary of the report.

Assessment 2

1. Prepare a concordance file as illustrated in the two-column table (figure 12.20) below to be used as a concordance file in creating an index for the report created in assessment 1. Pay careful attention to capitalization and punctuation. When keying the words in the first column, Word may automatically capitalize the first letter of the word. To turn this feature off, click Tools, then AutoCorrect. Click in the Capitalize first letter of sentences check box to remove the check mark. Click OK.

voice	Communication: voice
data	Communication: data
video	Communication: video
technology	Communication: technology
market potential	Communication: market potential
fiber optic	Communication: fiber optic
coaxial cable	Communication: coaxial cable
microwave	Communication: microwave
satellite	Communication: satellite
common	Carrier: common
value-added	Carrier: value-added
facility-based	Teleports: facility-based
real estate-based	Teleports: real estate-based
digital data reception	Transmission: digital data reception
encryption	Transmission: encryption
protocol	Transmission: protocol
conversion	Transmission: conversion
analog	Transmission: analog
digital	Transmission: digital
services	Integrated: services
benefits	Transmission: benefits

2. Save the file and name it c12sa02, concordance.
3. Close c12sa02, concordance.
4. Open c12sa01, communications report and save as c12sa02, index.
5. Create an index by completing the following steps:
   a. Move the insertion point to the end of the document, then insert a page break. (A section break is not necessary here.)
   b. Title the page *Index,* press Enter two times, and then apply the *Title* style to the index title.
   c. Position the insertion point below the title, then mark the text to be included in the index using the concordance file, c12sa02, concordance.doc.
   d. Turn off the display of nonprinting characters (Show/Hide ¶ button), then position the insertion point below the Index heading.
   e. Instruct Word to build the index using *Simple* as the formatting for the index.
   f. Position the insertion point to the left of the first indexed item, then change the column formatting to one column.
6. Update the table of contents to include the index just created by completing the following steps:
   a. Position the insertion point within the table of contents (should display with a gray background).
   b. Press F9 (Update Field key) to update the field.
   c. At the Update Table of Contents dialog box, choose Update entire table, then click OK.
   d. Select and delete the entire line containing the Table of Contents entry. (*Hint:* Position the insertion point at the end of the line, then press Backspace until the entire entry is deleted.)
   e. In the table of contents, remove italic formatting from any page number formatted with the *TOC 3* style.
7. Save the document again with the same name, c12sa02, index.
8. Print c12sa02, index. (Check with your instructor to see if you should print the entire document or just the index and table of contents pages.)

Assessment 3

1. At a clear document screen, format body text for a Bicycle Helmet Program Resources manual by completing the following steps:
   a. Open *program manual text.doc* located on your student data disk. (The text in this file is divided into three sections. Each section contains a Word table, providing a side-by-side column layout for this manual.)
   b. Save the document with Save As and name it c12sa03, program manual.
2. Select all the text in the third column in each table and change the font to 11-point Garamond. (Formatting text within the tables with the table gridlines displayed may be easier. Click Table, then Show Gridlines.)
3. Format the section titles by completing the following steps:
   a. Format the first section title, *Section 1: Most Commonly Asked Questions,* in 16-point Arial Bold, then create a style named *Section Heading*

from this formatting. (This could also be done with Format Painter. However, using styles for the formatting makes compiling a table of contents for the document easier.)

   b. Apply the *Section Heading* style to the remaining section titles.

4. Format the headings in the left column by completing the following steps:
   a. Format the first heading in the left column, *1. What do ANSI, ASTM, and Snell mean?*, in 14-point Arial Bold, then create a style named *Side Heading* from this formatting.
   b. Apply the *Side heading* style to the remaining headings in the left column.
   c. Remove the hanging indent paragraph formatting from the side headings on pages 4 and 5.
5. Create a footer that prints at the bottom of each page, with the following specifications:
   a. Position the insertion point on the first page, then display the Footer pane.
   b. At the Footer pane, create a single horizontal line with a weight of 4½ points. (*Hint:* Use the Borders and Shading feature.)
   c. Position the insertion point below the line, change the font to 10-point Arial Bold, then key BICYCLE HELMET PROGRAM RESOURCES.
   d. Set a right tab to align text with the right side of the horizontal line.
   e. Press Tab, key **Page**, press the space bar once, then click the Insert Page Number button on the Header and Footer toolbar.
   f. Select the page number and change the font size to 10-point Arial Bold.
   g. Click the Page Setup button on the Header and Footer toolbar, then click the Layout tab. In the Headers and Footers section, click the Different first page check box to insert a checkmark, then click OK.
   h. When the First Page Footer-Section 1 pane displays, leave it blank to eliminate the page number on the first page, then click Close on the Header and Footer toolbar.
   i. Use Print Preview to check the appearance of the footers. If any footers are not visible or only partially visible, access the Page Setup dialog box, then click the Margins tab. In the From edge section, change the Footer distance from the edge of the paper to 0.7 inches. Change this setting in each section of the document or select the whole document first and then change this setting.
   j. Check the page numbering throughout the whole document. Make sure page numbering is continuous from one section to another.
6. Create a header that prints a 2¼-point horizontal line on all pages except the first page of section 1. (*Hint:* Leave the First Page Header-Section 1 blank, then click Show Next on the Header and Footer toolbar. Create the header at the Header-Section 1 pane.)
7. Check page breaks in the documents for any widow and orphans and, if necessary, make adjustments.
8. Save the document with the same name, c12sa03, program manual.
9. Create a table of contents according to the following specifications:
   a. Create a separate page for the table of contents.
   b. Change the style to *Normal*, key **TABLE OF CONTENTS** as the title, and then press Enter two times. (The title will be formatted later.)

c. Mark the text for a table of contents according to the following specifications:
   (1) Use the *Section Heading* style as a level-one table of contents heading.
   (2) Use the *Side Heading* style as a level-two table of contents heading.
   (3) Delete any other TOC level numbers that may exist in the Available styles list at the Table of Contents Options dialog box.

d. Compile the table of contents using *Classic* as the table of contents formatting.

e. Apply the *Section Heading* style to the table of contents heading.

f. Adjust page numbering so that the table of contents is numbered with Roman numerals starting with *ii*.

g. Make sure the remaining page numbering is correct.

10. Save the document again with the same name, c12sa03, program manual.
11. Print and then close c12sa03.

Optional: Write a notice to all students at your local elementary school telling them why wearing a bicycle helmet is important.

Assessment 4

1. Create a cover for the Bicycle Helmet Program Resources manual prepared in assessment 3 according to the following specifications:
   a. Use any of the Ride Safe logo graphics included on your student data disk or any appropriate graphic image that you may have available to you.
   b. Create thumbnail sketches to formulate your design and layout.
   c. Title the manual **BICYCLE HELMET PROGRAM RESOURCES**.
   d. You decide on an appropriate font, font size, and font style. (*Hint:* Remember to be consistent with the elements that you have already established in the manual.)
   e. You may incorporate WordArt, graphic lines, color, rotated text, reverse text, borders and shading, text boxes, AutoShapes, etc.
2. Save the document and name it c12sa04, cover.
3. Print and then close c12sa04, cover.
4. Evaluate your booklet by using the Document Evaluation Checklist found on your student data disk.

creative activity

Find two examples of a report, manual, booklet, etc. Use the Document Evaluation Checklist located on your student data disk to evaluate the two examples. Hand in the checklists along with a list of suggested improvements for each of the documents.

Unit three

PERFORMANCE ASSESSMENTS

Assessment one

At a clear document window, create a one-page newsletter by completing the following instructions. This newsletter may be a holiday, personal, or family newsletter that you would like to duplicate and mail to your friends or relatives. Write four or five short paragraphs describing the highlights of this year and your expectations for next year. You may include items about your accomplishments, awards, talents, skills, hobbies, or any vacations you may have taken. Use the thesaurus and spelling features to assist you. Also, be sure to create your own styles, use any appropriate built-in styles, or use the Format Painter to assist you in repetitive formatting.

1. Create a thumbnail sketch of your newsletter.
2. Incorporate the following in your newsletter:
   a. Use appropriate typefaces and type sizes for all of the elements in your newsletter.
   b. Use em spaces for any indented text.
   c. The nameplate should include your last name (e.g., Smith Family Newsletter).
   d. Create a subtitle.
   e. Create a folio.
   f. Use appropriate column numbers and widths.
   g. Apply the desktop publishing concepts of focus, balance, proportion, contrast, directional flow, and consistency to your newsletter design and layout.
   h. Use kerning and character spacing.
   i. Use appropriate leading (paragraph spacing) before and after the headline and all subheads.
   j. Use a graphic, symbol, WordArt object, clip art, or a scanned picture. (A photograph would add a nice personal touch!)
   k. Be creative.
3. Save the newsletter and name it u03pa01, newsletter.
4. After completing u03pa01, newsletter, exchange newsletters in the classroom and evaluate them using the Document Evaluation Checklist

(document evaluation checklist.doc). Write any additional comments or suggestions, discussing weaknesses and strengths, on the bottom of the second page of the evaluation form.

Optional: Write and create a newsletter about the program in your major area of study. Research your program and include course descriptions, course learning objectives, certificate and degree options, prerequisites, etc. Relate your program's course of study to current trends in business.

Assessment two

In chapter 11, skill assessment 2, you redesigned the first page of an accounting firm's newsletter. In this assessment, you will create a two-page newsletter using the same text from your student data disk.

1. At a clear document window, open *redesign text.doc*, located on your student data disk.
2. Save the document with Save As and name it u03pa02, disclosures.
3. Redesign *both* pages of the newsletter and include the following items:
   a. Nameplate
   b. Folio
   c. Heading and subheading styles
   d. Header and footer
   e. Table of contents
   f. Sidebar
   g. Pull quote
   h. Graphic image with caption
   i. Spot color
   j. A kicker, end signs, jump lines, graphic images, etc., if desired or needed for copy fitting.
   k. Tracking, leading (paragraph spacing), etc., to set the body copy attractively on the page.
   l. Any design elements necessary to achieve consistency and unity between the two pages.
4. When completed, save the document again with the same name (u03pa02, disclosures).
5. Print and then close u03pa02, disclosures. (Ask your instructor about printing each page separately or printing the pages back to back.)
6. Evaluate your own work using the Document Evaluation Checklist *(document evaluation checklist.doc.)* located on your student data disk. Revise your document if any areas need improvement.

Assessment three

1. At a clear document window, create a cover for your portfolio with the following specifications:
   a. Create a thumbnail sketch of your cover.
   b. Use at least one graphic element such as WordArt, a watermark, ruled lines, a graphic image, or a scanned image.

   c. Consider balance, focus, contrast, directional flow, and proportion when creating the cover.
2. Save the completed cover and name it u03pa03, cover.
3. Print and then close u03pa03, cover.

Optional: Create a new cover for your portfolio. Assume you are applying for a government position or for a job in a comedy gallery and try to convey a tone that is appropriate to your purpose.

Assessment four

1. Prepare a benefits manual for Grant County Medical using the document *benefits manual.doc* that is located on your student data disk. Format the manual with the following specifications:
   a. Set the body text in a serif typeface and in a point size appropriate for a text-intensive document.
   b. Set the section headings and side headings in a sans serif typeface in a size larger than the body text.
   c. Create styles for the section headings and side headings.
   d. Create appropriate headers and/or footers.
   e. Include page numbering (this can be part of a header or footer).
   f. Prepare a table of contents using a customized style list, including the styles you created for the section headings and side headings. (*Hint:* When creating a separate page for the table of contents, use a Next Page section break.)
   g. Adjust the page numbering format to include Roman numerals for the table of contents page. (Check the page numbering in the remainder of your document to make sure the pages are numbered correctly.)
2. Save the manual and name it u03pa04, manual.
3. Print and then close u03pa04, manual.

Assessment five

1. At a clear document window, create a manual cover for the manual created in assessment 4. Consider these elements when creating the cover:
   a. Balance
   b. Directional flow
   c. Focus (use lines, fonts, and/or a graphic image as a focal point)
   d. Color
   e. Include the following text in the cover:
      Grant County Medical
      Benefits Plan
      Beginning September 1, 1999
2. Save the completed cover and name it u03pa05, benefits cover.
3. Print and then close c03pa05, benefits cover.

Optional: Read the manual and write a memo telling your employees what information this manual provides and why they should keep it readily available.

index

U